Routledge H
South As

Now available in paperback, the *Routledge Handbook of South Asian Politics* examines key issues in politics of the five independent states of the South Asian region: India, Pakistan, Bangladesh, Sri Lanka, and Nepal. Written by experts in their respective areas, this Handbook introduces the reader to the politics of South Asia by presenting the prevailing agreements and disagreements in the literature.

In the first two sections, the Handbook provides a comprehensive introduction to the modern political history of the states of the region and an overview of the independence movements in the former colonial states. The other sections focus on the political changes that have occurred in the postcolonial states since independence, as well as the successive political changes in Nepal during the same period, and the structure and functioning of the main governmental and non-governmental institutions, including the structure of the state itself (unitary or federal), political parties, the judiciary, and the military. Further, the contributors explore several aspects of the political process and political and economic change, especially issues of pluralism and national integration, political economy, corruption and criminalization of politics, radical and violent political movements, and the international politics of the region as a whole.

This unique reference work provides a comprehensive survey of the state of the field and is an invaluable resource for students and academics interested in South Asian Studies, South Asian Politics, Comparative Politics and International Relations.

Paul R. Brass is Professor (Emeritus) of Political Science and International Studies at the University of Washington, Seattle. His most recent books are *Forms of Collective Violence: Riots, Pogroms, and Genocide in Modern India* (2006) and *The Production of Hindu-Muslim Violence in Contemporary India* (2003).

Routledge Handbook of South Asian Politics

India, Pakistan, Bangladesh, Sri Lanka, and Nepal

Edited by
Paul R. Brass

Routledge
Taylor & Francis Group

LONDON AND NEW YORK

First published in paperback 2013

First published 2010
by Routledge
2 Park Square, Milton Park, Abingdon, Oxon OX14 4RN

Simultaneously published in the USA and Canada
by Routledge
711 Third Avenue, New York, NY 10017

Routledge is an imprint of the Taylor & Francis Group, an informa business

British Library Cataloguing in Publication Data
A catalogue record for this book is available from the British Library

Library of Congress Cataloging in Publication Data
A catalog record for this book has been requested

ISBN: 978–0–415–43429–4 (hbk)
ISBN: 978–0–415–71649–9 (pbk)
ISBN: 978–0–203–87818–7 (ebk)

Typeset in Bembo by
Swales & Willis Ltd, Exeter, Devon

Contents

Illustrations

List of figures

List of tables

Abbreviations

ACC	Anti-Corruption Commission
ADAB	Association of Development Agencies in Bangladesh
AIADMK	All-India Dravida Munnetra Kazhagam
AITC	All India Trinamool Congress
AL	Awami League
ANP	Awami National Party
ASEAN	Association of South East Asian Nations
B-C Pact	Bandaranaike-Chelvanayakam Pact
BCS	Bangladesh Civil Service
BCS (Admin)	Bangladesh Civil Service (Administration)
BHT	Baloch Haq Talwar
BILIA	Bangladesh Institute of Law and International Affairs
BJP	Bharatiya Janata Party
BLA	Baloch Liberation Army
BNP	Baloch National Party; Bangladesh National Party
BPL	below poverty line
BRAC	Bangladesh Rural Advancement Committee
BSP	Bahujan Samaj Party
CA	constituent assembly
CBI	Confederation of British Industry
CC	Constitutional Council (Sri Lanka)
CFA	ceasefire agreement
CHA	Cessation of Hostilities Agreement
CHT	Chittagong Hill Tracts
CIC	Ceylon Indian Congress
CII	Confederation of Indian Industry
CJ	chief justice
CJI	Chief Justice of India
CP	Communist Party
CPA	Comprehensive Peace Agreement

CPI	Communist Party of India; Corruption Perception Index
CPI (M)	Communist Party of India (Marxist)
CPI (Maoist)	Communist Party of India (Maoist)
CPI (M-L)	Communist Party of India (Marxist-Leninist)
CPN-M	Communist Party of Nepal (Maoist)
CSDS	Centre for the Study of Developing Societies
CSP	Civil Service of Pakistan
CSS	centrally sponsored schemes
CWC	Ceylon Workers' Congress
DDC	district development council
DMK	Dravida Munnetra Kazhagam
DWC	Democratic Workers' Congress
EFC	Eleventh Finance Commission
EPDP	Eelam People's Democratic Party
EPRLF	Eelam People's Revolutionary Liberation Front
EPW	*Economic and Political Weekly*
EROS	Eelam Revolutionary Organization of Students
FICCI	Federation of Indian Chambers of Commerce and Industry
FNB	Federation of NGOs in Bangladesh
FP	Federal Party
FRBM	Fiscal Responsibility and Budget Management Act
GDP	gross domestic product
GOI	Government of India
GRC	Gram Rajya Committee
HDI	human development index
HSS	*Halpati Seva Sangh*
IAS	Indian Administrative Service
ICES	International Centre for Ethnic Studies (Sri Lanka)
ICS	Indian Civil Service
ILO	International Labor Office
IMF	International Monetary Fund
IPKF	Indian Peace Keeping Force
IR	international relations
ISGA	interim self-governing authority
ISI	Inter-Services Intelligence Agency; import-substitution industrialization
IT	information technology
JD(S)	Janata Dal (Secular)
JHU	Jathika Hela Urumaya
JI	Jamaat-I-Islami
JKLF	Jammu & Kashmir Liberation Front
JMB	Jamaat ul-Mujahideen Bangladesh
JUI	Jamiat Ulema-e-Islam
JUI (F)	Jamiat Ulema-e-Islam (Fazlur Rehman)
JUP	Jamiat Ulema Pakistan
JVP	Janatha Vimukthi Peramuna
JWP	Jamhoori Watan Party
KHAM	intercaste alliance in Gujarat of Kshatriyas, Harijans, Adivasis, and Muslims
KKC	Krantikari Kishan Committee

LSSP	Lanka Sama Samaj Party
LTTE	Liberation Tigers of Tamil Eelam
MCC	Maoist Communist Centre
MDG	millennium development goal
MGP	Maharashtrawadi Gomantak Party
MJF	Madhes Janadhikar Forum
MMA	Muttahida Majlis Amal
MP	member of parliament
MQM	Muhajir Qaumi Mahaz
MRD	Movement for Restoration of Democracy
MRPS	Madiga Reservation Porata Samithi
NAP	National Awami Party
NC	Nepali Congress
NCA	normal central assistance
NCEUS	National Commission of Enterprises in the Unorganized Sector
NCG	neutral caretaker government
NDA	National Democratic Alliance
NGO	non-governmental organization
NL	National List
NPC	National Planning Committee
NPT	non-proliferation treaty
NREGS	National Rural Employment Guarantee Scheme
NRI	non-resident Indian
NRO	national reconciliation ordinance
NSCI (Isak-Muvia)	National Safety Council of India
NSS	national sample survey
NWFP	North-West Frontier Province
NWS	nuclear weapons state
OBC	other backward classes
OECD	Organization for Economic Cooperation and Development
OIC	Organization of the Islamic Conference
PA	People's Alliance
PCO	provisional constitutional order
PCs	provincial councils
PDB	Power Development Board
PDP	People's Democratic Party
PDS	Public Distribution System
PIL	public interest litigation
PLA	People's Liberation Army
PLOTE	People's Liberation Organization of Tamil Eelam
PLQR	permit-license-quota Raj
PML (N)	Pakistan Muslim League (Nawaz)
PMO	Prime Minister's Office
PNE	peaceful nuclear explosion
PPP	Pakistan People's Party; purchasing power parity
PQLI	physical quality of life index
PR	proportional representation
PSUs	public sector units

P-TOM	post-tsunami operational mechanism
PWG	People's War Group
RSS	Rashtriya Swayamsevak Sangh
SAARC	South Asian Regional Cooperation Council
SAD	Shiromani Akali Dal
SC	scheduled caste(s)
SLFP	Sri Lanka Freedom Party
SLMC	Sri Lanka Muslim Congress
SLMM	Sri Lanka Monitoring Mission
SMP	single member district plurality system
SPA	Seven Party Alliance
SSP	Sipah Sahaba Pakistan
SU	Sinhala Heritage Party
TADA	Terrorist and Disruptive Activities Act
TC	Tamil Congress
TDP	Telugu Desam Party
TFC	Twelfth Finance Commission
TMLP	Tarai Madhes Loktantrik Party
TMVP	Tamileela Makkal Viduthalaip Pulikal
TNA	Tamil National Alliance
TULF	Tamil United Liberation Front
US (or USA)	United States
UCC	Uniform Civil Code
UK	United Kingdom
ULFA	United Liberation Front of Assam
UML	Communist Party of Nepal (Unified Marxist-Leninist)
UN	United Nations
UNF	United National Front
UNMIN	United Nations Mission in Nepal
UNP	United National Party
UP	Uttar Pradesh (formerly United Provinces)
UPA	United Progressive Alliance
UPFA	United People's Freedom Alliance
WTO	World Trade Organization

Contributors

Editor

Paul R. Brass is Professor (Emeritus) of Political Science and International Studies at the University of Washington, Seattle. His most recent books are *Forms of Collective Violence: Riots, Pogroms, and Genocide in Modern India* (2006), *The Production of Hindu-Muslim Violence in Contemporary India* (2003), and *Theft of an Idol* (1997). His current research is on a multi-volume history of north Indian politics from 1937 to 2007.

Editorial board

Harry Blair, Yale University, US
Stephen P. Cohen, Brookings Institution, Washington, DC, US
David Gellner, Oxford University, UK
John Harriss, Simon Fraser University, Canada
Gary Jacobsohn, University of Texas, Austin, US
Tariq Rahman, Quaid-i-Azam University, Islamabad, Pakistan
Gurharpal Singh, University of Birmingham, UK
Ian Talbot, University of Southampton, UK
Jayadev Uyangoda, University of Colombo, Sri Lanka

Contributors

E. Annamalai was Visiting Professor at Yale University and Director of the Central Institute of Indian Languages, Mysore, India. His research areas include language policy and planning and language diversity and contact. He is currently working on the modernization of languages in India and the impact of English on them. His recent publications include *Managing Multilingualism in India: Political and Linguistic Manifestations* (2001).

Sumanta Banerjee is an independent researcher based in Dehradun, India, specializing in the areas of contemporary Indian Left politics and the popular culture and social history of nineteenth-century Bengal. His publications include *Crime and Urbanization: Calcutta in the Nineteenth Century* (2006), *The Parlour and the Streets: Elite and Popular Culture in Nineteenth-Century Calcutta* (1989) and *In the Wake of Naxalbari: A History of the Naxalite Movement* (1980).

Harry Blair is Professor (Emeritus) of Political Science at Bucknell University and presently serves as Associate Chair, Senior Research Scholar and Lecturer in Political Science at Yale University. He currently works on democratization, focusing in particular on civil society and local governance in South and Southeast Asia, and the Balkans.

Jan Breman is Professor (Emeritus) of Comparative Sociology at the University of Amsterdam and Fellow at the Amsterdam School for Social Science Research. He has conducted fieldwork-based research since 1961, mainly in India and Indonesia. Some of his recent books are *The Jan Breman Omnibus* (2007), *The Poverty Regime in Village India: Half-a-Century of Work and Life at the Bottom of the Rural Economy in Gujarat* (2007), and *The Making and Unmaking of an Industrial Working Class: Sliding Down the Labour Hierarchy in Ahmedabad, India* (2003).

Shahid Javed Burki is former Vice-President of the World Bank and former Finance Minister of Pakistan. He is currently Chairman of the Lahore-based Institute of Public Policy. His most recent book is *Changing Perceptions, Altered Reality: Pakistan's Economy under Musharraf, 1999–2006* (2007).

Stephen P. Cohen is Senior Fellow at the Brookings Institution, Washington, DC. His most recent books include *Four Crises and a Peace Process* (2007), *The Idea of Pakistan* (2004), and *India: Emerging Power* (2002). He has taught at the University of Illinois and also at universities in India, Japan, and Singapore. He was a member of the US Department of State Policy Planning Staff from 1985 to 1987. He is currently writing a book on Indian military modernization.

Stuart Corbridge is Professor of Development Studies at the London School of Economics and Political Science. His most recent books are *Seeing the State: Governance and Governmentality in India* (2005, with Glyn Williams, Manoj Srivastava, and René Veron) and *Reinventing India: Liberalization, Hindu Nationalism and Popular Democracy* (2000, with John Harriss).

Neil DeVotta is Associate Professor of Political Science at Wake Forest University. He is the author of *Blowback: Linguistic Nationalism, Institutional Decay, and Ethnic Conflict in Sri Lanka* (2004), co-author of *Politics of Conflict and Peace in Sri Lanka* (2006), and co-editor of *Understanding Contemporary India* (2003).

David N. Gellner is Professor of Social Anthropology at the University of Oxford. His publications include *The Theravada Movement in Twentieth-Century Nepal* (2005, with Sarah LeVine), *The Anthropology of Buddhism and Hinduism: Weberian Themes* (2001), and the edited books *Local Democracy in South Asia: The Micropolitics of Democratization in Nepal and its Neighbours* (2008, with Krishna Hachhethu), and *Resistance and the State: Nepalese Experiences* (2003).

Krishna Hachhethu is associated with the Centre for Nepal and Asian Studies (CNAS), Tribhuvan University. His publications include *Nepal in Transition: A Study on the State of Democracy* (2008), *Party Building in Nepal: Organization, Leadership and People* (2002), and the edited book *Local Democracy in South Asia: The Micropolitics of Democratization in Nepal and its Neighbours* (2008, with David Gellner).

John Harriss is Professor of International Studies at Simon Fraser University, Canada, having previously researched and taught at the universities of Cambridge and East Anglia and the London School of Economics. His publications include *Depoliticizing Development: The World Bank and Social Capital* (2001) and *Reinventing India: Economic Liberalization, Hindu Nationalism and Popular Democracy* (2000, with Stuart Corbridge). His current research concerns India's social policy in the context of liberalization.

Vernon Hewitt is a Senior Lecturer in the Department of Politics at the University of Bristol, UK. His most recent books include *Political Mobilisation and Democracy in India: States of Emergency* (2008), and *Development and Colonialism: The Past in the Present* (forthcoming, co-edited with Mark Duffield).

Sara Hossain is a barrister practicing at the Supreme Court of Bangladesh. Her recent publications include *"Honour": Crimes, Paradigms and Violence against Women* (2005, co-edited with Lynn Welchman). Her main areas of research and activism concern public interest law, access to justice, women's rights, freedom of expression, and the religious right.

Stanley A. Kochanek is Professor (Emeritus) at Pennsylvania State University, University Park. His most recent book is *India: Government and Politics in a Developing Nation* (2008). He is currently working on a comparative study of business and politics in India, Pakistan, and Bangladesh.

Professor W. D. Lakshman is Professor (Emeritus) at the University of Colombo. A former Vice-Chancellor of the University of Colombo, he currently serves as Senior Economic Advisor to the Ministry of Finance, Sri Lanka. His edited publications, *Sri Lanka's Development since Independence: Socio-Economic Perspectives and Analyses* (2000) and *Dilemmas of Development: Fifty Years of Economic Change in Sri Lanka* (1997), are among widely consulted recent studies in the economic development of Sri Lanka.

Paula R. Newberg is the Executive Director of Georgetown University's Institute for the Study of Diplomacy, and is a specialist in governance, development, and democracy in transition and crisis states. She is a former special advisor to the United Nations, a regular contributor to *Yale Global*, and *The Globe and Mail*. Her publications include *Double Betrayal: Human Rights and Insurgency in Kashmir* (1995) and *Judging the State: Courts and Constitutional Politics in Pakistan* (1995).

Tariq Rahman is Distinguished National Professor of Linguistic History in the National Institute of Pakistan Studies, Quaid-i-Azam University, Islamabad. His best known book is *Language and Politics in Pakistan* (1996). Other books include *Denizens of Alien Worlds: A Study of Education, Inequality and Polarization in Pakistan* (2004) and *Language, Ideology and Power: Language-learning among the Muslims of Pakistan and North India* (2002).

Lloyd I. Rudolph is Professor (Emeritus) of Political Science, University of Chicago. His recent books, co-authored with Susanne Hoeber Rudolph, include *Making U.S. Foreign Policy towards South Asia: Regional Imperatives and the Imperial Presidency* (2008) and *Postmodern Gandhi and Other Essays: Gandhi in the World* (2006).

Susanne Hoeber Rudolph is the William Benton Distinguished Service Professor (Emeritus) of Political Science, University of Chicago. She is co-author, with Lloyd I. Rudolph, of *Explaining Indian Democracy: A Fifty Year Perspective* (2008) and *Reversing the Gaze: The Amar Singh Diary, A Colonial Subject's Narrative of Imperial India* (1999).

Shylashri Shankar is a Senior Research Fellow at the Centre for Policy Research, New Delhi. She is the author of *Scaling Justice: India's Supreme Court, Anti-Terror Laws, and Social Rights* (2009). Her current research includes the medical jurisprudence of torture claims by detainees under criminal and anti-terror laws, and a study of district and village-level politics underlying an employment guarantee scheme in India.

Gurharpal Singh is the Nadir Dinshaw Chair in Inter-religious Relations at the University of Birmingham. His recent publications include *The Partition of India* (forthcoming, 2009, with Ian Talbot), and *Sikhs in Britain* (2006, with Dashan S. Tatla). He is currently working on a volume on India's democracy. He is the Deputy Director of the UK Department for International Development-funded Religions and Development research program.

Ian A. Talbot is Professor of British History at the University of Southampton. He is the editor of *The Deadly Embrace: Religion, Politics and Violence in India and Pakistan 1947–2002* (2007) and the author of *Divided Cities: Partition and Its Aftermath in Lahore and Amritsar 1947–1957* (2006). His current research is on Partition and violence.

Jayadeva Uyangoda is Professor and Head of the Department of Political Science and Public Policy, University of Colombo, and Founder-Director of the Centre for Policy Research and Analysis. He has written extensively and authoritatively on the civil war in Sri Lanka for many years and on ethnic conflict, minority rights, and conflict resolution. His most recent major publication is *Ethnic Conflict in Sri Lanka: Changing Dynamics* (2007).

Virginia Van Dyke is currently teaching in the South Asia Center, University of Washington, Seattle. She was formerly an Assistant Professor of Political Science at the University of Wisconsin-Milwaukee. She has published on the topics of religion and politics, religious violence, and electoral politics. Her current research project is a comparison of coalition politics in four Indian states.

Mohammad Waseem is Professor of Political Science at the Lahore University of Management Sciences (LUMS) Lahore. His most recent book is *Democratization in Pakistan: A Study of the 2002 Elections* (2006). His current research is on political conflict in Pakistan, covering electoral, civil-military, ethnic, religious, and sectarian conflicts.

Nira Wickramasinghe is Professor of Modern South Asian Studies, Leiden University. Her most recent book is *Sri Lanka in the Modern Age: A History of Contested Identities* (2006). She is presently a research fellow at the Shelby Cullom Davis Center for Historical Studies where she is writing a history of the reception of the Singer sewing machine in colonial Sri Lanka.

Steven I. Wilkinson is Associate Professor of Political Science and Chair of the Committee on Southern Asian Studies at the University of Chicago. He is the author of *Patrons, Clients or Policies* (2007, co-edited with Herbert Kitschelt) and *Votes and Violence: Electoral Competition and Communal Riots in India* (2005). His current research interests include colonial legacies for democracy, governance and conflict, and the causes of the Partition violence.

1

Introduction

Paul R. Brass

Part 1: Colonialism, nationalism, and Independence in South Asia: India, Pakistan, and Sri Lanka

The states of the South Asian region are often thought to have shared a common colonial experience through British rule and/or dominance, which has since profoundly influenced their political trajectories. Most notably, from a political standpoint, is the adherence, at least in form, and in some measure in actuality as well, of the leaders and the public in India and Sri Lanka to the basic principles of parliamentary rule through competitive elections, and the repeated striving, less successfully in the other states, towards the same end. Yet, it should be obvious by now that the differences in these respects are profound. First of all, of the five independent states in the South Asian region, only three—India, Pakistan, and Sri Lanka—arrived at Independence through a transfer of power from the British. A fourth, Bangladesh, achieved its Independence only a quarter century later after a traumatic civil war that left countless numbers of its citizens dead. As for Nepal, it never experienced direct British rule and has followed a quite different trajectory in the 55 years since its termination. Bhutan, touched on only very briefly

in this volume, has remained an independent protectorate of India.

So, the differences are profound, but, at the same time, the striving for open politics, civil liberties, and parliamentary rule has remained alive, active, and renewable in every state in the region. The similarities and differences in these and every other respect are brought out in every section of this volume, which has been organized to encourage comparison. With regard to most topics, the differences among the several countries are so great that a separate chapter on each topic has been required. In other cases, where there are important similarities or where differences have arisen despite a common heritage, the relevant topics have been analyzed in comparative chapters.

With regard to the transition from British rule to Independence, Chapter 2 (Talbot) addresses directly the similarities and differences in the inheritances and legacies that derive from British rule, the nationalist movement, and the partition of the subcontinent. Among those inheritances and legacies, the catastrophe of Partition that occurred simultaneously with the achievement of Independence for both states stands out. It remains a living legacy that has affected both the internal development and the external relations of both states, persistently endangering the peace of the region and retarding its common development. It is a common legacy, but even here there is a profound difference in its meaning for the two countries. For India, Partition destroyed the dream of its leaders for a unified subcontinent. For Pakistan, Partition signified freedom from Indian and Hindu dominance.

Also profound were the differences in the nationalist movement that brought Independence to each country upon the withdrawal of the British. In this case, there are three trajectories: the non-violent Congress movement built over three quarters of a century on the base of a strong, nearly subcontinent-wide organization and led by Mohandas K. Gandhi during the quarter century preceding Independence; the militant Pakistan movement led by Mohammad Ali Jinnah, with a history of a mere decade of organization, and with very weak roots in the politically dominant, western parts of the country; and the peaceful granting of Independence to Ceylon that limited the building of a strong nationalist movement.

Further, the nationalist movements in the three countries suffered from different degrees of noninclusiveness. The Indian National Congress, the broadest of the three, did not have equal strength in all regions of the country, and had little or none in some. Pakistan, of course, was created out of two entirely different cultural regions, united only nominally by the predominance of Islam in both. Moreover, within the western region of the country as well, as in India, there were major regional, cultural, and ethnic differences. Sri Lanka (then Ceylon) arrived at Independence with a thin veneer of elite cooperation—which soon collapsed—among the predominant Sinhala population; the minority, regionally concentrated Tamil population; and yet another minority group of Tamils of relatively recent South Indian origin, most of whom the new government promptly sought to disenfranchise and expel from the country.

At the same time, all three countries arrived at Independence with shared commitments to slogans of "democracy" and "secularism," although they differed on other fundamentals. The latter included, for example, the centrality of the state in development: greatest in India; least in Sri Lanka where the state commitment was not to development in the Indian sense, but, as Wickramasinghe notes in Chapter 3, to "social welfare"; and Pakistan, lacking any ideology of state development, rather more concerned with building an army capable of confronting India as needed. But, all states in the South Asian region, in common with most states everywhere, share an unshakable determination to retain at all costs the boundaries bequeathed to them at Independence in the face of several movements demanding separation. Only in the case of Pakistan—and there only because of the intervention of India—has the division of a South Asian state occurred.

Moreover, in all states in the region, the original commitment to secularism as an ideology has been battered and largely displaced with the rise of Hindu nationalism in India, recognition of Islam as the state religion and the rise of Islamic movements in Pakistan, and Buddhist demands for official recognition in Sri Lanka, accepted soon after Independence. Gellner, however, notes that: "Nepal, on the other hand, which was an officially Hindu state from 1962 to 2006, has, with the establishment of a secular republic, gone in the other direction."[1]

Part II: Political change, political parties, and the issue of unitary vs federal forms of government

India

In the years since Independence, dramatic changes have taken place, affecting all the countries of the region in substantially different ways. India has passed from a political order dominated by the Indian National

Congress through a brief period of emergency authoritarian rule under Indira Gandhi to a functioning multiparty system. Moreover, all these periods have been marked by intense political activity, involving an array of political parties across the entire spectrum of ideological differences in competitive elections based on universal franchise, with large voter turnouts in virtually every election. India, it can be safely said, has long ago passed the conventional tests of a stable, functioning democracy, namely, frequent passing of power to alternative political formations, complete and unchallenged civilian control over the military, and massive popular participation in electoral politics. Moreover, the forms of party mobilization and popular participation have been distinctive in India, building on and extending the many forms of nonviolent protest against government policies and actions that were developed during the movement for Independence. Further, these developments have also been accompanied by the gradual incorporation of the middle and lower castes into the electoral process and, in recent years, the capture of political power in several states by parties based on their support.

These changes have been brought about through the agency of vibrant, but highly fragmented, political parties and the struggles for power among them, in the course of which both the predominant parties and the relations among them have changed dramatically. The national one-party dominant system under the Indian National Congress prevailed from Independence until the late 1980s, since when it has been replaced by a multiparty system reshaped into a three-front, but dual coalitional system with the Congress and the Bharatiya Janata Party (BJP) the principal protagonists. The rise of the militant Hindu party, the BJP, has been the driving force in this competitive realignment.

But the national system is not simply replicated in the several states. Rather, most state party systems have a distinctive character. Indian politics at both state and national levels

also have adapted to various forms of coalition politics (Virginia Van Dyke, in Chapter 5) on which there is an increasing literature. At the same time, there has been a general movement in most states towards forms of bipolar competition, that is to say, predominantly two party or two front.

Beneath the veneer of conventional parliamentary democracy in India lie several other features: a political-electoral order increasingly based on money and muscle in which the primary aim of most elected representatives is to gain control over public institutions in order to enrich themselves; in many states also, a further degradation of the political order through the outright criminalization of politics; the move away from nonviolent protest movements to mobilizations that lead to considerable violence, often intended;[2] the continued, indeed in some ways increased reliance of politicians on what Harriss (Chapter 4) calls the social "identities of caste and religion" to garner votes; and, most importantly, the still limited ability of the vast population of miserably poor people to benefit from the political process, even to achieve a measure of dignity and self-respect.

The literature on electoral politics in India is fast becoming one of the richest in the world that elucidates the great changes that have taken place in popular participation and the composition of the electorate.[3] Not only has there been a considerable increase in the voting population (with variations over time and from state to state), but whole new groups of voters have been incorporated into electoral politics through a process that I have described elsewhere as "caste succession."[4] Whereas, in the early years after Independence, upper castes dominated as candidates and voters (often bringing their lower caste dependents along with them), the "backward" and "lower" castes now are well represented by persons from their own groups and dominate state governments in many of the Indian states. Moreover, despite occasional literature to the contrary, it is not the case that the importance of caste voting has declined.

Far from it, for the drive to garner benefits of all sorts, available from state agencies, on the part of caste groups, and the increased capture of state power by leaders from castes newly incorporated into the political process, has been so central to the politicization of the Indian population that one scholar has characterized India as a "patronage democracy."[5] Although the term is one that applies to many states in the past as well as the contemporary world, its distinctive character in India is the extent to which it implies a high degree of cohesive voting on the part of particular caste groups for persons from their own caste, who alone can be relied on to accommodate their needs and demands.

Pakistan

Pakistan's post-Independence political history has been markedly different from that of India. Whereas in India there was marked continuity of political leadership under Nehru—and even beyond under both Indira and Rajiv Gandhi—Pakistan lost both its founding leaders, Jinnah and Liaquat Ali Khan within a few years after Independence, the former through natural causes and the latter by assassination. Neither did the political parties have any substantial base in the electorate at Independence that would enable the firm establishment of parliamentary government or even, for that matter, the promulgation of a constitutional framework. In contrast to India, therefore, it is the military that has been the predominant political force in Pakistan since the initial displacement of the parliamentary regime by Ayub Khan in 1958.

A further profound difference between these two polities has been the deleterious influence of the United States that has repeatedly and disastrously influenced the course of Pakistani politics by supporting and feeding successive military regimes with massive "foreign aid," most of it used by the military to fortify its armaments and wage wars against India over Kashmir. Moreover, latterly, the United States has been using the country as a reluctant ally in the fruitless war in Afghanistan. Neither has American intervention changed at all the primary focus of the Pakistan military towards confrontation with India.

At the same time, it deserves mention that in Pakistan, as everywhere else in South Asia, there is a mass base that rejects military rule and supports parliamentary government that has twice been decisive in altering the country's history: the first time in the mass movement that led to the resignation of Ayub Khan in 1969 and the second occasion in 2007–08 that brought down the military regime of Pervez Musharaf and reinstituted civilian government. However, the crux of the problem of the failure of civilian rule in Pakistan, apart from the persisting virtual independence of the military from civilian control, has been, as Burki notes (Chapter 6), the inability of "the civilian leadership, when exercising power . . . to institutionalize the base of their support."

Bangladesh

Like Pakistan, Bangladesh belongs in the category of a society in which aspirations for the establishment of a democratic political order based on free, competitive elections have remained, but have been repeatedly undermined by violent conflict, including assassinations of heads of state, repeated military takeovers, and deep hatreds between the leaders of the two principal contending parties, the surviving spouses of former assassinated heads of state. Aspirations for independence and democracy arose in Bangladesh initially during one of undivided Pakistan's longest periods of military rule. The movement was crushed by the Pakistani army, but ultimately prevailed through the military intervention of India in 1971.

But none of the elected regimes in Bangladesh has lasted long. Even in the case of the country's first leader, Sheikh Mujibur Rahman, who had nearly total electoral support, democratic rule did not prevail.

Mired in corruption, soon losing respect and support while attempting to shore up his rule by building his own military force, Mujib and most members of his large family were finally slaughtered in 1975 during a military coup. However, one daughter was left alive, Sheikh Hasina, who was abroad at the time, and who ultimately matured into one of the principal contenders for power in Bangladesh politics up to the present day.

One of the leaders of the military coup, General Ziaur Rahman, emerged at the head of a new military regime, which lasted only until his own assassination in 1981. Since the killing of Sheikh Mujib and General Zia, it can be fairly said that politics in Bangladesh has been a form of vendetta, in which Sheikh Hasina, Zia's wife, Khaleda, and successive military leaders have struggled for power and the support of the people of the country through a series of competitive elections, coups, countercoups, and military takeovers that have persisted up to the present. At the same time, these struggles have often involved the mobilization of large numbers of people from all walks of life in mass movements that continue to testify to the aspirations in Bangladesh society for popular government or, at least, for competitive elections and "civil liberties"(Harry Blair, in Chapter 7).

Indeed, one of the shared characteristics of political behavior in the three states that were formerly part of British-ruled India has been the centrality of mass mobilizations as vehicles for political change, transformation, and even overthrow of military regimes to reestablish elections as the proper mode of achieving the power to rule. It is a curiosity, however, of Bangladesh politics that, although elections are considered the only valid means of attaining power, the losers invariably cry foul, insisting that the elections were marred by fraud or even rigged, often protesting the results by a return to the streets, as Blair puts it. Moreover, no matter which party wins power, the winner takes all the spoils that include especially the corrupt income and the control over the police to protect one's friends

and harass one's enemies. Indeed, both Blair and Kochanek (see Chapter 25) point out that Bangladesh has most often sur-passed all other countries in the world in Transparency International's corruption index. Yet, public faith in the idea of popular rule through elections continues to be high in Bangladesh as elsewhere in South Asia, where turnout rates consistently surpass anything in the United States, self-reputedly the world's "greatest democracy." Indeed, parliamentary government was again restored and elections called for December 2008. Sheikh Hasina and the Awami League emerged triumphant in a "landslide" victory in an election with more than 80 percent turnout in which the party won a two-thirds majority in parliament,

Throughout all the dramatic changes in Bangladesh politics, however, there has been one persistent feature, namely, the predominance of the bureaucracy in policymaking. This partly reflects the common experience of the pivotal role of the bureaucracy during British rule that has carried over to some extent in all three states. But it also reflects the fact that the parties and the politicians actually have little interest in policy, their primary concerns being in amassing corrupt income for themselves and distributing patronage to their supporters. Moreover, as in Pakistan, the bureaucracy maintains cordial relations with the military whenever the military reasserts its dominance in Bangladesh politics. But, the military in Bangladesh has by no means the power or the resources of its counterpart in Pakistan.

Sri Lanka

Like India, Sri Lanka has had an unbroken post-Independence history of civilian government in which, despite repeated changes in the constitution of the country, popular elections have always determined which parties and leaders are to govern the country. In fact, Sri Lanka was the first country in South Asia to pass the conventional test of a nonviolent change of government from one

5

party or set of parties to another. Moreover, it passed that test repeatedly in election after election between 1948 and 1977 (DeVotta, Chapter 8). Moreover, despite the existence in earlier periods of a multiplicity of minor parties, the basic pattern over time in Sri Lanka has been alternation between two main parties, the SLFP and the UNP, plus their allies. At the same time, repeated changes in the constitution of the country have shifted the balance of power in the political system to the president rather than to parliament. Further, DeVotta has argued that, despite the façade of a model democratic state, Sri Lanka has not been a liberal democracy, but rather an "illiberal democracy," in which the basic rules of democratic governance have been repeatedly violated. The violations have included refusal on the part of the ruling party "to hold scheduled elections in 1975," extending its rule by two additional years; the use and abuse of the Prevention of Terrorism Act of 1979 to victimize "innocent Tamils" as the government sought to suppress the rise of ethnic separatism and "manifold human rights violations" justified by the need to defeat the Tamil rebellion led by the Liberation Tigers of Tamil Eelam (LTTE); "voting irregularities" and "malpractices" during elections, including the outright "rigging" of a national referendum in 1982 by which the government of the day extended its rule "for another term"; and the "disappearance" of "over 40,000 Sinhalese" during the suppression of an "uprising" by the militant JVP. As in all the other South Asian countries as well, nepotism, favoritism, corruption, and "gangsterism" have been prevalent features in governance in Sri Lanka.

In addition, in common with all the other countries of South Asia, dynastic competition among prominent families for succession in power has been a recurrent aspect of politics. Also, as in Bangladesh, the competition between dynasties provides the basic core of political opposition in a system in which there is otherwise little loyalty of politicians to the parties on whose labels they

contest elections. For, as in India and the other countries of the region as well, it is the desire for a ministerial portfolio or the directorship of a public corporation that motivates politicians, who will barter their votes in parliament to the party that will provide them the portfolios or directorships from which they will garner corrupt income. The scramble for such opportunities provides an edge to politics both in Sri Lanka and elsewhere in the region that encourages as well resort to violent means to win elections and gain power.

Also of note is the fact that in none of the countries of South Asia, despite bows to secularist ideals, has there been a separation between religion and politics. In Sri Lanka, Buddhism has been declared the state religion and Buddhist monks have been active in numerous political movements, including that for the establishment of Sinhalese as the sole official language of the country in the 1950s, for the suppression of the Tamil revolt, and for strengthening the "unitary state."

The consequences of the failures of Sri Lankan politicians to accommodate the differences among the several ethnic groups on the island have been great: 70,000 people killed, nearly 600,000 "internally displaced, between 800,000 and one million Tamils" fled from the country during the past quarter century culminating in a humanitarian disaster with the victory of the Sri Lankan army terminating the civil war and, in the process, adding thousands more killed and perhaps another 300,000 persons displaced in its wake. Neither are these figures exceptional for the countries of South Asia, where slogans of national unity and ethnic supremacy justify the carnage and appear quite compatible with competitive regimes that proclaim their devotion to the ideals of democratic participation and governance.

Nepal

In a region where the unexpected is ordinary and fundamental changes have been taking place everywhere, recent events in Nepal stand out, namely, the overthrow of the monarchy through the success of a Maoist revolution after a ten-year war from 1996 to 2006; the victory of the Maoists in a free, competitive election; and the elevation of Prachanda, the leader of the Maoists, to the position of prime minister. In the process, Nepal has moved dramatically, as Hachhethu and Gellner note (in Chapter 9), from a state whose leaders proudly proclaimed that they were the only true Hindu state left in the world to a "secular state," towards the transformation of the government from its unitary form to federalism, and towards an "inclusive democracy" in contrast to the high-caste dominated polity that preceded it. Proposals for a mixture of ethnic and territorial federal units are currently (2008) under lively and controversial discussion.

Federalism and center–state relations

Most postcolonial states have opted for unitary rule by a central government, which has often turned into nothing more than military rule. However, the enormous cultural, linguistic, ethnic, and religious diversity of the states of South Asia has naturally led to demands from many groups for constitutional arrangements to accommodate and mediate actual or potential conflicts among them. Federalism, combined with various forms of local self-government, has been the method of choice for India, but it has been resisted in all other states in the region. Pakistan early discarded federalism in favor of a unitary state with two wings, east and west, in order to counter the much greater unity of the eastern wing of the country compared to the western part comprised of several major ethnic and linguistic groups. The failure to adopt a federal solution as a means of accommodation, however, was an important factor in the ultimate breakup of the country, with the separation of the eastern wing and the formation of Bangladesh. The latter state has felt no need for federalism since the principal minority group is the remnant population of Hindus who remained there after Partition,

then fled during the civil war and returned again after the division of Pakistan. They have no significant regional concentration. Neither would any demands from that quarter for any special institutional recognition be likely to be accepted. Further, no government of Bangladesh has expressed the wish to make significant concessions for institutional change to the small minority of hill tribal peoples who live in the southeastern parts of the country. As for Sri Lanka, various forms of so-called devolution have been discussed and even partly implemented in the northern and eastern provinces as a solution to the civil war that raged there from 1983 to 2009. The government of Sri Lanka steadfastly resisted a federal solution to the conflict in favor of military suppression of the Tamil rebels. Neither was federalism ever seriously considered by the king in Nepal, a situation that has changed dramatically with the victory of the Maoists and the proposed adoption there of a federalist framework.

India has been exceptional in this regard, and has developed distinctive forms of federalism, in which state and national politics have been intertwined and in which the balance of powers between what is called in India, the "center," and the states has undergone significant changes over time. In fact, federalism in India, perhaps more than in any other federal system, has involved "continuous negotiation" (Rudolph and Rudolph, in Chapter 10) concerning the relations between the center and the states.

India began as a unitary-biased federal system, with a strong center and weak states. That bias was especially evident in two respects: the center retained and used the powers "to create, abolish, divide, or combine states" (Rudolph and Rudolph). It also (mis)used regulary and increasingly, in the first several decades after Independence, its powers to take over governance of the states directly from the center under the constitutional provision known as the imposition of President's Rule. Moreover, during the heyday of Indira Gandhi, the governing Congress party at the Center virtually controlled the selection of Congress candidates to contest state legislative assembly elections, selected the chief ministers of the Congress-ruled states, and dismissed those who in any way became troublesome to Indira Gandhi herself and to the dominance of the Congress.

Nevertheless, the predominant pattern of shift over the past half century has been towards pluralism, regionalism, and decentralization.[6] With the shift in the balance of central and state powers, as well as intervention from the supreme court, the imposition of President's Rule has been much less frequent. That tendency has been reinforced in the last two decades with the decline of the Congress as the sole ruling party at the Center and its decline as well into permanent minority status in most of the states. Multipartism nationally and multipartism in the states—or forms of bipolar competition with parties that differ from state to state—have been largely responsible for these changes. The fragility of ruling coalitions at the Center has increased the power of parties based in particular states at times—now regularly—when they have sufficient members in parliament to bring down the central government, quite the opposite situation from the days of dominance by Nehru and his daughter. Additionally, the gradual shift since 1991 from a "command economy" directed by the Center and its planning commission to a liberalization regime—which, in India as the Rudolphs describe it, has become a "federal market economy"—has also reduced the levers of control formerly held by the center to influence state governments. The more enterprising and energetic leaders in the states have also used the opportunities opened up by the liberalization regime to directly solicit investments in their states by global corporations.

It is not the case, however, that the central government lacks significant power to influence state powers and politics. It still controls vast resources as a consequence of its continued dominance in revenue collection, which allows it to distribute funds for, and monitor development programs in the states. While a return to the days of central government dominance of the policy process and state politics is unlikely, the relations between the Center and the states continue in "flux" (Rudolph and Rudolph) and continue also to be based on negotiation, bargaining, and the relative political weight of particular states in national political coalitions.

Part III: The judiciary

Chapter 11 on the Indian judiciary (by Shylashri Shankar) documents a further aspect of political change and development of Indian institutions, namely, the gradual assertion and reassertion of the authority of the supreme court to oversee and limit, albeit rarely to invalidate, laws passed by parliament. Although it does not in this respect approach the powers of the US Supreme Court, yet, after many setbacks, including strong efforts to control, suppress, and overturn its judgments and interfere in its functioning, especially during Indira Gandhi's years in power, it has emerged with a stable, authoritative position in the Indian political order and has carved out niches for itself in several areas of public law, in which it has adopted assertive positions, notably, as Shankar has pointed out, in areas involving "social and economic rights."

Once again, the contrast with Pakistan is stark, illustrated clearly by Newberg (Chapter 12). Whereas, in India, the supreme court has gradually asserted its separate domain of authority against attempts to undermine it, in Pakistan, in contrast, the supreme court—and the judiciary in general—continue to struggle to formulate a set of criteria that would enable it to challenge effectively and consistently the repeated assertions of executive power. Successive political regimes, whether under military or civilian control, have dismissed judges and/or packed the courts with their own, compliant judges. The court, for its part, has repeatedly bowed to executive authority through decisions justifying authoritarian rule and/or dubious transfers of executive authority from the military to civilian leaders and vice versa on the grounds of such doctrines as "necessity" and "revolutionary legality." It has also repeatedly accepted the legality of granting immunity from judicial judgment and indemnity for the repeated abuse and misuse of power by the executive authority or, contrarily, has accepted the legality of the execution of a former prime minister, Zulfikar Ali Bhutto, ordered by his successor, General Mohammed Zia ul Haq.

Yet, even in Pakistan, the striving for legitimate authority not only of the courts but of all state institutions has continued from time to time to involve intense conflict, mass movements, and violence. The current crisis of authority in Pakistan (2007–08), as yet far from definitively resolved, has put the supreme court at the very center of the struggle for power and legitimate authority of all its institutions (except the Army, which continues to maintain—in reserve at the moment—its separate and often decisive role in the course of political change). The current struggle for power in Pakistan has placed the courts, especially the supreme court, in an extraordinary position. President Musharraf dismissed the chief justice and packed the courts with his own men. However, the dismissed chief justice then succeeded, along with his colleagues in the judiciary and the bar, and with the support of a mass public, in launching a movement that led to the restoration of free elections, the participation of previously banned leaders and parties, and the marginalization of Musharraf himself, and finally (2008) his forced resignation. Yet, neither Musharraf nor the country's prime minister, brought to power by the movement, or even the new president, Benazir Bhutto's widower, Asif Ali Zardari, wished to see the power and authority of the judiciary restored. Musharraf was forced to retire as president under threat of impeachment, but Zardari resisted the restoration of the judges until March 2009.

The position of the supreme court—and the judiciary in general—in Bangladesh since the achievement of Independence from Pakistan has been similar to that of Pakistan. Despite the assertion in the Constitution of 1972 of the "principle of judicial Independence" (Hossain, in Chapter 13), and periodic assertions of that principle by the court itself, it has experienced politicization during parliamentary periods, on the one hand, and subordination during alternating periods of military rule, on the other hand. Attempts to reassert the independence of the judiciary have relied on a stance articulated first in India, namely, asserting that certain features of the constitution (in this case, judicial independence) cannot be altered by parliament since they affect the "basic structure" of the constitution itself. However, the upshot of the struggles for judicial independence in Bangladesh has been the reduction of the independence of the judiciary and its politicization by both "full-blown military governments" as well as "autocratic presidents and elected parliaments."

The authority and performance of the Sri Lankan judiciary are intermediate between the respective positions of the courts in India, on the one hand, and Pakistan and Bangladesh, on the other hand, but rather closer to India than to Pakistan and Bangladesh. The three successive constitutions of Sri Lanka have, in several ways, limited the powers of the judiciary, especially with regard to judicial review of laws passed by parliament and the powers of the president. Not surprisingly, therefore, the judiciary in Sri Lanka has accorded "deference to the other state institutions," and avoided direct conflict with the executive and parliament (Shankar) and has not been free from "politicization." Nevertheless, it has not subordinated its decisions to the whims of the ruling power. Neither has it engaged in "judicial activism" in the manner of the Indian Supreme Court. In practice, however, its deference to other state institutions has also meant that it has provided no protection to the Tamil minorities in the country against discrimination and harassment by the state. Similarly, its decisions on religious freedom have been biased in favor of Buddhism and against the interests of Christians and Muslims especially, for example, with regard to the right to proselytize. Most important, in common with all institutions, policies, and procedures of the Sri Lankan state, judicial decisions on matters of human rights, including the right not to be tortured, have been negatively affected by the debilitating civil war, which has moved Sri Lanka's polity increasingly towards "executive sovereignty."

Part IV: Pluralism and national integration: language issues

Issues concerning pluralism and national integration have been at the forefront in virtually every multiethnic, multilingual, multicultural postcolonial state. They have been especially difficult and longlasting in India, Pakistan, and Sri Lanka. Bangladesh itself was created as a consequence of the politicization of linguistic issues concerning the official language of the state, which, in turn, overlay conflict over broader cultural differences between Bengalis and West Pakistanis. Equally extreme in its consequences has been the civil war in Sri Lanka between the Sinhalese-dominated state and the territorially concentrated Tamil minority. For their part, India and Pakistan, far more diverse in all respects than the other states in the region, have had to confront multiple issues concerning the status of ethnolinguistic and religiously distinct groups.

The Indian state has been largely successful in coping with demands for recognition on behalf of the multiplicity of language groups comprised within its boundaries. India's leaders resolved the issues of official language for the central government through a compromise between Hindi and English as the two official languages of state. Moreover, all the major regional languages of India have

also been accommodated through the federal system in a process that began with the reorganization of states in the 1950s and 1960s, but continues in some respects up to the present. Various other accommodations have also been made, including recognition of all regional languages as media of examination for entry into the central government services and the addition of other languages into the Eighth Schedule of the Constitution of India, which grants their speakers certain rights and privileges. Problems remain, nevertheless, with regard to minority language speakers within the reorganized states, particularly concerning the provision of educational facilities for such speakers. Further, there is also a considerable differentiation with regard to status and possibilities for advancement among the speakers of the various languages of India such that English remains the preeminent language of the educated elite of the country, who dominate the central government bureaucracy while speakers of the principal vernacular languages, who do not know English, remain confined to opportunities available within their home states. In effect, although there remain movements for recognition of several language groups, the language issue in India as a whole has become less a matter of official recognition and more a socioeconomic and status "issue of differential access to English education" (Annamalai, in Chapter 15).

Pakistan's solutions to the problems posed by a multiplicity of languages were initially quite different from India's and had disastrous results. Initial attempts to impose Urdu as the national and official language for the entire country derived from the symbolic importance of the rivalry between Urdu and Hindi language promoters in India before Independence, even though in Pakistan itself only the refugees (*mohajirs*) from India spoke Urdu as their mother tongue. Lacking any other language that could make a claim as the "national" language of the country, Jinnah chose Urdu on the mistaken belief that it would unite rather than divide the country.

However, the attempt foundered against Bengali opposition and provided the symbolic basis for the secessionist movement that ultimately resulted in the Independence of Bangladesh.

The 1973 Constitution of Pakistan, however, provides a similar solution to that of India for the question of the national/official languages of the country, namely, Urdu formally declared as the "national language," while allowing for the indefinite use of English "for official purposes" in the country as a whole and for the provincial languages in the several provinces (Rahman, in Chapter 16). Yet, movements demanding greater recognition of the regional languages of West Pakistan, such as Sindhi and Balochi, have persisted. Why? In most cases, language is the emblem for uniting ethnic collectivities against other ethnic groups perceived as dominant in a province (such as the Urdu-speaking *mohajirs* in Sindh) or against the Pakistani state itself (as in Balochistan). In other words, as Rahman has put it, in such cases language "serves as an identity symbol" for movements that have other ends beyond development and promotion of the use of the language itself.

But there has also been a curious twist in the symbolic and instrumental uses of language identification for political ends in Pakistan, namely, the preference of elite Punjabis—who form the largest and the dominant ethnic collectivity in Pakistan—for English and Urdu, including their resistance to the teaching of their own mother tongue in the primary schools of the province. It is a curious twist that has a parallel in the post-Independence Indian province of Punjab as well where, in order to resist the demands of Punjabi-speaking Sikhs for a separate province in which Sikhs would have a majority, Punjabi-speaking Hindus disowned their own language in favor of Hindi to such an extent that an entire generation switched their language both of identification and actual practical usage.[7] These two cases in themselves provide the most striking evidence for the proposition that language movements may be, and often are, symbolic representations of other interests than the protection of the language itself. Those interests everywhere concern primarily power (Rahman) and economic advantage.

One further issue of identity concerns the question of "national language" itself. India has wisely avoided using that term for either Hindi or English, which conveys a sense of superiority for one language among many, preferring instead to characterize all the widespread and predominant regional languages as "national languages," with those given preference being designated only as "official languages." Pakistan, however, less sure of its own national identity, made the mistake of attempting to assert it by elevating one language to the emotively powerful status of "national language." The obvious solution, however, as Rahman points out, is essentially an Indian one for Pakistan, namely, designating "five national languages in the country with Urdu as a language of inter-provincial communication and English for international communication."

The feature of language use that is most clearly shared by both Pakistanis and Indians is the high status associated with English and the class differentiation in its adoption. It is in both countries the language of the dominant elites in "private sector employment" and in "the upper echelons of Pakistani society" (Rahman). This, indeed, has become the most important consequence of language policies in both countries in the context of "a failed educational system," that is to say, one that relegates the vast mass of the populations of both countries to utterly inferior, decrepit, and poorly funded government schools while the rich and well-born attend English-medium schools of high standard, the latter even subsidized in Pakistan by government. In Pakistan, there is yet a further consequence, namely the spread of *madrasahs* as alternatives to totally inadequate government-funded vernacular schools. Although there is no evidence that these *madrasahs* are producing more anti-American "terrorists" than the ordinary government schools, they are most obviously producing generations of persons for whom religion provides their primary loyalty while the dominant English-educated elites constitute a "secular" governing minority. Rahman concludes his chapter with the very powerful statement that "the present language policies have the cumulative effect of increasing inequality and polarization in the country." That polarization would seem to place those who have political power, economic security, and secular values on one side in contrast to those disempowered, economically insecure, and oriented towards religious values as a primary identification.

Part V: Crises of national unity

India

All the countries of the region have, to greater or lesser degree, faced crises of national unity, greatest, of course, in the case of the disintegration of Pakistan. But all have had to confront, placate, or crush by military means demands for secession made by militant organizations on behalf of minority ethnic, linguistic, or religious groups. In the case of India, aside from a secessionist demand long ago abandoned in Tamil Nadu in south India, there have been three regions where violent secessionist movements have either continued since Independence or have recurred from time to time, namely, Jammu and Kashmir, Punjab, and the northeastern states. In all cases, the government of India over the past 60 years has made it abundantly clear that it will not tolerate any demand whatsoever for secession from the country while, at the same time, always being open to considering demands that fall short of secession, including the creation of separate states and/or autonomous regions within the Indian Union. Those movements that persist in making secessionist demands, however, have met with massive violence at the hands of the various military and paramilitary forces of the Indian state.

Further, in the case of Jammu and Kashmir, where support or safe haven has been provided to insurgents against the Indian state by Pakistan, India has gone to war to put a stop to its intervention, notably after Independence in 1947–48 and again in 1965 and, for different reasons, in the short Kargil war of 1999, fought at an altitude of 16,000 feet over the issue of the "line of control" in Kashmir. It also intervened directly to bring about the secession of Bangladesh from Pakistan in the 1971 war. While India's intervention might, on the face of it, appear to undermine its own adherence to the principle of the virtually sacred unity of postcolonial states, from another point of view it is wholly consistent with that principle, for it has never accepted the legitimacy of the original partition of the subcontinent, and especially its basis in religious separatism. Its intervention against Pakistan in that case, therefore, was propelled in part by the opportunity to demonstrate the illegitimacy of the original partition and of a state whose creation was based on such a claim.

Indian leaders never tire of making claims for their status as the "world's largest democracy." As indicated already, there is much to sustain such a view of India's democratic politics, but it is a rare kind of democracy whose military forces have killed so many of its own people, perhaps 25,000 in squashing the Punjab insurrection and another 25,000 in Kashmir, and perhaps 100,000 altogether against all insurrectionary movements since Independence. As Gurharpal Singh notes (in Chapter 17), this is a democracy that uses what he calls "hegemonic control," including "cooption, accommodation and symbolic agreements" in dealing with secessionist movements, but will also resort to "violent control" whenever necessary. Nowhere has this alternation been more apparent than in the northeastern region of the country where agreement after agreement has been reached through compromises with rebel groups that never hold and are inevitably followed by renewed violence and the unbending resolve of the government of India to use in response the utmost force to suppress secessionist movements.

Secessionist movements have not been the only types that have led to strident and often violent conflicts in Indian politics. More a part of everyday politics, in fact, have been issues pertaining to the status, political power, and access to state resources of caste formations, on the one hand, and the place of the two principal religious communities, Hindus and Muslims, on the other hand. In the latter case, the issue has also increasingly become one not of secession, but of the definition of the Indian state, whether it is to be defined as a Hindu state or a secular state. While intercaste conflicts have from time to time led to intercaste violence, such violence has been sporadic and mostly local in character. Communal conflicts, in contrast, while often arising out of local conflicts, have frequently been magnified deliberately for political purposes, and have been responsible for many thousands of deaths since Independence up to the present in what are labeled Hindu–Muslim "riots." These riots have been produced or instigated by politicians from many political parties for local advantage in electoral contests since Independence. In the past 15 years, however, the BJP and its sister organizations in the RSS family of organizations have been the principal promoters of such violence in calculated efforts to demonize the Muslim population of the country and mobilize the Hindu population in order to capture power in the several states and in the Indian Union itself. It has had substantial success in doing so in the past, notably in the massive mobilization that led to the destruction of the mosque at Ayodhya in 1992. It has also been responsible for the pogrom against Muslims in the state of Gujarat in 2002, under a BJP government that deliberately instigated and promoted the violence for the purpose of shoring up its electoral base in the upcoming state election. Wilkinson (Chapter 18) and others have demonstrated clearly that the strategy did, in fact, work to produce "a crushing victory" for the BJP in the December 2002 elections. The government, and the chief minister who orchestrated the violence, remain in power to this day (2008). Wilkinson, however, argues that communal politics in India have only limited and sporadic uses whereas caste politics are central to Indian politics on an everyday basis and, one should add, remain the most important factors in most elections in most states of the country up to the present.

Indeed, there have been innumerable movements based on caste solidarities and caste antagonisms over the past century, ranging from the non-Brahman movements in southern and western India to the movements of so-called "backward classes" (a term commonly used for the middle status castes) throughout the country, and the more recent rise of "dalit" ("oppressed") and other movements of low caste groups for recognition, government employment, and access to state resources and political patronage. Indeed, the preferred method of advancing the interests of all the less privileged caste groups in Indian society has been to demand "reservations" of places for designated caste groups in the legislatures and in government service. As a result, various forms of reservation for such groups have been adopted both in the central government and in most, if not all the Indian states. While intercaste conflicts have, as noted, sometimes led to violence, for the most part the jockeying has taken place through the political process, with bidding common among political parties for the support of the more numerous caste groups during elections.

It should not, however, be imagined that the status hierarchy that has always pervaded Indian life will soon be eliminated in consequence of such policies for the benefit of the less privileged classes. In fact, the rise of a vibrant private sector economy associated with the economic liberalization process has made it possible for the upper castes, displaced from positions of power in many Indian states,

13

to retain their eminence in Indian society, for it is the upper castes who get the lucrative jobs in the fast developing private sector while government jobs—especially at the lower levels—and the lower status accompanying them are reserved for the less privileged.

It is also important to note that the primacy of caste politics in India has an effect on communal politics, mainly to undermine it. The BJP's use of communal politics in elections has been designed to consolidate the Hindu vote in areas where there is a large Muslim population that can be demonized and blamed for the riots that are, in fact, produced by BJP or BJP-recruited Hindu activists. But such unification of the Hindu castes cannot be sustained indefinitely even in particular electoral constituencies and is untenable most of the time in most constituencies in most states in the country. Further, Wilkinson notes that, in states where there are highly competitive electoral contests in which Muslims hold the potential balance in determining the outcomes, the benefits of polarizing Hindu and Muslim votes turn negative for the political parties, thereby decreasing the likelihood of Hindu–Muslim riots produced for political reasons.

Pakistan

The scale and intensity of violence in Pakistan has sometimes seemed to threaten the viability of the state itself, which, after all, was one of the very few states in the world to split apart during the period of bipolar political dominance by the United States and the Soviet Union, when it was in the interest of neither great power to allow such dramatic political changes. Yet, it remains in the interest of none at this time, with the exception of al-Qaeda, to allow such a development in Pakistan. The paradox in all this is that powerful forces remain at work internally and externally to undermine Pakistan's stability and unity, including those two states that have the greatest interest in maintaining it, namely, India and the United States: India, by its refusal even

to consider seriously any kind of settlement in Jammu and Kashmir that would involve significant concessions to Pakistan, and the United States, by its bungling, inadequate, and incompetent intervention in Afghanistan that has added to the destabilization of Pakistan and, as any knowledgeable South Asian specialist could have predicted, to the intensification of the hostile relationship between the two major South Asian countries.

But, Pakistan's issues of national unity are not at all the creations of other countries—which merely exacerbate them—but arise from the very conditions that led to its foundation and its failures to accommodate successfully regional, ethnic, and Islamic movements and their demands. The status of the Pakhtun population in the North-West Province was a problem from the beginning since its predominant leadership preferred to remain part of India, but, in the midst of the turmoil of 1947, could only boycott the referendum, which resulted in a favorable vote for Pakistan, although with a low turnout. The Khudai Khidmatgars then demanded a semi-autonomous status for the region, which was denied.[8] Many Balochistan tribal leaders, for their part, have never accepted the legitimacy of Pakistan's rule over the province, which has been a site of unending insurgency since the creation of Pakistan, although this huge territory also is internally divided by conflicts between the Baloch and Pakhtun groups. Waseem (Chapter 19) attributes the persistent conflict there and elsewhere in Pakistan to the general preference of all ruling parties and the military for "coercive strategies for unification across ethnic divisions" that stand in sharp contrast to the general policy in India of accommodation of all ethnopolitical movements that stop short of demanding secession and independence. In contrast to India, for example, Pakistan has never seriously considered federal solutions as a means of accommodating ethnonationalist demands. Banned, jailed, and otherwise disrupted by the new Pakistan state, the secular, pro-India Pakhtun movement was ultimately displaced in the NWFP by Islamist movements. Islamist movements have also been supported in Punjab and Sindh by the *mohajirs*, migrants from India, and their offspring.

Further problems have arisen as a consequence of the very basis for the creation of Pakistan, namely, the idea that it was to be a homeland for the Muslims of India. Although its founder, Mohammad Ali Jinnah, never wished for a homogenous Muslim state, that was the result of the Partition violence that led to the total transfer of the Hindu and Sikh populations from western Punjab to India and of the entire Muslim population from Punjab to Pakistan. Despite Jinnah's declaration that Pakistan was to be a secular state, not a Muslim state, the result has been the opposite. Although, in fact, most Pakistanis, like most Indians, do not wish to see Pakistan become a state based on religion, the circumstances of Pakistan's creation have enhanced the influence of the *ulema* in policy formation and encouraged the proliferation of intolerant Islamist political movements.

A further difference from India has been the predominance of one province and one ethnic collectivity, Punjab and the Punjabis, with 58 percent of the country's population. In India, in contrast, although the north Indian Hindi speakers constitute the largest single linguistic conglomeration, they have never been able to consolidate into a unified political force that would dominate the rest of the country. It never emerged "as the power base" (Waseem, in Chapter 19) of the country as has Punjab, which is also the most economically dynamic region of the country.

There is, however, in all this a commonality between India and Pakistan in one very important sense, namely, the drive in both countries to find a basis for achieving a political majority to rule in countries that are multireligious, multiethnic, and multilingual and lack an overarching sense of cultural identity. In India, that drive has been most strongly articulated by the Hindu nationalist movement of the BJP. In Pakistan, it takes the form of Islamist movements that seek to override or suppress regional, linguistic, religious, and other cultural identities— including the Islamic faultline of Sunni-Shi'a difference— and are especially favored by those groups that lack an indigenous identity, namely, the non-Punjabi *mohajirs*, most of whom settled in Sindh where "they remained unassimilated in the host community" (Waseem). Their numbers were later increased by a second influx of so-called Bihari migrants from Bangladesh after its separation from Pakistan.

Sri Lanka

The longevity and scale of killing that has arisen out of ethnic, communal, and interstate conflicts in South Asia—including the states conventionally classed as "democracies," namely, India and Sri Lanka—should give pause to their apologists. In the sorry tale of seemingly unending violent conflicts in South Asia, the civil war in Sri Lanka requires attention. The civil war itself was a direct consequence of the nationalist idea that has overtaken the world especially in the past two centuries, namely, that every territory has its rightful nation and every nation has a territory of its own. Since there are no territories in the entire world that fit such a description, this nationalist idea requires that those who do not fit the ethnic definition of the rightful owners of a particular territory be defined as minorities who are either allowed to remain on that territory at the sufferance of the rightful owners or must be evicted, if not destroyed.

The ideological backdrop to the conflicts that arise from this exclusivism are usually ignored in favor of interpretations that stress their origins in inequalities that favor one group over another or in religious or ethnic or other antagonisms. But such differences become irresolvable mainly when the issue of "right" comes to the fore, namely, who has the right to the resources and the privileges and the status of equal citizens of a common territory.

15

In Sri Lanka, conflicts that arose in part out of resentments—or better, the creation of resentments by a political elite—against the alleged inequalities in Sri Lankan society that favored Tamils over the rightful indigenous owners of the island, the Sinhalese people, became irresolvable not because the issues themselves could not be resolved, but because the dominant Sinhalese elites of all parties found it politically helpful to make use of them to gain power through elections. That there were concrete ways of resolving the conflicts was evident very early in Sri Lanka's post-Independence history in the agreements reached between Tamil and Sinhalese leaders to resolve the language issue that was the surrogate for the dispute. Those agreements, especially in 1957 and 1965, however, were never implemented because they immediately became hostage to the cries of opposing political formations that the rightful place of the Sinhalese as the dominant people on the island was being undermined.

So, what began as an "ethnic conflict" over language rights—and behind that access to government jobs—in Sri Lanka ultimately turned "into a civil war between the state and Tamil nationalist groups . . . in the late 1970s" (Uyangoda, in Chapter 20). In the intervening years, so-called ethnic riots in which mostly Tamils were killed, often with the complicity of state leaders, prepared the ground for the final transformation of the conflict. But the progression, Uyangoda notes, arose on account of the "inflexibility of Sinhalese nationalism in responding to minority ethnic grievances" and was fed in a political process whose central feature was "ethnic outbidding."

The failure to end this civil war through negotiations continued to founder on the issue of whether or not the Sinhalese people own the entire island. Its specific form revolved around whether or not the war could be ended by transforming Sri Lanka into a federal state or agreeing to regional autonomy in the Tamil regions. The possibility of agreement, however, always foundered on

the fears of the Sinhalese leaders that any such concession would be but a prelude to secession, with the unstated fear that the party that allowed such a compromise would be wiped out in the next election. By the same token, the Tamil leaders proclaimed their insistence on the right of "national self-determination" (Uyangoda) which, of course, fed the Sinhalese fears.

India's failed intervention in the conflict in the mid-1980s was itself tarnished by the same brush. Intervening in reality to protect the Tamil population of the island in order to satisfy the feelings of the Tamil politicians and people in Tamil Nadu itself, it evolved into a failed effort to crush the armed Tamil revolt in Sri Lanka. The effort itself, however, was motivated by cross-purposes: protecting Tamils while absolutely rejecting any secessionist ideas that might also cross the waters and thereby revive the long ago abandoned dream in Tamil Nadu for secession and independence from India.

That all such dreams of ethnonational homogeneity of a people and a territory are chimeras is evident in the course of the civil war itself. In every such situation, there are inevitably small or large groups of people interspersed in the contending groups, but who do not belong to either. Such is the case of the Muslims in parts of Sri Lanka, including especially the Eastern Province where they have sizable populations, but also in parts of the Northern Province. The conflict between the Sri Lankan state and the Tamils thus led to a further demand, now from the Muslims, forced, in effect, to discover their "ethnic and political identity" (Uyangoda) as well. As Rupert Emerson put it many years ago: "Who can say the nations nay, and yet who can say what nations are and when and how they may assert themselves?"[9] In the meantime, the Sri Lankan civil war continued at the highest level of intensity yet seen until the Tamil insurrection was finally crushed with huge loss of life and displacement of Tamil civilians, "with life going on pretty much 'as normal' in most of the Sinhala-dominated parts of the island."[10]

Part VI: Political economy

Discussion of issues of politics and economic development in the South Asian countries have been handled differently by the several contributors to this volume. As a result, there are two chapters specifically concerning the political economy of India (Corbridge, Chapter 21, and Breman, Chapter 22) and one on Sri Lanka (Lakshman, Chapter 23), but the discussion of economic issues in Pakistan (Burki, Chapter 6) and Bangladesh (Blair, Chapter 7) have been included within the chapters on the politics of those two countries, referenced briefly later in this chapter.

India

Major transformations are occurring in the political economy of India, heralded in the press and business magazines as the latest addition to the new global capitalist world of high growth. In India itself, the former BJP government adopted the slogan of "India Shining" to proclaim its entry into that new world. Corbridge (in Chapter 21) examines these claims as well as the explanations for the changes that have occurred. That the Indian economy (before the current (2008–09) world economic crash) had been growing at a high and steady pace not previously seen since Independence is clear. That its benefits have not reached in significant measure the poorest of India's citizens—several hundreds of millions by any measure—who continue to live in the utmost poverty and degradation is also clear. That the changes have increased, rather than lessened, inequalities in a society historically based on one of the most rigid hierarchical systems the world has ever seen is not surprising.

Most observers would probably find little to disagree with these statements. What is mainly contested are the reasons for the new growth and the means for extending its benefits to the population as a whole. Outside India, it is generally assumed that it is economic liberalization, the freeing of the Indian economy from the constraints of state-directed, planned economic growth that is responsible for these changes. Within India, however, where the Left is not dead, it is argued that the earlier stage of planned economic growth laid the basis for the current surge, which would not have been possible without the previous public investments. The argument itself may appear academic, but it carries forward to the present in policy debates concerning the second issue of extending the benefits of the new growth. Can it really be believed, in the jargon of the acolytes of Milton Friedman, that the rising tide of growth and prosperity will "lift all boats," that public spending on health, education, and other forms of welfare cannot do the trick and that all these matters are best left for the private sector to resolve?

In fact, these are issues of ideological belief that cannot be resolved theoretically. What can be shown are the specific consequences of past and present economic policies for categories of people. Who benefited and who lost or were left behind by the developmental policies of the first decades after Indian Independence and what groups in the population are benefiting or losing now from the new liberalization policies? There is a consensus that crosses ideological dispositions that the beneficiaries of the developmental regime were the "richer farmers," the "industrial bourgeoisie," and "the country's leading bureaucrats" who profited from the corrupt income generated through the "permit-license-quota Raj" (Corbridge). The losers and those who gained little or nothing were mainly the poor and landless in the countryside. With regard to the present, under the liberalization regime, it is clear enough already that the main beneficiaries are the global

17

corporations, the high caste English-speaking Indians who find jobs in those corporations, indigenous entrepreneurs freed from the restraints of the development regime, a loosely defined urban middle class with rising incomes that enable them at last to obtain easily the cherished goods of modernity—refrigerators, TVs, automobiles for the richer among them, and the like. The losers remain the same: the poor, the landless, the "lower" castes, those displaced from their land by land grabs supported by the state to construct large dams or to benefit entrepreneurs and corporations, safely ensconced in "special economic zones." In brief, as Corbridge summarizes the matter: "The net effect of the reforms has been to widen the gulf between rich and poor people in India, and between rich and poor regions, but that was always going to be the case."

Another way of putting the matter is to say that the *varna* system is constantly reproduced in India, that the benefits of economic growth will go virtually exclusively to the upper castes, that the political order will become increasingly marginalized with the economy dominated by the ruling classes and the vast majority of rural and urban poor experiencing marginal benefits and continued grinding poverty.

In this context, Breman (Chapter 22) provides a reality check. What really are the conditions of life in "Shining India" for the wretched of the earth, the poorest of the poor, the laborers in agriculture? Agricultural policy in India in the post-Independence period focused primarily on eliminating the dominant tax farmers in the countryside and replacing them with a countryside dominated by a self-sufficient middle peasantry. Very little was done to improve the living and working conditions of the landless poor. Instead, they were offered a *chapati* in the sky of a bright future as factory laborers in a soon to be developed urban economy. In fact, however, most of those who have moved to the cities have merely shifted their underclass status to an equally wretched urban environment,

while those, the vast majority, who have remained in the countryside, continue to live a bleak subaltern life of labor for pay insufficient for decent nourishment of themselves and their families while faced with physical beatings from their overlords should they dare to protest or demand higher wages or even the legally mandated wage. Many of those who leave the land do not migrate to the city, but to backbreaking "unskilled jobs such as digging, hauling and lifting work" for which they get paid little more than the prevailing wage for agricultural labor (Breman).

Yet, however wretched the contemporary existence of the landless, there has been some improvement in their condition from the 1960s and 1970s: marginally better living quarters and nourishment, some elementary education, and some improvement in health care. Many of these improvements, however minimal, have come about through the political process as the Congress, especially during the heyday of Indira Gandhi, provided specific benefits for the landless laborers, including tiny plots of land on which to build their homes. In Uttar Pradesh, where the BSP, under the leadership of Mayawati, has provided considerable funding for the improvement of the lives of the lowest castes in the villages as well as employment opportunities in government service (including most significantly in the police) the status and assertiveness of the lowest castes has decidedly increased.

Yet, the bulk of the population classified as living below the famous "poverty line" continues to come from this class of landless poor. How then to summarize the improvement in living conditions for the poorest compared to their past wretchedness? In a word, however much conditions have improved, the gap between the poorest and those who live a comfortable—or luxurious—life has increased so that there is "even greater inequity than before" (Breman). Not only that, the Indian countryside continues to harbor large "landless colonies" whose populations consist of paupers and lumpen elements, living a "sub-human existence" without hope of any improvement for themselves or their children. Neither can the statistics of the government of India concerning the reduction in poverty in India be taken at face value for two reasons: first, they ignore the question of how decent life is, in fact, just above the poverty line. Second, as Breman has suggested, it is very likely that the data are being cooked to fit the image of "Shining India." Finally, Breman argues very strongly that a combination of a policy of "market fundamentalism" in a society with "an ingrained ideology of social inequality are a deadly combination" that offers little or no improvement in any near future for the poorest of the poor.

Sri Lanka

The political economy of Sri Lanka has differed in many ways from that of India and the other countries in the South Asian region. For one thing, a small island republic, it was, during British rule, a classic "tropical" export economy, "an export economy par excellence" (Lakshman, Chapter 23) based on estate tea cultivation and "other primary commodities" such as coconut and rubber. Sri Lanka's social economy has also differed significantly from that of India in its emphasis on "social expenditures programs," namely, education, health, and food subsidies. In consequence, Sri Lanka, in sharp contrast to the rest of South Asia has had a very high PQLI (Physical Quality of Life Index), as high as 82 in the early 1980s.

In other respects, however, Sri Lanka has followed a somewhat similar track to that of India and other developing economies, namely, a movement from "import substitution" to liberalization. Throughout the post-Independence period, however, the performance of the Sri Lankan economy has been, as Lakshman puts it, "lackluster." Meanwhile, however, there has been a significant reduction in the share of the economy contributed by primary agricultural production, although

it remains relatively high even now in both percentage of GDP and total employment in the country. The social consequences of the shift to liberalization policies has, of course, increased income inequalities, enriching the already rich and the newly rich and concentrating wealth in the hands of entrepreneurs, politicians, and high level bureaucrats. Contrariwise, the poverty ratio has hardly changed during the past 20 years, remaining at "around 20–25 percent." Overall, however, the Sri Lankan combination of a liberalization regime with significant social welfare benefits stands in sharp contrast to the tremendous inequalities and degradation of life for the poorest in most of India, a contrast that is starkly visible in the obvious differences in the quality of human life to anyone who spends some time in both countries. That the same combination could work in India is evident also in the Indian state of Kerala, where the quality of life is at least equal to that of Sri Lanka, if not even better.

Pakistan

In Chapter 6, Burki has noted that, in the repeated alternations of power between the military and the politicians in Pakistan, the latter have failed miserably to promote either responsible government or economic development. All the political leaders of the last several decades, from Bhutto *père* to Bhutto *fille* to Zardari and Nawaz Sharif have amassed enormous wealth and property by—to put it mildly—quite dubious means. Burki has placed great importance on the failures of the regimes led by the politicians to produce economic results as favorable as those produced by the military regimes (with, of course, American economic aid) as a factor in the acceptance by the public of the repeated interventions by the military.

Bangladesh

Throughout all the political changes, at least since the 1990s, and despite the instability and corruption, the Bangladesh economy, still overwhelmingly dominated by the agricultural sector, has done well, a paradox (Blair, Chapter 7) for which there is no easy explanation, although clearly massive foreign aid has had a great deal to do with it. Whatever the reasons, Blair notes that there has been a significant rise in foodgrain production during the past two decades, which translates into greater "food availability per capita" at reduced prices; some movement in "off-farm" sectors such as "transportation, construction, [and] retailing," leading to some upswing in wages; and a significant overall drop in "the proportion of rural workers whose primary occupation was in agriculture." Blair attributes these favorable results to a combination of policy changes towards a liberalization regime, fortified initially by massive foreign aid, both of which overrode—providing the paradox—the obvious "misgovernance" in the country since Independence.

Part VII: Comparative chapters

Civil–military relations

The similarities and differences among the states of South Asia are brought out especially clearly in the comparative chapters in this volume. One of the most distressing features of "development" in virtually all postcolonial countries has been the growth in importance of the military, not only or even especially to prepare for battle with foreign enemies, but for the purpose of controlling their own populations and quelling protest movements amongst them.

India and Pakistan inherited substantial military forces (Cohen, Chapter 24), including considerable elements with experience in battle in the Second World War. The Bangladesh component of those forces, however, was quite

minimal. Sri Lanka had only very small military forces. However, in the latter cases, the military have vastly expanded in size, power, and importance since Independence, decisive in politics in Bangladesh in fact, although firmly under the control of the civilian power in Sri Lanka. Moreover, the two largest countries in the region, India and Pakistan, have been engaged for many years in a nuclear arms race, subterranean for decades, but marked by blatant displays of their existence from time to time, beginning with the travesty of India's first "peaceful nuclear explosion" in 1974 and culminating in the successive nuclear explosions by both India and Pakistan in 1998. Neither have the two enemies shrunk on several occasions from making outright nuclear threats (Cohen).

The dispersion of military forces in South Asia has, moreover, gone far beyond traditional forms in Weberian states that maintain a monopoly of the legitimate use of force. There has been, in addition, a proliferation of paramilitary forces, some under the control of the state, others maintained surreptitiously by the state, and still others engaged in rebellion against the state, and in some cases, especially Sri Lanka, in the form of outright civil war. In Nepal, a Maoist insurrectionary force succeeded in 2007 in holding their own[11] against the weak and "ineffective" (Cohen) Royal Nepal Army, thereby bringing about the downfall of the king and the transformation of the political regime towards parliamentary rule.

Although India has experienced the proliferation and dispersion of various military elements, it has maintained absolute and unchallenged civilian control over the state military forces. Sri Lanka, too, has largely maintained civilian control over the military, with the exception of one farcical near coup d'état attempt in 1962 that was "called off" at the eleventh hour.[12] At the same time, the very extensive use of the military in dealing with "domestic violence" (Cohen) in both these countries and the very considerable military expenditures lavished on the military forces in them is part of the common pattern in the region. Moreover, it is rather a well-kept secret that Sikh forces posted in northern India engaged in outright mutiny at the time of the Indian army's assault on the Golden Temple in Amritsar in 1984 and had to be rounded up as they sought to head towards Amritsar.[13]

Corruption and criminalization

The differences among the South Asian countries with regard to corruption and the criminalization of politics are rather less than their differences with regard to the role of the military. All countries in the region rank high on the various indexes of global corruption, although Pakistan, Bangladesh, and Nepal persistently rank higher than either India or Sri Lanka. The literature on corruption in South Asia differs in its assessment of its consequences. Kochanek (Chapter 25) argues that it has negative consequences for economic growth, while others suggest that corruption has it uses, not merely in greasing palms, but in greasing the wheels of government to speed up economic development projects. Thus, the term "speed money" has been used in South Asia, as elsewhere, to summarize its positive effects.

Right-wing and laissez-faire economists, of course, blame the developmental state for the high incidence of corruption in postcolonial societies. Kochanek agrees. Further, the stakes have become sufficiently high in the developmental states of South Asia, where control over the distributional resources of the state has become the primary aim of nearly all politicians, so much so that the political process itself has become increasingly criminalized.

Any assessment of the state of democratic politics in South Asia that fails to note the pervasiveness of corruption and criminality that permeates all levels of the state and the electoral process itself must be considered deficient. In Bangladesh, criminality and violence are integral to ensuring success in elections. In Pakistan, several of its heads of state have had well-established records of massive corruption. Even India, where most heads of state have had reputations for honesty, Indira Gandhi, Rajiv Gandhi, and Narasimha Rao all had dubious records in these respects.

Like all other features of the developmental state, the corruption system promotes inequality. The principal beneficiaries are those who have "money, status, and connections" (Kochanek). Those who cannot pay, the poorest, are unlikely to receive even those benefits that are specifically designated for them.

Radical and violent political movements

The states of South Asia, in common with other postcolonial states, have all faced, and continue to face violent insurrectionary movements that challenge the authority, legitimacy, and/or the boundaries of the existing states. The parliamentary systems, India and Sri Lanka—as the chapters on pluralism and national integration illustrate—have been no different in this regard from the others. But there have been other forms of violent challenge to the states of South Asia, common primarily to India and Nepal, namely, challenges to state authority coming from radical leftist and Communist movements, called in India "Naxalites" and also, in both India and Nepal, "Maoists." Nor, as Banerjee points out in Chapter 26, has India been able "to resolve them through a democratic process," whereas, in Nepal (2008), such a process is already underway (Hachhethu and Gellner; see Chapter 9).

But the rebellions against state authority in India do not threaten the authority and power of the Indian state to anything like the extent they have in Nepal. In fact, the earliest rebellions, including especially those promoted by the Communist parties in Telangana and elsewhere, were either defeated by Indian armed force or their leadership was integrated into the parliamentary process. Both the earlier and the current anti-state violence has come from "the most desperate segments of the population who have remained deprived of the benefits of development following Independence, and who find that the prevailing ruling system has failed to fulfill its promises" (Banerjee). They have also drawn support disproportionately from the most marginal segments of society—especially tribal populations living in the more remote areas of the country—while articulating the broader "demands of the poor and landless peasantry" in general (Banerjee).

Reports are periodically published by various groups showing that a large swath of territory down through the middle of the country has been experiencing or is continuing to experience violent insurrectionary movements, including the assertion of control over isolated pockets. There is even a weekly death count for the states of Andhra Pradesh, Bihar, Chattisgarh, Jharkand, and Orissa—areas said to be infested by "left-wing extremism"—published by the right-wing, authoritarian online journal, *South Asia Intelligence*. Banerjee also asserts that the current leading organization promoting "guerilla war" against the Indian state maintains effective control over large swaths of Indian territory, exceeding even the area under the effective control of rebel groups in the northeastern part of India discussed by Gurharpal Singh (Chapter 17). As yet, however, these violent, mostly agrarian movements, pose no serious threat to the stability and power of the Indian state, which retains the capacity, if it chooses to exercise it with full force, to decimate, if not crush them all. The government of India also retains the nonviolent ability, successfully exercised from time to time, to adopt "reformist measures" (Banerjee) that undercut movements against its authority. At present, however, the tendency on the part of the GOI is more towards the use of increased force that includes the tried and tested Indian police tactic of cornering and killing groups

of rebels and "their sympathizers" in what are euphemistically called "encounters," but in which the gunfire is only in one direction. The Indian government has also perfected a tactic in the northeast that was used by the United States in Vietnam: village "pacification," which, of course, translates into "razing of tribal hamlets," just as the US burned Vietnamese villages to the ground. For these and so many other reasons noted by Banerjee, the Maoists in India cannot achieve the success of their counterparts in Nepal.

International politics of South Asia

Perhaps the most striking feature of international politics and interstate relations in South Asia is the extent to which they arise and are overwhelmingly influenced by domestic considerations. That is to say not that popular domestic opinion influences policy so much as that issues concerning the sovereignty and boundaries of the states of the region are all contested. It is also to say that even relations between the states of South Asia and extra-regional actors during most of the period since Independence have revolved around domestic issues. Although Nehru and his successors sought to formulate a distinctive foreign policy in relation to the world system, namely, nonalignment, even these efforts turned into another aspect of interstate relations in the region. For, whatever India did, Pakistan did the opposite, in this case turning towards outright alignment with the United States in the Cold War. This in turn influenced India's own policies, which increasingly then "tilted" towards semi-alignment with the Soviet Union, culminating in the 1971 Friendship Treaty, which also arose at a time when India was about to go to war to dismember Pakistan.

The states of the region, the least integrated region in the world, where even trade relations and travel from one state to the other have often been highly restricted, have sought external relations and alliances not only or even primarily for their own sake, but to counter the moves of regional enemies and/or dependencies.

The linchpin around which so much has turned in South Asian history and international politics is, of course, the unending conflict between India and Pakistan over the status of Kashmir, which, in turn, has been so bitter because it reflects the fundamental conflict over the very definition of the two states and even—in the eyes of many in India—not just who should have sovereignty over Kashmir but whether Pakistan itself even has the right to exist. This conflict alone has spawned four wars between the two countries, including one that led to the breakup of Pakistan and the creation of Bangladesh as an independent state.

Further, the policies of the states are heavily influenced by internal domestic conflicts such as those described in several chapters in this volume, and discussed earlier. As Hewitt has put it: "The states of South Asia . . . must be concerned as much with securing the state from its own populations as from other states, and from competing sub-nationalist claims and ethnic separatism" (see Chapter 27).

Moreover, the interplay between domestic and international considerations in South Asia, most especially between India and Pakistan, continues to be reflected in the current "War on Terror," which, like the older Cold War, draws into its net states around the world that make use of it to pursue their own interests. So, India now seeks to tar Pakistan with the brush of support for "terrorists" in what its leaders describe as cross-border attacks in Indian-held Kashmir and bomb attacks within India itself while Pakistan, as always, supports American interests largely for the sake of feeding the insatiable demands of its army, whose eyes are always turned primarily towards India and Kashmir and preparation for the next war with India. In this contest, the "subtext," as it were, in America's war against terrorism in Afghanistan is the struggle between India and Pakistan for influence and control in that country.

Neither has this interpenetration of domestic concerns and regional interstate relations been restricted to Indo-Pakistan relations. They affect as well relations between these two countries with the other states of the region, each of the two large states opposing whatever action the other takes in Bangladesh, Sri Lanka, Nepal, Bhutan or even in the Maldives. However, in relation to all these states, India remains the predominant power, far overshadowing Pakistan, despite the fact that relations between India and Bangladesh have deteriorated considerably since the halcyon days of India's support for Bangladesh's Independence and that India's dominance and intervention have also been resented in Nepal and Sri Lanka from time to time.

Notes

1 Personal communication.
2 Especially important in this regard have been the movements launched by the militant Hindu organizations that are ostensibly non-violent, but are in fact deliberately provocative and generally productive either of violence between Hindus and Muslims or outright victimization and killing of Muslims, with the aid of the police.
3 The leading source of such writings is the Center for the Study of Developing Societies (CSDS) in Delhi, and especially those of Yogendra Yadav.
4 Paul R. Brass, *Caste, Faction, and Party in Indian Politics*, Vol. II: *Election Studies* (New Delhi: Chanakya, 1985).
5 Kanchan Chandra, *Why Ethnic Parties Succeed, Patronage and Ethnic Head Counts in India* (Cambridge: University Press, 2004).
6 Paul R. Brass, "Pluralism, Regionalism and Decentralizing Tendencies in Contemporary Indian Politics," in A. Jeyaratnam Wilson and Dennis Dalton (eds), *The States of South Asia: Problems of National Integration* (London: Hurst, 1982), pp. 223–64; revised and updated in Paul R. Brass, *Ethnicity and Nationalism: Theory and Comparison* (New Delhi: Sage, 1991), pp. 114–66.

7 Paul R. Brass, *Language, Religion, and Politics in North India* (Cambridge: University Press, 1974).

8 Mukulika Banerjee, *The Pathan Unarmed* (Oxford: James Currey, 2000).

9 Rupert Emerson, *From Empire to Nation: The Rise to Self-Assertion of Asian and African Peoples* (Boston: Beacon, 1960), p. 297.

10 Comment from David Gellner.

11 In a personal communication, Gellner notes that the Maoists "held their own" against the Nepal army, "but they were not capable of overrunning it—and it was the realization that military victory was not possible, along with strong pressure from India, which persuaded the Maoist leaders to join the parties in overthrowing the King."

12 Donald Horowitz, *Coup Theories and Officers' Motives: Sri Lanka in Comparative Perspective* (Princeton, NJ: University Press, 1980).

13 Personal interview.

Part I

Colonialism, Nationalism, and Independence in South Asia

India, Pakistan, and Sri Lanka

2

India and Pakistan

Ian Talbot

Contemporary political developments, in the Indian subcontinent as elsewhere, can only be fully appreciated in their historical context. Whether it is the case of the predominance of the army in Pakistan politics, or the periodical outbreaks of communal rioting in some north Indian towns and cities, understanding requires an assessment of the inheritances from the colonial era. These encompass not only the ideas and institutions the British bequeathed, but the legacies arising from the nationalist struggle and from the 1947 division of the subcontinent. These three legacies form the focus of this article. We will turn first to the colonial inheritance.

The colonial impact

The colonial state introduced educated Indians to western concerns with progress, technological mastery over nature and the ideals of democracy and nationhood. These were made available through the medium of English which, for the elite, enabled communication across regional and religious barriers to a much greater extent than either the Mughal court language of Persian or the hybrid Hindustani had previously done. New institutions included not just an intrusive state

organized around the principles of bureaucratic rationalism, but representative political bodies at local, district, provincial, and national levels. At the heart of socioeconomic transformation was a communications revolution resulting from improved roads, the introduction of railways, and the explosion of print.[1] This impact was qualitatively different from the earlier Mughal construction of canals and the fabled Grand Trunk Road, which helped to unify the subcontinent. Under the British, not only goods and people, but ideas circulated more rapidly than ever before. Western notions of community and nation were so powerful precisely because they were linked with European technological accomplishments.

The early generation of western-educated Indians regarded the British presence as progressive. For this reason, they distanced themselves from the "traditionalist" uprising of 1857, which the British ruthlessly crushed. It was only a later generation of educated Indians who sought to portray the uprising as the first war of Indian national liberation. They had become disillusioned by the British failure to live up to their self-proclaimed virtues of justice and fair play. Illiberalism and racism, in fact, lay barely concealed behind the façade of high moral purpose. It was only in the wake of Gandhi's rise to power, however, that nationalist struggle was transformed from an elite to a mass undertaking. Non-violent struggle exposed the Raj's authoritarianism to the world's gaze.

The colonial state differed from its Mughal predecessor both in terms of its coercive capacity and the relationship between knowledge and power. "Orientalist empiricism," with its plethora of land settlement reports, caste handbooks, and census reports provided the knowledge to control the colonized. It also bolstered "traditional" institutions and social structures by, for example, codifying customary law. It could be argued that British rule had a "traditionalizing" as well as a modernizing effect by bolstering patriarchy, caste, and tribal identity. It is undoubtedly true that despite colonial stereotypes of a "changeless" India, many of the hierarchies that were in place by 1947 were of modern rather than ancient origin.

Orientalist philological studies provided the basis for ideas of both a Vedic and Dravidian golden age. The later developments of Hindu and Tamil nationalism cannot be fully appreciated without reference to the legacies of such Orientalist scholars as Max Müller and Robert Caldwell. The German-born Müller, who never set foot in the subcontinent, maintained that an "instinctive monotheism" was present in the early hymns of the Rigveda and that modern forms of Hinduism were the result of subsequent "decadent opulence." Such ideas were taken up by Indian writers, who contrasted current degradation with the golden Vedic past and linked a return to its "pristine" Hinduism with the recovery of national glory. The lesser known Reverend Robert Caldwell argued for the antiquity of Tamil and maintained that Aryan colonists had introduced idol worship to South India and had termed the indigenous Tamilian chieftains, soldiers and cultivators as sudras. The demand that the term sudra should be dropped for the Tamil castes was to become a major element of the later non-Brahman movement. It was soon to espouse

a new radicalism with the foundation of the *Suyamariyatai iyakkam*, the self-respect movement.

Considerable scholarly interest has focused on the effects of the introduction of the decennial census.[2] This was the crowning glory of the colonial rational bureaucratic state and of "Orientalist empiricism." The censuses that were conducted throughout India from 1881 onwards can be understood in Saidean terms as the "expropriation" of knowledge in order to sustain colonial control. Their greatest significance was to solidify previously "fuzzy" boundaries between different group identities. Multiple identities and fluid boundaries were replaced by essentialized categories of caste and religious community. The process was graphically illustrated in 1911 when Indian Census Commissioner E. A. Gait rapped the Bombay census superintendent over the knuckles for using the hybrid term "Hindu-Muhammadans" for groups that did not fit easily into any category. The persons concerned, Gait remarked, should have been assigned to "one religion or the other as best he could." Census requirements for clear self-definition were key elements in encouraging religious revivalisms, which attacked what Harjot Oberoi has termed the "enchanted world" of pluralism.[3]

Simultaneously, patronage was disbursed in terms of defined religious categories and demographic strength was for the first time linked with political power following the introduction of representative politics. Good governance was primarily to be secured through the activities of the civil administration. Nevertheless, part of the rationale for British rule was the tutelage of Indians in the democratic arts. Moreover, the recurring financial crises of the 1880s encouraged the establishment of a system of elective local government to secure consent for additional taxation. Local bodies could form new "arenas of conflict" for communal rivalries, especially where socioeconomic change was unsettling old power arrangements. This process could be seen at work in a number of towns in western UP where elected Hindu majorities on district boards used sanitation regulations to control butchers' shops and slaughterhouses to further their religious interests by protecting cows. Such actions offended the local Muslim religious sensibilities in such places as Moradabad, Chandpur, and Bijnor and revealed the perils they faced as a religious minority.[4]

British ideas of monolithically constituted religious communities were institutionalized in the granting of separate electorates for Muslims in 1909 and, later, following the 1932 Communal Award for Sikhs. The historical debate still rages whether this was part of a Machiavellian divide and rule policy or merely reflected a colonial balancing act. While the creation of Muslim separate electorates did not make Pakistan inevitable, it encouraged the premise lying behind communalism that people following a particular religion naturally shared common interests from which others were excluded. Those seeking power took their cue and mobilized politically around the symbols of religion, which had received state recognition as important community markers. For many scholars, communalism which culminated in the 1947 Partition is seen as an important legacy of colonial rule.[5]

Less contentious is the claim that important institutional inheritances from the Raj smoothed the path of nation building in India and Pakistan. Both the Indian and the Pakistan Administrative Services inherited the traditions of the so-called "steel frame" of the Raj, the Indian Civil Service. Until the two countries introduced their first post-Independence constitutions, they were governed under the terms of the 1935 Government of India Act. India's 1950 constitution retained the federal structure of government it had established.

The differential impact of imperial rule

A number of writers have found India and Pakistan's contrasting democratic experiences striking, given the assumption that they acquired almost identical intellectual and administrative inheritances from the colonial state.[6] The colonial impacts we have been considering in the preceding paragraphs were not, however, spread evenly. The differential effects of colonial rule with respect to both socioeconomic transformation and administrative systems were to exert a profound influence. The politics of Muslim separatism in colonial north India and of the anti-Brahman movement in the south, for example, were influenced by the domination of Hindu upper caste males over the new educational opportunities. Those regions and communities which lagged behind in the processes of socioeconomic change in late nineteenth-century India have struggled to catch up since Independence. West Bengal was at one stage a leading commercial region, but its relative post-Independence decline dates back to the decision to move the imperial capital from Calcutta to New Delhi in 1911. It is possible to argue that contemporary Pakistan's "overdeveloped" administrative and military institutions in comparison with India's stronger political institutionalization are rooted, at least in part, in differences in the colonial impact. Khalid bin Sayeed first summed up the greater British emphasis on the requirements of law and order rather than those of popular representation in the future Pakistan areas in terms of the concept of "viceregalism."[7] I have expanded this argument to conceptualize the inheritance of a British security state in northwest India in which political participation was far less developed than in other areas of the subcontinent.[8] The colonial priority in this region was to maintain law and order; the encouragement of political representation was a secondary consideration. Hence elected bodies came into being later, if at all in the case of Balochistan.

With the notable exception of Bengal, the future Pakistan areas lay in the security state region. They had been acquired for strategic rather than commercial reasons in the face of a threat of Russian expansion from Central Asia and Afghanistan and were accordingly administered along "viceregal" lines.[9] Adjoining both British Balochistan and the North-West Frontier Province was a buffer zone of tribal states and tribal areas. The former were under the exclusive jurisdiction of their hereditary rulers and were among the most backward areas of the subcontinent at the time of Independence. The latter were overseen by a British political agent. Control was maintained by tribal levies with the carrot of cash subsidies and the stick of punitive expeditions and collective fines. Customary law enforced through tribal *jirgas* was the order of the day. A similar system of administrative authoritarianism and the co-opting of traditional elites was followed in the directly administered provinces of Balochistan and the North-West Frontier Province. The latter was eventually to achieve responsible government, after widespread unrest in 1930–32, but Balochistan remained tied to the apron strings of its commissioner down to Independence. Within the Frontier, deputy commissioners wielded immense authority under the terms of the Frontier Crimes Regulation. They could refer civil and criminal cases to *jirgas*, which they had appointed, and they were also empowered to impose collective punishments. The loyalty of the large Khan clan was secured though a mix of "political pensions," honorific titles, and cash and land grants.

Punjab landowners were the recipients of similar rewards. The region's strategic significance increased when it became the main recruiting area of the Indian Army from the 1880s.[10] The decision to shift recruiting operations to Punjab was based on a variety of strategic, political and financial implications. It was rationalized in the martial castes ideology. The belief that the Muslim Rajputs, Sikh Jats and Hindu Dogras of Punjab were naturally suited for military service was based on "empirical" ethnographic research. Recruiting officers produced detailed caste handbooks that provided genealogies and histories of the martial castes, all set within a fashionable late nineteenth-century Social Darwinist framework. While the post-Independence Indian Army has widened its recruiting base, the bulk of the Pakistan Army recruits are drawn from a narrow range of communities and districts within Punjab. This has exerted a profound impact on political developments in terms both of sections of Punjabi society's identification with the military and in the encouragement it has given to the idea held by non-recruited communities that there has been a "Punjabization" of Pakistan.[11]

The simultaneous development of the vast canal colony areas in late nineteenth-century Punjab dramatically increased the resources with which the colonial state could patronize its rural allies.[12] In Punjab, and also in the Frontier, the colonial state abandoned economic laissez-faire principles to curb the predatory activities of moneylenders, which threatened the growing prosperity of its local allies. Moreover, whenever the principle of election was conceded, the British safeguarded the position of their rural allies by linking the right to vote with property qualifications and introducing special landholders' constituencies. Significantly, ex-servicemen were disproportionately represented both as landowners in the rich canal colony areas and as voters. The entrenchment of elites considered loyal to the Raj continues to influence contemporary Pakistan politics. This undermined the development of a strong political party system. It also reinforced a culture of political clientelism and placed insuperable barriers in the way of future socioeconomic reform by establishing the basis for a dominant landlord political interest. This was to form a marked contrast with the inheritance of those areas which went to India at the time of the 1947 Partition. In those areas, it was rich peasants rather than feudal landowners who dominated rural politics.

The shadow side of British paternalism was the violent repression of any perceived challenge to the status quo. Provincial administrations of the future West Pakistan areas all had blood on their hands and a tradition of calling on the army to aid civil power. The most infamous incident was, of course, the firing on an unarmed crowd in the walled area of Jallianwala Bagh in Amritsar on 13 April, 1919.

In sum, in much of what was to become Pakistan, a tradition of bureaucratic authoritarianism, along with the upholding of traditional elites, was deeply rooted by the time of the British departure. In Punjab, the future heartland of Pakistan, a special relationship between the peasantry and the army had been established which, as Clive Dewey has forcefully argued, holds the key to understanding military dominance in independent Pakistan.[13] The tradition of ruthless repression of unrest had also been established. Significantly, such leading Pakistani administrative and political figures of the 1950s as Chaudhri Muhammad Ali, Ghulam Muhammad, and Iskander Mirza had spent the formative parts of their careers in this atmosphere.[14] The differential inheritances in the future Indian and Pakistan areas of the subcontinent thus explain in part the variations in political experience of the two successors to the Raj.

The legacy of nationalist struggle

India's democratic "exceptionalism" among former European colonies has been linked by some writers to legacies from the nationalist struggle.[15] These included a highly institutionalized political party in the Indian National Congress, which reached down into the villages. The narrow support base of the nineteenth century had been transformed by Gandhi's leadership. At the same time, his genius in fundraising had allowed the establishment of a cadre of paid political workers.

The adherence of Congress to both the electoral politics of legislative council entry, on the one hand, and mass agitation, on the other hand, had ensured that it was not merely an oppositional force, but had produced leaders schooled in the arts of government. Finally, the post-independence ability to oversee nation building was enhanced by the legitimacy of its leaders who had been prepared to spend years in prison as part of their sacrifice for the greater cause of freedom.

Gandhi lay at the heart of both the institutional transformation of Congress at the 1920 Nagpur Session and of the widening of its popular appeal.[16] He was a charismatic figure who embodied the unique philosophy of non-violence that he brought to the struggle. Non-violence was remarkably successful as a strategy against a ruling power that prided itself on the moral authority to govern. It also allayed the fears of the propertied classes that independence would go hand in hand with social revolution. Significantly, the upper caste business and industrial classes under Gandhi's moral sway bankrolled Congress. Between 1921 and 1923, Congress collected over Rs 13 million. This huge war chest funded Gandhi's "constructive program" of khadi (the production and wearing of homespun cloth) and the removal of Untouchability as well as Congress political campaigns under his leadership. It made possible the new phenomenon of the full-time Congressite political worker. By the eve of the Second World War, the Congress possessed a membership of over four and a half million. No anti-colonial nationalist movement elsewhere was ever to attain this level of support. Gandhi introduced new groups and regions into the nationalist struggle. D. A. Low has seen the alliance between the rich peasants, the educated classes and the commercial classes as being of crucial importance.[17] Gandhi also appealed for female support as he believed that women naturally possessed the ability to suffer and the moral strength required in non-violent struggle.[18]

Women were especially drawn to the idealism of the nationalist struggle, whether this was expressed in terms of Gandhian philosophy, or in the socialism of Nehru and the Congress left wing. Thousands of Congress activists had demonstrated their commitment to a free India by submitting to the blows of the police and to extended periods of imprisonment. As Gopal Krishna has remarked:

> The significant difference between the pre-1920 and the post-1920 Congress leadership lay in the fact that before 1920 it was social position which automatically conferred a leading position in the movement; after 1920 it was the renunciation of social position and the demonstration of willingness to accept that sacrifice was demanded of those who aspired to lead.[19]

Jawaharlal Nehru, independent India's first prime minister, spent several periods of imprisonment in the early 1920s and 1930s. His longest incarceration following the Quit India Resolution of 1942 lasted for three years. During this period he wrote his most important work, *The Discovery of India*. Nehru's imprisonment, as well as that of countless lower rank Congressmen, created a high public service ethos when India attained freedom in August 1947. It also ensured that the prestige of the Congress surpassed that of all other parties. This, in part, explains its electoral successes throughout the 1950s.

Congress had combined agitation with the working of the legislatures in the provinces which the British had introduced from the time of the 1919 Government of India Act. This approach to politics has been dubbed a "struggle–truce–struggle" strategy. It enabled Congress to wear down the Raj's stock of moral and political capital while at the same time providing Indian politicians with the opportunity to acquire experience of government. This was one factor in the greater success of Congress, compared with many of its counterparts in Asia and Africa, in making the postcolonial switch from an oppositional force to a party of government. Council entry was, however, not without its drawbacks, as it opened the way for factional rivalries between the so-called ministerial and organizational wings of the party. Indeed, the decision of the High Command to ask for the resignation of the provincial ministries in the wake of Viceroy Lord Linlithgow's unilateral declaration in 1939 that India was at war, proclaimed without consulting Indian opinion, can be understood as a useful release from these growing tensions.

The visions of Nehru and Gandhi for an independent India were markedly different. The possibility of conflict was terminated by Gandhi's assassination on 30 January, 1948. His anarchist vision of a decentralized polity and economy based on the village was reduced to the margins of the nationalist enterprise, although the Mahatma was mythologized as the founder of the nation. Nehru based his nation-building enterprise on the vision first articulated during the independence movement. It sought to clothe the country in the "garb of modernity." At the heart of the Nehruvian vision was commitment to democracy, secularism, statism, and socialism. In the international arena, he espoused a commitment to non-alignment. By the 1980s all these foundational ideas had been challenged by the rise of militant Hinduism, which articulated concerns about Islamization in Iran and Pakistan, increasing Indian Muslim linkages with the oil-rich Gulf region, and resentment about the alleged "pampering" of the Muslim minority. But the clear vision of the early post-independence period was undoubtedly a factor in ensuring stability. Unlike many other nationalist movements, power had been seized from the departing rulers not for its own sake, but to bring about a major transformation. Despite their conflicting ideas, Gandhi and Nehru shared the belief that independence should mean a major break with the colonial past and that India's freedom could act as a source of inspiration well beyond its national borders.

While the seeds for India's democratic success were sown during the nationalist struggle, there were also warning signs for the future. Hindu nationalist sentiments had always been coeval with the territorial nationalism of Congress. Many within the organization's broad tent profoundly differed from Nehru's secularist approach. Congress also contained hegemonic tendencies that made it difficult for the minorities to be accepted on anything other than the majority's terms. The partition-related upheavals were to increase hostility to the Muslim "other" well beyond the narrow bounds of such communal organizations as the Hindu Mahasabha.[20] Indeed, for Gandhi, at least, partition represented a defeat for all that he believed in, causing him to dub freedom a "bitter loaf."

The legacy of the Pakistan movement

The movement for Pakistan, like that for Indian independence, was to provide an important political inheritance. It was not, however, to exert as favourable an impact for future democratic consolidation and nation building. The Muslim League was not as firmly institutionalized as Congress. Neither did its leaders possess a similar experience of government. In the key areas that were to form Pakistan, the Muslim League was a relative latecomer. Apart from Bengal, the party had failed dismally in the Muslim majority provinces in the 1937 provincial elections. In order to achieve a breakthrough in the 1946 polls, it had been forced to compromise with traditionalist systems of clientelist politics. Within its ranks there was much greater opportunism and lack of a public service ideal than was evident in Congress. The party was thus less well equipped on a number of counts to perform the tasks of political development. This was a crucial weakness in the light of the

"democratic deficit" that had accrued as a result of viceregal traditions inherited in the areas that were to form Pakistan.

It was only in Bengal that the Muslim League possessed a mass base of support and an organization of full-time workers similar to that of Congress. This was the result of the efforts of its dynamic secretary, Abul Hashim. Full-time workers were trained and accommodated in party houses. By the eve of the 1946 elections the Bengal Muslim League had one million members. Over a decade and a half later, Ayub Khan, Pakistan's first military ruler, was to turn to Abul Hashim's organizing genius to establish the Convention Muslim League in East Pakistan. The efforts of the 1940s could not, however, be reproduced in a much more politically hostile environment, with an increasingly frail Abul Hashim deputing the work to Shamsul Huda. There was some organizational development in other "Pakistan areas" after 1944, but in many districts, League branches existed only on paper. In Punjab, the corner-stone of Pakistan, its membership stood at just 150,000. Factional infighting in the Frontier League prompted an enquiry by the All-India Committee of Action in June 1944 which admitted that "there was no organization worth the name" in the province. The Sindh Muslim League had just 48,500 members. Its annual report for 1943–44 acknowledged that: "We should require years to create political consciousness among [the] Muslim masses in the province, where on account of long distances, scattered villages, illiteracy and local influence it is rather difficult to easily approach the people."[21]

The pyramid of branches stretching from the localities to the All-India level, which was the hallmark of Congress, was thus noticeably absent throughout most of the future Pakistan areas. The Muslim League was thus far less able to form a democratic pillar of the post-colonial state than its Congress counterpart.

In 1946 the Muslim League achieved the victories it required to lend credibility to the Pakistan demand, despite this organizational

33

weakness. It had to compromise to do so. This involved accepting opportunistic converts from rival parties such as the Punjab Unionists. It also had to mobilize support through existing power structures such as *biradari* (kinship groups) and sufi networks. Loyal party officials were bypassed for election tickets in favor of elite power holders. In Sindh, the Muslim League had to adapt itself to the power of the large landowners (*waderos*) who dominated the lives of their labourers (*haris*). Votes could not be obtained in Sindh's interior without the support of the *waderos*, but they were primarily concerned with their own factional rivalries, rather than mobilizing support for the Pakistan ideal. The Muslim League's approach to electioneering in future Pakistan areas was to be crucial in legitimizing its demand, but stored up problems for the future. It endorsed clientelist politics with its accompanying opportunism, factionalism, and corruption.

Of equal concern was the inexperience of the provincial Muslim League leaderships. The League never formed a government in Punjab before Independence. Its politics were dominated by the cross-communal Unionist Party, whose power relied on a combination of the personal influence of the rural elites and legislative enactments to prevent expropriation by the moneylenders. When the Coalition Unionist Government finally resigned in March 1947, Punjab remained under governor's rule until the end of the Raj. While the Muslim Leaguers in Punjab entered the post-Independence era with little experience of office, their counterparts in Sindh were already well versed in using power to feather their own nests through the manipulation of wartime contracts and the control of rationed and requisitioned goods.[22] In the Frontier, it was only after the imprisonment of many Congress representatives that it was able to form its first government in May 1943. What ensued was an undignified scramble for power and profit marked by bitter rivalries between the ministerial and organizational wings of the

party, rather than schooling in the arts of government. Factionalism, corruption, and violence formed part of the League's everyday experience. Together, inexperience, institutional weakness, and the low level of political culture inherited from the freedom struggle militated against Pakistan's future democratic consolidation.

The legacy of the freedom movement was ironically most problematic in Bengal where the Muslim League had put down the most roots. There was incipient conflict between the Urdu- and Bengali-speaking elites even at the height of the freedom struggle. The former remained loyal to Jinnah's conception of an East Pakistan zone within a single Pakistan state. They also subscribed to the belief, expressed as early as July 1933 by the All-Bengal Urdu association, that "Bengali is a Hinduized and Sanskritized language" and that, "in the interests of the Muslims themselves it is necessary that they should try to have one language which cannot be but Urdu."[23] This was, of course, in keeping with the Muslim League's official two nation theory, an ideology that viewed the community as monolithic and set apart from the Hindus. These views were challenged by Bengali-speaking Muslim Leaguers. In his May 1944 Presidential address, the Muslim League journalist-cum-politician Abul Manser Ahmed maintained that Bengali Muslims were not only different from Hindus but from Muslims of other provinces. He declared this position as follows:

> Religion and culture are not the same thing; religion transgresses [sic] the geographical boundary but *tamaddum* (culture) cannot go beyond the geographical boundary . . . here only lies the differences between *Purba* (Eastern) Pakistan and Pakistan. For this reason the people of *Purba* Pakistan are a different nation from the people of the other provinces of India and from the "religious brothers" of Pakistan.[24]

It was, however, the Urdu-speaking Bengalis who wielded influence in the All-India

Muslim League. Jinnah never nominated Abul Hashim to its working committee. He preferred to deal with such trusted lieutenants as Hasan and Ahmed Ispahani,[25] who knew little of Bengal outside Calcutta, or with the conservative Nawab of Dhaka whose newspapers dubbed Hashim and his supporters as communists. They indeed fought for liberation "from all forms of oppression." Moreover, their vision was for a sovereign East Pakistan state. Indeed, Hashim prophetically warned that a united Pakistan would result in the imposition both of Urdu and an alien bureaucracy and reduce East Bengal to a stagnant backwater.[26] Both the language issue and the marginalization of Bengali political influence were subsequently to dominate East–West Pakistan relations and contribute to the Bangladesh breakaway of 1971.

The clash between regional and Pakistani identities was most pronounced in Bengal, but it was present also in Sindh and the Frontier. In both provinces the Muslim League's popular base of support rested on local allegiances that were difficult to harmonize with Jinnah's All-India understanding of the Pakistan demand. In these circumstances, it was hardly surprising that provincialism, as it was termed, became a barrier to nation building almost immediately after Independence.

Finally, the freedom struggle had gained it popular support by being deliberately vague about the nature of a future Pakistan state. Nevertheless, many of the leading Deobandi 'ulama (Islamic scholars) had opposed the "secularist" Muslim League leadership. Syed Abul A'la Maudoodi, who founded the Islamist Jamaat-i-Islami in August 1941, opposed the Pakistan campaign because it was based on the notion of nationalism, which, in turn, was opposed to the solidarity of the worldwide Muslim community, the umma. Maudoodi migrated from India at the time of Partition and thereafter worked assiduously to bring Pakistan's laws into conformity with Islam. But this goal of Islamization conflicted with Jinnah's famous speech on the eve of

Independence when he presented a vision of Pakistan to the Constituent Assembly on 11 August that envisioned the goal of a plural secular state. The debate about the role of Islam in Pakistan has raged ever since. It is rooted in the fact that the freedom struggle itself was variously conceived as a movement of Islam and a movement of Muslims.

The legacy of partition

Partition divided the Muslim majority provinces of Punjab and Bengal and was accompanied by mass migrations and killings. The number of casualties has been estimated at anything from around 200,000, as put forward by the colonial official Penderel Moon, to the MQM's grossly inflated figure of two million. Upwards of 100,000 women were kidnapped on both sides of the border. The epicenter of the social dislocation was in Punjab, but much of north India was affected. After uncontrollable spontaneous flight, the two dominion governments oversaw a virtually total exchange of populations in Punjab. This involved the greatest refugee migration of the twentieth century. Some seven million people migrated to Pakistan. Around five and a half million Hindus and Sikhs crossed the new international boundary in the opposite direction. In Bengal, despite government efforts to assure minority populations, waves of migration continued throughout the opening decades of Independence whenever there were outbreaks of violence or rumors of communal conflict.

Social dislocation on this scale inevitably influenced political developments within India and Pakistan as well as affecting deeply their relations. The fledgling states had to devote huge resources to refugee resettlement. In the case of Pakistan, which was disproportionately affected and had inherited weaker political institutions, it has been argued that the refugee problem was an important factor in the strengthening of the bureaucracy and the army to the detriment

35

of political parties.[27] Muhammad Waseem has further maintained that the undercutting of parliament resulted from the refugees' loss of their political base. "Recourse to elections," he states, "was considered suicidal by the migrant-led government at Karachi because there was no way it could win elections and return to power in the center. Elections were considered dysfunctional for the political system of Pakistan in the immediate post-independence period."[28]

Political tensions were generated in both dominions by the huge refugee influx. Nehru's insistence that the large numbers of Muslims left behind after the creation of Pakistan were not a "fifth column" but equal citizens led to a clash with Deputy Prime Minister Sardar Patel. The latter was regarded as the strongman of Congress. He had always leaned towards Hindu nationalist sentiment. According to US reports, relations between the two men became so embittered that the impression prevailed that Patel was "determined to get Nehru out of government." According to Matthai, the Minister of Transport who was the Americans' New Delhi informant, Gandhi came to Nehru's rescue, making it clear that if Patel took any steps against Nehru, he "would be finished with him for life."[29] Such an admonishment could not be taken lightly by Patel, who had been the Mahatma's associate since the 1920s. Nevertheless, accounts of Muslim atrocities in Pakistan raised the communal temperature in India.[30] The state's secular policy would certainly have been in greater peril had it not been for the salutary lessons drawn in the aftermath of Gandhi's assassination by a Hindu fanatic. Refugees from Pakistan in such cities as Delhi have continued to provide support for Hindu nationalist parties and causes.[31] Similarly, the politics of Pakistan Punjab cities like Lahore, Sialkot, Multan, and Gujranwala, of whose population around half were enumerated as migrants at the time of the 1951 Census, cannot be understood without reference to the refugee dimension.

The issue of refugee resettlement increased tensions between the center and the provinces in Pakistan. They became most marked in Sindh where Prime Minister Muhammad Ayub Khuhro strongly opposed the demand that it should accept those refugees who could not be absorbed in West Punjab. By December 1947 Sindh had resettled only 244,000 displaced persons, while West Punjab had accepted over four million.[32] Raja Ghazanfar Ali, Pakistani minister for refugees and rehabilitation, severely upbraided Khuhro at a subcommittee of the Pakistan Muslim League Council held on 23 February, 1948. He dismissed the Sindh Prime Minister's defense that the local populace was suffering from the refugee burden as raising the "virus of provincialism."[33] Khuhro's stance was a contributory factor in his dismissal.[34] This not only strengthened Sindhi sentiment against the center, but also encouraged the precedent of executive action against elected representatives, which boded ill for the future.

Refugee resettlement not only created political tensions, but also provided an opportunity for the new Indian and Pakistan states to assert their authority. They were able to prove their paternalistic credentials by establishing a range of relief measures. The tentacles of refugee rehabilitation spread far into the economy with support for small businesses, custodianship of evacuee property, and a range of grants and loans and training schemes. Both states built satellite towns and colonies to help accommodate refugees.[35] State provision differentiated among classes of refugees, with the result that its overall impact was to re-establish community and gendered hierarchies.[36]

The state could never meet all refugee demands. The Hindu nationalist discourse seized on this. Failure to protect the symbolic body of Mother India, which had been vivisected, was linked with the reality of the violation of countless Hindu and Sikh women. Such Hindu nationalist writers as Chaman Lal called for a "strong and virile state backed up by a powerful army" to respond to the aggressor Pakistan state.[37] Stereotypes of the Muslim "other" as a sexually rapacious and violent aggressor have been drawn from the stories, memories, and distorted history of Partition and have been repeated at times of communal conflict. There is also evidence in the Partition-related violence of the prototype of what Paul Brass has termed the "institutionalized riot system."[38] Just as in large-scale post-Independence Hindu–Muslim violence, the 1947 killings display evidence of organized political intent and were made possible by the acquiescence of officials and police authorities.

Gyanendra Pandey has revealed how communities in both India and Pakistan have built identities around mythologized accounts of the partition.[39] Common to these accounts by both Brass and Pandey is blame displacement for the violence, the emphasis on stereotypical traits of courage and valor and a retelling of stories of "victimhood." Self-identity is strengthened by the demonization of the "other." These community narratives, along with the long-lasting personal scars and material and psychological losses have meant that Partition, rather than being a past event, continues to be a living reality and reference point at both societal and state levels.

Despite the ambiguities for Pakistan of the division of the Muslim population of the subcontinent, the state has used the event for nation-building purposes by emphasizing the sacrifices it entailed. Official histories have also linked its attendant violence with stereotypes of Hindu "treachery" and the desire to destroy Muslim culture. These are expressed most clearly in school textbooks sanctioned by the state, which distort the events leading up to Partition and the upheavals themselves. Such distortions find their counterparts in India where BJP-led governments have influenced textbook production.

The Urdu-speaking refugee community in Karachi and the East Bengal *bhadralok* refugees now settled in Calcutta have experienced the greatest problems of adjustment that are common to all those displaced in 1947. Both communities weigh their perceived post-independence marginalization against their sacrifices and losses. The political geography of both the metropolises is inexplicable without reference to the refugee influence. In Karachi, this has resulted in the dominance of the ethno-nationalist MQM, which appealed directly to the *mohajirs*.[40] In Calcutta, the educated refugees who were reduced to illegal occupations of land formed the main base of support for the Communist Party.[41]

The responses of the Indian and Pakistan governments both to autonomy demands and to each other were profoundly influenced by Partition. It has given birth to what has been termed the "fearful South Asian state" by some scholars,[42] expressive of the determination to prevent future divisions. Demands for greater autonomy by subnational groups are thus viewed with suspicion. This is especially the case in India if these are associated with religious interests. The Khalistan movement of the 1980s is sometimes referred to as part of the unfinished business of Partition because of the Sikh failure to acquire a Sikhistan in 1947. The way the Indian government responded to the Akali Dal movement in the 1980s also requires reference to the Partition era, as no less does the Pakistan authorities' response to the insurgency in urban Sindh a decade later.[43] Neither state has displayed mercy towards what they have deemed to be secessionist movements, even when repression has been counterproductive in radicalizing domestic opposition and arousing international condemnation of human rights abuses.

For some writers, the long-running Kashmir dispute is the single most important legacy of Partition in that it not only has had a major impact on relations between India and Pakistan, but has distorted the latter's domestic political development. It is well established that the conflict over the territory has adversely affected the economic and human development of the subcontinent because the two rivals have traded less with each other and have spent great resources on weapons. Another consequence has been the introduction of great power rivalries in the region. Kashmir was not the only factor in souring the Indo-Pakistan relationship at the time of independence. Distrust mounted over the division of assets, water management and water sharing between the two dominions. The Partition-related massacres and mass migrations also embittered relations. Nevertheless, events in Kashmir in 1947–49 provided a defining moment both in Indo-Pakistan relations and for Pakistan's domestic priorities.

Any lingering hopes for continued economic or military interdependence of the two dominions were snuffed out in Jammu's killing fields from where a flood of Muslim refugees migrated to such bordering Pakistani cities as Sialkot where they formed an important anti-India lobby. Although the military conflict was confined to Kashmir, it highlighted the strategic dangers for Pakistan. The priority of building up the armed forces led to the establishment of a "political economy of defense." The years 1947 to 1950 saw up to 70 percent of the national budget allocated for defense. Funds were diverted from nation-building activities at the same time that the state's administrative machinery was expanded to ensure the center's control over the finances of the provinces. The long-term repercussions were a strengthening of the non-elected institutions of the state—the bureaucracy and the army—at the expense of political accountability. This process contributed not only to the failure to consolidate democracy, but to the alienation of the eastern wing of the country. Bengali politicians' priorities were of a different order and did not involve sacrificing democratic politics on the altar of the Kashmiri Muslim cause. The army increasingly acquired an almost insatiable appetite for new technology, which became ever more expensive. By 1958 an American intelligence report attested that the "Pakistani army had developed as a pressure

group" and would continue to have priority over economic development for appropriations," irrespective of the Indian factor.[44]

Conclusion

Post-Independence India and Pakistan have experienced rapid socioeconomic change and other significant developments in both their regional and international political environment. These have introduced important discontinuities seen in postcolonial ethnicization and regionalization of politics; the growing middle-class influence in Indian politics; the establishment of large overseas communities with a range of transnational linkages with the homeland; and the growing strategic asymmetry in the subcontinent. South Asia's political environment is thus very different from what it was six decades ago.

Nevertheless, the foregoing analysis has revealed that unresolved conflicts, competing sources of identity and political cultures inherited from the Raj, and the nationalist struggle still resonate. Moreover, the crisis period of 1947–48 continues to influence Indo–Pakistan relations and has undoubtedly affected strongly the response of both states to ethno-nationalist movements. In the case of Pakistan, crisis management at its birth shaped the state's future political trajectory. Contemporary South Asia is not fully explicable without reference to this past.

Notes

1 The number of miles of railway track increased from 34 in 1854 to 8,500 in 1880. By the beginning of the twentieth century there were nearly 1,400 newspapers with a total all-India subscription of two million. Effective readership was much greater, as newspapers were read aloud and passed from hand to hand.
2 See Ian Talbot, *India and Pakistan: Inventing the Nation* (London: Arnold, 2000), pp. 12–16.

3   The revivalist activities of the Singh Sabha movement were undoubtedly spurred on not just by the attempts of the rival Arya Samaj to reconvert Sikhs to Hinduism, but by the fact that, until the 1901 Census, only the orthodox Khalsa Sikhs were enumerated as Sikhs. See, Harjot Oberoi, *The Construction of Religious Boundaries: Culture, Identity and Diversity in the Sikh Tradition* (Chicago: University Press, 1994).

4   See Francis Robinson, *Separatism Among Indian Muslims: The Politics of the United Provinces' Mulims, 1860–1923* (Cambridge: University Press, 1975), p. 82.

5   See Gyanendra Pandey, *The Construction of Communalism in Colonial India* (Delhi: Oxford University Press, 1990).

6   See Asma Barlas, *Democracy, Nationalism and Communalism: The Colonial Legacy in South Asia* (Boulder, CO: Westview Press, 1995).

7   K. B. Sayeed, *Pakistan: The Formative Phase, 1857–1948* (London: Oxford University Press, 1968).

8   See Ian Talbot, *Pakistan: A Modern History* (London: Hurst, 1998).

9   The East India Company assumed the *diwani* or revenue collectorship in Bengal as early as 1765. The areas that formed British Balochistan were acquired for strategic reasons from 1876 onwards. Sindh had been seized from its Baloch Talpur rulers in 1843. Six years later the British annexed the whole of Punjab and the Frontier region, which had been part of the Sikh kingdom.

10 Ian Talbot, *Punjab and the Raj, 1849–1947* (New Delhi: Manohar, 1988) and *Khizr Tiwana, the Punjab Unionist Party and the Partition of India* (London: Curzon, 1996).

11 See Yunas Samad, "Pakistan or Punjabistan: Crisis of National Identity," in Gurharpal Singh and Ian Talbot (eds), *Punjabi Identity: Continuity and Change* (New Delhi: Manohar, 1995), pp. 61–87.

12 Imran Ali, *The Punjab under Imperialism, 1885–1947* (Princeton, NJ: University Press, 1988).

13 Clive Dewey, "The Rural Roots of Pakistani Militarism," in D. A. Low (ed.), *The Political Inheritance of Pakistan* (Basingstoke: Macmillan, 1991), pp. 255–84.

14 See Allen McGrath, *The Destruction of Pakistan's Democracy* (Karachi: Oxford University Press, 1996).

15 See Judith M. Brown, *Modern India: The Origins Of An Asian Democracy*, 2nd edn (Oxford: University Press, 1995).

16 See Judith M. Brown, *Gandhi's Rise to Power: Indian Politics, 1915–1922* (Cambridge: University Press, 1972).

17 D. A. Low, "The Forgotten Bania: Merchant Communities and the Indian National Congress," in D. A. Low (ed.), *Eclipse of Empire* (Cambridge: University Press, 1991), pp. 101–19.

18 Contemporary Indian feminists decry this as perpetuating sexual stereotypes. They point out that female participation was linked with the traditional role models such as Sita and with women's sense of devotion and duty, which was extended from the family to the nation; Madhu Kishwar, "Gandhi on Women," *Economic and Political Weekly*, Vol. 20, No. 40 (5 October, 1985), pp. 1, 691–702.

19 Gopal Krishna, "The Development of the Indian National Congress as a Mass Organisation, 1918–1923," in Thomas E. Metcalf (ed.), *Modern India: An Interpretive Anthology* (London: Collier, 1971), p. 267.

20 The Hindu Mahasabha was founded in 1915 to safeguard Hindu interests, which its leaders claimed were being sacrificed by Congress. Its main concern was resistance to the Muslim "other" rather than colonial rule. It sought to overcome weaknesses arising from the disunity of the caste system and from an alleged lack of physical strength.

21 *Annual Report of the Sindh Provincial Muslim League for 1943–4*, Shamsul Hasan Collection 1:24 (Karachi).

22 S. F. Kucchi, member of the Working Committee Sindh Provincial Muslim League to G. M. Syed, Shamsul Hasan Collection, Sindh 11:37.

23 Harun-or-Rashid, *The Foreshadowing of Bangladesh: Bengal Muslim League and Muslim League Politics, 1936–1947* (Dhaka: Research Society of Bangladesh, 1987), p. 45.

24 Harun-or-Rashid, p. 181.

25 The Ispahani family originated in Persia. It moved to Calcutta from its original trading centers in Madras and Bombay at the beginning of the twentieth century.

26 Yunas Samad, *A Nation in Turmoil: Nationalism and Ethnicity in Pakistan, 1937–58* (New Delhi: Sage, 1995), p. 106.

27 See Ayesha Jalal, *The State of Martial Rule: The Origins of Pakistan's Political Economy of Defence* (Cambridge: University Press, 1990).

28 Muhammad Waseem, *The 1993 Elections in Pakistan* (Lahore: Vanguard, 1994), p. 163.

29 Ian Talbot, *India and Pakistan: Inventing the Nation* (London: Arnold, 2000), p. 164.

30 Mushirul Hasan has chronicled the economic, political and emotional depression of the Indian Muslim community left leaderless and traumatized by Partition. Even in the Nehruvian era, the Muslims' relations with the Hindu majority were marked by a sense of insecurity and desire to disprove any charges that they represented a fifth column. See Mushirul Hasan, *Legacy of a Divided Nation: India's Muslims since Independence* (Delhi: Oxford University Press, 1997).

31 See Christophe Jaffrelot, "The Hindu Nationalist Movement in Delhi: From 'Locals' to Refugees and Towards Peripheral Groups?," in Veronique Dupont, Emma Tarlo and Denis Vidal (eds), *Delhi: Urban Spaces and Human Destinies* (Delhi: Manohar, 2000), pp. 181–203.

32 *Dawn* (Karachi), 12 December, 1947.

33 *Statesman* (Calcutta), 25 February, 1948.

34 For further details, see Sarah Ansari, *Life After Partition: Migration, Community and Strife in Sindh 1947–1962* (Karachi: Oxford University Press, 2005).

35 See Ian Talbot, *Divided Cities: Partition and its Aftermath in Lahore and Amritsar 1947–1957* (Karachi: Oxford University Press, 2006).

36 See Ravinder Kaur, *Since 1947: Partition Narratives among Punjabi Migrants of Delhi* (New Delhi: Oxford University Press, 2007).

37 Urvashi Butalia, *The Other Side of Silence: Voices From the Partition of India* (New Delhi: Penguin, 1998), pp. 183–84.

38 Paul R. Brass, *The Production of Hindu-Muslim Violence in Contemporary India* (Seattle, WA: University of Washington Press, 2003).

39 Gyanendra Pandey, *Remembering Partition: Violence, Nationalism and History in India* (Cambridge: University Press, 2001).

40 See I. H. Malik, "Ethno-Nationalism in Pakistan: A Commentary on Muhajir Qaumi Mahaz (MQM) in Sindh," *South Asia* Vol. 18, No. 2 (1995), 49–72.

41 Prafulla Chakrabarty, *The Marginal Men: The Refugees and the Left Political Syndrome in West Bengal* (Kalyani: Lumiere Books, 1990).

42 S. Mahmud Ali, *The Fearful State: Power, People and Internal Wars in South Asia* (London: Zed 1993).

43 See Gurharpal Singh, *Ethnic Conflict in India: A Case-Study of Punjab* (Basingstoke: Macmillan, 2000).

44 Jalal, *The State of Martial Rule*, p. 238.

3

Sri Lanka's independence

Shadows over a colonial graft

Nira Wickramasinghe

Introduction

Sri Lanka's independence process is generally described as "the conversion of a colony into an independent state by peaceful means"[1] or as a "transfer of power" from British administration to the representatives of the new independent state of Ceylon, a phrase that implies considerable continuity with a colonial era that lasted 400 years.[2] Portuguese and Dutch rule left an imprint but not as marked as the British (1796–1948), the first power to conquer the entire island. The British attempted to intervene at the level of what Eric Stokes calls "society itself."[3] The exceptional depth of the colonial impact on Ceylon, particularly in the coastal areas, radically modified the social and economic structures of the island. In some respects, the colonial impact oriented the economy outward, overturned traditional streams of trade, and distorted links with India, while introducing into society new elements of heterogeneity: Christianity, the languages of the conqueror, new communities such as the Burghers (mixed European and native descent) and, later, Indian immigrant plantation workers. It also imposed unifying factors: modern modes of communication, a unified administrative system, a common language of

domination, and monetarization of exchanges. However, this depth should not be overestimated: family structures, the caste system, and Buddhism were maintained, especially in the center of the island where foreign domination was resisted for three centuries. Traditions were transformed by reshaping or adapting to features of modernity.[4]

There are many ways of reading the moment of the foundation of the state of Ceylon on 4 February, 1948: few would see it as a fundamental disjuncture from colonial rule, the image of a continuum or a nexus being more suitable. When reflecting on this critical moment one needs, however, to go beyond the conventional reading of Ceylon in 1948 as a "satellite of Britain,"[5] or as the theater of a consensual transition to independence. What I hope to provide in this chapter is a more shadowy picture of a state whose legitimacy was weak as it derived neither from a political body bound by nationalist sentiment nor from a nationalist struggle against colonial autocracy in the name of deeply felt democratic principles.

The transfer of power, occurring, as it did, in two stages (1931 and 1948) took place within the institutional framework of a dominion. This chapter will first look at the years immediately before independence that

41

paved the way for independence and witnessed the nurturing of leaders for the new state. It will then analyze the institutional continuities in practice between the British colonial state and the newly founded state. Finally, it will address the legacies of unsolved issues—dominion status, citizenship, ethnic mistrust—that persisted into the following decades.

Towards independence: The democratic graft of 1931

The two decades that preceded independence constitute a formative period for the future statesmen of independent Ceylon: they gained experience in statecraft in the state councils and introduced important and lasting legislation in areas where power was delegated: namely agriculture, industry, education, health care, and local administration.

The Donoughmore experience in self-rule

Since 1915, the year of violent intercommunal riots, the island had been enjoying a relative calm, unlike its larger neighbor. In the decades that followed, the island's westernized elite was introduced to the ideals of parliamentary debate within the confines of a system similar to that of India, with limited franchise and communal representation. In 1926, Sir Hugh Clifford, Governor of Ceylon, sent a dispatch to the Colonial Office that contributed to convincing the Under-Secretary of State of the urgency for sending a small royal commission to examine on the spot the actual effect of the constitutional changes already granted.[6] The arrival of the Donoughmore Commission had the effect of stimulating political activity in the country and spawned a number of new associations based on region, caste, and community as well as yearnings for greater political participation. Within a year following the sittings of the Donoughmore Commission, a report was

drawn up and published. Instead of the expected cabinet system, a scheme for executive committees modeled on those of the League of Nations and the London County Council was proposed. The Executive Council was abolished. Instead of a ministry and an opposition, the unicameral legislature, the State Council would divide into seven committees, each of which would be concerned with a particular public department. The main recommendation of the commission was the abolition of communal representation and the extension of the franchise to all males over 21 and females over 30 domiciled in Ceylon. Eventually universal suffrage was adopted, with some restrictions.

The abolition of communal representation and the adherence to the principle of equality between individuals signified—in effect—Sinhalese rule. The aim of the commissioners, in accord with the view prevailing at the Colonial Office, was most probably to ensure a gradual and limited transfer of power to the moderates of the Ceylon National Congress,[7] while keeping a strong minority group which was apprehensive of any more advances towards self-government as a safety valve against any potential radical moves by the majority. It was also a way of reinforcing the power of the conservative leaders of the Ceylon National Congress, many of whom were rural notables, at the expense of the labor leader A. E. Goonesinha who, the British felt, was gaining too much prominence in the political life of the country. The project exceeded the demands of the Ceylonese elites, who had asked for less democracy, but more autonomy. However, Britain retained authority over finance, justice, law and order, and foreign relations.

During the Donoughmore period the transfer of power to a moderate Ceylonese leadership was accompanied by a similar transfer of power in the administration. The period of the second State Council from 1936 onwards saw the near completion of a program of Ceylonization of the administration There was no formal policy of

"Sinhalization," although the number of Sinhalese increased dramatically in the administration. A possible explanation is the increase in the English literacy rate for the whole population and consequently a higher output of English-educated Sinhalese than Burghers and Tamils. It is also possible that many Sinhalese turned to employment in the public service as a result of economic trends in the 1930s. More importantly, however, the officials who first served in the Ceylon Civil Service were inculcated with a sense of the public domain that transcended belonging to particular communal groups.

The Donoughmore years entrenched the idea that the state had a responsibility towards its citizens. In the late 1940s, the principle of collective provision for common human and social needs through state intervention was firmly established through the implementation of the Education Act of 1943 and the establishment of the department of social services in 1948. As early as the end of the nineteenth century, some initiatives relating to labor welfare had been forthcoming, motivated essentially by the need of the state to safeguard the highly profitable plantation sector by giving special treatment to indentured Indian labor. In 1927, for instance, minimum wage legislation was enacted for Indian estate workers.

The origins of welfarism can be more clearly traced to the Donoughmore years when social legislation laws relating to a wide number of issues such as child and family welfare, poverty alleviation, education, and health and social security were promulgated. The commitment to improving living standards through education and health policies surfaced in these transition years of semi-self-government as a concomitant of universal franchise. However, the 1930s were especially hard on the poorer sections of the population, as those years were further plagued by a severe drought and a devastating malaria epidemic. Thus, it was necessity too that sparked a number of measures, among them the introduction of a Poor Law in 1939

following the Wedderburn Report of 1934, which attempted to deal with poverty by recommending state assistance, a measure that was not, however, continued in the years that followed. During the Second World War, except for a food subsidy for the entire population, social welfare was accorded little priority.[8] The Kannangara Report of 1943 recommended a system of universal and compulsory free education from kindergarten to university that led to a national system of education founded on the principle of equal opportunity.[9]

Another important welfare measure directed at a particular segment of the population, namely the peasantry, needs to be mentioned. Under the leadership of Don Stephen Senanayake, Minister of Agriculture and Lands and Leader of the State Council, an important program of state-sponsored land colonization was initiated to provide landless peasants with opportunities to settle in the "dry zone," the old Rajarata, or Land of Kings.[10] This issue would later become a thorn in the relations between Sinhalese and Tamils, since the latter saw this measure as an attempt by a majoritarian state to conquer lands where they themselves had lived for a number of generations.

The nationalist movement

The British transferred power in 1948 to a conservative multiethnic elite that had spearheaded a reformist nationalist movement. The British felt that this group would offer the best resistance to the forces of cultural nationalism and Marxism then gaining momentum in the country. The westernized elites had, on the whole, been willing partners of the British.

What resistance there had been had occurred in the first two decades of the century when the temperance movement rallied Sinhalese Buddhists against the imposition of Christian values. It was also a means through which the newly emergent middle classes could challenge the social values of foreign Christian rulers and British rule as a whole. The social and religious reformers, Anagarika Dharmapala and Walisinha Harischandra, led a campaign to protect places of Buddhist worship. They were also leaders of the temperance movement. This endeavor, which peaked first in 1903–05 and, more importantly, in 1911–14, had a dual purpose: first to reassert Buddhist strictures against alcohol, which amounted to the renewed assertion of the validity and relevance of Buddhist values in general after years of acquiescence in the values of foreign rulers; second, on the political plane, to attack excise duties as an important source of British revenue. The impact of this movement was not confined to the urban intelligentsia, but spread to the rural middle class and urban workers. Dharmapala appealed to the middle classes when he stressed the doctrinal tradition and rejected peasant religiosity, especially the worship of deities. After severe Sinhalese–Muslim rioting in a number of locations in 1915, the British colonial authorities clamped down on men associated with the temperance movement, arbitrarily arresting many members. Subsequently, the pattern of political agitation underwent a distinct change. The shift started with the death of W. Harischandra in 1913 and was consolidated by the exile of Anagarika Dharmapala to India. From this time, the constitutional reform movement adopted a secular outlook and religion became of secondary importance.

Reform and state councils, 1931–36

During the 1930s and until the mid-1940s, the political space was occupied by a multi-ethnic elite group that belonged to a variety of political formations: the Ceylon National Congress was essentially a Sinhalese moderate movement with a few minority Muslim and Tamil members; the Sinhala Maha Sabha created by S. W. R. D. Bandaranaike, the heir

to a line of wealthy landowners from the Colombo region was a more virulently Sinhalese nationalist organization. Bandaranaike had received an English and Protestant education, but learnt Sinhala and converted to Buddhism on his return from Oxford. The Lanka Sama Samaja Party, a Marxist organization formed in 1935, was nonsectarian in nature and led by members of the Sinhalese elite. Minority groups were represented by vocal individuals such as G. G. Ponnambalam. There was, however, no united front of minorities to combat the increasingly majoritarian features of the State Council era. In 1944, the minority coalition was restricted to the Ceylon Tamils and Ceylon Indians (plantation Tamils, often referred to as Estate Tamils).

On the whole, the state councils saw an under-representation of minority communities. In 1931, a Tamil boycott of the elections instigated by a Tamil radical group called the Youth Congress further aggravated the situation. This was rectified in 1934 with the entry of four northern members. The relations between communities soured further when, in 1936, all seven ministers elected were Sinhalese. From then on, minority leaders presented their own solutions for political reform—such as balanced representation for minorities—quite separately from the reform demands which the State Council, under the leadership of D. S. Senanayake, were crafting.

D. S. Senanayake was heir to a rich family whose fortune came from graphite mines and coconut plantations. He was very popular with the peasant class, to whom he distributed lands as Minister of Agriculture after 1931, as well as with the upper classes who were reassured by his social conservatism. The British saw him as an ideal ally.

It would be incorrect to suggest, however, that the political space was limited to the conservative native elite in the State Councils. Many young village monks, who had studied at seats of monastic learning such as Vidyoda Pirivena and Vidyalankara Pirivena, returned to their villages with high ideals of uplifting the lot of the peasants. In the 1947 elections many would work under the banner of the Marxist parties.[11]

Lineages of the colonial past: Soulbury constitution and continuities in political practices

In July 1944, Lord Soulbury was appointed head of a commission charged with the task of examining a new constitutional draft that the Sri Lankan ministers had proposed but that was, in fact, the creation of Sir Ivor Jennings, the Vice-Chancellor of the University of Ceylon and the unofficial advisor to D. S. Senanayake. After the fall of Singapore to the Japanese, under pressure from Sri Lankan politicians, the British finally agreed to concede full participatory government after the war, which meant full responsible government in all matters of internal civil administration. The Soulbury Report, published in September 1945, provided a bicameral parliamentary government based on the Whitehall model. Universal suffrage was retained. The executive committees and the posts of three officers of state were abolished. Executive power was to be vested in a prime minister and a cabinet appointed by the governor-general but responsible to the lower house of the bicameral legislature. The governor-general was given overriding powers in matters of defense, external affairs, and constitutional amendments, but on all other matters could only act on the advice of his ministers. He would also appoint 15 of the 30 members of the senate or upper chamber. The first chamber or House of Representatives would consist of 101 members, 95 of whom would be elected, with six nominated by the governor-general. The London *Times* quite accurately described the treatment of the issues by the Soulbury Commission as "unimaginative."[12] Indeed, except for the addition of a second chamber, it amounted to an endorsement of the main principles of the constitutional scheme formulated in 1944.

Provision was made in the Soulbury Report and in the Ceylon (Constitution) Order in Council for the protection of minority rights, but the assumption was that the minority communities constituted a large and powerful enough bloc to be able to counter majoritarian initiatives. The Soulbury Report ensured that the governor-general would exercise his discretion on any bill that evoked serious opposition by any racial or religious community and that, in his opinion, was likely to involve oppression or serious injustice to any such community. The Soulbury Report contained a clause, which later became Section (29)2 in the 1946 Constitution modeled on clause 8 of the ministers' draft constitution, that prohibited legislation infringing on religious freedom or discriminating against persons of any community or religion. The incorporation of the principle of weightage in representation was the chief safeguard against majority domination. Area, as well as population, was taken into account in the delimitation of constituencies so that minorities scattered in various parts of the country would be represented. Minority rights were also to be protected by the requirement of a two-thirds majority in the house for any change in the constitution or any piece of legislation aimed at discriminating against a racial or religious minority. There were multiple checks: if by chance such legislation came to parliament, the two-thirds requirement provided another check against it. The concurrence of at least 68 members in a House of 95 elected members and six nominated members was thus needed. The second chamber could check and revise legislation of a discriminatory character but not obstruct a bill.

The institutional safeguards for minorities embodied in the Soulbury Report lagged far behind the demands put forward by the minorities at the commission's sittings. While other minorities gradually ceased their protests and prepared to collaborate with the majority, the Ceylon Tamil and Ceylon Indian leadership remained aloof.

Hazards of instability: Strikes

In the years following the end of the war, after the publication of the Soulbury Report and the subsequent framing of a constitution, political activity was renewed with the holding of elections for a new parliament. The end of the artificial prosperity that had prevailed during the war years when troops were stationed in Ceylon, together with the announcement of future elections, created conditions of social unrest throughout the island, instigated in the main by the three Marxist parties

Although the widely felt fear that the moderate leadership of the nationalist movement was being submerged by the left had no real substance, it had a double effect. First, it led the moderates of all ethnic groups to join hands and form the United National Party (UNP) in April 1946. The UNP rallied non-Marxists of all communities except the Tamil Congress. Second, it acted as a bargaining card for D. S. Senanayake, the leader of the State Council, to compel Whitehall to make a decisive statement regarding the status of Ceylon in order to reinforce the position of the moderates. The British, indeed, had no desire to see Ceylon ruled by what they considered "extremists." Class politics then made a shattering entry into the otherwise dormant political scene of post-war Ceylon. Unrest started in October 1946 with the bank clerks' strike led by the Ceylon Bank Clerks Union. The Union was more influenced by Goonesinha's ideas than by the Marxist parties. It then spread to government workers and municipal employees, paralyzing essential services. The government treated the strike as a major emergency. The *hartal* was eventually suspended but it acted as a warning to the Board of Ministers.

At the beginning of 1947 agitation for an increase in wages among government daily paid workers reached another climax. The military was eventually called in; on 5 June the police opened fire on a crowd of strikers near Kolonnawa, killing one of them, a government clerk by the name of Kandasamy. The strike was broken after a month.

Elections 1947

The general elections of 1947 for Ceylon's First House of Representatives was the third held since the bestowal of universal suffrage by the Donoughmore Constitution in 1931. The main parties that contested the elections were the UNP, the Lanka Sama Samaj Party (LSSP), the Bolshevik Leninist Party (BLP), the Communist Party (CP), the Labour Party, the Ceylon Indian Congress (CIC) and the Tamil Congress. There were also two minor parties, the Lanka Swaraj and the United Lanka Party. The 1947 elections were the first in which class conflict was a factor, taking the form of a UNP-Left duel in the Sinhalese areas of the country. The Lake House newspapers, the country's major written media, joined by the nationalist *Sinhala Jatiya* and *Sinhala Bauddhaya* (founded by Dharmapala) constituted the main forces opposed to Marxism. In the two decades preceding these elections, numerous Buddhist societies— the Sri Sanandhara Society (Society for the Support of the Buddhist Priesthood), Buddhagaya Defense League, and the All Ceylon Buddhist Congress were some of the main ones—had emerged in response to the newly felt need for organizing the largest religious community in the island. These developments prepared the terrain for Bhikku involvement in politics. The conservative forces were supported by the rural petit bourgeoisie and many monks inspired by the Vidyodaya Pirivena (Vidyoda monastic school), who travelled around the countryside with a message of disaster should the Marxists capture power.

The left, with the help of Vidyalankara monks, had succeeded in winning to its side a significant number of radical Buddhists, who believed socialism was not alien to the spirit of Buddhism as the sangha was a community in which private property was non-existent.

The election results were a disappointment for the UNP, which secured only 42 of 95 seats. The LSSP won ten seats, the BLP five seats, the CP three seats and Labour one seat. Left-wing parties, which secured 20.5 percent of the votes, dominated the low country, from Colombo to the southwestern coast to Matara at the southern tip. At the time, the success of the left was explained as a consequence of the post-war economic slump. There was also a caste dimension to the Marxist power base. The coastal fringe of the country contained a heavy concentration of the Karava, Salagama, and Durava castes, castes that occupied an intermediate place in the social hierarchy dominated by the majority Goyigama (farmer) caste. The left did not make any headway in non-Sinhalese areas.[13] Interestingly, the northern part of the country was the only area where the LSSP won fewer votes than its Marxist rivals. Clearly the nonsectarian language of the LSSP was not attractive to the Tamil voter.

Independents had secured 21 seats while the Tamil Congress and Ceylon Indian Congress gained seven and six seats respectively. As the UNP had not secured a majority, anti-UNP forces gathered to try to form a government at what is known as the Yamuna Conference.[14] But no agreement was reached and D. S. Senanayake lured enough independents in support to form a cabinet. The left parties would never come closer to forming a government.

Economy, bureaucracy, army

At Independence, the island remained heir to a colonial system in which the economy was tied to the export of tropical goods and the import of food products such as rice. First established with cinnamon, the export trade turned successively to coffee in the 1840s, tea and coconuts in the 1880s, and rubber in the 1900s. The plantation structure remained, based on the exploitation of an Indian labor force in vast plantations of several hundred hectares, overseen by a British managerial class, and with well-established commercial networks: "Over 40 percent of the Gross Domestic Product in 1948 came from agriculture and the share of tea, rubber and coconut in the agricultural output was over 60 percent."[15] The smallholding sector produced mainly for the domestic market at relatively low levels of productivity. At Independence, economic indicators were largely favorable. The balance of payments recorded a sizeable current account surplus while external reserves were sufficient to finance imports for about one year.[16] The standard of living, owing to well-entrenched welfare policies in education, health, and food, was among the highest of the South and Southeast Asian countries.

Although legislation passed in 1949 authorized the creation of the Royal Ceylon Army, Royal Ceylon Navy and Royal Ceylon Air Force and although, in the years that followed, an independent military force was established, the organization of the armed forces in existence during colonial times did not change. Most officers continued to be trained in military academies in Britain. The basic structure of the colonial forces was retained, as were the symbolic trappings—the flags, banners, and regimental ceremonies. At that time, the army served a purely ceremonial function and took up less than 4 percent of the national budget.[17]

The Ceylon Civil Service had been Ceylonized to the extent of 90 percent by 1949, but a small minority of administrative officers remained as a vestige of colonialism and social privilege. After independence, its 200 members continued to enjoy special advantages and status. The new middle classes continued to feed into the Ceylon Civil service for another decade and a half. This anomalous status would last until 1963 when the Ceylon

47

Civil Service was incorporated into a unified administrative service of 1,030 officers.[18]

Unfinished legacies: The citizenship issue

While the Soulbury constitution avoided all matters relating to citizenship, three pieces of legislation, namely, the Ceylon Citizenship Act of 1948, the Indian and Pakistani Residents Act No. 3 of 1948, and the Ceylon Parliamentary Elections Amendment Act No. 48 of 1949, clearly demarcated those considered sons of the soil from those considered aliens. The first law deprived the Estate Indian Tamils, constituting 12 percent of the population, of their citizenship, the second made it possible for those with property and education within the community to obtain citizenship, and the third deprived those without citizenship of the right to vote.

The Ceylon Citizenship Act No. 18 of 1948 created two types of citizenship: citizenship by descent and citizenship by registration. In both cases, documentary proof was required for applicants, a procedure that disqualified the majority of Indian Tamil workers who were illiterate. Citizenship would be given only to those who satisfied the government concerning the intensity of their desire to adopt Sri Lanka as their home.[19] Citizenship by descent was restricted to persons who could prove that at least two generations had been born on the island. Citizenship by registration was open to those residents who could prove that either parent had been a citizen by descent and that the individual had been a resident of Ceylon for seven years, if married, or ten years, if unmarried. The minister in charge was given discretionary power to register 25 persons a year for distinguished public service.

The Indian and Pakistani Residents (Citizenship) Act No. 3 of 1949 was based on Senanayake's proposals at the December 1947 negotiations, the only change being the decision to take 1 January, 1948 as the qualifying date for completion of residence. Senanayake had proposed stringent conditions, including a residence qualification of seven years for married and ten years for unmarried adults, calculated since 31 December, 1945, together with proof that the applicant had adequate means of livelihood and conformed to Ceylonese marriage laws. Application would have to be made within two years of the date of legislation.

The new citizenship and franchise laws altered the balance of power between the various communities and helped consolidate a majority within the polity. Through these laws, Estate Tamils were defined as an alien and marginal group. The laws in many ways also embodied a class position on the part of a group in society which was closer in cultural terms to a middle- or upper-class Briton than to a Sinhala or Tamil worker. Documentary proof such as registration of birth was required for applicants. In this sense it was not surprising that the elites in Ceylon had absorbed one of the main myth models of European cultures, which implied that writing epitomized learning, civilization, and all that distinguished the west from the rest.

The urgency for passing such stringent laws lay in the links that had been forged between the estate population and the Left parties before Independence. This became a concern for the conservative elite to whom power had been transferred. The laws just described had shattered any possibility of stronger interethnic and class alliances by excluding the entire Estate Tamil population from participating in the polity. They also pandered to fears of the Kandyan constituency that they would be swamped by the ever-growing Tamil population. D. S. Senanayake's position was consolidated both within the UNP, where the threat of his rival, S. W. R. D. Bandaranaike, a favorite of the Kandyans owing to his marriage to a Kandyan woman, lessened, and in the state as a whole at the expense of 10 percent of the population that was cast out as not belonging to the nation state.[20]

The trade unions that represented the Estate Tamils in the late 1940s and early 1950s—the Ceylon Workers Congress (CWC) and the Democratic Workers' Congress (DWC)—issued conflicting instructions to members. Tales of application forms that were requested but never arrived because of the connivance of postmasters, and of a climate of suspicion and fear on the part of illiterate workers, are part of the collective memory of plantation labor workers.[21] The result was that most estate workers became stateless.

The citizenship acts spelled the end of any sort of trust between the Estate Tamils and the Jaffna Tamils. Indeed, the leader of the Tamil Congress, representing the Jaffna Tamils, accepted a ministry in the UNP government that had just disenfranchised nearly one million Tamil plantation workers. The stand taken on behalf of the Estate Tamils by the newly created federal party leader, S. J. V. Chelvanayakam, did not create much of an impact among the isolated Estate Tamils. The relative isolation of the Indian Tamils from the rest of society, whether Ceylon Tamil or Sinhala, as well as their low caste status and poverty, ensured their lack of political representation and mobilization and their rapid marginalization in national politics.

Ethnic issues: Divide and rule?

The reconquest of political power by the Sinhalese majority was supported by the British and excesses on their part did not lead the British government to adopt a more conciliatory attitude towards minority demands. This was in keeping with the Colonial Office preference for gradualism. An overview of the Soulbury Report's treatment of minority grievances issued in 1945 is revealing. On the whole, it appears that the Soulbury Commission felt the minorities were exaggerating the precariousness of their situation. They agreed that there

had been minor instances of discriminatory action by the Sinhalese. However, the report on discrimination concluded that there was no substantial indication of a general policy on the part of the government of Ceylon to discriminate against minority communities.

Apart from remaining closed to the political demands of the minorities, the British played a role in the process of Sinhalese national affirmation which was not negligible. During the 1930s and 1940s, the colonial rulers participated in defining what they thought was the uniqueness of Sinhalese civilization. The study, preservation, translation and publication of Sinhalese texts were encouraged. State sponsorship was given to indigenous systems of medicine. Thus, in the last decades of British rule, a "divide and rule" policy designed to suppress nationalism by fostering ethnic tensions was more mythic than real. The urgency was on another plane: left-wing parties such as the LSSP were fomenting social unrest and threatening the old order. The British policy of alliances was one supporting moderates against "extremists." The main concern of the British was to hand over power peacefully. The near completion of the program of Ceylonization of the administration was motivated by the same concern.

Dominion status: A flawed independence

On 18 June, 1947 the British government made the official announcement that Ceylon would receive "fully responsible status within the British Commonwealth of Nations."[22] Contemporaries as well as scholars in the decades that followed have debated whether dominion status meant the continuation of colonial rule under another name. Among the main critics of dominion status in the 1940s were supporters of the leftist parties of Ceylon. On Independence Day they made sure that black flags were displayed in various parts of the island as a protest against the Rs

800,000 allegedly spent on the celebrations. The leftist newspaper *Nidahasa* (freedom) recalled occasions when students were caned by their teacher for refusing to participate in Independence Day festivities or to bring flags to schools.[23] Historians of the immediate post-independence decades took positions on the issue, although today few people would feel it is something worth debating. K. M. de Silva, for instance, argued that D. S. Senanayake's emphasis on moderation and pragmatism was tactical and that Sri Lanka only followed the constitutional approach of memoranda and talks that had brought Australia, Canada, and New Zealand to independence status without the bloodshed that, he argued, had occurred in India where independence was said to have been won by a mass-based nationalist movement.[24] It was, however, the Defense Agreement signed by Ceylon and Britain in 1948 that was most criticized by the leftists, who called D. S. Senanayake a traitor for allowing the British to continue to maintain naval, air, and land forces on the island and use naval bases, airports, and other facilities.[25] Leftists also regarded the agreements as "badges of inferiority" and "checks on full sovereignty in external affairs."[26] By this agreement the government of Sri Lanka and the government of the United Kingdom would give each other "military assistance for the security of their territories, for defense against external aggression and for the protection of essential communications." Wriggins makes the important point, however, that Ceylon retained the right to terminate the arrangement.[27] Further, Jennings notes that D. S. Senanayake signed the Defense Agreement rather as an inducement to Britain to hasten Sri Lanka's independence than for any military purpose.[28] These agreements that gave credibility to the argument made by Marxists that Sri Lanka's independence was flawed must be understood as an integral part of the independence package of the British that aimed at keeping Sri Lanka free from Soviet influences as far as possible. The regime of the 1950s would not disappoint its proponents: it would be the most conservative and pro-western regime Sri Lanka ever would know.

Conclusion

In 1948 the colonial power departed Ceylon, but left behind real and important traces. The transfer of power within the framework of a dominion allowed the country to avoid the necessity or human costs of struggling for a national cause, but it also denied its ruling class a founding myth comparable to that which accompanied the birth of the Indian Union and, to a lesser extent, Pakistan. For a founding myth, politicians would look back to a much more distant past that did not embody democratic ideals but conjured up images of violence, exclusiveness, and parricide. The Sinhala myth of Vijaya and the people of the Lion would fill the symbolic void created by an ineffective nationalist movement.

The vestiges of colonialism remained in the army, the civil service, the constitution, and the Anglicized middle class, whose members continued to rule in all walks of life. The island's dominant political models and idioms, including Marxism in its most intellectual form, were also imported from the west. The absence of legitimacy of politicians, who cut themselves away from the culture of the rural people, led to the institutionalizing of a system of vote catching that emphasized dynastic loyalty with regard to the Senanayake and Bandaranaike clans. In the next decade, S. W. R. D. Bandaranaike would ride the rising wave of dissatisfaction of the common man with a regime from which he felt alienated and leaders for whom he had little regard.

Notes

1 W. Ivor Jennings, "The Dominion of Ceylon," *Pacific Affairs*, Vol. 22, No. 1 (March 1949), p. 1.

2 See the mainstream historical works on the British period, especially K. M. de Silva (ed.), *History of Ceylon*, Vol. III (Colombo: Colombo Apothecaries, 1973); Robert N. Kearney, *The Politics of Ceylon* (Ithaca, NY, and London: Cornell University Press, 1973); Howard Wriggins, *Ceylon: Dilemmas of a New Nation*, (Princeton, NJ: University Press, 1960).

3 David Scott, *Refashioning Futures: Criticism after Postcoloniality* (Princeton, NJ: University Press, 1999), citing Eric Stokes, *The English Utilitarians and India* (New Delhi: Oxford University Press, 1989).

4 Eric Meyer makes this point very convincingly in his latest book, *Sri Lanka: Entre Particularisme et Mondialisation* (Paris: La Documentation Française, 2001).

5 See, for example, S. Arasaratnam, review of *Sri Lanka: From Dominion to Republic*, by Lucy M. Jacob, in *Pacific Affairs*, Vol. 47, No. 4 (Winter 1974–75), pp. 567–68.

6 Command papers 3131. 1928. Ceylon: *Report of the Special Commission on the Constitution of Ceylon*, July 1928 (London: His Majesty's Stationery Office, 1928), pp. 11–12.

7 The Ceylon National Congress formed in 1919 was constituted by notables belonging to all ethnic and religious communities of Ceylon to push for reforms of the constitution. See Michael Roberts (ed.), *Documents of the Ceylon National Congress and Nationalist Politics in Ceylon 1929–1950*, 4 vols (Colombo: Department of National Archives, 1977).

8 Nira Wickramasinghe, *Sri Lanka in the Modern Age: A History of Contested Identities* (London: C. Hurst 2006), pp. 306–307.

9 Wickramasinghe, *Sri Lanka*, p. 306.

10 Nira Wickramasinghe, "Politics of Nostalgia: The Citizen as peasant," *Delhi School of Economics Occasional Paper*, (New Series), No. 2, 2005.

11 H. L. Seneviratne, *The Work of Kings: New Buddhism in Sri Lanka* (Chicago: University of Chicago Press, 1999).

12 Cited in *The Hindu Organ* (a daily English-language paper published in Jaffna). Seneviratne, pp. 228–43.

13 Seneviratne, pp. 228–43.

14 N. Sanmugathasan, *Political Memoirs of an Unrepentant Communist* (Colombo: Colombo Apothecaries, 1989), p. 70.

15 Godfrey Gunatilleke, *Welfare and Growth in Sri Lanka*, Marga Research. Studies No. 2. (Colombo: Marga Institute, 1974), pp. 1–2.

16 Godfrey Gunatilleke, *Development and Liberalisation in Sri Lanka. Trends and Prospects* (Colombo: Marga Institute, 1993), pp. 5–6.

17 http//ieweb2.loc.gov/frd/cs/cs.

18 James Jupp, "Constitutional Development in Ceylon since Independence," *Pacific Affairs*, Vol. 41, No. 2 (Summer 1968), pp. 169–83; Robert N. Kearney, "Ceylon: A Year of Consolidation," *Asian Survey*, Vol. 4, No. 2 (1964), pp. 729–34.

19 A. Aziz, CIC President, *Hindu Organ*, 18 May, 1948.

20 See the excellent analysis of Amita Shastri, "Estate Tamils, the Ceylon Citizenship Act of 1948 and Sri Lankan politics," *Contemporary South Asia*, 8, 1 (1999), pp. 65–86. For more conventional approaches, see I. D. S. Weerawardena, "The Minorities and the Citizenship Act," *Ceylon Historical Journal*, 1, 3 (1951); S. U. Kodikara, *Indo–Ceylon Relations Since Independence* (Colombo: Colombo Apothecaries, 1965).

21 E. Valentine Daniel, *Charred Lullabies: Chapters in an Anthropography of Violence: Sri Lankans, Sinhalas, and Tamils* (Princeton, NJ: University Press and New Delhi: Oxford University Press, 1997), pp. 110–13.

22 See K. M. de Silva (ed.), *British Documents on the End of Empire. Sri Lanka. Part II. Towards Independence (series B Volume 2) 1945–1948* (London: Institute for Commonwealth Studies, 1997), pp. 350–51.

23 *Nidahasa*, 25 February, 1948.

24 K. M. de Silva, "Ivor Jennings and Sri Lanka's passage to Independence," in K. M. de Silva (ed.), *Sri Lanka's Troubled Inheritance* (Kandy: ICES, 2007), p. 106.

25 For the full text of the defense requirements of the British government, see K. M. de Silva (ed.), *British Documents*, pp. 299–305; H. S. S. Nissanka, *Sri Lanka's Foreign Policy—A Study in Non-Alignment* (New Delhi: Vikas, 1984), pp. 9–11.

26 K. M. de Silva, "Sri Lanka—D. S. Senanayake and the Passage to Dominion Status, 1942–1947," *Sri Lanka Journal of Social Sciences*, Vol. 3, No. 2 (December 1980), p. 14.

27 Howard Wriggins, *Ceylon*, p. 385.

28 Cited in Shelton Kodikara, *Foreign Policy of Sri Lanka: A Third World Perspective* (Delhi: Chanakya, 1982), pp. 84–86.

Part II

Political change, political parties, and the issue of unitary vs federal forms of government

4

Political change, political structure, and the Indian state since Independence

John Harriss

India is, famously, the biggest democracy in the world. And, given the failures of democratic political systems in so many other former colonies, a good many commentators have found it remarkable that the country should have remained a democracy—except for the brief period between 1975 and 1977 when the then prime minister, Indira Gandhi, declared an "emergency" and suspended the Constitution. This chapter traces the history of Indian democracy and the implications of political changes for the functioning of the key institutions of government.

In 1990 a leading writer on the politics of India, Atul Kohli, published a book entitled *Democracy and Discontent: India's Growing Crisis of Governability*. The idea of "crisis" in his title accurately reflected views that were generally held at the time. By the end of the 1980s the long period of the almost absolute dominance of Indian politics by the Congress Party was coming to an end. Rajiv Gandhi, Indira's son, who had won an overwhelming victory in the 1984 General Election, following her assassination, had failed in his efforts to renew the organization of the party. His government had drifted, its programmes in disarray, and it had become embroiled in damaging charges of corruption at the highest levels, notably in the "Bofors affair";[1]

insurgencies had gathered momentum in Punjab and Assam, and latterly in Kashmir, and there appeared to be growing violence and instability across the country, whether in an "advanced" state like Gujarat, or a "backward" one like Bihar (states to which Kohli devoted chapters in his book). Shortly thereafter the fabric of the Indian polity was torn as never before, at the moment in December 1992 when a mob of supporters of the movement of Hindu cultural nationalism, spurred but not overtly led by the Bharatiya Janata Party—that had by this time emerged as the major force of opposition nationally to the Congress Party—tore down an old mosque in the north Indian town of Ayodhya. The 1990s then saw, on one level at least, greater political instability than India had ever known. There were five general elections in ten years in the 1990s (in 1989, 1991, 1996, 1998, and 1999) whereas there had been only eight such elections in the previous 40 years, and the country experienced minority governments for the first time (starting with the government of V. P. Singh in 1989–90). Yet this was also the decade in which India changed course in terms of economic policy, as reforms that began to be instituted in 1991 brought in moderate liberalization. This, building on the earlier

55

development of a policy environment more sympathetic to private business, has borne fruit in recent years in exceptionally high rates of economic growth. Even before the end of the decade Kohli apparently reached a different judgment about the state of India's government from that which he had held earlier, according to the title of an edited book, *The Success of India's Democracy*. The counterpoint between Kohli's two titles suggests the enduring puzzle of the governance of India: how is that a country with so many contending social forces, characterized by high levels of everyday violence, has nonetheless remained united, politically a fairly stable parliamentary democracy, and lately economically successful? The answer lies in large part in India's constitutional design.

India's parliamentary democracy

The Preamble to the Constitution of India that came into force on 26 January, 1950 declared: "WE, THE PEOPLE OF INDIA [have] solemnly resolved to constitute India into a SOVEREIGN DEMOCRATIC REPUBLIC." It seems that by the late 1940s it was almost a foregone conclusion that independent India would be a parliamentary democracy, and there was little debate on this point in the Constituent Assembly that drew up the constitution. It is sometimes thought that this was a natural inheritance from the British colonial rulers, but such a viewpoint discounts the extent to which a commitment to a universal franchise, and also to federalism and to secularism, became a necessary part of the struggle for independence. The leaders of the Congress movement needed to build national unity amidst the enormous diversity of India in terms of caste, language, religion, and local patriotisms,[2] and to manage the groundswell of popular opposition to colonial rule that built up after 1920. Their commitment to democracy was instrumental in the creation of national consciousness.[3]

Democracy under a universal franchise (extending also to women in India well before a number of western countries) was, in a sense, the gift of a small and privileged, mainly upper caste, professional elite. Certainly India does not fit at all well with structural theories about the social basis of movements of democratization, which hold, alternatively, that democratization depends on the existence of a developed middle class, or of a significant organized working class. Although India by the late 1940s did have an influential industrial bourgeoisie, and a politically mobilized proletariat in the major urban centres, it remained overwhelmingly a hierarchical agrarian society in which the power of large landholders remained pervasive, together with the subtle and not so subtle forms of social exclusion and oppression associated with caste. Pratap Bhanu Mehta has argued that although the nationalist movement and the impulse of social reform that "sometimes accompanied it" delegitimized the more extreme forms of oppression of Hindu society, it did not eliminate them:

> [T]he structure of what we might call India's ancient social regime . . . survived into democracy relatively intact . . . The contradiction, between proclaimed political equality on the one hand, and deep social and economic inequality on the other, was too obvious to go unnoticed. But this feature, in part, constituted the uniqueness of the Indian experiment. Rather than political democracy following at least a social transformation of sorts, ultimately it was going to be the instrument of this transformation.[4]

It is not inconceivable that political democracy should be the instrument of social transformation—and the experience of certain regions of India, notably that of Kerala, shows that sometimes it has been.[5] But with regard to India as a whole, as Mehta notes perceptively: "The irony is that the more unequal the background institutions and practices of society, the more likely it is that politics will be a struggle to displace the holders of power rather than an ambition to bring about social transformation."[6] This point aptly reflects differences across India, and the character of politics in the Hindi heartland as opposed to parts of the south and the west.[7] Formal political democracy has generally proved to be a limited instrument of social transformation in modern India where, however, Kerala, West Bengal and, perhaps, Tamil Nadu are exceptions to the general rule. Sudipta Kaviraj and Partha Chatterjee have both referred to Gramsci's idea of "passive revolution" in explaining the process of social change in modern India, and have shown how, under the authority of India's first prime minister, Jawaharlal Nehru, it was believed that social transformation could be brought about from above through state–bureaucratic agency.[8] Chatterjee argues, however, that even after more than 50 years of independence, it remains the case that the rights of democratic citizenship are meaningful only for a minority of Indians. Only a minority have a role in "civil society," the sphere in which citizens come together on terms of political equality in voluntary associations through which they are able to deliberate on matters of public concern. The great majority of Indians are left still to struggle for their rights as citizens of democratic India.[9] Even now the structure of India's "ancien régime" remains strong.

Act one in the political drama of independent India: The Nehruvian state and the era of Congress dominance

The Indian National Congress, the organization that led the movement for Indian independence, was—it has been said—already "becoming the Raj" even before the end of British rule, as its leaders, notably Sardar Patel, Nehru's powerful home minister in the first post-independence Congress government, were careful to preserve key institutions of the colonial government such as the bureaucracy and the police. The Congress was the unifying force of the new India. Nehru could proclaim with justice at the time of the first general election to the Indian parliament, the Lok Sabha, in 1952, the slogan that "India is the Congress, the Congress is India." By this time, following the death of Patel in 1950, he himself held a position of undisputed authority in both party and government, though he was constrained by the majority of Congress conservatives within the Congress Working Committee.

The governments that Nehru headed pursued policies intended to build a broadly socialist, secular, modern state through central planning, but in the context of an accommodative political system. This was what he once proclaimed as India's "third way," namely, "planning under a democratic pattern of socialism."[10] Although India was far from being a one-party state, since the Congress was opposed by parties of both the left and the right throughout the 1950s and into the 1960s, the dominance of Congress was rarely threatened either in the central government or in the states. The lone exception was when the Communist Party of India won control of the state government of Kerala in 1957. India's political setup was described by W. H. Morris-Jones as a one-party dominant system and by Rajni Kothari, in similar terms, as a "dominant party system," in which dominance coexisted with competition but without a trace of alternation of parties.[11] The central government bargained with state governments led by powerful state leaders from the Congress, although, ultimately, authority lay in New Delhi.[12]

Still, Kaviraj argued in 1991 that the political elite of the new Indian state in the 1950s and 1960s largely failed to develop a "common political language" shared with the masses.[13] In the main, in the context of Indian society in the first 25 years of Independence, the Congress-dominant party system operated through a structure of clientelistic relations extending from local levels, both urban and rural, up to the apex of the pyramid of power. Those who were locally powerful, commonly the larger landholders and the dominant peasant proprietors, became, over much of the country, critical brokers, mediating between the mass of the people and politicians.[14] In the end these local power holders were able to defeat the reforming intentions of the Nehruvian elite.[15]

Act II: Congress dominance contested under the regimes of Indira and Rajiv Gandhi

Nehru's authority was declining even before his death in May 1964, partly as a result of India's defeat in a war with China over borders in 1962, while the modernizing efforts of the Nehruvian state were checked by the failures of planned economic development. Declining electoral support for Congress showed that these failures called into question the legitimacy of the exercise of power by the government that Nehru headed.

Nehru was followed in the office of prime minister by Lal Bahadur Shastri and then, after Shastri's death in 1966, by Nehru's daughter Indira, who the senior leaders of the Congress mistakenly thought would be the pliant instrument of their will. In 1967, in the fourth general election to the Lok Sabha, the Congress majority was drastically reduced, and the party also failed to win majorities in no fewer than eight states. The era of Congress dominance was over, although it would take another 20 years before it was finally replaced at the end of the twentieth century by an apparently quite stable political system of opposing party coalitions (see Table 4.1 for a listing of India's prime ministers).

Indira Gandhi split the Congress party in 1969 in her struggle for authority with its senior leaders, the immediate cause being a dispute over the election of a new president of India. In the general election that she then called in 1971, she was successful in winning a convincing victory, in spite of having lost control of much of the Congress organization. She was successful, as observers noted at the time, in reaching voters "over the heads" of the local notables who mostly remained stalwarts of the party machine that had continued to be in the hands of Indira's opponents.[16] Thereafter, the Congress organization that had served Nehru well, was broken—and it has remained so to the present.

Table 4.1 Prime ministers of India

	Period of office	Party
Jawaharlal Nehru	1947–1964	Congress
Lal Bahadur Shastri	1964–1966	Congress
Indira Gandhi	1966–1977	Congress
Morarji Desai*	1977–1979	Janata
Choudhary Charan Singh	1979–1980	Janata
Indira Gandhi	1980–1984	Congress (I)
Rajiv Gandhi	1984–1989	Congress (I)
Vishwanath Pratap Singh*	1989–1990	Janata Dal
Chandra Sekhar	1990–1991	Janata Dal
P. V. Narasimha Rao	1991–1996	Congress (I)
Atal Behari Vajpayee*	1996 (for 13 days)	Bharatiya Janata Party
H. D. Deve Gowda*	1996–1997	Janata Dal/United Front
Inder Kumar Gujral	1997–1998	Janata Dal/United Front
Atal Behari Vajpayee	1998–2004	Bharatiya Janata Party/National Democratic Alliance
Manmohan Singh	2004–	Congress (I)/United Progressive Alliance

Note: * indicates that tenure of office ended with resignation (rather than electoral defeat or death).

Atul Kohli revisited in the 1980s the constituencies studied 20 years earlier by Myron Weiner, who had found that the Congress Party had local organization and some semblance at least of internal party democracy. Both organization and internal democracy had withered,[17] and nothing has been done since then to restore the party as an organization. What political scientists have described as the "deinstitutionalization" of Indian politics extends to most other party political formations, which are little more (if at all) than loose followings of more or less charismatic political leaders. Elections in individual states and in the country as a whole have commonly been subject to "wave" effects, and incumbents, more often than not, have been booted out of office by the electorate after one term. Politics has become a kind of business, calling for significant investments in order to win office, but with the prospect then of making major gains from kickbacks of various kinds.[18]

When opposition to her mounted in the mid-1970s, in a context of increasing economic failure and political unrest, Indira Gandhi used a clause of the last major act of the British, the Government of India Act 1935, that had been incorporated into the Indian Constitution, to suspend that constitution, with the declaration of an "emergency." Democracy was suppressed for 20 months. In the elections that followed, in 1977, Indira was defeated, although less comprehensively than some had expected, since Congress remained strong in parts of the south and the west of the country. But, for the first time, India had a non-Congress government. The Janata Party was a coalition in which the Jan Sangh, founded in 1952 as the party of those sympathetic to arguments for Hindu nationalism, held the most seats. The Janata government appears, with the advantage of hindsight, to have been significant for this reason, and also because it saw a much greater share of members of the Lok Sabha than ever before who were drawn from among the peasantry. But the Janata government and the broad-based Janata Party itself did not last, both broken by petty squabbles among their leaders. As a result, Mrs Gandhi was returned to office in January 1980, an event that had seemed almost inconceivable only shortly before.

In the 1980s, as James Manor put it: "India became increasingly democratic and increasingly difficult to govern."[19] Despite their electoral majorities, the authority of the Congress governments of both Indira Gandhi and then of Rajiv were fragile, being dependent on the personalities of their leaders. Both were leaders with attitudes rather than policies,[20] points of view rather than coherent ideology. Indira developed a highly personalized and centralized strategy of rule, destabilizing state governments if ever a political leader appeared to be developing an independent power base. In the process, however, she created opportunities for regional parties, like the new Telugu Desam Party in Andhra Pradesh. The Telugu Desam won success very quickly in 1983 after a year in which, because of Indira's interventions, the state had as many as three different chief ministers. In one way, the Indian central state appeared to gain in strength, and yet its capacity to realize its will was weaker than before, so that it was described by Lloyd and Susanne Rudolph as a "weak–strong state"[21]—a far cry indeed from the Nehruvian state.

Indian politics became increasingly criminalized, too, in this time, with more and more elected representatives having criminal records. There is sometimes an unholy alliance between politicians of this ilk and the police.[22] And both Indira and Rajiv Gandhi made increasing concessions, in their efforts to maintain political support, to the Hindu nationalist constituency. Rajiv, in spite of winning the most crushing victory that Congress has ever contrived, taking advantage of the "sympathy wave" that followed his mother's murder in 1984, signally failed to restore the Congress organizations and his government drifted. By the end of the 1980s there was a political vacuum in India.

Act III: Towards a new political order

Into the vacuum there stepped at first the Janata Dal, a political grouping formed mainly by politicians who had at one time or another been on the left of Congress, which won office in 1989 under the leadership of Vishwanath Pratap Singh. However, in order to govern, the Janata Dal government depended on the support from the outside of the successor to the Jan Sangh, the Bharatiya Janata Party (BJP), which had won 86 seats, and of the communist parties. In the following year, V. P. Singh provoked opposition over his proposal to implement the recommendations of the Second Backward Classes Commission (the Mandal Commission, as it was commonly known, from the name of the senior politician who had headed it), and lost the support of the BJP. In the meantime, the BJP had won control of two state governments for the first time, those of Madhya Pradesh and Himachal Pradesh, in January 1990.

The Mandal Commission proposals called for an expansion of reservation of jobs in central government services and public undertakings for people from the officially defined "other backward classes," that is, those castes and classes held to have been socially and educationally disadvantaged and who had not had the benefit of such reservations previously granted to persons from the lowest castes in Indian society, categorized as scheduled castes. In the outcry that followed from members of higher castes, V. P. Singh was soon forced to resign, to be replaced as prime minister by Chandrasekhar, at the head of a minority government that relied on Congress support. The latter government in turn lasted for less than six months before a fresh general election had to be called.

The most significant event at this moment, however, was the Rath Yatra ("chariot procession") across the country undertaken by the BJP leader L. K. Advani, intended to culminate in "rebuilding the temple" in Ayodhya, in Uttar Pradesh, on the site occupied by an old mosque, the Babri Masjid, that is held to be the birthplace of the Hindu god, Rama. The Babri Masjid had become the object of increasing controversy since 1984, when a movement for the "liberation" of a number of holy sites in various parts of India had been launched on the grounds that they had been forcibly occupied by Muslim conquerors and converted to use as Islamic sites. The Rath Yatra was only the most recent in a series of carefully staged political dramas through which the BJP, together with its sister organizations of the sangh parivar—the "family" of associations pursuing Hindu cultural nationalism—were successful in winning wider support. From now on, the BJP, a well-organized force that recommended itself to the expanding middle classes as a party of order, in contrast to the fractious Janata Dal, became the center of opposition to Congress.

Through the 1990s, Indian politics eventually settled into a new pattern, not so much of stable two-party politics, but rather of stable "two-coalition" politics, albeit one in which shifts in the balance of power depend on the changing allegiances of minority, mainly regionally based parties. The general election of 1991 saw Congress returned to power, partly as a result of the sympathy vote brought about by the assassination of Rajiv Gandhi in the midst of the election campaign, but with the BJP, now with 120 seats and 20 percent of the popular vote, clearly in second place. Rather against the odds, the minority government of P. V. Narasimha Rao survived for a full term, but then, in 1996, the BJP emerged as the largest single party even though it did not succeed in expanding its support base. The government that the party formed survived for only 13 days, to be replaced by a 13-party United Front government, which was kept going under two prime ministers (Deve Gowda and I. K. Gujral) with the outside support of Congress. When this support was withdrawn in 1998 and fresh elections were held, the BJP won more seats, and the largest share that it has won so far of the popular vote (25 percent). However, the coalition that it headed failed in April 1999, and it was only after the thirteenth Lok Sabha elections of October 1999 that the party succeeded in managing the support of coalition partners in the National Democratic Alliance in such a way as to run the government through a full term. Then, in 2004, amidst the hubris of its claims to have made "India Shining," the BJP lost power to Congress, which, on this occasion, managed the coalition arithmetic more effectively, and contrived to remain in office for five years and to win power again in the 2009 elections.

The third phase in the history of Indian democracy has, therefore, at last seen the establishment of a "competitive multiparty system which can no longer be defined with [exclusive] reference to Congress."[23] In this new system, state-based parties have become nationally significant as never before,[24] their rise marking a definite shift away from the centralizing thrust of the Constitution. This change is reflected in the much more sparing use of Article 356, authorizing "President's Rule," through which governments at the centre have regularly dissolved state governments (Indira Gandhi used this instrument 39 times between 1966 and 1977; and it was used altogether upwards of 100 times before the end of the last century).

Another very important development in this phase has been what Yogendra Yadav has described as "the second democratic upsurge." He refers to the way in which certain historically subordinated communities from among the other backward classes, and even some of the scheduled castes, have become politically mobilized and empowered through the electoral process, yet behind political leaders[25] and party political groupings that are far from being democratic in their own functioning.[26] The most recent, striking expression of this tendency is the majority won by the dalit leader, Mayawati, and her Bahujan Samaj Party in state elections in Uttar Pradesh in 2007. But, as Sunil Khilnani has put it, democracy

in India has come to mean little more than "elections":

> As the sole bridge between state and society, they have come metonymically to stand for democracy itself . . . . This . . . has altered how political parties now muster support. The most recent period of India's democracy has shown a tenacity of community identities, in the form of caste and religion, as groups struggle to construct majorities that can rule . . . But the fact that such identities were less significant for four decades after independence . . . only shows how much they are creations of modern politics.[27]

So, as Khilnani says further, democracy has reconstituted social identities in modern India, but identities of caste and religion have also "bent the democratic idea to their own purposes."[28]

The compromised character of Indian democracy now, therefore, is that while representative electoral politics do represent the means whereby the mass of the people can hope to realize the self-respect that is, as Pratap Mehta argues,[29] democracy's deepest aspiration, these politics provide for only the most limited kind of agency on the part of poor people. There is now strong evidence for the first proposition, for example in the work of Javeed Alam,[30] on the reasons why in India, alone among major democracies, there should be an inverse relationship between income and social status and electoral participation. Yet electoral politics provide for only the most limited kind of agency on the part of poor people, if they actually have to enter into relationships of dependence with powerful intermediaries in order to secure their entitlements as citizens of the country.[31]

The institutions and functioning of the Government of India

Lloyd and Susanne Rudolph have argued that, alongside the political changes that have taken place over the last 20 years, the character of government has undergone quite radical change:

> After 1989 both the planned economy and the centralized state have gradually given way to a regulatory state more suited to coalition governments in a multiparty system, to economic decentralization, and to more independent and competitive federal states.[32]

An important part of this change in the character of the Indian state, they argue, is that there has come about a shift in the balance of power between the key institutions of government, in favor of the president, the supreme court, and the election commission, and at the expense of parliament, the prime minister, and the cabinet. These arguments are examined here, in the context of a review of India's government institutions.

Parliament

The Indian parliament is bicameral. The 552 members of the lower house, the Lok Sabha, which is the supreme legislative body, are elected under a universal franchise from single member constituencies in a first-past-the-post system. The ratio between the number of seats allotted to each state and the population of the state is supposed to be constant—although there are now concerns that this principle is giving an unhealthy weight to the more populous and socially "backward" states of the north.[33] Turnout in elections has on average been between 50 and 65 percent. The upper house, the Rajya Sabha ("Council of States"), has 250 members, 238 of them elected by state legislatures and 12 of them nominated by the president. The members, who sit for six-year terms (with one-third retiring every two years), can, and on occasion, have blocked legislation passed by the Lok Sabha. It is co-equal with the lower house in the electoral college for the election of the president.

Arun Agrawal concludes his recent analysis of the Indian parliament with the argument that it is "able to ensure executive accountability to only a limited extent."[34] There has been a steady erosion of procedural norms in the Lok Sabha over the last 30 years, and it has had a poor record in controlling the exercise of executive power. A striking demonstration of this weakness occurred in the ninth Lok Sabha when "19 bills, including one on constitutional amendment, were passed by members on a single day in March, without referral to any committee or any discussion."[35] By now, as we have seen, there has emerged a vocal opposition in India, but because of the disunity of both governing and opposing coalitions, the result "has been less the establishment of accountability, more a pervasive concern for office among those who seek to represent the Indian people."[36]

The prime minister and the cabinet

India's system of government was set up following the conventions of British cabinet government of the time, which gave a leading position to the prime minister, but along with the principle of the collective responsibility of the cabinet. And this was how Nehru operated. Then, under his successor, Shastri, and more so under Indira Gandhi, the prime minister's personal secretariat (now the Prime Minister's Office), became an alternative source of influence to the cabinet. Mrs Gandhi's secretariat became an independent executive force; and the pattern of prime ministerial dominance of a weak cabinet[37] has continued and developed further. The personal authority of prime ministers has been weaker, however, since the time of Indira and of Rajiv Gandhi, with the series of hung parliaments (following the 1989, 1991, 1996, and 1998 elections) with minority governments. Atal Behari Vajpayee, a powerful prime minister in 1999–2004, was, however, constrained by parliament not nearly so much as by the influence on him of the other organizations of the sangh parivar, while Prime Minister Manmohan Singh (2004–) is constrained by dependence for his personal authority on the sanction of Sonia Gandhi, Rajiv's widow, as the effective leader of the Congress Party and of what is sometimes called India's "ruling [Nehru] family," as well as by the dependence of his government until mid-2008 on the support of the communist parties.

President[38]

Under the constitution, virtually all executive powers are vested in the president, although they are supposed to be exercised on the advice of the prime minister and the cabinet. There have been longstanding concerns about the possibility of a president exercising discretionary power, but for most of the time, up until 1989, successive presidents of India restrained themselves.[39] Certain of the actions of Sanjiva Reddy during the misadventures of the Janata government in the late 1970s were controversial, and it is known that President Zail Singh considered dismissing the government of Rajiv Gandhi over the Bofors affair,[40] but these were exceptions to the general rule (see Table 4.2 for a listing of India's presidents). The era of hung parliaments since 1989, however, has created opportunities and even the necessity for assertive action by presidents because s/he is the referee in the game of government formation, while the perception of spreading corruption has pro-

Table 4.2 Presidents of India

Election	President
1950	Rajendra Prasad
1952	Rajendra Prasad
1957	Rajendra Prasad
1962	Dr. S. Radhakrishnan
1967	Zakir Hussain (died 1969)
1969	V. V. Giri
1974	Fakhruddin Ali Ahmed (died 1977)
1977	Sanjiva Reddy
1982	Zail Singh
1987	R. Venkatraman
1992	Shankar Dayal Sharma
1997	K. R. Narayanan
2002	Dr Abdul Kalam
2007	Smt. Pratiba Patil

vided space for presidents to act as guardians of fairness and constitutional balance.

Ramaswamy Venkataraman established an important precedent concerning the president's role in the formation of governments in hung parliaments when, in 1989, he first asked the largest single party (Congress, following that election) to form the government, a principle that has been followed by his successors. Among them, the one who most clearly asserted his independence, in the defense of what he saw as constitutional propriety, was K. R. Narayanan. In 1998 he refused a request from the Janata government of I. K. Gujral to impose President's Rule in the state of Uttar Pradesh. Following the election later that year of a government headed by the BJP, he appeared, through several actions, to criticize that government in a way that was unprecedented. He then pushed his powers to the limit in requesting Prime Minister Vajpayee in 1999 to establish, through a vote in the Lok Sabha, that he still had majority support (when he might have been expected to have waited for the opposition parties to table a non-confidence motion). In January 2000 his address on the occasion of the fiftieth anniversary of the establishment of the republic questioned the BJP government's efforts to change the 1950 Constitution by providing for a directly elected president. Narayanan, and his predecessor Shankar Dayal Sharma, did much to ensure that the use of Article 356 of the Constitution, authorizing President's Rule, has come closer to the position Dr B. R. Ambedkar (generally identified as the principal draughtsman of the constitution) intended for it, "a matter of last resort." More generally and most importantly, these two presidents "found constitutional grounds and appropriate occasions to act independently of the union executive in the public interest."[41]

The bureaucracy[42]

It has been found that one of the critical features of those polities that have been more successful in terms of economic development is the quality of their bureaucracies, in which it is considered that merit-based recruitment plays an important part.[43] The "higher" civil services of India in which the Indian Administrative Service (IAS) is the senior body, are recruited through stiff competitive examination. So, the principle of merit obtains in recruitment—modified by the operation of reservations—although subsequent promotion is based very largely on seniority. The IAS is an all-India service and the practice of allocating large numbers of outsiders to a state cadre is intended to secure a higher level of impartiality. The service continues to be prestigious, and the quality of many officers is undoubtedly exceptionally high, but it is known that whereas it was formerly the preferred career for the most able, now many of the best young people opt rather for careers in the private sector.

The advent of the developmental state of independent India in the 1950s meant that members of the civil service, especially in the higher echelons, were expected to take on a much wider range of functions, and the service continues to face problems having to do with multiple goals. It remains capable of high-quality delivery but there are concerns about the deterioration of its general performance that is thought to have come about as a result of the reduced independence of senior bureaucrats and increased political interference. Political–bureaucratic relationships have been transformed, Brass argues, in a patrimonial direction, with the political leadership selecting officers who are personally loyal and will serve their narrow interests.[44] The system of transfers of civil servants is manipulated by politicians and is one basis for corruption,[45] while one of the results of the frequency with which even senior officers are transferred is their very short average tenure in any one post.

Below the senior levels of the civil service there is an enormous army of minor civil servants whose salaries constitute a huge drain on the public exchequer, who are notoriously inefficient and mired in petty corruption. The extent to which the IAS is involved in corruption is disputed, but senior officials, who can exercise a great deal of influence on public decision making, are certainly part of the dominant class of India and important beneficiaries of the actions of the state.[46]

Conclusion

This review of political change and the functioning of the institutions of government in India suggests two strong conclusions, in answer to the "puzzle of governance" set out in the introduction. First—in line with the Rudolphs' argument concerning the shift to the "regulatory state"—it seems clear that increased political competition, and the instability of the 1990s, have strengthened some institutions (the president, the Supreme Court and the election commission) and weakened others. The weakening of the centralizing thrust of the Indian Constitution has probably had positive consequences. The fact that the constitutional design sets up many "veto points"—checks on change, ranging from the formal requirements for judicial review to the informal checks of procedural delay within the bureaucracy—has negative consequences, no doubt, but provides defenses against the abuse of power.[47] This points to the second conclusion. The Indian state remains, it is said, "excessively procedural and rule bound." This makes for inertia, for sure, but also limits the capacity of particular social forces to manipulate the state. As Kapur and Mehta argue, it makes in the end for the systemic stability that has puzzled so many observers of Indian politics and the state.[48]

Notes

1 The "Bofors affair" was a major corruption scandal in which Rajiv Gandhi was among those accused of having taken illegal commissions from the Swedish firm Bofors, for

winning a bid to supply field guns to the Indian Army.

2 On the formation of regional patriotisms in India see Christopher Bayly, *Origins of Nationality in South Asia* (Delhi: Oxford University Press, 1998).

3 Nehru wrote, for instance, in 1938 that a directly elected assembly would "represent the people as a whole"; cited by Stuart Corbridge and John Harriss, *Reinventing India* (Cambridge: Polity Press, 2000), p. 27. And see Sumit Sarkar, "Indian Democracy: The Historical Inheritance," in Atul Kohli (ed.), *The Success of India's Democracy* (Cambridge: University Press, 2001).

4 Pratap Bhanu Mehta, *The Burden of Democracy* (Delhi: Penguin Books, 2003), pp. 52–53.

5 On Kerala, see Patrick Heller, "Social Capital as Product of Class Mobilization and State Intervention: Industrial Workers in Kerala, India," *World Development*, Vol. 24, No. 6 (1996), pp. 1055–71; and V. K. Ramachandran, "On Kerala's Development Achievements," in Jean Drèze and Amartya Sen, *Indian Development* (Delhi: Oxford University Press, 1996).

6 Mehta, p. 48.

7 On differences in political regimes across Indian states, see John Harriss, "Comparing Political Regimes Across Indian States," *Economic and Political Weekly*, Vol. 34, No. 48 (1999), pp. 3367–77; and Ashutosh Varshney, "Is India Becoming More Democratic?", *Journal of Asian Studies*, Vol. 59, No. 1 (2000), pp. 3–25.

8 See Partha Chatterjee, *The Nation and Its Fragments* (Princeton, NJ: University Press, 1993); Sudipta Kaviraj, "On the Crisis of Political Institutions in India," *Contributions to Indian Sociology*, 18 (1984), pp. 223–43; and "A Critique of the Passive Revolution," *Economic and Political Weekly*, 23 (1988), pp. 45–47.

9 Partha Chatterjee, *The Politics of the Governed: Reflections on Popular Politics in Most of the World* (New York: Columbia University Press, 2004).

10 Cited by Corbridge and Harriss, p. 43.

11 Rajni Kothari, *Politics in India* (New York: Little, Brown, 1970), Chapter v.

12 Paul R. Brass, *The Politics of India Since Independence* (Cambridge: University Press, 1994), p. 37.

13 Sudipta Kaviraj, "On State, Society and Discourse in India," in James Manor (ed.), *Rethinking Third World Politics* (Harlow: Longman, 1991).

14 F. G. Bailey showed this, seminally, in his work on the politics of Orissa in the 1950s. See "Politics and Society in Contemporary Orissa," in Cyril Phillips (ed.), *Politics and Society in India* (London: Allen & Unwin, 1963).

15 Francine Frankel, *India's Political Economy, 1947–1977: The Gradual Revolution*, 2nd edn (Princeton, NJ: University Press, 2004) provides a compelling analysis of the way in which the Nehruvian project was derailed by local power holders.

16 Marguerite Robinson is one commentator on this change in her observations of the electoral process in rural Andhra Pradesh. By 1977 electoral outcomes no longer depended on "vote banks" controlled by local notables. See her *Local Politics: The Law of the Fishes — Development through Political Change in Medak District, Andhra Pradesh (South India)* (Delhi: Oxford University Press, 1988).

17 See Atul Kohli, *Democracy and Discontent: India's Growing Crisis of Governability*, (Cambridge: University Press, 1990).

18 On which, see the chapter by Stanley Kochanek in this volume.

19 James Manor, "Parties and the Party System," in Atul Kohli (ed.), *India's Democracy: An Analysis of Changing State-Society Relations* (Princeton, NJ: University Press, 1988), p.72.

20 This paraphrases Myron Weiner, "Congress Restored: Continuities and Discontinuities in Indian Politics," *Asian Survey*, 22, p. 253.

21 See Lloyd Rudolph and Susanne Hoeber Rudolph, *In Pursuit of Lakshmi: The Political Economy of the Indian State* (Chicago: University of Chicago Press, 1987).

22 Brass, p. 56.

23 Yogendra Yadav, "Reconfiguration in Indian Politics: State Assembly Elections 1993–95," *Economic and Political Weekly*, 31 (1996), pp. 2–3.

24 The share of seats of national parties declined through the general elections of the 1990s from 78 percent in 1991 to 68 percent in 1999, while that of parties based in single states increased from 16 percent to 29 percent.

25 Examples of such political leaders are Mulayam Singh Yadav in Uttar Pradesh and Lalu Prasad Yadav in Bihar.

26 Yadav, p. 100.

27 Sunil Khilnani, *The Idea of India* (London: Hamish Hamilton, 1997), pp. 58–59.

28 Khilnani, p. 59.

29 Mehta.

30 Javeed Alam, *Who Wants Democracy?* (Delhi: Orient Longman, 2004).

31 Partha Chatterjee, *Politics of the Governed*, argues that this is frequently the case. See also S. Jha *et al.*, "Governance in the Gullies: Democratic Responsiveness and Leadership in Delhi Slums," *World Development*, 35, 2 (2007), pp. 230–46, on the slums of Delhi; and John Harriss, "Antinomies of Empowerment: Observations on Civil Society, Politics and Urban Governance," *Economic and Political Weekly*, Vol. 42, No. 26 (2007), pp. 2,716–24 on local politics in Chennai.

32 Lloyd Rudolph and Susanne Hoeber Rudolph, "Redoing the Constitutional Design: From an Interventionist to a Regulatory State," in Atul Kohli, *Success of India's Democracy*, p. 161

33 Ashish Bose, "Beyond Population Projections: Growing North–South Disparity," *Economic and Political Weekly*, Vol. 42, No. 15 (2007), pp. 1,327–29.

34 Arun Agrawal, "The Indian Parliament," in Devesh Kapur and Pratap Bhanu Mehta (eds), *Public Institutions in India: Performance and Design* (Delhi: Oxford University Press, 2005), p. 99.

35 Agrawal, p. 94.

36 Agrawal, p. 94.

37 Brass, p. 46.

38 This section draws extensively on Rudolph and Rudolph, "Redoing the Constitutional Design"; and on James Manor, "The Presidency," in Kapur and Mehta.

39 Brass, pp. 43–45.

40 See note 1.

41 Rudolph and Rudolph, "Redoing the Constitutional Design," p. 154.

42 A recent study of the civil service is by K. P. Krishnan and T. V. Somanathan, "Civil Service: An Institutional Perspective," in Kapur and Mehta.

43 See James Rauch and Peter Evans, "Bureaucratic Structure and Bureaucratic Performance in Less Developed Countries," *Journal of Public Economics*, Vol. 75, No. 1 (2000), pp. 49–71.

44 Brass, p. 52.

45 On the transfer system see Robert Wade, "The Market for Public Office: Why the Indian State is Not Better at Development," *World Development*, Vol. 13, No. 4 (1985), pp. 467–97.

46 Brass, p. 54; and Pranab Bardhan, *The Political Economy of Development in India*, 2nd edn (Delhi: Oxford University Press, 1998).

47 Devesh Kapur and Pratap Bhanu Mehta, "Introduction," in Kapur and Mehta.

48 Kapur and Mehta, p. 12.

5

State-level politics, coalitions, and rapid system change in India

Virginia Van Dyke

The Indian political party system has changed dramatically in the last two decades. These changes have included the rise of Hindu nationalism and the emergence of the Bharatiya Janata party as a true national party and a rival to the Congress party in electoral strength and ideology; the increase in strength of state-based parties; the ethnification[1] of politics in north India, that is, the emergence of caste-based parties; and the arrival on center stage of coalition governments at the national, state, and local levels. In 1994 Brass wrote of the "universal presence of the Congress" in all states, "even where Congress has been reduced to seemingly permanent minority status."[2] More recently, Yadav referred to a "post-Congress polity,"[3] and a number of states have no significant presence of Congress at all. While the BJP was for some time expected to be unable to move outside of north and northwest India, where its implicit slogan of "Hindi, Hindu, Hindustan" could resonate, it won the assembly elections in Karnataka, one of the southern states, in 2008.

On 22 July, 2008 a trust vote was held by the Congress-led United Progressive Alliance (UPA) to establish its majority after the left parties withdrew support to protest the India–United States agreement on sharing nuclear technology. The BJP-led National Democratic Alliance (NDA) joined the move to bring the government down, while some state-based parties attempted to establish a "third front" apart from the two main alliances. The maneuverings that went on as Congress attempted to secure the requisite numbers threw into relief some of the fundamental changes and tendencies of the Indian political party system. First, in terms of the coalition at the Center, the regional parties continue to tend towards forming a third front that cannot be written off, even though the members of that front are transient. That is, it is not so clear that India is moving towards a permanent two-front system at the Center, despite the fact that it has been the pattern since 1998. Second, regional parties are crucial at the Center, but participate there largely to extract benefits and support at the state level where their interests essentially lie.

There are numerous examples of this phenomenon of state-based politicians utilizing their participation in coalitions at the Center to accomplish goals at the state level. Mayawati's Bahujan Samaj Party had, in 2007, accomplished the surprising feat of coming to power in Uttar Pradesh in a one-party majority government in spite of all indications suggesting coalition governments would be the political configuration in that state in the foreseeable future. Mayawati was a leader of the proposed third front at the Center and projected as the prime ministerial candidate. Apparently as a result, her primary opponent and *bête noire* in the state, Mulayam Singh Yadav, then reversed his long-term previous policy, deciding to side with Congress. Suddenly, "disproportionate assets" charges were filed by the Central Bureau of Intelligence (CBI) against Mayawati, charges that she maintains were politically motivated and engineered by the Congress-led central government. The leader of another party, Ajit Singh, who controls a few MPs in UP, was wooed by all three sides, opting finally to back Mayawati who could offer berths in her cabinet and who would be most useful in electoral understandings that would benefit him in the next general as well as state-level assembly elections.

State-level parties

Many states have a unique configuration of parties; some states have parties which are specific to only that state. Chhibber and Petrocik have shown that even Congress is in some sense a different party in each region as its support base varies by caste, class, religion, or language,[4] while Yadav and Heath have demonstrated that Congress has different supporters depending on the nature of the opposition, that is, Congress is the party of the well-off in opposition to the Left and the party of the lower socioeconomic groups in opposition to the BJP (see Table 5.1).[5]

In constructing a typology of state party systems, one would need to move fast as the situation is in a state of extreme flux. Formerly one-party dominated states have over time become two-party systems and in some cases multiparty systems thereafter. Those fragmented multiparty systems with a history of coalition formation may become stabilized as two-party systems, as seems to be occurring in UP. States where the BJP was allied with a regional party have become states where the BJP is making inroads in the place of the regional party.

In contrast to what is seen at the Center, the state-level systems do seem to be tending towards a two-party system (or two coalitions) as would be suggested by "Duverger's law."[6] Coalitions are emerging as old party structures break down: for example as Congress declines, fragments of the Janata Party become regional parties and the BJP establishes itself. Over time then, the tendency is towards two-party systems once again, that is, in some states the coalition period looks like a transition period, much like the short-lived coalitions that emerged after Congress lost control of a number of states for the first time in 1967.

The desire to expand and the need for regional party allies for national level coalitions, has led the BJP to seek a presence in every state, as, of course, does Congress. Congress has been less successful in forging alliances with regional parties, as regional parties first emerged in opposition to Congress; this is changing under the new compulsions of politics. The importance of coalition building was clearly illustrated in the 2004 general election when one of the crucial factors responsible for shifting the election result from the expected BJP-led NDA victory to one for the Congress-led coalition was the move of the DMK (with 16 seats) from the former to the latter. An ongoing, important change in state politics involves the emergence of the BJP as at least an alliance partner in every state but one. In spite of continued efforts, it has not been able "to open its account," by winning a seat in Kerala, as will be discussed further later.

Two-party systems comprised of the BJP in opposition to Congress include:

- Chhattisgarh
- Delhi
- Gujarat
- Himachal Pradesh
- Madhya Pradesh
- Maharashtra
- Rajasthan
- Uttarakhand

Table 5.1 Party composition of state governments in India, 1998–2007

State	Party composition of government after last election	Pre-poll or post-poll arrangement	Party composition of previous government	Type of competition
Two-Party Competition: INC vs BJP				
Chattisgarh	BJP (2008)	One-party government	BJP (2003)	BJP vs INC
Delhi	INC (2008)	One-party government	INC (2003)	BJP vs INC
Gujarat	BJP (2007)	One-party government	BJP (2002)	BJP vs INC
Himachal Pradesh	BJP (2007)	One-party government	INC (2003)	BJP vs INC
Madhya Pradesh	BJP (2008)	One-party government	BJP (2003)	BJP vs INC
Maharashtra	INC/NCP (2004)	Pre-poll	INC/NCP post-poll alliance (1999)	BJP/Shiv Sena vs INC/NCP
Rajasthan	INC (2008)	One-party government	BJP (2003)	BJP vs INC
Uttarakhand	BJP (2007)	One-party government	BJP (2002)	BJP vs INC
Two-coalition competition: Left-led front vs INC-led front				
Kerala	LDF (2006)	Pre-poll	UDF (2001)	INC-led front vs Left-led front
Left front vs INC				
Tripura	CPM and allies (2008)	Pre-poll	CPM and allies (2003)	INC vs Left
West Bengal	Left front (2006)	Left front coalition	Left front (2001)	Left front has been in government since 1977. Now challenged by INC, BJP and state party in shifting coalitions
Multiparty competition with unstable coalitions				
Andhra Pradesh	INC (2009)	One-party government	INC/TRS/Left (2004)	Shifting coalitions: state parties that were allies of the BJP and Congress left them
Bihar	JD(U)/BJP (Oct. 2005)*	Pre-poll	RJD/INC (2000)	Multiparty with unstable coalitions
Jharkhand	First JMM/INC, then BJP/JD(U)(2005)	Pre-poll		Multiparty with unstable coalitions
Karnataka	BJP (2008)	One-party government	JD(S)/INC (2004) then JD(S)/BJP	Shifting alliances between state party and INC, BJP
Kashmir	INC/JKNC (2008)	Post-poll	INC/PDP (2002)	Newly multiparty with shifting coalitions. Elections held under threats by militants.

Table 5.1 continued

State	Party composition of government after last election	Pre-poll or post-poll arrangement	Party composition of previous government	Type of competition
Orissa	BJD (2009)	One-party government	BJP/BJD (2004)	State party that was in alliance with the BJP severed ties before most recent election
Uttar Pradesh	BSP (2007)	One-party government	Initially BJP/BSP (2002) then SP-led coalition	Four major parties; shifting alliances
INC vs state party/BJP				
Assam	INC (with independents) (2006)	Post-poll	INC (2001)	INC vs regional party allied with BJP
Goa	INC/NCP (2007)	Pre-poll	(BJP/UGDP (2002)	Unstable coalitions
Haryana	INC (merged with HVP before election) (2005)	One-party government	BJP/INLD (BJP did poorly) (2000)	INC vs state party (HVP or INLD) allied with BJP
Punjab	BJP/SAD (2007)	Pre-poll	INC (2002)	INC vs persisting alliance between state party and BJP
Two state parties in alliance with smaller state parties which form coalitions at the national level				
Tamil Nadu	DMK/INC/PMK/CPM/CPI (alliance known as the DPA-Democratic Progressive Alliance) (2006)	Pre-poll alliance	AIADMK/TMC/INC/PMK/CPN/CPI (2001)	Two state parties ally with smaller state parties and the BJP or INC

Note: * elections were held in Bihar twice in 2005: in February and in October.

Source: Compiled from http://www.indian-elections.com/assembly-elections/; and the Election Commission of India, available at: http://www.eci.gov.in/StatisticalReports/ ElectionStatistics.asp; "Tamil Nadu heading for a coalition government," *Rediff: India Abroad*, March 14, 2006, online at http://www.rediff.com/news/2006/mar/14tn.htm; Kalpana Sharma, "An election too close too call," *The Hindu*, September 3, 2004, online at http://www.hindu.com/2004/10/03/stories/2004100301461400.htm; Peter Ronald deSouza, "Democracy's inconvenient fact," 543, *Seminar* (Nov. 2004), online at http://www.india-seminar.com/2004/543.htm; Prakash Kamat, "Congress-NCP alliance set to form government in Goa," *The Hindu*, June 6, 2007, online at http://www.thehindu.com.2007/06/06/stories/2007060613320100.htm; Venkitesh Ramakrishnan, "Soren's turn," *Frontline*, September 13–26, 2008, online at http://www.frontlineonnet.com/stories/20080926251903500.htm; Yogendra Yadav and Dhananjai Joshi, "The wave and what caused it," *The Hindu*, March 6, 2005, online at http://www.hindu.com/2005/03/06/stories/2005030603371600.htm

In Maharashtra, the BJP has been in an alliance with a regional party, the Shiv Sena, while Congress may ally with its own breakaway faction, the Nationalist Congress Party, as it did in the last assembly elections. (Even in two-party systems, it is very common to have small parties—often breakaway factions—and independents contesting.)

Another type of two-party system is characterized by Congress in opposition to a left front. In Kerala, this takes the form of two opposing coalitions. In West Bengal, where the Left front has been in power since 1977, there is a third party, the All-India Trinamul Congress (AITC), led by the mercurial Mamata Banerjee, which has taken support from the BJP or from Congress at different times. In the last assembly elections, the BJP was in alliance with the All-India Trinamool Congress, but was not able to win a seat.

States which have multiparty systems include Bihar, Uttar Pradesh, and Jharkhand. In a fourth type of system, Congress is in opposition to a regional party. In many cases the BJP will strike up an alliance with a regional party; sometimes it is able to parley such alliances into a foothold in the state. That is, or has been, the case in Andhra Pradesh, Assam, Goa, Haryana, Karnataka, Orissa, and Punjab. In Goa, for example, the BJP and the Maharashtrawadi Gomantak Party (MGP) together contested the assembly elections in 1994, with the BJP gaining four seats and the MGP gaining 12. In 1999 Rubinoff suggested that the BJP had "displaced the MGP as the preferred party of the state's Hindu voters."[7] By the 2007 elections the BJP and Congress were splitting the votes and the regional parties were relegated to one or two seats each.

This strategy is not always completely successful. In 2000 the BJP had an alliance with the Indian National Lok Dal in Haryana. The INLD did very well in the elections, and its partner, the BJP, did very poorly.[8] During the 2009 state-level elections in Andhra Pradesh and Orissa, a state party in each that had been allied with the BJP abruptly decided to contest the elections alone to the detriment of the latter. The state party in Orissa, the Biju Janata Dal, then came to power on its own. Mayawati's Bahujan Samaj Party in UP is also an important exception to the BJP's strategy as Mayawati has utilized coalitions with the BJP to enable it to come to power on its own while the BJP's strength in Uttar Pradesh has been severely attenuated.

A fifth type of party system exists in Tamil Nadu, where two opposing regional parties drawing on Dravidian nationalism, the DMK and the AIADMK, trade power, and each also trades alliances at the national level between the BJP and Congress. The AIADMK had supported the BJP in its first attempt to establish a coalition government at the Center in 1998, and was responsible for bringing that government down by withdrawing support. In spite of the BJP's giving the AIADMK a prominent role, including the position of Lok Sabha speaker, the leader of that party was dissatisfied with the BJP's refusal to dismiss the state government in Tamil Nadu controlled by her primary rival.

Coalition politics

Different configurations of party systems have given rise to very different types of coalitions; fragmented multiparty systems involving less institutionalized parties (opportunistic and rapidly changing),[9] on the one hand, more stable relationships among parties, on the other hand. Kerala is the sole example of a system of two "fronts," which alternate in power, but each expect to last the full five-year term once in power. Coalitions differ in India from those in many other political systems in that they are characterized by factionalism and frequent party splitting. They tend not to be defined by ideology, except in the cases of religious nationalist and left parties. In fact, McMillan argues, drawing on Luebbert, parties may prefer to maintain their uniqueness by not allying with parties that are too similar. For this reason it would be rare to find in India the ideologically linked minimum winning

71

Table 5.2 Election results in India by state: number of seats won by largest party or coalition, 2003–2008

State	Date of most recent election	Seats won by largest party/coalition+	Seats won by 2nd largest party/coalition	Seats won by 3rd largest party/coalition
Andhra Pradesh	2009	157 (INC)	106 (TDP/TRS/Left)	18 (PRP)
Arunachal Pradesh	2004	34 (INC)	9 (BJP)	2 (NCP) and 2 (AC)
Assam	2006	52 (INC)	27 (AGP/Left)	10 (BJP) and 10 (AUDF)
Bihar	2005	143 (JD(U)/BJP)	65 (RJD/CPM/ INC/NCP)	13 (LJP/CPI)
Chhattisgarh	2008	50 (BJP)	38 (INC)	2 (BSP)
Delhi	2008	42 (INC)	23 (BJP)	2 (BSP)
Goa	2007	16 (INC)	14 (BJP)	3 (NCP)
Gujarat	2007	117 (BJP)	59 (INC)	3 (NCP)
Haryana	2005	67 (INC)	9 (INLD)	2 (BP)
Himachal Pradesh	2007	41 (BJP)	23 (INC)	1 (BSP)
Jammu & Kashmir	2008	28 (JKNC)	17 (INC)	21 PDP
Jharkhand	2005	30 (BJP)	17 (JMM)	9 (INC)
Karnataka	2008	110 (BJP)	80 (INC)	28 (JD[S])
Kerala	2006	98 (LDF)	42 (UDF)	0 others
Madhya Pradesh	2008	142 (BJP)	71 (INC)	7 (BSP)
Maharashtra	2004	140 (NCP/INC)	116 (BJP/SHS)	4 (JSS)
Manipur	2007	30 (INC)	5 (MPP)	
Meghalaya	2008	25 (INC)	14 (UDP)	11 (NCP)
Mizoram	2003	21 (MNF)	12 (INC)	3 (MZPC)
Nagaland	2008	26 (NPF)	24 (INC)	2 (BJP) and 2 (NCP)
Orissa	2009	103 (BJD)	27 (INC)	6 (BJP)
Pondicherry	2006	10 (INC)	7 (DMK)	3 (AIADMK) 3 (PMC)
Punjab	2007	67 (SAD/BJP)	44 (INC)	
Rajasthan	2008	96 (INC)	78 (BJP)	6 (BSP)
Sikkim	2009	32 (SDF)		
Tamil Nadu	2006	163 (DMK+)	69 (AIADMK+)	2 others
Tripura	2008	46 (CPM)	10 (INC)	2 (CPI)
Uttarakhand	2007	34 (BJP)	21 (INC)	8 (BSP)
Uttar Pradesh	2007	206 (BSP)	97 (SP)	51 (BJP)
West Bengal	2006	227 (Left front)	30 (AITC/BJP)	21 (INC)

Notes: + Coalition here refers to pre-poll alliance; *BJP won 2 seats.

AC	=	Arunachal Congress	JSS	=	Jan Surajya Shakti
AGP	=	Asom Gana Parishad	LEF	=	Left Democratic Front; CPM-led alliance
AIADMK	=	All India Anna Dravida Munnetra Kazhagam	LJP	=	Lok Janshakti Party
AIMIM	=	All India Majlis-E-Ittehadul Muslimeen	MNF	=	Mizo National Front
AITC	=	All India Trinamool Congress	MPP	=	Manipur People's Party
AUDF	=	Assam United Democratic Front	MZPC	=	Mizoram People's Conference
BJD	=	Biju Janata Dal	NCP	=	Nationalist Congress Party
BJP	=	Bharatiya Janata Party	NPF	=	Nagaland People's Front
BSP	=	Bahujan Samaj Party	PDP	=	People's Democratic Party
CPI	=	Communist Party of India	PMC	=	Pudhucherry Munnetra Congress
CPM	=	Communist Party of India (Marxist)	PMK	=	Pattali Makkal Katchi
DMK	=	Dravida Munnetra Kazhagam	SDF	=	Sikkim Democratic Front
INC	=	Indian National Congress	SHS	=	Shiv Sena
INLD	=	Indian National Lok Dal	SP	=	Samajwadi Party
JD(S)	=	Janata Dal (Secular)	TDP	=	Telugu Desam Party
JKNC	=	Jammu & Kashmir National Conference	TRS	=	Telangana Rashtra Samithi
JMM	=	Jharkhand Mukti Morcha	UDF	=	United Democratic Front; Congress-led alliances

Sources: http://www.indian-elections.com/assembly-elections/; Election Commission of India, available at http://www.eci.gov.in/StatisticalReports/ElectionStatistics.asp

coalition proposed by theorists as the most likely result of post-electoral coalition negotiations in multiparty systems.[10] Further, because of factionalism and the strong likelihood of party splits, governments with excess parties are common, also challenging the ideal of the minimum winning coalition (see Table 5.2).

As Sridharan notes, India's first-past-the-post electoral system, also known as a single member district plurality (SMP) system, creates a situation whereby a small swing in the percentage of votes can produce a large swing in seats, thereby encouraging brinksmanship behavior among politicians.[11] Parties tend to gamble that their opponents might be decimated in the next election; they do not assume that they will be negotiating with the same party leaders in a few years, as would be the case in a more stable proportional representation system. Further, the intentions of the coalition partners are often not to establish a stable cabinet that can facilitate "good governance." Coalitions are formed with very short-term goals in mind, positioning themselves to be ready for the next election and to be in power long enough to reap some patronage benefits from that as well. Often, not many resources are expended in creating or running a coalition that is expected to be short-lived.[12] Further, politicians are aware that if they are never in power only the most ideologically dedicated supporters will continue to vote for them; they need to establish themselves as leaders of parties that may actually run the government. As Luebbert argues, party "leaders are motivated above all by their desire to remain party leaders."[13] One cannot remain a party leader long as the head of a party that is never in the government, particularly given its patronage nature of the system.

State politics cannot be considered in isolation from the government at the Center. Through the actions of the state governor, appointed by the party in power at the Center, and through the ability of the central government to utilize the imposition of "Presidents Rule" to dismiss state governments, state-level governments led by a party that is not the party at the Center sometimes have a limited lifespan. So, parties ally with Congress or the BJP at the national level to derive benefits, but also to ensure the longevity of their governments. However, power in India's federal system is shifting in the direction of the states for several reasons, including the dislike of state parties for a policy that may lead to their dismissal for partisan purposes (see Rudolph and Rudolph, this volume).

The rise of the BJP and its impact on state politics

1947–1967

Both at the national level and in many states a one-party dominant system characterized this time period. This term was developed by Rajni Kothari to describe a political system in which, although there were opposition parties along with free, competitive elections, the same party won every election. Part of the success of Congress at this time can be attributed to the fragmented opposition. Parties such as Swatantra, a party of large landowners advocating a more capitalist economic system, and the Praja Socialist Party had limited support in terms of constituency and geographical spread. Another advantage of Congress was its ability to absorb the opposition. The Shiromani Akali Dal, for example, actually merged with Congress on two separate occasions. Congress, through its domination of the national government could also control the states. In 1959, when a Communist-led government was elected in Kerala, the Congress-controlled central government was complicit in organizing massive protests, and then dismissing the state government, based on argument that public sentiment had changed, as evidenced, allegedly, by the protests.

Aiding in the development of regional identities and regional parties was the government policy of redrawing state boundaries along linguistic lines, known as the linguistic reorganization of states. This policy enabled parties that drew on a specific regional identity tied to language to have its likely constituency defined in one electoral arena. To use the Akali Dal as an example again, it was never able to win an election until the boundaries of Punjab were redrawn to give Sikhs a majority of the population in the reorganized unit.

1967–1977

In 1967, following the death of Jawaharlal Nehru in 1964 and the beginning of a long succession struggle which included a split in the party, Congress lost power in eight states. Coalition governments emerged in many states. These tended to be unstable and few lasted long, but it portended a future when Congress would not be the dominant party. In 1967 in Tamil Nadu, a non-Congress government emerged and two regional parties, the DMK and its offshoot, the AIADMK, have alternated in power ever since. Two-party systems emerged in Punjab and Uttar Pradesh the same year. In 1977 a Communist government came to power in West Bengal and has held power from that date.

Indira Gandhi, Nehru's daughter, gaining popularity for backing Bangladesh in the Pakistan civil war, solidified her leadership of the party in the elections of 1971. She restructured and centralized the party organ-ization; she began personally to make decisions regarding state-level politics, undermining institutional support for state Congress leaders. Although originally admired for her populist and pro-poor measures, a series of economic and political challenges led to her declaring the "emergency," involving a suspension of civil liberties that gave her the opportunity to jail many of her political opponents. However, while in jail, opposition leaders were then able to network with each other. After elections were called in 1977, a conglomeration of opposition parties came together to form the Janata Party, which won a decisive victory, allowing the first non-Congress government to take power at the center, as well as in a number of states.

1977–1989

The Janata Party fell apart due to infighting arising out of competing ambitions. The next elections brought Congress back to power as the "party that works." However, Indira Gandhi faced militant anti-state movements in both Punjab and Assam. The latter was a protest by Assamese-speaking Hindus against a lack of government control over an influx of Bengali speakers, largely Muslims, from Bangladesh. The former was a movement led by Sikhs for greater economic, political, and social auto-nomy for their state, which grew into a demand for outright secession about the same time as Indira Gandhi sent the Indian army into the Sikh central religious site to rout the militants. Indira Gandhi was assassinated in retaliation for this course of action, and her son, Rajiv Gandhi, assumed the position of prime minister in 1984. Concerns about Rajiv Gandhi's alleged corruption and elitism brought another "third front" government to power in 1989, the Janata Dal led by V. P. Singh, supported from the outside by the BJP.

1989–2008

The beginning of the BJP's electoral success dates to 1989. Although its predecessor party, the Bharatiya Jan Sangh, was a presence in Uttar Pradesh, it was never able to gather significant strength elsewhere. The Jan Sangh had been part of the Janata Party that provided an opposition to Congress at the Center and in many states in the 1970s. It established its new identity as the BJP in 1980. In the general election of 1984, in the midst of the sympathy wave after Indira Gandhi's assassination, the BJP won a mere two seats. In 1989 it won 86; in 1991, 120; and, by 1996, it had become the largest party (although far from a majority) and was asked to form the government. This it was unable to do because of its "majestic isolation," shunned as a coalition partner by most parties at that time because of its *Hindutva* ideology. However, in 1998, they were at last able to form a government at the center.

It also won state-level elections for the first time: in Madhya Pradesh, Rajasthan, and Himachal Pradesh in 1990; in UP in 1991; Delhi in 1993; and Maharashtra and Gujarat in 1995. There are a number of explanations as to why this party was able to make these phenomenal gains.

BJP politicians and ideologues refer to the BJP as "the party with a difference," by which they mean they are guided by an ideology and a vision; they are not simply seeking the *gaddi* or a powerful position. They are, in fact, a party with a difference in that they are part of a larger structure. The BJP grew out of a pre-existing organization called the Rashtriya Swayamsewak Sangh (RSS), which was founded in 1925 in a context of Hindu–Muslim riots. The intention of the organization was to train young men, ideologically and physically, to defend Hinduism against the perceived Muslim threat, as well as to construct a nation grounded in a specifically Hindu culture. A women's wing was added, somewhat reluctantly, later. The RSS has spawned a number of organizations, which are collectively referred to as the *Sangh Parivar* [Sangh family]. The Vishwa Hindu Parishad (VHP) and its offshoot, the Bajrang Dal, are active in advancing what they view as Hindu causes, from creating agitations around "disputed sites" such as the mosque in Ayodhya, or a Sufi shrine in Karnataka, to protesting so-called forced conversions and organizing attacks on Christian Churches in Gujarat, Orissa, and even Kerala.

All these organizations are closely intertwined; many members of the VHP and the BJP were trained by the RSS and hold joint membership. A particularly esteemed position within the RSS structure is that of a *pracharak*; an individual who is supposed to be a dedicated celibate lifetime worker. The head of the VHP is an RSS *pracharak*, as is former BJP Prime Minister, Atal Bihari Vajpayee.

Jaffrelot argues that over time the BJP has moved back and forth between agitation as a method of creating support and a focus on building up its grassroots organization.[14] In the late 1980s, the BJP committed itself to agitational methods, joining a VHP campaign to build a Hindu temple to Lord Ram on what was said to be the site of his birth, then occupied by a sixteenth-century mosque. The grand processions and ceremonies that accompanied this demand, along with favorable media coverage in much of the vernacular press, and the fortuitous timing of a television series on the life of Ram, created what was referred to as the *Ram Lahar*, or "Ram Wave." This emotional response to an upsurge of Hindu nationalist sentiment challenged the ideals of secularism associated with Nehru and the Congress.

The BJP utilized a number of other strategies to build its support, such as incorporating and promoting—even creating—Hindu religious figures to represent its message articulated through vitriolic speeches, some distributed on cassette tapes. Despite its rhetoric of a Hindu society undivided by castes, like other parties, it created a support base comprised of specific caste groups. For example, in UP, it gained the support of the Lodhi Rajputs along with its usual base of high caste voters, by promoting individuals from this caste into high positions in the party including that of chief minister. Again in common with other parties, it incorporated local notables who have the support of voters in their local area no matter to which party they belong.[15] Hansen argues that one of the primary reasons for its success in gaining the votes of the upper castes was that, in an era of Congress decline and aggressive caste-based mobilization by the backward castes and the scheduled castes, this party articulated an ideology of order and nationalistic pride in India that attracted them, particularly police officers and military personnel.[16]

Post-Ram Wave, other tactics have been used. Although, the BJP has played down Hindutva issues in the interests of coalition formation, communal tension and violence have continued to work to the BJP's advantage.[17] Horrific anti-Muslim riots in Gujarat were followed by a resounding BJP victory in the subsequent elections in that state in 2007.

But, the BJP has been particularly adept at coalition building, adopting this strategy when it was still disdained by Congress. Coalition formation with smaller parties at the state level, in conjunction with accommodating the state-based party at the Center, has been a useful policy. As a national, well-organized party, with ideologically motivated extra-parliamentary activists, the BJP can erode the support base of smaller regional parties, who see their primary opponent as the Congress.[18]

Karnataka: The BJP's "southern beachhead"[19]

Karnataka is an example of a state which moved from a one-party-dominant system to a competitive two-party system to a multiparty system after the entry of the BJP into this state's politics. After a series of unstable coalitions, a BJP-led one-party government took power in 2008. Its success in Karnataka demonstrates the BJP's ability to parlay short-lived alliances or coalitions into an expanded presence.

Karnataka is a southern state, former bastion of the Congress party, which evolved into a two-party system in 1983 when Ramakrishna Hegde of the Janata Party became chief minister with the support of the BJP. The Janata Party split, but the three faction leaders—H. D. Deve Gowda, Ramakrishna Hegde, and S.R. Bommai—were reunited in the 1990s and the party won the assembly elections in 1994, along with the general elections in 1996. It built its strength by combining the support of the two major castes, the Vokkaligas and the Lingayats, along with "other backwards, scheduled castes, and Muslims."[20] In 1998, the Janata Dal split again, and Hegde, who was a Brahman, but whose support base was among the Lingayat community, fashioned an alliance with the BJP with his newly formed Lok Shakti party. According to Gould, the BJP, whose state-level leader was a Lingayat, successfully combined "standard Hindutva appeal[s]" and appeals around farmers' issues to split the "Lingayat–Vokkaliga

axis," the basis for the Janata Dal's success. In so doing, the BJP was able to make inroads into the state.[21]

Before the assembly elections in 2004, the Lok Shakti had become the Janata Dal (United) while Deve Gowda's faction had become the Janata Dal (Secular), perceived as promoting Vokkaligas and also dynastic rule.[22] In the state elections in 2004 the BJP won the largest number of seats and two former adversaries, the Congress and the JD(S), formed a coalition government, although there were some talks between the BJP and the JD(S), as well. The Congress party nominally controlled the post of chief minister, but Congress Chief Minister M. Dharam Singh was very solicitous of taking the advice and recommendations of Deve Gowda, head of the JD(S), who was seen as inordinately powerful. After the *panchayat* (local-level) elections, however, Congress moved toward setting up joint councils with a dissident from the JD(S), the former Deputy Chief Minister Siddaramaiah, who had chief ministerial aspirations, and who had also made joint appearances with Congress leaders at backward caste forums. This was perceived by the JD (S) as an attempt to split the party and absorb MLAs, as Congress had done during the previous Congress-led administration. Deve Gowda's son, Kumaraswamy, abruptly resigned from the government, in spite of Deve Gowda's assurances to Congress that he would rein in his son, took the majority of MLAs with him, and formed a coalition government with the BJP. This was a shocking move considering the party's secular stance. It appears to have been done in order to secure the post of chief minister for Kumaraswamy; what is still not clear is whether the outspokenly secular Deve Gowda's protests were sincere or whether the split in the family was but a drama for the press and public.[23]

The BJP and the JD (S) agreed that each party would have a turn at the chief minister's post for 20 months; an arrangement identical to that which had *not* worked out for the BJP with Mayawati previously, an ominous sign for them. When Kumaraswamy was supposed to turn over the position to the BJP, complaints against the BJP were concocted and the deadline came and went. Much to the JD (S)'s surprise, however, the BJP, rather than continuing to support the alliance, withdrew its support to the government, and President's Rule was imposed. Second-tier party leaders then went back to Congress, attempting to negotiate a new tie-up with the party that they had snapped ties with so abruptly. When those talks failed, the government was formed once again with the BJP and the JD (S), but the BJP chief minister resigned his position after a week when the JD (S) would not commit to supporting him in a confidence motion while raising new conditions which were not part of the original arrangement. Deve Gowda certainly did not want to be the person who facilitated the establishment of a BJP government in Karnataka. However, the unpopular move of ending the government led to the exodus of a number of party leaders, mainly to Congress, but also to the BSP and the BJP. The BJP capitalized on being the "injured party"; in the 2008 elections, the BJP came to power largely on its own, with the assistance of a few independents. In spite of painstaking organizational work in the state by the Sangh Parivar, and an emotive issue as well, that of the "disputed" Sufi shrine of Bababudangiri, it was playing the factional politics game that enabled the BJP to achieve its "beachhead."[24]

Coalition in Punjab

Punjab is a Sikh majority state, in which the party configuration includes a party that draws its support specifically from Sikhs. The Shiromani Akali Dal (SAD) was founded in 1920 as the action group to lead a nonviolent agitation to reclaim the historic Sikh gurdwaras (places of worship and gathering) from private hands into which they had devolved. This organization then became a political party which has led a number of campaigns to secure specific rights for the Sikh community. Since leadership of the community passed into the hands of a dominant cultivating caste, the Jats,

the latter have largely supported this party, while some urban and scheduled caste Sikhs have tended to support Congress.

In 1997, the normal electoral system was reestablished after more than a decade of a militant movement which disrupted elections and marginalized the mainstream parties in Punjab. No assembly elections were held between 1985 and 1992; the 1992 elections were held in the face of a militant-declared boycott, and few crossed that line, either out of sympathy or fear. Since 1997 the Akali Dal has been in coalition with the BJP, when the Akali Dal is in power in the state, or a BJP-led coalition is in power at the Center. This coalition works politically and socially on a number of different levels. At the national level, the BJP adds members of parliament from the Akali Dal to its own strength. At the state level, it establishes intercommunal harmony (as the BJP is supported by Hindus and the SAD by Sikhs) which helps to assure continued normal relations after an extended period of communal tension and violence.[25]

From a political aspect, the support base of each party is completely separate. As the two parties are not trying to entice each other's supporters, they reinforce rather than undermine each other. Ideologically, they are both religious nationalist parties. More than this, the BJP alliance supports the Akali Dal against factional splits that could undermine an Akali Dal-led government. Promoting factional splits was a way that Congress had been able to undermine Akali Dal governments in the past—and in fact is a strategy that Congress had used against regional parties elsewhere—and this alliance is a protection, particularly when the BJP is in power at the Center. So the Akali Dal has included the BJP in its government, even when they have had a clear majority on their own. Unlike in other states, where the BJP has eroded the support of a regional party with which it is allied, the Akali Dal is an institutionalized political party whose voters would be highly unlikely to vote for the BJP, except in the case of seat adjustments (and maybe not even then).

The Counterexample of Kerala

Kerala is a counterexample in a number of different ways: it has stable coalition governments made up of two fronts; it is one of only two major states where the communist parties have a strong presence; and it is the only major state where the BJP has virtually no presence. The BJP has done its best to penetrate the party system in Kerala: there is a network of RSS shakhas, particularly in the capital; other Sangh Parivar organizations are present; agitations over "Hindu issues" have taken place; and members of the RSS sometimes clash physically with Communist Party members. In spite of all this, the BJP has not had the ability to penetrate the two fronts that dominate Kerala politics, and there is little scope to contest outside these fronts, each of which receives more than 40 percent of the vote, with little margin between them.[26] Further, Chiriyankandath argues, the type of mobilization that leads to actual communal violence has had the effect of undermining the BJP's position rather than reinforcing it.[27]

Coalitions are more stable in Kerala than in many other states in India for a number of reasons. The two fronts are to some extent based on ideology, particularly the Left front, in contrast to other states in India. An early emergence of coalitions has led to the expectation of continued coalitions, rather than political parties indulging in brinksmanship behavior in an effort to establish one-party rule. Therefore, the coalitions themselves are more institutionalized, with coordination among parties. The party system itself is also institutionalized; parties in many cases have had long-term support in castes or communities in constituencies located in particular geographical regions.

Uttar Pradesh and "ethnic parties"

Religious nationalism and caste-based politics have been alternative forms of political mobilization since the BJP used the Ram Temple to build support at the same time that V. P. Singh introduced new job reservations in central government departments and seats in educational institutions for backward castes. This is referred to in India as Mandal (the name of the commission that recommended caste-based affirmative action for backward castes) versus Mandir (Hindu temple). Cleavage-based politics is a type of identity politics where parties compete to shape voters' perception of the primary group to which they belong. For example, the Kurmis, a "backward caste" in UP, some of whom have adopted the name, Patel, have been courted at election time by several parties:

1 the BJP, appealing to the idea of an "organic" Hindu whole
2 the Samajwadi Party attempting to put together a coalition of backward castes and Muslims, but perceived as dominated by Yadavs
3 Apna Dal (translates as "our own party") a caste-based party based on Kurmis/Patels
4 the BSP trying to form a coalition of the Bahujan Samaj (the majority of low castes), but perceived as promoting mostly Chamars.

Caste has, of course, always been important in Indian politics, which has had reserved constituencies for scheduled castes from its inception; in fact, some reservations stem from the colonial period. In the 1970s Congress utilized the KHAM strategy in Gujarat, which was an attempt to put together a coalition of castes: Kshatriyas, Harijans, Adivasis, and Muslims. In UP, Charan Singh challenged Congress by putting together a coalition of backward agrarian-based castes. What has evolved since then, and represents a change, is what Kanchan Chandra has referred to as the "ethnification" of politics or the tailored appeal to a specific caste by an "ethnic party" that explicitly excludes other castes.[28] While Charan Singh, although himself a Jat, appealed to OBCs in general, his son, Ajit Singh, appeals specifically to Jats. While the KHAM strategy referred to "Harijans" as a category to be included, the scheduled caste leader from Uttar Pradesh, Mayawati, originally appealed only to Harijans while vehemently criticizing upper castes, and, in fact, her appeal was most specifically to her own caste, the Chamars. Meanwhile, Mulayam Singh Yadav's party has been so perceived as responding specifically to the Yadav caste—despite the fact that he also had broad support from Muslims—that a new term emerged, the "Yadavization" of politics in UP.

Caste-based parties are emerging because of the heightened competition for government benefits as more groups become politically mobilized and come to include a strata of educated, ambitious individuals. While scheduled caste/low caste voters once voted for their higher caste patrons, and landless laborers voted as the landowners directed them to vote, castes have begun to vote for their own parties. That is, rather than patronage links being vertical, linkages are now horizontal. As India is a "patronage democracy," status recognition, and material goods have both come from the state, not from achievement in the private sector, although this is changing rapidly. Those who can do so, opt for careers in government service, those who cannot, gain "material and psychic benefits" from their "proximity" to the state.[29] Political parties gain the support of groups by incorporating their members in important positions. Further, Chandra argues that caste provides a shorthand way for voters to identity who is "one of them" and, therefore, likely to dispense government benefits in their direction; therefore, the tendency is to vote for parties that incorporate one's own caste,[30] if, in fact, the party is large enough to have an actual chance at office.[31]

The BSP, led by Mayawati, until its transformation in 2007 to a broad-based party, was the quintessential example of a caste-based party, and the state of UP an example of the impact caste-based parties have had. This state has moved from a one-party dominant system, to a basically two-party system to a multiparty

system in which Congress is by far the most junior member. As Yadav and Heath argue, wherever cleavage-based politics emerge, Congress changes from a "catch-all party" to "a catch-none party."[32] The BJP was able to draw away the high-caste voters, along with certain specific backward castes who supported the BJP in their competition with other backward castes; Mulayam Singh's Samajwadi Party was supported largely by Yadavs and Muslims; and the BSP initially drew its support from scheduled castes and some Muslims.

The BSP was founded by Kanchi Ram, a Dalit government employee who initially started the Backward and Minority Communities Employment Federation (BAMCEF), an organization of scheduled caste government workers who felt they were not getting due respect.[33] Mayawati, once second in command, but known for her autocratic leadership style, emerged as the chief minister-designate. After Kanchi Ram's death in 2004, Mayawati utilized a strategy that was focused unapologetically on gaining political power for Dalits, a name used by Kanshi Ram and Mayawati to broaden the party's appeal beyond its solid base among the Chamars, to all the scheduled castes. Mayawati allied first with the Samajwadi Party, then abruptly left that alliance in an acrimonious fashion when the SP seemed to be gaining strength because of its participation in the coalition. This led to the infamous guest house incident in which Mulayam Singh supporters surrounded the guest house where she was staying, leading her to believe they planned to kill her. Her response to this was to contact the BJP, a high caste-based party with which she never would have been expected to ally. She ultimately formed coalitions with the BJP on three occasions: June to October 1995; March to September 1997; and March to October 2002. The BJP supported her in the belief that she could and would transfer Dalit votes to them in upcoming elections. In each case, she unceremoniously pulled out of the alliance when it suited her purpose to do so, for reasons that often left analysts guessing as to her motives. She also forced the BJP to support her

Dalit-friendly policies, to the dismay of the BJP's high-caste supporters. Although the BJP was counting on gaining the support of scheduled caste voters, it really never reaped such benefits. While allying with a high caste-based party like the BJP could have dampened her supporters' enthusiasm, her clear upper hand in these relationships actually enthused those who supported her.

The BSP has successfully appropriated and utilized symbols of empowerment to an extent unmatched by other parties, transforming the political geography of the state. Ambedkar statues dot the countryside, the BSP head-quarters in Lucknow sits next to a large mausoleum containing very large statues of scheduled caste leaders, including Mayawati and Kanchi Ram, and some scheduled caste villages, or scheduled caste areas in villages contain "pucca" (brick) houses built with funds from the government. Mayawati has also constructed a very large park in the center of town, Ambedkar Park, containing statues of Dalit heroes. When the previous Mayawati-led government ended its tenure and a Mulayam Singh-led government took its place, work stopped on the Ambedkar Park and started instead on Ram Manohar Lohia Park, dedicated to Mulayam Singh's mentor.

In the most recent assembly elections in UP, in 2007, Mayawati expanded both her appeal and her distribution of tickets, granting official party support to candidates from higher castes, which suggests that the party has actually moved away from being an ethnic party. It was able to form the government on its own for the first time, ending, at least in the short term, a long period of coalition government.

Conclusion

The focus here on the ability of parties to form governments raises the question of what role ideology and policy play in state-level politics. Coalition theorists disagree on the degree to which policy or power drives the decision-making process among politicians forming coalitions. In India, ideology, or the desire to put into place particular policies, is less impor-tant than gaining control over the government for several reasons: policy issues are not the stuff of political campaigns; politicians' goals are often tied up with patronage distribution; and there is a consensus among the parties on some of the larger issues. For example, with the introduction of neoliberal economic reforms in the early 1990s, states have a larger dis-cretionary role in attempting to attract foreign investment, and even in independently taking out loans from the World Bank for various projects. Many parties approve of these policies although this is more contentious in the states controlled by the Left.

Further, the less policy is discussed, the easier it is to keep a party together; in fact, once a state government is in power, it typically avoids being in session to the extent legally permissible. Much of what passes for policy-making has more to do with patronage distribution, such as the decision by a state government to add a particular caste to the list of castes that qualify for affirmative action benefits, or contesting over water distribution among states, which primarily affects farmers.

There are specific powers that are granted to the states by the constitution; among these are education and law and order. In both these areas, the BJP has clearly made decisions unique to its interests. Certainly, the strategy of the BJP to attract coalition partners has compelled it to place some of its most contentious issues on the backburner, such as the demand for a uniform civil code and building a grand temple to the god Ram on the site of the demolished mosque. Lall argues that it was in education policy that the NDA government made its most distinc-tive mark on the Indian polity. However, efforts by Murli Manohar Joshi, Human Resource Development Minister, to promote new textbooks that "saffronized" Indian history while removing the work of prominent historians, were resisted by state-level coalition partners who were opposed to accepting the new textbooks, insisting that education is a state subject.[34] Mitra argues that, with regard to minorities, the BJP's policies represent less of a break with the past than many expected. Policies that the BJP has attempted to implement have, again, been blocked by coalition partners at the state level,[35] none of whom, with the exception of the Shiv Sena, supports a Hindutva ideology. Further, many state-level parties are concerned about alienating Muslims or other minorities. The most egregious failings of the BJP governments at both the central and state levels have been in the area of violence against minority groups.

Notes

1 On which, see Kanchan Chandra, *Why Ethnic Parties Succeed: Patronage and Ethnic Head Counts in India* (Cambridge: University Press, 2004).

2 Paul R. Brass, *The Politics of India since Independence*, 2nd ed. (Cambridge: University Press, 1994), p. 125.

3 Yogendra Yadav, "The New Congress Voter," *Seminar* 2003, No. 526 (http://www.india-seminar.com/2003/526/526%20yogendra%20yadav.htm).

4 Pradeep Chhibber and John R. Petrocik, "Social Cleavages, Elections, and the Indian Party System," in Richard Sisson and Ramashray Roy (eds.), *Diversity and Dominance in Indian Politics*, vol. 1 (New Delhi: Sage, 1990), reprinted in Zoya Hasan (ed.), *Parties and Party Politics in India* (New Delhi: Oxford University Press, 2002).

5 Anthony Heath and Yogendra Yadav, "The United Colors of Congress: Social Profile of Congress Voters, 1996 and 1998," *Economic and Political Weekly [EPW]*, (21–28 August, 1999), reprinted in ibid.

6 This is argued by Eswaran Sridharan, in "Coalitions and Party Strategies in India's Parliamentary Federation," *Publius: The Journal of Federalism*, Vol. 33, No. 4 (Fall 2003), p. 136.

7 Arthur G. Rubinoff, "Conflicting Ambitions in Goa's Parliamentary Elections," in Ramashray Roy and Paul Wallace (eds.), *Indian Politics and the 1998 Election: Regionalism, Hindutva and State Politics* (New Delhi: Sage Publications, 1999), p. 266.

8 Yogendra Yadav and Oliver Heath, "A Split Verdict in Haryana," *Frontline*, Vol. 17, No. 7

(1–14 April, 2000). http://www.hinduonnet.com/fline/fl1707/17070490.htm.

9 Brass has defined an institutionalized party system as one that encompasses "parties [that] persist over time, that regularly win a number of seats, and that know their areas of strength." He argues that the degree of institutionalization of a political party system correlates strongly with stable coalitions; Paul R. Brass, "Party Systems and Government Stability in the Indian States," *The American Political Science Review*, Vol. 71, No. 4 (December 1977), p. 1,396.

10 Alistair McMillan, "The BJP Coalition: Partisanship and Power-Sharing in Government," in Katharine Adeney and Lawrence Saez (eds.), *Coalition Politics and Hindu Nationalism* (London and New York: Routledge, 2005), pp. 20–21.

11 E. Sridharan, "Principles, Power and Coalition Politics in India: Lessons from Theory, Comparison and Recent History," in D. D. Khanna and Gert W. Kueck (eds.), *Principles, Power and Politics* (New Delhi: Macmillan, 1999).

12 Virginia Van Dyke, "'Jumbo Cabinets,' Factionalism, and the Impact of Federalism: Comparing Coalition Governments in Kerala, Punjab, and Uttar Pradesh," in Paul Wallace and Ramashroy Roy (eds.), *India's 2004 Elections: Grassroots and National Perspectives* (New Delhi: Sage Publications, 2007).

13 Gregory M. Luebbert, *Comparative Democracy: Policymaking and Governing Coalitions in Europe and Israel* (New York: Columbia University Press, 1986), p. 46.

14 Christophe Jaffrelot, *The Hindu Nationalist Movement in India* (New York: Columbia University Press, 1996).

15 Bangarappa in Karnataka, for example, has been a Congress CM twice, started two of his own parties, and then won a seat in parliament on a BJP ticket. When he left the BJP to join the Samajwadi Party, he resigned his seat in the Lok Sabha and stood for election again in 2005. Once again, he won.

16 Thomas Blom Hansen, *The Saffron Wave: Democracy and Hindu Nationalism in Modern India* (Princeton, NJ: University Press, 1999).

17 Steven Wilkinson, *Votes and Violence: Electoral Competition and Ethnic Riots in India* (Cambridge: University Press, 2004).

18 Sridharan, "Coalitions and Party Strategies." pp. 150–52.

19 Term borrowed from Harold A. Gould, "The 12th General Election in Karnataka: The BJP Achieves its Southern Beachhead," in Ramashray Roy and Paul Wallace (eds.), *Indian Politics and the 1998 Election: Regionalism, Hindutva and State Politics* (New Delhi: Sage Publications, 1999).

20 Gould, p. 189.

21 Gould, pp. 204–208.

22 The following two paragraphs are based on interviews with politicians and political party workers in Karnataka in 2006. I am grateful to Mohan Kondajji for allowing me access to his extensive private collection of newspaper clippings.

23 Interviews in Karnataka; and "A Clever Ploy by a Humble Farmer?" *Indian Express*, 18 January, 2006.

24 As predicted by James Manor in 1998, the BJP's success in Karnataka depended on the Janata Dal self-destructing; James Manor, "Southern Discomfort: The BJP in Karnataka," in Thomas Blom Hansen and Christophe Jaffrelot (eds.), *The BJP and the Compulsions of Politics in India* (Delhi: Oxford University Press, 1998).

25 Ashutosh Kumar, "Electoral Politics in Punjab: Study of Akali Dal", *Economic and Political Weekly* (3–10 April, 2004).

26 James Chiriyankandath, "Bounded Nationalism: Kerala and the Social and Regional Limits of Hindutva," in Thomas Blom Hansen and Christophe Jaffrelot (eds.), *The BJP and the Compulsions of Politics in India* (Delhi: Oxford University Press, 1998), p. 203.

27 Chiriyankandath, p. 216.

28 Chandra, pp. 3–5.

29 Chandra, p. 12.

30 Chandra, pp. 57–60.

31 Chandra, p. 13.

32 Yadav and Heath, "The United Colors of Congress," pp. 136–45.

33 This section draws on Van Dyke, "'Jumbo Cabinets,' Factionalism and the Impact of Federalism."

34 Marie Lall, "Indian Education Policy under the NDA Government," in Katherine Adeney and Lawrence Saez (eds.), *Coalition Politics and Hindu Nationalism* (London and New York: Routledge, 2005).

35 Subrata K. Mitra, "The NDA and the Politics of 'Minorities' in India," in Katherine Adeney and Lawrence Saez (eds.), *Coalition Politics and Hindu Nationalism* (London and New York: Routledge, 2005).

6

Pakistan's politics and its economy

Shahid Javed Burki

Introduction

This chapter has three parts. The first lays out the main argument on which the analysis of the chapter is based. It is followed by the listing and then development of some of the themes that help to explain the country's economic, social, and political development in the past. The third part examines the current situation and indicates what might happen if the country's political and economic leaders do not act to move the country in the right direction at this critical juncture in its history.

Intertwining of politics and economics: The case of Pakistan

Political and economic developments are intertwined processes, with the one affecting the other. Economists, particularly economic historians, have begun to recognize that it is difficult to map the economic progress of a society without fully understanding its political evolution. That the relationship also works in the other direction is now being appreciated by political scientists as well.

Politics and economics have had a more profound impact on one another in Pakistan than in most developing countries. Why that is,

has been and will continue to be the case will be a recurrent theme of this chapter. In Pakistan's case, this interaction between economics and politics is further complicated by the enormous influence over the country of external forces and the changes in the external environment in which the policymakers must operate. Both economics and politics are affected by the changes that are taking place outside the country's borders and over which policymakers have little or no control. The most important of these is, of course, the rise of Islamic extremism in the part of the world in which Pakistan is situated. There is a developing consensus that, for a variety of reasons, Pakistan is now at the epicenter of this movement.

Pakistan's politics, its economy, and its external relations have been on a rollercoaster ride ever since the country gained independence on 14 August, 1947, some six decades ago. It ran into turbulence within a year of its birth when Muhammad Ali Jinnah, the country's founding father, withdrew from active politics on account of ill health. His death on 11 September, 1948 left a political void that was not filled for a decade. It was the extreme turbulence and confusion that prevailed during the decade after Jinnah's death that created an opportunity for General

Muhammad Ayub Khan, the first Pakistani to be appointed to the position of commander-in-chief, to bring the military into politics.[1] Ayub Khan's intervention created a precedent that was followed by three other army commanders.

Pakistan became politically stable only when the military was in charge. That was for 33 years in the country's 61-year history. Only four leaders governed during the time the military was in control. Only in one case did power directly flow from one military leader to another. That was when General Yahya Khan forced the politically and physically weakened Ayub Khan out of office in 1969 and became president himself.

Economics played an important role in Ayub Khan's departure. His economic model, appreciated in particular by the community of foreign donors, had produced impressive macroeconomic results.[2] GDP increased by 6.1 percent a year and income per head of the population by 3.8 percent per annum. But an impression was created that the rewards of economic growth ended up concentrated in a few hands. There was considerable discontent in the country's eastern wing which first led to a popular political movement against the regime and finally to the breakup of the country.

Economics was also the reason for the demise of the administration of Zulfikar Ali Bhutto that succeeded two successive military regimes and created the expectation that the economy would deliver more to the masses than had happened during the Ayub Khan period. Bhutto adopted an entirely different model of economic management from that followed by his military predecessors. He placed the public rather than the private sector at the commanding heights of the economy. However, the expanded role of the state created different kinds of exploitation, this time by government functionaries who were prepared to oblige their political masters by using the economic entities they controlled for granting favors. The result was growing discontent and a sharp slow down of the economy. There was once again a popular movement which led to

regime change and brought the military back to power in 1977, this time under General Zia ul-Haq.

Economics contributed to regime change once again—albeit somewhat less significantly—in the late 1990s when General Pervez Musharraf forced an elected prime minister out of office. Had the economy fared better economically under a succession of civilian prime ministers, the military's intervention in 1999 might not have been as welcomed as was the case when Musharraf assumed control.

Another transition from military to civilian control has now (2008) occurred, but in circumstances very different from those that prevailed on previous occasions. The military was forced to yield control not because of economic difficulties but because of the extraordinary mobilization of some segments of civil society. On 18 August, 2008, four days after President Pervez Musharraf celebrated Pakistan's birthday, he resigned after coming under intense pressure from the political parties that had won massive victories in the elections held on 18 February, 2008. The parties threatened to impeach the president in case he did not surrender his position. After resisting for a few days, he tendered his resignation.

Economic difficulties followed the change in the governing order rather than preceding it.[3] What will happen now will depend on how the various forces that have had important roles in the past will affect the new, evolving situation. In order to anticipate how the current situation is likely to evolve, we will lay out some of the themes that explore the interaction between economic and political forces and how both are affected by the country's external environment. However, before spelling out these themes it would be useful to underscore one other feature of Pakistan's political history.

In the two relatively long periods of civilian rule, each lasting eleven years, more than a dozen persons held power, but derived it not from such political institutions as the parliament or political parties. Most of them gained positions of power because of the alliances they were able to forge outside the formal political structure. There was much political turmoil in the decade immediately after independence when seven prime ministers held power. In 1988– 99, another period of long civilian rule, power changed hands seven times as well (see Table 6.1). The only time the country gained political stability during civilian rule was in the six-year-period when Zulfikar Ali Bhutto was in control. However, even Bhutto ruled as a quasi-dictator rather than as the head of a political party. In other words, the civilian leadership, when exercising power, failed to institutionalize the base of their support. Had they done that, the military would have found it more difficult to intervene.

During the time the military held the reins of power, the economy also did well economically, growing at an average yearly rate of 6.5 percent (see Table 6.2). Rapid economic progress was often used by the military to claim legitimacy for governing the country.

This rollercoaster history raises two important questions—important not only to develop a better understanding of Pakistan's exceptionally turbulent history but also to lay down some markers for the future. The questions are: why did the military intervene so frequently in the country's political life? And, why did the economy perform so well during the period of military domination compared to the time the civilians were in charge? Finding some answers to these questions will be the main subject of this chapter.

Themes to understand Pakistan's development: state, society, and economy

We will structure the story of political, social and economic change in Pakistan around a number of themes concerning politics, economics, and relations with the world outside. These will be brought together into a fabric

Table 6.1 Political periods in Pakistan's history

Period	Type of governance
August 1947–October 1958	Competitive politics
October 1958–December 1971	Military control
December 1971–July 1977	Quasi-dictatorship
July 1977–August 1988	Military control
August 1988–October 1999	Competitive politics
October 1999–March 2008	Military control
March 2008–	Competitive politics

Table 6.2 United States' assistance to Pakistan

Period	Amount ($ million)	Yearly average ($ million)
Pre-first Plan	181.2	30.2
First Plan 1955–60	472.9	94.6
Second Plan 1960–65	504.1	100.8
Third Plan 1965–70	197.4	39.5
Fourth Plan 1970–75	141.1	28.2
Pre-first Afghan War 1975–1981	23.3	3.9
First Afghan War 1982–1989	1,517.2	216.7
Post-Afghan War 1990–98	2,216.4	246.3
Post-nuclear tests 1999–2001	303.3	75.8
Support for war on terror 2001–07	1,695.4	333.1

Source: various issues of *Pakistan Survey*

that will keep on changing its weave and color as time progresses. Some of these themes were developed in my earlier works;[4] the rest are the product of reflections on the way Pakistan has once again, at the time of yet another transfer of power from the military to the civil, plunged into a serious economic and political crisis.

I will first list these themes and then go on to develop them at some length:

- There were constant changes in Pakistan's social landscape. These led to the emergence of new social and economic groups that competed for power with those that were already established. Demography played an important role in this development.

- Transfer of population following the partition of British India "Muslimized" Pakistan with the proportion of Muslims in the population increasing from 72 to 93 percent. This demographic event laid the ground for the later radicalization of the society. Islam may not have developed such a prominent place in the society had there been a larger presence of non-Muslims in the population of the country.

- There was an absence of an institutional structure that could have helped the socio-economic groups to engage in dialogue with one another in order to reach an understanding on the sharing of economic power as well as the economic rewards that come from access to power.

- The group conflict took place outside the confines of a formal political structure. This produced conflict that, in the eyes of the military, seemed to threaten national security and justified its repeated ventures into the political space.

- The first generation of Indian leaders took time to come to terms with the partition of British India and the creation of a new state on the basis of religion. This led to a serious conflict between what some scholars have called the idea of India[5]— that a state could accommodate diverse cultures, religions, and languages provided institutions were built that would give voice to each of these groups, and the idea of Pakistan[6]—that the Muslims of British India needed a state of their own to preserve their distinct identity. An impression was created that India wished to undo Partition and create the unified state for which its leaders had campaigned during the independence movement. Thus threatened, the Pakistani establishment, in particular the country's military, placed protecting the country's integrity and survival above issues concerning nation building.[7]

- The preoccupation with India's real or perceived intentions towards the country led to the creation of a triangular relationship involving Islamabad, New Delhi, and Washington. This was to be tested a number of times and is once again at the center of attention.

- It was an accident of history that the opportunities for crafting close relations with Washington occurred mostly when the military was in power in Islamabad. The military's preoccupation with India gave an edge to the relations between Islamabad and New Delhi.

- On the surface, the military's economic performance was impressive. However, that performance was not based on urgently needed structural reforms that could have placed economic progress on a growth trajectory that was continuous and ensured large and sustainable increases in national income. Instead, the military leadership relied on the economic sustenance provided by the United States.

- The military used political power to improve its economic base. This was done mostly to keep in line the senior officers.[8]

- Long periods of rule by the military led to a highly centralized system of governance that made the provinces totally subservient to the center. This contributed to the emergence of serious tensions among the provinces. It was this conflict between the military-dominated center and the province of East Pakistan that led to a bloody civil war between East and West Pakistan in 1971 and to the emergence of the country's eastern wing as Bangladesh.

I will now develop in some detail each of these eight themes and then discuss what may lie in the country's future if the current leadership groups do not develop a strong political–institutional base.

Changing social fabric

The continuous evolution of the social landscape with the emergence of new groups was an extraordinary feature of Pakistan's economic, social, and political development. In that respect, Pakistan presents a more dynamic picture than other countries of South Asia. The creation of new social structures was the consequence of at least three circumstances. The first of these was the social composition of the leadership that led the movement for the creation of a Muslim state once the British left India. The political elite that spearheaded the movement came from the provinces in which the Muslims were in a minority. It was economically and socially very different from the political elites who were dominant in the areas that were to constitute the state of Pakistan. A clash between the two groups—the outsiders and the insiders—was inevitable. It was only under President Ayub Khan that the landed aristocracy won back its position in the political system it had lost to the newcomers.

Also responsible for the enormous social flux in the country was a number of profound demographic developments, among them the massive transfer of population that accompanied Partition; the flow of workers into Karachi from the country's northern areas to help build the nation's first capital; the migration of millions of workers to the Middle East during the first economic boom in that part of the world that lasted for a decade and a half (1974–91); the creation of three Pakistani diasporas in Britain, the Middle East, and North America; and the arrival of three to four million refugees from Afghanistan in the 1980s.

"Muslimization" of Pakistani society and increase in Islamic radicalism

An important consequence of the transfer of population that accompanied Partition when eight million Muslims moved from India to Pakistan and six million Hindus and Sikhs went in the other direction left a deep imprint on Pakistani society. One of these was the "Muslimization" of Pakistan's population. In the mid-1940s, when the campaign for the creation of Pakistan was conducted, Muslims constituted 72.5 percent of the population of the areas that now make up Pakistan. After the transfer, the proportion of Muslims in the country's population increased to 93 percent. Punjab, the most affected of Pakistan's four provinces, was thoroughly "cleansed" of the non-Muslim minorities. One of the important "what if?" questions about Pakistan's history is the impact the presence of a large non-Muslim population would have had on the country's political and social development. It would not have moved the country so far towards Islamic radicalization as happened first gradually in the 1960s and 1970s and later more rapidly. The fact that Pakistan today has become the epicenter of Islamic extremism is, in part, because of the Muslimization of society following the partition of British India.

This process was given a further boost by the temporary movement of millions of Pakistanis to provide labor for the first economic boom in the oil-exporting countries of the Middle East. This boom lasted for a decade and a half, from the oil embargo in the mid-1970s to the first Gulf War in 1991. During this time, some 12 to 15 million workers from Pakistan went to the Middle East, mostly as construction workers on three- to five-year contracts. A very large number of them were from the North-West Frontier Province (NWFP) and the adjoining tribal belt as well as from the northern districts of Punjab. The workers lived in camps where they were exposed to Wahabism, the conservative form of Islam that was and remains the state religion of Saudi Arabia. They brought the teachings of this brand of Islam back to Pakistan. This contributed to the radicalization of this part of the country.

This move towards Islamic radicalism was reinforced by the way the allies, led by the United States, fought the Soviet Union's occupation of Afghanistan in 1979–89. During this time Pakistan, one of the two US allies actively involved in this struggle—the other being Saudi Arabia—was led by General Zia ul-Haq, who was deeply committed to turning the country he led into an Islamic state. The campaign against the Soviets was centered around training and indoctrinating tens of thousands of young men, a large number of whom came from the Afghan refugee camps located in Pakistan, to become mujahideen, Islamic holy warriors. While the US supplied weapons for the fighters, the Saudis provided finance for their procurement and Pakistan set up hundreds of *madrasahs* in which the warriors were trained.[9] These moves resulted in the defeat and withdrawal of the Soviet Union from Afghanistan, but it left Pakistan and southeastern Afghanistan with a legacy that the two countries are still dealing with two decades after the Soviet departure. The Taliban, who overran Afghanistan in the late 1990s, gave sanctuary to Osama bin Laden's al-Qaeda, and allowed Saudi renegades to mount an attack on the United States, were the product of these *madrasahs*. With Islamic radical groups digging their roots deep into Pakistani soil, the country's social fabric became even more complicated.

Failure to develop formal political structures

Pakistan's inability to develop robust political institutions was in part a consequence of the enormous powers that remained concentrated in the hands of the members of a few social groups. These groups competed with one another, causing great turbulence in the political life of the country. That turbulence would not have been so disruptive had competition among the groups taken place within institutional confines, as happened in India. In Pakistan, the political system did not create an institutional base within which political discourse could take place. Consequently, group politics became sharply defined because of the absence of institutions that could have helped to establish a dialogue among the various competing groups. The groups contending for power included the refugees from India who had settled in Karachi and Hyderabad and had dominated politics for a decade after independence, the refugees who had settled in Punjab's countryside and were given the land vacated by the Sikh smallholders and peasants who had migrated to India, the large landlords of Punjab and Sindh who had been politically powerful when the British ruled India, the tribal chiefs of Balochistan and the NWFP and the religious leaders in Punjab and NWFP.

The emergence of Islamic groups has further complicated institution building in Pakistan. Most of these groups do not subscribe to western notions of democracy, the rule of law based on a legal system devised by the elected representatives of the people, and tolerance of groups that do not accept their interpretation of the Koran and the Hadith. While many scholars, including several from the West,[10] have argued that Islam and democracy are not incompatible, this is not accepted by more radical Islamist groups. They maintain that, in the Islamic system, there is no place for man-made laws and institutions. Some of these groups are now engaged in military campaigns in parts of the northwest—in particular in the Swat valley—to impose Islamic *sharia* on the population.

Wherever competition among the social groups became so intense that it adversely affected the quality of governance, the military intervened. In other words, political underdevelopment and a persistent feeling of insecurity created the space for the military to act on the political stage.

India's perceived intentions and concerns about the survival of the state and the rise of the military as a political force

Right from the time of its birth, the non-military groups that had political power were anxious over the country's survival as a separate entity in South Asia. This feeling of insecurity was initially fed by the actions of the first generation of India's leaders, who took time to come to terms with the partition of the subcontinent and the creation of a separate homeland for the Muslim community. As Pakistan was struggling to find its feet, the Indians took a number of steps designed to cripple the country economically. These included the refusal to pay the "sterling balances" Britain provided New Delhi to compensate for the effort India made during the Second World War, a part of which was owed to Pakistan. The Indians also refused to accept the new rate of exchange between their currency and that of Pakistan. In 1949 the rate changed from parity to 144 Indian rupees for 100 Pakistani rupees when Pakistan refused to devalue its currency in relation to the US dollar as was done by all countries of what was then called the "sterling area" (now the Commonwealth). India sought to punish Pakistan by halting all trade with its neighbor.[11] This action was to have a profound impact on the development of the Pakistani economy. In 1950 India began to divert water in the eastern rivers of the Indus system for use in its state of Punjab. It used the canal head works located on its territory to block water from flowing into Pakistan. This act was considered hostile enough for Liaqat Ali Khan, Pakistan's first prime minister, to appear on the balcony of his house in Karachi, raise his fist, and threaten war, if India persisted in its designs. This dispute was resolved a decade later when the World Bank intervened and the two countries signed the Indus Rivers Water Treaty in 1960.

One consequence of these moves by India was to create a deep fear in Pakistan about the intentions of its much larger neighbor. This fear was used by the military leadership as one reason for intervening in the country's politics. The military's appearance on the political stage, therefore, was not the result of ambition on the part of those who were its leaders.[12] General Ayub Khan was perhaps the most politically ambitious military chief, but even he would not have ventured into politics had the politicians not created an opportunity for him to act and had India not continued to pose a threat to Pakistan's survival.

While the failure of the Pakistani political establishment to create political institutions within which it could function without resorting to the politics of the street created the space for the military to operate, the military, once in power, did not consolidate its position by systematically undermining the political structure. All four generals-turned-presidents used the political process and the politicians to buy political longevity for themselves. Three of the four did not succeed; the fourth, General Zia ul-Haq, died in an aircrash while still engaged in an attempt to manipulate the political system to win more time for himself. In other words, the failure to institutionalize politics, has to be placed at the door of the political establishment.

While the military establishment may not have actively engineered its entry into the political system, it used its position when it did attain power to strengthen its economic base. This was done mostly by those who held the reins of power to keep in line the senior members of the military. By now the military has created an elaborate system for providing economic benefits to its senior officers. General Pervez Musharraf went the furthest in this regard, appointing military personnel to a large number of senior positions in the bureaucracy. This led to much resentment and persuaded General Ashfaq Pervez Kayani, Musharraf's successor as the head of the army, to order military officers back to the barracks. Kayani also made it clear that the civilian leadership was fully in charge in all spheres of policymaking and that the military's role was to be confined to that of an implementer of the policies made by the civilian administration. This resolve was put to the test when, on 7 August, 2008, the political parties issued an ultimatum to President Pervez Musharraf to vacate his office. The military refused to intervene openly, confining its role to ensuring that the former chief of the army staff was not humiliated in the process.

Close relations with the United States

Once in power, the military leadership managed the country's foreign affairs to bring it closer to the west, in particular the United States. During the long periods of its rule— 1958 to 1969, 1977 to 1988, and 1999 to 2008—it was able to forge close relations with the United States. This resulted in the flow of significant amounts of US assistance to the country (see Table 6.2).

This was one reason why the economy did so much better during the time the military held the reins of political power (see Table 6.3). It was able to obtain large flows of assistance from the United States to augment paltry domestic savings. These remained low and did not establish a sustainable structure that could ensure growth on a long-term basis without resort to external savings.

The easy availability of foreign assistance created a situation that economists describe as a "moral hazard." That Pakistan was able to obtain large amounts of foreign flows to augment domestic savings was one reason why important structural reforms were not taken

up and why no effort was made to develop robust political institutions. Pakistan's political leadership was prepared to take risks with the economy in the expectation that the country would be bailed out should it land in serious crises: and this happened time and again.

There was serious talk in American policy circles in the spring and summer of 2008 about changing the relationship with Pakistan and moving towards an association that placed much greater emphasis on a long-term arrangement. Such an arrangement would not only provide assistance for strengthening Pakistan's security forces but also help with economic development. It was finally recognized that there was no military solution to Pakistan's problems, especially those that emanated from the increasingly disaffected populations of the tribal belt and the NWFP.

There was a deep and growing resentment among the people of the tribal belt and the NWFP that the world, in particular the US, had not treated them well. This, it was felt, was especially the case since 9/11 when the US, supported by Pakistan, launched an intensive military campaign against the Taliban regime in Afghanistan. The impression, widely held for some time in Washington, that the Taliban had been decisively beaten, turned out to be wrong. The Taliban began, to reassert themselves after the snows melted in 2008 and revived their campaign not only against the US but also its NATO allies, who had an active presence in Afghanistan. What went wrong?

Table 6.3 Economic performance in various political periods in Pakistan, 1947–2008

	GDP growth rate (%)	Population growth rate (%)	GDP per capita increase (%)
1947–58	2.7	1.8	0.9
1958–69	6.1	2.3	3.8
1969–71	5.8	2.8	3.0
1971–77	3.9	3.1	0.8
1977–88	6.5	3.1	3.4
1988–99	4.7	2.7	2.0
1999–2008	6.1	2.3	3.8

The Taliban's defeat brought to power in Kabul the ethnic groups who had never been comfortable with the much larger Pakhtun population that had economically and politically dominated Afghanistan for decades. Political power brings economic rewards; the non-Pakhtun groups benefited from the economic revival, albeit slightly, that followed the occupation of Afghanistan by the US and NATO. The Pakhtun were largely marginalized even though Hamid Karzai, the country's president, belonged to that community. In the absence of secure sources of income, the Pakhtun population in the southern and eastern parts of the country turned to the cultivation of poppy and Afghanistan became the world's largest producer and provider of heroin. A close relationship developed between the people who ran the country's drug economy and the dissidents who constituted the Taliban.

Since the majority of the Pakhtun population lived on the Pakistani side of the border —Pakistan has an estimated 25 million of the 40 million people who identify themselves as Pakhtun—it should not have come as a surprise that the country's tribal areas would join in the fight. Their discontent began to seep into the rest of Pakistan, which also became restive. The economic downturn in the country in 2007–08 provided an added impetus to the groups operating out of the northwestern hills to increase their activities not only in their own areas but also in other parts of Pakistan. The only way to counter these trends was to ensure that the Pakistani economy did not suffer a severe and long-term decline, that economic revival was not concentrated in the areas that benefited from the short-lived prosperity that marked the second part of the period of President Pervez Musharraf, that a broad-based program of economic development was initiated that provided employment and incomes to the country's young population, and that a special effort was made to bring the tribal areas and the NWFP into the economic mainstream.

The US seemed to agree with this approach. A bill was prepared by two powerful senators to reflect this change in sentiment. Its authors were Joe Biden, a Democrat, who headed the Senate's Foreign Relations Committee, and Richard Lugar, a Republican, who was the senior most member representing his party on the same committee. The bill was aimed at providing Pakistan $7.5 billion over a five-year period with the assistance to be directed towards the country's economic and social development. "Our bill represents a genuine seachange—one which will set the US' Pakistan policy on a safer and more successful course. For too long our policy towards Pakistan has been in desperate need of serious overhaul," said Senator Biden, while introducing the bill. "While our bill envisions sustained cooperation with Pakistan for the long haul, it is not a blank check," added Senator Lugar, the bill's co-sponsor. The two senators believed that the bill would have the support of the House of Representatives, the lower house of the Congress and, once passed, would be signed into law by President George W. Bush. However, the bill died, having failed to reach the Senate floor before the end of its term in January 2009. At the same time, the Americans indicated that they would continue to provide between one and $1.5 billion a year for military purposes, an amount that included the logistics support Islamabad was giving for Washington's efforts in Afghanistan.

The data presented in Table 6.2 show how fickle the US has been in the past in aiding Pakistan. It provided large amounts of support when the country was ruled by the military; on average $100 million a year during the first part of the period of Ayub Khan, $217 million a year during the period of Zia ul-Haq and $333 million a year when Pervez Musharraf held the reins of power. While it is true that American strategic interests were strong in the area in which Pakistan is located when the latter was governed by the military, it is also the case that Washington felt more comfortable in working with the military than with the civilian leadership.

As Pakistan enters into a new and possibly economically more productive relationship with the US, it is important that the civilian leaders prepare themselves to deliver the expected results. Their actions in the economic arena have not given confidence that they will be able to do that. While many economic problems the country faced at the time Musharraf resigned his position as president were inherited from the Musharraf period, it should be recognized that more than four months elapsed between the effective transfer of power from the military ruler to the elected representatives of the people without any action having been taken to address either the deteriorating economic situation or the worsening situation with respect to the insurgency in the tribal areas. This was a long enough time to display competence, confidence in economic matters, and willingness to take hard decisions.

Pakistan has a long tradition of postponing reform when large foreign capital flows become available. There is also the feeling in the Pakistani political and economic establishments that the country will be rescued by its friends when the times are really difficult. This has happened in the past on several occasions. It was happening again in the summer of 2008. As previously noted, the world of finance has a phrase for this phenomenon: "moral hazard" is the term financial people use when managers postpone action and take risks in the belief that their enterprises will not be allowed to sink. Policymakers in Pakistan have behaved in much the same way. It has been recognized for many years that Pakistan needs deep structural reforms in its political system and economy. In many countries, such reforms have been undertaken when there was a crisis. In Pakistan's case, this was not done since crises opened up foreign coffers. It could be different this time around if the new leaders study the country's history and draw some lessons from it.

There are two other aspects of Pakistan's history that should be briefly discussed— one with a long tradition and the other more recent in origin—before we turn to the final part of this chapter.

Centralization of governance

That Pakistan was governed for long periods by the military, which relied on the civil services—initially on the powerful Civil Service of Pakistan (CSP)—for support brought power to two groups that were comfortable with centralized command and control. This led to the concentration of power in the hands of the federal government located at Islamabad. This happened in spite of the fact that the constitution of 1973, written and adopted in the aftermath of the civil war in East Pakistan, opted for provincial autonomy. The schedule to the constitution provided two lists of government's responsibilities: the first listed the responsibilities of the federal government, the second spelled out those that were initially "concurrent"—to be performed by both the center and the provinces—but were to be fully transferred to the provinces. This did not happen. Zulfikar Ali Bhutto, the author of the constitution, sabotaged the system the moment it came into being. He fired the two provincial governments that were not controlled by his political party, the Pakistan People's Party, on flimsy grounds and forced the parliament to postpone for a ten-year period most requirements of the constitution that would have seen greater exercise of provincial autonomy. His successor, yet another military leader, had even less interest in sharing power with the provinces. After the death of General Zia ul-Haq when the country was governed by a succession of democratically elected governments, they made no attempt to invoke the federal features of the constitution. The country continued to be governed from Islamabad.

Under General Pervez Musharraf, the governing system became more centralized. The provinces were given little power and, even within the center, the prime minister gathered an enormous amount of authority in his own hands, building a secretariat that became all powerful. The only initiative taken by the Musharraf government towards decentralization was to establish a new system of local government which, at least on paper, was allowed to exercise considerable authority in a number of areas previously under the control of the federal and provincial governments.

Pakistan had failed to develop a viable system of local government in spite of the many efforts made by different regimes over a period of six decades. It had tried five different systems since its birth, starting with the system of *panchayats* inherited from the British period. In the 1950s, this system was replaced by "Village Aid," a local government structure that had the moral and financial support of the US. Ayub Khan introduced the system of "basic democracies." This was a multi-tiered system that had elected councilors at the bottom who then elected representatives to the higher tiers. Government officials serving in the areas over which the councils had jurisdiction were also represented. This system worked well for promoting development but it was also entrusted with political responsibilities. The 80,000 "basic democrats," 40,000 from each of the two provinces, constituted the electoral college for the election of the president and the members of the national and provincial assemblies. The system was discarded by General Yahya Khan who succeeded Ayub Khan as president in 1969. The military government headed by General Zia ul Haq which took office in 1977 introduced another system of local government which borrowed heavily from the structure of Ayub Khan's "basic democracies." This too was discarded by the political governments that held the reins of power in the 1990s.

Pakistan's current situation: how it might evolve with and without appropriate public policy choices

At time timing of writing (early fall 2008), Pakistan once again stood at a crossroads. This situation arose on account of several events that took place within the space of 17 months, from March 2007 to August 2008. They destroyed the government headed by General Pervez Musharraf and brought the economy to its knees. Although the rate of growth of GDP was high during the Musharraf period it was based on the growth of the sectors that did little for employment creation and for the poor. The government also let serious shortages develop in the supply of such vital goods and services as food grains, electric power, and natural gas. While Islamabad's policymakers were responsible for some of these developments, a number of them were the result of happenings over which they had no control. It may be useful to describe the internal developments briefly since they illustrate a number of themes that were identified in this chapter.

On 8 March, 2007 President Musharraf summoned Chief Justice Iftikhar Chaudhry of the Supreme Court to his "camp office" in Rawalpindi, the city that had the headquarters of the Pakistani army, and asked him to resign from his position. The meeting between the two men was filmed by Pakistan Television, the official news channel, which showed Musharraf in his army uniform facing the chief justice. Several other senior generals were present in the room, all in uniform. That the meeting was held in the camp office used by Musharraf when he operated as the army chief was also significant. It is not clear whether the intention was to communicate to the judiciary the army's displeasure at its conduct, but that was the way it was perceived. Chief Justice Chaudhry, to the surprise of General Musharraf and his colleagues, refused to oblige. The authorities were clearly not prepared for this development; it was their assumption that Chaudhry would quietly walk away, accepting whatever compensation was being offered to him. The government's response to the developing situation was panic. The chief justice was prevented from returning to his office; instead he was taken to his official residence and was prevented from leaving or meeting with anybody from the outside world. His family was held with him in the house.

This drama was played out on the TV screens by dozens of private channels the government had not only allowed but encouraged to operate. This was a part of the government's policy to modernize the political and communication systems. The government's objectives succeeded but not in the way it had hoped. The treatment meted out to the chief judicial officer of the country incensed the legal community whose members launched a countrywide campaign to have him reinstated. The government changed course and allowed Chaudhry to leave his house and meet with his supporters. He took this opportunity to travel widely and address various bar associations around the country. The "contact the people" campaign was inaugurated by a procession that started from Islamabad and took 25 hours to cover the distance of 175 miles to Lahore. While this campaign was drawing hundreds of thousands of supporters out on the streets of urban Pakistan, a case was filed against Chaudhry's dismissal which was adjudged in his favor by his erstwhile colleagues in the court. The chief justice took his position on the bench.

Chaudhry lost no time to assert himself. He allowed the case against Musharraf to proceed and he also took on board the challenge to the passage of the National Reconciliation Ordinance (NRO) that gave blanket amnesty to a large number of people who had been charged with corruption by the Musharraf government. Notable among these was Asif Ali Zirdari, the husband of Benazir Bhutto. It was well known that the administration of US President George W. Bush had encouraged the two sides—Bhutto and Musharraf—to conclude this deal. Washington was of the view that by gaining the support of the country's largest and most popular party, Pervez Musharraf would be able to gain legitimacy and thus be able to fight al-Qaeda and the Taliban more effectively. These two groups had established themselves in the country's tribal belt and had begun to inflict heavy casualties on the American and NATO forces fighting in Afghanistan.

The case against Musharraf was based on the constitutional provision that a person who was in the employ of the government could not contest for political office within two years of leaving the service of the government. Musharraf had won the second term as president while still holding the office of the chief of army staff. By the time these cases began to be heard Bhutto had returned to Pakistan. On 18 October, when she arrived in Karachi, her cavalcade was attacked by suicide bombers, resulting in the death of more than 140 people. She was the target of the attack but escaped unhurt.

Fearing that the Supreme Court would nullify his election, Musharraf, as the chief of the army staff, moved on 3 November to issue a proclamation setting aside the constitution and promulgating in its place a provisional constitutional order (PCO). Sixty judges of the Supreme Court were not invited to take the oath of office under the PCO. Musharraf's desperate action was termed as a "coup against himself." Widespread condemnation of the move by several foreign governments and by an energized civil society led Musharraf to withdraw the PCO, restore the Constitution, and announce that general elections would be held in the first half of January. Nawaz Sharif, the other former prime minister, who had spent eight years in exile, was also allowed to return. However, while the country was in the grip of election fever, on 27 December, Benazir Bhutto was assassinated after addressing a public meeting in Rawalpindi. A total breakdown of law and order followed for three days as Bhutto's supporters expressed their anger by coming out on the streets and attacking government property. The government reacted by postponing the election to 18 February, 2008.

The elections produced unexpected results. While Benazir Bhutto's Pakistan People's Party was expected to do well, especially after her assassination, Pakistan Muslim League (Nawaz) (PML(N)) performed better than expected even by the party's senior leaders.[13] The

Pakistan Muslim League (Quaid), the party that had supported Musharraf and had governed as his partner for five years after the elections of 2002, did very poorly. The Islamic parties also lost the support they had picked up in 2002.

The PPP and PML (N) were able to set aside their traditional differences and form a coalition government at the federal level as well as in Punjab. The old rivals were prepared to work together for different reasons. The PPP wished to ensure that its senior leaders would be cleared of the charges of corruption that had been leveled against them by both Nawaz Sharif when he was prime minister and then by the administration headed by General Pervez Musharraf. The PML (N) wanted all the judges removed by Musharraf on 3 November to be reinstated. These differences could not be resolved. The only common ground the two sides could walk on was to force Musharraf to leave office. On 7 August they announced their agreement to launch impeachment proceedings against the president. On 18 August Musharraf resigned from office. On 6 September Asif Ali Zirdari, Bhutto's widower, was elected president by an overwhelming majority of the electoral college. Zirdari's election was not supported by the PML(N) that moved across to the opposition benches in the national assembly. Not only did the coalition fall apart; the two parties declared open war in February 2009. The president responded by dismissing the provincial government in the Punjab after the supreme court issued an order barring the Sharif brothers from holding public office. The PML(N) reacted by ordering its supporters to march on Islamabad starting 12 March. The party leaders ordered a *dharna* (sit in) in front of the supreme court building for 16 March. This is where the situation stood at the time of writing.

Which way Pakistan will proceed depends on a number of things. Among them, the leaders will have to find the right answers to a number of difficult questions. Whether the leadership groups that now have poli-

tical power will be able to institutionalize it? Whether the civil society that was responsible for forcing political change by having the military withdraw from center stage and allow the elected leaders to occupy that space will find a way of becoming a part of the evolving political structure? Whether the new leaders will find a way for resolving the difficult economic situation the country now faces will depend on how much attention they will be prepared to give to economic management and how much external support they will receive to deal with some of the macroeconomic imbalances that had materialized.

The economic situation worsened rapidly in 2008 with severe power shortages, increase in the prices of various foodgrains, and increases in the fiscal, external trade, and external accounts deficits. The strain on the economy was partly the consequence of the sharp increases in the prices of fuel oil, edible oil, and foodgrains in the international markets and also because of the spending spree by the Musharraf government as it prepared for the elections of February 2008. The new leaders will need to find solutions to the problems the economy faces without sacrificing long-term growth and by changing the structure of the economy in order to place it on a trajectory of high rate of growth that can be sustained over time without an excessive dependence on external flows. These problems raise further questions for the future. Whether the economy can be developed in a way to provide productive job opportunities to a very young and increasingly restive workforce? Whether the capital the country needs over the short term will become available from the traditional donors? Whether a strategy for dealing with the rise of Islamic fundamentalism can be developed that will have the confidence of a world that is getting increasingly worried about developments in the areas adjacent to the border with Afghanistan? And whether the political establishment will find political as well as economic answers to deal with the growing discomfort the provinces have with the government at the center? Whether positive answers can be found to these questions will depend on how well the new set of policymakers understand the dozen themes explored in the previous section.

While it is difficult to be positive about Pakistan's future in these dark times for the country, there are a number of developments that may lead the country to develop sustainable institutions of political governance and to set the economy on a trajectory of high level growth that can also be sustained over time. The reasons that give hope include the following. The military has withdrawn from politics, placing its faith in the development of political institutions. A two-party political order is emerging with the Centre-Left PPP and the Centre-Right PML (N) accounting for most of the political support. A few regional parties operating in the troubled provinces of Balochistan, the NWFP, and Sindh are prepared to work with the mainstream parties. A number of donors with interest in Pakistan's economic survival are getting ready to provide emergency assistance. Punjab remains well governed and, given its size and dynamism, may become the engine of growth for the rest of the country. There is now a growing consensus in the country that the problems posed by the rise of Islamic extremism need to be resolved. And finally there is a genuine interest on the part of the new leadership groups to reach a settlement with India on the most difficult issues that have caused so much damaging hostility in the past.

Notes

1 Ayub Khan provided a detailed account for his move in his autobiography published at the height of the campaign his administration launched to celebrate what it called the "decade of development." See Muhammad Ayub Khan, *Friends not Masters: A Political Autobiography* (London: Oxford University Press, 1967).

2 Several books were written on Pakistan's development experience during the period of Ayub Khan. Most of the authors had served in Pakistan as advisors to the government. See, for instance, Gustav F. Papanek, *Pakistan's Development; Social Goals and Private Incentives* (Cambridge, MA: Harvard University Press, 1967).

3 These were analyzed in some detail by a group of six senior economists, including this author, in the maiden report of the Institute of Public Policy, *Status of the Economy: Challenges and Opportunities* (Lahore: IPP, 2008).

4 Shahid Javed Burki, *Pakistan under Bhutto, 1971–77* (London: Macmillan, 1980) and *Pakistan: A Nation in the Making* (Boulder, CO: Westview Press, 1983).

5 Anil Khilnani, *The Idea of India* (London: Hamish Hamilton, 1997).

6 Stephen Cohen, *The Idea of Pakistan* (New Delhi: Oxford University Press, 2004).

7 For a detailed history of the Pakistan Army and how it affected the country's political development, see Shuja Nawaz, *Crossed Swords: Pakistan: Its Army, and the Wars Within* (Karachi: Oxford University Press, 2008).

8 For an assessment of how the military used its political power to build its economic strength as an institution and the roles played by several senior military officials, see Ayesha Siddiqa, *Military Inc.: Inside Pakistan's Military Economy* (London: Pluto Press, 2007).

9 This story is well told by Steve Coll in *Ghost Wars: The Secret History of the CIA, Afghanistan, and Bin Laden, from the Soviet Invasion to 10 September, 2001* (New York: Penguin, 2004).

10 See, for instance, Noah Feldman, *Fall and Rise of the Islamic State* (Princeton, NJ: University Press 2008).

11 For a detailed account of this episode, see Chaudhri Muhammad Ali, *The Emergence of*

Pakistan (New York: Columbia University Press, 1967). Ali, a senior civil servant at the time of Independence, went on to become prime minister in 1956.

12 The subject of the military in Pakistan's politics has attracted some analytical attention in recent years. See, for instance, in addition to Nawaz, Husain Haqqani, *Pakistan: Between Mosque and Military* (Washington, DC: Carnegie Endowment for International Peace, 2005).

13 I met Shahbaz Sharif, the chairman of PML (N) and the younger brother of Mian Nawaz Sharif, a couple of weeks before the elections. His prediction about the number of seats his party was likely to win was less than the number actually won.

7

Party overinstitutionalization, contestation, and democratic degradation in Bangladesh[1]

Harry Blair

[P]olitical parties [controlled in very hierarchical fashion by entrenched leaderships] have monopolized the political process and thus so pervasively penetrated state and organizational life that they have robbed interest groups and other political institutions of their autonomy ... This extreme domination and institutionalization of political parties ... has been a central factor in eroding the effectiveness, legitimacy and stability of democracy.

Larry Diamond made these observations about Venezuela's party system in the late 1990s,[2] but his observations on party "over-institutionalization" could as well have been written about Bangladesh in the middle of the first decade of the twenty-first century. Other examples are not hard to find: Colombia in the later 1940s, Pakistan in the 1990s. All ended unhappily. Some terminated severely—a Colombian civil war in the 1950s that killed more than 200,000 people; others came to a halt with less turmoil—a populist Venezuelan autocrat stifling civil liberties; a repressive Pakistani general continuing to postpone a promised democratic restoration in the present decade. The Bangladesh experience has yet to play out, with a military-backed emergency rule declared in January 2007, followed by the restoration of electoral politics in December 2008 being the latest chapters.

Electoral democracies like those in many developing countries are always incomplete, as Diamond and others point out at some length, but they can function, and some serve as a transitional phase on the way toward liberal democracy and democratic consolidation.[3] But where party contestation becomes so entrenched and ferocious that it precludes all other aspects of the polity, a self-destructive pathology can set in. This is what happened in Venezuela, Colombia, and Pakistan, and, by the middle of the present decade, it is what had appeared to have overtaken Bangladesh.

For a while, it looked as if democracy might take permanent hold in Bangladesh following its restoration in 1991. There was a near-death experience for the democratic experiment in 1996, but afterward the two major parties recovered with enough sobriety to agree on an electoral mechanism that steered the system through a first turnover that year and then a second one in 2001. Thus the polity passed Samuel Huntington's "two turnover test"—the ruling party was removed from office by the voters and peacefully turned over charge to its successor not once but twice.[4]

By the beginning of 2007, however, the country's political system appeared headed into an unstoppable downward spiral when the military intervened to stop the political clock for the third time since independence had been won in 1971.[5] As always with such takeovers, a quick return to democracy was promised, but within short order the timetable had already been extended to a minimal 18 months before a new national election would be allowed.

How did politics and political parties in Bangladesh come to such a sorry pass? This question will form the central query of this chapter. We begin with a brief account of the origins of the country's principal political parties and their history during the largely authoritarian decades of the 1970s and 1980s. But the main focus will be on the democratic era beginning in 1990, and the debilitating pathologies that came to hobble the political system during that period, paradoxically at a time when the economy was doing quite well for the first time since independence.

Political parties and political history during the first two decades: 1971–1990[6]

The dominant party at Bangladesh's birth was the Awami League (AL), founded in the mid-1950s by Husain Shaheed Suhrawardy. After his death in 1963 the party's leadership passed to the charismatic Sheikh Mujibur Rahman (known generally as Sheikh Mujib or just Mujib), who became the major leader of the provincial autonomy movement for East Bengal within united Pakistan. The movement picked up momentum during the authoritarian rule of Ayub Khan, culminating twice in massive outpourings of protest against rule from the west wing of united Pakistan, interrupted on both occasions by military intervention.[7] The first time came in 1969 when agitation led by the AL resulted in a crackdown from West Pakistan, imposition of martial law, and the ouster of Ayub, to be replaced by another general, Yahya Khan.

Yahya promised national elections to form a national government that would replace Ayub's indirect rule scheme, and, in the ensuing poll of December 1970, Mujib's AL won 75 percent of the East Bengal votes and all but two of the province's 162 seats to the Pakistan Constituent Assembly.[8] This overwhelming victory in the East gave Mujib's party an absolute majority at the national level, but negotiations to form a government soon broke down over how much autonomy the country's eastern wing should get and, on 25 March, 1971, Yahya had Mujib arrested and ordered his army to crack down on the AL. His move immediately led to a bloody civil war between the West Pakistan-dominated army and a pro-independence force composed of those Bengali soldiers who had revolted and allied with a much larger contingent of guerillas, collectively known as the *Mukti Bahini*. The *songram* (struggle or conflict) lasted into December, when the Indian army invaded on behalf of the freedom fighters, captured the provincial capital at Dhaka, and received the surrender of the Pakistan army. Bangladesh became independent on 16 December, 1971.

The AL winners of the 1970 elections (to both the Pakistan National Assembly and the East Pakistan Provincial Assembly) formed the new parliament, which drew up a new constitution creating a Westminster-type parliamentary system and a polity based on the four pillars of *Mujibbad* (Mujibism): nationalism, socialism, secularism, and democracy. New elections held in early 1973 for the *jatiyo sangsad* (parliament) turned out to be a de facto ratification of Mujib's leadership role, awarding the AL some 73 percent of the vote and 292 out of the 300 seats at stake (see Table 7.1).

But by the time of the election, corruption, nepotism, favoritism, and incompetence had seeped into the Mujib regime, and, compounded by a severe and badly mismanaged famine in 1974, popular confidence in the *Bangabondhu* (Friend of Bengal, Mujib's self-assumed title) rapidly eroded, the economy declined and security deteriorated. Mujib responded to the crisis by building a parallel military force alongside the army, declaring a state of emergency in December 1974,

Table 7.1 Votes and seats in Bangladesh elections, 1973–2001

		1973	1979	1986	1988	1991	1996	2001
AL (Awami League)	Votes	**73.2**	24.5	26.2		30.1	**37.4**	40.2
	Seats	**97.7**	13.0	25.3		29.3	**48.7**	20.8
BNP (Bangladesh National Party)	Votes		**41.2**			**30.8**	33.6	**42.3**
	Seats		**69.0**			**46.7**	38.7	**64.1**
JP (Jatiya Party)	Votes			**42.3**	**83.7**	11.9	**16.4**	6.5
	Seats			**51.0**	**68.4**	11.7	**10.6**	4.7
JI (Jamaat-i-Islam)	Votes			4.6		12.1	8.6	**4.2**
	Seats			3.3		**6.0**	1.0	**5.7**
Others and independents	Votes	26.8	34.3	26.9	16.3	15.1	4.0	6.8
	Seats	2.3	18.0	20.4	31.6	6.3	1.0	4.7

Notes: 1996 results pertain to the June election of that year, not the repudiated February election. Figures are in percentages; votes in normal typeface, *seats in italics*, ruling party or alliance in boldface.

Source: Nizam Ahmed, "Bangladesh," in Dieter Nohlen, Florian Grotz and Christof Hartmann (eds), *Elections in Asia and the Pacific: A Data Handbook*, vol. 1, *Middle East, Central Asia, and South Asia* (New York: Oxford University Press, 2001), 515–52; Nizam Ahmed and Sheikh Z. Ahmad, "The parliamentary elections in Bangladesh, October 2001," *Electoral Studies*, Vol. 22, No. 3 (2003), pp. 503–509

nationalizing the major newspapers and, the next month, amending the Constitution to make himself head of a presidential system of government. He then abolished all political parties in favor of a new one of his own and in effect declared the country his personal fiefdom. In democratization terms, Bangladesh took a rapid downward tumble, as is reflected in the Freedom House scores for political rights and civil liberties (see Figure 7.1). Reaction was not long in coming, and, in mid-August 1975, a group of army officers organized a coup in which Mujib and most of his family were assassinated.

A period of uncertainty followed, replete with coups and countercoups, but within a few months, General Ziaur Rahman (known as Zia), who had been a hero in the *songram*, emerged as leader of a military-headed government. After surviving several coup attempts, Zia tried popularizing his rule, founding a political party that became the Bangladesh National Party (BNP), and contesting a presidential election in 1978 as well as a parliamentary election in 1979, both of which he won handily (see Table 7.1). There were, of course, charges of poll rigging, but evidence indicates that Zia proved able to transform himself into a genuinely popular

leader by the end of the 1970s. Democratization measures reflected this change, as indicated in Figure 7.1.

Unrest continued to infest the military, however, resulting in Zia's assassination in May 1981. His vice president, Abdus Sattar, succeeded him in office and then won a mandate on his own in a presidential election held in November of the same year. But his victory proved to be short-lived, as a new general, Hussain Muhammad Ershad, seized power in a bloodless coup the following March.

Like Zia before him, Ershad launched a political organization, the Jatiya Party, and in the spring of 1986 held a parliamentary election. The BNP, now headed by Zia's widow Khaleda, boycotted the poll, but under the leadership of Mujib's daughter, Sheikh Hasina Wajid, the AL, which had been cooperating with the BNP in opposing the Ershad regime, broke ranks with it, and decided to contest amid cries of betrayal from the BNP side. The ensuing election saw the Jatiya Party win a bare majority of the parliamentary seats, but the victory was enough to give a patina of legitimacy to the Ershad government. The AL took about a quarter of the seats (see Table 7.1), but then boycotted the parliament. An addition to the political spectrum this time was the

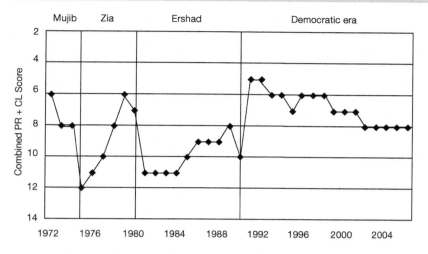

Figure 7.1 Bangladesh Freedom House democracy scores, 1972–2006.

Note: PR = Political Rights. CL = Civil Liberties. Each score ranges from 1 (most democratic) to 7 (least democratic). When combined, the scores thus range from 2 to 14.

fundamentalist Jamaat-i-Islam, which had been banned as a collaborationist organization after the civil war but which Ershad allowed to resume. It won only ten seats.

Despite winning what were essentially uncontested presidential and parliamentary elections in October 1986 and March 1988 respectively—the AL and BNP boycotted both campaigns—the Jatiya Party never matured into anything more solid. Opposition intensified with frequent processions, demonstrations, and *hartal*s (strikes) which at times shut down Dhaka for several days running.[9] This drama ebbed and flowed over the Ershad years, rising to a crescendo in late 1990, when an expanding movement composed of political parties, student groups, professional associations, non-governmental organizations, trade unions and government workers demanded Ershad's resignation. In a scenario reminiscent of Ferdinand Marcos' ouster in the Philippines several years before, Ershad was rebuffed by the military when he attempted to impose martial law and resigned office on 4 December, 1990.

An interim caretaker government was set up to superintend a new election, which was held in February 1991, ushering in a period of almost 16 years of what might be called

"punctuated democracy," in which more or less free and fair national elections were held,[10] and the print media were essentially free, but a virtually total hostility between the two major parties almost completely debilitated political life, corroded the bureaucracy, encouraged corruption, and fostered criminal behavior to the point of gangsterism. In democratization terms, the period began on a highly optimistic note but soon began declining, as is reflected in Figure 7.1. Exploring this pathology will take up the bulk of this chapter, but first it would be appropriate to sum up the condition of the political parties at the outset of the democratic era.

Party ideologies and practical differences

In 1972 when it took power, the AL adopted a somewhat vague ideology centering around the "four pillars of *mujibbad*" noted earlier. It saw itself as the party spearheading the drive for independence from Pakistan, placed the industry and banks owned by Pakistanis under state control, emphasized the Bengali aspect of the country's character rather than its Muslim

101

dimension, and professed popular sovereignty in contrast with the military dictatorships that had dominated Pakistan for most of the time since Partition in 1947. In addition, largely because India had offered refuge to its leadership cadres during the 1971 civil war and had secured Bangladesh's independence with its military intervention, the AL looked to India as an ally rather than as an antagonist. And it was less friendly toward the US, which had, after all, sided with Pakistan during the civil war.

For its part, the BNP at its birth in the late 1970s emphasized the Bangladeshi nationalist aspect of the new country, as opposed to its Bengali cultural character. It expressed no interest in socialism, neither was it much concerned with secularism (which meant essentially the fate of the minority Hindu population). It was "democratic" in the sense that, like the AL, it demanded elections and was willing to support civil liberties while evincing little enthusiasm for transparency or the rule of law. In contrast with the AL, it looked on India with some hostility but with relative favor on the United States.

When it came into existence, in 1986, H. M. Ershad's Jatiya Party more resembled the BNP in its ideology, but tried to play the Muslim card slightly more strongly by declaring Islam the state religion (although not proclaiming Bangladesh to be an Islamic state) in 1988. As the fourth party of consequence, the Jamaat-i-Islam projected a very conservative Islamic ideology and pro-Pakistan political stance when it was allowed to resume operations in 1986.

By the 1990s, however, differences between the two major parties had largely disappeared in practice, although they continued to surface rhetorically as the BNP would accuse the AL of being beholden to India, which would be countered with charges that the BNP was oppressing Hindus. The real difference between the major parties was not ideological at all but personal, in the form of the enmity between the "two begums"—party leaders Sheikh Hasina and Khaleda Zia. Hasina built her life and her party around an obsession with

avenging her father's murder, convinced that Zia had a hand in it and that Khaleda was an apologist for his complicity. Khaleda saw herself as continuing the legacy left by her husband and duty-bound to oppose the opportunist megalomania displayed by Sheikh Mujib in his later days and (in Khaleda's eyes) replicated by his daughter when she agreed to contest the 1986 parliamentary elections allied with Ershad. The two leaders cooperated rarely, as in the campaign to oust Ershad in the late 1980s and during the first days after the 1991 election; otherwise they remained implacable enemies, continuously "at daggers drawn" in the subcontinental English idiom.

Lower-level leaders, party loyalists, and camp followers in these two top-down organizations had successively less ideological inclination as time went on, working mainly for the rewards of power and patronage. Neither party showed any inclination toward intraparty democracy, with upward loyalty being the strongest requirement for participation in party affairs.

The Jatiya Party and Jamaat-i-Islam both hung on into the new era, but very definitely in a subordinate role. The Jatiya became a regional enterprise, strong in Rangpur (Ershad's home district) and Sylhet but almost non-existent elsewhere, while the Jamaat managed to establish something of a regional base in the Khulna region. The Jatiya Party, never very strong on ideology in power, became even less so in opposition, but uncompromising Islam continued to be the Jamaat's principal raison d'être.[11]

Launching the democratic era

After Ershad's ouster in December 1990, the combined opposition parties agreed on Chief Justice Shahabuddin Ahmed as a caretaker president to preside over a new election, held in February 1991. Although the two major parties were extremely close in the popular vote (see Table 7.1), the BNP won 140 of the 300 seats at stake, far more than the AL's 88, but not enough to form a government, so it pulled the Jamaat (18 seats) into a coalition—a portent of things to come in the next decade.

In an initial—although, as it turned out, brief—show of comity, the two major parties agreed to change the constitution to replace the presidential system with a parliamentary model. After that, cooperation broke down, and, by the spring of 1994, a dispute over a by-election precipitated an opposition boycott of parliament and then the obstructionism and paralysis that came to plague the political system thenceforward. The AL and the minor opposition parties initiated demonstrations, processions, and *hartals* reminiscent of the final months of the Ershad dictatorship, in the hope of bringing about a similar outcome: a collapse of public confidence in the government, desertion of its supporters, and (probably, although this was not articulated) a military decision to intervene and start the political clock again with a new national election.

This scenario failed to unfold, but the opposition was not deterred, and the major cities continued to be roiled with strikes and shutdowns. As the five-year lifetime for the incumbent parliament began to reach its end, the AL focused its demands on a caretaker government to supervise the upcoming elections, employing the model established during the interim between the Ershad government's collapse in December 1990 and the election held the following February. Posturing on both sides precluded any compromise, and an election was held in February 1996 with the opposition boycotting. Voters boycotted as well, with a turnout estimated at 5–10 percent. Although the unopposed BNP won almost all the seats, the outcry at home and abroad proved so strenuous and embarrassing that Khaleda agreed to a neutral caretaker regime, which supervised an election held in June and widely regarded as free and fair.[12] In the June election (see Table 7.1), the AL won 146 of the 300 seats, as against 116 for the BNP, and it allied with the Jatiya Party (whose leader Ershad was in jail) to form the government. As the AL did in 1991, so too in 1996 the BNP protested the

results as unfair and rigged, but this time the BNP did not wait as long to launch processions, demonstrations, and *hartals* that disrupted social and economic life throughout the country.[13] As the BNP did before it, while in power, now the AL shut out the opposition from any role except that of raising trouble in the streets.

In 2001 the AL government came to the end of its five-year maximum lifetime, and turned over state power to a new caretaker government, now made standard procedure through a constitutional amendment passed shortly after the 1996 election. This time the BNP won substantially (see Table 7.1), taking 64 percent of the seats and attaining, in combination with its electoral ally the Jamaat (which won 17 seats or almost 6 percent) a supermajority sufficient to amend the constitution over the objections of the opposition.[14] True to form, the AL claimed fraud, rejecting the results and initially refusing to take its seats in the new parliament. Later, party leaders did allow their newly elected MPs to join the parliament, but soon returned to the "politics of the streets," replete with the same processions, demonstrations, and *hartals* that the BNP had deployed against it previously. The AL continued essentially the same disruptive behavior right down to the time the next election was to be held in January 2007.[15]

Flouting "the rules of the game" or following different rules?

One frequently heard during the three successive democratically elected governments in 1991–2007 that both ruling party and opposition conspicuously failed to follow "the rules of the game" prescribed for a Westminster political system.[16] The party in power totally excluded the opposition from any role in politics and used the power of the state, in particular the police, to harass and undermine it in every possible way. For its part, the opposition used every possible means short of outright insurrection to disrupt normal life, to provoke the state into retaliating with force. The political scene—and indeed the economic

103

and social scene—was continually interrupted, often seemingly without any rules of behavior.

In fact, however, there was in place a very definite—but never publicly articulated—set of rules for the political game, well understood by the parties, the police, and general public. The rules were more or less as follows:[17]

- Elections are more or less free and fair. Considerable fraud (ballot box stuffing, bogus voting, manipulation of voters' lists, etc.) occurs, and some parliamentary seats undoubtedly go to the wrong candidate, but the overall outcome is legitimate.
- Election winners take all political power, leaving nothing for the opposition party. Once in power, the ruling party enjoys a mandate to do essentially whatever it wants over the next five years, which generally means fostering corruption, skimming foreign aid, diverting contracts to relatives, and the like. The police become a political arm of the ruling party, which uses them to harass the opposition, break up opposition rallies while protecting its own, and so on.
- The opposition party claims that the election was rigged and launches an intermittent five-year campaign of disruption. It boycotts parliament, mobilizes huge processions, shuts down the major urban areas with *hartals*, demands that the government resign, and calls for its overthrow. But there are distinct limits on the agitation. The opposition rants and raves, but never really mounts the barricades or engages in actual insurrectionary activities. Instead, its purpose is to call attention to itself as a viable alternative in a system where it has no other way to generate publicity.
- Parties develop extensive networks of thugs on call generally known as *mastaans*, who act as enforcers. The *mastaans* support themselves through exacting protection money and "tolls" from merchants and contractors, under the patronage of their party bosses. Needless to say, *mastaans* identifying with the ruling party do better

than those allied with the opposition, for they can operate under the protection (and often with the connivance) of the police.
- Both major parties (as well as the minor parties, to the extent that they are able) endeavor to commandeer organized life in Bangladesh, politicizing professional associations, trade unions, and most notoriously the universities. All these sectors become colonized by party "panels," that is, associations affiliated with one party or another. On university campuses, gangsters infiltrate the associations, and gunfights become common.
- Press freedom exists (with some harassment of journalists), although the print media are weak in investigative journalism, fact checking, and the like. A generally unrecognized factor in freedom for the print media is their small circulation (especially the English language media), which reaches only the elite strata. Radio remains a state monopoly, and while there are several independent TV stations, their efforts at news have not progressed beyond the embryonic stage. Even so, the media do bring into public debate many of the worst excesses of government and parties.
- An independent higher court system gives some protection to political rights and civil liberties, though access tends to be restricted to those who can afford to lodge complaints with it, and this protection does not extend to the lower court system, which has continued since colonial times to be part of the executive branch and is thus subject to direction from the law ministry. Still, the safeguards maintained by the high court and supreme court do provide a significant warning that limits exist on what the state can do to impede or obstruct political participation.
- A new cycle begins with each successive election. The opposition that has been making its case through the cacophonous protest of the street will have a reasonably fair chance at the ballot box to oust the incumbent regime. After the election, the

losing side will replicate the obstructionism exercised by the opposition in the previous cycle.

These *de facto* rules of the game were observed for the most part through the 1991–2007 period, and they gave the political system a certain degree of popular legitimacy. After a turnout of 55 percent in the 1991 national election, the second (i.e., the valid) election of 1996 saw 75 percent of the electorate vote, a figure duplicated almost exactly in the 2001 election. Some of the large turnout can surely be explained by ballot box stuffing, but most of it appears to reflect a genuine popular interest in political participation. A 2004 survey, for example, found fully 80 percent of respondents saying they would vote in the next election.[18] But, though they maintained the system, the rules contained an inherent instability, given the strong incentives for the ruling party to tilt the game in its favor. Indeed, it was just such an attempt on the part of the BNP in the 1996 election that led the AL to resort to its only remaining weapon, a boycott of the election, which, in turn, led to instituting the caretaker setup. Beginning part way through the BNP's second term in power, signs began to appear that the game was unraveling again.

A metastasizing pathology: The run-up to 2007

Within a couple of years of the 2001 election, evidence began to accumulate that the BNP was again yielding to the temptation to reconfigure the de facto rules to give it an unimpeded route to victory in the next election, which constitutionally would have to come by the beginning of 2007. There were several symptoms of the unfolding pathology.[19]

To the average citizen, undoubtedly the most distressing signs of the deterioration were the increase in violence and criminal behavior, manifested in extortion (often referred to as "tolls"), kidnappings, campus violence, death threats, cinema house fire bombings, and the like. In many ways, it seemed that the *mastaan*s, as often as not in alliance with the police, had taken charge of public life.[20] On occasion, the state did more than symbolically condemn the violence. Responding to intense criticism, the ruling BNP ordered the army to crack down on criminal elements in "Operation Clean Heart," which lasted from October 2002 to the following January. Thousands were rounded up, reports of human rights abuses mushroomed, crime rates went down briefly (whether because the perpetrators had been arrested or were just lying low for a while was never clear), the army was given amnesty for any excesses committed, and crime rates shortly resumed their upward climb. The nexus between the *mastaan*s and the politicians was evidently not interrupted for long, if at all.[21]

Violence affected the political sphere directly as well. In May 2004 Ahsanullah Master, a prominent Awami League MP, was assassinated in broad daylight, followed later the same month by a bomb attack on the British high commissioner. The next January, Shah A. M. S. Kibria, an Awami Leaguer and former finance minister, was assassinated.[22] These high-profile incidents apart, numerous lower ranking party operatives were also killed, on both sides.

Islamic fundamentalism became wrapped up in the violence also. On 17 August, 2005 over 400 small bombs went off in 63 of the country's 64 districts within the space of an hour. Carefully planned to minimize harm (only three people were killed) while broadcasting the existence of a countrywide network, the attack seized worldwide attention.[23] A group calling itself Jamaat ul-Mujahedeen Bangladesh (JMB or Assembly of Holy Warriors of Bangladesh) claimed responsibility in leaflets distributed at the time. Shortly afterward, several suicide bombers, apparently from the same group, targeted the judiciary, setting off bombs in courthouses and killing perhaps two dozen people.[24]

Most notoriously, during this time an Islamist militant calling himself Bangla Bhai (Brother of Bengal) set up operations as a local religious warlord in the countryside near Rajshahi, imposing dress codes (burqas for women and beards for men), enforcing daily prayers and Ramadan fasting rules, torturing malingerers, and executing opponents in public displays. Although he gave interviews to journalists, the government claimed alternately that either he did not exist or that he could not be located.[25] It seemed clear that Bangla Bhai was getting local police protection, and there was much speculation that his ideas of justice found favor with BNP bosses, who were anxious to co-opt any challenge from the religious right by adding an active Islamic militant tone to the alliance they had built with the Jamaat from the 2001 election onward.[26] International concern mounted and pressure grew on the government to rein him in, fanned by a feature story in the *New York Times Magazine*, appearing in January 2005.[27]

Over a year later, in March 2006, the government finally moved in to arrest him and other militant leaders, claiming a major triumph for an act that could easily have taken place a year or two sooner.[28] Violence did diminish after the crackdown, but few believed that Islamist militancy had withered away. Rather, the speculation was that the movement's members were lying low, hoping that a BNP return to power after the 2007 elections would free their leaders.[29]

Less dramatic but likely portending a more profound long-term impact, *madrasah*s expanded rapidly in Bangladesh during the first part of the present decade, growing with state support by 22 percent between 2001 and 2005, as against a 10 percent growth in state schools over the same period.[30] But it was widely believed that most of the support for them came not from the public budget but from the Persian Gulf, in particular from Saudi Arabia, which was also thought to be bankrolling the Jamaat and perhaps even JMB and Bangla Bhai.

Politicization of the bureaucracy proceeded apace. Whereas earlier some officers had sided with one party or another, there were significant numbers who remained neutral, still adhering to the esprit de corps of the Civil Service of Pakistan members (the "CSP-wallahs") who signed on with the independence cause in 1971 and became the inner core of the Bangladesh bureaucracy. By the early 2000s, however, there were few if any bureaucrats left who had not joined (or been forced to join) one side or the other.[31]

The bureaucratic politicization facilitated corruption by making it easier for government officials and political leaders to work together in siphoning off funds from the public purse. With the ruling party exercising an uncontrolled (and between elections unaccountable) access to procurement, regulation of the economy, and the police power, corruption expanded. Transparency International's Corruption Perception Index, when it began including Bangladesh annually in 2001, ranked the country as globally most corrupt and then continued it in last place for five years running—an unparalleled achievement during the Index's lifetime. Finally, in 2006, the Index "graduated" Bangladesh to the third place from last out of 163.[32] The World Bank's *Governance Matters* report for 2007 gave Bangladesh a slightly more generous ranking among the more than 200 countries ranked—a berth in the 4.9 percentile—but its rating system showed the country declining more or less steadily from the 35th percentile in 1996 to its 4.9 rating in 2006.[33]

Along with the bureaucracy's politicization came a similar calamity within the NGO community—actually a greater tragedy, in a sense, because the NGOs had maintained their neutrality more or less untainted by politics for much longer. With few exceptions, the NGO sector had retreated from politics after some unhappy experiments in the flush of new independence in the 1970s to an almost exclusively service delivery mode for the 1980s and 1990s. There were exceptions. On two occasions in particular, the sector had entered the political arena through its apex organization, the Association of Development Agencies in Bangladesh (ADAB), once in 1990 to join the movement to oust the Ershad regime and then again in 1996 to protest the bogus election in February of that year.[34] Otherwise, it had stayed clear, working its own terrain quite successfully.

In 2003, however, the second largest NGO in Bangladesh, Proshika, was accused by the BNP government of having embarked on an outright political campaign on behalf of the AL. Many in the NGO sector thought the charges were in significant degree (if by no means completely) true, and left ADAB (of which Proshika's president had then assumed the presidency by rotation) under the leadership of BRAC (the largest single NGO in the country) to form a new apex body, now called the Federation of NGOs in Bangladesh (FNB). Inasmuch as Proshika and ADAB were perceived to be pro-AL, the new FNB came to be seen by many as a BNP front. The NGO sector's neutrality (and not a little of its legitimacy, which had remained very high as long as it refrained from politics) had been lost.[35] With the politicization of the NGOs, it seemed that there was no sector of public life that had not been sucked into the maelstrom of the parties.

The mechanics of elections also came to be perceived as badly compromised. In early May 2004, the BNP, relying on the help of the Jamaat-i-Islam for a two-thirds parliamentary majority, passed the 14th Amendment to the Constitution, which specified inter alia that the mandatory retirement age for the chief justice of the supreme court would be extended from 65 to 67 years of age. This seemingly innocuous change had huge implications for the next national election, for the 13th Amendment passed after the 1996 election had declared that the Chief Adviser (i.e., administrator) of a caretaker government superintending the hiatus between parliaments would be the most recently retired chief justice. Advancing the retirement age meant that by the time of the 2007 election, the incumbent chief justice would not have retired and so his predecessor, widely recognized as a BNP partisan, would take over the chief advisor post and be in a position to condone

electoral malpractice, if not actually manipulate it himself.

A second source of concern with election mechanics arose in May 2006 with the appointment of the Chief Election Commissioner. The BNP government's appointee and his deputies were generally believed to be BNP sympathizers, and the election commission was soon charged with padding the voters' rolls by adding millions of bogus names.[36] In addition, the government was alleged to have stacked the election deck through secondments of pro-BNP officers to supervise the elections themselves.[37]

When the time came in October 2006 for the BNP government to step down and turn over charge to a caretaker administration until the January 2007 election, the AL raised a storm of opposition to retired Chief Justice K. M. Hasan's becoming Chief Adviser. Bowing to the pressure, Hasan withdrew, and after some jockeying President Iajuddin Ahmed appointed himself to the post. Agitation then shifted to the election commission, and after a month the President (and now chief advisor) announced that the chief election commissioner would go on leave until after the election, which was to be held on 22 January, 2007.

Along with these manoeuvers, the protests, demonstrations and counterdemonstrations continued, with the AL playing its last card, announcing that it would boycott the election and organize a "siege program" against the government, at which point three-fifths of the parliamentary candidates withdrew their candidacies.[38] In early January, matters were clearly building toward a crisis, and the donor community made strenuous representations to the caretaker government concerning the dangers of an uncontested election and a breakdown of the polity. The American Embassy and British High Commission, along with the European Union issued strong statements, the American ambassador pronounced a one-sided election unacceptable, and international election-monitoring bodies

107

declared they would not act as observers for a flawed poll.[39]

Then, on 11 January, three things happened. Envoys from the United States, United Kingdom, Japan, the European Commission, Canada and Australia all held closed-door meetings with both the AL and BNP alliances. The United Nations resident coordinator announced that Bangladesh participation in future UN peacekeeping operations could be jeopardized if the military supported a one-sided election.[40] And President Iajuddin Ahmed declared a state of emergency while at the same time announcing that he was resigning his position as chief adviser to the caretaker government.[41] The next day, Fakhruddin Ahmed, a former governor of the Bangladesh central bank, took office as chief adviser to the caretaker government.

Within a few days, it became widely known that the military had masterminded the sudden change,[42] with the UN letter (or at least the sentiments behind it) thought to be a major precipitating factor. Bangladesh had for some years been a major supplier of UN peace-keeping troops; in January 2007, the country had about 9,000 on UN duty, roughly 8 percent of active duty army strength.[43] The special pay and allowances the military received for its UN tasks had come to form a major part of its perquisites and would have been difficult indeed to give up.[44]

The military-backed caretaker regime shut down public political party activity and arrested leading politicians from the major parties with accusations of various criminal activities, but it steered clear of declaring martial law and allowed fairly open press freedom (although the press appeared to avoid any direct criticism of the military, perhaps practicing a degree of self-censorship). At one point the caretaker government moved to exile Khaleda Zia and prevent Sheikh Hasina's return from abroad, replicating, in effect, Pervez Musharraf's actions against Pakistan's two feuding ex-prime ministers, Benazir Bhutto and Nawaz Sharif, but a combination of domestic and international pressure led the

government to back down, and the "two begums" were not banned, although open politicking was not allowed to resume. Elections were postponed indefinitely, and eventually the government declared they would be held in December 2008, holding that it would take that long to establish a new voters' registration system based on ID cards.

In February, Mohammed Yunus, founder–director of the world-renowned Grameen Bank and 2006 winner of the Nobel Peace Prize, publicly floated the idea of starting a new political party, but finding support lukewarm, he had dropped the project by May.[45] Bangla Bhai was convicted and executed in April, more than a year after his arrest, and Islamist militancy appeared to have taken a holiday for the duration of the caretaker regime, at least for its first several months. General Moeen U. Ahmed, the army chief of staff, declared on numerous occasions his intent to return the country to democratically elected civilian rule, yet he also mused publicly about the need for Bangladesh to have its "own brand of democracy."[46] But, as the months wore on, popular speculation increased about the likelihood of the Bangladesh military follow-ing the example of General Musharraf in Pakistan, who was by the summer of 2007 in his eighth year of power.

Discussion

The management of the polity in Bangladesh has gone through several distinct phases.[47] The first phase, illustrated in Figure 7.2, lasted a full 19 years, from Independence in December 1971 until the ouster of the Ershad dictatorship in December 1990. The bureaucracy, led by the "CSP-wallahs" carried over from the Civil Service of Pakistan, formed the centerpiece, operating in a partnership with either the ruling party elite or the military. The "either . . . or" term is key here, for the bureaucracy had only one partner at a time. Initially, it was the Mujib regime and then most of the time thereafter the military, though part way into the Zia era, the BNP basically displaced it as Zia transformed his authoritarian rule into a more popular one. Ershad attempted the same kind of transformation with his Jatiya Party, but never succeeded. Over the whole period, the bureaucracy remained at the center: strategic policy decisions might be made by the political or military managers, but owing to its experience at operating the state's machinery, the bureaucracy was critical and at times the dominant partner in the management of state affairs. As for the NGOs, although a number of them got their start with social change agendas in the early 1970s, within a few years they had largely concluded that trying to introduce fundamental change into the socioeconomic structure was too difficult and so reverted to a neutral service delivery role.

Essentially the same pattern prevailed at the outset of the democratic era in 1991, now with the political class and the bureaucracy aligned. The military stayed out of the picture, even during the critical period of the first 1996 election, when most elements of civil society (including the major NGOs) did involve themselves. As the enmity between the two

major parties began to strain the political system, however, especially after 2001, the picture changed, as shown in Figure 7.3. The political class had subordinated the bureaucracy by dividing it into factions allied to the main parties, and it had begun to make similar inroads into the hitherto neutral NGO community. The military continued to remain outside the political sphere, enjoying a gradually rising budget along with the perquisites and monetary rewards of being among the top two or three providers of UN peacekeeping forces.

In 2007, the picture changed to that depicted in Figure 7.4. After the emergency proclaimed in January, the military formed the caretaker government and provided broad policy instructions to it (although presumably allowing it considerable latitude). In turn, the caretaker government directed the bureaucracy while totally sidelining the political class. Relations between the military/caretaker government and the NGO sector remained uncertain.

Ultimately, the military followed through on its repeated promises to turn over charge to a democratically elected government by the

Figure 7.2 Bureaucracy + one ally, NGOs outside, 1972–1991

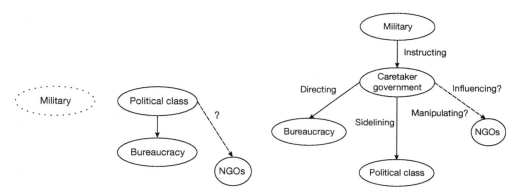

Figure 7.3 Military distracted, bureaucracy subordinated, NGOs likewise?, early 2000s

Figure 7.4 Military in charge, others subordinated, 2007

109

end of 2008. It did not succumb to a temptation to follow the Musharraf route and find ways to hang onto power, even long past any semblance of popular support.[48] At least three factors would seem to have argued against long-term military control of the polity, two of them acts of the regime and the third a long-term pattern. First, the caretaker government committed itself to separating the judicial from the executive branch. In India, the two functions have long been separated, but Bangladesh followed the path it had inherited from Pakistan and, before it, Britain, in that it maintained the lower judiciary[49] under the executive branch through the law ministry. Although the constitution specified a separation for the entire judiciary, and the supreme court had required it, successive governments had found it expedient to maintain control over the lower branches.[50] In May 2007 the Supreme Court again required a separation, but this time the caretaker government appeared to take the order seriously, and in November 2007 the caretaker government did, in fact, order the lower judiciary separated.[51]

Second, the caretaker regime launched the massive process of establishing a totally new voter registration system with individual ID cards, a move that indicated a degree of seriousness not exhibited by any previous government.

Third, the military has nothing like the cosseted status enjoyed by Pakistan's defense establishment over the years—a privileged position the military there would go to serious lengths to protect. Bangladesh's military has had budgetary support rising at the same level as GNP during the present decade, similar to the pattern in Pakistan. But this has meant about 1.4 percent of the gross domestic product while Pakistan's military was being allotted 3.5 percent—about two-and-a-half times as much—and Pakistan's GDP in 2006 was roughly twice that of Bangladesh, so the military rested on a much larger base. In addition, there is the huge economic enterprise that Pakistan's military has built up, consisting of industries, banks and businesses, all funneling in

their profits to the military.[52] Beyond that, Pakistan has become the beneficiary of an immense US government largesse in the post 9/11 era, to the extent of some US\$ 10 billion by the beginning of 2007. The likelihood is that this generosity will continue for some time to come, given American dependence on Pakistan in connection with its ongoing operations in neighboring Afghanistan.[53] In short, the Bangladesh military has nothing like the vested interest in maintaining control of the political system to feed its own demands that exists in Pakistan.

The developmental paradox

In spite of corruption, unaccountability, and frequent disruptions caused by the many *hartal*s, Bangladesh enjoyed a long period of economic growth during the years after the democratic restoration in 1991, especially in agriculture, which still absorbs roughly half the active labor force. In marked contrast with the country's earlier years, when it was often referred to in terms of Henry Kissinger's reported "international basket case" remark, Bangladesh began to do quite well economically. Over the period since 1990, foodgrain production grew significantly, rising from about 18–19 million tons to more than 28 million tons in 2006–07. In the process, food availability per capita rose from about 0.46 kg/day to at least 0.55 kg by the middle of the present decade. In consequence, foodgrain prices dropped in Bangladesh as elsewhere in the world over this time. Meanwhile, growing off-farm economic activity in sectors like transportation, construction, retailing, and small enterprises generally were exerting an upward pressure on wages. Between the late 1980s and 2000, the proportion of rural workers whose primary occupation was in agriculture dropped from 66 percent to less than 48 percent, while those working mainly outside agriculture rose from 34 percent to 52 percent—a quite remarkable shift. Not surprisingly, agricultural wages (generally the baseline measure of rural welfare for the bottom strata) rose, and the terms of rental for agricultural land moved in favor of the tenant/sharecropper.[54]

A good part of the explanation for these favorable trends has to be accounted for by food policy reforms adopted in the late 1980s and continued in the early 1990s, including privatizing inputs like tubewells and fertilizers, allowing international foodgrain trading, investing in infrastructure (especially transportation), paring back subsidies in the food sector, and supporting microcredit institutions. Donor pressure, reinforced by decreasing foreign aid helped induce the state to take up these reforms, many of which were elements of the "Washington Consensus" then in vogue in the international development community. But the reforms also found a ready partner in the BNP and Awami League governments in power. For, during this time, the state increased its own revenue by about the same level that had been lost in foreign aid—roughly 2 percent of GDP.[55] In other words, the state could have afforded to continue with its subsidies but chose instead to undertake a reform path.

While all these economic trends were unfolding, Bangladesh became something of a poster child in family planning circles as its crude birth rate dropped by about one-third. Total fertility rate, which had earlier dropped from an estimated 6.3 in the mid-1970s to 5.1 by the end of the 1980s, continued to decrease in the 1990s to 3.3 by 2000—still well above replacement level (a rate of 2.2), but showing substantial advancement along the demographic transition. Much of the explanation for such progress lies in the changing economics of household management, as the benefits of child labor declined in an increasingly nonagricultural economy while the costs of childrearing increased. But state commitment to family planning had to play a strong role.[56] In addition, child mortality decreased and primary education increased.

As the decade wore on, the Bangladesh economic boom began to unravel. Fertilizer shortages began to appear, and rice prices began to creep upward. The poverty rate, which had decreased from 68 percent to 44

percent between 1988 and 2004, had returned to 55 percent by 2008.[57] Still, the good times had a long run before beginning to sag.

How could all these beneficial developments have happened with such misgovernance at the helm of the polity, where almost every measure of good governance in the World Bank's reckoning ranked among the world's lowest?[58] A large, energetic, and effective NGO sector working in agricultural extension, education, health, and microcredit can explain a good part of the country's success here,[59] but there is more than a smattering of paradox. At the least one is moved to ponder whether good governance in the sense of accountable democratic management of the state's business is necessary in the short or even middle run.

Conclusion

Bangladesh has had several chances to develop a viable political party system since achieving its independence in 1971. So far, the country's political leaders have squandered them all in their obsession to demolish opposition parties and sequester all the spoils of office for themselves. Sheikh Mujibur Rahman turned 1971's promise of a democratic *Sonar Bangla*[60] into a one-party dictatorship in 1975. The BNP's blatantly rigged February 1996 election virtually ended the democratic experiment of 1991 before rescue came in the form of the caretaker government scheme. And the BNP's attempts at rigging the 2007 election led in the end to the military-supported emergency declared in January of that year.

Can a genuine multiparty system ever take hold in Bangladesh? Can the perverse and degraded "rules of the game" that guided politics from 1991 to 2007 be replaced by something approximating a genuine Westminster model? Perhaps the 18-month emergency rule that ended with elections in December 2008 can begin seriously to separate the *mastaans* from the parties and from the police, depoliticize the bureaucracy and the NGO sector, curb corruption, and defuse the militant Islamist threat. The multitude of tasks seems overwhelming, but even to achieve significant success in just a couple of these spheres might be sufficient to set a "virtuous cycle" into motion. If so, a country that has managed to attain a very respectable rate of economic growth under severe malgovernance in recent years might well become a real development success story.

Postscript

In December 2008 the Caretaker Government made good on its promise to hold a national election, which took place on the 29th of the month. Amid intense international attention and under the scrutiny of a large deployment of foreign and domestic monitors (the author served as a member of the National Democratic Institute's team), a peaceful and orderly election transpired. Some 70.5 million voters went to the polls (87 percent of those registered, a record turnout). The results surprised virtually everyone, not least the political parties themselves. The Awami League captured fully 49.0 percent of the vote, translating into 230 seats or 76.7 percent of the total—the largest majority since Sheikh Mujib's victory in 1973 just after independence. The BNP won only 32.7 percent of the vote, giving it 29 seats or 9.7 percent.

The BNP's loss was so stunning—"tsunami" was the word most frequently used to describe it—and the verdict of the monitors so uniform as to the election's fairness that the party lodged only minor claims of fraud and rigging, turning quickly to a mode of self-reflection on how to regroup and reposition itself. A row soon developed over seating in the new parliament and the BNP began boycotting, but the efforts seemed only half-hearted as the party licked its wounds. At the end of February 2009, two months after the election, it was not clear whether the BNP would use its time in the political wilderness to refashion itself as the British Labour Party did after its successive drubbings at the hands of Margaret Thatcher in

the 1980s (and the Canadian Conservatives did after being reduced to two seats in the country's 1992 elections), or whether it would return to the politics of disruption and obstruction as had been the norm for losing parties over the previous 18 years. To say that the better part of Bangladesh's political future rides on the BNP's decision would not be an overstatement.

Notes

1   This chapter is based largely on my own experience of some 20 visits to Bangladesh beginning in April 1973, with the most recent ending in June 2004. My work there as an academic and a consultant has been sponsored by Cornell University, the Department for International Development (UK), the Ford Foundation, the Social Science Research Council, the Swedish International Development Authority, the United States Agency for International Development, and the World Bank, to all of which I am most grateful. I would also like to thank C. Christine Fair of RAND and Nawreen Sattar of Yale for comments. None of these organizations or individuals bears any responsibility for the interpretations and views expressed here, which are my own.

2   Larry Diamond, *Developing Democracy: Toward Consolidation* (Baltimore, MA: Johns Hopkins University Press, 1999), pp. 96–97, referencing Michael Coppedge, *Strong Parties and Lame Ducks: Presidential Partyarchy and Factionalism in Venezuela* (Stanford, CA: University Press, 1994).

3   "Electoral democracies" refer to countries that do have regular elections with real competition, but fall far short when it comes to other critical components of democracy such as civil liberties, guaranteed minority rights, and the like. "Liberal democracy" requires an absence of unaccountable actors (especially the military) and the presence of horizontal accountability between major actors (e.g., executive and legislature), extensive provisions establishing pluralism, and perhaps most importantly the "rule of law" guaranteeing political rights and civil liberties through an independent judiciary. See Diamond, *Developing Democracy*, for an extensive analysis; also Larry Diamond,

"Thinking about Hybrid Regimes: Elections without Democracy," *Journal of Democracy*, Vol. 13, No. 2 (2002), pp. 21–35. "Democratic consolidation" can be said to obtain when all significant actors in a political system—winners and losers—accept democracy as "the only game in town" (see Juan J. Linz and Alfred Stepan, *Problems of Democratic Transition and Consolidation: Southern Europe, South America, and Post-Communist Europe* (Baltimore, MA: Johns Hopkins University Press, 1996), pp. 5–6). On the incompleteness of democracy, in addition to Diamond's works just cited, see for instance Guillermo O'Donnell, "The Perpetual Crises of Democracy," *Journal of Democracy*, Vol. 18, No. 1 (2007), pp. 5–11.

4   See Samuel P. Huntington, *The Third Wave: Democratization in the Late Twentieth Century* (Norman, OK: University of Oklahoma Press, 1991), pp. 266ff.

5   The first time came after Sheikh Mujibur Rahman's assassination in 1975; the second occurred with the coup that brought General Hussein Muhammad Ershad to power in 1982.

6   There are many accounts of this period. Three very good ones are Craig Baxter, *Bangladesh: From a Nation to a State* (Boulder, CO: Westview Press, 1997); Lawrence Ziring, *Bangladesh from Mujib to Ershad: An Interpretive Study* (Dhaka: University Press Limited, 1992); and Talukder Maniruzzaman, *The Bangladesh Revolution and Its Aftermath*, 2nd edn (Dhaka: University Press Limited, 1988). Except where noted, most of this section on the 1971–90 period has been taken from these three sources.

7   For an analysis of the two sequences, the first leading to a change in Pakistan's government and the second to the disintegration of Pakistan itself, see Harry Blair, "Sheikh Mujib and Déjà vu in East Bengal: The Tragedies of 25 March," *Economic and Political Weekly*, Vol. 6, No. 52 (1971), pp. 2,555–62.

8   In contrast with West Pakistan and its four provinces, East Pakistan consisted solely of the province of East Bengal, so the two designations were used interchangeably.

9   On *hartals* and their political uses, see M. Rashiduzzaman, "Political Unrest and Democracy in Bangladesh," *Asian Survey*, Vol. 37, No. 3 (1997), pp. 254–68.

10 With one very notable but ultimately redeemed exception, the national election of February 1996, about which more later on.

11 On the place of Islamic parties in Bangladesh, see Ali Riaz, "Islamist Parties and Democracy in Bangladesh," paper prepared for annual meeting of the American Political Science Association, Chicago, 30 August–2 September, 2007.

12 For an account of the two 1996 elections, see Zillur R. Khan, "Bangladesh's Experiments with Parliamentary Democracy," *Asian Survey*, Vol. 37, No. 6 (1997), pp. 575–89; also Stanley Kochanek, "Bangladesh in 1996: The 25th Year of Independence," *Asian Survey*, Vol. 37, No. 2 (1997), pp. 136–42.

13 See Rashiduzzaman, "Political Unrest," on the quick resumption of *hartals* after the 1996 election.

14 In return for joining the ruling alliance, the Jamaat received two important portfolios, agriculture and social welfare. In the election itself, the BNP won only 2 percent more of the popular vote than the AL, as shown in Table 7.1.

15 The saga can be tracked most easily in *Asian Survey's* annual recap of Bangladesh politics published in its first issue each year, e.g., M. Rashiduzzaman, "Bangladesh in 2001: The Election and a New Political Reality?" *Asian Survey*, Vol. 42, No. 1 (2002), pp. 183–91, and Rounaq Jahan, "Bangladesh in 2003: Vibrant Democracy or Destructive Politics," *Asian Survey*, Vol. 44, No. 1 (2004), pp. 56–61.

16 See, e.g., N. Ahmed and Sheikh Z. Ahmad, "The Parliamentary Elections in Bangladesh, October 2001," *Electoral Studies*, Vol. 22, No. 3 (4 September, 2003), pp. 503–509.

17 This account of the "rules" is based largely on Harry Blair, Robert Charlick, Rezaul Haque, Manzoor Hasan and Nazmul Lalimullah, "Democracy and Governance: Strategic Assessment of Bangladesh," report for USAID, Bangladesh (Burlington, VT: ARD, Inc., October 2004). But see also Rehman Sobhan, "Structural Dimensions of Malgovernance in Bangladesh," *Economic and Political Weekly*, 39 (4 September, 2004), pp. 4,101–08.

18 See Associates in Rural Development, "Bangladesh: Knowledge, Attitudes and Practices: National Survey Covering Democracy and Governance Issues" (Burlington, VT: ARD, Inc., for USAID/Bangladesh, 2004).

19 There have been several insightful overviews of the decline. See, inter alia, Mohammad Mohabbat Khan, "State of Governance in Bangladesh," *The Round Table*, 370 (July 2003), pp. 391–405; Rehman Sobhan, "Structural

Dimensions of Malgovernance"; also Moazzem Hossain, "Bangladesh: 'Home-Grown' Democracy," *Economic and Political Weekly*, 41 (2006), pp. 791–93. The account given in the present essay is based in large measure on Blair *et al.*, "Democracy and Governance: Strategic Assessment of Bangladesh."

20 At times the police substituted for the *mastaans*. One account of the Eid season in 2005 reported that a heavy presence of uniformed police to keep order during Eid had displaced the usual extortionists from retail business establishments in Dhaka but had filled in the gap by charging their own "tolls" on the vendors. See Shaheem Mollah, "Cops in Extortionists' Role on Streets: Regular Thugs Stay Away in Fear of Rab," *Daily Star* (Dhaka), 1 November, 2005.

21 For a perceptive analysis of the linkages between *mastaans* and politics in rural Bangladesh, see Joe Devine, "Wellbeing, Democracy and Political Violence in Bangladesh," paper for the 57th Political Studies Association Annual Conference, University of Bath, UK, 11–13 April, 2007.

22 Despite rhetorical demands from the prime minister to find the culprits, no one was ever apprehended.

23 See, for instance, Associated Press, "Concerted Bombs Hit 100 Bangladesh Sites," *New York Times*, 18 August, 2005; Nora Boustany, "Bombings Force Bangladesh Envoy Home," *Washington Post*, 19 August, 2005; and Raekha Prasad, "Cities Shaken by 350 Co-ordinated Attacks," *The Times* (London), 18 August, 2005.

24 See David Montero and Somini Sengupta, "Bangladesh Blast Kills 1 and Hurts 100: 3rd Attack in Days on Legal System," *New York Times*, 2 December, 2005; also Rounaq Jahan, "Bangladesh in 2005: Standing at a Crossroads," *Asian Survey*, Vol. 46, No. 1 (2006), pp. 107–13.

25 See the several accounts in the Dhaka *Daily Star* at the time of his capture http://www.the dailystar.net/2006/03/07/d6030701011.htm (accessed 10 August, 2007).

26 For a detailed account of the machinations apparently involved, see International Crisis Group, "Bangladesh Today," Asia Report No. 121 (Brussels: ICG, 23 October, 2006).

27 See Eliza Griswold, "The Next Islamist Revolution?" *New York Times Magazine*, 23 January, 2005.

28 Julfikar Ali Manik and Shamim Ashraf, "Tyrant Bangla Bhai Finally Captured," *Daily Star* (Dhaka), 7 March, 2006.

29 After his arrest in March 2006, the BNP government did not press a legal prosecution up to the time of its leaving office in October.

30 See Rejaul Karim Byron and Shameen Mahmud, "Madrassas Mushroom with State Favour," *Daily Star* (Dhaka), 4 August, 2005.

31 For an assessment of trends in relations between politicians and bureaucrats since 1971, see Ahmed Shafiqul Huque and M. Taiabur Rahman, "From Domination to Alliance: Shifting Strategies and Accumulation of Power by the Bureaucracy of Bangladesh," *Public Organization Review: A Global Journal*, 3 (2003), pp. 403–18.

32 There were many ties at the bottom of the scale, so that Bangladesh actually shared the third from bottom rank with three other countries in 2006. Burma, Guinea, and Iraq tied for next to bottom, and Haiti rested by itself in last place. See Transparency International "Corruption Perceptions Index 2006," annual publication available at http://www.transparency.org. For further details, see the chapter by Kochanek in this volume.

33 See Daniel Kaufmann, Aart Kraay, and Massimo Mastruzzi, *Governance Matters VI: Aggregate and Individual Governance Indicators 1996–2006*, World Bank Policy Research Paper 4280 (Washington: World Bank, July 2007). Actually, Bangladesh had fallen to the 4.9th percentile in 2004, then showed an uptick to 7.8 in 2005 before settling back to the 4.9 level in 2006.

34 The NGO sector had also involved itself in political decision making during the Ershad regime when the latter sought to establish control over the sector in the mid-1980s. And there were at least a couple of prominent NGOs that did become involved in local level politics quite explicitly, viz., Gonoshahajjo Sangstha, which sponsored specific candidates in local elections, and Nijera Kori, which explicitly pursued advocacy for social change at village level. On the latter prospect, see Harry Blair, "Civil Society and Pro-poor Initiatives at the Local Level in Bangladesh: Finding a Workable Strategy," *World Development*, Vol. 33, No. 6 (2005), pp. 921–36.

35 Data from interviews. See also World Bank, "Bangladesh Economics and Governance of Nongovernmental Organizations in Bangladesh," Report No. 35861-BD

(Washington: World Bank, 16 April, 2006); and S. M. Nurul Alam, "Whose Public Action? Analyzing Inter-sectoral Collaboration for Service Delivery" (Dhaka: International Development Department, 2007).

36 The voters' list prepared in 2006 contained about 10 million more names than demographic estimates based on the last census could support, according to a pre-election assessment team preparing for international monitoring, headed by ex-US senator Thomas Daschle and sponsored by the National Democratic Institute (see National Democratic Institute, "Report of the National Democratic Institute (NDI) pre-election delegation to Bangladesh's 2006/07 Parliamentary Elections" (Dhaka: NDI, 11 September, 2006), p. 6. Also International Crisis Group, "Bangladesh Today;" and Karim and Fair, "Bangladesh at the Crossroads." The Election Commission ignored High Court rulings to remedy the inaccuracies. See Pavithra Banavar and Nicholas Howenstein, "The Future of Democracy in Bangladesh," USIPeace Briefing (Washington: United States Institute of Peace, March 2007).

37 As in other South Asian countries, the state posts ("seconds") large numbers of government servants temporarily to conduct elections as returning officers, ballot counters, security guards, etc. For the 2001 election, the Awami League as ruling party was generally believed to have attempted the same approach, moving a party sympathizer into the presidency and chief adviser positions, as well as posting its bureaucratic favorites into slots where they could supervise the polling and ballot counting. These efforts notwithstanding, however, the AL lost the election, and proceeded to claim that it had been rigged.

38 *Daily Star* (Dhaka), 4 January, 2007 (several stories). Some 2,370 out of 3,935 parliamentary candidates were said to have withdrawn (ibid.).

39 See *Daily Star* (Dhaka), "US, UK, EC disappointed," 4 January, 2007; "Act Swiftly, Impartially to Create Conditions for All-Party Polls, US Urges CG," 6 January, 2007; "One-sided Polls won't be Credible, Acceptable, says US Envoy," 9 January, 2007; "EU Poll Mission May not Go Ahead if Crisis Persists," 11 January, 2007; "NDI, IRI won't Watch Jan 22 Elections," 11 January, 2007.

40 The resident coordinator's letter came in the form of a press release, so it attained maximum publicity. See Renata Lok Dessallien, "Press Statement by UN Resident Coordinator, Ms Renata Lok Dessallien, Dhaka," Media release (Dhaka: Office of the United Nations Resident Coordinator in Bangladesh, 11 January, 2007).

41 The two daily newspapers *Daily Star* and *New Age* provided detailed coverage of the tumultuous period during early January as these various threads were unfolding. See web page archives at www.thedailystar.net and www.newagebd.com. A good summary of the international pressure can be found in Nazrul Islam, "Military Role May Bear on Dhaka's Peacekeeping," *New Age* (Dhaka), 12 January, 2007.

42 See Jo Johnson's articles in the *Financial Times* (London), on 15 and 17 January, 2007: "Ex-bank chief heads Bangladesh government," and "Bangladesh generals plan anti-corruption drive: The military leaders now controlling the government in Dhaka want to cleanse the political system." The Bangladesh press did not note any army involvement with the emergency until some days later, although it was surely understood.

43 Data from UN Department of Peacekeeping Operations. See United Nations, "Contributions to United Nations Peacekeeping Operations, as of 31 January, 2007." The Bangladesh contingent amounted to about one-eighth of all UN troops on peacekeeping service in January 2007. Total army size from International Institute for Strategic Studies, *The Military Balance*, 107 (London: IISS, January 2007).

44 There is some question about how serious the UN would have been about cutting back or eliminating Bangladesh as a peacekeeper. After all, Pervez Musharraf's 1999 coup and establishment of a dictatorship did not lead to any penalties on peacekeeping assignments. Pakistan maintained roughly the same number of peacekeeping troops in the field as Bangladesh. All this was known to the Bangladesh military, of course, and raises the question as to whether the army took advantage of the uncertainty created by the letter to launch the declaration of emergency.

45 See Muhammad Yunus, "Yunus' second letter," *Daily Star* (Dhaka), 23 February, 2007; "Yunus writes letter to all," ibid., 4 May, 2007.

46 On returning to democratic government and denying political ambitions, see e.g., *Daily Star* (Dhaka), "Moeen again Rules out Army's Role in Politics," 13 August, 2007; and "Moeen says Polls by 2008 end," 18 August, 2007; also "Moeen says Army has no Plan for Martial Law," 24 May, 2007. For an example of Moeen's speculation about governance, see *New Age* (Dhaka), "Army Chief calls for 'Own Brand of Democracy,'" 3 April, 2007. For a good general overview of political events over the emergency period, see Economist Intelligence Unit, "Bangladesh Country Report, April 2007" (London: EIU, 2007); and "Bangladesh Country Report, July 2007" (London: EIU, 2007).

47 The discussion here represents a further elaboration and development of thinking I began in Blair, "Politics, Civil Society and Governance in Bangladesh" and continued in Blair *et al.*, "Democracy and Governance: Strategic Assessment of Bangladesh."

48 For an example of the speculation on this question, see Farid Bakht, "Army Entrenches Itself in Bangladesh," *Economic and Political Weekly*, Vol. 42, No. 29 (2007), pp. 2,991–92.

49 The lower judiciary comprises the entire court system save for the supreme court and high court, which had become independent during the Pakistan period and continued this status through successive governments since the 1972 Constitution. But as in other countries, the higher courts hear only a minute percentage of the total cases.

50 The supreme court, presumably anxious to avoid direct confrontation, continued allowing extensions for the government to comply with the constitutional requirement. The twenty-first such extension, for example, was allowed in October 2005.

51 Julfikar Ali Manik, "Judiciary Freed from the Executive Fetters Today," *Daily Star* (Dhaka), 1 November, 2007.

52 See Ayesha Saddiqa, *Military Inc. Inside Pakistan's Military Economy* (London: Pluto Press, 2007). The Bangladesh military has some business operations as well, but they are small scale compared to those in Pakistan. See Siddiqa, ibid., p. 50; also *New Age* (Dhaka), "Gen Moeen contradicts law adviser," 29 August, 2007.

53 Data on budgetary allotments from International Institute for Strategic Studies, *The Military Balance*, 102 (2002) and 107 (2007). (London: IISS). For an account of US military aid to

Pakistan, see Craig Cohen and Derek Chollet, "When $10 Billion Is Not Enough: Rethinking U.S. Strategy toward Pakistan," *Washington Quarterly*, Vol. 30, No. 2 (2007), pp. 7–19.

54 These developments are presented and analyzed in an excellent series of articles in *Economic and Political Weekly* edited by Isher Ahluwalia and Wahiduddin Mahmud, "Economic Transformation and Social Development in Bangladesh," *Economic and Political Weekly*, 39 (2004), pp. 4,009–52. See, in particular, Raisuddin Ahmed, "Rice Economy of Bangladesh: Progress and Prospects," *EPW*, 4,043–52; Paul A. Dorosh, "Trade, Food Aid and Food Security: Evolving Rice and Wheat Markets," *EPW*, 4,033–42; and Mahabub Hossain, "Rural Non-Farm Economy: Evidence from Household Surveys," *EPW*, 4,053–58. Some data in this paragraph were derived from the website maintained by the Bangladesh Bureau of Statistics: http://www.bbs.gov.bd/. The agricultural side is analyzed in greater detail in Raisuddin Ahmed, Steven Haggblade, and Tawfiq-e-Elahi Chowdhury (eds), *Out of the Shadow of Famine: Evolving Food Markets and Food Policy in Bangladesh* (Baltimore, MD: Johns Hopkins University Press, 2000). Some of the political impact of these trends at local level are explored in Blair, "Civil Society and Pro-poor Initiatives at the Local Level in Bangladesh."

55 See Wahiduddin Mahmed, "Macroeconomic Management: From Stabilization to Growth?" *Economic and Political Weekly*, 39 (2004), pp. 4023–32.

56 Considerable argument exists as to whether a changing economic calculus or family planning intervention played the greater role here. See Simeen Mahmud, "Health and Population: Making Progress under Poverty," *Economic and Political Weekly*, 39 (2004), pp. 4,081–91; and Shihidur R. Khandker and M. Abdul Latif, "The Role of Family Planning and Targeted Credit Programs in Demographic Change in Bangladesh," World Bank Discussion Paper No. 337 (Washington: World Bank, 1996).

57 For a summary of these less happy trends, see Abdul Bayes, "Beneath the Surface: Why is the Price of Rice Still so High?" *Daily Star*, 24 August, 2008.

58 The conundrum is aptly summed up in Shantayanan Devarajan, "Two Comments on 'Governance Indicators: Where Are We, Where

Should We Be Going?' by Daniel Kaufmann and Aart Kraay," *World Bank Research Observer,* Vol. 23, No. 1 (2008), pp. 31–6.

59 On the NGO sector as a formidable engine of development, see Sajjad Zohir, "NGO Sector in Bangladesh: An Overview," *Economic and Political Weekly,* 39 (2004), pp. 4,109–13.

60 "Golden Bengal"—the title of a poem by Rabindranath Tagore and the country's national anthem.

8

Politics and governance in post-independence Sri Lanka

Neil DeVotta

Sri Lanka was long considered a model colony, and when Britain granted the island independence in February 1948 many believed it was the post-colonial state with "the best chance of making a successful transition to modern statehood."[1] The optimism was well founded: universal franchise preceded independence in 1931, just three years after being instituted in Britain; the country ranked relatively high on various socioeconomic indices, especially when compared to other Asian and African states undergoing decolonization; and, most important, ethnic tension between the majority Sinhalese and minority Tamils notwithstanding, the country's polyethnic and multi-religious elites had agreed to the transfer of power and the constitutional structure the British left behind.[2] Yet within eight years of independence the island adopted a trajectory that led to ethnocentrism, illiberal governance, and a gruesome civil war.[3]

Post-independence politics

From 1931 to 1946 the Donoughmore Constitution, with its unitary structure, governed Sri Lanka (then called Ceylon). Communal electorates that preceded Donoughmore and parity of representation with the Sinhalese

allowed the Tamils to operate as a second "majority" community, despite Tamils being about 12 percent of the population (in comparison to nearly 70 percent Sinhalese).[4] The Donoughmore Constitution, however, discarded communal electorates and introduced universal franchise; both measures vitiated the political influence of Tamils and encouraged attempts to minimize Sinhalese domination and majoritarian politics. Strong camaraderie between Sinhalese and Tamil elites, however, enabled the 1946 Soulbury Constitution, which lacked stringent minority guarantees: Article 29(2) merely required the government to treat all ethnoreligious communities dispassionately. The article and minority input were disregarded when Sinhalese elites crafted the 1972 and 1978 constitutions that consolidated the unitary state structure.

Sri Lanka's transition from colonialism to independence was a tepid affair that contrasted with the pre-independence mobilization and ruckus in neighboring India. Indeed, the transfer of power was so seamless that people in rural areas hardly realized a major political change had taken place. The country's mainly western-educated elite was well versed in parliamentary traditions and practice, which partly ensured that the two main political parties would respect subsequent electoral verdicts. Indeed, between 1948 and 1977, power was transferred six times between the United National Party (UNP) and Sri Lanka Freedom Party (SLFP). If two turn-overs between opposition parties mark the consolidation of democracy,[5] Sri Lanka achieved such vaunted status in March 1960. But, in a true liberal democracy, the rules, laws, norms, and conventions governing formal democratic processes are scrupulously and consistently observed; in this sense Sri Lanka represents a classic illiberal democracy.

The most revolutionary post-independence event took place in 1956, when Solomon West Ridgeway Dias Bandaranaike and his SLFP-led coalition championed a "Sinhala-only" policy to win parliamentary elections. English had operated as the national language despite the fact that only around 10 percent of the population spoke it fluently. Initially the SLFP, UNP, Tamil elites within the UNP, and the main Tamil parties supported the replacement of English by Sinhala and Tamil as national languages. But when a grassroots move-ment began clamoring for Sinhala only, Bandaranaike—who had left the UNP in July 1951 on realizing that Prime Minister D. S. Senanayake was grooming his son, Dudley, to assume the party's leadership—recognized that he could use the issue to capture the premiership. When the UNP, led by the abrasive and hyper-westernized Sir John Kotelawala, belatedly acknowledged that the party could not win elections by championing linguistic parity, it too embraced a Sinhala-only policy. The UNP and SLFP thereafter resorted to "ethnic outbidding," trying to outdo each other on who best could promote Sinhalese preferences.[6] Bandaranaike won the contest, but the Sinhala Only Bill of 1956 led to Tamil protests and the first ever anti-Tamil riots. These riots were followed by more severe Sinhalese–Tamil riots in 1958.[7]

The Sinhala-only movement was not merely about defending language and culture; it also had to do with socioeconomic realit-ies and perceived opportunities. For instance, northern Tamils had utilized missionary schools to excel in English and become overrepresented in the civil service, military, and universities. Sinhalese were goaded into believing that Sinhala only would expedi-tiously and radically transform their fortunes. This did not happen and it led to dis-enchantment with Bandaranaike. The prime minister's attempts to accommodate the Tamil language also upset Sinhalese Buddhist extremists, and in September 1959 a Buddhist monk assassinated him.

Bandaranaike's wife, Sirimavo, soon thereafter took over the SLFP and became the first ever elected woman head of state in the world, in July 1960. Her first government (July 1960–March 1965) claimed it was furthering the revolution her husband had begun, but the numerous anti-Tamil practices it embraced further marginalized the Tamil minority.[8] The Dudley Senanayake-led UNP government that followed (March 1965–May 1970) failed to alleviate Tamil grievances, although neither did it aggravate them.

Sirimavo Bandaranaike returned to power in May 1970. In 1971 disgruntled Sinhalese Marxist students belonging to the Janatha Vimukthi Peramuna (People's Liberation Front—JVP) unleashed an insurgency that nearly toppled the government. The insur-gency was violently suppressed, but it spurred the government toward an even more radical pro-Sinhalese Buddhist and anti-Tamil agenda. Tamils were required to score higher than Sinhalese to get into university and they were more or less blocked from entering govern-ment service; furthermore, a new constitu-tion was introduced in 1972 that gave Buddhism "foremost status," thereby relegating Hinduism, Christianity, and Islam to second-class status. In relation to the economy, the government embraced *dirigisme* and autarky. This led to the most basic goods becoming scarce and rationed. The government also nationalized mostly foreign-owned plantations and corporations, insurance companies, and banks. Furthermore, the government refused to hold scheduled elections in 1975 and extended its rule until 1977.

119

The SLFP became so discredited that not only did the J. R. Jayewardene-led UNP win the July 1977 elections with a five-sixths majority, but the Tamil United Liberation Front (TULF), comprising several Tamil parties, won more seats than the SLFP to become the country's principal opposition. Sri Lankans vote in high numbers during parliamentary and presidential elections, and voter turnout for the 1977 elections was a stratospheric 86.7 percent, the highest thus far. The TULF, citing widespread discrimination against Tamils, had issued a resolution in 1976 (the so-called Vaddukoddai Resolution) calling for the predominantly Tamil northeast to secede from the rest of Sri Lanka. The resolution was likely designed to appease increasingly militaristic Tamil youth mobilizing against the Sri Lankan state, but many Sinhalese considered the party a separatist entity and treated it with hostility. This partly contributed to the August 1977 anti-Tamil riots.

Given the majority he commanded in parliament, Jayewardene was best equipped to accommodate legitimate Tamil grievances; instead, he sought to use the ethnic problem to consolidate his position. The increased restiveness in the northeast caused the government to institute the draconian Prevention of Terrorism Act of 1979, which allowed security forces to arrest, imprison, and leave incommunicado for 18 months without trial anyone deemed threatening to the state. Hundreds of innocent Tamils were caught in its dragnet and the torture and humiliation encountered radicalized them further. The worsening ethnic problem stymied the government's development plans, marginalized moderate Tamil leaders, emboldened extremist radical Tamil youth and their Sinhalese Buddhist counterparts, and contributed to the 1981 and 1983 anti-Tamil riots.[9]

J. R. Jayewardene used the massive UNP majority in parliament to introduce the 1978 constitution. It created an all-powerful executive president.[10] To deal with the discrepancy between the percentage of votes parties polled and the number of seats won,[11] it jettisoned the first-past-the-post electoral system for a complicated proportional representation-cum-preferential voting system. It was believed the latter would increase the weight of the votes of minorities.[12] Other features—such as a high qualifying threshold and a bonus vote for the party that won a district—seemed designed to ensure that the UNP stayed dominant and to limit the proliferation of parties, which proportional representation typically facilitates.[13] The constitution continued with the unitary state structure, ensured Buddhism's special status, and made Tamil a national language although little was done to eradicate the entrenched linguistic discrimination. Such discrimination continued even after the Thirteenth Amendment, passed in November 1987, made Tamil an official language and the Sixteenth Amendment, passed in December 1988, consolidated this status.[14]

Jayewardene bragged that the only thing he could not do under the new constitution was change a man into a woman and vice versa whereas his prime minister lamented he was nothing more than a peon under the new setup. In this spirit, Jayewardene amended the constitution 16 times between 1978 and 1988, often in a partisan and whimsical fashion, and ruled in an autocratic manner. In 1980 he vindictively stripped Mrs Bandaranaike of her civic rights for seven years (in retaliation for her previous extension of SLFP rule by two years until 1977) and expelled her from parliament, thereby ensuring that his most effective opponent could not challenge him for reelection in 1982. Jayewardene thus set a precedent for presidential rule that his successors emulated.

The new constitution's electoral provisions were not tested until the October 1982 presidential elections, which Jayewardene won. This election evidenced voting irregularities: the most glaring was when the SLFP candidate for president went to the polls and found that someone had already cast his vote! The government also used its majority in parliament to pass the fourth amendment, through which it justified holding the first and only national referendum in place of scheduled parliamentary elections. This allowed the regime to use a simple electoral majority to extend the party's nearly five-sixths parliamentary majority for another term. The December 1982 referendum saw rigging on a grand scale, with UNP supporters—especially those in the party's trade union—resorting to ballot stuffing, intimidation, and violence to ensure a UNP victory.

The same forces harassed and beat up Buddhist monks, Catholic clergy, civil society activists, academics, opposition supporters, and supreme court justices who dared speak out or protest against government policies. They were also mostly responsible for the 1983 pogrom targeting Tamils.

Proclaiming "let the robber barons in," Jayewardene collaborated with the IMF, World Bank, and western governments to introduce structural adjustment policies. Sri Lanka thus embraced open market reforms two years before China and 14 years before India. The policies led to the creation of a class of nouveau riche; but they also contributed to economic disparity and disgruntlement. Overall, the Jayewardene years saw more development than under any previous Sri Lankan leader, and the open market economy and 1978 constitution remain his most important legacies. But he also instituted a political culture smacking of illiberal governance that was exacerbated under his successors.

In December 1988 Ranasinghe Premadasa, Jayewardene's prime minister, became president. Premadasa remains the first and only Sri Lankan leader not from the dominant *govigama* (cultivator) caste. Caste politics among Sinhalese was more pronounced in pre-independence times. However, there were some senior UNP politicos who begrudged and resented Premadasa for his low-caste status, and this was one reason they sought to impeach him in August 1991. Premadasa stripped these detractors of membership in the UNP and inducted many parliamentarians into his cabinet, thereby buying their loyalty. Thus it was under Premadasa that the so-called

"jumbo cabinet," whereby most members of the ruling party end up with ministerial or deputy ministerial portfolios, took hold and it has only magnified inefficiency, malpractice, and corruption.

A second murderous uprising by the JVP between 1988 and 1990 forced Premadasa to retaliate in brutal fashion. Estimates suggest that over 40,000 Sinhalese were disappeared as state-sponsored paramilitary forces eradicated the JVP leadership and suspected sympathizers.[15] Prime Minister Premadasa was responsible for a popular program called *gam udawa* (village reawakening), which centered on rural development and the building of thousands of homes. He continued doing so as president and was quite popular among the masses. The crackdown against the JVP, however, led to his being vilified, so much so that many Sinhalese celebrated by lighting firecrackers when a Liberation Tigers of Tamil Eelam (LTTE) suicide bomber killed Premadasa in May 1993 and the location of his death was referred to as "*balla marapu thanna*" (the place where the dog was killed).

The lackluster but dignified Dingiribanda Wigetunga succeeded Premadasa as president, but the electorate was ready for political change after 17 years of UNP rule. Chandrika Bandaranaike Kumaratunga, daughter of S. W. R. D. and Sirimavo Bandaranaike who had become prime minister in August 1994, became president in November 1994. Kumaratunga was supported enthusiastically by civil society groups and Tamils who saw her as the best bet to end the country's civil war, and she captured 62.3 percent of the votes cast. She survived an LTTE assassination attempt and was reelected in December 1999. A solution to the country's ethnic conflict, however, eluded her partly because of the LTTE's intransigence as well as her belief that no peace was possible unless the LTTE's leader, Vellupillai Prabhakaran, was killed and the LTTE militarily defeated. The upshot was a dubious "War for Peace" campaign that saw thousands killed and the military suffer humiliating reversals.

121

President Kumaratunga failed most where she could have succeeded rather easily: crafting a common peace agenda with an opposition that was, in the main, prepared to work with her. But hostility toward UNP leader Ranil Wickremasinghe precluded consensus politics, and her tenure was marked by moderate economic growth, corruption, favoritism, political legerdemain, and further institutional decay.

The SLFP under Kumaratunga also resorted to vote rigging and violence to win elections. The January 1999 Northwestern Provincial Council elections saw her supporters resort to blatant and even depraved electoral malpractices, making it the most violent election in Sri Lanka's history. For instance, SLFP cadres "not only assaulted UNP supporters but stripped men and women naked and paraded them on public roads!"[16] The October 2000 and December 2001 parliamentary elections were also conducted amidst widespread electoral malpractice, mostly perpetrated by Kumaratunga's party members and supporters.[17] The October 2000 election was the most violent parliamentary election hitherto conducted. The Elections Commissioner apologetically noted that "the allegations of vote-rigging have to be seen in the context of electoral systems in the developing world in general and the subcontinent in particular," thereby inadvertently highlighting how Sri Lanka is more an "electoral" as opposed to a "liberal" democracy.[18]

The UNP-led United National Front (UNF) coalition won the December 2001 parliamentary elections; its biggest achievement was the ceasefire agreement reached with the LTTE in February 2002. But "cohabitation" between president and parliament failed to take hold, and President Kumaratunga used her powers to dissolve the legislature and conduct new elections in April 2004. The SLFP-led United People's Freedom Alliance (UPFA) coalition won the elections, the fourth national election conducted in five years.

In November 2005 the SLFP's Mahinda Rajapaksa became Sri Lanka's fifth president.

The vast majority of Tamils now do not vote for the SLFP, and Rajapaksa may have bribed the LTTE to prevent Tamils in rebel-controlled areas from voting in the presidential elections.[19] This likely disenfranchisement led to the defeat of the UNP's Ranil Wickremasinghe. Within a year of coming to power Rajapaksa's government began a new war against the LTTE, although the latter's repeated aggression provided the president ample reason to justify renewed hostilities.[20] The government unilaterally abandoned the ceasefire in January 2008, with the president claiming the LTTE had to be destroyed for peace and development to take root. In January 2009, with the LTTE close to being defeated, the government also proscribed the group, thereby signaling that it was averse to holding any discussions with the rebels.

Sri Lanka has been plagued with extremist ethnic ideologues: the LTTE refused to settle for anything short of a separate state, while Sinhalese Buddhist nationalists refused to acknowledge legitimate Tamil grievances. Their maximalist demands are responsible for the carnage experienced in the past quarter century. Mahinda Rajapaksa is the first president to subscribe wholeheartedly to the Sinhalese Buddhist nationalist ideology, which is rooted in the belief that Sri Lanka is *Sihadipa* and *Dhammadipa* (island of the Sinhalese ennobled to preserve and propagate Theravada Buddhism) and that all minorities live there thanks to Sinhalese Buddhist sufferance.[21] Indeed, Rajapaksa even claims that he must embrace Sinhalese Buddhist preferences since Sinhalese Buddhists were the ones who mostly voted for him. With defeating the LTTE taking precedence, Rajapaksa's government tolerated manifold human rights violations, especially against Tamils, including murder, rape, arson, torture, kidnapping, extortion, and disappearances.[22] No one has been charged for any of the violations committed.

President Mahinda Rajapaksa has also resorted to blatant nepotism, appointing his three brothers to highly influential positions in government and nearly 130 relatives to other prominent governmental positions. Sri Lankans complain that the Rajapaksa brothers control over 80 percent of the country's budget through their ministerial portfolios; although the president's relative success in waging war against the LTTE has made him popular. His government, however, has taken to new heights the culture of impunity prevalent in Sri Lanka and has become adept at branding detractors "traitors." Furthermore, Rajapaksa has refused to install the Constitutional Council, which was created by the seventeenth amendment in October 2001 to ensure independent commissions to oversee the police, elections, bribery and corruption, human rights, and judiciary. This has allowed the president to appoint his supporters and favorites to these commissions. All evidence suggests that the Rajapaksas plan to rule the country for the foreseeable future by hook or by crook.

The ethnic politics that began to take shape in the late 1950s gradually marginalized minorities, seeking only to accommodate Sinhalese, especially Sinhalese Buddhists. Thus, Sinhalese, despite comprising around 75 percent of the population, now control over 95 percent of government jobs. Likewise, over 98 percent of military personnel are Sinhalese. Over time, competence and merit were discarded, and appointments to both low and high government positions were based on nepotism and favoritism. The attendant mediocrity and corruption led to shambolic governance that was tolerated at the highest levels. A culture of violence also took root. The majority Sinhalese initially tolerated illiberalism and violence insofar as they were directed toward Tamils; it became even easier to do so when the LTTE resorted to terrorism to attain its separatist goal. But illiberal governance cannot be compartmentalized, and over time the gangsterism and other malpractices accompanying such governance spread to the entire island. Today, a deadly nexus has taken shape among politicians, security personnel, and criminal elements.[23] In short, Sri Lanka's post-Independence ethnocentric politics has led not only to institutional decay and illiberal democracy, but could well also lead to dictatorship.

Parties and politics

Under the Donoughmore Constitution, legislators were divided among seven executive committees in the state council and committee chairmen, who together formed the board of ministers, oversaw certain government functions. It was a structure designed for independents and discouraged the formation of political parties. Nevertheless, leftists motivated by trade union politicking created the Trotskyist Lanka Sama Samaja Party (Lanka Equal Society Party—LSSP) in 1935 and the pro-Moscow Communist Party (CP) in 1943. Sri Lanka's conservative electorate never fully warmed up to either the LSSP or the CP, which reached their apogee in the early 1970s when they joined Mrs. Bandaranaike's second government.

The United National Party was created only in April 1946 in anticipation of independence. A two-party system took effect when S. W. R. D. Bandaranaike joined the opposition and soon thereafter formed the Sri Lanka Freedom Party. The SLFP has consistently appealed to Sinhalese Buddhists and drawn support mainly from rural areas, while the UNP has enjoyed a more urban base, appealing to those with western proclivities, and still draws strong support among minorities during presidential elections. Minorities also supported the party in large numbers during parliamentary elections until minority parties took hold.

The SLFP has operated as a dynasty, with three family members—Mr and Mrs Bandaranaike and their daughter, Chandrika Kumaratunga—serving as the country's leaders. Mahinda Rajapaksa's takeover of the SLFP heralds an end to the Bandaranaike's dominance. Indeed, some in the Rajapaksa camp now confidently talk about a Rajapaksa dynasty.

The UNP, by way of contrast, has been labeled the "Uncle–Nephew Party," given that

123

four of the party's six leaders have been related to its founder (and Sri Lanka's first prime minister) D. S. Senanayake: Dudley Senanayake took over from his father D. S., and Dudley's cousin, Sir John Kotelawala, succeeded him; J. R. Jayewardene was closely related to D. S. Senanayake, and the UNP's present leader, Ranil Wickremasinghe, is Jayewardene's nephew.

During the post-Second World War period many western European countries, including the United Kingdom, adopted socialist policies. This no doubt influenced newly independent states like Sri Lanka. Consequently, while the UNP is considered right of center and has traditionally embraced pro-western and pro-market policies and the SLFP has preferred a left-of-center platform that embraced state centrism, both resorted to populist, socialist practices until 1977. Socialist rhetoric notwithstanding, both Chandrika Kumaratunga and Mahinda Rajapaksa have continued Jayewardene's open market policies.

Ethnic outbidding between the UNP and SLFP caused Sri Lanka to miss numerous windows of opportunity to solve its ethnic imbroglio. As the ethnic conflict intensified, finding a solution became more difficult. During the late 1980s and 1990s, the JVP and other nationalist parties adopted a more uncompromising ethnic stance. However, with Mahinda Rajapaksa's election, the SLFP is now as nationalist and uncompromising as any other pro-Sinhalese Buddhist party.

The mainly Sinhalese Buddhist JVP first gained prominence through the 1971 insurgency. J. R. Jayewardene released the party's leadership from prison and tolerated its reentry into politics, believing correctly that the JVP would draw support away from the SLFP. However, seeking to absolve UNP cadres involved in the 1983 anti-Tamil pogrom, Jayewardene, adopting the Indian term for radical, violent formations, claimed there was a "Naxalite" connection to the riots and banned the JVP. The party went underground, only to resurface violently after Jayewardene, in July 1987, signed the Indo-Lanka Peace Accord, which stationed the Indian Peace Keeping Force (IPKF) in the northeast.

The JVP began as a Maoist organization in the 1960s. In its early years it sympathized with the plight of the Tamils and even acknowledged the community's right to self-determination; but post-IPKF, it morphed into a rabid nationalist party. The Premadasa government killed all in the JVP's politburo except Somawansa Amarasinghe, who fled to London and now heads the party. The JVP reentered the political mainstream in 1994 and has allied with the SLFP in recent years. It clamored for a military solution to the ethnic conflict and opposes devolution. The party won ten seats in the October 2000 parliamentary elections and 16 seats in the December 2001 elections. In the April 2004 elections it campaigned as part of the SLFP-led United People's Freedom Alliance and won 39 seats. The JVP draws most of its support from the Sinhalese Buddhist lower classes in the south and is unlikely on its own to fare better than it did in April 2004. The April 2008 split within the party is also bound to weaken it. But the JVP enjoys strong support among lower ranks in the military, and this can have adverse ramifications down the road.

In recent years the JVP has had to compete for the nationalist vote with the Sinhala Urumaya (Sinhala Heritage Party—SU) and the Jathika Hela Urumaya (National Sinhalese Heritage Party—JHU), which succeeded the SU. The JHU is a party almost exclusively based on Buddhist monks, and its formation caused Buddhists to debate whether the *vinaya* (monastic law code) permitted monks to participate directly in politics and how doing so may tarnish the clergy's image.[24] The party stunned most observers by winning nine seats in the April 2004 elections. The JHU supports the Mahinda Rajapaksa government and, like the JVP, called for a military solution to the ethnic conflict and a strong unitary state. It opposed vociferously the ceasefire agreement with the LTTE and Norwegian involvement in the peace process. The party thus applauded when the Rajapaksa government unilaterally abrogated the ceasefire and terminated Scandinavian involvement in the peace process.

The country's Muslims used to vote for the UNP and SLFP, but many now vote for the Sri Lanka Muslim Congress (SLMC), which began contesting elections in 1989. The SLMC originated in the Eastern Province but gradually spread its influence to the south. The party has fared well over the years, winning four, seven, eleven, and ten parliamentary seats in 1989, 1994, 2001, and 2004, respectively. With the UNP and SLFP increasingly dependent on coalitions to govern, the SLMC and other ethnic parties wield influence disproportionate to their small parliamentary representations. The SLMC split after its founder, M. H. M. Ashraff, died in a helicopter crash in September 2000. The new faction, called the National Unity Alliance, is led by Ashraff's wife, and it has allied with the SLFP. The rural Muslims of the Eastern Province have different preferences from those in urban areas like Colombo, and this dictates party loyalty. However, during presidential elections the vast majority of Muslims vote for the UNP candidate.[25]

The Ceylon Worker's Congress represents the interests of the Indian Tamils, and their leaders have usually allied with the governing party. The Sri Lankan Tamils mostly voted for the Ceylon Tamil Congress and the Federal Party. These moderate parties became marginalized as they achieved little by engaging with Sinhalese politicians. Anti-LTTE Tamil militant groups like the Eelam People's Democratic Party now operate as part of government coalitions. The March 2004 split in the LTTE has led to the Tamileela Makkal Viduthalaip Pulikal (Tamileela People's Liberation Tigers—TMVP), which operates as a state-sponsored paramilitary group and political party, dominating (often via intimidation and force) Tamil areas in the Eastern Province. With the loss of the territories controlled by the LTTE, the TMVP and other anti-LTTE parties will certainly undermine the pro-LTTE Tamil National Alliance (TNA). The TNA, with 22

seats in parliament, is presently the largest Tamil party because the LTTE ensured that Tamils in the northeast voted for it.

Tamil party leaders are often targeted by their Tamil rivals. In the TNA's case, government forces may have also colluded in assassinating its members. With anti-LTTE forces targeting TNA parliamentarians and the LTTE targeting Sinhalese and pro-government Tamil legislators, it is not surprising that as of April 2008 seven parliamentarians elected in the 2004 elections were assassinated (with four killed in the first three-and-a-half months of 2008).

As of January 2008 there were 53 registered parties in Sri Lanka. With fewer than a dozen having a fair chance of winning even a single seat in parliament, most have apparently been organized to try to make money by selling television and radio time allotted to them.[26] For example, 52 parties/coalitions contested the April 2004 parliamentary elections, yet only seven won at least a single seat.

A sense of noblesse oblige once influenced some Sri Lankan politicians, who forfeited personal fortunes to run for office. With ministerial portfolios akin to sinecures full of perks sweetened by commissions and kickbacks, it is the venal and predatory who, in the main, seek political office today. This has also affected the quality of candidates standing for election. Furthermore, the quest for acquiring wealth, prestige, and power via politics has undermined party loyalty as opposition politicians eagerly cross over to the governing party provided they are afforded ministerial portfolios. Some have done so four and five times. Indeed, one irony in Sri Lankan politics is that voters are more loyal to parties than are the party candidates. For instance, soon after Mahinda Rajapaksa became president, 11 UNP parliamentarians (including some senior party members) crossed over to the government, claiming they wanted to ensure good governance. All were provided ministerial portfolios. Indeed, as of April 2008, 24 UNP members elected through the April 2004 parliamentary elections had crossed over to the

125

government while nearly 50 parliamentarians had bolted their parties to join the government or operate independently. Thus, as of February 2008 the Mahinda Rajapaksa government comprised 51 ministers, 35 non-cabinet ministers, and 21 deputy ministers. Frustrated Sri Lankans bemoan how an island with 21 million people is saddled with 51 cabinet ministers while nearby India with 1.1 billion people manages relatively well with 32 cabinet ministers. Indeed, the Rajapaksa government had to postpone its first cabinet meeting since it could not find a room large enough to accommodate the ministers, and newspaper editorials suggested derisively that the government rent a hotel ballroom.

The island's unicameral legislature has 225 members. Of these, 196 are elected in multimember districts, while 29 are reserved for National List (NL) members. A party's national vote determines the number of NL members it may have, thereby allowing a party to nominate prominent supporters and highly skilled and qualified citizens to parliament. Yet most NL appointees have been as opportunistic as elected parliamentarians and have crossed over eagerly to government ranks when provided portfolios. For instance, the opposition UNP had 11 NL members, but ten had crossed over to government ranks as of February 2008. In fact, only four NL members currently sit with the opposition; the rest belong to the government.

Violence and deadly weapons are part and parcel of Sri Lankan politics, and there are three main reasons for their proliferation. The civil war forced the government to recruit Sinhalese home guards from villagers bordering LTTE-controlled areas, and the arms provided them have been used to settle personal and political scores. When the second JVP insurgency targeted politicians, the UNP distributed nearly 15,000 weapons among political parties. Very few of these were returned; politicians and their supporters now use them to perpetrate violence. Finally, in the past two decades, nearly 60,000 personnel have deserted the military. Many absconded with their arms

and ammunition and some now work for politicians as bodyguards and storm troopers.

Elections won by corrupt practices are rarely overturned in Sri Lanka, which discourages free and fair polls. Furthermore, preferential voting forces politicians to compete against party colleagues in their districts, adding intraparty violence to the existing interparty violence. Some student unions in the universities are affiliated with political parties; the JVP's Inter-University Student Federation is especially notorious for its politically influenced gangsterism on campuses. The upshot is that parties and their candidates now increasingly rely on violence to influence politics and win elections.

Devolution and state and local politics

Sri Lanka has nine provinces and 25 districts. In July 1981 J. R. Jayewardene and the UNP discarded the existing village and town councils and instituted a district development council (DDC) scheme, hoping to palliate Tamil demands for broad devolution. Rather than promoting autonomy, the DDCs reiterated the state's predilection for centralization. The DDCs that operated between 1981 and 1987 are thought to have played a minor role facilitating economic development,[27] but these and subsequent local/regional institutions have hardly come close to satisfying Tamil demands for autonomy. As of 1978 the president had appointed as district ministers parliamentarians whose constituencies fell outside the district. While district ministers are not included in the cabinet, the position generates the same perks as does a cabinet portfolio.

Most Tamils consider the Northern and Eastern Provinces to be their homeland, and it is here that the LTTE wanted to create the state of Eelam. The Indo-Lanka Peace Accord of 1987 recognized the historical presence of the Tamils in the northeast and necessitated the Thirteenth Amendment to the constitution, which merged the two provinces. That same year, the supreme court upheld the thirteenth amendment. Sri Lanka thus consisted of eight provinces between 1987 and 2006, when a different Supreme Court ruled that the merger was invalid. The decision was hailed by Sinhalese nationalists who viewed the merger and any devolution as precursors to the island's dismemberment.

Provincial Council elections were first held in 1987 throughout the island and have since been conducted with regularity outside the northeast; but the state's embedded paternalistic and centripetal tendencies have prevented the sharing of power between the central government and the regions.[28] Currently, the provincial councils are white elephants beloved by party leaders desperate to accommodate loyal supporters within the government echelon. Thus, today national party leaders, not provincial leaders, mostly choose provincial councilors; and the country currently has over 4,000 representatives of the people at local, provincial, and national levels. A further irony is that a system that was primarily passed off as one to ensure some Tamil autonomy has, in the main, functioned throughout the island *except* in the predominantly Tamil northeast.

Currently there are 18 municipal councils, 42 urban councils, and 270 *pradeshiya sabhas* (local councils incorporating several old village councils) overseeing local public health, beautification, voter registration lists, and postal services. Unsurprisingly, some units function more efficiently than others. Overall, however, lack of funding, widespread corruption, ambitious provincial councilors, and overbearing parliamentarians combine to undermine the responsibilities and effectiveness of these units.[29]

In 1949 S. J. V. Chelvanayakam and others left the Tamil Congress (TC) and formed the Federal Party (FP) because of concerns over government-sanctioned Sinhalese colonization of historically Tamil areas and disagreement concerning the entry of the TC leader, G. G. Ponnambalam, into the UNP Cabinet. As its name indicates, the FP mainly clamored for a federal structure, but Sinhalese nationalists opposed federalism, claiming it would be the first step toward separatism. The FP won ten seats in the April 1956 elections to become the largest Tamil party. This, combined with Tamil protests over the Sinhala Only Act, led S. W. R. D. Bandaranaike to meet with Chelvanayakam to try and accommodate Tamil grievances. The result was the July 1957 Bandaranaike-Chelvanayakam (B-C) Pact, under which the FP agreed to drop its demand for linguistic parity and the government agreed to permit the use of Tamil for all administrative purposes in the northeast and to create regional councils to deal with education, agriculture, and Sinhalese colonization of Tamil areas. The B-C Pact provided Tamil leaders a way out of their demands for devolution, but it was vilified by Sinhalese Buddhist nationalists and the UNP. Under pressure, Bandaranaike abrogated the pact in April 1958. After Bandaranaike's assassination, his wife worked to consolidate the unitary state structure.

The FP provided support in parliament to Dudley Senanayake's UNP government during March 1965 and May 1970. The two parties had agreed to the Senanayake-Chelvanayakam Pact of 1965, under which the UNP promised to recognize the Northern and Eastern Provinces as Tamil speaking, amend the previous government's Language of the Court's Act of 1961 so that both Sinhala and Tamil could be used in the courts system, and provide Tamils first preference when colonizing Tamil areas while placing district governments under national authority. Yet the UNP failed to honor the pact. Thus for the second time a Sri Lankan government discarded an agreement reached with Tamils and provided a fillip to the budding separatist tendencies among disenchanted Tamil youth.

Constitutional change and devolution are related issues, with which Sri Lanka has grappled especially since the mid-1990s. Presidents typically eschew relinquishing presidential powers whenever constitutional engineering is contemplated. The devolution

127

debate, contrariwise, has ranged between perpetuating the unitary state and introducing a federal structure, with further debates on whether devolution should only be extended to the northeast or all nine provinces, and, if the latter, whether devolution ought to be symmetrical or asymmetrical. Chandrika Kumaratunga's People's Alliance (PA) government released a draft constitution in October 1997 that sought to do away with the executive presidency and devolve power to the regions. The attempt failed. In July 2000 the PA and UNP agreed to a watered-down version of the 1997 draft constitution only to have the UNP back off amidst stiff opposition from Buddhist clergy and Sinhalese nationalist forces. The possibility that the Northern and Eastern Provinces may not remain merged caused Tamil parties also to oppose the parliamentary bill to amend the constitution. Kumaratunga's insistence that she should be allowed to complete her presidential term irrespective of when the new constitution took effect did not help.

Chandrika Kumaratunga's malpractices notwithstanding, she promoted a federal solution to the ethnic conflict and even castigated those Sinhalese opposing devolution as "racists." Mahinda Rajapaksa's government, however, contemptuously abandoned any discourse on federalism. This suits the nationalist mindset of the Rajapaksa regime, which ardently believed in a military solution to the ethnic conflict and opposed meaningful devolution. For instance, the regime's first devolution proposals mooted in April 2007 called for creating 30 districts from the extant 25 districts and devolving power to these miniaturized units. Under international pressure, the government thereafter embraced the Thirteenth Amendment to the constitution as a potential solution, notwithstanding that the provincial council system created by the amendment had failed to meet even basic expectations. The Rajapaksa regime was merely posturing, while adhering to its belief the LTTE could be defeated militarily; for when this eventuates, the government knows

minorities will have no choice but tolerate the existing unitary state and Sinhalese Buddhist dominance.

Conclusion

If relative consensus and compromise between Sri Lanka's two principal ethnic groups facilitated a peaceful transition to independence, the island's opportunistic and ethnocentric post-Independence politics promoted institutional decay and ethnonational extremism. Consequently, a country once renowned for its tea and beaches is now just as famous for suicide bombings and civil war: over 70,000 people were killed, nearly 600,000 were internally displaced, and between 800,000 and one million Tamils had fled the island during the past 25 years. The United Nations, western governments, and rights groups consider the country to be a serial human rights abuser. In 2006 and 2007 paramilitary forces and government soldiers were responsible for disappearing more people in Sri Lanka than anywhere else in the world. In its Global Press Freedom report for 2007, Freedom House branded the country "not free" and ranked it below Pakistan, Angola, and Egypt, although it ranked higher in the combined average rating on all measures, a rank of 4, whereas Pakistan, Angola, and Egypt are ranked far below at 5.5. When combined with the anomie, corruption, and predatory politics outlined in this chapter, Sri Lanka has by almost any measure regressed radically from the polyethnic and liberal democratic promise evidenced in 1948.[30]

Notes

1 Howard W. Wriggins, "Impediments to Unity in New Nations: The Case of Ceylon," *American Political Science Review*, Vol. 55, No. 2 (June 1961), p. 316.
2 For an account of politics leading to independence, see Nira Wickramasinghe, *Ethnic Politics of Colonial Sri Lanka, 1927–47* (New Delhi: Vikas, 1995).

3 Neil DeVotta, "Illiberalism and Ethnic Conflict in Sri Lanka," *Journal of Democracy*, Vol. 13, No. 1 (January 2002), pp. 84–98.

4 There are two principal Tamil communities in the island: the Sri Lankan (Ceylon) Tamils and Indian Tamils. The British transplanted the latter to work on plantations starting in the 1830s. Just prior to independence the Indian Tamils outnumbered the Sri Lankan Tamils (11.73 percent to 11.01 percent of the total population of the island), but disenfranchisement and a repatriation treaty with India have reduced their numbers to just over 5 percent. The Indian Tamils are not involved in Sri Lanka's separatist conflict.

5 Samuel P. Huntington, *The Third Wave: Democratization in the Late Twentieth Century*. (Norman, OK: University of Oklahoma Press, 1991), pp. 266–67.

6 Neil DeVotta, *Blowback: Linguistic Nationalism, Institutional Decay, and Ethnic Conflict in Sri Lanka* (Stanford, CA: University Press, 2004).

7 For a good account of these riots see Tarzie Vittachi, *Emergency '58: The Story of the Ceylon Race Riots* (London: André Deutsch, 1958).

8 For details, see DeVotta, *Blowback*, pp. 122–30.

9 The latter was one of the most violent ethnic riots in South Asia and marks the beginning of the ongoing civil war. It also created the vast Tamil diaspora that now supports the Liberation Tigers of Tamil Eelam, which seeks to create a Tamil state in the northeast and is branded a terrorist outfit by many countries.

10 For details of the 1978 constitution, see A. Jeyaratnam Wilson, *The Gaullist System in Asia: The Constitution of Sri Lanka (1978)* (London: Macmillan, 1980).

11 For instance, in the 1970 elections, the UNP received 37.9 percent of votes cast but won just 17 seats, while the SLFP captured 36.9 percent of votes and won 91 seats. Similarly, in the 1977 elections, the UNP received 50.9 percent of votes cast and won 140 seats, while the SLFP received 29.7 percent of votes, yet garnered just eight seats.

12 The effect has been insignificant. See Amita Shastri, "Channelling Ethnicity through Electoral Reform in Sri Lanka," *Journal of Commonwealth and Comparative Politics*, Vol. 43, No. 1 (March 2005), pp. 34–60.

13 This has not prevented parties from proliferating, although the country, in the main, may be characterized as a two-party system, in which each of the two main parties is assisted by coalition partners. See Matthew Shugart and John Carey, *Presidents and Assemblies: Constitutional Design and Electoral Dynamics* (Cambridge: University Press, 1992), p. 67; Robert C. Oberst, "Proportional Representation and Electoral System Change in Sri Lanka," in James Manor (ed.), *Sri Lanka in Change and Crisis* (London: Croom Helm, 1984), pp. 118–33.

14 For instance, Tamils dealing with state bureaucracies are forced to operate in Sinhala and most southern police stations have no personnel fluent in Tamil, causing Tamils who seek redress at such stations to authorize entries written in a language they do not read. Likewise, Tamils living in the south have their birth, marriage, and death certificates registered in Sinhala even though the vast majority does not read the language.

15 Mick Moore, "Thoroughly Modern Revolutionaries: The JVP in Sri Lanka," *Modern Asian Studies*, Vol. 27, No. 3 (July 1993), p. 593, fn. 2.

16 See *The Island*, "When Political Pots and Kettles Disparage One Another . . . ," 13 March, 2008.

17 See Neil DeVotta, "Sri Lanka's Political Decay: Analysing the October 2000 and December 2001 Parliamentary Elections," *Journal of Commonwealth and Comparative Politics*, Vol. 41, No. 2 (July 2003), pp. 115–42.

18 For a distinction between the two, see Larry Diamond, "The Democratic Rollback: The Resurgence of the Predatory State," *Foreign Affairs*, Vol. 87, No. 2 (March–April 2008), pp. 36–48.

19 The likely reason that the LTTE consented to this ploy is because Ranil Wickremasinghe deftly internationalized the peace process to the point where the LTTE felt trapped. The group believes that the Sinhalese Buddhists cannot be trusted. It also believed correctly that a jingoistic Mahinda Rajapaksa regime would highlight Sinhalese Buddhist intransigence more than would a Wickremasinghe-led UNP regime.

20 The LTTE used the ceasefire to target anti-LTTE Tamils allied with the government, military intelligence officers and soldiers. It also violated the ceasefire agreement by continuing to tax Tamils and Muslims in the northeast and smuggling in weapons. The Rajapaksa regime began full scale military action against the LTTE after the group shut down the Mavil Aru anicut in July 2006 and thereby deprived villagers of water, although President Rajapaksa and his advisors had in any case come into power

129

believing that military victory, as opposed to a political solution, was the best way to end the civil war.

21 See Neil DeVotta, *Sinhalese Buddhist Nationalist Ideology: Implications for Politics and Conflict Resolution in Sri Lanka*, Policy Studies 40 (Washington, DC: East West Center, 2007).

22 See Human Rights Watch, *Recurring Nightmare: State Responsibility for "Disappearances" and Abductions in Sri Lanka*, http://hrw.org/reports/2008/srilanka0308/ (accessed 8 March, 2008); U.S. Department of State, *Sri Lanka: Country Reports on Human Rights Practices—2007*, Bureau of Democracy, Human Rights, and Labor, 11 March, 2008, at http://www.state.gov/g/drl/rls/hrrpt/2007/100620.htm (accessed 12 March, 2008).

23 Neil DeVotta, "Explaining Political and Societal Violence in Sri Lanka," in Laksiri Fernando and Shermal Wijewardene (eds), *Sri Lanka's Ethnic Conflict in the Global Context* (Colombo: University of Colombo Faculty of Graduate Studies, 2006). pp. 113–26.

24 See Neil DeVotta and Jason Stone, "Jathika Hela Urumaya and Ethno-Religious Politics in Sri Lanka," *Pacific Affairs*, Vol. 81, No. 1 (April 2008), pp. 31–51.

25 For details on Muslim politics see, Dennis B. McGilvray and Mirak Raheem, *Muslim Perspectives on the Sri Lankan Conflict*, Policy Studies 41 (Washington, DC: East West Center, 2007).

26 See *The Island*, "Beggar Woman's Quintuplets and the Multitude as Kings," 24 January, 2008.

27 For details on the DDCs, see Bruce Matthews, "District Development Councils in Sri Lanka," *Asian Survey*, Vol. 22, No. 11 (November 1982), pp. 1,117–34.

28 For details on the provincial council system, see Amita Shastri, "Sri Lanka's Provincial Council System: A Solution to the Ethnic Problem?" *Asian Survey*, Vol. 32, No. 8 (August 1992), pp. 723–43.

29 This negative appraisal contrasts with Robert C. Oberst, "Government Structure," in Craig Baxter *et al.* (eds), *Government and Politics in South Asia*, 5th edn (Boulder, CO: Westview Press, 2002).

30 For further details in this regard, see Neil DeVotta, "Sri Lanka at Sixty: A Legacy of Ethnocentrism and Degeneration," *Economic and Political Weekly*, Vol. 44, No. 5 (31 January–6 February, 2009), pp. 46–53.

9

Nepal

Trajectories of democracy and restructuring of the state

Krishna Hachhethu and David N. Gellner

On 10 April, 2008 Nepal held wholly unprecedented and epochal nationwide elections— the most peaceful in its history[1]—for a 601-member constituent assembly (CA). Two hundred and forty representatives were elected in "winner-takes-all" or "first-past-the-post" constituencies, 26 were to be nominated later by the Council of Ministers, and 335 were elected by proportional representation with the whole country as a single constituency. Under strict rules about representativeness, parties were obliged to ensure, both on their submitted lists, and in their selection of successful candidates, that there would be 50 percent women within each of the following categories: 13 percent Dalits, 31.2 percent Madhesis, 37.8 percent Janajatis, 30 percent "others," and 4 percent from nine backward districts.[2]

The previous 60 years of Nepal's history, starting with the overthrow of the Rana autocracy in 1951, were marked by zigzags and contention—numerous strikes, demonstrations, revolts, and uprisings, followed by periods of peace based on compromises between different forces. Until 2006 the palace had always been an important, usually decisive, factor in the equation. In April 2006, for the first time, no compromise was made with the monarchy, and in the year and a half that followed, step by step its every symbolic presence was removed from events and edifices connected to the state.

The monarch, held a prisoner by the Rana Prime Ministers before 1951, had been an asset in the 1950–51 armed struggle against the century-old Rana oligarchy. Consequently, the post-revolution period gave birth to a hybrid system of sovereign monarchy and democratic structures. Even after 1960, when parties were banned, King Mahendra could plausibly represent the monarchy as a defender of democracy thanks to his father's role in the 1950–51 revolution. Public faith in royal leadership and an active king finally ran out in the late 1980s. The 1990 mass movement against the Panchayat system was called jointly by the Nepali Congress (NC), a liberal democratic party, and several communist parties. The rise of an educated middle class and rapid urbanization were the forces behind the success of the 1990 mass movement. The people's representatives in the elected bodies of the 1990s were, therefore, predominantly middle class, unlike the rural-based landowning classes who dominated in the 1950s and 1960s. The April 2006 popular uprising against monarchical rule was a shared effort, backed both by the parliamentary political parties and by the Communist Party of Nepal (Maoist) (CPN-M). It was the Maoists who had given most succor to ethnic and regional movements.

The changes on which Nepal is about to embark are radical and comprehensive. The key areas of departure from its past are: from monarchy to republic, from Hindu state to secular state, from unitary government to federalism, and from the monopoly of political power by high-caste Hindus from the hills (the Bahuns and Chhetris, who together make up 31 percent of the population) to inclusive democracy with guaranteed representation for all segments of Nepali society (hill people and Madhesis; high castes, Janajatis, and Dalits; men and women).

This chapter is organized in two parts. The first provides a historical survey of the development of democracy in Nepal with a very brief account of the internal and external situations during and after each of the major political developments between 1950 and 2006. The second deals with the three major agendas—peacebuilding, republicanism, and inclusive democracy—that Nepal faces today.

The dawn of democracy: The 1950s

Nepal entered the world community with democratic aspirations in the early 1950s. For other South Asian countries, as for most of the third world, the advent of democracy was intertwined with the achievement of independence. Nepal, by contrast, was never colonized, despite its dependent relationship with the British Raj in India. Thus, democracy was intimately connected to liberation from the native despotic rule of the Ranas. Inspiration came from the general Asian resurgence of the 1940s and, in particular, from the Indian independence movement in which several early NC leaders participated. However, the structural conditions of Nepal's internal environment of the time could not be said to be highly conducive to democracy.

Nepal under the Rana oligarchy (1846–1950) was what South Asians call highly feudal in its social order, with a subsistence agricultural economy, a society governed by an orthodox Hindu social and legal code (the caste division of labor and differential punishments by caste had the force of law), and a political system founded on *hukum* or peremptory command. Confounding those who believe that modernization must precede democracy, Nepal had a democratic revolution when its literacy rate was less than 5 percent; having only a few kilometers of motorable road in the capital; lacking any mass media except for one government-run newspaper, the *Gorkhapatra*; and in the absence of any of the features of a capitalist economy, with the exception of one bank in Kathmandu and two factories in the eastern Tarai. Contrariwise, the ease with which the king was able to outmanoeuver democratic politicians during the 1950s may be said to have had its roots in these very conditions of economic and social backwardness. The Ranas had themselves fully understood the connection between modernization and political opposition, and had therefore sedulously attempted to keep their population isolated from foreign influences. The Ranas' policy of isolation had a loophole, however—allowing the movement of people across the open border with India for education, pilgrimage, political exile, and recruitment into the British Army. A small group of educated middle-class Nepalis living in India and ex-Gurkha soldiers were the catalysts in the formation of political parties opposed to the rule of the Ranas.

The NC, supported by other parties, launched a three-month armed revolution in November 1950 that succeeded in winning control of much of the eastern hills, as well as the towns of Birganj and Tansen in the west. But the insurrection did not culminate in military victory, as some Congress activists had hoped. Rather: "[T]he decisive battles of the revolution were fought in New Delhi between the Indian government and the Rana government, at the diplomatic level."[3] This indicates how powerful external factors behind the dawn of democracy in Nepal were. Despite their isolationist policies, the Ranas had failed to check the global trend towards national independence and democracy. Independent

India backed the democracy struggle in Nepal in several ways: providing asylum to dissidents, including King Tribhuvan; allowing space for the organization of anti-Rana activities; transmitting the ideology of democracy; and exerting diplomatic pressure on the Ranas to compromise with the King and the NC. India's predominant role was acknowledged by all contending political forces in the country, and it was India's solution that was accepted, although the Ranas initially resisted it: the return of King Tribhuvan to the throne in place of his grandson Gyanendra who had been crowned in his absence, a coalition government of the Ranas and the NC, and a new constitution to be framed by an elected constituent assembly.[4]

The restoration of the Shah monarchy and advent of democracy were the twin goals of the 1950–51 armed revolution and so the Interim Government of Nepal Act 1951 provided for a polity based on the principle of the King in Council of Ministers; this was later modified to the model of King in Parliament by the Constitution of the Kingdom of Nepal 1959. Alongside these constitutional arrangements, the basic principles of democracy were also adopted, i.e., the rule of law, a multiparty competitive system, periodic elections, fundamental rights, an independent judiciary, a modern bureaucracy, and so on. But, against the spirit of the 1951 and 1959 constitutions, which posited the monarchy and democracy as complementary to each other, actual politics in the post-Rana period moved in the direction of a zero-sum game between traditional forces led by the king, on the one side, and modern forces led by political parties, on the other.[5] The 1950s were, in effect, a prolonged interim period with ten governments in eight years (including direct rule by the king). King Mahendra, who ascended the throne following his father's demise in 1955, gradually consolidated the bases of royal rule. The often-postponed elections were finally held in February 1959. The NC won two thirds of the seats on 37 percent of the vote. Their popular leader B. P. Koirala became

prime minister, but he was unable to check King Mahendra's ambition. Mahendra dismantled democracy by means of a bloodless coup in December 1960.

Restoring democracy, 1960–2002

The movement for the restoration of democracy (MRD)—although its roots go right back to 1960 when King Mahendra introduced absolute monarchy under the banner of the partyless Panchayat democracy—reached its climax with the 1990 mass movement (called "Jan Andolan I"). King Mahendra introduced a new constitution in 1962, which for the first time explicitly designated Nepal as a Hindu kingdom. On the one hand, Nepal joined the ranks of many "guided democracies" such as Pakistan, Egypt, Indonesia, and so on. On the other hand, in the early days, Mahendra and his ideological supporters imagined that they could "unleash the energies of the country for development," as they often put it, by mobilizing youth and imitating some of the methods of Chairman Mao. However, sending Master's students to the villages as a compulsory part of their education turned out to be a way to radicalize the villagers, and the regime quickly put a stop to it.

Opposition to the authoritarian Panchayat regime began with small-scale armed resistance by the NC in the early 1960s and the early 1970s (including raids across the border and the hijacking of a plane). Initially the regime concentrated on its main opponent, the NC, and did not attempt to repress communist activity so severely; subsequently many communists also spent long periods in jail. In 1972–73 there was a short-lived communist revolt (a series of targeted assassinations of landlords) in Jhapa, east Nepal, inspired by the Naxalite uprising just over the border in India six years earlier. The Panchayat regime was able to suppress these struggles effectively for three main reasons. First, India gave priority to its security interests, in maintaining its supremacy over the southern flanks of the Himalayas, especially during and after its humiliation in the India–China war of 1962. This correlated with the primacy of strategic interest over ideological interest on the part of the superpowers during the Cold War, although it fit less well with the high moral tone adopted by India in arguing for nonalignment on the world stage. (Nepal's strategy in response to this was to attempt to cultivate ties also with China, and later, under King Birendra, to attempt to win agreement from neighbors to declare Nepal a zone of peace. However, India never agreed to this.) Second, as a consequence of the adverse external situation, anti-establishment forces, in particular the NC, were reduced to seeking strategies for survival. Thus in 1968 Subarna Shamsher, the leader of the NC in exile offered "loyal cooperation [with the king]." B.P. Koirala was then released from jail and went into exile in India. Similarly, in 1977, the NC adopted a policy of "national reconciliation": in 1975, after Mrs Gandhi declared her emergency, staying in exile in India became problematic for B.P. Koirala and his lieutenant, Ganeshman Singh; both of them were arrested on their return to Nepal in 1976. Third, despite some internal tensions and conflicts, the elite in Kathmandu was essentially united around the king in his determination to rule and to suppress violent opposition, a unity and determination which contrasted strongly with the attitude of the center when it was faced by armed rebellion again in the late 1990s. This determination gradually dissipated in the 1980s.

King Mahendra's son Birendra, whose rule began in 1972, was certainly a softer and more compromising character than either his father or his brother Gyanendra. In 1980, following violent student protests sparked by the hanging of Zulfikar Bhutto in Pakistan, but clearly aimed at authoritarian government nearer home, the king conceded a referendum on the future of the Panchayat system. The Panchayat side, making full use of the advantages of government incumbency and also, according to its opponents, thanks to considerable corruption in the form of selling forests

and buying votes, won by 55 percent to 45 percent. Despite losing the referendum, the parties had been allowed the freedom to organize during the campaign, a freedom that was hard to reverse after it was over. The Panchayat system itself moved in a more democratic direction with direct elections to the national legislature, explicit responsibility of the cabinet to the legislature, and limited political freedom. Thus, both the internal and external situations developed in the direction of greater democratization in the 1980s. Increasingly, the legitimacy of the partyless system became eroded; its incumbents were mired in repeated corruption scandals, including some which were widely believed to reach right up into the royal palaces.

Although democracy suffered a setback in 1960, it was a key part of the legitimacy sought by King Mahendra that he aimed to be a democratic, modernizing, and reforming king— for all that he simultaneously sought to portray himself as an authentic Hindu monarch and to enlist the support of pro-Hindu groups in India. Thus, the process of modernization, begun in 1951, was continued under the partyless Panchayat system. A new civil code in 1963 established equality before the law regardless of caste, creed, and sex, and the implementation of the Land Reform Act 1964, with its provisions for ceilings on landholdings, the protection of tenancy rights, and the regulation of land rents, over time fundamentally undermined hierarchical dependencies on upper-caste landholding families in most areas of the country. This was complemented by rapid progress in infrastructure developments, i.e., education, health, road transportation, communications, and so on, which in turn produced a critical mass of educated middle-class and urbanized Nepalis. By the end of the decade of 1980s the literacy rate in Nepal had reached around 39 percent; the road network was 7,330 kilometers long; the number of cities was 35; and communication media, including television, had proliferated. Progress was evident in infrastructure and education, but jobs and income generation opportunities were much harder to come by. This led to the problem of educated unemployment, combined with price rises, as well as, for many, perceived ethnic inequalities. The result was a frustrated middle class, which, especially in the 1980s, began to seek redress through various civil society forms. "Nepali civil society originated and revived as a part of [the] democratic movement"[6] and it was the backbone of "extra systemic opposition" during the Panchayat period.[7] The 1990 mass movement was largely a middle-class urban movement; it combined student radicalism, support from professional groups, such as doctors, and an unacknowledged ethnic element, since the revolts were based in the old Newar cities of the Kathmandu Valley and mobilized both men and women of the Newar peasant caste. The young people of this caste are suspended between a peasant (and pro-communist) elder generation and past, on the one side, and incipient middle-class identity, on the other side, since they are urban dwellers who have, for the most part, prospered from the development of the capital.[8]

The 1990 mass movement in Nepal formed one small part of the global "third wave" of democracy. The fall of dictators in Eastern Europe, Asia, Africa, and Latin America boosted the morale of democratic forces of Nepal. The international environment—the global relaxation in east–west tensions, as well as the détente in Sino–Indian relations—reduced the room for maneuver of the authoritarian Panchayat system. Moreover, relations between Nepal and India in the late 1980s were strained for several reasons: in particular, India took umbrage at Nepal's import of arms from China, which it held to be in violation of the 1950 Friendship Treaty. The semi-blockade imposed by the Indian government in 1989 when Nepal tried to renegotiate the Trade and Transit Treaty was in part retaliation for this; the economic hardships experienced in Nepal's cities added to dissatisfaction with the regime that boiled over in 1990. However, in contrast to its decisive and directing role in 1950–51,

the Indian government adopted a "non-interference" attitude in 1990. Nonetheless, Chandra Shekhar—at that time a leading figure in the National Front government of India, who became prime minister the following year—provided very significant moral support by visiting Nepal in January 1990 and publicly speaking out in favor of the overthrow of tyrannical rule by democratic forces. A similar role was played by US Senator Stephen Solarz in mobilizing support from American and other western human rights activists and non-governmental organizations.

At the outset of the 1990 mass movement, unity between two different ideological streams—the NC, on the one side, and several splinter communist parties, on the other— was remarkable. Unlike in 1950–51, when the Communist party was relatively insignificant, the leftist forces had developed in size and strength during the Panchayat period and so they were able to play a prominent and active role in 1990, which was duly acknowledged in post-movement political arrangements. A coalition government led by the NC, comprising representatives of both the Left and the king, brought forward a new constitution, namely, the Constitution of the Kingdom of Nepal 1990, which adopted a Westminster model of parliamentary democracy and constitutional monarchy. This new constitution, although vesting sovereignty in the people, kept the king as head of state and of the armed forces, and gave him the power, in the fateful article 127, to take power in an emergency "in order to remove difficulties." Contentiously also, the constitution continued to designate Nepal as "a Hindu Kingdom," even though it also dubbed it "multiethnic" and "multilingual" (the adjectives "multireligious" and "secular" were conspicuously absent). Finally, the fact that the constitution, although vesting sovereignty in the people, had been granted by the king, gave legitimacy to the Maoists' demand for a constituent assembly. Had the king and those in the palace been convinced of the need to help make constitutional monarchy work, none of these problems would have been insuperable.

135

In a context where many in the palace sought a return to the monarchical preeminence of the Panchayat era, they turned out to be fatal flaws in the constitutional design.

Three successive parliamentary elections were held in 1991, 1994, and 1999, and two nationwide elections for local government institutions in 1992 and 1997. The NC and the Communist Party of Nepal (Unified Marxist-Leninist), usually known by the initials UML, emerged as the two major parties. The former formed a majority government after the 1991 and 1999 general elections (on the latter occasion thanks to a split in the UML). After the 1994 mid-term elections, the UML was the largest party in a hung parliament and formed a minority government. This was soon brought down, however, by a vote of no confidence, and the pattern of unstable, indecisive, coalition governments that characterized the mid-1990s and gave the political parties such a bad name, was set (see Tables 9.1 and 9.2).

Although the second experiment with party democracy lasted longer than in 1959, it was likewise full of stress and strains.[9] The political parties began with a huge fund of goodwill, which they rapidly squandered. Adopting neoliberal solutions to Nepal's deep-seated economic and ecological problems (selling off nationalized industries, inviting foreign business in to run major infrastructure projects) neither generated employment nor inspired confidence in transparency and good governance. The disparities between the remote rural areas and the cities were exacerbated. The country only remained afloat economically because of the growing remittances sent from abroad (India, the Gulf countries, Southeast Asia, South Korea) by poor Nepalis working in construction and security; this was ironic since the elite was at the same time exporting capital, either to invest abroad directly or in the form of school and college fees for their offspring in India, the USA, and other Western countries.

The problem of underdevelopment and uneven development was further exacerbated by disparities along caste/ethnic and regional lines. Ethnic difference had been downplayed in the Panchayat era of nation building. People of Indian origin living in the southern strip, the Tarai, were in a particularly sensitive position. The border with India is completely open: Nepalis may cross and work in India without papers and vice versa. In many border areas, Nepalis own fields in India and vice versa. Nepali citizens marry, shop, go to college, and carry out business in India—and vice versa. In other words, it is a border that, in many of the modern understandings of the term, is

Table 9.1 Political party positions in the first, second, and third parliamentary elections in Nepal

Parties	Number of seats elected			% of popular vote		
	1991	1994	1999	1991	1994	1999
Nepali Congress (NC)	110	83	112	37.75	33.38	36.14
Unified Marxist-Leninist (NCP-UML)	69	88	70	27.98	30.85	30.74
Rashtriya Prajatantra Party (RPP)	4	20	11	11.94	17.93	13.46
Nepal Sadbhawana Party (NSP)	6	3	5	4.10	3.49	3.13
National People's Front	–	–	5	–	–	1.36
Nepal Worker and Peasant Party (NWPP)	2	4	1	1.25	0.98	0.54
United People's Front (UPF)	9	0	1	4.35	1.32	0.83
Communist Party of Nepal (Democratic)	2	0	0	2.43	0.38	0.06
Independents	3	7	0	4.17	6.18	2.83
Other small parties	0	0	0	6.04	5.49	10.92
Total	205	205	205	100.00	100.00	100.00

Source: Election Commission, *House of Representative Members, 2048 (1991): Final Results*; *House of Representative Members, 2051 (1994): Election Results*; *House of Representative Members, 2056 (1999): Election Results*

Table 9.2 Governments of Nepal, 1990–2005

	PM	Parties	Length	Dates
1	KP Bhattarai	Congress + ULF interim	13 months	19/04/90–25/05/91

First general election (1991) Congress 110 seats (37.8% votes), UML 69 (28%)

	PM	Parties	Length	Dates
2	GP Koirala	Congress majority	42 months	26/05/91–28/11/94

Second general election (1994) Congress 83 seats (33.4%), UML 88 (30.9%)

	PM	Parties	Length	Dates
3	MM Adhikari	UML minority	9 months	29/11/94–10/09/95
4	SB Deuba	Congress–NDP–NSP coalition	18 months	11/09/95–11/03/97
5	LB Chand	RPP–UML coalition	7 months	12/03/97–05/10/97
6	SB Thapa	RPP–Congress–NSP coalition	6 months	06/10/97–25/03/98
7	GP Koirala	Congress minority	5 months	26/03/98–25/08/98
8	GP Koirala	Congress–ML coalition	4 months	26/08/98–22/12/98
9	GP Koirala	Congress–UML–NSP coalition	5 months	23/12/98–26/05/99

Third general election (1999) Congress 112 seats (36.1%), UML 70 (30.7%)

	PM	Parties	Length	Dates
10	KP Bhattarai	Congress	9 months	27/05/99–09/03/00
11	GP Koirala	Congress	16 months	10/03/00–22/07/01
12	SB Deuba	Congress, later Congress (D)	14 months	23/07/01–04/10/02
13	LB Chand	Non-party	8 months	11/10/02–31/05/03
14	SB Thapa	Non-party (in practice RPP)	11 months	04/06/03–07/05/04
15	SB Deuba	Cong (D) + NSP(Mandal) + UML + RPP	8 months	01/06/04–01/02/05

not a border. The fact that Madhesis, as Nepalis of Indian ethnicity and language are called, are indistinguishable culturally from Indians means that their loyalty to Nepal is always suspected by hill people (Pahades or Parbatiyas). Madhesis know and resent this. For many years they have felt that they have been treated like a colony of the hills, despite the fact that the Tarai is now home to 50 percent of Nepal's population, most of its industry, and the great bulk of its agriculturally productive land, and despite the fact that the educational level and capabilities of many Madhesis is high.

The other big cleavages are between the hill high castes, the Bahuns (Brahmans) and Chhetris (Kshatriyas), and those groups that used to be called hill tribes and are now known as Janajatis, and between all these and the Dalits (former untouchables). None of these differences was acknowledged in the Panchayat period (it was considered that simply declaring formal equality before the law was enough). Following the 1991 census, which recorded and published the results, ethnic difference emerged into the public sphere and was increasingly politicized. The extent to which all the major

offices of state and society were dominated by Bahuns, Chhetris, and Newars could now be documented and demonstrated (see Tables 9.3 and 9.4). For the first time, reservations (affirmative action) became possible, politically feasible, and increasingly unavoidable.[10]

Frequent changes of government (see Table 9.2) meant that governments were unable to address underlying issues. Neither were they able to deal with the Maoist insurgency, which was launched in the western hills in February 1996. Instability and division at the center were in marked contrast to the force and determination with which the Panchayat regime had been defended in its heyday. Each competing power center in Kathmandu sought to use the growing insurgency to bolster its own position: the NC hoped that it would split the left and undermine its main competitor, the UML; the UML hoped that the main targets would remain NC- and RPP-aligned landlords; the palace hoped that the political parties would be undermined. The first force to benefit from increasing weakness and instability at the Center was the palace. The king seized power in two steps, first in October

Table 9.3 Population breakdown of Nepal (2001 census) (total: 23.15 million) with figures for hill minority language loss

Parbatiyas ("hill people")		Hill minorities (Janajatis)		Language loss among minorities	Madhesis ("plains people")		Others
Bahun	13%	Magar	7.2%	52.1% (67.9)	Tharu	6.7%	Muslims 4.2%
Chhetri (incl.		Newar	5.5%	34.5% (33.7)	Yadav	4%	
Thakuri)	18%						
Dalit	9%	Tamang	5.6%	7.1% (11.2)	(+ many small castes incl. Dalits and Janajatis)		
		Rai	3%	23.2% (16.4)			
		Gurung	2.4%	47.5% (49.5)			
		Limbu	1.6%	6.2% (14.5)			
Total	40%		25%			30%	5%

Notes: Dalit = former untouchables; Janajatis (underlined) are mainly those who were formerly called hill tribes (many Tharus, as noted, reject the label "Madhesi"): 59 groups were officially designated as Janajatis in February 2002, not all of which had been included in the 2001 census. Estimated figures for language loss are courtesy of John Whelpton, with the 1991 figures given in parentheses (see Whelpton 1997: 59). All figures are likely to be disputed. Those for language loss require particular care. The apparent increase in minorities speaking "their" language since 1991 may be ascribed to the increased politicization of the issue and the fact that many Magar activists, for example, campaigned for people to return their language as "Magar" regardless of what they spoke at home.

Table 9.4 Presence (percentage) of different groups in leadership positions in Nepal, 1999

		Dominant groups		Marginalized groups					
		Bahun/ Chhetri	Newar	Madhesi	Janajati	Dalit	Other	No. of individuals
1	Court	77	13.6	7.6	1.7	0	0	235
2	Constitutional bodies	56	24	12	2.8	0	0	25
3	Cabinet	62.5	9.4	15.6	12.5	0	0	32
4	Parliament	60	7.6	17.4	13.6	1.5	0	265
5	Public administration	77.6	17.6	3.7	1.2	0	0	245
6	Party leadership	58.8	10.9	15.8	15.2	0	0	165
7	Local elected bodies	55.5	15.7	16.2	12	0	0	191
8	Commerce and industry	16.7	47.6	35.7	0	0	0	42
9	Educational arena	77.3	11.3	7.2	2.1	1	1	97
10	Cultural arena	69.1	17.9	0	4.9	0	0	123
11	Science/technology	58.1	29	9.7	3.2	0	0	62
12	Civil society leadership	75.9	14.8	7.4	1.9	0	0	54
	Total	66.5	15.2	11.2	7.1	0.3	1	
	Population %	31.6	5.6	30.9	22.2	8.7	1	
	Difference with population %	+34.9	+9.6	−19.7	−15.1	−8.4	−1	

Note: Although Newars are officially included in the Janajati category, in practice their "advanced" position, as the inhabitants of the capital with a higher HDI than any group in the country, makes it sensible to treat them separately.

Source: Neupane, Govinda, Nepalko Jatiya Prashna (The Caste/Ethnicity Question in Nepal) (Kathmandu: Centre for Development Studies, 2000)

2002, when he dismissed Prime Minister Deuba and called for a technocratic government of those with a "clean image," and subsequently with a full-blown coup d'état in February 2005, when phone and internet connections were shut down for a week and the King himself became the chair of the Council of Ministers.

Reinventing democracy after 2002

Until the royal coup of February 2005 political struggle took the form of a triangular conflict with different roles and motives for each of the key actors. The king, while sidelining the political parties, attempted to tackle the Maoist insurgency alternately by negotiation or suppression (the army is said to have promised to deal with the insurgency within six months, which it signally failed to do).[11] The mainstream parties, united under the banner of the Seven Party Alliance (SPA), launched a series of street protests against the King's "regression" (*pratigaman*), while keeping their distance from the Maoists and their violent methods. The standing of Girija Prasad Koirala (the younger brother of B.P.) in the post-2006 period stemmed from his outspoken and unwavering opposition to the king from October 2002 onwards, whereas other leading politicians allowed themselves to be tempted into compromise and accepting participation in the king's governments. Finally, the CPN (Maoist) was able to escalate its "People's War" more intensely during the time of the royal regime, winning some important morale-boosting battles, such as over-running Beni, the district headquarters of Myagdi, in March 2004 and the hill town of Tansen in January 2006.

The king's coup of 1 February, 2005, in which the major leaders were all put under house arrest and the leaders of civil society and political activists were taken into military barracks and in some cases tortured, forced the parties closer to the CPN-M. The Maoist leaders, aware that they would not be able to

conquer the cities militarily, were also looking at the possibility of alliance with the parties. This turning point in oppositional politics was reflected in the 12-point understanding made between the SPA and the CPN-M in Delhi in November 2005. It contained three key commitments: first, the SPA endorsed the CPN-M fundamental demand for elections to a CA; second, the Maoists reciprocated with an assurance that they accepted a multiparty competitive political system, the prime concern of the SPA; third, both the SPA and the Maoists agreed to launch a peaceful mass movement against the monarchy.

The 12-point pact was agreed with the active involvement of India. As in previous democracy movements, the external factor in the April 2006 Jan Andolan II was extremely important, although unlike 1951 or 1990 it did not correspond to any global "wave." The change of government in India in May 2004, with a Congress-led alliance replacing the BJP, limited the king's ability to play on Hindu sentiment in India or to mobilize his kin links with Indian royal families. Sita Ram Yechuri, a leader of the Communist Party of India (Marxist), a major supporter of the ruling coalition in India, played a similar role to that of Chandra Shekhar in 1990. Disappointed by King Gyanendra's attempt to bring in China as an observer in SAARC, and frustrated by his repeated rejection of Indian advice to compromise with the political parties, India took a tough stand against the king's coup. The international community had been sympathetic to King Gyanendra's post-October 2002 political project of combining the monarchy and democracy to counter the Maoist "terrorist" threat, but it unequivocally condemned the King's seizure of power in February 2005. The principal suppliers of military aid—India, the US, and the UK—postponed their shipments. Many donors withdrew or cut their earlier commitments to development aid as well. There were attempts in the international community to persuade the leaders of the April 2006 popular movement to accept a return to the status quo ante

February 2005, i.e., retaining the monarchy as an important actor. Such moves were rejected outright. Unlike the 1950–51 revolution, but in some ways similar to 1990, it was internal forces, rather than external pressures, that determined the course and outcome of the April 2006 movement.

The April 2006 Jan Andolan II was unique and unprecedented both in terms of the degree of the people's participation and the nature of the political demands. It was the most powerful anti-establishment struggle that Nepal has witnessed. The 1950–51 revolution was fought by the NC's cadres as a guerrilla war, like the Maoist insurgency of 1996–2006, though on a much smaller scale. The 1990 MRD was a largely urban and middle-class movement, with a specifically Newar ethnic element. By contrast, the April 2006 Jan Andolan II was rural in the specific sense that many among the millions of people who participated in this 19-day popular uprising were rural dwellers who had come (or, as many claimed, had been sent by the Maoists) to the cities for this very purpose. In Kathmandu the main sites of opposition were around the ring road, i.e., close to the new poor suburbs settled by migrants from the hills; the old city cores were very quiet by comparison.

The post-April 2006 transition ushered in important political developments, namely reinstatement of the dissolved parliament along with formation of a government led by NC leader G. P. Koirala in April 2006, signing of a comprehensive peace agreement (CPA) between the government and the CPN-M in November 2006 followed by placement of the CPN-M's combatants in cantonments, promulgation of the interim constitution of Nepal in January 2007 and subsequent participation by the CPN-M in the interim parliament and government in January–April 2007, and the Madhes uprising in January 2007, which recurred in January 2008. The frequent *bandh*s, bombs, and assassinations, and the emergence of a plethora of small armed groups hiding over the border in India, established that the strategically important Tarai can no longer be ignored or taken for granted by Kathmandu. Amendments to the interim constitution had to be made three times to take into account the demands of the Madhes activists, as well as those of the Janajatis and the Maoists, incorporating the provisions of federalism, delimitation of constituencies according to the principle of population size, and adaptation of a mixed electoral system weighted more to proportional representation (PR) than to first-past-the-post (FPTP) in the distribution of CA seats.

The CA election was held peacefully and in a relatively free and fair manner despite massive pre-election apprehension about violence and rigging. (There was certainly some intimidation in districts where the Maoists are strong, such as Rukum and Gorkha, but not enough to invalidate the result as a whole.) As expected the election produced a hung assembly but what was unexpected and surprising, even to the winners themselves, was that the CPN-M—a former insurgent group—should come out on top with a total strength of 220 out of 575 elected seats, putting its rivals—the NC and the UML—far behind. The NC, which expected to win, came second with 110. The UML, which was also confident—evidently over-confident—of winning, came third with 103 seats. The rise of regional ethnic parties was confirmed by the fact that the Madhes Janadhikar Forum (MJF)—a party created from the Madhes uprising of January 2007 — won 52 seats and another Tarai party, the Tarai Madhes Loktantrik Party (TMLP), led by Mahantha Thakur who had defected from the NC, scored 20 seats.

Simply to hold the elections was itself a major achievement. The other accomplishments of the transitional period (April 2006 to April 2008) flowed from the aim of restructuring the state. The three key elements of this project are the transformation of the armed conflict, the end of monarchical rule forever, and the advancement of inclusive democracy.

The transformation of armed conflict

The restoration of democracy in April 2006—against the background of a decade-long war (1996–2006) between the Maoist guerrillas and the state security forces in which around 13,000 people lost their lives[12]—is closely associated with the peace project. After the 1950–51 revolution, conflict transformation was not a big challenge either technically or politically. The NC *Mukti Sena* (liberation army) was simply turned into the Nepal police as Nepal did not have a proper police force at that time. The NC's intentions were not in doubt because the political system introduced after the 1950–51 revolution conformed to its ideology of multiparty democracy. Today's parallel situation is not so simple, even though the People's Liberation Army (PLA) is in cantonments, its arms are locked in containers, and the United Nations Mission in Nepal (UNMIN) is monitoring the arms management process. The CPN-M disclosed only 3,428 weapons, whereas the number of its combatants living in the cantonments is 19,601. Moreover, the Nepal Army is firmly against any integration with the PLA whereas the CPN-M is unlikely to revise its proposal for the integration of the Nepal Army and the PLA. The PLA was constituted and trained according to communist principles; clearly, the restructuring of the state will require both the party and the PLA to adapt to a multiparty political system.

To the surprise of many observers, the CPN-M as a party began to adapt in this direction, even in 2003 when the insurgency was at its peak. At this stage, it was running a parallel administration in the many areas under its control.[13] Perhaps the decision was taken in realization of the impossibility of military victory over the state army, and with a plan for collaboration with the mainstream parties in order to consolidate all anti-monarchy forces. After signing the 12-point understanding with the SPA in November 2005, the CPN-M publicly reaffirmed its faith in the multiparty system, provided the SPA backed its demands for a CA and a republic. In conformity with its changed ideological position, the party was actively involved in every important decision taken in the post-Jan Andolan II transitional process. Despite some ambivalence and inconsistency in words and deeds, the CPN-M has basically been moving towards a new commitment to peaceful politics. The crux of the matter is that the transformation of the CPN-M may very well be a necessary condition of the survival of multiparty democracy in Nepal.

Establishment of a republic

Jan Andolan II was the final showdown in a half-century-long confrontation between democracy and monarchy. King Gyanendra ascended the throne against the background of the royal massacre of 1 June, 2001 in which King Birendra along with all his immediate family members and five other royals were killed. The then Crown Prince Dipendra was the culprit according to the official version. However, because King Gyanendra was absent and both his wife and his son Paras, who were present, survived, the vast majority of Nepali people became convinced that it was a conspiracy. The personal unpopularity of both Gyanendra and Paras fueled republican sentiment and massively undermined people's faith in the institution of monarchy. The rise of ethnic activism, accompanied by demands for a secular state, also had a negative impact on the traditional legitimacy of the Nepali monarchy. Since the unification of Nepal in 1768, the Shah dynasty had made concerted efforts to blend inherent rights with divine authority, promoting Hinduism as a symbol of the Nepali nation. Now the whole package of Hinduism and monarchy—far from being a bulwark of democracy as Gyanendra's father Mahendra had claimed—was seen as inimical to it.

Gyanendra's own political ambitions were also to blame for the rise of republicanism.

The February 2005 royal coup—the logical culmination of the series of royal takeovers begun in October 2002—was primarily justified by the failure of the party regime to counter the Maoist insurgency. But people's initial hopes that there was to be a rapid improvement in the situation were quickly dashed by the lack of any plan— economic, political, or military. Instead, the CPN-M's violent "People's War" rapidly intensified and spread all over the country. By systematically opposing and undermining the political parties, King Gyanendra pushed them into the arms of the Maoists. The single biggest reason for the success of republicanism in Nepal has been the shortsightedness of the monarch. Unlike his father's assertion of authoritarian rule in 1960, Gyanendra's attempt cannot be said to have corresponded to any worldwide movement or tendency; Gyanendra himself lacked either the toughness or the military experience that would have enabled him to follow such unhappy regional examples as Pakistan or Burma, and it was the army generals who went to him in April 2006 and told him the game was up.

Jan Andolan II was, in fact, a republican movement in spirit, even though the 12-point pact explicitly claimed only to be aiming at "the end of the absolute monarchical system." The post-Andolan period saw the rapid removal of monarchical relevance. The May 2006 Declaration—considered the Nepali Magna Carta—made by the reinstated House of Representatives, formally cut off the monarchy's two arms—the Hindu religion and the army's loyalty—by declaring Nepal a secular state and deleting the title "royal" from the military and all other state organizations. The change in the popular mood was so radical that support for a republican system of government increased from 15 percent in 2004 to 59 percent in 2007.[14] Consequently, the interim Prime Minister G. P. Koirala was forced to withdraw his proposal to save the monarchy by installing a "baby king" through the voluntary abdication of both king and crown prince in favor of Gyanendra's grandson Hridayendra.

The CPN-M's relentless campaigns for a republic eventually forced the government, in November 2007, to insert a provision into the interim constitution declaring Nepal a federal republic. The original provision that the fate of monarchy would be decided by a simple majority of the CA members in its first meeting was retained and it was understood, certainly by the Maoists, that this meant simply that the CA would put the already taken decision into operation. As parties contesting on a republican platform swept the CA election and the CPN-M, long the leading champion of republicanism, went on to head the post-CA election government, it was clear that the days of the Shah dynasty, which had ruled Nepal for nearly 240 years, were numbered.

Inclusive democracy

The government of post-2006 Nepal will be radically different from anything that has gone before. The 1990 constitution, though it permitted reservations and designated the state as "multiethnic" and "multilingual," neither built measures of positive discrimination into the structure of the state nor gave any consideration to the introduction of proportional representation. This very weak support for restructuring was, it became apparent, not going to be sufficient to satisfy the demands of ethnic and regional activists as they became increasingly better organized and mobilized throughout the 1990s. Post-Jan Andolan II politics include much more radical measures. The declaration of Nepal as a secular state, the adoption of bilingualism, a new provision of 45 percent reservations in the bureaucracy for excluded groups, a provision ensuring 33 percent representation for women in all state machinery, including elected bodies and political parties, distribution of 335 PR seats in the CA as per the size of the population of different social segments, and political and constitutional commitments to federalism are some of the concrete decisions in favor of inclusive democracy made during the transitional period.

The restoration of multiparty democracy in 1990 coincided with an ethnic revival. As one of us has written: "If the period 1960 to 1990 was one of *nation*-building, the [period] since then has been a time of *ethnicity*-building."[15] The principles of popular sovereignty, equality, freedom, cultural rights, and the right to organize provided a platform for ethnic activism. The disadvantaged of Nepal fall into three large blocs: the Janajatis, Madhesis, and Dalits and each of these groups has its own organizations aiming to speak on behalf of the bloc as a whole. Of all the political forces seeking to cash in on post-1990 ethnic mobilization, the CPN-M seems to have been the most successful. It is certainly thanks to the Maoists that the maximum ethnic demands — for autonomy and federalism—have been adopted into the political agenda. The CPN-M's concerted effort to blend ethnic rights and class war was evident both in its opening of ethnic "front organizations" and in its division of the country into nine ethnic and region-based "regional governments," eight of which were declared in the first half of 2004 at mass meetings and heavily publicized afterwards.

The experience of the transitional period, 2006–08, suggests that street demonstrations, *bandh*s, and other forms of political protest will not stop just because the CA has been elected. Dalits, women, Janajatis, Madhesis, and other regional groups are all likely to protest if their demands are not met, and some expectations are bound to be disappointed. The NC and UML may themselves turn to the politics of the street now that they find themselves in opposition. The Madhesi movement of January–February 2007 was the strongest, most violent, and most effective set of street protests Nepal has seen—and the lesson has surely not been lost on others. During the 21 most intense days of the Madhesi movement, 27 people lost their lives, more than the 21 people who died in April 2006. A further 27 Maoists were massacred in Gaur, the capital of Rautahat, right on the Indian border, when

a Madhes and a Maoist meeting were called at the same place on the same day. It was the sheer ferocity and persistence of the Madhes uprising that convinced the interim government that there was no alternative but to accede to demands for federalism, the redistribution of electoral constituencies on the basis of the size of population, and ethnic representation for the CA members elected under the PR system.

For the first time in Nepali history, the hill high castes will find their representation reduced in the national legislature to their own population size 31 to 32 percent, where previously it had been between 54 and 63 percent. For the first time in the electoral history of Nepal, the Janajatis, Dalits, and Madhesis will be represented approximately in proportion to the size of their population. Having one-third women in the CA will also be a new phenomenon. This may have a massive demonstration effect on the whole country.

Conclusion: A comparison with recent developments in Bhutan

For those looking from afar, Nepal is often bracketed with Bhutan since both are (or, in Nepal's case, were) Himalayan kingdoms. There are some fairly radical differences, however. Nepal's population is heading towards 30 million, half of whom live in the Tarai bordering India and sharing much with the neighboring Indian states of UP, Bihar, and West Bengal. Bhutan's population is less than 1 million. The ruling elite of Nepal is and has always been Hindu and pro-Indian in outlook; Nepali is close to Hindi and most Nepalis can understand Hindi fairly easily. The ruling elite and dynasty of Bhutan are Tibetan Buddhists and the national language of Bhutan is a dialect of Tibetan.

Despite these highly significant differences of scale, culture, and history, there is a striking (albeit inverted) structural similarity between the problems faced by the two countries. Nepal's key ethnic problem—although most

Nepalis only woke up to the fact in January 2007—is the presence of a sizeable minority of Nepali citizens (over 30 percent) who are ethnically Indian and who are no longer willing to accept second-class citizenship or being ruled by non-Madhesis. Bhutan's key ethnic problem was the presence of a similarly sized minority of Nepali origin, likewise based in the fertile south, the so-called Lhotshampas ("southerners"). Bhutan has, in the short term, attempted to solve this problem by a degree of ethnic cleansing, expelling over 100,000 Lhotshampas in 1990, who ended up crossing the short span of Indian territory and being settled in UNHCR-run camps inside Nepal.

The achievements of Nepal's Maoists are arguably unparalleled in world history. What other Maoist movement has gone from armed movement to success in national polls in 12 short years? (Ironically, had they not pushed so hard, along with ethnic activists, for the PR system, they would, after the April 2008 elections, have had 50 percent of the seats, instead of 229 out of 601.) These achievements, which produced a secular republic in Nepal, have had a powerful demonstration effect on Bhutan's Lhotshampa population, among whom the Bhutanese Maoist Party (founded 2003) started to become quite powerful. In 2008 it issued death threats to any Bhutanese refugee who came out openly in favor of accepting the US offer to resettle 60,000 of them,[16] and in some cases carried them out. By January 2009 these threats had died away as the process of resettlement got under way.

Nepal's trajectory towards democracy has been, as we have shown, highly chequered and marked by several phases of violent opposition. Only in the latter phases has mobilization on ethnic grounds been overwhelmingly significant. In Bhutan, by contrast, developments have been far more controlled. Violence has been less open and the regime's concern, whether in politics, tourism, or development projects, has been to avoid taking the Nepali path.

It is possible to write the history of democracy in Nepal and Bhutan in terms of a conflict between four models of democracy: guided

monarchical "democracy," liberal party-based democracy, communist "people's democracy," and multiculturalism.[17] Bhutan has attempted to shortcircuit further internal dissent by moving from guided democracy without elections (somewhat similar to Nepal's early Panchayat regime) to a form of guided party elections. The first elections under this system were held in March 2008. Only two parties were allowed to run. To the surprise of many, the Bhutan Peace and Prosperity Party, led by Jigme Y. Thinley, won over two thirds of the votes and 45 out of 47 seats in the new Parliament. In short, Bhutan is attempting to combine the first two models (monarchical guided and liberal democracy), while firmly rejecting the latter two. Nepal, by contrast, has seen the definitive defeat of the first model and a rapprochement between the other three.

[We would like to thank John Whelpton for helpful comments on an earlier draft. This chapter was composed in the immediate aftermath of the April 2008 elections, with minor amendments made in March 2009.]

Notes

1 "Peaceful" is a relative term, and the judgment could, of course, be disputed. INSEC, one of the leading human rights organizations in Nepal, recorded that, in 2007, 37 people were killed by the state, 15 by the Maoists, and 108 by nine different Madhesi groups (inseconline.org); 75 persons died from the date of enforcement of the election code of conduct (16 January) to the CA election day (Mahendra Lawoti, "Aspiration to Change and Threat Factor" (in Nepali), *Himal Khabar Patrika*, 29 April–13 May, 2008, p. 53).

2 The category "other," originally intended to protect groups not explicitly named, such as Muslims, was adopted as a reserved category for the high castes (i.e., Bahuns, Chhetris, Thakuris, and Sanyasis). In 1996 a government committee published a list of 23 castes (by surname) that would be recognized as Dalits. Fifty-nine officially recognized Janajatis ("nationalities," what in India are called "tribes") are listed in a

government document published on 10 February, 2002; (see D. N. Gellner and M.B. Karki, "Democracy and Ethnic Organizations in Nepal", in D. N. Gellner and K. Hachhethu (eds), *Local Democracy in South Asia* (Delhi: Sage, 2008, p. 111) ; there is also a national confederal body bringing together one representative organization from each group, the Nepal Federation of Indigenous Nationalities (see nefin.org.np). Madhesis are the ethnically Indian Nepali citizens who inhabit principally the flat Tarai belt in the south of the country bordering India. Some groups such as Tharus, Santals, and Rajvamshis are both Janajati and Madhesi, although they often do not wish to be included in the Madhesi category. It is essential for some double-counting of the PR candidates in order for all the required percentages (which sum to 116 percent) to be fulfilled. Whether Muslims are to be included in the Madhesi category is controversial. The nine backward districts (those lowest on human development indices) are Achham, Kalikot, Jajarkot, Jumla, Dolpa, Bajhang, Bajura, Mugu, and Humla. All are either in the far west or on the northern fringe, or both.

3 Bhuwan Lal Joshi and Leo Rose, *Democratic Innovations in Nepal* (Berkeley, CA: University of California Press, 1966), p. 79; cf. Martin Hoftun, William Raeper, and John Whelpton, *People, Politics, and Ideology: Democracy and Social Change in Nepal* (Kathmandu: Mandala Book Point, 1999), ch. 1.

4 Anirudha Gupta, *Politics in Nepal* (Bombay: Allied Publishers, 1964), pp. 46–47. The constituent assembly was never held and the election of a new one became one of the key demands of the Maoist insurgency launched in 1996.

5 R. S. Chauhan, *The Political Development in Nepal 1950–70* (Delhi: Associated Publishing House, 1971).

6 Krishna Hachhethu, "Civil Society and Political Participation," in Lok Raj Baral (ed.), *Nepal: Quest for Participatory Democracy* (New Delhi: Adroit Publishers, 2006), p. 128.

7 Lok Raj Baral, *Oppositional Politics in Nepal* (New Delhi: Abhinav Publishing House, 1977). For Nepali politics during the Panchayat period, see also Rishikesh Shah, *Essays in the Practices of Government in Nepal* (New Delhi: Manohar Publishing House, 1982).

8 Krishna Hachhethu, "Mass Movement 1990," *Contributions to Nepalese Studies*, 17, 2 (1990), p. 190. See Vincanne Adams, *Doctors for Democracy* (Cambridge: University Press, 1998) on the involvement of the doctors, and David N. Gellner, "Caste, Communalism, and Communism: Newars and the Nepalese State," in D. N. Gellner, J. Pfaff-Czarnecka, and J. Whelpton (eds), *Nationalism and Ethnicity in a Hindu Kingdom* (Amsterdam: Harwood, 1997) on the unacknowledged ethnic background to the 1990 uprisings in the cities of Lalitpur (Patan) and Bhaktapur.

9 For details of Nepali politics in the post-1990 period, see Lok Raj Baral, *Nepal: Problems of Governance* (New Delhi: Konark Publishers Pvt. Ltd., 1993); Lok Raj Baral, *The Regional Paradox: Essays in Nepali and South Asian Affairs* (Delhi: Adroit Publishers, 2000); Lok Raj Baral, Krishna Hachhethu, and Hari Sharma, *Leadership in Nepal* (New Delhi: Adroit Publishers, 2001); Michael Hutt (ed.), *Nepal in the Nineties* (Delhi: Oxford University Press, 1994); Martin Hoftun, William Raeper, and John Whelpton *People, Politics and Ideology* (Kathmandu: Mandala Book Point, 1999); POLSAN, *Political Parties and the Parliamentary Process in Nepal: A Study of the Transitional Phase* (Kathmandu: Political Science Association of Nepal, 1992); Ole Borre, Sushil Raj Pandey, and Chitra Krishna Tiwari, *Nepalese Political Behaviour* (New Delhi: Sterling, 1994); Dhruba Kumar (ed.), *State, Leadership and Politics in Nepal* (Kathmandu: Centre for Nepal and Asian Studies, 1995); Dhruba Kumar (ed.), *Domestic Conflict and Crisis of Governability in Nepal* (Kathmandu: Centre for Nepal and Asian Studies, 2000); T. Louise Brown, *The Challenge to Democracy in Nepal: A Political History* (Routledge, 1996); Krishna Hachhethu, *Party Building in Nepal: Organization, Leadership and People, A Comparative Study of the Nepali Congress and the Communist Party of Nepal (Unified Marxist-Leninist)* (Kathmandu: Mandala Book Point: 2002).

10 On ethnic aspects of Nepali politics, see Frederick H. Gaige, *Regionalism and National Unity in Nepal* (New Delhi: Vikas, 1975); David N. Gellner, Joanna Pfaff-Czarnecka, and John Whelpton (eds), *Nationalism and Ethnicity in a Hindu Kingdom* (Amsterdam: Harwood, 1997); Prayag Raj Sharma, "Ethnicity and National Integration in Nepal: A Statement of the Problem," *Journal of Nepalese Studies*, 1

(July–December 1987), pp. 23–30; "How to Tend This Garden," *Himal* (May–June 1992), pp. 7–9; Harka Gurung, "Representing An Ethnic Mosaic," *Himal* (May–June 1992), pp. 19–21; Marie Lecomte-Tilouine and Pascale Dollfus (eds), *Ethnic Revival and Religious Turmoil* (New Delhi: Oxford University Press, 2003); Mahendra Lawoti, *Towards a Democratic Nepal: Inclusive Political Institutions for a Multicultural Society* (New Delhi: Sage, 2005); Susan I. Hangen, *Creating a "New Nepal": The Ethnic Dimension* (Washington: East-West Center, 2007); G. Toffin, M. S. Tamang, P. Onta, and S. Sato, *Studies in Nepali History and Society*, Vol. 11, No. 2 (2006).

11 On censorship and self-censorship during the period of the king's rule, see Michael Hutt, "Things that Should not be Said: Censorship and Self-censorship in the Nepali Press Media, 2001–2," *Journal of Asian Studies*, 65 (2006), pp. 361–92. For information on the way in which internet blogs kept the outside world informed of what was going on inside Nepal, see James Sharrock, "Nepali Blogging and Democracy," *Studies in Nepali History and Society*, Vol. 12, No. 1 (2007), pp. 55–94.

12 For details of the Maoist insurgency, see Arjun Karki and David Seddon (eds), *The People's War in Nepal: Left Perspectives* (New Delhi: Adroit Publishers, 2003); Michael Hutt (ed.), *Himalayan People's War: Nepal's Maoist Rebellion* (London: Hurst, 2004); Deepak Thapa and Bandana Sijapati, *A Kingdom under Siege: Nepal's Maoist Insurgency, 1996 to 2003* (Kathmandu: The Print House, 2003); Deepak Thapa (ed.), *Understanding the Maoist Movement of Nepal* (Kathmandu: Martin Chautari, 2003); S. D.

Muni, *The Maoist Insurgency in Nepal: The Challenge and The Response* (New Delhi: Rupa, 2003); Arjun Karki and Binod Bhattarai (eds), *Whose War? Economic and Social-Cultural Impacts of Nepal's Maoist-Government Conflict* (Kathmandu: NGO Federation of Nepal, n.d.); and Kiyoko Ogura, "Maoists, People, and the State as seen from Rolpa and Rukum," in H. Ishii, D. Gellner, and K. Nawa (eds), *Political and Social Transformations in North India and Nepal* (New Delhi: Manohar, 2007).

13 See Kiyoko Ogura, "Maoists' People's Governments, 2001–05: The Power in Wartime," in D. N. Gellner and K. Hachhethu (eds), *Local Democracy in South Asia* (Delhi: Sage, 2008).

14 Krishna Hachhethu, *State of Democracy in Nepal: A Survey Report* (Kathmandu: SDSA/Nepal and International IDEA, 2004); and Krishna Hachhethu with Sanjay Kumar and Jiwan Subedi, *Nepal in Transition: A Study on the State of Democracy* (Stockholm: International IDEA, 2008).

15 David N. Gellner, "Caste, Ethnicity and Inequality in Nepal," *Economic and Political Weekly*, Vol. 42, No. 20 (2007), p. 1,823.

16 On the US offer, see http://hrw.org/english/docs/2007/05/17/bhutan15936_txt.htm. For an article about the appeal of Maoism to refugee youth in the camps, see R. Evans, "The Two Faces of Empowerment in Conflict," *Research in Comparative and International Education*, 3 (2008), pp. 50–64 (doi:10.2304/rcie.2008.3.1.50).

17 See David N. Gellner, "Democracy in Nepal: Four Models," *Seminar*, 576 (2007), pp. 50–56 (available at http://ora.ouls.ox.ac.uk).

10

The old and the new federalism in independent India

Lloyd I. Rudolph and Susanne Hoeber Rudolph

Introduction

We start our consideration of federalism in independent India by contrasting the formal characteristics and political dynamics of an "old" or founding federalism with those of a "new" or post-1990s federalism. We begin with the federalism that emerged from the writing of the 1950 constitution by the constituent assembly that sat between 9 December, 1946 and 26 January, 1950, when the constitution came into effect.

For some analysts, the text of the 1950 constitution has a transparently essential nature. It can tell us, for example, whether India is or is not a federal state. Ashok Chanda, a "heaven-born" ICS officer and one of the first to write a book on the Indian constitution, stated: "A Constitution is either federal or unitary; the test is whether its provisions give it a unitary bias or maintain fully the equality of the national and state governments in their demarcated fields of authority and jurisdiction."[1] Another early critic was the distinguished constitutional scholar, Sir Ivor Jennings. In his 1953 appraisal, *Some Characteristics of the Indian Constitution*,[2] he declared that the Indian constitution, admittedly the world's longest written constitution, was ruinously long, detailed, and rigid. For us these charac-terizations are too static, lacking a sense of historical process. Federalism is better concep-tualized as a continuous negotiation about how sovereignty can be shared and layered.

Both historical trajectories and individual actors motivated by interests and ideologies shaped the Indian state. The most important person in shaping the Indian state, including its federal dimension, was Jawaharlal Nehru, Gandhi's designated heir, prime minister of the 1946–47 interim government, India's first prime minister (1948–64) and advocate of a strong state capable of executing a socialist agenda. As the leader of a Congress party that held 74 percent of the seats in the Constituent Assembly, he and his Congress colleagues, Vallabhai Patel, Maulana Azad, and Rajendra Prasad, constituted an inner circle that dominated the work of the assembly.[3] Nehru's view of the kind of federalism proposed by the cabinet mission is captured by a remark attributed to him in early 1947 after Lord Mountbatten, the newly appointed viceroy, had indicated that the multilayered federal state with a weak center and strong provinces of the Cabinet Mission Plan would not work and that India would be partitioned. "Thank God we are out of that bag at last," said Nehru. Initially, Nehru had accepted the Cabinet Mission Plan, but backed out for several reasons, not least because he "wanted a strong center so that development could be done in a planned manner and landlordism could be abolished."[4]

Nehru was happy to be rid of the strong states and weak center of the Cabinet Mission Plan. Dr B. R. Ambedkar, the law minister who guided the constitution through the assembly, too made the case for a "union" rather than a "federal" government.[5] That said, the 1950 constitution's strongest institutional inheritance from the act of 1935 was federalism. The drive for a unitary state by the leaders of the constitutional assembly was countered by the template of the 1935 Government of India Act, an act whose dominant characteristic was a federal state. The 1935 act reflected not only the federal experience of the 1919 Montagu-Chelmsford reforms era and the 12 years when it served as India's constitution, but also the centuries of historical experience, from Mughal to East India Company (EIC) to British rule, with the *de facto* federalism of shared and layered sovereignty. Its federal features were overdetermined by the attempt to accommodate the princely states, a need that faded when the princes acceded to independent India.

With only minor alterations, the 1935 act's constitutional provisions became those of the 1950 constitution. Closely following provisions of the 1935 act, article 246 of the 1950 constitution deals with the distribution of legislative powers as between the union and the state legislatures in terms of the three lists found in the 1935 act and given in the seventh schedule of the 1950 constitution, viz., list I, the union list (97 items), including defense of India, foreign affairs, intelligence; foreign and interstate trade; finance; custom duties and corporation and income taxes; list II, the state list (66 items), including public order and police; public health; education; agriculture, land, land revenue and taxes on agricultural income; and list III, the concurrent list (47), including criminal and civil law and procedure; marriage and divorce; transfer of property other than agricultural land; economic and social planning; labor and trade unions.[6] Clause

1 of article 246 provides for "federal supremacy" by stating "that in case of inevitable conflict between union and state powers, the union powers as enumerated in list I shall prevail over the state powers as enumerated in lists II and III."[7] Contestation over legislative authority in many arenas of policy, mostly in the courts but also in party politics and the public sphere, has been continuous.

India's former provinces, now states (as of 2008, there were 28) are represented in an upper house known as the Rajya Sabha or Council of States. Seats are allocated on the basis of population,[8] and not equality as is the case in the US senate. For example, India's most populous state, Uttar Pradesh, occupies 31 of 241 seats in the Rajya Sabha. This feature of Indian federalism not only favors big over small states but also majoritarian democracy over minority representation and rights.

Members of the constituent assembly used the American example to distinguish Indian from American federalism. India's federal government was not constituted by independent states yielding up powers to a center, a metaphor that implies the power might revert and that residual powers lie with the contracting states. "One thing is very certain," said Justice A. M. Ahmadi, "that it is not a federation like the United States, where it was the states that created the federal or central government and invested it with some of their powers."[9] The constituent assembly reversed this process by making the states creatures of the center. Articles 2 and 3 give parliament the authority to create, abolish, divide, or combine states.

Paradoxically, the power of the center to create and divide states has enhanced the Indian union's capacity to represent difference by sharing sovereignty. In the face of Jawaharlal Nehru's majoritarian and rationalist resistance to the reorganization of the states on linguistic lines[10] and warnings from influential observers[11] that linguistic nationalism would lead to balkanization or authoritarian rule, sharing sovereignty through linguistic states has strengthened the Indian state's stability and legitimacy. As Sanjib Baruah has observed: "Federations can prevent the tyranny of the majority by a variety of means, including constitutionally guaranteed meaningful autonomous spheres of action for the territorial units."[12] And Katherine Adeney sums up the effects of sharing sovereignty via linguistic reorganization of India's states by observing that it "accommodated conflicts and stabilized the federation."[13]

The constitution's emergency powers, particularly article 356, provided an opening for the center to intimidate and control state governments as well as to deal with its stated purpose, emergencies in the states. The article 356 procedure calls for the report of a governor—appointed by the government of the day and often beholden to it— "that the government of the state cannot be carried on in accordance with the provisions of the constitution." The center, acting through the president, can remove a state government by imposing "President's Rule," i.e., a government appointed and controlled by the center.

Article 356 was intended as a measure of last resort in times of severe governmental crisis. Starting in 1957, when Indira Gandhi as Congress president arranged for the dismissal of a CPI-M [Communist] government in Kerala, Congress governments began using Article 356 routinely to remove troublesome opposition state governments. Perhaps its most constitutionally problematic use was in 1977 by the Janata government, which took power after Indira Gandhi's emergency regime. Claiming that Congress "opposition" governments of nine northern states that had been independently elected in separate state elections had lost their mandate as a result of the Janata Party's parliamentary victory, the Janata government used Article 356 to impose President's Rule on all nine. When a Congress government under Indira Gandhi was returned to power in 1980, it used the Janata government precedent to justify the dismissal of nine independently elected Janata state governments.

The abuse of the provisions of article 356 has been mitigated not only by the Bommai Supreme Court judgment of 1994,[14] but also because India entered an era of coalition politics, in which regional parties are generally unwilling to support the use of article 356 because future administrations may sanction its use to dismiss their own state governments.[15] Thus, a constitutional provision once thought to advantage the center over the states now no longer seems to do so.

State powers under the old federalism

Discussion of the old and new federalism proceeds in the context of our understanding of federalism as a form of state formation characterized by sharing, layering, and contesting sovereignty. Our analysis of a movement from an old to a new federalism involves state and political actors negotiating sovereignty relationships in the context of a formal constitution and changing political, economic and ideological conditions. Beginning about 20 years ago, with the transformation of the party system in 1989 and of the economy in 1991, an old federalism associated with Nehruvian planned development and Congress party domination was challenged by a federalism associated with a multiparty system and a market-oriented economy. Constitutional amendments can not account for this change. Changes in the informal constitution, such as the decline of the planning commission and the transformation of the party system, help explain the shift in the balance of power from the center to the states.

The transformation from the old to the new federalism was hardly abrupt. During the first two five-year plans—1951–56 and 1956–61—Jawaharlal Nehru was able to marshal the resources of the center, particularly those commanded by the planning commission, to carry through "basic industrialization" of the economy and, in his phrase, "occupy the economy's commanding heights." He was also able to use Congress' political capital and his own to convince state governments, most of which were Congress governments, to use their constitutional authority over agriculture to eliminate "intermediaries," *zamindars* and *jagirdars*, and to vest operational control of the land in tillers of the soil. The result was to bring into being a vast voting population of cultivators in India's states.[16] Nehru's soon-to-be nemesis in India's most populous state, Charan Singh, compared this new class of cultivators to western yeoman farmers, fiercely independent and committed to self-cultivation and remunerative prices.

By 1958, Nehru, like Karl Marx, a city boy who reviled the "idiocy of rural life" and thought the countryside could pay for industrialization, moved to collectivize Indian agriculture under the rubric of "joint cooperative farming." He had been inspired by the results being claimed in China for Mao Tse-tung's collectivization policy. At Congress' annual session at Nagpur in 1959, he proposed that the party adopt "joint cooperative farming," a proposal sharply opposed by Charan Singh, the principal architect of the UP Zamindari Abolition Act. Speaking for the self-employed cultivators, he argued that joint cooperative farming was the first step toward a collectivized and industrialized agricultural sector. The Nagpur resolution threatened to split Congress, and created a political climate that enabled Congress governments at the state level to stymie Congress efforts at the center to implement land ceilings legislation.

Another manifestation of power at the state level under the old federalism is the fate of what had been the largest source of provincial revenue under the British Raj, the land revenue. With agricultural producers being by far the most numerous voters in the states of independent India, it is not surprising that state-level politicians seeking their support quickly lowered the land revenue to a nominal amount. Although it is notorious that incomes in the agricultural sector are substantial, it has been impossible to date for state governments to institute a tax on agricultural income.

Equally notorious are state government subsidies to cultivators for electricity, water and fertilizer.

It seems that even in the heyday of the old federalism, the federalism of Congress dominance and of the command economy, the states sat at the bargaining table with the center, carrying enough political clout to scuttle central government policy initiatives and to introduce their own.[17]

Economic pre-conditions of the new federalism: From a planned to a market economy

Dramatic shifts in the nature of the India's economic policy help account for the changing nature of Indian federalism. As we have seen, Jawaharlal Nehru welcomed the strong center that partition made possible because it was a necessary condition for realizing his goal of industrializing India. He spoke of "occupying the commanding heights" of the economy—basic and heavy industry and infrastructure—what the former Soviet Union referred to as primary industrialization. Consumer goods, the agricultural sector, and the bazaar and service economy remained in private hands. Investment was, for the most part, state-funded and channeled through a planning commission created and chaired by Nehru.

In 1950 Nehru had the cabinet authorize the creation of a planning commission with the prime minister as its *ex officio* chairman. Unknown to the constitution and an "advisory body" without legislative standing, it became the most powerful institution of a "developmental state" and a command economy. A. H. Hanson, who wrote the definitive study of the planning commission in its heyday, characterized its role this way:

> Gradually, the Commission . . . became, in fact, the supreme arbiter of future development in all fields of administration except defence. Not only were the states required to submit projections of

150

their revenue and expenditure budgets for the five years covered by the plan, but they had also to submit their capital programmes for approval. The coordination of state plans, decision on establishment and location of industries, character of education and health programmes and assistance to be given to the states, all came under the overall scrutiny and control of the Commission.[18]

The policy succeeded in the short run but failed in the long run. It achieved a modicum of basic industrialization but the economy grew at an annual rate of only 3.5 percent in the 1960s, in what the late Raj Krishna mockingly called "the Hindu rate of growth." This compared with the double digit growth experienced by the export-oriented East Asian Tigers—South Korea, Taiwan, Hong Kong, and Singapore. Investment in public sector enterprises was massive and furnished India with the heavy industry that characterizes modern economies. But, year after year, public sector enterprises operated at a loss, showing themselves incapable of generating the surpluses needed for economic growth.

By 1991, when India changed course, the system was literally broke. The planning commission had no public funds to invest and India could not pay its current account balance. The crisis in India's "socialist" economy coincided with and was reinforced by the collapse of the Soviet Union, its client states, and their socialist economies, events that were perceived as the victory of market economies over planned economies. India changed course.

The radical reduction of public investment by the center created a need for private investment to replace it that was quickly met by the more enterprising state governments. As Raja Chelliah put it: "The relative spheres of the two levels of the government have been thrown into flux. The scope for real decentralization of economic power has been greatly increased and new vistas have opened for creative and innovative activities by the subnational level of government."[19]

Rob Jenkins added another dimension by observing that "when the center, due to economic reforms, gave up its vast discretionary power over industrial licensing, the states became the crucial point of contact for entrepreneurs."[20] State chief ministers began to play leading roles in what we have called India's emergent "federal market economy."[21] State chief ministers could be found in New York, Chicago and Dallas, Frankfurt, London, and Tokyo, as well as in Davos, convincing investors of the opportunities and incentives available in their respective states. Whether led by high-tech reformers such as Andhra's Chandrababu Naidu or market converts such as Bengal's Communist chief minister, Jyoti Basu, the more enterprising states became the engines of economic liberalization and growth. Although much remains to be remedied and accomplished, by 2007, India's GDP grew by 9.6 percent, thanks in large measure to state-level initiatives and entrepreneurship.

Political conditions of the new federalism: From a one-party dominant to a multiparty system

Another important condition for a new federalism was the transformation of the party system from one dominated by a single party, Congress, to a federalized multiparty system. Congress entered the independence era with a huge amount of political capital from its active leadership during the nationalist era. From Independence in 1947 until the ninth national election in 1989, Congress, with two exceptions,[22] was India's dominant party. Its dominance in most state legislatures as well as in the central parliament enabled it to manage policy at both the center and in the states. Party political power countered the constitutional division of function. So, for example, agriculture and land revenue were state subjects, but the leadership for land reform was provided by Nehru in his role as the national leader of the Congress Party. Facing a divided opposition in a first-past-the-post electoral system, Congress was able to win about 70 percent of the seats with roughly 45 percent of the vote in India's first three national elections.

However, the year 1989 was a watershed. For the first time since independence, a national election resulted in a hung parliament in which no party won a majority. This event marked the end of the one-party-dominant system and majority governments and the beginning of a multiparty system of coalition governments.

The multiparty system was "federalized" by the rise of regional parties. State parties such as the Dravida Munnetra Kazagam, (DMK), in the state of Tamil Nadu (formerly Madras), the Telegu Desam Party (TDP) in the state of Andhra Pradesh, and other state parties, began to play a key role in the formation of coalition governments *at the center*, and in the making of policy.

In the tenth national election in 1991, it became apparent that state parties were gaining on national parties. The national parties, of which the Congress and the Hindu nationalist Bharatiya Janata Party (BJP), were by far the largest, together won 78 percent of the seats and 76 percent of the votes. By the 2004 election the share of the vote garnered by national parties had dropped to 63 percent and their seats to 67 percent. In contrast, both the vote and seat shares held by regional parties had risen between 1991 and 2004 from 16 to 29 percent. It is these changed percentages that enable us to speak of a federalized multiparty system as a key component in the new federalism.

State chief ministers push back: Reshaping federal consciousness

If a new federalism in the form of a federal market economy and a federalized multiparty system did not come into being until the 1990s, it was not for want of trying by state leaders provoked by Prime Minister Indira Gandhi's arbitrary and authoritarian actions.

State-level opposition became visible as early as 1969, three years after she was chosen by the "syndicate"—an informal collective of weighty Congress state leaders led by Kamaraj Nadar of Tamil Nadu—to succeed Lal Bahadur Shastri, Jawaharlal Nehru's successor, as prime minister. In August 1969, she successfully defied syndicate domination by having her candidate, V. V. Giri, elected president of India over Sanjiva Reddy, the Congress candidate picked by the syndicate. By November, the Congress split, with Indira Gandhi leading a majority faction, the Congress-I (for Indira), that went on to electoral success in both the 1970 state assembly and the national election of 1971.

After Indira Gandhi returned to power in 1980 following her emergency rule (1975–77) and the Janata Party government that turned her out of office (1977–79), Bhagwan D. Dua could say:

> [She] perceived the security and durability of a chief minister as more of a threat than an assurance to the continuity of her paramount powers, made and unmade chief ministers and undermined the operation of the Indian federal system in particular, and the Indian political system in general. [She] operated with a different calculus of power to ensure (1) that there was sufficient factionalism in the Congress-ruled states so that the Congress provincial leaders could not dispense with her mediating ploys; and (2) that no state chief developed a local power base strong enough to challenge her supremacy or circumvent a smooth dynastic succession to her son [Rajiv Gandhi] to the office of prime minister.[23]

It is not surprising that the movement to redo India's federal constitutional design arose in the first instance in Tamil Nadu. Its history of resistance to northern Sanskritic language and culture was personalized in the Justice Party's anti-Brahman movement in the 1920s and later under E. V. Ramaswami Naicker ("Periyar" or Great Sage). As India approached independence, Periyar called for a sovereign

Dravidistan, a state composed of those who shared Dravidian culture and languages in Madras, Kerala, and today's Andhra and Karnataka. His anti-Brahmanism went beyond challenging the fact that 3 percent of Madras's population—the Brahmans—occupied 70 percent of the high-level posts in government; to trashing the *Laws of Manu* (the *ur* text of the purity and pollution caste hierarchy); to creating reservations ("communal government orders") in government jobs and universities for lower castes; to opposition to the Sanskrit-based northern language of Hindi being taught in the schools of Madras; to a retelling of the great Hindu epic, the *Ramayana*, so that Ravana, a southern hero-king is the conqueror of Rama, the northern hero-king, and Sita, Rama's wife, Ravana's willing paramour, not Rama's devoted faithful wife.[24]

By 1967, the DMK under Annadurai had transformed itself from a secessionist movement[25] to a well-established regional party that could win a landside victory over the Congress. "Anna" died in 1969 and was succeeded by another film writer and director, M. Karunanidhi. One of his first acts was to set up the Rajamannar Committee on Center–State Relations.[26] Its report called for the radical transformation of center–state relations, including creating an interstate council to advise parliament on all decisions of national importance or that affect one or more states, abolishing articles 249, 356, and 357 which allowed the president (acting, of course, on behalf of the government of the day) to dissolve state governments and place them under the central government, and transferring certain crucial items from the central list of legislative powers to the state list.

It took a decade under Indira Gandhi's centralized rule, including two years under the Emergency (1975–77), for Tamil Nadu's efforts to gain a footing in other states. In 1978, the CPI-M government of West Bengal published a statement critical of center– state relations.[27] Five years later, in 1983, the Janata government of Karnataka, under the dynamic leadership of Ramakrishna Hegde, held a highly visible

seminar on center–state relations that helped to put reform of the constitutional balance of power between the central and state governments on the national agenda.[28] When Punjab's Akali Dal-led government followed Hegde's lead by calling for a national commission on center–state relations, Indira Gandhi tried to preempt the issue by doing just that, thereby taking the wind out of the opposition sails, and making the inquiry to an extent the creature of government.

The interventions of opposition chief ministers intensified the rising drumbeat of criticism that placed the federal question front and center. Indira Gandhi, now re-established and somewhat chastened was forced to respond. On 24 March, 1983 she called for a commission to examine center–state relations and in June asked Rajinder Singh Sarkaria, a retired supreme court justice from Punjab, to head it.[29]

Momentous events soon followed, all relevant to the federal story: the rise of violence, including an insurrectionary movement in Punjab; Operation Blue Star (3–6 June, 1984), an assault ordered by Indira Gandhi on the Golden Temple, the Sikh's holiest shrine, by the Indian Army to capture and kill Jarnail Singh Bhindranwale, the leader of the Khalistan rebellion; and Indira Gandhi's assassination by trusted Sikh bodyguards with automatic weapons on 31 October, 1984 while walking in her garden at No. 1 Safdarjung Road.

It was not until 1988 toward the end of Rajiv Gandhi's prime ministership that the commission submitted its 1,600-page final report.[30] It contained 247 recommendations but none that fundamentally challenged the center–state status quo with respect to the distribution of legislative authority between the center and the states, the role of governors or the use of article 356. The efforts of the states to compel the center via constitutional amendment to change the balance of power between the center and the states had raised consciousness but come to naught in their stated objective. We have shown, however, that the federal system *was* ultimately transformed in the 1990s, not by constitutional amendment but by a shift from a planned to a "federal market economy" and from a one-party dominant to a "federalized multiparty system."

The transformation is illustrated by the access coalition politics has given enterprising state chief ministers and their governments to central government bureaucratic networks that manage procedure and policy. Aseema Sinha has shown that, in 1999 and 2000, regional parties accounted for 24 and 23 percent of shares in national cabinet membership,[31] and that they are likely to hold a substantial number of key ministries. Their insider status, she argues, gives them access to information and opportunities that had previously been unavailable to them. The need for their support to maintain the coalition's viability means that they can influence, sometimes disproportionately, policy decisions and the allocation of resources in federalized central governments. On the negative side, the chronic political weakness of the lead parties in coalitions can make it possible for state parties, even those with few seats, to practice extortion.

There is a question mark that hovers over what appears to be a well-established federalized multiparty system. The dominant party system of the Nehru-Gandhi eras depended on Congress winning 40 percent or more of the vote to claim 60 percent or better of parliamentary seats. Similarly, the viability of the federalized multi-party system has depended for its effectiveness on the two largest national parties, Congress and BJP, whose organizations are built to address a national electorate, being able to win enough seats/votes between them to overshadow the state parties.

To do so, the Congress and the BJP separately need to average between 25 to 33 percent of the vote in the typically three- and four-cornered first-past-the-post contests for parliamentary seats. If they drop below those levels in three- and four-cornered contests they will not be able to win the plurality of seats they need to form and lead coalition governments that rely on the participation or backing of state parties. As we

have shown, over the past 15 years state parties have increased their share of votes and seats from 16 to 29 percent, percentages that come close to threatening the capacity of the two largest national parties to form governing coalitions. Will the center hold? Will the Congress or BJP be able to capture a high enough proportion of the votes and seats in the face of the challenge from state parties to maintain the viability of India's federalized multiparty system?

Beyond the new federalism? The transformations of fiscal federalism

Our story about the transformations of fiscal federalism in India starts with the finance commission that lies at its heart. The principles the commission invokes to distribute the federally collected taxes among the states are central to defining the nature of the federal system. Shall all regions be brought to an equal level? Shall the more prosperous states subsidize the less prosperous? Or shall the allocation of revenue reward effort, fiscal discipline, economic growth? In 2001, chief ministers of the more prosperous and disciplined states challenged distribution by population and level of development. Their challenge was encouraged by the spirit of the new market economy. In consequence, they modified the operation of the finance commission.

The constituent assembly framed provisions that made the union government the collecting agent for most of the state governments' revenues. In accepting article 246 and its seventh schedule dividing legislative power, including the power to tax and spend, into three lists—union, state, and concurrent—the states accepted not having tax heads adequate to meet expenditures because they knew that the financial provisions of the constitution would "resemble very closely their predecessors in the 1935 Act."[32] The Government of India Act of 1935 included a finance commission whose track record under the Raj made it clear that the revenues collected by the center would be divided fairly between itself and the [then] provinces.[33]

From the first finance commission until the eleventh, the guiding principle of its division of revenues was "need," i.e., redistributing revenues from the richer to the poorer states with a view to the latter's "development"— including infrastructure, investment in human and physical capital and remunerative employment. According to Austin, the constituent assembly provided that "the most lucrative tax heads [income, corporate, excise duties] should be levied and collected by the union and distributed among the provinces according to their need." In addition, the union was to distribute some of the proceeds from its own revenues, or make grants-in-aid to the provincial governments "again on the basis of need."[34] "If federation means anything," said Pandit Kunzru, "it means there should be a transfer of wealth from the richer to the poorer provinces."

The first finance commission recommended that revenues be distributed in ways that "attempt to lessen the inequalities between states" and the second that 10 percent of divisible revenue should be distributed on the basis of collection and the remaining 90 percent according to population.[35] The agent of this policy, the institution expected to realize distribution of revenue according to need, was a finance commission. Appointed every five years, finance commissions were to make recommendations to the president (and thus the government of the day) indicating the share of the union and the states, respectively, in the divisible taxes and to prescribe the principles for the distribution of the states' shares among the states themselves. The expectation was that the recommendations in finance commission reports would be accepted "without question." And so they were until the year 2000, when the Eleventh Finance Commission submitted its report to the president. It is a commentary on the solidarity of the consensus on socialist economic policy, and/or on the durability of ingrained bureaucratic habits, that the there was no earlier challenge to the unquestioned

nature of the reports when so many of the opposition governments were challenging other aspects of the federal pattern.

Chandra Babu Naidu, Andhra Pradesh's entrepreneurial, high-tech chief minister and a key player in Atal Behari Vajpayee's National Democratic Alliance coalition government, led the prosperous, high-performing states from the south and west in a challenge to the Eleventh Finance Commission's Report. As the influential *Business Line* put it:

> The recommendations of the Eleventh Finance Commission [EFC] appear to be heavily loaded in favour of States whose level of effort in terms of taxation, development and Plan performance has continued to be poor … The issue of devolution of funds to the States is snowballing into a major controversy between the Centre and the States.
>
> The acceptance by the centre of the EFC's recommendations militate against the spirit of fiscal federalism and the concept of cooperative federalism advocated in recent years. *All southern states and Maharashtra and Gujarat are at the receiving end of the recommendations and are, obviously, upset.* [emphasis in original][36]

Business Line went on to warn that "the entire framework of fiscal cooperation between the Centre and the States is now out of alignment …Many states may worry about whether they should be more efficient in the national interest if the potential gains are all to be immediately redistributed."[37]

Writing in the spirit of the new market culture spawned by the economic reforms of 1991, *Business Line* also asked whether the finance commissions' concept of equity— taking from the richer, efficient states and giving to the poorer, profligate states—had become obsolete. The "normative and prescriptive" method of assessing post-devolution state deficits (sometimes called "gap-filling") "appears to be loaded in favour of fiscally-imprudent States."[38] In the new era popular perception, the EFC seemed to be rewarding the improvident *bimaru*[39] or sick states (Bihar,

Madhya Pradesh, Rajasthan, Uttar Pradesh) of the north at the expense of the six prudent, disciplined southern and western states. From the latter's perspective, they were being penalized for their successes and the *bimaru* states were being rewarded for their failures. Particularly galling was the EFC's continued reliance on population as a metric of "need," a policy that seemed to reward the *bimaru* states for their failure to control their libidos and the consequent population growth while penalizing the southern and western states for controlling theirs.

In the context of challenging population as a measure of need, *Business Line* called for a new concept of equity based on a "Rawlsian approach to justice" that treated efficiency as part of equity. It is only when some states are more efficient, *Business Line* argued, that, overall, "the income of the economy can be larger, and potentially larger resources can be transferred to the worst-off regions."[40]

Naidu's initiative was indicative of the changing federal balance of power in favor of the states under the new federalism. The BJP-led National Democratic Alliance government responded with alacrity to Naidu's challenge to the convention that finance commission reports, like supreme court judgments, are the law of the land. Many sage heads warned that if this were not so, the finance commission's capacity to make fiscal federalism work in India would be hopelessly politicized and the system ruined. In retrospect, this seemingly well-grounded fear did not prove justified.

The NDA government responded positively to the Naidu initiative for the good reason that the stability of its government was dependent on the support of the TDP, Naidu's party. Although the EFC had delivered its report to the president, the government of India charged the commission with the task of writing a supplementary report. It should address the possibility of making finance commission grants to an extent dependent on the kind of fiscal discipline and efficient use of resources which the southern and western states had exhibited. The commission was asked to make

its grants conditional, to "draw a monitorable fiscal reform programme aimed at reduction of revenue deficit of the States and to recommend the manner in which the grants to States to cover the assessed deficit in their non-plan revenue account may be linked to the progress in implementing the programme."[41] The commission responded by recommending that 15 percent should be deducted from the grants allocated to deficit states, that the government match this amount, and that the total sum should be placed in an incentive fund for which all the states, both deficit and non-deficit, could compete by showing progress.

The charge by the NDA government to the EFC and the modifications it made represented a startling change in the way finance commission reports were perceived and treated. Previously, they were thought of as insulated from, and immune to political forces. The EFC's supplementary report reflected the new federal balance between the states and the center and the inadequacy of the finance commission's concepts of social justice and equity. The goal of equalization had seemed to be integral to the finance commission as a constitutional body dealing with the practical meaning of federalism. To impose conditions on the allocation of revenues seemed alien to its mission. But times had changed and with them the mission of finance commissions.

The finance commission's move toward merit and conditionality altered the dominant discourse. It highlighted the fact that the 1991 economic liberalization and the consequent shift from a planned to a market economy had changed priorities from "need" and social justice to effective use of resources and economic growth. The change was not uncontested; influential commentators questioned whether subjecting finance commission allocations to conditionality were compatible with Article 289 of the constitution.[42]

Paradoxically, the Naidu-led challenge to the Report of the Eleventh Finance Commission (EFC) resulted in the unintended consequence of strengthening the center's recently found role as a regulatory state.[43] The shift from plan to market brought about by the 1991 and subsequent economic reforms had the effect of dismantling an interventionist state and contributing to the creation of a regulatory state, a shift that seemed to strengthen the states against the center. But regulation too is a form of control. In the case of fiscal federalism, regulation took the form of the Fiscal Responsibility and Budget Management Act of 2003 or FRBM, the principles of which attempt to implement the performance clause of the EFC-amended report. Another instrument strengthening the center against the states is a stealth-like return to the interventionist strategy via centrally sponsored schemes (CSSs). To the extent that the centrally sponsored schemes induct the policy priorities of the center into policy priorities of the state governments, they give the center a strong counterforce to the new federalism.

The main aim of the 2004 FRBM legislation was to eliminate the center's revenue and fiscal deficits by 2009.[44] The states were persuaded, by the threat of losing the debt waiver facility offered by the Twelfth Finance Commission, hurriedly to pass similar state legislation, and to specify steps that would lead to the deficit reductions goal.[45] The states are now subject to two kinds of central regulation: the regulation imposed by the finance commission conditionalities on central transfers to the states and the constraint of the self-imposed FRBM legislation. Critics from across the political spectrum fear that meeting the deficit elimination targets will suffocate social expenditure and new development initiatives.[46]

Centrally sponsored schemes (CSS) have become a powerful instrument of central intervention in the states. They are changing the federal balance of power by making it possible for the center to assume functions on the state list. When the center makes transfers to support the states' five-year plans, that is, freshly introduced developmental projects, it can do so via normal central assistance (NCA), i.e., block grants that may be spent at the discretion of the state. This funding is plainly under state control. It can also make transfers via CSS. The latter grants are for a specific purpose; the state must spend them as designated. The most conspicuous instance of such a scheme is the National Rural Employment Guarantee Act launched by the Congress-led United Progressive Alliance (UPA) government soon after it took power in 2004 and "hailed as a major initiative in the Government of India's commitment to providing an economic safety net to India's rural poor."[47]

CSS make it possible for the center to shape state policy preferences and priorities even in fields that are constitutionally placed under state jurisdiction, such as education and health.[48] State ministries, departments, local bodies, and externally funded autonomous state societies and district societies registered under the Societies Registration Act become de facto agents of the center in ways that subvert state autonomy. Needless to say, the states prefer block grants that they control whereas the center favors specific purpose assistance, which implements the Center's priorities *du jour*.

The struggle between the states and the center over control of funds to implement their respective policy preferences is a longstanding one. In 1969, the National Development Council, a forum of state chief ministers and central government ministers, determined that CSS should not exceed one-sixth of the amount to be given as NCA. CSS would be an exception, to be used to fund projects of national or regional importance that fall in the domain of the states. The limit was observed for a few years, but soon CSS expanded enormously, outgrowing the level of NCA assistance.

This growth was not the result of any consensus achieved between the center and the states. There was no second pronouncement by the National Development Council to ratchet up the level of acceptable CSS. Rather, it appears to have been the result of a silent, subterranean process that Rob Jenkins in another context has characterized as "stealth."

157

Central government officials, in alliance with state-level departments or civil society associations (NGOs) that share program objectives and/or funding have acted below the radar screen of the constitutional distribution of powers to "normalize" the use of CSS. By 2005–06 CSS funding stood at Rs 54,580 crores and NCA funding at Rs 15,451 crores of central government plan expenditures.[49] As one observer put it: "These schemes have provided a major financial lever to the central government to change states' choices in these subjects, which are constitutionally almost exclusively their mandates,"[50] that is, of the state governments, not the center. Whether Article 282 of the constitution authorizing the union [or a state] to make grants "for any public purpose" validates CSS grants that encroach on or displace activities that are given on the state list in the seventh schedule seems to be the current frontier in the ongoing struggle between the center and the states in India's federal system.[51]

Conclusion

In our examination of the major characteristics of Indian federalism and of the dynamics and crises of negotiated or bargaining federalism, we have contrasted two ideal typical versions of federalism, a relatively centralized "old" and a relatively decentralized "new" federalism. We then examined the provenances of the models of federalism and the changing conditions that led from about 1990 onward to a shift from the old to the new federalism, the replacement of a planned economy by a "federal market economy," and the replacement of a one party dominant by a federalized multiparty system.

As an editorial in the 8 March, 2008 issue of the *Economic and Political Weekly* makes clear, federalism remains at the center of the state formation and policy stories in India. An *EPW* editor inquires, "How federal is the Union budget for 2008–9?" and then proceeds to elaborate the issues:

On the one hand, a mitigation of regional imbalances in development would need a stronger redistributive role for the Union. On the other, many of the areas that call for intervention to realize greater inclusiveness [such as] agriculture, irrigation, local development and health-care . . . are the domain of the states . . . Even in such areas, where the optimal response is much more likely to differ locally, the increase of resources to the states so that they can explore their own solutions, be they private, public or in-between, do not seem to be an option that the Union deems worthy of consideration.[52]

The current condition of federalism is indeed in flux. At the same time, the center, as represented by both the BJP-led NDA and the Congress-led UPA governments, has exploited the relative failure of the states to address the needs of the constituencies at the bottom of the pyramid with development programs. The decline of the interventionist state epitomized by the relative bankruptcy of planning commission public investment has been countered by the rise of a regulatory state epitomized by the center's fiscal monitoring of state revenues and spending via the FRBM of 2003. At the same time, there has been a stealth-like return to an interventionist state via CSS that implement the center's policy preferences in the guise of state programs. Paradoxically, opposition BJP state governments have claimed political capital for successfully implementing Congress' most important CSS, the National Rural Employment Guarantee Act. We are left to ponder whether the CSS should be counted as strengthening the center or the states.

Notes

1 Ashok Chanda, *Federalism in India: A Study of Union–State Relations* (London: Allen & Unwin, 1965), p. 41.
2 See Sir Ivor Jennings, *Some Characteristics of the Indian Constitution* (Madras: Oxford University Press, 1953).

3 See Granville Austin, *The Indian Constitution: Cornerstone of a Nation* (Oxford: Clarendon Press, 1966), pp. 1–25; also Ralph Retzlaff, "The Indian Constituent Assembly and the Problem of Indian Unity," PhD dissertation, Cornell University, 1959.

4 Ram Puniyani. "Social Roots of Partition Process," *Issues in Secular Politics*, Vol 1, No. 2 (11 January, 2002). www.sacw.net, February 2002.

5 Dr. B. R. Ambedkar, known as the "father of the Indian Constitution," preferred to characterize the newly constituted state as "unitary" rather than federal. He explained that the word "union," as in "union of India" in Article 1 of the constitution had been self-consciously chosen over the weaker "federation." Minutes of the Union Constitution Committee, 7 June, 1947, Indian National Archives.

6 Continuity between the 1935 Act and the 1950 Constitution is suggested by the fact that when the Union Powers Committee's report was presented in the constituent assembly by N. G. Ayyangar there was "only a brief debate on union subjects – only the first 37 items of the union list and neither of the other two lists was discussed." See Austin, *The Indian Constitution,* p. 197.

7 These provisions are spelled out in detail in Durga Das Basu, *Shorter Constitution of India*, 13th edn (Agra: Wadhwa, 2001). The provisions of article 246 are dealt with on pp. 1164–71 and the seventh schedule listing the subjects specified in the three lists of article 246, along with extensive citations of relevant cases, are given on pp. 1,732–1,826.

8 Members are elected by the legislative assembly of each state. Elections in the state legislatures are held by using single transferable votes with proportional representation. In 2006, with the addition of Chhattisgarh, Jharkhand and Uttarakhand, and one member from Pondicherry and 12 nominated members, the Rajya Sabha had 242 members. Its power over money bills, which must originate in the Lok Sabha, is consultative; it has no power to dismiss the prime minister or any minister, such authority being the sole prerogative of the Lok Sabha. In all other respects, the two houses of parliament are equal.

9 Justice A. M. Ahmadi, "Federalism Revisited," in Pran Chopra, *The Supreme Court versus the Constitution; A Challenge to Federalism* (New Delhi: Sage, 2006), p. 147. As Dr. B. R. Ambedkar told the Constituent Assembly, "the Federation not being the result of an agreement [among states], no State has the right to secede from it"; Austin, *The Indian Constitution.*

10 Adeney observes that Nehru's and Congress' initial rejection of linguistic reorganization of the Indian states was "a specific extension of the majoritarian nature of of the Indian federation . . . Although Nehru ultimately reversed his position, he did so reluctantly and only after overwhelming pressure from within the Congress"; Katherine Adeney, *Federalism and Ethnic Conflict Regulation in India and Pakistan* (New York: Palgrave Macmillan, 2007), p. 77.

11 Selig Harrison, *India: the Most Dangerous Decades* (Princeton, NJ: University Press, 1960).

12 Sanjib Baruah, *India Against Itself: Assam and the Politics of Nationality* (Philadelphia, PA: University of Pennsylvania Press, 1999), p. 11.

13 Adeney, p. 78.

14 *S. R. Bommai and others v Union of India.* A.I.R. 1994 Supreme Court 1918.

15 Adeney, p. 115 and fn.10, p. 203, says of the Bommai judgment that it "restricts the ability of the center to dismiss state governments without following procedures, such as giving the state government a chance to prove its majority on the floor of the Legislative Assembly . . . this has radically restricted the power of the center to use it."

16 We have discussed land reform in greater detail in Lloyd I. Rudolph and Susanne Hoeber Rudolph, *In Pursuit of Lakshmi: The Political Economy of the Indian State* (Chicago: University Press, 1967), ch. 12; see esp., pp. 314–15.

17 Aseema Sinha has pointed out that under the old federalism, too, the states were able to influence the then much more empowered center; see *The Regional Roots of Developmental Politics in India* (Bloomington, IN: Indiana University Press, 2005), pp. 83–88.

18 Albert H. Hanson, *The Process of Planning: A Study of India's Five Year Plans, 1950–1966* (London: Oxford University Press, 1966), p. 97.

19 Rajah Chelliah, *Towards Sustainable Growth: Essay in Fiscal and Financial Reforms in India* (New Delhi: Oxford University Press, 1996), p. 19.

20 Rob Jenkins, *Democratic Politics and Economic Reform in India* (Cambridge: University Press, 1999), p. 132.

21 See Lloyd I. Rudolph and Susanne Hoeber Rudolph, "The Iconization of Chandrababu: Sharing Sovereignty in India's Federal Market Economy," in Lloyd I. Rudolph and Susanne Hoeber Rudolph, *Explaining Indian Democracy: A Fifty-Year Perspective*, II. *The Realm of Institutions: State Formation and Institutional Change* (New Delhi: Oxford University Press, 2006).

22 The first exception was the fourth national election in 1967, after Nehru's death in May 1964, when his relatively inexperienced daughter, Indira Gandhi, led the party. The second exception was in 1977, the election after Indira Gandhi imposed the "emergency" of 1975–77. Congress lost that election to the Janata Party.

23 Bhagwan D. Dua, "Federalism or Patrimonialism: The Making and Unmaking of Chief Ministers in India," *Asian Survey*, Vol. 25, No. 8 (August 1985), p. 794.

24 For E.V.R. and the non-Brahman movement and the Justice Party, see Eugene F. Irschick, *Politics and Social Conflict in South India: The Non-Brahman Movement and Tamil Separatism, 1916–1929* (Berkeley, CA: University of California Press, 1969) and Robert L. Hardgrave, *The Dravidian Movement* (Bombay: Popular Prakashan, 1965). For Dravidian ideology and politics in Madras, see Marguerite Ross Barnett, *The Politics of Cultural Nationalism in South India* (Princeton, NJ: University Press, 1976). For retelling of the *Ramayana* from a Dravidian perspective, see Lloyd I. Rudolph, "Dravidian Politics in Madras," *Journal of Asian Studies*, Vol. 20, No. 3 (May 1961), pp. 283–97, where, inter alia, Aubrey Menon's best-selling *Ramayana Retold* (London: Chatto & Windus, 1949), is discussed.

25 For other subsequent secessionist movements and violent conflicts in Punjab, Assam, Nagaland, Mizoram, and Kashmir, see the chapter in this volume by Gurharpal Singh. For an excellent discussion of the factors contributing to secessionist conflicts see the chapter in Adeney, "Federal Instability in India," particularly at pp. 114–15 and 120–24. Two principal factors cited by Adeney as contributing to secessionist politics, language and religion, were theorized and examined in Paul R. Brass, *Language, Religion and Politics in North India* (New York: Cambridge University Press, 1974).

26 Government of Tamil Nadu, *Rajamannar Report on Centre–State Relations* (Madras: Inquiry Committee, Government of Tamil Nadu, 1971). The citation is from www.interstate council.nic.in/CHAPTER1.3.htm, accessed 5 February, 2008.

27 Government of West Bengal, *Views on Centre–State Relations* (Calcutta: Department of Information and Cultural Affairs, 1978).

28 Government of Karnataka, *Seminar on Centre–State Relations, Bangalore, 5–7 August, 1983*, organized by the Economic and Planning Council, Government of Karnataka, in association with the Institute for Social and Economic Change, Bangalore and the Centre for Policy Research (New Delhi and Bangalore: Government of Karnataka Press, 1983). See also Sati Sahni, *Center–State Relations: Proceedings of a Meeting of Leaders* (New Delhi: Vikas, 1984).

29 *Indian Express*, 25 March, 1983. The Sarkaria Commission is referenced as Government of India, *Commission on Centre-State Relations*, 2 vols (Delhi: Government of India Press, 1988).

30 For a discussion of the Sarkaria Commission and the Inter-State Council (ISC) established in its wake under article 263 of the constitution by the V. P. Singh government in 1990, see Lawrence Saez, *Federalism Without a Centre* (New Delhi: Sage, 2002). For accounts of the functioning of the ISC, see two articles by V. Venkatesan, "Centre–State Relations: A Blow for Federalism," *Frontline*, Vol. 18, No. 25 (8–21 December, 2001); and "Inter–State Council: A Blow for Federalism," *Frontline*, Vol. 20, No. 19 (13–26 September, 2003).

31 Sinha, p. 87.

32 Austin, p. 226.

33 See Austin, pp. 217–34. The quote is at p. 218 and is from *The Report of the Expert Committee on the Financial Provisions of the Constitution*, para 28. According to M. M. Sury, the finance commission is a feature unique to the Indian constitution, "having no parallel in the existing federal constitutions of the world." M. M. Sury, *Fiscal Federalism in India* (Delhi: Indian Tax Institute, 1998), pp. 80–81.

34 The constitution makes it possible for the union government to provide for grants-in-aid to states that have a deficit on their revenue accounts. Called "gap-filling," such grants-in-aid acquired a bad name because more often than not deficits were the result not of "need"

but rather of wasteful expenditure and weak revenue effort.

35 *Report of the Finance Commission [1952]*, 7, and *Report of the Finance Commission [1957]*, 40, cited in Austin, p. 224.

36 *Business Line*, "Eleventh Finance Commission," 25 August, 2000.

37 *Business Line*, "Report of the Eleventh Finance Commission: Implications and Re-examination," 12 August, 2000.

38 *Business Line*, "Eleventh Finance Commission," 25 August, 2000.

39 *Bimar* means sick in Hindi. The adjective, *bimaru*, is formed out of the initial one or two letters of the backward northern states mentioned in the text.

40 *Business Line*, "Report of the Eleventh Finance Commission," 12 August, 2000.

41 "Explanatory Memorandum as to the action taken on the recommendations made by the 11th Finance Commission Report submitted to the President on 30 August, 2000." www.fincomindia.nic.in/eleventh.ernet.htm, accessed May 2008.

42 Amiya Bagchi, a member of the Commission, dissented from the modified report. Isaac and Kumar argued that the Twelfth Finance Commission exceeded its constitutional brief by proposing conditions on federal transfers. T. M. Thomas Isaac and R. Ramakumar, "Why Do the States not Spend?" *Economic and Political Weekly*, Vol. 46, No. 48 (2 December, 2006), p. 4,972.

43 The shift from an interventionist state to a regulatory state is a principal theme of our article, "Re-doing the Constitutional Design: From the Interventionist to the Regulatory State," in Atul Kohli (ed.), *The Success of India's Democracy* (Cambridge: University Press, 2001).

44 For a critical analysis of the FRBMA, see C. P. Chandrasekhar and Jayati Ghosh, "Fiscal Responsibility versus Democratic Accountability," *Business Line*, 27 July, 2004.

45 Among the steps were limits to state government guarantees on debt; and limits to overall liabilities that could be incurred; Isaac and Ramakumar, p. 4971. Communist-ruled Bengal refused to pass FRBM legislation.

46 Isaac and Ramakumar, p. 4,973.

47 Arnab Basu *et al.*, "The National Rural Guarantee Act of India, 2005," in *Oxford Companion to Economics in India* (New Delhi: Oxford University Press, 2007), p. 1.

48 Subhas Chandra Garg, "Transformation of Central Grants to States: Growing Conditionality and Bypassing State Budgets," *Economic and Political Weekly*, Vol. 46, No. 48 (2 December, 2006), p. 4,982. See also J. V. R. Prasada Rao, "State Participation in the Centrally Sponsored Schemes," *Family Welfare*, 5 May, 2003.

49 Garg, "Transformation," Table 4, p. 4,981.

50 Garg, "Transformation," p. 4,982.

51 See B. P. R. Vithal and M. L. Shastry, *Fiscal Federalism in India* (New Delhi: Oxford University Press, 2001), p. 229.

52 "Is the Union Budget a Federal Budget?" *Economic and Political Weekly*, Vol. 43, No. 10 (8 March, 2008).

Part III

The judiciary

11

India's judiciary

Imperium in imperio?

Shylashri Shankar

We do not want to create an "imperium in imperio" and at the same time we want to give the judiciary ample independence so that it can act without fear or favor.

(Speech by B. R. Ambedkar, India, *Constituent Assembly Debates*, Vol. 8, Book 3, p. 397)

No court in the world—not the House of Lords, nor the US Supreme Court put together—has such vast jurisdiction, wide powers and final authority as the Indian Supreme Court.

(Iyer 1987), *Our Courts on Trial*, New Delhi: B. R. Publishing, p. 38)

Introduction

India's supreme court is, to paraphrase George Gadbois, the "most powerful court in the world", having virtually become an *imperium in imperio*, an order within an order. In the past two decades, the higher judiciary transformed constitutionally non-justiciable economic, and social rights to basic education, health, food, and shelter, among others, into legally enforceable rights.[1] In a famous judgment giving all children the right to elementary education, the court said that a right could be treated as fundamental even if it were not present in the justiciable section of the constitution.[2]

According to economist Jean Drèze, the introduction of cooked midday meals in primary schools would not have happened without the supreme court cracking the whip. The Indian courts illustrate scholarly characterizations of this century as the global age of "decline and fall of parliamentary sovereignty," the "global expansion of judicial power," and even a "juristocracy."[3]

How did India's judiciary become so powerful? How does it use its power? Does it legitimate the majority coalition's decisions, as American political scientist Robert Dahl[4] famously said about the American supreme court? Or do the judges diverge from the ruling party's political preferences as they discover and use broad powers of judicial review to constitutionally protect new rights? Have India's courts strayed into legislative and executive space or have they played a supporting role to the other branches of the state? The chapter addresses these questions.

On 25 June, 1975, Prime Minister Indira Gandhi suspended Article 21 and imprisoned hundreds of people (mainly political opponents and members of civil society groups) under an executive order proclaiming a state of emergency. When these detentions were challenged, nine high courts rejected the constitutionality of the order. The supreme court, except for the lone dissenting voice of Justice Hans Raj Khanna, overruled the lower courts and, in the process, experienced a dent in its authority for allowing Indira Gandhi and her associates to violate the civil liberties of citizens.[5] Legal scholars argue that the entry of courts into new domains was a redemptive move by the apex court to atone for its capitulation during the emergency.[6] Most agree that the genesis of the judiciary's activity on social rights can be traced to the immediate post-emergency era when Justices P. N. Bhagwati and Krishna Iyer evolved user-friendly approaches like public interest litigation (PIL).

I argue that the history of judicial activity in India is predominantly a story of judicial pragmatism rather than activism (defined as overturning laws), evident in the weak compliance mechanisms favored by judges who are aware of their dependence on political and bureaucratic wings of the state. The judiciary remains, to paraphrase political scientist Gerald Rosenberg, a hollow hope because of constraints imposed by institutional, ideological, and structural factors.[7]

The chapter first charts the path to power of the judiciary through an analysis of the constitutional role envisaged for (and appropriated) by the supreme court. I argue that the judiciary's growing clout was a product of three factors: the ambiguity of the constitution on the extent of judicial power; a crisis of legitimacy induced by court-curbing moves of the executive in the 1970s, which coincided with a third factor, the fragmentation of political power in the 1990s.

The second section assesses the use by judges of their expanded powers. Scholars like Tate and Vallinder contend that among parliamentary democracies a high degree of party competition within the legislature tends to invite challenges from the judiciary because these systems produce weak governing coalitions.[8] The evidence, culled from an analysis of judgments on religious freedom and social rights, suggests that the relationship between courts and political configurations in a parlia-mentary system is less coherent. Having appropriated the power of judicial review and independence through its own judgments,[9] the court has struggled to find ways to exercise the power meaningfully.

I argue that the categorization of Indian courts as activist and over-activist are premature if we assess their track record in health and education. Like Choudhary and Hunter, I define activism in quantitative terms: the more decisions that find government actions unconstitutional, the more activist the courts.[10] While the supreme court has expanded its power of judicial review, it has neither overturned laws frequently nor become a habitual policymaker. Rather, judges have preferred to adopt what Tushnet[11] calls "weak remedies," such as setting up committees and negotiation channels to deal with negligence by the state. The court's reluctance to overturn legislative actions or even penalize the government stems from its institutional rules emphasizing restraint, confirmed in the words of a former justice that the higher courts "have unwittingly become conscience keepers of the status-quo except in exceptional cases."[12]

The final section highlights the critical challenges faced by the institution. The irony is that the court's power to have an impact on the lives of citizens rests with the same government and bureaucracy that judges and others chastise for having been negligent. In the last five years or so, because of structural and political factors, the judiciary (particularly the high courts) has become an overseer of governance, in addition to its task of balancing citizen's rights with the state's goals of social justice and harmonising relations with minorities. I argue that the recent spurt in judicial activity in areas reserved for executive and legislative actions is an alarming development that will undercut the court's authority because of its inability to deliver on the content of the right.

The path to judicial power

The characteristics of a powerful judiciary include the authority to review legislation and relative immunity from political machinations. There are two sets of theories on how courts become powerful. Juristocracy theories argue that political elites transfer power to judges in hopes that they will be conservative and/or protective of rights.[13] Conversely, others attribute judicial empowerment to the legal choices of judges.[14] India's experience validates the second theory; the supreme court seized autonomy by appropriating (through its judgments) the power to appoint itself; political elites did not transfer power to judges.

The Constitution of India (1950) established a federal republic with a parliamentary system, a strong central government and a unified judiciary under an apex court. The supreme court, which is on top of a three-tiered system, has original jurisdiction over disputes between the center and the states, and between states; appellate function over criminal and civil courts involving substantial questions of law; advisory functions on matters referred by the president; and special leave jurisdiction that allows it to hear any issue in politics, except for issues concerning the armed forces. At the intermediate appellate level, the high court stands at the head of a state's judicial administration.[15] The decision of the supreme court is binding on all courts in India (article 141) and non-compliance invites contempt of court. Litigants can also approach a parallel statutory system, the Lok Adalat (People's Court), to resolve disputes in a conciliatory manner.

Seizing the power of judicial review

The constitution's ambiguity on whether it explicitly endorsed parliamentary sovereignty, implicitly allowed judicial review, or did both arose from struggles in the constituent assembly (CA) on the best way to ensure a separation of powers among the executive, legislature, and judiciary.[16] The CA ultimately emphasized balance rather than checks but

agreed with the chairman of the drafting committee, B. R. Ambedkar, that the constitution had to walk the fine line between creating a Leviathan and giving the judiciary adequate power to act without fear or favor. The majority decided that the supreme court's powers would be determined by law, i.e., those made by parliament rather than by the constitution, but left room for ambiguity on the extent of judicial scrutiny of legislation, the powers of the federal court, the appointments and removal process, and whether judges could take post-retirement jobs.

Scholars argue that federalism (which provides built-in opportunities for jurisdictional conflict), a written constitution (which provides judges with the basis for rights-based decisions), judicial independence, and a competitive party system (which could produce weak governing coalitions) all invite challenges from the judiciary.[17] India has a federal setup, a written constitution, de jure judicial independence, and, in the late 1980s, shifted from one-party rule to coalition governments—all the structural conditions that can produce judicial review.

An empirical examination, however, shows that the court incrementally appropriated the power to review legislation irrespective of the political or structural conditions. The supreme court enshrined judicial review by creating a basic structure doctrine in 1973. The judgment, which was a response to the twenty-fourth and twenty-fifth amendments reducing the level of judicial review of legislation, held that parliament could not alter the basic structure or framework of the constitution—a structure that was undefined but knowable only by the court.[18] This occurred when the Congress party had a dominant majority in parliament, and the executive exercised influence on judicial appointments. The basic structure doctrine has been called anti-democratic, used "mostly to protect judicial power" by giving the final say to an unelected body of judges.[19]

But the use of the basic structure doctrine in later judgments was "haphazard" and "not doctrinal or a general principle";[20] definitional problems plagued concepts like secularism, separation of powers, equality, rule of law and judicial review, which were seen as part of the basic structure.[21] In *S. R. Bommai vs Union of India*, the court upheld the president's authority, in the aftermath of the destruction of the Babri Masjid mosque in Ayodhya, to dismiss three elected state governments for failing to comply with the secular provisions of the constitution, but, as Rajeev Dhavan notes, a "clear judicial statement of what constitutes secularism continues to elude us."[22] The failure to evolve a consistent jurisprudence on the basic structure has become a recurrent theme in how the court exercises its powers.

The Indian experience also challenges the argument that strong single-party majorities produce weak courts. The supreme court fought with Prime Minister Jawaharlal Nehru's government (a single-party majority government) in the 1950s and 1960s on the extent to which social reform legislation, including property and land reforms, could impinge on fundamental rights. After Nehru's death in 1964, the judiciary clashed with the governments of Lal Bahadur Shastri and Indira Gandhi over populist measures such as the nationalization of banks and abolition of privy purses. The supreme court appropriated the power of judicial review through decisions in the Golak Nath, bank nationalization and privy purses cases.[23] In response, and unlike her father, Indira Gandhi set out to pack the court with "committed judges," prompting legal analysts to hark back wistfully to the Nehruvian era as a period when the court cautiously expanded its own authority while maintaining a balance of power with the other two branches. In the cabinet, Nehru had successfully fought against the worst anti-judiciary sentiment, saying that a socialist program could be pursued without striking at the judiciary's roots.[24]

Clashes with the executive and parliament

The court's growing clout evolved from clashes with parliament over the extent of judicial review of some of the 104 constitutional amendments. The first amendment inserted a ninth schedule into the constitution, providing that any law placed in the schedule would be immune to challenges asserting violation of fundamental rights. The parliament got into the habit of inserting controversial laws in this schedule which, as Granville Austin (1999) points out,[25] would develop into a predilection for undermining judicial powers broadly and even attacks on the judiciary as an institution during the prime ministership of Indira Gandhi (1966–77; 1980–84).[26] But, as Sathe rightly notes, the Supreme Court exercised "maximum restraint" in using the basic structure doctrine against constitutional amendments and was "reticent" in striking down an amendment.[27]

Crisis of legitimacy

Judicial review was severely curtailed by the Indira Gandhi regime in the period preceding and during the emergency (1975–77). The forty-second amendment in 1976 excluded constitutional amendments from the purview of judicial review.

The judiciary had some respite during the Janata Party coalition (1977–80), which offered return transfers to those judges who had been summarily transferred during the emergency and reinstated the convention of appointing the most senior judge as chief justice. Emboldened by these moves, the court reasserted judicial scrutiny (assessed against the basic structure doctrine) of amendments and laws inserted into the ninth schedule after 24 April, 1973 (the date of the Kesavananda judgment), saying that the constitution allowed parliament only "limited amending power."[28] In 2007, a nine-judge constitution bench reiterated the right of the court to review the law in the ninth schedule.[29] Although several legal observers and the media criticized the ruling "for weakening constitutional protection given to progressive laws" and having devastating results for judicial accountability, the court's self-aggrandized power of judicial review is now firmly part of the basic structure of the constitution.[30]

Judicial independence and political influence

The apex court's judgments seizing independence in appointments coincided with the fragmentation of political power in parliament as minority and coalition rule became the norm. Judicial independence refers to the autonomy of courts (institutionally and personally) from political influences.

India's courts had some degree of institutional autonomy written into the constitution. Only parliament has the power to remove high court and supreme court judges; no judge has been impeached so far.[31] The constitution empowered the president (acting on the advice of the prime minister and cabinet) to appoint judges of the supreme court and the high courts, after consultation with the CJI and CJs of the lower courts (articles 124 and 217). But consultation did not mean concurrence of the CJI, since it was "a dangerous proposition" to allow the CJI "a veto" because it would amount to a "transfer of authority."[32]

Initially, judges agreed with Ambedkar's intent to keep the judiciary from appointing its own members. When the Congress party led by Indira Gandhi returned to power in 1980, several high court judges were transferred, while the renewal or non-renewal of tenures of others was rumored to have involved political considerations. Petitions questioning these transfers were decided in the first judges case: a four-judge majority held that a judge's consent was not necessary for his transfer but that such transfers ought not to be punitive, and that the CJI's concurrence was not mandatory.[33]

A decade later, a majority led by Justice Verma reversed the ruling by holding that the CJI's views on appointments and transfers must be supreme for independence and separation of powers to operate.[34] The third judges case outlined the process of consultation, which now included the CJI and four of his most senior colleagues. Thus, structurally, the Indian supreme court made itself virtually independent of the executive and legislature with regard to entry procedures.[35]

However, the extent of political influence on the judiciary depended on the strength and predilections of the prime minister. During Nehru's leadership, the executive "by and large respected the wishes of the Chief Justice,"[36] who had "virtually a veto over appointments, a result of the conventions and practices of the time, and the Chief Justice's strength of character."[37] But Indira Gandhi even abandoned the seniority convention in choosing a chief justice in 1973 and 1977.[38] The selection process allegedly involved "communal and political considerations,"[39] leading to "havoc with judicial decisions in crucial and sensitive cases."[40] Some of the judges appointed during the Janata regime "would not have sat on the bench had the Congress (I) been in office at that time and vice versa."[41]

So, when the political actor was strong (single-party majority), prepared to take on the courts, and had a policy agenda (as Indira Gandhi's government did), the supreme court was more constrained by the political milieu. When the political actor was strong and had a policy, but was not prepared to strike at the court's autonomy (the Nehruvian regime), or if there was a weak governing coalition/minority government (post-1988 governments), the supreme court had more room to maneuver. A variation on this is that single party-dominated political systems will accord courts less independence because of the governing party's expectation that it will continue to win elections, whereas competitive parties favor greater judicial independence in order to preserve a party's legislative gains made while in office after it has lost power.[42]

169

This could explain why the 1977–80 Janata Party (coalition) government removed some of the court-curbing amendments of the previous government, emboldening the court to reintroduce due process in 1978, and appropriate vast powers over administrative action. Even the timing of the judgments that expanded judicial autonomy over the appointments process came during minority and coalition governments in 1993 and 1998. But the expanded autonomy for judges did not imply that they would support social rights; in fact, one study shows that judges were more conservative on the rights to health and education after 1993.[43]

Even after the court seized the power to appoint its members, the political branches continued to retain influence through the power to allot post-retirement jobs.[44] According to a retired judge, the court favored the state in the Prevention of Terrorist and Disruptive Activities Act (TADA) 1985 cases because a district judge on the verge of retirement could be appointed by the government (with the CJ's consent) to hear the case in the relevant court, thus allowing him to continue working even after retirement. "One who is obliged to the state by extension beyond superannuation is less than impartial in a 'terrorist' trial."[45] This is partly substantiated by data on TADA and preventive detention cases where almost all appeals to the Supreme Court had the state as a defendant, implying that the state won in the lower courts.[46]

The judiciary's decision-making process emphasizes collaboration and seniority, thus making it difficult for us to gauge the effect of political influences.[47] Institutional rules such as short stints of four to six years at the apex court prior to retirement at the age of 65 deter *sustained* clashes with the government. "Institutional accommodation is crucial for preservation of democratic rights; attempts to preserve rights at the cost of endemic conflict between the executive, legislature, and the judiciary are, according to Chief Justice Chandrachud, self defeating," a statement that sums up the attitude of the post-emergency

supreme court.[48] Overt dissent is low, because of fragmented bench structures of decision making (two and three judge panels), the norm of assigning opinion writing responsibiliy to a senior judge, quick rotation of judges on different panels, and heavy workload.[49]

It is debatable, however, whether executive interference in appointments before 1993 actually occurred for a vast number of cases *and* reduced the quality of judges.[50] The author's analysis of the biographies of 116 supreme court judges from 1950–2005 shows that over 50 percent had worked for the state government at some point prior to their induction in the high court, but less than half (46 percent) had worked for a state or central government just prior to their induction into the high court. Over 72 percent of supreme court judges had served in the high court for 11–16 years, indicating that those elevated to the supreme court were senior judges.

What has the court done with its powers?

The promise and perils of judicial interventions

Religious freedom and gender equality

In 1985 the supreme court played a key role in the clash between two constitutional rights: religious freedom (articles 25–30) and gender equality (articles 14 and 15 on equality and nondiscrimination) through a ruling that privileged civil law over religious laws. India allows citizens to choose between religious and civil laws in matters relating to personal law issues of marriage, divorce, inheritance, and adoption. Muslims can choose to marry under *sharia* law, Hindus under the Hindu Marriage Act 1955, and so on. The court issued a ruling in the Shah Bano case giving Muslim women the right to receive maintenance (available to non-Muslim women under civil laws) even if they had married under Muslim religious laws.[51]

Like the Dreyfus affair in late nineteenth-century France, the Shah Bano case became a lodestone for warring groups. The Congress party-dominated parliament immediately passed the Muslim Women's (Protection of Rights on Divorce) Act in 1986 reversing the Shah Bano ruling, drawing protests from feminist groups and jubilation among Muslim religious leaders. The act provided Muslim women "a reasonable and fair provision of maintenance" at the time of divorce but forbade them to appeal to Section 125(8) of the Criminal Procedure Code for such maintenance unless their husbands consented to it. Lower court judges (later endorsed by the supreme court) interpreted the new act in ways that awarded Muslim divorcees large lump sums that would maintain them for a lifetime, showing that the concerns of the act's opponents were unfounded.[52]

Muslim religious leaders were particularly incensed with the CJI's call for legislating an uniform civil code (UCC), which was in the directive principles, the non-justiciable section of the constitution. They saw the court's recommendations, which were made in reference to national integration, as an attack on Muslim law, and as implicitly creating the fiction that Hindus were governed by a secular and egalitarian code. But as Agnes points out, the court's attitude towards bigamy by Hindus has been lax.[53] Scholars have also questioned whether the enactment of a UCC can itself bring about gender equality.[54] However, judges have not given up on the UCC; in October 2007, the supreme court set a new deadline for states to frame rules making the registration of marriages compulsory.

As several scholars point out, the judiciary thus played a negative role through its bias in favor of Hindu laws in the UCC debate, a controversial role in the Shah Bano case where it privileged group interpretations at the cost of individual rights, and a positive role in its interpretations of the 1986 Act allowing Muslim divorcees to gain the substance of their rights. The supreme court has been "high sounding" in the area of group rights such as affirmative action, gender justice and personal laws, while "adroitly avoiding a too courageous pursuit" of egalitarian social justice.[55] We see a similar pattern in the domain of social rights

where judges have struggled to reconcile their power with effective delivery of the substance of the right.

Social rights[56]

The often-cited cases of judicial activism pertain to judgments from the 1980s onward, transforming several directive principles such as the right to a clean environment, health, education, shelter, among others, into fundamental rights through an expanded notion of the right to life (article 21).[57] These judgments came in the wake of innovations like public interest litigation (PIL), which allow citizens and NGOs to appeal directly to either the high courts or the apex court.[58] Sathe argues that post-emergency judicial activism, which was the liberal interpretation of articles 21 (right to life) and 14 (right to equality), reconceptualized the basic rules of the judicial process with a view to making it more accessible and participatory.[59]

Indian judges have not been activist in health and education, and even on environmental issues if we define activism as finding government actions unconstitutional. Instead, the judiciary played a more supportive role in line with its inherent tendency to avoid conflict with the government. Most of the judgments legalizing social rights came in the wake of the emphasis—and legislation—on redistribution and social justice. For instance, in 1971 and 1976, Mrs Gandhi's government amended the constitution to force the courts to take more notice of the directive principles.[60]

Judges focused on making the government perform its statutory tasks and highlighted legislative actions as the basis for the shift towards justiciability of some social rights. Our data on compliance mechanisms in 384 judgments in health and education show that judges were more likely to prefer committee-style collaborative measures (rather than strong penalties) to elicit actions from the government. The government complied with the court's directives in high-profile cases such as those pertaining to clean air in Delhi or the use of safe water by cola companies, but most other cases and complex issues involving multiple agencies such as public sanitation and administration of hospitals were left unresolved. Even when the court instituted time limits, enforcement depended more on monitoring by litigants, such as the NGOs, for a right to food and education. Not surprisingly, the court's impact on a citizen's ability to enjoy the substance of the right was low. Despite judicial support, the right to food campaign is looking beyond legal tools to carry out and sustain its work because of the manpower and funding needed for litigation. Judges were aware of the disconnect between their directives and the propensity for compliance or noncompliance by the government, but could do little about it.[61] Even when the judgments found fault with the government, the phrases employed were "unfortunate," "policy matter," "conscious attempts must be made to increase budgetary allocations," "moral and social obligation of the state," and the like.[62]

The judiciary thus had a strong impact on the legal dimension of social and economic rights. Judges had a selectively significant impact on some policies such as those that expanded free access to anti-retro virals (ARVs) for AIDS patients, created a right to food, enabled anti-pollution policies in Delhi, provided part of the justification for an education guarantee scheme, and helped create new regulatory mechanisms for blood banks and for processing medical negligence claims. But such contributions were not tantamount to judges becoming policymakers since, for the most part, the institution or government acted only when it was ready to do so, not because the court demanded it. The constitutional right to education was introduced ten years after the judgment. The judiciary had the weakest impact in ensuring the effective delivery of these rights, leading us to the question whether the judicial arena provides the best site for improving the realization of social rights.

Judicial woes

Overloaded dockets arising from the vast jurisdiction, inadequate staff, and funding, have compromised the capacity of the court to deliver prompt justice. The supreme court's docket had 2,614 cases in 1951 (67 percent disposal rate), registered a spike in 1977 with 30,168 cases (34 percent disposal rate), 139,796 cases in 1985 (36 percent disposal rate), and 80,691 cases in 2005 (57 percent disposal rate).[63] One report estimates that 24 million cases are pending in different courts, with high courts producing the biggest bottlenecks.[64] Persistent vacancies (with levels reaching 30 percent in Delhi over the last 12 years in district and subordinate courts) and the tendency of judges to allow adjournments without valid reasons add to the delay.[65]

Corruption in the judiciary is another source of concern. One retiring chief justice provided a shocking indictment of India's judges, saying that more than 20 percent of judges were corrupt. Among the causes of corruption are the low pay scales of the subordinate judiciary. In December 2006 the cabinet approved a bill to amend the Judges Inquiry Act and create a national judicial council that would examine all complaints of corruption and misdemeanors against judges. But the problem is that judiciary will police itself, thus creating only an "illusion of accountability."[66]

However, as Baxi points out, it is unfair to put all the blame on judges; the state, lawyers, and litigants also have to shoulder some of the responsibility. With a ratio of just 10.5 judges per million population, when at least 50 judges are required, it is not surprising that there are tremendous delays in lower courts. Contrast this with the US, where there are 107 judges per million citizens. Only 0.2 percent of the GNP is spent on the judiciary. The Malimath Committee, and more recently the supreme court directed the state governments to fill vacancies in subordinate courts by 31 March, 2003 and increase the number of judges to 50 per million citizens by 2007.[67] Unfortunately, the deadline has not been met.

Conclusion

Scholarly studies and newspaper reports give us contradictory images of the judge: activist, political, confrontational, policymaker, corrupt, apolitical, impartial, and inefficient. Our analysis shows that they are not the puppets of political masters, but neither are they strategists nor idiosyncratic. Rather, Indian judges are more likely to engage in a constant process of negotiation with their identities as judges, citizens, and as members of a state institution.

Rosenberg's view that constitutional rights are more likely to be implemented if they reflect the preexisting beliefs of politicians, policymakers and the public is an apt characterization of the actual power of the Indian judiciary. "Courts do not exist in a vacuum. Supreme court decisions, even those finding constitutional rights, are not implemented automatically or in any straightforward or simple way. They are merely one part of the broader political picture. At best, they can contribute to the process of change. In and of themselves, they accomplish little."[68] The Indian Supreme court's effect on policy has been indirect for the most part. Even the "right to education" that the court articulated in a 1992 judgment became a constitutional amendment only after it appeared as an election promise of a political party and was finally passed ten years later. The Indian experience reinforces the theoretical and empirical evidence from other countries that there is no intrinsic link between judicial independence and the expansion of rights.[69]

So what does our report card say about the Indian judiciary? First, though Sathe[70] is right that the Indian supreme court has moved beyond the traditional separation of powers approach, the evidence from social rights litigation suggests that, until recently, the judiciary neither appropriated a policymaking role nor was it activist in the sense of overturning laws. Even in environmental cases, the court provided temporary solutions, while nudging the government to address pressing issues such as cleanliness in cities. The

allocation of cases by the chief justice, lack of enforcement capacity, the emphasis on collaboration rather than dissent in the two- or three-judge panels encourage conformity and status quo behavior by judges.

Second, the relationship between courts and political configurations in a parliamentary system is less coherent than is commonly assumed. When the political actor was strong (single-party majority), prepared to take on the courts (as Indira Gandhi did), and had a policy agenda, the supreme court was more constrained by the political milieu. If the political actor was strong and had a policy, but was not prepared to strike at the court's autonomy (the Nehruvian regime), or if there was a weak governing coalition/minority government (post-1988 governments), the supreme court had more room to maneuver. But the judges predominantly played a supporting role to the government.[71]

Third, theories of legal mobilization rightly argue that the emergence and strength of support structures within civil society enable a rights revolution,[72] provide critical support to the courts against a belligerent executive,[73] but also constrain the court's potential contribution in the area of civil rights and liberties.[74] The low rates of litigation by NGOs and the minimal use of PILs in these sectors confirm the argument by Epp that social rights litigation (except environmental cases) lacks the support structures for a full-fledged rights revolution in India. Other studies show that India's higher judiciary at best provided temporary solutions to complex problems of public health and primary education, but were more effective on simpler issues dealing with government regulation of private providers and obligations of private providers to citizens.[75] The higher courts often used declaratory language that focused on the strength of the right rather than the remedies.

The evidence raises concerns about whether the court is the right arena to ensure the provision of social goods. Judges are not qualified to assess the implications of their judgments. For instance, a recent interim ruling by the supreme court allowing a

pharmaceutical policy that facilitated government intervention when prices of essential
drugs behaved abnormally was interpreted by
the government as allowing a drug price
control policy. Even PILs have come under a
huge strain; the Prime Minister cautioned the
bench that PILs could not become vehicles for
settling political or other scores.[76]

While the courts have been used in the past
by India's political elites to decide thorny
political issues such as the beneficiaries of
affirmative action, the recent decade has
increased this propensity—in line with the
global trend—of promoting judicial intervention and even policymaking to avoid
responsibility for controversial decisions.[77]
Plagued by fractured political support and
squabbling coalition partners, the executive
and legislature have shifted the burden of
governance to the judiciary. The judges seem
willing, and even justify their intervention on
grounds of growing lawlessness and ineffective
administration. But the court would do well
to heed the words of Justice Pathak that "it
possesses the sanction of neither the sword nor
the purse and that its strength lies basically in
public confidence and support, and that
consequently the legitimacy of its acts and
decisions must remain beyond all doubt."[78]
Judicial intrusion may be well motivated, but
the resulting workload, the incapacity of the
judiciary as an institution to make policies, the
stop-gap nature of the solutions devised by
courts, and the destabilizing campaigns initiated by the political branches may overwhelm
the judiciary.

Notes

1 The Indian constitution distinguishes between justiciable fundamental rights and non-enforceable directive principles; see H. M. Seervai, Constitutional Law of India, 3rd edn (New Delhi: N. M. Tripathy, 1983); and B. N. Rau, India's Constitution in the Making (Bombay: Orient Longmans, 1960).

2 Unnikrishnan vs State of AP (1993) 1 SCC 645.

3 C. Neal Tate and Torbjörn Vallinder, "The Global Expansion of Judicial Power: The Judicialization of Politics," in C. Neal Tate and Torbjörn Vallinder (eds), The Global Expansion of Judicial Power (New York: University Press, 1995), pp. 1–24; Ran Hirschl, Towards Juristocracy —The Origins and Consequences of the New Constitutionalism (Cambridge, MA: Harvard University Press, 2004).

4 Robert Dahl, "Decision-Making in a Democracy: The Supreme Court as a National Policy-Maker," Journal of Public Law, Vol. 6, No. 2 (1957), pp. 279–95.

5 ADM Jabalpur vs Shiv Kant Shukla (1976) 2 SCC 52.

6 Upendra Baxi, "Taking Suffering Seriously: Social Action Litigation in the Supreme Court of India," in R. Sudarshan et al. (eds), Judges and the Judicial Power (Bombay: Tripathi, 1985); S. P. Sathe, Judicial Activism in India (Delhi: Oxford University Press, 2002).

7 Gerald N. Rosenberg, The Hollow Hope: Can Courts Bring About Social Change? (Chicago: University of Chicago Press, 1991). For a similar argument on the pragmatic bent of India's judiciary, see Pratap Bhanu Mehta, "India's Judiciary," in Devesh Kapur and Pratap Bhanu Mehta (eds), Public Institutions in India (New Delhi: Oxford University Press, 2005).

8 Tate and Vallinder.

9 Pratap Bhanu Mehta, "India's Judiciary," in Devesh Kapur and Pratap Bhanu Mehta (eds), Public Institutions in India (New Delhi: Oxford University Press, 2005).

10 Sujit Choudhary and Claire E. Hunter, "Measuring Judicial Activism on the Supreme Court of Canada: A Comment on Newfoundland (Treasury Board) V. Nape," McGill Law Journal, 48, 2003.

11 Mark Tushnet, Symposium: "Constitutional Courts in the Field of Power Politics: Social Welfare Rights and the Forms of Judicial Review," Texas Law Review, Vol. 82 (2004).

12 V. R. Krishna Iyer, Our Courts on Trial (New Delhi: B. R. Publishing, 1987), p. 144.

13 Hirschl.

14 Tate and Vallinder.

15 Apart from writ jurisdiction, the 21 high courts have jurisdiction over all lower courts in its territory. There are 3,150 district level courts, 4,816 munsif/magistrate courts and 1,964 magistrate II and equivalent courts at the

bottom of the integrated judiciary. Arnab Kumar Hazra and Bibek Debroy (eds), *Judicial Reforms in India— Issues and Aspects* (New Delhi: Academic Foundation, 2007).

16 Sathe, p. 39; Susanne Rudolph and Lloyd Rudolph, *In Pursuit of Lakshmi* (Chicago, IL: University of Chicago Press, 1996).

17 Tate and Vallinder, p. 30.

18 *Keshavananda Bharati vs State of Kerala*, AIR (1973) SC 1461.

19 Raju Ramachandran, "The Supreme Court and the Basic Structure Doctrine," in B. N. Kirpal *et al.* (eds), *Supreme But Not Infallible* (Delhi: Oxford University Press, 2000), pp. 107–33.

20 Mehta; Gary Jacobsohn, *The Wheel of Law: India's Secularism in Comparative Constitutional Perspective* (Princeton, NJ: University Press, 2005).

21 *Bommai vs Union of India* (1994) 3 SCC 1, *IR Coelho (dead) by LRs vs State of Tamil Nadu and Ors* (2007) 2 SCC 1.

22 Rajeev Dhavan, "The Supreme Court and Group Life," in Kirpal, p. 275.

23 In the Golak Nath case, a 6:5 majority held that parliament was not competent to amend the chapter on fundamental rights; in the Bank Nationalization Case, the majority held that the right to property was a very important fundamental right; the Privy Purse Case held that the claim to receive a privy purse was part of the right to property; and the Kesavananda Bharti Case outlined the "basic structure of the constitution doctrine"; Gobind Das, "The Supreme Court: An Overview," in Kirpal.

24 George Gadbois, "The Supreme Court of India as a Political Institution," in R. Dhavan *et al.* (eds), *Judges and the Judicial Power: Essays in Honour of Justice V. R. Krishna Iyer* (London: Sweet & Maxwell and Bombay: N. M. Tripathi, 1985).

25 Granville Austin, *Working a Democratic Institution; The Indian Experience* (Delhi: Oxford University Press, 1999).

26 Two hundred and eighty-four laws were inserted into the ninth schedule up to 2007, of which 217 were enacted after 1973.

27 Sathe, p. 88.

28 *Minerva Mills vs Union of India* (1980) 3 SCC 625, para 22, *Waman Rao vs Union of India* (1981) 2 SCC 362.

29 *IR Coelho (dead) by LRs vs State of Tamil Nadu and Ors* (2007) 2 SCC 1.

30 V. Venkatesan, "Judicial Challenge," *Frontline* (9 February, 2007).

31 Even investigations into judicial conduct cannot occur without prior written consent of the CJI, who will not consent unless there is clinching evidence, which the police cannot get unless they investigate.

32 B. R. Ambedkar, CA Debates, Volume 8, Book 3, p. 258.

33 *S. P. Gupta vs Union of India*, AIR (1982) SC 149.

34 *Supreme Court Advocates on Record Association vs Union of India* (1993) Supp 2 SCR 659. For a critique, see Lord Cooke of Thorndon, "Where Angels Fear to Tread," in Kirpal.

35 See Rajeev Dhavan, *Justice on Trial: The Supreme Court Today* (Allahabad: Wheeler, 1980); and Vijay K. Gupta, *Decision Making in the Supreme Court of India* (Delhi: Kaveri, 1995) for detailed analyses of decision making in the supreme court.

36 Gupta, p. 37.

37 Austin, p. 125.

38 On 25 April, 1973, Justice Ray was appointed CJI, superseding three senior judges (Shelat, Hegde, and Grover), who subsequently resigned. In January 1977 Justice H. L. Khanna was superseded for dissenting in the habeas corpus case.

39 Iyer, p. 13.

40 Lawyer Indira Jaising, quoted by Iyer, p. 16.

41 Iyer, p. 30. This practice is the norm in the USA where supreme court judges are political appointees.

42 Mark J. Ramseyer, "The Puzzling (In)dependence of Courts: A Comparative Approach," *Journal of Legal Studies*, Vol. 23 (1994), pp. 721–47 and J. Mark Ramseyer and Eric Rasmusen, "Judicial Independence in Civil Law Regimes: Econometrics from Japan," *Journal of Law, Economics, and Organization*, Vol. 13 (1997), pp. 259–86.

43 Shylashri Shankar, *Scaling Justice: India's Supreme Court, Anti-Terror Laws and Social Rights* (Delhi: Oxford University Press, 2008).

44 Supreme Court judges retire at the age of 65, high court judges at 62.

45 Iyer, p. 64.

46 Shankar.

47 Order VII of the Supreme Court Rules.

48 Baxi, p. 81.

49 Gupta, p. 147, reports that the two major dissenters between 1973–81 were Justice

Bhagwati (seven dissents), and Justice A. P. Sen (six dissents).

50 Mehta, p. 176, points out that a government affidavit in 1993, filed in the second judges case, noted that, of 575 appointments, the government had rejected the chief justice's opinion in only a handful of cases; also see Gupta.

51 *Mohd. Ahmad Khan vs Shah Bano Begum*, AIR (1985) SC 945

52 *Arab Ahmadhia Abdulla vs Arab Bail Humuna Saiyadbhai*, AIA (1988) Guj 141 and *Daniel Latifi vs Union of India*, AIR (2001) SC 3958.

53 *Bhaurao Lokhande vs State of Maharashtra*, AIA (1965) SC 1564 and *Sarla Mudgal vs Union of India* (1995) SCC 635.

54 Upendra Baxi, "The Rule of Law in India," *SUR – Revista Internacional de Direitos Humanos*, Vol. 6, No. 4 (2007).

55 Dhavan, in Kirpal, p. 274.

56 This section is based on an analysis by the author of 384 judgments in the higher courts on the "rights to health/education."

57 Article 21 states that no person shall be deprived of his life or personal liberty except according to the procedure established by law.

58 Common law systems (adversarial) permit only a person whose rights are directly affected to approach the court. The PIL, which is non-adversarial, allows any member of the public acting in a bona fide manner to espouse public interest causes by sending a letter or petition to the supreme court in case of a violation of a fundamental right (article 32), and to the high court for violations of legal rights (article 226).

59 Sathe, pp. 100 and 107.

60 Dhavan, *Justice on Trial*, p. 128.

61 *Koolwal vs State of Rajasthan*, AIR (1988) Raj 2.

62 *Ravindra Kumar, Advocate and Anr vs State of UP* (Writ Petition M/S 1746 of 1998, Allahabad HC).

63 Supreme Court Registrar under an RTI request from the author.

64 Eighty-fifth Report of the Parliamentary Standing Committee on Home Affairs on Legal Delays. The high courts of Allahabad (800,000), Madras (650,000), Kerala (300,000) and Bombay (240,000) were the worst offenders.

65 Hazra and Debroy.

66 Prashant Bhushan, "Judicial Accountability or Illusion?" *Economic and Political Weekly*, Vol. 46, No. 47 (25 November, 2006), pp. 4,847–48.

67 *All India Judge's Association vs Union of India* (2002) 4 SCC 247.

68 Gerald N. Rosenberg, "The Real World of Constitutional Rights: the Supreme Court and the Implementation of the Abortion Decisions," in Lee Epstein (ed.), *Contemplating Courts* (Washington, DC: CQ Press, 1995), p. 417.

69 Tamir Moustafa, "Law versus the State: The Judicialization of Politics in Egypt," *Law & Social Inquiry*, Vol. 28, No. 4 (Fall, 2003), pp. 883–930; Hirschl; Ceren Belge, "Friends of the Court: The Republican Alliance and Selective Activism of the Constitutional Court of Turkey," *Law and Society Review*, Vol. 40, No. 3 (2006), pp. 653–92.

70 Sathe, passim.

71 Also see S. Muralidhar, "Implementation of Court Orders in the Area of Economic, Social and Cultural Rights: An Overview of the Experience of the Indian Judiciary," First South Asian Regional Judicial Colloquium on Access to Justice, New Delhi, 1–3 November, 2002.

72 Charles Epp, *The Rights Revolution* (Chicago, IL: University of Chicago Press, 1998).

73 Moustafa.

74 Belge.

75 Shankar, *Scaling Justice*.

76 *Indian Express*, 7 April, 2007, "Line Dividing Activism and Over-reach is a Thin One: PM's Caution to Bench."

77 Tate and Vallinder; Hirschl.

78 Justice Pathak, in *Bandhua Mukti Morcha vs Union of India* (1984) 3 SCC 161 76.

12

Balancing act

Prudence, impunity, and Pakistan's jurisprudence

Paula R. Newberg

We seek to inculcate the belief that laws are not meant to be jealously preserved in jurisprudential tomes but to be applied, by activist judges, for the protection of the common man, and that the rule of law is an idea worth fighting for.

> Muneer A. Malik, Supreme Court Bar Association, *Dawn*, June 2007

Whereas the Government is committed to the independence of the judiciary and the rule of law and holds the superior judiciary in high esteem, it is nonetheless of paramount importance that the Honourable Judges confine the scope of their activity to the judiciary function and not assume charge of administration . . . I hereby order and proclaim that the Constitution of the Islamic Republic of Pakistan shall remain in abeyance.

> *Proclamation of Emergency*, November 2007

By legitimizing military takeovers, the judges have abdicated their role to defend the Constitution.

> Justice (Retd) Saeeduzzaman Siddiqui, *Newsline*, May 2007

Introduction

In the sixtieth year of Pakistan's independence, its president, General Pervez Musharraf, went to war against its courts and judges. As the Supreme Court took up petitions challenging the disappearances of citizens,[1] corruption in the privatization of state enterprises,[2] the conduct of police and security forces, and finally, the questionable legitimacy of Musharraf's tenure and re-election bid, Musharraf took on the judiciary.

Within a short period of time, Musharraf removed the chief justice of the supreme court in March 2007, but was forced to return him to the court after public protests from the legal community and a formal restoration mandated by the Supreme Judicial Council.[3] A few months later, fearing that the court would thwart his re-election bid, Musharraf declared a state of emergency, suspended the constitution, and promulgated a provisional constitutional order (PCO). He then fired more than 60 percent of the country's superior court justices, stacked the courts with loyalists who were willing to swear their oaths to the PCO, and placed several lawyers and Supreme Court justices under house arrest. To cement his power, he removed the licensing of lawyers from professional associations, arrested lawyers who protested these attacks on the courts, and amended the Army Act to negate fundamental rights otherwise guaranteed in the constitution. The newly constituted supreme court validated Musharraf's constitutional revisions and on his re-election as president.[4] In one short year, the safety of judges and lawyers, the integrity of judicial institutions and the foundations of the country's jurisprudence were grievously compromised.

This was not the first time that the courts ran afoul of the executive. Musharraf had issued a previous PCO when he seized power in 1999, and in 2000 had promulgated an Oath of Offices (Judges) Order that required judges of the higher judiciary to swear allegiance to that PCO. General Zia ul Haq had done the same after imposing martial law in 1977. In both instances, the courts were cleansed of opponents to the ruling executives, providing pliant judges to rule on the legality of military-led governments. As a result, through the 1980s under General Zia, and for much of General Musharraf's tenure as well, Pakistan's superior judiciary was not only assumed to be in league with the military, but also to be responsible for maintaining an executive-oriented judicial culture.

Pakistan's judicial history reflects a calculus of conflict and convenience that highlights the incomplete resolution of the country's fundamental political disputes and deep structural tensions between the judiciary and the executive. Since independence, Pakistan's courts have lived in a juridical universe defined by a heavily bureaucratized, praetorian state that has never completed a transition to representative government. The regular imposition of military or emergency rule has consistently skewered constitutions for short-term political gain, systematically undercutting citizen rights as generals and presidents (often the same individuals) have strengthened their role in the state. As parliamentary leaders have sparred with presidents and military leaders in their continual efforts to re-equilibrate executive–legislative relations, the courts have been left to dangle between them, sometimes as victims

of intra-governmental strife, occasionally as arbiters in the cause of constitutionality. When they have failed, the courts have contributed to an evolving culture of executive impunity in which anti-constitutional behavior regularly overrides promises of future good governance. This poisonous combination has repeatedly diminished the rule of law, limited access to justice, and deeply injured democratic development.

In the frequent absence of freely elected governing bodies, the superior courts have repeatedly turned their attention to the executive—whether civilian or military— and judicial dockets have consistently attended not only to the unfinished business of the state, but also to the soundness and validity of executive action. The judiciary has often functioned without a valid constitution, and Pakistan's jurisprudence reflects a constant struggle to arbitrate in its absence. Under military rule, the courts have often acquiesced in executive actions that might otherwise be rendered unconstitutional. Under civilian governments, judges have occasionally tried, in their rulings, to impart a sense of judicial responsibility for the stability of the state, although that has meant devaluing participatory politics. In so doing, they have lurched from between active and reactive roles, in each instance under-scoring the uncertain sources of their institutional powers and, too often, reducing their potential strengths.

Pakistan's jurisprudence therefore remains inconsistent and idiosyncratic—long on prudence, occasionally short on justice, often intellectually compromised and always intensely, if retrospectively, political. When courts disagree with ruling authorities, they are considered independent—politically, if not jurisprudentially—but judgments contrary to presidents and parliaments often boomerang, leaving the judiciary under greater duress than before. When judging the executive-centered state, however, the courts have often found themselves complicit in its actions, and Pakistan's jurisprudence understandably reflects this strained juridical environment. In all these senses, the judiciary has mirrored the weaknesses of the Pakistani state, even as political society has called on the courts to solve the problems that such weaknesses have inevitably provoked.

Musharraf's antipathy toward the judiciary reflected his difficulties governing the fragile Pakistani state. In particular, his commitment to the global anti-terrorism campaign led to significant abuses of fundamental rights in the name of strong executive rule. The court's so-called "activism" on this and other matters became Musharraf's excuse to thwart the courts and, by extension, Pakistan's vocal legal community. As it contested the sitting government, the 2007 supreme court's docket and demeanor reflected 60 years of accumulated frustration about executive prerogatives, and the problematic role of the judiciary and judicial rulings.

Constitutions and courts

The script for Pakistan's troubled judiciary and jurisprudence has been written on the pages of discarded constitutions.[5] Even when the superior courts have been allowed to function without explicit direction from the executive, a cumbersome state bureaucracy often tied to seemingly capricious politicians has limited formal judicial capacities and the breadth of court rulings. Motion has often been mistaken for progress: frequent changes in political leadership long ago turned the courts into interpreters for political systems whose constitutions did not, or could not, anchor the state. Over and again, the executive, the military or politicians have overstepped their roles, making the courts part of the problematic of the state, at the same time that they have been cast as the assumed arbiters of the damage done by the state, and even more tenuously, as catalysts for the state's transformation. These tasks have been impossible to accomplish, whether separately or together, and have led alternately to contradictory rulings, timidity, self-justification, or creative fence sitting. Only recently have the superior courts turned their

inclinations to expand the judicial role into sustained, outright confrontation about the substance of policy.

Courts create and respect precedent, and their formal interpretations of the juridical past influence, and are influenced by, their informal interpretations of the political and constitutional environments in which they work. For Pakistan's courts, the foundation on which its early decisions were drafted was the disputed territory, ideology, and political practice of the country's early independent years. Pakistan struggled to overcome the combined legacies of the 1935 Government of India Act, the 1940 Lahore Resolution, and the 1947 Indian Independence Act and the 1956 Constitution mirrored conflicted efforts of both the governor-general and a sequence of constituent assemblies to identify the political and legal theories that could and should ground the state. With the western provinces divided, and separated by India from Bengal in the east, the assemblies found it difficult to reconcile the diverse and potential meanings of political sovereignty, provincial autonomy, political representation and citizen rights, and religious and communal identity. Then as now, religious conservatives sought to ensure that *sharia* law would be supreme—that is, that secular law would comply with the Quran and Sunnah— and liberals sought to organize a pluralist state that can accommodate all religions and ethnicities. By 1956, after sustained litigation in the nine-year absence of a constitution, agreement was reached to amalgamate the western provinces into one unit, limit parliamentary authority, and define the powers of a strong governor-general, whose authority was meant to echo the colonial role inherited from the 1935 Government of India Act. The Objectives Resolution, a preamble that has been included in subsequent constitutions, paid respect to the ideas of Islam in an otherwise secular constitution. Fundamental rights were guaranteed and the judiciary was made nominally independent, but neither stipulation could ensure that the constitutional provisions would be respected.

The gap between constitutional ideal and political circumstance helped to divide a fractious polity. Neither the bureaucracy nor the military had much patience with politics, although both meddled quite freely with appointments, emoluments and policies, and experiments with emergency rule in lieu of electoral reform. This ensured that a consistent jurisprudence would not easily develop. Drafting constitutional text is a parliamentary, not a judicial responsibility, but as weak and changeable parliaments conflated their constitution-drafting and legislative roles, the electorate—and often, disgruntled politicians—turned to the courts to solve governance problems that would otherwise be outside the judicial ambit.

In 1958 martial law was declared through a coup d'état, adapting an emergency model used briefly in Lahore in 1953 to quell sectarian disturbances, and again by Governor General Ghulam Mohammed in 1954 to dissolve a constituent assembly. Although the period of formal martial law was relatively brief, it quickly led to the erosion of judicial autonomy under Field Marshal Mohammed Ayub Khan, who ruled from 1958 until 1969. After obtaining court validation of his coup d'état, and promulgating ordinances to indemnify his regime, Ayub Khan took on the task of creating a new constitution to replace the "amorphous document" of 1956. Among his goals for the 1962 Constitution were to reinforce presidential powers over representative bodies, limit provincial rights (while strengthening the hand of West Pakistan in the federation), and notably, circumscribe the power of the courts. Although Ayub Khan declared that "the courts are . . . the final arbiters of what is legal and binding," his rule under the 1962 Constitution was designed to ensure the control of the executive over the judiciary: he allowed only circumspect dissent, whether from political parties or the courts, whose capacity to protect basic rights was limited. This rigid resistance to political debate became the constitution's, and Ayub Khan's, undoing.

Widespread agitation in both East and West Pakistan led to an extra-constitutional transfer of power in 1969 to General Agha Mohammed Yahya Khan, with a concomitant reversion to martial law. He confirmed past practice by limiting legislative authority, constrained advocates for provincial autonomy, and after gaining temporary judicial sanction for his rule, palpably restricted the role of the courts—actions that nonetheless did not persuade judges to resign their posts.[6] As increasing public discord met with executive intransigence, the space for negotiation between East Pakistan and the center over provincial rights decreased. Although the 1970 elections were among Pakistan's fairest, dissension between the provinces in their aftermath—West Pakistan would not cede the election to the majority from East Pakistan—led to the abrogation of the existing legal framework, devastating war, and finally, the independence of Bangladesh.

First as civilian martial law administrator, then as president and finally as prime minister, Bhutto oversaw the drafting of a new constitution, which was approved by parliament in 1973. Its passage was not easy, and dissenting voices raised issues that remain unresolved today: devolution and decentralization, the relationship between parliament and the president, and, by implication, the independence of the courts. For the first time, constitutional text unambiguously raised the status of the prime minister relative to the president, and guaranteed the separation of judicial and executive powers, even if the path to achieving court autonomy was not clarified. Almost concurrent with the passage of the new constitution, the supreme court partially reversed its earlier rulings on the validity of executive power transfers and, at the same time, expanded its concepts of judicial autonomy and power to ensure, in a sense, that constitutionalism would be given a firmer footing for the future. But conflict arose almost immediately: provincial rights advocates sought greater power in the federal relationship, setting the stage for armed struggle in Balochistan through the 1970s and constitutional amendments restricting civil rights. Civil libertarians warned that the uneasy relationship between president and parliament could fail, and that the government's quick constitutional amendments restricting minority rights would easily undermine rights protections more generally. Both predictions proved to be accurate, and the end of the populist Bhutto era came four years later with General Mohammed Zia ul Haq's coup d'état, and Bhutto's subsequent, court-sanctioned, execution.[7]

Zia ul Haq's malign manipulation of the political system set a juridical context from which Pakistan has yet to recover. His provisional constitutional order replaced the 1973 Constitution—euphemistically placing the constitution "in abeyance"—by martial law regulations and ordinances that were unequivocally exempted from judicial contest. Once again, ordinances were promulgated to ensure that the regime would be indemnified, leaving martial law authorities to function freely in pursuit of the military's goals.[8] So-called disloyal judges were removed from their positions, further politicizing the administration of a rapidly waning justice system as civilian institutions—including the courts—were replaced by the military. The 1973 Constitution was partially restored in 1985, but just as political society was becoming more restive in the late 1980s, and before he was able to amend or substantially redraft the constitution to ensure the primacy of the executive, Zia ul Haq and almost all his top military leaders died in a plane crash. Surprisingly, open elections were allowed, and civilian government—and the 1973 Constitution—returned to Pakistan under the rule of Prime Minister Benazir Bhutto.

None of the four civilian, elected governments between 1988 and 1999 completed a full term. Prime Ministers Bhutto and Mian Nawaz Sharif were thwarted by the unworkable relationships between military and civilian institutions, and both proved unable to redress the accumulated grievances that four decades of uneven governance had brought to the country. Neither confrontation nor accommodation with the military could save political rule: the troika of president, prime minister, and army chief proved to be self-defeating, and a constitutional amendment to provide titular primacy to the parliament further alienated the military. Conflicts between prime ministers and presidents about appointments, procedures and rulings once again burdened the courts.[9] Bhutto profoundly distrusted those judges who had validated her father's execution, and when the Supreme Court did not acquiesce in Sharif's power politics, his party members stormed the supreme court.[10]

By the late 1990s, four contentious problems plagued political competition: political corruption that led cumulatively to a growing sense that governance had eroded beyond repair; economic weaknesses, magnified after Pakistan's 1998 nuclear tests that led to international sanctions; the rise of sectarianism, the parallel evolution of the Taliban movement in neighboring Afghanistan, and renewed tensions surrounding the prospects of *sharia* law in Pakistan; and continued conflicts along all Pakistan's borders.

Unsurprisingly, Pakistan's pendular parliamentary politics, which swung from liberal to conservative, secular to religious, and across the entire spectrum of economic and foreign policies, were often at odds with the army. This led Army Chief Pervez Musharraf to justify his coup d'état in 1999 as a critique of the 1973 Constitution, erroneous state policy, and of course, politicians.[11] Musharraf's wariness of rough-and-tumble politics led to political manipulation, constitutional amendments to extend his regime's tenure, rigged elections and, as with earlier regimes, disputes with the Supreme Court over the judiciary's docket and judgments. The counterpoint to this domestic wrangling was the toll that terrorism took on the judicial system and individual rights protections in the wake of the events of September 2001, the resumption of war in Afghanistan, and perilous cross-border militancy and insurgency. Pakistan's foreign and domestic politics converged in the denial of rights to the

181

accused, including disappearances overseen by the military and intelligence agencies in presumed collaboration with foreign governments. All these actions underlined the fullness of the civil-military alliance symbolized by Musharraf's dual role as army chief and president, and embodied in a legal framework order that he shepherded through parliament as the Seventeenth Amendment to the 1973 Constitution.

These actions inevitably complicated the judiciary's role, for once again the actions of the state were declared immune to judicial scrutiny or judgment. With parliament's strength derived only from presidential patronage, and weary of imposed judicial subservience, Pakistan's legal community forced the issues of constitutionality and judicial autonomy onto the public agenda. In late 2007, Musharraf assailed the presumption of the superior judiciary to review the propriety of his re-election, removed anti-government cases from the courts and, following past practice, unilaterally indemnified the emergency government against future legal challenge.

Dockets and doctrines

Despite the limits on its role, Pakistan's superior courts have played critical—although rarely incisive, transformative, or progressive—roles in formulating or judging the arrangement of state power and authority. The courts have rarely acted as impartially as constitutions might have optimally decreed, but they have equally rarely submitted fully to the strictures imposed on them by overweening executives. Unsurprisingly, the country's contingent, conflicted jurisprudence has provided unclear guidance for the state. Its signal jurisprudential principles—articulated in the double-barreled doctrines of necessity and revolutionary legality that justified coups d'état and the retrospective validation of unconstitutional appropriations of power—have been fundamentally detrimental to the development of a democratic state. Although it can be argued

that the courts have helped to maintain a state whose powers are based on coercion rather than participation or consensus, they have also been outlets for public discussions that were unavailable elsewhere: even when the courts have validated the misuse of power, they have, sometimes counter-intuitively and unexpectedly, provided arenas for open discussions of pressing matters of state policy when presidents, parliaments and generals have continued to disappoint or silence the electorate.

Pakistan's difficult first years gave the judiciary unenviable tasks: negotiating the shoals of postcolonial governance meant setting a foundation for the rule of law while constitutionalism remained a distant aspiration. The 1950s judicial docket unwittingly set the ground for subsequent decades in two distinctive ways: first, by ruling on government actions in the absence of a constitution (and thus with startlingly insufficient legal grounding), and, second, by agreeing to validate government actions in ways that presaged its later legitimating roles for military governments and extra-constitutional actions. In their efforts to craft a legal language for the new state, they dealt with questions of justiciability and standing, and struggled with questions of legal doctrine that continue to color politics today.

From the first cases of the 1950s, Pakistan's higher courts were occupied with matters that went beyond the usual judicial ambit, forcing judges to define their own roles in complex transitional environments. In quick succession, they ruled on the propriety of actions of the governor-general and the constituent assemblies, the contested nature of constitution making and the role of parliamentary prerogative, the rights of the executive to exclude opposing political voices, and more generally, the relationships between political power and legal authority.[12] Responding to a reference on the governor-general's power to dissolve an elected assembly and declare a state of emergency, the court raised (but did not resolve) three questions that remain salient—and largely unanswered—today: what counts as the normal functioning of the state, when does a political authority have the right to use power to alter state institutions, and how do laws and judicial institutions determine whether power has been exercised rightly?

These questions, regrettable in their provenance, proved to be even more unfortunate in their resolution, for they presaged two essentially contested questions about the state: the nature of democracy in the evolving polity—a choice articulated in 1955 "between the substance and the shadow" of democratic rule[13]—and the role of the courts in setting a political course. Perhaps most important, when the Supreme Court chose to define its authority and independence as separate from politics—meaning, perhaps, impartiality between and among political parties—it implicitly aligned itself with the executive rather than the legislative branch and in so doing, sullied the institutional neutrality it was trying to establish for itself.

These early cases also provided opportunities for the Supreme Court to articulate a self-justifying doctrine of state necessity that has shadowed Pakistan's jurisprudence and politics ever since. Its 1955 advisory ruling confirmed that "an act which would otherwise be illegal becomes legal if it is done bona fide under the stress of necessity." The court thus accepted not only the primacy of executive action but also the right of the executive—in this instance the governor-general, but in subsequent years almost any executive— to arrogate to himself powers well beyond those articulated in the state's constituting documents.[14]

This implied alliance between court and executive set the stage for the court's actions in the wake of the declaration of martial law in 1958. The constitution became disposable, democracy reverted to a theoretical end of governance rather than a means to achieve good government, and on the day after Ayub Khan's coup d'état, the supreme court agreed—sadly, although inevitably—to adjudicate a constitutional problem in the absence of a formal constitution.[15] It ruled that

the usurpation of power was legally valid, thus equating force, efficacy and legality under the cover of a legal order promulgated by the usurping power itself. The doctrine of revolutionary legality, as it was then coined, took as its basis not the constitution—which had already been abrogated by Ayub Khan's coup—but the seeming fact that the coup had been a successful way to challenge a constitutional order: "The revolution itself becomes a law-creating fact," the court wrote, underscoring politically risky judicial functionalism even as it eschewed any serious analysis of the political events that brought the case to the bench, and reinforcing the notion that the court had allied itself against representative, rights-protecting governance.

With time, however, the high courts, particularly in East Pakistan, began to rule against the legal framework established by Ayub Khan's 1962 Constitution. They posed serious questions about the laxity with which the legislature interpreted its constitutional mandate, the individual rights of citizens, and the assumptions about provincial autonomy and representation on which the state was based—in particular, Ayub Khan's devolutionary basic democracies policy, the disqualification of politicians, and the civilianizing of martial law.[16] Their rulings argued for the expansion of judicial review while at the same time accepting the government's arguments for limiting political participation. In this way, the courts enlarged their formal purview, while leaving the substance of rights protections to legislatures (both national and provincial) whose powers to give substance to democracy remained disturbingly limited.[17]

This vacillating judicial approach was undercut by the extra-constitutional transfer of power from Ayub Khan to Yahya Khan in 1969, the resumption of military rule, and the imposition of a self-defeating legal framework order that became the prelude to the separation of East and West Pakistan. The end of war between the two wings of the state brought a new, albeit temporary, jurisprudence when the courts ruled belatedly against the discredited doctrine of revolutionary legality in *Asma Jilani's case*.[18] But power seeks its closest mooring. Although the supreme court retrospectively challenged Yahya Khan's regime and the many instances of constitutional usurpation that preceded it, the new Bhutto government—which came into power under the aegis of military rule, and, against judicial advice, only later legitimated its authority and drafted a new constitution—nonetheless supported the doctrine of necessity as a way to anchor its own legality and legitimacy.

Pakistan's supreme court was nothing if not cautious. Although it disavowed the rationale of revolutionary legality —one amicus curia called it "a standing menace"—it did not declare the 1958 coup d'état to be illegal, opting to offer Ayub Khan retrospective validation via the constitution he drafted after the fact. Instead, the court turned its attention to its future role: to distinguish good laws from bad, ensure the public welfare, and differentiate judgments about legality from those about political legitimacy. These were hardly viable tasks under circumstances of profound, post-civil war uncertainty, but from the point of the view of the courts, optimistic ones that put the new Bhutto government on notice that the courts were willing to play a significant role in the reconstituted Pakistani state.[19]

Once again, however, the superior courts found themselves navigating an unfamiliar and distressingly brief political transition. In the four years between the passage of the 1973 Constitution and its abrogation in 1977, the judiciary ruled on an enormous range of issues for which it was only partially prepared: economic and political federalism, democracy and emergency, and the prerogatives of an ideological government inclined to politicize state institutions. Pakistan's first federal—rather than Westminster—constitution proved to be a challenge to adjudicate.[20]

Bhutto held military and civilian powers concurrently—not the first Pakistani leader to do so, and, of course, not the last—and the intersections of civil and military law under emergency rule impelled the courts to

delineate carefully, in a series of habeas corpus petitions and challenges to preventive detention, the respective powers of the civil and military courts in order to ensure that the reach of the Army Act would be limited.[21] In its later judgment in a case brought by the government against an opposition political party, however, the Supreme Court once again tried to be clever rather than consistent. It interpreted its role expansively—too much so, it seemed, for Bhutto—while at the same time accepting the government's version of explicitly political issues rather than return them to the legislature.[22] Paradox resulted: keen to underscore its own broad powers, the court aligned itself with government actions that were bound to redound negatively on judicial prerogative. The unfortunate habit of hewing to the will of extra-constitutional authority, even when costumed as valid law, eroded the necessary boundaries between civil and military law. As a national security state began to take shape under Bhutto, civil cases were transferred to military tribunals that, in turn, set aside judicial precedents intended, for example, to proscribe the use of torture.

Indeed, in a ruling on the expanding purview of the Army Act, the Supreme Court foreshadowed the opportunities for extra-constitutional authority in the 1973 Constitution. In a judgment published shortly after Zia ul Haq's coup d'état, the chief justice reaffirmed the constitutional prohibition against the imposition of martial law, but speculated that, "if the Constitution is abrogated, set aside or placed in a state of suspended animation or hibernation, it might be possible to impose Martial Law *outside* the Constitution."[23] Such an action, he commented, "may or may not be justified by the doctrine of necessity."

It was as if the supreme court was offering instruction to the military, and when the court was once again asked to judge the validity of the military takeover, it returned to old practice: the doctrine of necessity returned, almost without limit, and the doctrine of revolutionary legality was ignored.[24] Zia ul

Haq promised the courts that they would continue to operate, and in return the supreme court granted him the power to limit their jurisdiction to a degree hitherto almost unknown in Pakistan. In time, the peregrinations of misapplied doctrine took their toll. In 1981, when Zia ul Haq abruptly canceled the civil court powers that had been assumed in the necessity case, his rule was by implication legitimized by the otherwise discredited doctrine of revolutionary legality.

Had the court ruled differently, it is hard to imagine that the military government would have changed its course. Judges, after all, do not command army divisions. As years of martial law continued, however, it was hard to escape the conclusion that the superior courts had validated the execution of an elected prime minister and then presided over the near death of civilian justice. The longer term effects of judicial compliance were made clear when Zia ul Haq premised a 1984 referendum and a controlled election in 1985 on constitutional revisions that gave continuing legal effect to martial law, and provided immunity of unprecedented scope to all actions and persons involved in the martial law government.

However, stubborn politicians gave the high courts some opportunities to reverse themselves and reclaim some authority. The Karachi High Court had upheld the immunity of martial law regulations from judicial questioning, but in 1987, it decided that some military convictions could be challenged in civilian courts, and the Lahore High Court ruled further that Zia ul Haq had violated the doctrine of necessity by going beyond the promises he made when he seized power.[25] In the same year, the supreme court heard a petition from Benazir Bhutto, the leader of the People's Party, in its effort to reinstate the rights of political parties. The court underscored the inconsistencies of Zia ul Haq's revived, mixed government constitution, a decision that pointed the way toward the reinstatement of political and electoral rights.[26]

Zia ul Haq died in the following year, shortly after dissolving parliament, and only after his death did the courts begin to assert that the constitution—in some form, never quite specified—should take precedence over any regime or administration, and the courts should be the constitution's protector and interpreter.[27] It was a shallow response to a deep problem, however, for both politics and law were left almost irretrievably tangled in Zia's wake. Former parliamentarians wanted to be reinstated, new contestants sought polls, and the elected parliament led by Prime Minister Benazir Bhutto lacked sufficient power to override the martial law constitution. The best the courts could do, it seemed, was validate the fact of political change—an ironic nod to the old theme of revolutionary legality—and hope that a new political order would represent a step forward for constitutionalism and judicial autonomy.

The transition to civilian rule was a critical step in the evolution of the Pakistani state. When viewed through the retrospective lens of the law, however, hope triumphed over progress. Bhutto quickly tried to cleanse the supreme court of justices she deemed unworthy of appointment, setting the judiciary on edge before the real work of constitutional revision could begin, and giving rise to renewed suspicion that her party was keen to meddle with the instruments of justice. Neither Bhutto nor Sharif was able to transcend the complexities that four decades of civil-military rule had created; both were keen to create a new culture of parliamentary supremacy that, intentional or not, had the effect of vesting inadequate authority in the courts. The signal case during this period came early in Bhutto's tenure, when the supreme court reviewed the eighth constitutional amendment.[28] This was the law that Zia ul Haq had demanded as the price for lifting martial law in 1985, and that gave sanction to the president's right to dissolve parliament.[29] In step with popular sentiment to strengthen the legislative branch, the court sent the matter of the amendment's validity back to parliament, where it languished until Sharif became prime minister. When it was finally revoked—a major piece of legislation, supported in rare concord by parliamentarians in both major parties—it set off a political confrontation between the presidency and parliament that contributed to the army's growing distaste for parliamentary rule. Sharif tried as well to enact a constitutional amendment that would arm the prime minister with emergency powers equal to those of the President. Combined with disagreements over foreign policy, the economy and alleged corruption, these legislative efforts led almost inexorably to the end of Sharif's government.

Throughout the 1990s, therefore, the courts struggled with overtly political issues: the nature and limits of parliamentary rule, the problems that arise if courts ignore politics when judging constitutional issues, the intractable problems of parliamentary sovereignty, and the selective application of laws by beleaguered and weak governments.[30] Equally important, judges came to realize that their own tenures were no more stable under civilian than military governments, and indeed, that the intensely political nature of even routine hearings could pose as many dangers to them personally as to the law and constitution.

The decade of parliamentary government came to a close in 1999, when Musharraf took the opportunities offered by disputes about foreign policy and domestic governance to depose Sharif and impose emergency rule.[31] He followed Zia ul Haq's model by combining the roles of army chief and president (initially calling himself chief executive), and Ayub Khan's lead by refashioning governing bodies to cleanse them of traditional political leadership. The supreme court set a deadline for elections—a generous three years—but found itself nonetheless hampered by the new government's curbs on the judiciary. The PCO of 1999 gave the president the authority to issue ordinances, overriding all other laws, including the constitution and, predictably, immunizing him from prosecution. Judges were required to take new oaths of office— although dissidents were instead removed or retired—and to agree "not to call into question

or permit to be called into question" the validity of the PCO. When the PCO was challenged in *Zafar Ali Shah's case*, an obliging Supreme Court cited the familiar doctrine of necessity to validate the coup d'état and subsequent constitutional amendments that did not "change (its) basic features." The court, it seems, was immune to irony, for among those basic features was a chimera: the independence of the judiciary.

Like Zia ul Haq, Musharraf then choreographed a presidential referendum to ensure his tenure, and followed it with a Legal Framework Order in 2002 that restored the president's powers to dissolve parliament, extended his term as both president and army chief for five years, and provided immunity to all actions taken since the coup.[32] Some elements of this law were then included in the seventeenth amendment to the constitution, duly passed by the parliament—in return for a promise, later broken, that Musharraf would step down as army chief in 2004.[33] A challenge to the seventeenth amendment failed when the court fully supported the government and agreed to the constrained democracy put in place by rigged elections.[34]

The supreme court's prospective docket rather than its rulings were therefore the cause for renewed tensions between the executive and the judiciary in 2007, and, from Musharraf's point of view, with good reason. The supreme court's last opinion, published after the 2007 emergency proclamation, took up the constitutionality of the new PCO. Its short opinion warned against the government's taking actions contrary to the constitution and the independence of the judiciary, including the issuing of fresh oaths to the PCO.[35] By the time the opinion was issued, judges had been sacked, a new roster of compliant justices had indeed taken such an oath, and the deposed judges had assumed an unaccustomed place at the vanguard of a movement to return Pakistan to constitutional rule.[36] Their first target was Musharraf; their movement was critical in forcing him to step down as army chief after engineering his re-election as president.

Questions of justice

The election of a new parliament in February 2008 was framed by a year-long boycott of the courts by the legal community that followed the dismissal and arrest of the chief justice and later, his colleagues. In that sense, the election underscored the importance of the judiciary's status and independence, but it left many questions unanswered. Although the new ruling coalition initially promised to restore deposed judges and return to the 1973 Constitution, each party interpreted its intention differently: the politically ambitious Muslim League favored the unequivocal restoration of all deposed judges, while the majority People's Party, negotiating with Musharraf (who retained the office of president) preferred partial restoration as part of a larger package of political promises and constitutional reforms that included indemnity for the emergency of 2007.[37]

Underlying debates about political efficacy were serious, if unspoken, questions about the meanings of justice in a state whose constitutions have been compromised for so long, the role of judges whose actions were complicit in the steady diminution of judicial independence, the proper venue for reviewing the content of legislation (including the federal *sharia* court), and the proper balance among the executive, legislative and judicial branches of government. Although the organization of state power has been the particular province of the superior courts, it has also affected the ways that Pakistanis have been able to redress grievances and secure their rights. In many ways, access to lower courts has for the most part been of only peripheral interest to those in power. As a result, Pakistan's class chasms are reflected in the justice system, where corruption and inattention are rampant in the delivery of justice to the poor, and where defendants and lawyers assume that the abuse of state authority among the police is replicated in the judicial system.[38]

As if to correct these problems—but primarily to ensure that order is maintained

even when the rule of law is not—special courts have occasionally been added to the civilian judicial system. Speedy trial courts were created in the 1990s, but were soon shown to deliver judgments (if not justice) at a slower rate than the regular courts. Special courts, used to dispense justice under special rules, seemed to bypass the rule of law, and many observers referred to them instead as "conviction" courts. Anti-terrorist courts, most evident during states of emergency, and particularly since 2001, have been used either to remove defendants from the ambit of civil law and rights protections, to secure convictions, or to sequester detainees when the rule of law is absent. Qazi courts—local level religious courts—have been peripheral, but the Musharraf government's campaign to add them to the conflicted tribal agencies has led to suspicions that they would be instruments of the executive rather than voices for justice

The issues of injustice that permeate these systems of adjudication are of paramount importance as future parliaments take up questions of justice in Pakistan. It is the role of elected bodies, not the courts, to set aside Pakistan's sad history of indemnity in cases of abuse of power so that the state can chart a clear course toward the democracy promised in the 1973 Constitution. The juridical doctrines of necessity and revolutionary legality that have permeated political discourse reflect the profound weaknesses of Pakistan's governments, but they have offered little more than a language with which a distressed, disempowered and often alienated public has been able to voice its dissatisfactions with the state and its governing elites.

No matter how unsatisfactory the hand dealt to the courts by parliaments, presidents and the laws they have enacted, the judiciary—or at least, those judges who have chosen to remain on the bench during the worst of times—remains responsible for the misleading pragmatism and awkward prudence that has governed its rulings for six decades. A new compact is therefore essential for the country's legal future, for no matter how firm the exhortations of judicial autonomy might be, they are meaningful only if governments and citizens follow judicial rulings. If they are ignored—as they will be ignored if the courts do not craft incisive, constructive rulings that look to Pakistan's future rather than its past—then Pakistan's judiciary will revert to its accustomed role as historian for a weak, and weakly governed state.

Notes

1 "Pakistan's Supreme Court Takes Government to Task Over Missing Persons Issue," 5 July, 2007, available at Open Source Center SAP 20070705094002.

2 Constitutional Petition No. 9 of 2006 and Civil Petitions Nos. 345 and 394 of 2006 (*Pakistan Steel Mills Case*).

3 Under Article 209 of the 1973 Constitution, the Supreme Judicial Council is a body comprised of supreme court and high court justices to whom the president must refer all issues concerning the performance or possible misconduct of superior court judges. No superior court justices can be removed from office without the concurrence of the council.

4 Masood Rehman, "Rebirth of doctrine of necessity: Emergency and PCO validated," *Daily Times* (Lahore), 24 November, 2007; Nasir Iqbal, "SC hands out clean chit to Musharraf," *Daily Times* (Lahore), 24 November, 2007.

5 For a full discussion of these issues, see Paula R. Newberg, *Judging the State: Courts and Constitutional Politics in Pakistan* (Cambridge: University Press, 1994).

6 Dorab Patel, *Testament of a Liberal* (Karachi: Oxford University Press, 2000), p.101.

7 See *Begum Nusrat Bhutto vs The Chief of Army Staff and Federation of Pakistan*, PLD (1977) SC 657.

8 On the night of his coup d'état, Zia ul Haq promulgated The Laws (Continuance in Force) Order, 1977 (C.M.L.A. Order No. 1 of 1977). Article 1(2) mandated the continued functioning of the courts, but article 1(3) suspended the fundamental rights portion of the constitution, as well as "all proceedings pending in any court, insofar as they are for the enforcement of any of these rights." Judicial powers were undercut as well by Order No. 2, which stated that "provided that the Supreme Court or a High Court shall not have the power to make any order of the nature mentioned in Article 199 of the Constitution against the Chief Martial Law Administrator or a Martial Law Administrator or any person exercising powers or jurisdiction under the authority of either." See *The Chief Martial Law Administrator & All the Zonal Martial Law Administrators, Martial Law Regulations, Orders and Instructions*, 4th edn (Lahore: Paw Publishing Company, 1983).

9 For example, the so-called Judges Case of 1996: *Al Jehad Trust vs Federation of Pakistan*, PLD (1996) SC 324 at pp. 363–67. See also Sajjad Ali Shah, *Law Courts in a Glass House: An Autobiography* (Karachi: Oxford University Press, 2001), ch. ix.

10 See Ardeshir Cowasjee, "Storming of the Supreme Court," *Dawn* (Karachi), 31 October, 1999.

11 Sajjad Ali Shah, p. 671: Musharraf's military takeover came about "because the constitution did not provide any solution for the crisis with which the country was beset."

12 For example, in *Mohammed Ayub Khuro vs Federation of Pakistan*, PLD (1950) Sind 49, the Sind High Court ruled that while the constituent assembly held powers both to legislate and to write a constitution, "there is no limit imposed upon the legislative powers of the Constituent Assembly sitting as a constitution making body." In the Reference by His Excellency the Governor-General, PLD 1955 Federal Court 435, as well as in *Maulvi Tamizuddin Khan vs The Federation of Pakistan*, PLD (1955) Sind 96 and *Federation of Pakistan et al., vs Moulvi Tamizuddin Khan*, the courts ruled on the relative roles of the governor-general, the extent of the legislature's powers, and the judiciary's authority to limit executive authority. In *Usif Patel and Two Others vs The Crown*, PLD (1955) Federal Court 387 (Appellate Jurisdiction), the court limited the scope of the governor-general's powers. These cases, and many others, highlighted not only the indeterminacy of popular politics at the time, but the inadequacies of state institutions at this early stage of independence.

13 "Pakistan's Dilemma," *Civil and Military Gazette*, 6 March, 1955, p. 4.

14 In *Muhammad Umar Khan vs The Crown* PLD (1953) Lahore 528, High Court Justice Mohammed Munir (later Supreme Court Chief Justice in the 1955 *Reference*) equated the declaration of military necessity by a military ruler with civil necessity by a civilian ruler. By 1958 the two forms of necessity were joined in a military coup d'état justified by a doctrine of civil necessity.

15 *Dosso and Another vs the State and Others*, PLD (1957) (W.P.) Quetta 9.

16 In Ayub Khan's first years, the court acknowledged the absence of justifiable rights and accepted its reduced power in *The Province of East Pakistan vs Md. Mehdi Ali Khan Panni*, PLD (1959) Supreme Court (Pak) 387, and in *Mian Iftikhar-ud-Din and Arif Iftikhar vs Muhammaed Sarfraz and the Government of Pakistan*, and vice versa, PLD (1961) Supreme Court 85, found it impossible to extend its jurisdiction under Ayub Khan's writ. Once a written constitution was in force, however, the court found it easier to push for more balanced powers and the beginnings of rights protections. On conflicts between the executive and parliament, and the right to judicial review, see *Fazlul Quader Chowdhry and others vs Mr. Muhammad Abdul Haque*, PLD (1963) Supreme Court 486; on freedom of political speech, see *Saiyyid Abul A'la Maudoodi et al., vs The Government of West Pakistan and the Government of Pakistan*, PLD (1964) SC 673. In *Government of East Pakistan vs Mrs. Rowshan Bijaya Shaukat Ali Khan*, PLD (1966) Supreme Court 286, the Court reiterated the right of habeas corpus, despite deep divisions among justices about the effects of rights protections on executive prerogative. This debate continued in *Malik Ghulam Jilani vs The Government of West Pakistan*, PLD (1967) Supreme Court 373, which deepened the court's debate about judicial prerogative and political speech.

17 When the Supreme Court in *Snelson's Case* declared "the law of the country is what the judiciary says it is," Ayub Khan responded that "any government worth its name should be in a position to control its Executive officers and rectify their errors." *Sir Edward Snelson vs The Judges of the High Court of West Pakistan, Lahore and The Central Government of Pakistan*, PLD (1961) Supreme Court 237.

18 *Zia-ur Rahman vs The State*, PLD (1972) Lahore 382.

19 The revocation of revolutionary legality in *Asma Jilani's Case* (*Miss Asma Jilani vs The Government of the Punjab [sic]* and *Mrs Zarina Gauhar vs the Province of Sind and Two Others*, PLD (1972) SC 139) became a reference point for the courts through the Bhutto years.

20 See *Debates: Official Report*, 10 April, 1973, and 1973 Constitution, Preamble and Article 2(A).

21 *State vs Yusaf Lodhi*, PLD (1973) Peshawar 25; *Fakhre Alam vs The State and Another*, PLD (1973) SC 525; *Liaqat Ali vs Government of Sind through Secretary, Home Department*, PLD (1973) Karachi 78. In the most important case concerning civil law and military practice, *F. B. Ali vs The State*, PLD (1975) SC 506, the Court claimed the traditional power of judicial review and allowed courts martial to keep powers provided by subsequent constitutional amendments.

22 See *Zafar Iqbal vs Province of Sind and Two Others*, PLD (1973), Karachi 243; *Islamic Republic of Pakistan through Secretary, Ministry of Interior and Kashmir Affairs, Islamabad vs Mr. Abdul Wali Khan MNA* (Reference No. 1 of 1975).

23 *Darwesh M. Arbey, Advocate vs Federation of Pakistan through the Law Secretary and Two Others*, PLD (1980) Lahore 206, and earlier, *F. B. Ali vs The State*, PLD (1975) Lahore 999.

24 *Begum Nusrat Bhutto vs The Chief of Army Staff and Federation of Pakistan*, PLD (1974) Lahore 7.

25 *Nazar Muhammad Khan vs Pakistan and Two Others*, PLD (1986) Karachi 516; Muhammad Bachal Memon vs Government of Sind, PLD (1987) Karachi 296.

26 *Benazir Bhutto vs Federation of Pakistan and Another*, PLD (1988) Supreme Court 416, and *Benazir Bhutto vs Federation of Pakistan and Another*, PLD (1989) Supreme Court 66; on indemnity, *Federation of Pakistan and others vs Haji Muhammad Saifullah Khan and Others*, (1988) PSC 338.

27 *Benazir Bhutto vs Federation of Pakistan and Another*, PLD (1989) SC 66.

28 *Haji Ahmed vs Federation of Pakistan through Secretary, Ministry of Justice and Parliamentary Affairs and 88 Others*, Constitutional Petitions D-76, 163, 168 of (1989).

29 See previously, *Reference No. 1 of 1988, made by the President of Pakistan Under Article 186 of the Constitution*, PLD (1989) SC 75, regarding the question of dissolution at the time of Zia ul Haq's death.

30 On questions of judicial independence, see *Government of Sind vs Sharif Faridi*, PLD (1994) SC 105, on divesting district government officials of their judicial powers, and *Mehram Ali vs Federation of Pakistan*, PLD (1998) SC 1445; on the contentious questions involving appointment of justices, see *Al Jehad Trust vs Federation of Pakistan*, PLD (1996) SC 324 (the Judges Case), and *Asad Ali vs Federation of Pakistan*, PLD (1998) SC 161.

31 Former Justice Sajjad Ali Shah later noted that the military took power "because the constitution did not provide any solution for the crises with which the country was beset," the same justification used by previous military governments in Pakistan and, more recently, in Bangladesh; Shah, p. 671.

32 *Zafar Ali Shah vs Pervez Musharraf*, PLD (2000) SC 869 unsuccessfully challenged the coup d'état, and *Hussain Ahmed vs Pervez Mushrraf*, PLD (2002) SC 853 unsuccessfully challenged the referendum. See also *Qazi Hussein Ahmed, Ameer Jamaat-I-Islami, Pakistan vs General Pervez Musharraf, Chief Executive and Another*, Constitutional Petition No, 15, 17–24 and 512/2002. *Supreme Court Bar Association vs Federation of Pakistan*, Constitutional Petition No, 1 of 2002 unsuccessfully challenged Musharraf's appointment of judges.

33 Zahid Hussain, "A Military State," *Newsline* (Karachi), October 2004.

34 The case also challenged the "President to Hold Another Office Act of 2004" which was intended to clarify the relationship between Musharraf's two roles.

35 Proclamation of Emergency and Provisional Constitutional Order, *Gazette of Pakistan*, 3 November, 2007; Order to Further Amend the Constitution, *Gazette of Pakistan*, 20 November, 2007.

36 See Library of Congress (US), "Suspension and Reinstatement of the Chief Justice of Pakistan; From Judicial Crisis to Restoring Judicial Independence," Current Legal Topics (web), 20 March, 2008.

37 "Article Inserted by Musharraf," and "New Article in PPP Amendment Bill," *Dawn* (Karachi), 2 June, 2008. See also International Crisis Group, *Winding Back Martial Law in Pakistan*, Asia Briefing #70 (Islamabad and Brussels) 12 November, 2007.

38 http://www.adb.org/Documents/Periodicals/ADB_Review/2005/vol37–2/justice-all.asp# delays. See also Ali Saleem, "Inaccessible justice in Pakistan," Asian Legal Resource Center, Hong Kong, 11 August, 2004.

13

Confronting constitutional curtailments

Attempts to rebuild independence of the judiciary in Bangladesh

Sara Hossain

The independence of the Judiciary . . . is one of the basic pillars of the Constitution and cannot be demolished, whittled down, curtailed or diminished in any manner whatsoever, *except under the existing provisions of the Constitution* . . . we find no provision in the Constitution which curtails, diminishes or otherwise abridges this independence.

(*Masdar Hossain vs Bangladesh* 2000 BLD (AD) 104 Per Mostafa Kamal J. [emphasis added])

Introduction

In the almost four decades since Bangladesh became an independent nation, through periods of continuing transition, from immediate post-war aftermath through parliamentary to presidential to outright military rule and back again, the supreme court has repeatedly been the focus of public attention, providing a forum not only for redress of rights against a repressive state, but carving out, with greater or lesser caution, parameters for determining relations between the state and political parties and, more recently, the duties and obligations of the state to the people at large and to the public interest.

The court's approach has oscillated between permitting full frontal challenges followed by correctives to executive action and inaction in the face of flagrantly arbitrary action and clear constitutional breaches. This approach has also marked the efforts made to safeguard the court's own autonomy and independence.

Experiences of executive control and interference, which marked both the colonial and the Pakistan periods, informed the framing of explicit provisions in the post-independence Constitution of 1972, mandating independence of the judiciary and its separation from the executive at all levels. However, amendments to the original constitutional provisions made under autocratic and military rule, the failure to overhaul the inherited institutional structure, and the continued intervention of deeply embedded vested interests, further exacerbated by overt politicization of the court, and new constitutional arrangements enabling involvement of the senior most members of the judiciary in the executive, have—if not as yet demolished—certainly diminished and curtailed the scope for the court to operate with full independence.

This chapter examines the legal and institutional framework for safeguarding the independence of the judiciary in Bangladesh, focusing in particular on the role of the supreme court in this regard. It first outlines the provisions of the 1972 constitution, which articulated the principle and promised the potential for securing judicial independence at all levels. It then describes how these principles were eroded through law and practice, most significantly through enhancing the president's powers to the detriment of the chief justice under the fourth amendment (accompanying the imposition of one-party rule), fragmentation of the supreme court by the eighth amendment (under effective military rule) and then further—albeit more indirectly—by the thirteenth amendment (under an elected government introducing the caretaker government system), which envisaged a role for the judiciary in the executive, as well as through interference with the appointments process. The discussion then traces the Supreme Court's assertions of judicial independence, focusing in particular on the landmark judgments in Anwar Hossain's case (which laid down the doctrine of the basic structure of the constitution), and the more recent Masdar Hossain case, which elaborated a framework for separation of the lower judiciary from the executive, and its outcomes. (A third judgment, in *Idrisur Rahman's Case*, which may ultimately join these in significance, is currently under appeal in the appellate division and therefore not discussed here.) The discussion concludes with a reflection on the continuing legacy of the politicization of the judiciary with regard to its effective functioning as well as current institutional challenges to the delivery of justice. It also considers the approaches available to the court as it seeks to put its own house in order, not merely by asserting autonomy, but examining whether it is as yet prepared for ensuring its accountability.

Constructing the pillar: The 1972 constitution

In the immediate aftermath of the independence of Bangladesh, the members of the constituent assembly charged with drafting the constitution were fully alive to the need to safeguard the judiciary from politicization and executive control, the impact of which many of them had suffered directly during both the British and Pakistan periods.

Consequently, the 1972 Constitution, in its original incarnation, articulated a principle of judicial independence (art. 22) as a principle of state policy, and explicitly guaranteed that the chief justice and the other judges of the supreme court would be independent in the exercise of their functions (art. 22, read with art. 94 4). This constitutional mandate for independence at every level was buttressed with specific provisions addressing the appointment, removal, and other terms and conditions of service of members of both the higher and lower judiciary.[1] Under this framework, the Supreme Court enjoyed an unprecedented degree of administrative and financial control over itself. Supreme Court justices could only be appointed by the president, subject to consultation with the chief justice (art. 95). The retirement age was 62, and no judge could be removed following confirmation, except by the Supreme Judicial Council by president's order after a parliamentary resolution with a two-thirds majority and on grounds of proved misbehavior or incapacity (art. 96). Their remuneration, privileges and terms and conditions of service could not be varied to their disadvantage during their term of office.[2] Additional judges were to be appointed by the president for two years, if the president was satisfied, after consultation with the chief justice, of a need for increase (art. 98). Retired judges (except additional judges) were barred from acting before any court/authority or being appointed to service of the republic (art. 99).

The supreme court also had powers of superintendence and control over all courts subordinate to it.[3] The chief justice was empowered to appoint all district judges, and the president all other judicial officers and magistrates exercising judicial functions according to rules made by him in consultation with the Public Service Commission and the Supreme Court. The Supreme Court also had powers of control (including posting/promotion/grant of leave) and discipline of such judicial officers and magistrates exercising judicial functions (art. 116). While the regulation of appointment and conditions of service was to be by law made by parliament, subject to the constitution, it was also provided that the president may make rules until such laws were framed, which would be effective subject to the law's provisions (art. 133). Significantly, there was a clear mandate that separation "shall be implemented as soon as practicable," set out as a "transitory provision" (see Fourth Schedule, art. 6 [6]).

This framework proved impermanent, and the almost four decades since independence saw major encroachments, by autocratic and military rulers and indeed by democratic governments, on the relevant constitutional provisions, both through legal amendments and in practice, as we shall see later.

Attempts at demolition

Within barely three years of the adoption of the constitution, in 1975, the then Awami League Government enacted the Fourth Amendment to the Constitution,[4] resulting in extensive reworking, and virtual undoing, of the major provisions concerning the judiciary (Part VI, Chapters I and II). Most critically, this amendment curtailed the powers of the chief justice and the Supreme Court in the matter of appointments of both the superior and subordinate judiciary (arts 95 and 115). It removed the express constitutional requirement to consult with the supreme court or the chief justice in either case. It also provided scope for the president not to confirm the appointment of additional judges of the Supreme Court (art. 98), and to remove Supreme Court judges simply on grounds of misbehavior or incapacity following the decision taken by the Supreme Judicial Council (comprising the chief justice and two other judges). The amendment also resulted in the president taking over the

Supreme Court's powers of control (including posting, promotion, and grant of leave) and discipline of the subordinate courts (art. 116). The consequence—as noted by a respected former judge of the Supreme Court—was that "Article 116, as it stands now, is the insurmountable block against separation of the judiciary from executive control."

Within the year, in 1976, martial law was proclaimed, and the Supreme Court was divided into the appellate division and High Court division, only to be reunited again barely a year later.[5] More positively, however, the requirement for the president to consult with the Supreme Court regarding the control and discipline of subordinate judges and magistrates exercising judicial functions was restored (art. 116).[6]

Further incursions into judicial independence—in particular of the superior judiciary—were made during the military rule of Lt. General Ershad. First, the retirement age of Supreme Court justices was changed to 62 or on completion of three years as chief justice, whichever were earlier, in a deliberate design to affect the sitting chief justice. This provision was equally cavalierly repealed three years later, to enable the next chief justice to continue in office. By further martial law proclamations, Ershad then sought to denude the Supreme Court—a major source of resistance to his rule—of its strength. He established "permanent benches" of the high court in six district towns and transferred judges from the High Court to preside over them,[7] measures which faced massive protests from lawyers across the country. Following elections that were widely questioned, parliament then adopted the Constitution (Eighth Amendment) Act 1988, which provided for establishing six permanent benches outside Dhaka and empowered the president (now Ershad) to determine their territorial jurisdiction (art. 100). The political and legal challenge against the breakup of the High Court, and this effort to diminish its powers, were ultimately to catalyze the popular movement against the Ershad "autocracy."

193

Following Ershad's fall in a popular cross-party movement, which demanded transfer of power to a caretaker government headed by a nonpartisan person, he appointed the sitting chief justice, Mr. Justice Shahabuddin Ahmed as vice president and then handed over power to him. Justice Shahabuddin headed the caretaker government and oversaw the return to a parliamentary system in 1991, and also the adoption of the Constitution (Twelfth Amendment) Act, which extended the high court's supervision and control over subordinate courts to include tribunals (art. 109). Attempts were made to restore the original provisions of the 1972 Constitution but failed in the face of parliamentary deadlock.[8]

Subsequently, in 1996, following renewal of demands for a caretaker government arrangement in the wake of reports of massive vote rigging under Khaleda Zia's government, the Thirteenth Amendment to the constitution introduced the system of a caretaker government overseeing parliamentary elections every five years, and allowed for a retired chief justice to be appointed as the chief advisor to each caretaker government. This provision blurred the lines regarding separation from the executive, this time at the highest levels of the judiciary (art. 58C).

This series of constitutional amendments curtailed the scope for the court to operate independently, enabling executive controls to be manifested over the powers of appointments and removals, and their administration. The legacy of the Fourth Amendment bore out the prescient remarks of a former judge: "The possibility of entry of political factors into the question of appointment of judges of the Supreme Court cannot be ruled out."[9] Following the restoration of the parliamentary system, and under the elected governments in place from 1990, several significant crises regarding appointments and non-confirmation of ad hoc judges of the Supreme Court took place. These incurred protests from the bar and criticism from civil society, and also faced constitutional challenges, resulting in a series of damaging standoffs with potentially very grave and long-term implications for the Supreme Court's ability to act as a "competent, impartial and independent" forum of justice.

In each of these incidents, the issue of consultation with the chief justice was central. As noted by one leading lawyer, such consultation was meant to be "effective, meaningful, consensus-oriented, leaving no room for complaint of arbitrariness or unfair play in appointment of judges."[10] Although the constitutional provision requiring consultation with the chief justice had been obliterated through the Fourth Amendment, there had never been any deviation from the actual process of such consultation. This process was followed as an unbroken convention until 1992 when, for the first time, the president appointed nine additional judges without consultation with the chief justice. The then chief justice (Shahabuddin Ahmed) declined to administer the oath to them and the legal community considered the matter as a threat to the independence of the judiciary. The then prime minister had to comply with the demand of the lawyers and canceled the appointment. The process of consultation with the chief justice was established as a cornerstone to the independence of the judiciary.[11] However, lack of consultation recurred as a concern over the coming years and increasingly became mired in partisan disputes. Further appointments under the BNP-led government were questioned on this basis, as were some of the Awami League government's appointments of additional judges to the high court division, and the next BNP-led government's refusal to confirm the appointments of these nine additional judges. The nadir was reached in the wholesale appointment on a single day of 19 judges to the high court under the BNP-led government in 2004 (one of whom later resigned when facing a proceeding before the Supreme Judicial Council in relation to the allegation of his having tampered with his mark sheets and obtained a third-class LLB degree). In several instances, judges were appointed to the apex court by supercession of others, in derogation of the tradition of appointment of the senior most judge. Such appointments under the Awami League-led government were followed by physical attacks launched by lawyers supporting the opposition Bangladesh National Party (BNP) on the members of the apex court itself, and ultimately to counter–supercessions by the BNP-led government.

Reconstructing the basic structure

A number of these constitutional amendments and executive practices curtailing independence faced challenges before the Supreme Court, mainly by way of writ petitions filed by lawyers acting in the public interest, members of the subordinate judiciary, and most recently by former Supreme Court judges. The first major challenge in *Anwar Hossain's case* resulted in perhaps the most important judgment of the appellate division to date (declaring judicial independence to be part of the basic structure of the constitution).[12] Subsequently, following the return to the parliamentary system, the Masdar Hossain judgment laid out the legal and institutional framework for ending subordination of the lower judiciary to the executive. Most recently, a challenge by several former ad hoc judges of the high court to the then president's non-confirmation of their appointment has been held to be wholly unconstitutional, and currently faces final determination before the appellate division.[13] It is too early to review this last judgment, which may have long-lasting implications for the court, but the next two sections will discuss how, through Anwar Hossain's and Masdar Hossain's case, the judiciary laid down some fundamental principles for guiding relations between the legislature, judiciary and executive as well as asserting its own autonomy and independence.

Anwar Hossain's case

As noted already, seven "permanent benches" of the high court had been set up under martial law in 1982, and then when the constitution was revived, following a constitutional amendment in 1988, the permanent benches were treated as sessions of the high court outside the capital. Each of these benches was given a fixed territorial jurisdiction while the high court was given a "residual" jurisdiction. The chief justice also framed rules for transfer of proceedings out of the high court to the permanent benches. In 1988, three petitioners challenged the refusal of the concerned court official to allow them to affirm affidavits in Dhaka on the ground that the main writ petition had been transferred to a "permanent bench" outside Dhaka under the Eighth Amendment to the constitution.[14] It was argued that the constitutional amendment and the rules had damaged the basic structure of the constitution, which envisages the high court as having plenary judicial power. The high court rejected the petition, but the appellate division, by a majority of three to one—and for the only time in Bangladesh's history—held that the constitutional amendment was void and that the structural pillar of the judiciary is basic and fundamental to the scheme of the constitution. They found in essence that the permanent benches of the high court, which the martial law authorities had sought to justify—and later the government and also the chief justice—as means of expanding access to justice to litigants beyond the capital, had in practice contributed to reducing significantly the quality of justice. Reflecting on the political context and the strains—and indeed dominance of the executive—within which the judiciary was compelled to operate, Justice M. H. Rahman remarked as follows:

> The doctrine of basic structure . . . developed in
> a climate where the executive, commanding an
> overwhelming majority in the legislature, gets
> snap amendments of the Constitution passed

without a Green Paper or White Paper, without eliciting any public opinion, without sending the Bill to any Select Committee and without giving sufficient time to members of Parliament for deliberation on the Bill for amendment.

The court proceeded to ground the basic structure doctrine by reference to Article 7 that all powers in the Republic belong to the people which, as noted by Justice Shahabuddin Ahmed:

> [S]tands between the Preamble and Article 8 as the statue of liberty, supremacy of law and rule of law and to put it in the words of an American judge . . . it is the pole star of our Constitution. No Parliament can amend it because Parliament is the creation of this Constitution and all powers follow from this Article, namely, Article 7.
>
> (at paras 183, 184)

The judgment resulted in the termination of the "permanent benches," return of all judges to the Dhaka High Court, and restoration of the full plenary powers of the high court, which went on to become the forum in which many aspects of Ershad's regime were to face challenge until his ultimate downfall in 1990, and his handover of power— in a pleasant irony—to the then Chief Justice, Shahabuddin Ahmed.

Masdar Hossain's case

In 1996, Masdar Hossain, a district judge, along with several others, challenged a law[15] that purported to include judicial officers within the Bangladesh Civil Service. As in *Anwar Hossain's case*, the high court rejected the petition but, on appeal, Masdar Hossain won a landmark judgment, in which the appellate division directed establishment of a separate judicial service, distinct from the executive and from the administrative cadres of the Bangladesh Civil Service, to include both judicial officers and magistrates exercising judicial functions. It stated that members of both the judicial services and magistrates

exercising judicial functions formed a class distinct from other services of the republic, and that they could not be "treated alike or merged or amalgamated with any other service, except a service of an allied nature." The apex court addressed head on longstanding concerns regarding executive control over the subordinate judiciary, reaffirmed the principle of independence of the judiciary, elaborated on the constitutional position and practice regarding separation of the judiciary from the executive, and laid down a series of 12 declarations and directions for implementation by the government in this regard.[16]

This judgment addressed the larger colonial legacy, perpetuated by succeeding regimes both in Pakistan and independent Bangladesh, involving an overlap and blurring of judicial and executive functions. In the lower criminal courts, the area where executive control was most apparent and most problematic, the pattern for lack of separation was set early on. The colonial view, happily adopted by the postcolonial state, that administration could only be effective with a centralization of authority and the power to punish and discipline, informed these arrangements. Thus, the chief executive officer at the district level, the deputy commissioner, was also responsible for judicial functions as the district magistrate. Similarly, magistrates, appointed and controlled by the executive, who performed executive functions (for example issuance of licenses or orders of detention) were also empowered to exercise judicial powers including, among others, taking witness statements, entertaining bail applications, conducting trials and passing sentences in respect of certain offences. (These arrangements were embedded in the *Criminal Procedure Code of 1898* ["the Code"].) The dilemma so eloquently expressed by John Eames, serving in Chittagong as a magistrate in the early 1920s, thus continued to plague all his successors into the century ahead: "It is troubling to be the executive officer in the morning, and then wear a judicial hat and sit in judgment on my own decisions in the afternoon!"[17]

196

While attempts at separation were made in the Pakistan period, they were either not maintained, or never implemented.[18] Immediately after liberation, new members of the constituent assembly—who had directly or indirectly faced unfair trials, arbitrary arrests, denial of bail and prolonged periods of incommunicado detention, resulting from extensive use and abuse of magisterial powers—acting at the behest of the executive of the day, sought to chart a new path by embedding a clear mandate for separation of the lower judiciary. However, as noted earlier, the onslaught on the original letter and spirit of the constitution effected by the Fourth Amendment, swiftly followed by 15 years of direct and indirect military rule, put paid to the hope and potential for reform in this area.

As noted already, prior to the Fourth Amendment, the president could appoint officers in judicial service and magistrates exercising judicial functions "in accordance with rules made by him" (art. 115), which could be framed only following consultation with the supreme court and Public Service Commission. The president was also vested with direct *control* (including the power of posting, promotion, and granting of leave) and *discipline* of the subordinate courts, although this remained subject to his or her exercising it in consultation with the Supreme Court. Following the Fourth Amendment, and in the absence of any rules having been framed, the president appointed all judges of the subordinate courts as well as magistrates. These recruitments were made from the judicial cadre of the Bangladesh Civil Service (BCS Judicial) and the administrative cadre of the civil service (BCS Admin) respectively. By delegation of the president's powers under the constitution, the Ministry of Law was responsible for initiating the process with regard to appointments, and also for transfer, promotion, leave and discipline of the subordinate courts. After preparing the files, the ministry, in a nod to the consultation requirement, would send these on to the Supreme Court for approval. The executive was thus placed in an extraordinarily strong position of control over the lower judiciary, and was able to use its power of appointments, promotions, and postings as a carrot or stick as necessary to manipulate both the composition of the lower judiciary and its functioning. These powers were in turn routinely abused by all regimes as a tool to cement their authority, and, too often, to control their respective political oppositions.

Another arena for confusion between judicial and executive functions was with respect to the practice of deputation, whereby judicial officers could be posted to purely administrative or executive posts, as the law officers of various ministries, including the Ministry of Law.[19]

When Masdar Hossain challenged the recruitment rules for judicial officers, he set in motion a process that enabled the court to examine each of the aspects of lack of separation between the executive and judiciary already discussed. It also resulted in a clear exposition of the contours of judicial independence, and a realistic and pragmatic understanding of its current constitutional limits. Thus, the court identified five key characteristics of independence of the judiciary: security of tenure; recruitment to the judicial service as a permanent posting and through a transparent Judicial Service Commission; security of emoluments, including pension, etc.; institutional functional independence of the subordinate judiciary from parliament and the executive and, finally, financial autonomy within the sphere of funds allocated. The court further held that every institution, authority and individual associated with the judicial administration is required to advance, strengthen and achieve these measures. In one of its "12 commandments," the court required the government to set up two separate bodies, the Judicial Service Commission (to recruit members of the judicial service), and the Judicial Pay Commission (to fix pay scales for members of the judicial service), specifying the nature of their composition, powers, and functions, and to separate the executive and judicial functions of the magistracy. To this end, it required the government to adopt two sets of laws, one set requiring regulation of the terms and conditions of service of judicial officers,[20] and the other requiring replacement of all references to "magistrates" in existing laws by the term "judicial magistrates," and amendment of all laws that empower magistrates to try criminal cases.

For almost ten years after the Masdar judgment, it remained virtually unimplemented. In 2001, the then caretaker government ensured that all the draft rules were prepared and was on the brink of approving these at its last meeting prior to handing over power to the newly elected government, but did not proceed on receiving an assurance from Khaleda Zia, prime minister-elect, that her government would do so in fulfilment of their manifesto commitment. Once in power, however, Begum Zia's government took no steps other than to adopt one set of rules for establishing the Judicial Service Commission[21] and to provide for financial autonomy of the Supreme Court, and otherwise took adjournment after adjournment before the Supreme Court, claiming that the process was underway.

It was to take another five years and another caretaker government for all the rules to be finalized and adopted.[22] In 2007, the caretaker government ultimately adopted the remaining rules regarding the terms and conditions of judicial officers, as well as legislation amending the Code of Criminal Procedure regarding the nomenclature, powers and functions of the magistracy. The amended code replaced all existing references to "magistrate," without any qualifying word, by the term "judicial magistrate." It provided for appointment of executive magistrates from among persons employed in the BCS (Admin) and appointment of judicial magistrates from among persons employed in the (newly created) Bangladesh Judicial Service. It also set out the powers and functions of executive and judicial magistrates both under the code and other laws. These functions are now clearly identified, with judicial magistrates being responsible for the appreciation or shifting of evidence or the formulation of any decision that exposes any person to any punishment or penalty or detention in custody pending investigation, inquiry or trial or other proceeding or would have the effect of sending him for trial before any court, while executive magistrates are responsible for functions which are administrative or executive in nature, such as licensing matters, or decisions to sanction or withdraw a prosecution.

Despite the institutional and legal framework for separation having now been established, several concerns have arisen in regard to whether this framework is fully compliant with the letter and spirit of the judgment. One set of concerns relate to the continuing overlap between the powers of the judiciary and executive regarding appointments. With regard to appointments, control, and discipline of judicial officers, the Ministry of Law still initiates this process and thereby continues to exert influence over it. This has already given rise to critical questions in the media regarding how the ministry had nominated judicial officers for promotion overlooking "adverse remarks" in their confidential records, and the Supreme Court had approved this list of nominations without further scrutiny. In one case currently (2008) pending hearing, a national newspaper published reports highlighting the continued dependence of the Supreme Court on the executive, that is, the Ministry of Law, in relation to the appointment of district judges. Following publication, a lawyer filed a contempt of court petition against the newspaper alleging interference in the functioning of the supreme court.[23]

Another set of concerns relates to the practice of deputation. Deputation is a condition of service; but the apex court in Masdar Hossain clearly held that "judicial service" falls outside this definition of service, and thus there can be no deputation from judicial service, observing that "as oil and water cannot mix, the judicial and civil administrative executive services are non amalgamable."[24] Thus, the continuing practice of deputation—in respect of posting judicial officers to executive posts—appears contrary to the spirit of the judgment as well as the constitution. One concern is that the long-term effect of such "executive posting" might undermine the impartiality and independence of the judicial service by allowing judicial officers to operate within an executive environment, thereby affecting their capacity to operate neutrally and free of executive influence. However, judicial officers are continuing to demand that this facility be allowed. This question has been highlighted in litigation on the appointment of the Secretary to the Ministry of Law, Justice and Parliamentary Affairs, a member of the BCS (Judicial) cadre who chose to opt out of the judicial service and into the executive, but whose appointment has been challenged in a public interest petition brought by a former judge.[25]

The Masdar judgment has also been invoked to buttress long-standing demands from the bar for a law containing specific guidelines to prevent arbitrariness in appointments of Supreme Court judges, in order to strengthen the court as an institution. When the Supreme Judicial Commission Ordinance 2008 was promulgated, in apparent response to this demand, a public interest petition was filed challenging its constitutionality on the ground that the proposed commission was comprised of a majority of members from the executive branch.[26] While the petition was pending, the government amended the ordinance, ensuring that a majority of members were to be drawn from the judiciary.

The High Court Division also recently declared the Contempt of Court Ordinance 2008 to be unconstitutional on the grounds, inter alia, that certain provisions contravened the Masdar judgment, in particular regarding the definition of contempt. The ordinance had provided that non-compliance with a court order would not constitute contempt if such compliance was not practicable, and, further, if it would involve contravention of any existing laws, and would effectively have benefited members of the executive.

Other more practical concerns regarding implementation of the judgment relate to the nature of recruitment—in terms of numbers and quality—for both the civil and criminal courts. In respect of the former, the Judicial Service Commission has proceeded with recruitment after a hiatus of several years, during which many judicial posts had lain vacant, and appointed over 200 judicial officers, with some controversy arising regarding the nature of these appointments. With respect to the criminal justice system, the relatively small numbers of magistrates opting for the judicial service (presumably loath to abandon their proximity to power in the executive service) meant that there was, and will continue to be, a serious shortfall in judicial capacity at this level, compounding existing delays and difficulties to be faced by the users at the frontlines of the system.

Moving beyond Masdar: Questions of accountability

While the steps taken to date are significant, they are clearly only the beginning of a very long process required for effective separation and for full independence. As acknowledged in Masdar Hossain's case, without restoring the original Articles 115 and 116 of the constitution, the supreme court will be unable to exercise full control and discipline over the subordinate courts. Further amendment of the current rules may be necessary. Other more practical measures will also be needed, to supplement the formal and legal framework so that judicial officers and judicial magistrates can operate freely. These would require changes in their conditions of service to include more appropriate remuneration and benefits, raising the levels of competence, introducing systems of monitoring and evaluation, schemes for annual recognition and reward, as well as greater transparency and openness in the functioning of the courts, for example, by holding annual conferences, or the publication of annual reports containing case data. The most crucial change needed, and the one impossible to address through legislation alone, will require the cultivation of independence of mind and spirit immune to any kind of influence, whether from partisan political forces, or other powerful actors or agencies.

If the operation of the courts continues to give rise to fears that they are not able to operate free of "extraneous influences," and if there is no strong mechanism to check partisan decision making, then concerns regarding the accountability of the judiciary will also multiply.[27] The politicization of the appointment process, and the consequences of these appointments in terms of the patterns of judgments and orders in certain politically sensitive cases, have led to serious questioning of the image of the judiciary as an independent institution. These issues have, in turn, raised concerns regarding the capacity of the judiciary to ensure its own accountability. Recent experiences have heightened these concerns. These include the refusal of the court to investigate allegations raised in the media regarding the lack of qualifications of a person appointed as an additional judge (who later himself resigned when a proceeding was finally initiated before the Supreme Judicial Council); the continuing lack of inquiry into the nature of these appointments, and the lack of any self-corrective mechanism established by the court to address them. These questions are likely to come to the fore in a pending appeal before the supreme court against the high court's judgment holding unconstitutional the earlier non-confirmation by the BNP-led government of nine additional judges.[28] In this judgment, the appellants include 19 sitting judges of the high court, on the one hand, pitted against persons who had all served as additional judges, on the other. It establishes unprecedented and complex hurdles for the court to overcome on the road to establishing both judicial accountability and independence.

Conclusion: Repairing the rebuilding

The *Anwar Hossain case* involved reinsertion of bricks into the pillar of the independence of the judiciary, which had been flung out in four directions, and Masdar Hossain's has enabled rebuilding of a firm plinth in the form of separation of the judiciary. Clearly, there is much still to be done, and the constitutional petitions now pending before the courts raise important questions regarding the manner and mode of this rebuilding process, and what it will require if the foundation is to be solidly built. But most importantly, with Article 116 remaining in its present form, it is clear that there are major structural deficiencies in the pillar. And the new controversies regarding appointments and non-confirmation of Supreme Court judges now call in question whether the pillar is crumbling from within.

The discussion in this chapter has shown how movements for ensuring independence of the judiciary, and for reconstructing the applicable legal framework have been first catalyzed, and then driven from within the legal system by activist judges and lawyers with a commitment to maintaining the integrity of the system and enabling it to continue to deliver justice, within all existing constraints. It is equally evident that these movements have faced continued resistance from within the bureaucracy and, most important, from those holding political power at the highest levels (and elements partisan to them among both judges and lawyers), who have sought to retain executive controls over the judiciary, not only to manipulate the political opposition but in the more general expectation of favorable outcomes.

Sadly, while lawyers actively engaged in political life, and members of the Bar actively engaged in movements for democracy have advocated, inside and outside the courts, for the restoration of judicial independence, they have been less insistent on this demand once their favored political parties achieve office. And indeed the consistent pattern under all regimes—from full-blown military governments to autocratic presidents and elected parliaments—has been to reduce independence, on the one hand, and further politicize the judiciary, on the other. The fruits of this political patronage—exacerbated by the carrot and stick effect on the senior most judges of the possibility of their elevation to the highest office in the land as chief advisor of the caretaker government—have led to the current crisis. Today, the higher judiciary remains the forum of last resort against arbitrary executive action. But its capacity and ability to provide such protection is under question, and it is clear that its reputation has suffered serious erosion. The current confrontation between appointed and non-confirmed judges and sitting judges further threatens the integrity of the institution. It remains to be seen whether and how the apex court will steer itself through the crisis that looms.

Notes

1   The Chief Justice of Bangladesh presides over the supreme court and the subordinate courts. The supreme court itself has two divisions, the appellate division and the High Court division (see art. 94, Constitution). The subordinate courts include civil courts (established by the Civil Courts Act 1887), criminal courts (established by the Code of Criminal Procedure 1898) and other courts and tribunals as established by Parliament (art. 114, Constitution and specific laws).

2   Art. 147, Constitution of Bangladesh; see also Mahmudul Islam, *Constitutional Law of Bangladesh*, 2nd edition (Dhaka: Mullick Brothers, 2002), para 6.59B, and *Commissioner of Taxes v Justice S. Ahmed* 42 DLR (AD) 163 (exemption of Supreme Court judge's salary from payment of tax).

3   Art. 108-109 of the Constitution of 1972; see *Shahar Ali v AR Chowdhury, Sessions judge,* 32 DLR (1980) 142 (on the ambit of art. 109).

4   Justice Naimuddin, "The Problems of the Independence of the Judiciary in Bangladesh," in Bangladesh Institute of Law and International Affairs (BILIA), *Human Rights in*

Bangladesh: A Study of Standards and Practices (Dhaka: BILIA, 2001), p. 187. The Fourth Amendment inserted a new Article 116A providing that "subject to the provisions of this Constitution, judicial officers and magistrates shall be independent in the exercise of their judicial functions" described by Mahmudul Islam as "being without substance" in view of the removal of the consultation requirement (M. Islam, Constitutional Law of Bangladesh, supra, at p. 63).

5   Second Proclamation (Seventh Amendment) Order 1976, the effect of this being undone by the Second Proclamation (Tenth Amendment) Order 1977.

6   Proclamation (First Amendment) Order 1982, this part being repealed by Proclamation Order No. IV of 1985. The retirement age was later fixed at 65 in the Constitution (Seventh Amendment) Act 1986.

7   The Proclamation (Second Amendment) Order 1982 provided for the Chief Martial Law Administrator to establish permanent benches of the High Court at such places as he may fix. By the Proclamation (Third Amendment) Order 1986, these were renamed as Circuit Benches, and then later, after withdrawal of martial law, they were renamed as Sessions of the High Court.

8   Salahuddin Yusuf MP (AL) introduced a private member's bill in parliament in 1991 to re-introduce the original Articles 95, 98, 115 and 116, which was sent to the Select Committee, where it was considered until 1993, but not ultimately enacted. See discussion in M. I. Farooqui, infra, at p. 66.

9   Naimuddin, supra, at p. 177.

10 M. I. Farooqui, "Judiciary in Bangladesh: Past and Present," in 48 DLR (1996) Journal 65; see, in particular, discussion of pattern of appointments in 1992 onwards and references cited at p. 68 from *Dr. Ahmed Hossain v Shamsul Huq Chowdhury* 48 DLR. 155.

11 There were no specified criteria for such consultation relating, for example, to merit, competence, honesty, integrity although presumably it was required that such issues were to be taken into consideration.

12 1989 BLD (Spl) 1.

13 *Idrisur Rahman v Secretary, Minister of Law, Justice and Parliamentary Affairs,* Writ Petition No. 1543 of 2003, judgment dated 17 July, 2008

challenging the non-appointment by the President of Justice Abdus Salam and Justice Momtazuddin Ahmad, despite their having served over three years as additional judges of the high court, and despite the Chief Justice having recommended their appointment.

14 *Anwar Hossain Chowdhury v Bangladesh, Jalaluddin v Bangladesh, Ibrahim Shaikh v Bangladesh* (1989) BLD (1) Special.

15 Bangladesh Civil Service (Reorganisation) Order 1980.

16 The review petition was disposed of in *Secretary, Ministry of Finance v Md. Masdar Hossain and others (20 BLD (2000) (AD) 141)*, The judgment arose from an original petition filed by 218 members of the subordinate judiciary.

17 John Beames, *Memoirs of a Bengal Civilian* (London: Eland, 2003[1961]). Beames joined the Indian Civil Service in 1859; his last posting was in Chittagong. I am indebted to R. Sudarshan for recalling this reference.

18 See Art. 55(4), *Constitution of Bangladesh*, read with the Rules of Business, 1996.

19 In 2005, about 80 judicial officers were posted in various ministries, departments and statutory corporations. Judicial officers posted on deputation mostly serve as legal advisors or administrative officers. The administrative functions discharged by judicial officers while on deputation include serving in the registrar's office in the Supreme Court or in various tribunals; as solicitor or administrative officer at the Solicitors Office, the Ministry of Law, the Parliament Secretariat, the Judicial Administration Training Institute and in the Prime Minister's Secretariat.

20 The *Code of Criminal Procedure, 1898* provided for the classification and powers of different categories of magistrates.

21 The Judicial Service Commission Rules (JSC Rules) 2004. Masdar Hossain's counsel and others had noted that the JSC's composition was contrary to the requirements of the judgment, which required that it should comprise majority members from "the Senior Judiciary of the Supreme Court and the subordinate courts."

22 The Bangladesh Judicial Service Commission Rules, 2004 (notified on 28 January 2004), was thus finally followed by the Bangladesh Judicial Service (Pay Commission) Rules 2007, the Bangladesh Judicial Service (Service Constitution, Composition, Recruitment and Suspension, Dismissal & Removal) Rules 2007, the Bangladesh Judicial Service (Posting, Promotion, Leave, Control, Discipline and other Service Conditions) Rules 2007 and the Code of Criminal Procedure (Amendment) Ordinance 2007.

23 See report titled *Jela judge Podonnoti'r khetrey 16 joner biruddhey gurutoro obhijog* (Serious allegations against 16 persons recommended for appointment to District judge), *Daily Prothom Alo*, 24 May, 2008.

24 At para 41. Deputation is a service condition provided for in Art. 8 of the Bangladesh Civil Service Recruitment Rules, 1981 as follows: "Rule 8. Relaxation. – (1) Notwithstanding anything contained in these rules - (b) A person holding a specific post in a Service may be appointed by the Government to a specified post in another Service on deputation." This provision is applicable to a person who holds a specific post in a "Service" as defined in Schedule I to the Rules. A person in the BCS (Admin) Cadre may be sent on deputation to a judicial post for up to three years after the coming into force of the Composition Rules.

25 *Aftabuddin v Habibul Awal*, Writ Petition No. 6219 of 2007, judgment dated 18 February, 2007, upholding the challenge; the operation of the judgment has been stayed, pending appeal before the appellate division.

26 *Md. Idrisur Rahman v Bangladesh and others*, Writ Petition No. 3228 of 2008.

27 See discussion in Justice Latifur Rahman, "Judicial Independence and the Account-ability of Judges and the Constitution of Bangladesh," in 52 DLR (2000) Journal 65, at p. 68, noting that there had been no effective functioning of the Supreme Judicial Council till that date, nor had any effective measures been taken to improve the account-ability of subordinate courts nor had there been any implementation of the Code of Conduct of 2000.

28 *Idrisur Rahman v Bangladesh*, Writ Petition No. 1543 of 2003.

14

Executive sovereignty

The judiciary in Sri Lanka

Shylashri Shankar

Introduction

In January 2006 the supreme court resolved a case in favour of Sri Lankan President Mahinda Rajapaksa in his petition against an investigation of alleged fraudulent transfers of tsunami funds into his private bank account. The court ordered police officers conducting the investigation to personally pay a sum of money to the president as damages for their individual liability in violating his fundamental rights.[1] In October 2006 the apex court issued a judgment that the merger of the North and East Provinces, part of the 1987 Indo-Lanka Accord, was null and void from its inception. The ruling had "detrimental" implications for the peace process with the rebel Liberation Tigers for Tamil Eelam (LTTE) that wanted a separate state for the Tamil minority.[2] Since its independence from the British, the Sri Lankan state has grappled with the task of maintaining the hegemony of Sinhalese Buddhist national identity without undermining other ethnic (Tamil) and religious (Hindu, Muslim, and Christian) identities. Critics argued that the judgments showed a clear political bias of the apex court towards the ruling regime led by a Sinhalese nationalist president. Their argument is summarized in the following statement: "The timing of the court challenge, 17 years

after the merger's effect and at the height of renewed war, signalled a deliberate attempt to drive a political wedge into the ethnic issue."[3]

How are such decisions by the Supreme Court of Sri Lanka to be judged? Is the Sri Lankan judiciary merely a tool to carry out majoritarian impulses or has it championed the rule of law and fundamental rights?[4] I argue that the court's seeming bias towards the ruling regime and its inability to assuage the fears of the minority stems from its structural attributes inscribed in the constitution. Parliamentary sovereignty and the constitutional power of the executive over judicial appointments made the court less able to challenge the parliament. This, coupled with an ongoing civil war with the LTTE, ensured deference to the other state institutions in matters of national security and contributed to the court's failure "to restrain majoritarianism" and facilitate nation building.[5] Despite several opportunities, the Sri Lankan judiciary (unlike its Indian counterpart) remained committed to legal positivism rather than some form of judicial activism.

The first section of this chapter charts the erosion of judicial review and independence in three constitutional documents. I argue that the two later constitutions supported a Sinhalese majoritarian project at the expense of minority rights, with courts functioning as unwilling

203

accomplices. The second section discusses the implications of parliamentary sovereignty on the behaviour of the court towards fundamental rights and the rights of minorities. I argue that the executive's intervention in the appointments process created a higher judiciary that was more likely to be circumspect and avoid tussles with the president and parliament over minority freedoms. The conclusion highlights the detrimental implications of politicization of the judiciary for law, governance, and democracy in Sri Lanka.

Three constitutions and judicial independence: Executive control

Since independence from the British in 1948, Sri Lanka has formulated three constitutions. A comparison with the Indian constitution highlights the control wielded by the executive in Sri Lanka and explains the court's deferential attitude. First, the constitutions (particularly the 1972 and 1978 ones) were explicitly designed to preserve Sinhala majoritarianism, in contrast to the ameliorative bent of the Indian counterpart.[6] Second, unlike India, the constitution could be (and has been) amended or repealed by a two-thirds majority in the legislature, implying a view of the constitution "as a statute rather than as a special document."[7] Third, the notion that sovereignty was vested in the people, and, by implication, in parliament prevented judicial review of legislative acts—but not executive or administrative ones—with profound implications for minority rights.[8] The court has rarely challenged the executive. To understand the quiescence of the judiciary, we have to assess the nature of judicial independence in the three constitutions.

The first, the 1947 Soulbury Constitution, was a "product of positivist aspirations" and a legislative attempt to "reflect the necessary conditions for peace and security." Instead of a bill of rights, the Soulbury Constitution provided for minority protection (Section 29[2]) forbidding discrimination on the ground of race or religion and legislation infringing on

religious freedom.[9] The court saw it as an implicit power to declare such discriminatory legislation invalid, and did so, but not as effectively as the minorities hoped. We shall see later how courts interpreted this section. The constitution was also silent on the separation of powers, but allowed the judiciary a modicum of independence to control appointments, transfers, dismissals, and disciplinary actions against judicial officers, by vesting the power in a judicial service commission.

But the succeeding autochthonous constitution of 1972, also known as the first republican constitution, left no doubt about the dominance of the National State Assembly as the supreme instrument of state power. "We are trying to reject the theory of separation of powers," said Felix Dias Bandaranaike, the minister of justice during the constituent assembly deliberations.[10] "We are trying to say that nobody should be higher than the elected representatives of the people, nor should any person not elected by the people have the right to throw out decisions of the people elected by the people." The legislature made itself supreme with the power to take away the jurisdiction of any court, thus making the judiciary "the most crippled arm" of the government.[11]

The 1978 Constitution (the current one, as of 2010), which was designed in the wake of severe criticism of the previous constitution's restrictive provisions for judicial powers, widened the independence of the judiciary by recognizing the separation of powers (art. 4). But it continued to deny judicial review, thereby leaving the fundamental freedoms of all "open to governmental abuse and administrative non-compliance."[12] Significantly, it created a bill of rights which Peiris calls the most important single factor that allowed the supreme court constitutional jurisdiction over fundamental rights:

Today our Constitution recognises that there are certain matters, in respect of which, Parliament does not have the competence to legislate. There are things Parliament cannot do. Parliament cannot restrict the freedom of association, the freedom of publication, the freedom of movement and so on except in circumstances which fall in the provisos which form part and parcel of the constitutional document.[13]

The court did not use the entrenched articles, which were harder to amend, to fashion a basic structure doctrine, as their Indian counterparts did.[14] In the *Thirteenth Amendment Case*, permitting the repeal of entrenched articles, the Supreme Court said:

If the Constitution contemplates the repeal of any provision or provisions of the entire Constitution, there is no basis for the contention that some provisions which reflect fundamental principles or incorporate basic features are immune from amendment. Accordingly, we do not agree with the contention that some provisions of the Constitution are unamendable.[15]

What accounts for the reluctance of judges to challenge the executive? Let us assess the nature of judicial independence in the 1978 Constitution. Commenting on judicial independence from 1978–88, C. R. De Silva said that the judiciary was under great threat from the legislative and executive branches because they used select committees to inquire into the conduct of judges.[16] A parliamentary committee was set up to investigate the comments, made by the chief justice in a speech, that were critical of the government's policy on the anti-Tamil riots of 1983.[17] The establishment of a Special Presidential Commission of Inquiry by the president in 1978 to oversee the conduct of public officials including judges introduced political oversight and eroded the power of the Judicial Services Disciplinary Board.[18] In the same year, the president also used his appointing powers to ensure that seven apex court and several high court judges did not serve again in the reconstitued courts. In several instances, the government promoted police officers who were held guilty by the Supreme Court of violating freedom of speech,[19] and did not protect those judges hearing the case from mob

violence. Thus, the third constitution reinforced the president's control over judicial appointments, marring the capacity of judges to operate independently.[20] Not surprisingly, the court was restrained in its dealings with the executive, and allowed presidential authoritarianism to continue unchecked, which had severe implications for minority rights and religious freedom.

Implications of executive sovereignty

Minority rights

The underlying ethos of the 1972 and 1978 constitutions supported Sinhalese nationalism at the expense of minority aspirations.[21] Scholars have explained Sri Lanka's bloody struggle as a product of a religious divide between Tamil Hindus and Sinhalese Buddhists;[22] colonial practices of divide and rule which inscribed race, class, and religious categories (Wickramasinghe, 1995); shortsightedness of political elites owing to the need to accommodate minorities;[23] minority complex based on regional security considerations;[24] and Sinhalese linguistic nationalism.[25] The Sinhalese–Tamil ethnic relationship followed a sequence of ethnic cohabitation (1948–56), autonomy (1956–72), soft separatism (1972–83), and ethnic conflict and civil war (1983–present).

The judiciary played a significant role in the evolution of the conflict. Immediately after independence, the failure of legal challenges to three discriminatory pieces of legislation—the Citizenship Act of 1948 and the Franchise Legislation of 1949 depriving Tamil plantation workers of Indian descent of franchise, and the Official Language Act of 1956 making Sinhalese the only official language—eroded the faith of the minorities in the institutions of the state.[26] The Citizenship Act of 1948 was changed to deprive Tamil workers in up-country plantations of their franchise, but the court dismissed the subsequent appeal on grounds that it was not made explicit that the purpose of the legislation was to deprive a particular community of the franchise. As Peiris wryly points out, when the provisions required that one's grandfather and great-grandfather had to have been born in the country in order to have the right to vote, it would not have required a great degree of imagination or perception to arrive at a firm conclusion with regard to the objectives of the legislature. The judges, however, found the laws intra vires (within the power of the legislature) despite the Soulbury Constitution's prohibition on parliament to enact discriminatory legislation (art. 29(2)).

Legal theorist Rohan Edrisinha describes the approach of the court as "narrow and technical" because the judges refused to consider the motive and effect of the legislation. The reason for the court's position, argues political scientist Jayadeva Uyangoda, was that the political climate in the 1950s and 1960s favored the view that parliament could do no wrong. So, judicial invalidation of any law would be seen as a challenge to the very idea of parliamentary sovereignty. Not surprisingly, the judiciary avoided "crucial political issues" and disappointed Tamil minorities in "its blindness to assertions of discrimination."[27]

The formal constitutionalization of Sinhalese majoritarianism, according to constitutional theorist Asanga Welikala, occurred in the 1972 Constitution, which discontinued the special protection accorded to minorities by the 1947 Constitution, entrenched the unitary nature of the republic, impinged on the secular principle, and trampled on multicultural sensitivities by giving constitutional recognition to the preeminent position of Buddhism.[28] Any impulse for constitutional reform emanating from the Sinhalese political leadership was conceptualized not in terms of democratizing majority–minority relations within a pluralist framework, but as a way of giving juridical expression to the majority community's nationalist aspirations.[29] The legal positivist orientation of the court made it an unwilling accomplice in the majoritarian project, leading scholars like G. L. Peiris to

castigate the Sri Lankan judges for being "needlessly diffident" and "ambivalent"[30] and for taking a very "narrow view of their functions," while other critics condemned the court for failing to maintain a balance between majoritarianism and constitutional limitations to protect individual freedom and minority rights.[31]

The recent (2008–9) success of the Sri Lankan military in wresting its territories back from the LTTE, has been seen by powerful Sri Lankan elites as a victory for the Sinhalese against secessionist claims by Tamils. Such chauvinist sentiments carry a high price for the Tamil and Muslim minorities who face severe curtailment of their democratic liberties. Recent events (discussed in the conclusion) indicate that even if the judiciary supports their petitions, the government is not likely to implement court orders.

Religious freedom

The preamble to the 1978 constitution promises all citizens freedom, equality, justice, fundamental human rights, and an independent judiciary. Article 9, which was introduced in 1972 and continued in 1978, guarantee foremost place to Buddhism and made it the duty of the State to protect and foster the Buddhasasana, while assuring to all religions freedom of religion and worship, guaranteed by articles 10 and 14 (1)(a) and (e). This has resulted in imbalances between the rights of Buddhist and non-Buddhist citizens. When Buddhism was not involved, as in a bigamy case dealing with two minority religions (Christianity and Islam), the court adopted a strict legal interpretation of the marriage contract, rather than a cultural one. But when religious freedom had an adverse impact on the freedom of Buddhism, the judges upheld the concerns of Buddhists. In two judgments dealing with rights of Christian missionaries to propagate religion, the Supreme Court upheld the preeminent place for Buddhism and clarified that freedom of religion did not include freedom to propagate. Critics chastised the judgment as "clumsy" and said that it would exacerbate the fragmentation of the polity and weaken the credibility of state institutions.[32]

Thirteenth Amendment Case

The majority opinion in the *Thirteenth Amendment Case* exemplified the court's support for the ruling regime's interpretations and for majoritarian concerns. The Thirteenth Amendment arose from the decentralization agreement negotiated under Indian auspices in the Indo-Sri Lanka accord of 1987. The agreement, which came after years of bloody conflict between a guerrilla group, the LTTE, and the Sri Lankan government, necessitated changes to article 2, which had "entrenched" the unitary nature of the state. The nine judge bench of the supreme court considered whether the amendment was a breach of articles 2 (unitary state), article 3 (sovereignty of the people) and 9 (preeminent position of Buddhism). The shift towards federalism and India's role aroused violent protests from sections of Sinhalese society, who saw the agreement as eroding the sovereignty of the country. An armed insurgency, led by the Janatha Vimukthi Peramuna (JVP), erupted on the streets while Buddhist organizations challenged President J. R. Jayawardene in court. The court upheld the amendment by a whisker (5:4). Explanations for the tenor of the majority opinion emphasize the institutional and political pressure from the president, who had to implement devolution in order to please India, whereas the minority opinion was seen as reflecting the ethnic (rather than religious) fear of Tamil control by the Sinhalese Buddhist nationalists.

The debate on decentralization/devolution affected the rights of Sinhalese and Muslims living in the eastern part of Sri Lanka. Tamil Hindus formed a majority in the north, while the Eastern Province (at that time) had an equal representation of Hindu Tamils, Muslim Tamils, and Sinhalese. The new bill treated the Northern and Eastern Provinces as a single unit (the North–East province), which meant that Tamils would become the majority group, while earlier they were the majority only in the north. It triggered historical fears of creeping Dravidian hegemony over the whole country, and concerns about the future protection of Buddhist monuments and culture. Chief Justice Wanasundera's words (in the minority opinion) reflected the worry of the Sinhalese nationalists about the dismemberment of the country.

> It is a fact that the single provincial council for the North and East would be dominated by Tamils with an overwhelming Tamil-speaking majority. It would be controlled and administered by Tamils, who had for nearly a half century claimed this territory as their traditional homeland and resisted a Sinhala presence. They have subscribed to a two-nation theory and *not to an ideal of a Sri Lankan nationality* [author emphasis].[33]

Nineteen years later, in October 2006, the Supreme Court implicitly supported Wanasundera's position. The five-judge bench, headed by Chief Justice Sarath de Silva, unanimously agreed with the petitioners, representing the JVP, that the merger of the Northern and Eastern Provinces was invalid because two conditions of the accord had not been fulfilled, namely the cessation of hostilities and the demobilization of militant groups. The JVP's argument in court focused on debunking historical and current claims by Tamils to a northeastern homeland and highlighted the secessionist consequences of allowing it. In agreeing with the petitioners, the court risked being seen as a Sinhalese nationalist, anti-Tamil entity even though the judges used the rationale of a "right to equality."

Other cases

Although, overall, the tone of the judgments favored the positions adopted by the ruling regime, the legal positivist attitude of the judiciary had a silver lining for the victims of torture. The court evolved mechanisms to compensate the victims (usually Tamils suspected of links with the LTTE) when state agencies infringed on fundamental rights such as freedom from torture (art. 11). Similarly, environmental activists benefited from a ruling in November 2005 that Galle Face Green, a 14-acre seaside promenade in Colombo, was a public utility and could not be leased out to private developers.[34] The government was directed to pay costs of Rs 50,000 to the NGO plaintiff.

Conclusion

In September 2006, a five-judge bench of the apex court headed by the chief justice ruled that the accession of the government to the Optional Protocol of the International Covenant on Civil and Political rights was inconsistent with the constitution. The judgment came after a petition by a Tamil man who had been arrested and convicted on evidence that was coerced through torture; the United Nations Human Rights Commission validated the petitioner's claim of torture and found the Sri Lankan state responsible for violating the Optional Protocol.[35] Critics saw the judgment as further undermining public confidence—particularly that of minorities—in the state's (including the judiciary's) commitment to the rule of law and human rights and, in effect, removing the country from the international human rights community.[36]

Another worrying development has contributed to further politicization of the judiciary. The Seventeenth Amendment, enacted in 2001, decreed that the president's nominees to the higher judiciary had to be ratified by a constitutional council (CC), a body with six members appointed by parliamentary consensus, and four ex-officio members. The CC, however, has been defunct since 2005 because of the president's refusal to fill the vacancies.[37] Instead, the president bypassed the CC and appointed several judges on the recommendation of the chief justice.[38] Ruling on

a petition challenging the President's actions, the Supreme Court ordered the government to establish the CC by 15 January, 2009. The president lashed out at the court accusing it of undermining his powers and made veiled threats that the judges could find themselves the target of thugs.

In the name of national security, the Rajapakse government has curtailed basic democratic liberties, threatened the media and NGOs, and turned a blind eye to the hundreds of "disappearances" and murders of political opponents allegedly caused by death squads operating with security forces. The decision-making power is now concentrated in the hands of the president and his close associates, particularly his three brothers. With the success of the Rajapakse government in recapturing the eastern and the northern provinces from the LTTE, the judiciary has become the main arena for the battle between president and those political/civil society groups who fear that Rajapakse is using the argument of national security to become autocratic. Several recent judgments—removal of the treasury secretary for corruption, halting the sale of government land to private developers—supported the position of these groups against the president. But the government has ignored court orders or only partly implemented them (e.g. reduced the price of petrol but not to Rs 100 as mandated by the court). In January 2009, the supreme court terminated the proceedings on the oil case saying that the government was no longer implementing court orders on the issue. Executive sovereignty looks set to ring the death knell for the rule of law and democracy (particularly for minorities) in Sri Lanka.

Notes

1 *Mahinda Rajapakse vs Chandra Fernando and Ors*, S.C. (FR) Application No. 387/2005 (also known as the *Helping Hambantota Case*), reported in Center for Policy Alternatives, *War, Peace and Governance in Sri Lanka: Overview and Trends 2006*, p. 20.

2 Jayadev Uyangoda, *The State and the Process of Devolution in Sri Lanka*, in Sunil Bastian (ed.), *Devolution and Development in Sri Lanka* (Colombo: ICES, 1994); Neelan Tiruchelvam, *Federalism and Diversity in Sri Lanka*, in Yash Ghai (ed.), *Autonomy and Ethnicity* (Cambridge: University Press, 2000), pp. 198–200.

3 Center for Policy Alternatives, p. 21.

4 Sri Lanka has a professional judiciary, a strong executive (which is the directly elected head of the state and government), parliamentary sovereignty, and emergency/anti-terror laws to combat secessionism.

5 Rohan Edrisinha, "Sri Lanka, Constitutions without Constitutionalism—A Tale of Three and a Half Constitutions," unpublished paper.

6 Gary Jacobsohn and Shylashri Shankar, "Constitutional Borrowing in South Asia: India, Sri Lanka, and Secular Constitutional Identity," forthcoming.

7 Author's interview with Rohan Edrisinha, Professor of Law, University of Colombo, March 2006.

8 Article 80(3) which reads as follows: "[N]o court or tribunal shall inquire into, pronounce upon or in any manner call in question the validity of such Act on any ground whatsoever." But the court can vet executive and administrative infringements. R. Coomaraswamy (1994) *Devolution, the Law, and Judicial Construction* in Bastian, *Devolution and Development* and Sunil Bastian, *Ideology and the Constitution* (Colombo: ICES, 1996), ch. v.

9 Ivor Jennings reportedly said in a 1961 BBC interview that a comprehensive bill of rights should have been included: "If I knew then, as much about the problems of Ceylon, as I do now, some of the provisions would have been different"; Jayampathy Wickramaratne, *Fundamental Rights in Sri Lanka* (Pannipitiya: Stamford Lake, 2006), p. 18.

10 Quoted in Lal Wijenayake, *Independence of the Judiciary in Sri Lanka Since Independence* (Pannipitiya: Stamford Lake, 2005), p. 5.

11 Radhika Coomaraswamy, *Sri Lanka: The Crisis of Anglo-American Constitutional Traditions in a Developing Society* (New Delhi: Vikas, 1984).

12 Lakshman Marasinghe, "An Outline for a Constitutional Settlement in Sri Lanka," Address at the International Center for Ethnic Studies, Colombo, March 2003, p. 11.

13 G. L. Peiris, "Judicial Review of Legislative and Administrative Action," unpublished conference paper, 28 August, 1988, pp. 437–56.

14 Articles 1 (the State), 2 (Unitary State), 3 (Sovereignty of the People), 6 (National Flag), 7 (National Anthem), 8 (National Day), 9 (Buddhism), 10 (Freedom of Thought, Conscience, and Religion), and 11 (Freedom from Torture) are entrenched.

15 *In Re The Thirteenth Amendment to the Constitution and Provincial Councils Bill*, S. C. 7/87 (Spl) TO S.C. 48/87 (Spl), p. 329.

16 The 1978 Constitution adopted a three-tiered system of courts: the supreme court, court of appeal, and the high courts. All judges of the higher judiciary (supreme court and court of appeal) were appointed by the president and served until his/her retirement at the age of 63 in the case of supreme court judges and age 63 in the case of court of appeals judges *retired at 63*, unless removed by the president for misbehavior, which had to be endorsed by a majority of the parliament.

17 Cited from C. R. De Silva, "The Independence of the Judiciary under the Second Republic of Sri Lanka, 1978–88," unpublished paper presented at the Eleventh Conference of the International Association of Historians of Asia, 1–5 August, 1988, Colombo, p. 491.

18 Special Presidential Commission of Inquiry, Law No. 7, 1978. The parliament declared a judgment of the Court of Appeals (*Bandarnaike vs Weeraratne* (1981) 1 SLR 10) null and void.

19 *Daramitipola Ratnasara Thero vs P. Udugampola* (1983) 1 Sri LR 461; *Vivienne Gunawardene vs Hector Perera* (1983) S.C. Application 20/83.

20 The most recent example was the appointment of Justice Sarath Silva as the chief justice, overlooking Justice M. D. H. Fernando. See Wijenayake, pp. 16–22.

21 With a population of 19.4 million, approximately 70 percent of the population is Buddhist, 15 percent Hindu, 8 percent Christian (mainly Roman Catholics), and 7 percent Muslim (mainly Sunnis).

22 David Little, *The Invention of Enmity* (Washington, DC: United States Institute of Peace Press, 1993).

23 Jonathan Spencer (ed.), *Sri Lanka: History and the Roots of Conflict* (London: Routledge, 1990).

24 Stanley J. Tambiah, *Sri Lanka: Ethnic Fratricide and the Dismantling Of Democracy* (Chicago, IL: University of Chicago Press 1986).

25 Neil de Votta, *Blowback: Linguistic Nationalism, Institutional Decay, and Ethnic Conflict in Sri Lanka* (Stanford, CA: University Press 2004).

26 *Mudanayake vs Sivagnasunderam* (53 NLR 25); *Kodikam Pillai vs Mudanayake* (54 NLR 433); *Kodeswaran vs Attorney General* (70 NLR 121).

27 Jayadeva Uyangoda, *Questions of Sri Lanka's Minority Rights, Minority Protection* (Monograph, South Asia Series-2, International Center for Ethnic Studies, Colombo: Unie Arts 2001), p. 57.

28 Asanga Welikala, "Towards Two Nations in One State," unpublished conference paper, EURO Regions Summer University of the Institute of Federalism, University of Fribourg, Switzerland, 21 September, 2002.

29 Uyangoda, *Questions of Sri Lanka's Minority Rights*, points out that despite a clear victory in the Northern and Eastern provinces for a Tamil party fighting the 1977 elections on the idea of achieving separate statehood for Tamils, the new Sinhalese UNP government adopted a constitution reiterating all features of unitarism and centralization.

30 Radhika Coomaraswamy and Neelan Tiruchelvam, *The Role of the Judiciary in Plural Societies* (Delhi: Palgrave Macmillan, 1987).

31 Coomaraswamy and Tiruchelvam, *The Role of the Judiciary*; Rohan Edrisinha, "In Defence of Judicial Review and Judicial Activism," unpublished paper presented at the Eleventh Conference of the International Association of Historians of Asia, 1–5 August, 1988, Colombo, p. 476.

32 Asanga Welikala, "The Menzingen Determination and the Supreme Court—A Liberal Critique," Monograph, Center for Policy Alternatives, p. 10.

33 In *Re The Thirteenth Amendment to the Constitution and Provincial Councils Bill*, p. 377.

34 EFL vs UDA FR 47/2004.

35 *Sinharasa vs Sri Lanka*, Case No. 1033/2004.

36 *War, Peace and Governnance in Sri Lanka*, p. 21.

37 In June 2006 the Court of Appeals rejected the petition by two citizens in *J. Dandaniya and Edirimuni Samith de Silva v Sri Lanka*, C.A. Appeal 66/2006.

38 For a critique of the chief justice's actions, see http://www.alrc.net/doc/mainfile.php/alrc_statements/418/.

Part IV

Pluralism and national integration

Language issues

15

Politics of language in India

E. Annamalai

Framework

Throughout its history, the Indian sub-continent has been a place for many languages that are historically unrelated, but have interacted in geographical space. The political relationships among them did not remain constant, but the shaping of their inter-relationships through policies formulated and implemented by rulers is a phenomenon of the modern period beginning with colonial rule. The recent history of the politics of language has been marked by changes in language policy, but with some continuity across the colonial and postcolonial periods as well as within each period. The factors that motivate policy changes are multiple, encompassing both the goals of government and percep-tions of people concerning their interests, which include economic opportunities, social advancement, and cultural security. Language policies concern both the choice of languages that will be used in public domains, most importantly in government and education, by the state, and in private domains such as kin networks, recreational activities, and cultural practices, including religious practices by the people. A third domain, which overlaps the public and the private, is the market. This chapter is about language policy and language behavior in public domains, covering the historical period of colonial formation and its consolidation, as well as the transition to independence and social transformation in the new nation. The constant amidst change is the maintenance of some social, economic, and political relationships among languages. But changes in language policies are continually redefining these relationships. The continu-ously contested relationship of English with other languages, concerning its role in political control and socioeconomic transformation through the phases of its emergence, contain-ment, and reemergence in the Indian political scene, provides a vantage point to survey also the relationship among all the languages of the country.

The politics of language policy open a window to an understanding of the nature of the Indian nation and its differences from neighboring countries, whose national integ-rity was broken or is threatened on the issue of language dominance. Pakistan split into two and Sri Lanka has endured violent conflict over the division of the country, arising in both cases from issues of language dominance. Guha[1] characterizes India in relation to its linguistic diversity, among other aspects of diversity, as an "unnatural nation." The way language con-flicts, arising from the contested relationship among languages in India—which is a country of linguistic minorities in which even an amalgamated community of Hindi speakers make up less than half the population[2]—have been resolved through policy decisions has been an important factor in sustaining the integrity of this unnatural nation. It is unnatural from the classical European criterion of "one nation, one culture, one language," but is natural with respect to the traditional, historical existence of India as a country. India's linguistic diversity has not blocked its aspirations towards nationhood.

Language differentiation and norm building

The need of the colonists to equip themselves with knowledge of the country under their rule and the need to generate consent of the ruled for its legitimacy made it necessary for the colonial government to take a direct, political interest in the languages of the subcontinent.[3] This political interest manifested itself not only in learning the languages, but also in constructing knowledge about them by classifying them according to their historical relations and categorizing some as languages, others as dialects subordinate to the principal languages. This knowledge was required in order to decide which among them would be used as prescribed languages in government and education. The analytical task involved was identifying and naming languages and defining boundaries among them. The process of boundary making worked to change the perception of languages among the peoples of India from that of a mosaic with fluid relations to that of discrete entities with opaque boundaries. This opened the way as well towards a coupling of languages with other sociocultural entities, including religion. Language categorization by external actors, including colonial administrators, missionaries, and scholars, paved the way for language identification and grouping to be manipulated for political uses, including the exercise of

power by the rulers and mobilization for collective action by the ruled. The task of choosing a language for administration, and by extension for education, added a premium to demarcating languages by differentiating names. It created a need for standardizing languages, which culminated in a process of differentiating languages and distancing languages used in formal domains from the languages of everyday speech.

The conflict arising out of the differentiation of *khari boli*, a widely used speech form for communicating in the bazaar and in the army, into Hindi and Urdu and associating them with two religions, Hinduism and Islam, is a prime example of the political use of language categorization.[4] The policies of the colonial government and the actions of individual officers concerning the choice of language for local use in public domains such as courts of law were intended to support one side or the other in the Hindi–Urdu controversy, depending on government's political exigencies at the time.

Contrariwise, erasure of language boundaries in order to create an overarching language, build a political force around it, and form a political interest group based on language is exemplified by the projection of Hindi as the putative national language of the country. This political process was in turn aided by caste and religious calculations.[5]

Differentiating languages was essential for curriculum development and textbook production when they came to be controlled and administered centrally in the colonial period. The differentiation began in the language textbooks prepared for training colonial officers in the East India Company's trading posts in Calcutta and Madras and in the making of a canon of literary texts for language learning. These activities formalized the separation between languages, for example, between Hindi and Urdu; they also involved decisions with regard to literary disputes such as what constituted the earliest Bengali literary text, which could also be claimed to have been actually written in Oriya or Maithili, and so on. The dialect or language chosen as the language of textbooks and classrooms became the legitimate form of that language. Thus, it was the particular variety of a tribal language used by Christian missionaries to translate the Bible that then became the language of the tribe. All these factors enabled the emergence of a political consciousness of language distinct from cultural consciousness. This development of building political consciousness around language became manifest later in the post-colonial period in political agitations for redrawing the administrative boundaries of states to conform to new language boundaries.

Identity by mother tongue

A by-product of the political consciousness of language is the concept of mother tongue transplanted from its European origin in the age of reformation. This concept gave a new meaning to the conventional characterization of their speech by ethnic communities as "our speech," opposing it to "their speech." This popular distinction denoted different ways of speaking. The concept of mother tongue—*matru bhasha* or *thaay mozhi*—is not just a shift of *boli* (colloquial speech, as in *khari boli*) to *bhasha* (formal language, as in Hindi *bhasha*), but also an introduction of a powerful symbolism to characterize one's language. It shifted the opposition between any two languages to that of mother tongue versus other tongue. In the regions other than northern India, *bhasha* has been long in the consciousness of speakers, but it was a cultural consciousness rather than a political one. This is true even in southern India, where languages have a longer literary tradition.[6] Mother tongue came to denote the person claiming it as a different being culturally and politically. This symbolism became a convenient political tool to be used for inclusive or exclusive purposes to realize particular political goals. Many of the political debates as well as political conflicts in the colonial and post-colonial periods were framed around this way of conceptualizing one's language.

Language, characterized as mother tongue, with marked boundaries, became another group characteristic to define and categorize people along with others like caste, religion and ethnicity and to create new political formations. Beginning in 1917, with the formation of the Andhra Provincial Congress Committee to represent the Telugu region, the regional units of the Congress party were organized according to linguistic region.[7] This was done when the administrative units of the colonial government or the principalities were not coterminous with linguistic regions.

Language may provide an overarching group identity, although it may not supersede other characteristics for group formation such as religion when it serves some political purpose, as in the cases of Urdu (for Muslims) and Punjabi (for Sikhs). Alternatively, language unity may be undermined by caste differences, as in the case of Maithili.[8] The political potency of language as a marker of group identity multiplies when it is coupled with another characteristic like religion. Such a coupling, however, has not been witnessed in many states, notably Tamil Nadu and Kerala, where linguistic identity covers more than one religion and where castes do not align with different languages. Decennial variation in mother tongue figures recorded in censuses does not fluctuate significantly in such states, in contrast to others where political identifications based on religion, for example, have led millions of people to adopt a different name for their language or even to deny their own language identity. At the same time, mother tongue as a sign of social identity can be politically negotiable. For example, the political behavior of people with regard to their declared mother tongue may not match their actual linguistic behavior with regard to its use at home or their choice with regard to medium of instruction.

215

Ascendancy of English and the social divide

Colonial intervention in language identification and choice heightened the political consciousness of language in ways briefly described already. It also changed the nature of cultural, social, political, and economic relations among languages in the multilingual Indian constellation. The ascendancy of the English language, which started with the official policy of the colonial government, formulated in 1835, to support English as the language of education, reworked the relationship among languages. English replaced the classical languages, Sanskrit and Arabic, as the source and means of acquiring knowledge. With it, the nature of knowledge also changed to conform to what the colonial administrators and educationists called useful knowledge, which was meant to be the knowledge of European thought, science, and morals. English also relegated the vernaculars in education to a secondary role as carriers, through translation, of this useful knowledge to the masses, while these vernaculars continued to be repositories of their past literature for local consumption. Vernaculars were also a conduit for Christian theology to reach the masses through the activities of Christian priests and pastors from Europe inside and outside missionary schools.

The government schools, although notionally open to everyone, in fact provided education through the medium of English mostly to students from upper castes. The main contributor to this was the government's education policy, based on what was known as the filtration theory, to provide English education to a few, who, in turn, would transfer (filter down) European knowledge to the masses through the vernaculars. The evolution of this policy was shaped by the huge anticipated expenses in providing universal English education, shortage of teachers to provide this education, fear of social unrest from the frustration of a large number of English-educated youth not finding gainful

positions in the government, and the idea that the class of people with leisure and a tradition of learning are best equipped for intellectual pursuits.[9] One result of this policy was that students from lower castes were largely excluded from English education. They were attracted by the missionaries to their schools with the hope of proselytizing them. This fostered the public idea that English education, where English is the medium, is for those in the upper echelons of the society and vernacular education, where English is only a subject, is for those at lower echelons. English thus played, through differential access, a crucial role in the reproduction of social inequality through education. This turned into a political problem in the colonial period, which was more acute in western and southern India, engendering demands from the excluded lower castes for access to English, expressed through petitions, protests and formation of political parties. This issue of differential access to English education remains a political problem in postcolonial India.

English education took early roots in the presidency provinces of Bombay, Madras, and Bengal, which were under the direct control of the colonial government. The traditional elites living in the presidencies, by virtue of their ritual high status and land ownership granted to them for their ritual services to the ruling classes, transformed themselves into new elites through their access to the new temporal power, status, and wealth that English education gave them. The elite status traditionally sanctioned by knowledge of Sanskrit was augmented by a new sanction, namely, knowledge of English. Castes that were not ritually at the top, but provided administrative service to the pre-colonial governments, also adapted themselves to the needs of the colonial government. The middle level castes that owned lands and traditional industrial production, such as textiles, were behind in English education and the tillers and the low service castes were largely left out of it. The aspirations for upward mobility that were curtailed as a consequence of the regionally and socially differentiated access to English education, and hence to new economic opportunities, led to political action by the excluded people in the colonial period. But the issues were far from resolved and were carried over to the governments formed after independence. Political conflicts in independent India, arising out of regional differences in material progress created by the colonial economy, were fought in the name of language; much of it was framed in terms of "for or against English." The social differences in material progress have been echoed in the politics of affirmative action, in demands for reservation of seats in education and jobs for scheduled and backward castes in independent India. Language, however, figures in this conflict of social equalization only secondarily, and only recently in relation to the teaching of English.[10]

Search for a language as a national symbol

It has been claimed that acquisition of English by the new middle class helped communication across linguistic regions within this class, and thereby organization of the opposition to colonial rule and the fostering of nationalism.[11] However, English did not fill the need to communicate with the masses and mobilize them for political action against the British. It was the regional languages that were used for these purposes by political leaders in the respective regions—although not so much use was made of the minority languages in these regions. Every national movement for independence uses symbols by which people identify themselves to represent the nation and its elevation from the status of a colony. Under Gandhi's leadership, *khadi* (homespun cloth) was one such symbol. With regard to language, Gandhi sought to elevate Hindustani (which he saw as an amalgam of Hindi and Urdu) to such a national symbol.[12] However, this choice itself became a subject of political debate, particularly concerning its relationship to the Hindi and Urdu languages. Many in the

independence movement identified Hindi as the national language and promoted learning of Hindi as an expression of nationalism. This was not, however, embraced by all communities defined by religion or language. Ambivalence among the people concerning the desirability of having one language to symbolize the nation[13] and to develop citizen allegiance to that language, was reflected in the policy debates in the constituent assembly[14] and in the later political agitations concerning the choice of the official language of the government of the new nation.

Postcolonial questions of language

Two questions relating to language that the nation faced on the eve of its independence concerned the language of government and of education. The first is a question of administration and the second of development. A third question is dependent on these two. It concerns communication among people across the country to facilitate participation in the government both in its administrative tasks and developmental programs as well as to nurture a sense of sharing a language common to all. With regard to the search for answers to all three questions, policies were made, contested, and modified. Practice on the ground with regard to actual use of languages was guided by the policies at some levels and in some ways and was at variance with policies at other levels and in other ways. There is thus tangible divergence between policy and practice in the 60 years after independence. The story of the politics that has produced and continued this divergence is essentially the story of the politics of language in India.

Shift in multilingualism

One policy, however, where there is no divergence, is that of maintaining the multilingual and multicultural fabric of India. The kind of nationalism built on one language and one culture has not been accepted by the majority of people. The political parties that promote this ideology of a nation have not been able to make it a legitimate policy and the people who subscribe to it at an ideational level practice multilingualism in real life. While there is no divergence from this policy of defining the nation as multilingual in practice, there has been a difference in the nature of multilingualism as practiced in postcolonial India. The difference is in the public roles assigned to languages and, consequently, in the differential access of promoters of languages to the resources and patronage of the state. This influences the composition of the linguistic repertoire of people. This composition ultimately stems from the larger political and economic interests of the people. Education plays a major role in bringing in this difference in the linguistic repertoire. The shift in multilingualism since Independence is towards adding non-local languages, like English and Hindi, to the repertoire of speakers. The premium on such non-local languages is their literate variety taught in schools. This shift cuts across communities, with the result that the new multilingualism becomes less community-based and more class-based. Local variations in multilingualism that reflect local conditions and needs get subordinated to the national pattern.

Multilingualism as the national symbol

Taking up first the third question mentioned earlier (communication among people across the country), there is no officially mandated or constitutionally recognized national language of India. There is, however, a set of languages listed in the constitution, which are called scheduled languages, as they are placed in a schedule (numbered eighth) annexed to the constitution. The specified purposes of the list were to shape and monitor the development of Hindi as a pan-Indian language, drawing from the resources of the languages in the list, and to constitute an official language commission,

whose members would be drawn from the communities of languages in the list, to review the acceptance and performance of Hindi as the official language of the union. The list, at the time of writing the constitution, had 14 languages, representing different historical, linguistic and cultural traditions in the regions of India. The purpose of listing languages in the constitution changed, in the political perception of it at the ground level, soon after its adoption in 1950. The list was perceived at the popular level to be granting political recognition and entitlement to some languages over others, thereby placing those languages in a privileged position to receive a greater share of the patronage and resources of the state for their development and to acquire a political status superior to that of other languages. At the bureaucratic level, the list was viewed as providing a "natural" criterion for federal decisions concerning which languages, other than the two federal official languages, would be added to meet the language demands on the federal government. These demands concerned the languages that would be available for candidates for civil service examinations, those that could be taught as a third language in schools under the policy dubbed as three language formula, the languages that would be eligible to receive grants from the federal government earmarked for the development of modern Indian languages, and so forth.[15] Such uses of the list as a criterion for inclusion and exclusion of languages to benefit from major government decisions strengthened people's perceptions of the list as a mechanism for status elevation and material rewards for these languages. The languages included in the list are popularly believed—without any constitutional sanction for such belief—to be the national languages. Political demands to include new languages in the eighth schedule gradually increased in number and intensity. The first agitation for inclusion was in 1967 on behalf of Sindhi, which did not have a contiguous region of its own; the last four, added in 2004, are Dogri, Maithili, Santhali and Bodo, of which the second one is subsumed under Hindi as one of its 48 "mother tongues" or "dialects"[16] and denied an independent language status in the census, and the last two of which are tribal languages. The total number of languages in the list now stands at 22. The criterion for inclusion in the list is now political pressure by means permitted in a democratic polity, including bartering political support in elections, bargaining in coalition politics, and street demonstrations.

Language of wider communication

The other part of the third question concerns lingua franca. It is generally coterminous with the official language of a country, but not always. There are two languages of wider communication across linguistic regions in India, viz., English and Hindi, which run parallel along class lines. English is preferred by the educated middle and upper class in interactions among themselves. Hindi is used by the working classes for communication among themselves in situations such as labor migration to another linguistic region, travel to pilgrim centers, and with the middle and upper classes from different language backgrounds. English is the preferred language for air travelers to speak with stewardesses, whereas Hindi is the necessary one for train travelers to speak with vendors. The lingua franca Hindi is different from the official language Hindi in words and grammatical structures, but is closer to Hindustani in both respects. The English used by rural college graduates who travel to other regions or meet with people from other regions is likewise different from official English; it is also different from the pidgin variety of English used by people, who may be high school graduates or dropouts, for example, tourist and pilgrim guides, whose clients do not know any Hindi.

Hindi as a lingua franca is fostered and transmitted through popular cultural media, particularly feature films, rather than by any federal government effort, which is limited to supporting teaching of Hindi as a second language in the voluntary sector. The government's Hindi teaching programs serve the purposes mainly of increasing acceptance of, access to, and use of the official language, Hindi. The federal government's actions in displaying Hindi on signboards in areas of public use such as train stations, milestones on national highways, post offices, and national banks serve the dual function of using the official languages of the Union in federal facilities and of using a common language all over the county for people on the move across regions. These actions have been resisted on the political ground that the regional languages must have a status on par with Hindi in the regions or on the grounds that English and the regional language will suffice for the intended purpose, as in Tamil Nadu, where Hindi in name boards was erased by political parties subscribing to Dravidian ideology. The final political solution was to have sign boards in three languages in federal establishments, viz., English, regional language, and Hindi in that order. There have been erasure campaigns in some states, like Tamil Nadu and Karnataka, to remove English or demote it to a secondary place in commercial sign boards in bazaars. These are by and large fringe movements politically. The alphabet characters (and numbers) used in the registration plates of motorized vehicles are roman (and international), not in devanagari characters (and numbers). Some state governments allow the use of the script of the state official language for the characters (and numbers), but the enthusiasts who go for this option are a small minority. In the public transport systems run by state governments, destination signs on buses are posted in their official language only, and in English also in buses running to other states. It is clear that the contestation for status as a lingua franca is between Hindi and the regional language in the public sector in states, while English remains the unquestioned common language of choice. It is also clear that the question of lingua franca becomes salient politically when the issue is symbolic, as in sign boards, but it ceases to be so when it concerns actual practice, as in travels or recreation of people.

Acceptance and use of Hindi has increased since independence in the private domain of entertainment, specifically films and television. The language used in films is actually Hindustani, not the official language, Hindi. Hindi films and television programs, which are mostly clips from films, are watched in all linguistic regions. Music stores carry discs of Hindi light music in all regions, but newspaper and magazine stands carry minimal Hindi materials. The pop music programs in popular religious and other festivals in street corners have a component of Hindi songs along with the songs of the regional language and of the larger minority languages in the state. This is, however, more of an urban phenomenon. Learning basic Hindi in schools eliminates any inhibition in learning it as a language, but the real understanding of the language comes from hearing it spoken in the entertainment media. Such acceptance of Hindi, however, does not extend to getting information from the media or reading literature. It is more common for the educated non-Hindi speakers to read English fiction or watch English news in addition to those in the regional language. Among the second languages, Hindi is favored in oral pop culture and English in literate culture.

Language of the Federal Government

The first question mentioned earlier concerning the language of government in its three wings of administration, judiciary, and legislature is the most contentious one politically. This was one of the hotly debated questions in the constituent assembly[17] and required political compromises for a solution. With regard to the central government, the first part of the question concerned the choice of language. For ideological and sentimental reasons, it could not be English, which represented the colonial government and not the masses of the new nation. The real contest was between Hindustani, visualized by Gandhi as a language of the common people and as a bridge between the people of two religions, Hinduism and Islam, in northern India, and Hindi, visualized as the largest regional language and as a bridge to the ancient past symbolized by Sanskrit. These two languages, or two varieties of a language, differ more ideologically than grammatically. They were fostered in the anti-colonial movement with different political ideologies and goals and had developed different political bases. Political mobilization for Hindi involved the political incorporation of many geographically contiguous, but historically different, mother tongues into a language called Hindi and presumed the willingness of the people to surrender their distinct linguistic identities. Political mobilization for Hindustani envisioned an India united through a composite culture, by which was meant a culture incorporating ways of life in two religions, Hinduism and Islam. Hindi in devanagari script finally won the vote in the Congress Party and then in the constituent assembly.

The other part of the first question about the official language of the Indian Union concerned the timing for the replacement of the old official language, English, by the new official language, Hindi. After acrimonious debate concerning the time of the switch, it was decided that it would take place in 15 years after the constitution was adopted, which would have been the year 1965.[18] Until that period, Hindi and English would be the two official languages of the Union. The distribution of domains of use in the three branches of the government between the two languages and the levels in each domain were spelled out with the proviso that the use of Hindi will progressively expand to the domains and levels assigned to English.[19] Hindi, during this period of transition, was to equip itself with technical terms and translations that would make it functional in running the business of government.

The third part of the same question was how to make Hindi acceptable to all the regions of the country. To reframe this question, it became one of concern about how to elevate Hindi from a language of a region, however large, to a language of the national government. Hindi had a disadvantage compared to the languages of many regions in lacking a long literary tradition and previous use in royal courts. This disadvantage had to be made up to fortify its numerical strength. The solution hit upon, as mentioned earlier, was the creation of a list of languages of major regions and literary traditions from which Hindi was to draw nourishment. This solution took on a different purpose as those languages became competitors[20] to Hindi for official benefits from the federal government, which culminated in the amended Official Language of the Union Act, 1967 of organization of the party itself by linguistic units and previous party resolutions in favor of that principle for reorganizing the internal boundaries of the country as well.[21]

Languages of the State Governments

Regarding the official languages of the states, which were successors to the British presidencies and native states, the constitution provided that the then existing state legislatures could choose a language spoken in the state or Hindi. Most states chose the majority language of their state. There were a few exceptions. For example, Jammu and Kashmir chose the language associated with the majority religion, Urdu; Nagaland, when separated from Assam to become a new state (much later, in 1963), chose a language ordinarily not considered a native language, namely, English. Himachal Pradesh, where Hindi is not the majority language, nevertheless chose Hindi when it became a state later on, in 1971. The reasons for the different choices of official language in the states related to their different political orientations as well as their language demography.

Hindi or English were chosen as official languages in non-Hindi-speaking states that did not have an alternative majority language. The choice between the two was motivated by a political perception about the state's relationship with the central government or the nation defined in terms of relative political autonomy and economic advantage from the central government.

States based on language

Elevation of the political status of regional languages to official languages goes along with the claim that speakers of the language in question are predominant in one political territory under one government. Status elevation and territorial consolidation feed each other. This aspect of language-territory identification led to a major shift in the political organization of the states in the union, erasing the earlier one that reflected the colonial history of annexation of territories and divisions of them for administrative convenience. The first state carved out of the former Madras presidency and the Nizam's state of Hyderabad on the basis of this language-territory identification was Andhra Pradesh. The language was Telugu. The creation of Andhra Pradesh was conceded in 1956 after a violent agitation following the death of a regional congress leader and a disciple of Gandhi in 1952, who had gone on a fast unto death to achieve this demand.[22] The government of independent India put on hold the formation of linguistic states in the aftermath of partition of the country on the basis of religion in spite of the Congress Party's principle. After the creation of Andhra Pradesh, many other linguistic states followed, usually after agitations, often violent, based on the principle of "one state, one language" (not one language, one state in the case of Hindi, which was the official language of many states with Hindi as the majority language, and Bengali with two states (West Bengal and Tripura) in which it was the majority language).[23] With the formation of Haryana, carved out of Punjab in 1966, language was combined with religion in drawing the boundaries between the two states. In the case of the formation of new states carved out of Assam, language became secondary to ethnicity in defining those states. Thus, the principle of establishing states based on linguistic majority expanded in course of time to include establishment of new states based on the identity of religion or ethnicity of minorities with distinct languages of their own. However, the new ethnically defined states, such as Nagaland, either do not have a majority language at all or, as in the case of Meghalaya (created in 1972), have a bare language majority.

Linguistic states ended up becoming subnations identified with a language, which became the politically dominant language of the state. Those linguistic groups that contested the establishment of Hindi as the only dominant language in the union sought to promote the majority language of their states as the dominant language within them. In spite of this principle of single-language dominance, every linguistic state in fact is multilingual, containing minority languages of different demographic strengths. Depending on their political strength, some minority languages have been given the status of a second official language of the state, as, for example, Urdu in Uttar Pradesh and Andhra Pradesh, Bodo in Assam, or Kok Borok in Tripura. They are not called associate official languages, as in the case of English in the union, and often their status as second official language is restricted to particular districts in the state and to particular domains of government.

Emergence of dominant regional languages

The process of creating linguistic states also created boundary problems. Political campaigns were launched, some of which turned violent, to claim adjacent areas or to claim a preeminent cosmopolitan city in the region as the capital of the new state. The campaigns were for consolidation of language groups with a majority in one state, but having a minority status in neighboring states, thus leading to demands to alter the borders between states in order not to leave the majority language speakers of the new states as minorities in neighboring states. Nevertheless, such consolidation also has not solved the problems of a majority language community when majority language speakers in one state migrate to another state in search of work and become a linguistic minority there. They lobby the government of their "home state" from which they migrated for educational opportunities in their state of residence, especially in professional education for their children, and make other demands such as for waiver of residency conditions for allotment of house sites by municipal corporations. At the same time, in some states, such as Karnataka, an opposite form of political pressure has arisen to make the claim that only the "sons of the soil," that is, those who have resided in the state for generations, were entitled to full rights and privileges in the linguistic states. In other words, there are contradictory claims by those demanding rights in a state based on residency in it rather than language to ward off new linguistic communities that migrated into it in recent times from having rights to privileges in the state, and those demanding rights to privileges based on their natal affiliation to the dominant language community in the state they migrated from rather than residency. A mother tongue speaker of Kannada living in Maharashtra, to give an example, can claim a seat under the distributive control of the government in a professional college in Karnataka, but not a speaker of Hindi from Rajasthan who migrated to Karnataka in his generation and is living there.

The emergence of linguistic states with dominant languages effectively eliminated Hindi as an option for official language in those states. This option, provided in the constitution, was not even debated in any public forum in non-Hindi states. The debate was only about the timeframe for the transition from English as the official language to the dominant language(s). Nevertheless, as mentioned earlier, the number of states in which Hindi was declared the official language increased when some newly created states with no majority language chose Hindi, or when a Hindi majority state was bifurcated, as in the cases of Uttaranchal, Chhattisgarh, and Jharkhand. Hindi is now (in 2008) the official language of nine states, as well as of the capital territory of Delhi. Out of the 28 states of India, English was chosen by only one state, Nagaland, although it continues to be used—along with the official language of the state—for some intrastate and all interstate official purposes in many states. In some tribal states in north-eastern India, such as Arunachal Pradesh, whose legislature has not yet passed a bill establishing an official language, English remains the de facto official language.

Challenge to the dominance of Hindi

During the constitutionally mandated 15 years allowed for the switchover to Hindi, official use of Hindi in the central government gradually increased, despite political protests from southern and eastern states, particularly Tamil Nadu, whenever an increase in use was perceived to involve imposition of Hindi. Tamil Nadu (formerly part of the former Madras province), has had a long history of opposition since the colonial period towards giving Hindi any special status; such opposition has for long been an important part of the platform of the various political parties that have been associated with the Dravidian movement.[24] The first political agitation against Hindi occurred in 1938 against the decision of the Congress government of Madras presidency to make Hindi a compulsory subject in high schools. C. Rajagopalachari, the chief minister, implemented the national policy of his party. Congress had come to power winning the first election in 1937 after the dual government run together by the British and some Indian political leaders (called dyarchy) ended with

the Government of India Act of 1935. The Justice Party, which was in the government during dyarchy, had political reasons to strike against the new government. The 1938 anti-Hindi agitation (the first in Tamil Nadu) ended in loss of two lives from hardships in imprisonment and withdrawal of the order of compulsory Hindi by the government.

Opposition to Hindi was part of a political strategy to safeguard the interests of southern India against the feared dominant position of the numerically larger Hindi-speakers in northern India, on the one hand, and of the upper caste, southern Brahmans, who occupied leadership positions in the Congress party and were expected to fortify their advantage in mastery of English with the learning of Hindi as well, on the other. Organized political action against Hindi in the form of conferences, demonstrations, and agitations continued intermittently for the next three decades from the first agitation in 1938 whenever the provincial government reintroduced Hindi in the school curriculum or the central government issued an order for its employees to learn Hindi or to write sign boards in Hindi in its departments in the province or to give more time to Hindi programs in state-controlled television, and such other actions perceived as involving imposition of Hindi on unwilling Tamils.[25] Anti-Hindi agitations peaked in 1963 when an Official Language Act was being framed to carry out the constitutional provision to make Hindi the sole official language of the Union effective in 1965. The agitation continued through 1965 to 1967 when the Official Language Act was amended (see below). This drawn-out, widespread, student-led anti-Hindi agitation propelled the Dravida Munnetra Kazhagam (DMK) (an offshoot political party of the Dravidian Movement) to come to political power in 1967 in Madras. The new DMK government removed teaching of Hindi in school altogether, establishing a policy of two-language instruction in schools against the national policy of three-language instruction known as three language formula, which had been designed to accommodate a combination of the official language of the linguistic state and the two official languages of the country, one of which happens to be an international language.

Change in the official language policy

The amended Official Language Act of 1967 includes the assurance given by India's first prime minister, Jawaharlal Nehru in Parliament in 1963, in response to the sustained anti-Hindi agitation in Tamil Nadu, while piloting the Official Language Act of 1963, that English may continue to be an official language as long as the non-Hindi population of the country wants it. With this act, a reversal in official language policy was set in motion, namely, continuation of English, which made the policy of official language bilingual, not monolingual either with Hindi or with English. This act also wrested the final decision about Hindi becoming the only official language of the country from the Hindi-speaking majority and entrusted it to the collective of non-Hindi-speaking minorities.[26]

By this time, opposition to Hindi had found its place in the mainstream of politics in Tamil Nadu in the sense that no regional political party or unit of a national party in the state, including congress, could speak openly in support of Hindi.[27] Another development was the political realization that the battle of regional languages (the majority languages of the linguistic states) to contain the supremacy of Hindi has better chances of winning by having English as the contestant against Hindi rather than the regional languages themselves.[28] This realization was shared by many states in the southern, eastern, and northeastern parts of India besides Tamil Nadu.[29] It became possible because of the changed political equations, including the rise of regional political parties in many states and the changed attitudes towards English from being a language of political oppression to a language

of progress, from a language of economic deprivation of the rural masses to a language of centrally planned development for all, from a divisive language of the administration to a unifying language of the constitution, from a language of political inequality to a language of ethnic neutrality. The new Official Language Act also made the central government responsible for the development of regional languages in the states as languages of the nation, not just of their regions alone. The earlier policy position that the central government was responsible only for supporting development of its official language, Hindi, the country's classical language, Sanskrit, and the "stateless" languages, Urdu, and later Sindhi, changed with the allocation of money in the federal budget and the creation of institutions for the development of regional languages. Thus, the Official Language Act of 1967 was politically significant in two respects. First, along with the new meaning of the eighth schedule of the constitution (see earlier), the national status of the regional languages was enhanced. Second, the national role of English was restored in administration and made to be a crucial vehicle for economic development of the country.

Minority languages in states

The place of the official languages of states having been asserted in the national political arena, a further issue within the states concerned the claims for recognition from minority language groups. Their demands were for equal access to employment opportunities in the public sector and educational opportunities in government institutions, as well as assurances that native speakers of the majority language would not have any special advantage by virtue of their language. They sought to achieve these goals by limiting the dominance of the majority language through opposition to compulsory teaching of it in schools and to the requirement that knowledge of the state language be required prior to selection for government employment. Further, they sought to provide a place for English in education as medium of instruction on the basis of the constitutional provision (art. 30) that grants rights to minorities to establish and administer their own educational institutions. These institutions may choose not to teach the majority language and instead choose any other language, provided they do not receive any financial aid from the state government. They admit students from the majority language community also, subject to stipulations decreed by the Supreme Court, thus reducing the stake of the majority language to be the language learnt by everyone having school education. Students speaking the majority language could take this route to learn another language, Sanskrit or French, for example. This offers the possibility for students to finish school education without becoming literate in the official language of the state. The minority educational institutions more often follow the legal route, basing their claims on constitutional grounds, than the political route to preserve their rights to manage their educational institutions on their own terms.[30] Nevertheless, the success of the migrated or border linguistic minorities in a state (such as the Kannada-speaking community in Maharashtra) and the autochthonous minorities of a state (such as Tulu- or Urdu-speaking communities in Karnataka), depends on their political strength and leverage in the state. As at the level of the relations between the nation and the states, English plays the role of keeping the powerful in check at the level of relations between the majority and minorities within states.

Constitutional safeguard for minority languages

According to the constitution, the states have a responsibility with regard to the use of minority languages in government schools, including tribal languages, and in primary education under certain conditions, particularly concerning the numerical strength of students speaking those languages. Imple-

mentation of this provision, which does not fall under fundamental rights of citizens granted in the constitution (arts 350A, 350B), but is under the obligations of the states, has been cursory and fragmentary. The apathy and indifference of states in the implementation of this provision are described in the *Report of the Linguistic Minorities Commission*, which is submitted to parliament every year. But it does not lead to any governmental action when the linguistic minorities are politically weak. The political and bureaucratic reasoning for inaction is that promotion of minority languages in education, particularly the tribal languages in non-tribal states, will hinder the political process of integrating minorities with the mainstream. This is a reasoning rejected by these same politicians and bureaucrats when it concerns regional languages and national integration. That leaves the cause of minority languages in education to be taken up by the nonpolitical voluntary sector. This sector runs teaching centers for children left out or dropped out of school education, which often focus on children of tribal language communities and other poor linguistic minority children. These centers supplement mainstream education by running classes after school, or they provide alternative education that includes the teaching of tribal and other poor minority languages and using them as medium of instruction in the initial years before they are switched to mainstream education.

Language of education

The second question mentioned earlier, the question of language in education, is closely tied to the first question, the question of language in government, because the purpose of education policy was seen as building skills and knowledge for the development of the country. Skills include language skills. When national development takes precedence over personal development in education policy, the choice of language is made by the state. India developed a political consensus in 1961,[31] following deliberations with the chief ministers of states, that every child completing ten years of school must learn three languages: the regional language, English, and Hindi in the non-Hindi-speaking states, but another modern Indian language, preferably a south Indian language, for students in Hindi-speaking states. This policy sought to achieve three goals: the acquisition of skills to enable participation in the economics and politics of the nation, a perception of an integrated nation through language learning, and equal distribution of "language load" for students in all regions. Failure to include a place for the mother tongue in the formula (constitutionally mandated for teaching in primary schools, as mentioned above) and the classical language (Sanskrit and others) in the policy has led in practice either to adding a language or, more commonly, to substituting the minority mother tongue or a classical language in place of one of the three languages, often the regional language.[32] When it comes to implementation of this policy of language choice in education, insofar as the Hindi states are concerned, there is no instrumental motivation for students to learn a third, modern Indian language. The preferred choice in the Hindi states has been Sanskrit. Tamil Nadu follows a two-language policy, as mentioned above. It is clear that the national policy in regard to language education may not articulate well with state policies and with parental preferences in practice. Thus there is variation in language choice across the country in actual practice. Variation, it must be noted, is in the first language (which is by and large the official language of the state) and in the third language (which is mostly the primary official language of the Union, viz., Hindi); it is almost non-existent in the second language, viz., English throughout the country.

Medium of instruction in colleges

The greatest challenge to language policy concerns medium of instruction. As with regard to the language of government, the policy enshrined in the constitution with regard to education provides for Hindi or any Indian language of the state legislature's choice. The policy decision of the states was to provide for the official language of the state to be the medium of education as well. No state other than the states where Hindi is the official language chose Hindi as medium of instruction. There is thus consistency in the language policy in government and in education in the states and near uniformity in exercising the choice of language provided in the constitution.[33]

There is, however, one crucial difference in the language policy for government as opposed to education with regard to replacement of English. There is no timeline for switchover for the language of education as there was for switchover in official language. This, along with other factors mentioned earlier, including the change in perception about English, has contributed to the widest divergence between policy and practice and between policies in relation to education. Absence of a time line results in differential implementation of the policy in higher and lower levels of education. This, in turn, mars the cohesion in policy leading to lack of unity between policy and practice. It is possible, for example, to attribute the reluctance in using the national and provincial official languages at higher levels of administration in part to their non-use at higher levels of education, which supply bureaucrats who work at higher levels of government. It is possible also to explain partially the parental preference for the medium of English in school education by the failure to switch from English medium in higher education.

All governmental commissions on education hedge the time line for switching to indigenous languages with words like "as early as practicable"[34] when it comes to changing the medium of instruction in higher education. The National Policy on Education promulgated in 1976 says that "urgent steps should be taken" without specifying a time. The reasons for hesitancy are two: the speed with which English emerged after independence as the language of academic disciplines, particularly in science and technology, and the time needed for Indian languages to equip themselves with terms and translations for the new task.[35] The switchover time has remained the catch-up time with English, which does not close up. It is a fallacy that form precedes use; the belief that words and materials must be ready before the language can be used takes precedence over the fact that the use of a language in new domains creates words and materials. Another language ideology that informs policy is language purism, according to which the new state-controlled uses of the language must not borrow forms from another language, Persian in the case of Hindi, Sanskrit in the case of Tamil. This results in delay in use in the class room induced by the ideological debate, incomprehensibility of the new register of the language for students, and control over the materials going into the hands of language specialists rather than subject specialists. With the new knowledge-based, globally integrated economy that puts a premium on English, the policy of switchover of language medium in higher education will remain merely politically symbolic, not substantive. The symbolic offering of an option to have an Indian-language medium of education draws to these courses mainly students who are poor, scholastically and economically, which further corrodes the credibility of policies for Indian language change.

Reversal of medium in schools

During dyarchy (1919–35), Indian political parties shared power in the colonial governments in the presidencies and had the education portfolio under their charge. At their initiative, Indian languages were introduced as an alternative medium of instruction in government schools from 1921. By 1937, when the political arrangement with provincial autonomy was in force and the Congress party formed the government in Madras presidency, 51 percent of secondary schools offered an

Indian language as a medium of instruction.[36] The switchover of the medium at the school level became nearly universal after Independence. Indian language medium schools at present comprise 90 percent of all schools in India.[37] The switchover from English to an Indian language as the medium of instruction, however, has been partially reversed in the last few decades. The prestige and power of English as the medium of education at higher levels has percolated down to lower levels of education. The government's policy concerning school education remains that the official language of the state must also be the medium of instruction in the schools. This policy is implemented in government schools and those that receive financial aid from the government.[38] The government's policy of disallowing use of its funds in English medium schools is a reversal of the colonial government's education policy from 1835. The popular demand, however, is to have English as the medium for various reasons, including the desire for success in higher education in English medium and in the world of work where English dominates, as well as the desire of first-generation learners to catch up with others, who have had the benefit of English through education over two or more generations. The gap coincides with the divide between forward and backward castes and between working and middle classes. This takes the medium of education issue from pedagogy to politics. It becomes a matter of seeking government funds for English medium education, thus bringing about a reverse switchover from existing Indian language medium education. This demand amounts to a return to the colonial policy. This also amounts to reversal of the stated policy of extending the Indian-language medium available in schools to universities to one of extending the English medium from universities to schools.

Governments have changed their policies concerning the teaching of English as a subject by pushing downwards the starting year to the primary stage from the post-primary stage and in some states to the first year of education. They accommodate the popular demand with

227

regard to medium not by changing the policy, but by allowing manoeuverability in the policy through such means as providing parallel streams of medium in aided schools, or parallel structures of education such as matriculation schools in Tamil Nadu. The new structure added to the existing structures of the State Board of Education and the Central Board of Education, which implement government policy in education in Tamil Nadu, is the board of matriculation schools; the latter are in the private sector and have freedom in implementing the policy, although they are under the administrative (not financial) control of the state with regard to accreditation. In the name of increasing access to education, private schools are encouraged, which are not governed by the policy of the government with regard to medium of education, and some of which are accredited by bodies outside the country. These schools charge a heavy fee from students, thereby restricting access to those who can afford it. Schools run by minorities are another source for providing education through English medium, as mentioned already.

It is an intriguing political question why democratically elected governments do not change their policy to meet the popular demand for English-medium education. There is, of course, the pedagogical reason of the advantage of teaching children though the language of their childhood experience. But there is also the politics of symbols. Using the language of the state as the medium of education is an acknowledgement of its prestige and an expression of its power. This policy gets legitimacy for the government from cultural elites like littérateurs and language teachers and from the general public as the custodian of their language. But in their personal lives they, as well as the political leaders themselves, who make the policy, make their choices on substantive grounds, notably economic opportunities. Hence the dichotomy between policy and practice is not perceived by the people as contradictory.

Empowering the oppressed with English

The politics of preserving or promoting the economic and political interests of various groups was played out in the name of language soon after independence until it changed to one of promoting the interests of various designated castes in the second half of the period. But the English language continues to play a role in the pursuit of political interests, as it does in economic pursuits. Socially and economically advanced groups try to hold on to their advantages by holding on to English while the disadvantaged groups try to advance socially and economically by acquiring knowledge of English. The latter suspect that there is a conspiracy by the elites in control of government to keep them from mastering English through the government's language policy in education. English is believed to be a liberating force for them and a means of empowerment,[39] which is not different from their perception of English in colonial times. The politically active among them want their voice heard across the nation and beyond it and to have a common language to communicate with other *dalit*s (economically and socially deprived lower castes) in other states in the country to create a national political platform to fight oppression, just as the elites used English for interregional communication in their fight against British oppression[40] They believe that they have a right to English, which was denied them by the colonial policy and that they should get it from the government, since the fee for attending a private English medium school is beyond their reach. Clearly, in postcolonial times, the politics of language in India has taken a new trajectory with roles reworked for English.

Differential gains

The narrative of the politics of language in India suggests the following conclusions. The minority languages without political clout are orphaned. Regional languages have gained political dominance and retained their supremacy in the literate culture of the states. Hindi retains an edge in the competition for jobs nationally, for social networking in the national capital, and has gained acceptance as the language of entertainment and urban pop culture as well as a sign of *desi* (native) identity for the mobile youth in the globalized market. English, in contrast, has enhanced its status as the language of economic power, elite status and intellectual pursuits.

Notes

1 Ramachandra Guha, *India after Gandhi: The History of the World's Largest Democracy* (New York: HarperCollins, 2007), "Prologue," pp. 1–15.

2 This is true of religion also. Although Hinduism is the majority religion, it is a heterogeneous religion with no organized structure of control and designated authority. It does not have a common language; Sanskrit is not a language of religious practice or identity for all Hindus.

3 Bernard S. Cohn, "The Command of Language and The Language of Command," in Ranajit Guha (ed.), *Subaltern Studies IV: Writings on South Asian History and Society* (Delhi: Oxford University Press, 1988).

4 Christopher R. King, *One Language, Two Scripts: The Hindi Movement in Nineteenth Century North India* (Delhi: Oxford University Press, 1994) is a narrative of this differentiation. Distancing of formal Hindi from its popular base is described in Alok Rai, *Hindi Nationalism* (Hyderabad: Orient Longman, 2001).

5 Paul R. Brass, *Language Religion and Politics in North India* (Cambridge: University Press, 1974); reprint edn (Lincoln, NE: iUniverse, 2005).

6 Tamil may be an exception, but the relationship between Tamil and Sanskrit and the perception of Tamil as both a cultural icon and a political icon is complex in its relation to "Aryan" North India. See S. V. Shanmugam (in Tamil), *Mozhi vaLarcciyum mozhi uNarvum: canka kaalam (Language Development and Language Awareness: Sangam Period)* (Madras: Manivasagar Patippakam, 1989), p. 219.

7 Gandhi initially opposed this idea, but soon gave it his approval. See M. S. Thirumalai, "Early Gandhi and the Language Policy of the Indian National Congress," in the online journal, *Language in India*, Vol. 5, No. 4 (2005), www.languageinindia.com. The Congress Party, persuaded by Gandhi, adopted Hindustani as the language of its official deliberations, including proceedings of its conferences. Use of Hindustani had been increasing in party conference speeches from the time of Gandhi's association with the party despite resistance to it from some leaders from the south. But, by 1947, Gandhi had become an advocate of linguistic reorganization of the states of India, although he had a lurking suspicion that the regional languages may assert themselves, thereby threatening the unity of India that had been forged with Hindustani; see Ramachandra Guha, pp. 189–90.

8 Brass, pp. 78–90.

9 Gauri Viswanathan, *Masks of Conquest: Literary Study and British Rule in India* (New York: Columbia University Press, 1989), ch. vi, "The Failure of English," pp. 142–65. See also E. Annamalai, "Medium of Power: The Question of English in Education," in James W. Tollefson and Amy B. M. Tsui (eds), *Medium of Instruction Policies: Which Agenda? Whose Agenda?* (Mahwah, NJ: Lawrence Erlbaum, 2004), pp. 171–94.

10 The debate is about teaching English effectively to subaltern students from social groups who had missed out education. The demands vary from teaching English to them from class one to using English as the medium of instruction. One encounters a conspiracy theory also, according to which the educationists, who come from upper castes, teach a standard variety of English they speak, denying any role to subaltern English in order to make these students fail in English.

11 For example, Bruce McCully, *English Education and the Origins of Indian Nationalism* (New York: Columbia University Press, 1942).

12 Mohandas K. Gandhi, *Thoughts on National Language* (Ahmedabad: Navajivan, 1956); also Jawaharlal Nehru, *The Question of Language* (Allahabad: Congress Political and Economic Studies, 1937).

13 This question continued to be debated even after the constitution did not choose to designate any language as the national language;

see, for example, V. K. R. V. Rao, *Many Languages, One Nation: The Problem of Integration* (Bombay: Mahatma Gandhi Memorial Research and Library, 1978).

14 For the intensity and diversity of beliefs about language and nationhood, see Kuldip Nayar, "Bilingualism," in *Between the Lines* (Bombay: Allied Publishers, 1969), pp. 30–69. Nayar is a journalist who worked as the press information officer of the Government of India.

15 B. Mallikarjun, "The Eighth Schedule Languages: Critical Appraisal," in R. S. Gupta *et al.* (eds), *Language and the State: Perspectives on the Eighth Schedule* (New Delhi: Creative Books, 1995), pp. 61–83.

16 The census reports what the citizens tell the enumerators is their mother tongue, which is a token of social identity rather than a distinct language; neither is it a dialect in a linguistic sense. The reports group these mother tongues (raw data) into languages (processed data) on the basis of linguistic and political considerations. Mother tongues reported by less than 10,000 speakers are not counted. Hindi has the largest number of mother tongues grouped under it. The number will be more than 48, if these numerically smaller mother tongues are also included. The anomaly with Maithili is that it is not given a language status in the census but is on par with the country's major languages in the constitution. It is also recognized (along with Dogri) as a literary language by Sahitya Akademi (National Academy of Letters) for awards for best literary works.

17 See, for example, extracts from the Constituent Assembly Debates (1949) compiled by M. S. Thirumalai and B. Mallikarjun, "The Evolution of Language Policy in the Constituent Assembly of India," in *Language in India*, Vol. 6, No. 2 (2006).

18 This scheme of things, however, was modified with the Official Language Act of 1963 issued in response to agitations against Hindi becoming the sole official language from 1965. This Act provided for the continued use of English beyond 1965 in domains in which it was in use with the stipulation that all acts, government orders and such other documents made originally in English must be accompanied with their Hindi translation.

19 See "The Constitution of India: Provisions Relating to Language," compiled by M. S. Thirumalai, in *Language in India*, Vol. 2, No. 2 (2002).

20 At the level of political symbolism, the demand by the Dravidian parties in Tamil Nadu is to make all the scheduled languages the official languages of the Union. This demand, irrespective of its impracticality by the number of languages to be used and of the fact that the list is open-ended, was still alive in 2008, as can be seen in a speech of the chief minister of Tamil Nadu ruled by DMK on the seventieth anniversary of the first anti-Hindi agitation: "Other regional languages should also be made official languages at the Centre" (*The Hindu* online (Tamil Nadu section), 27 January, 2008). Note the implication of "other" in the sentence cited suggesting that Hindi is also a regional language that was elevated to be the official language of the central government, which elevation other regional languages also deserve. The idea is to have all regional languages including Hindi as the symbolic official languages of the country and English the working official language.

21 For the text of the act, see The Official Language Act, 1963 (as amended, 1967) in *Language in India*, Vol. 2, No. 2 (2002).

22 For detailed history, see *History of Andhra Movement* (2 vols) by Committee for History of Andhra Movement (Hyderabad: Goverment of Andhra Pradesh, 1985). After the Congress Party's electoral debacle in the Telugu region of the Madras state on the question of having a separate Telugu-speaking state, the central government constituted the *Commission on Linguistics Reorganization of States* (New Delhi: Government of India, 1955), which evolved criteria and recommendations for the formation of linguistic states. The linguistic basis of the formation of states yielded later to demands based on religion, ethnicity, and unequal economic development within a state. The demand for a separate state of Telangana, which is Telugu-speaking, to be carved out of Andhra Pradesh on the basis of economic underdevelopment is likely to be met by the compulsions of electoral politics.

23 B. R. Ambedkar, *Thoughts on Linguistic States* (Bombay: Popular Prakashan, 1955).

24 It should be pointed out that Hindi was first introduced as an optional subject in 1926 during the period of dyarchy and, a few years

later, was made a compulsory language in high schools in Madras presidency not by the government of the Congress Party, but by the government in which the Justice Party, the progenitor of the Dravidian movement, shared power and was in charge of the education portfolio. See Eugene F. Irschick, *Tamil Revivalism in the 1930s* (Madras: Cre-A Publishers, 1986), pp. 213–14.

25 For an analysis of anti-Hindi agitation from a point of view of dialectical materialism, see Mohan Kumaramangalam's *India's Language Crisis* (Madras: New Century Book House, 1965); and from a cultural–political point of view, see Mohan Ram's *Hindi vs. India: The Meaning of DMK* (New Delhi: Rachna Prakashan, 1968).

26 This assurance of Nehru was a long way from Gandhi's characterization, in 1931, of the Tamil Nadu Congress delegation's failure to use Hindi in the party conference as an act of tyranny by a minority; cited in Irschick, p. 212. For Nehru's pragmatic views and influential role in formulating and implementing official language policy, see Robert D. King, *Nehru and the Language Policy of India* (New York: Oxford University Press, 1997).

27 After he left the Congress, C. Rajagoplachari changed his earlier position in favor of Hindi and became an advocate of English against Hindi; see his *The Question of English* (Madras: Bharatan, 1962).

28 This political strategy is considered to be relevant even now in 2008. The current chief minister of Tamil Nadu said, in the speech cited in note 19, that "English will remain as our shield" against Hindi.

29 The choice of English as a political symbol by the northeastern states is based on a different reasoning, namely, that it gives their tribal communities a non-Hindu (and, for some, non-Indian) identity.

30 E. Annamalai, "Language Choice in Education: Conflict Resolution in Indian Courts," *Language Science*, Vol. 20, No. 1 (1998), pp. 29–43.

31 This was originally proposed by the Central Advisory Board of Education in 1957. It was incorporated in the National Policy on Education in 1968 and has been repeated in every new formulation of education policy since then.

32 S. Aggarwal, *Three Language Formula: An Educational Problem* (New Delhi: Gian, 1991).

33 As there are departments of the central government in the states, there are schools run by the central government in the states. These central schools have Hindi (along with English) as medium of instruction.

34 A phrase used by the University Education Commission, chaired by S. Radhakrishnan, in 1977.

35 For arguments for and against switchover see A. B. Shah (ed.), *The Great Debate* (Bombay: Lalvani, 1968).

36 S. Nurullah and J. P. Naik, *A History of Education in India (during the British Period)*, 2nd edn (Bombay: Macmillan, 1951), p. 650.

37 National Council for Educational Research and Training, *Sixth All India Educational Survey: Main Report* (New Delhi, 1999).

38 One section of a class in such aided schools may have English medium instruction, whose teachers' salary will be paid by the school management from its sources, not from grants given by the government.

39 S. Anand, "Sanskrit, English and Dalits," *EPW*, Vol. 34, No, 30 (24 July, 1999), pp. 2,053–56.

40 After Independence, the use of English by these elites increased in literary production promoted globally in the name of postcolonial literature. *Dalits* are beginning to participate in this literary culture after half a century of Independence. They have conflicting pulls between the desire to have their voice heard globally and locally, between participation through English in the national and international literary culture, and in the historically longer literary culture of the regional language they are born into. Meena Kandasamy, a Tamil-speaking *dalit* poet in English, says in an interview (*The Hindu* online, 6 January, 2008, magazine section), "*Dalits* need English for social empowerment, but English has become more or less another caste. In India, after caste and class, the next important thing is whether you are English-speaking, (but) unlike caste it is something you can change (into) by yourself. (But) I think you have to be very conscious of your background, of where your roots lie." She goes on to say: "Some activist–academics like Kancha Ilaiah tell us to bury our Indian language in favor of English; but somehow I am very scared of that."

16

Language problems and politics in Pakistan

Tariq Rahman

Introduction

There are two major kinds of language problems in Pakistan: those concerning the use of language as a symbol of identity; and those concerning its use as a medium of instruction. The first feeds into the ethnic politics of Pakistan; the second into the politics of social class, deprivation, marginalization and, increasingly, of political Islam. The first may be called horizontal, affecting as it does, collectivities or would-be collectivities dispersed over the geographical boundaries of the country. The second is vertical, affecting the way social mobility and class formation are affected by language. Both are connected with politics, i.e., the way in which power is distributed in society and how it is pursued to secure goods and services for collectivities (such as ethnic groups), social classes (such as the westernized elite), and individuals.

This chapter studies the use of language in both ethnic politics and the politics of social class in Pakistan. The first part owes its origin to my work, *Language and Politics in Pakistan* (1996),[1] but it has been updated to take into account subsequent developments. The second is based on recently published and still unpublished research.[2] There is also a brief discussion of the present language policy

on the indigenous (weaker) languages of Pakistan.

Review of literature

Paul Brass[3] and Jyotirindra Das Gupta[4] remain the paradigmatic models for the study of the relationship between language problems and politics in India. As Indian realities—brought out in many studies[5]—parallel those of Pakistan, these models remain valid for students of the language politics of Pakistan. Language, however, remains almost as under studied a variable in the ethnic politics of Pakistan as it was in 1995 when the present author's work on that subject just mentioned was published.

The pioneering scholarly work in those days were articles by Hamza Alavi,[6] articles on "regional imbalances and the national question" in a book edited by S. Akbar Zaidi[7] and Tahir Amin's full length study of the rise and fall of "ethnonational movements" in Pakistan.[8] Hamza Alavi's analysis deals with the over-developed state, which creates a "salariat" dependent on its patronage for goods, services and power. Ethnic struggle, in his view, is the struggle between the central and peripheral "salariats" for power. Although these contending elites "fracture (or align) along ethnic lines," they do not necessarily work in the interests of the subordinate classes.[9] Alavi was wary of ethnic politics and paid no attention to the role of language in constructing the subordinate group or personality in Pakistan. Akbar Zaidi's edited book includes articles not only on the language issue (Feroze Ahmed's) but also the underdevelopment of certain regions; they are among the pioneering empirical writings on this subject in Pakistan.[10] The pioneering book-length study of ethnicity, however, is by Tahir Amin. He gives a "dynamic picture of changing group identities"[11] with reference to internal and external factors without, however, paying much attention to language.

The work of Feroz Ahmed, published two years later, was a collection of his work on this subject from a Marxist point of view, all written earlier.[12] However, Feroz Ahmed was one of the first political scientists to study the alienation of the Urdu-speakers (*mohajirs*) of Sindh from the political process and to suggest that they should be accommodated.[13] After that the only major study of a language-based ethnic movement, based on the Siraiki language of Southern Punjab, is Hussain Ahmad Khan's *Re-Thinking Punjab: The Construction of Siraiki Identity* (2004).[14] Apart from that, though language has been touched on in studies of ethnicity in Pakistan after 1996—Ishtiaq Ahmed, Adeel Khan[15]—it is not the focus of these studies. Ishtiaq Ahmed offers a comparative analysis of ethnic politics in India, Pakistan, Bangladesh, and Sri Lanka. Language is given attention but, "since the invocation of language or religion as a basis for separatist national identity in contemporary South Asia has not been consistent,"[16] it is seen in the context of resistance to the state's project of modernization, which is perceived to benefit certain elitist groups at the expense of the resisting minorities. Adeel Khan points out that it is not only the economic disadvantages of modernization but the distance from the state structure of the ethnic groups that determines the degree of their resistance to the ruling elite. In his view, "culture, history

and language have been part of the symbolic and rhetorical armory of these movements but not of their actual political agendas."[17] This point, if interpreted to imply that languages have iconic significance and are used to express conflicts for power in a given political system, needs no emphasis. If, however, this becomes a justification for leaving language out of the analysis altogether, or treating it in an inadequate manner, it needs to be corrected. This chapter attempts to make this kind of correction in order to point out that language policies and practices, both of the ruling elites and those resisting them, have far-reaching consequences for the politics of a country.

Language policy in Pakistan

Pakistan is a multilingual state with six major languages—Punjabi (spoken by 44.15 percent out of a population of 160 million in 2007); Pashto (15.42); Sindhi (14.10); Siraiki (10.53); Urdu (7.57); Balochi (3.57)—and about 57 minor ones. Urdu is the national language and English the official one.[18] English is spoken spontaneously and fluently only by a small elite, which is estimated to comprise between 5–6 percent of the population.[19] The 1973 constitution of the country, which was suspended in part both during the military rule of Generals Zia ul Haq (1977–1988) and Pervez Musharraf (1999–2008), is again in force. It provides the following guidelines on language policy:

(a) The National language of Pakistan is Urdu, and arrangements shall be made for its being used for official and other purposes within fifteen years from the commencing day.

(b) Subject to clause (1) the English language may be used for official purposes until arrangements are made for its replacement by Urdu.

(c) Without prejudice to the status of the National language, a Provincial Assembly may by law prescribe measures for the teaching, promotion and use of a provincial language in addition to the national language.

(Article 251)[20]

233

This policy, as overtly declared and actually put in practice, has led to ethnic resistance using language as a symbol of identity, the continuation of a class-based, unequal system of education, and the weakening of the indigenous languages of the country. Let us take these issues one by one.

Language and ethnic politics

With the death of Nawab Akbar Bugti, a tribal leader of the Baloch, in August 2006, and the construction of the Gawadar port which is seen by the Baloch nationalists as an outpost of the Punjabis (and especially the army) in their motherland, the province of Balochistan has witnessed the re-emergence of a militant ethnic movement last seen there in the 1970s.[21] In Sindh, too, there is deep resentment against the army, ostensibly because of the construction of cantonments. Indeed, since the late 1990s, the ethnonationalists have formed an alliance called the Pakistan Oppressed Nations Movement (PONM), which held a meeting in Islamabad on the 1st and 2nd of November 1998. The declaration adopted there had eight demands, one of which was:

> Pushto, Siraiki, Balochi, Sindhi and Punjabi languages should be declared national languages and the culture of the federating nations should be given an equal opportunity to develop and prosper.[22]

However, language, though very much a part of rhetoric and declarations in conferences, is not as strong a force as it was in the first 25 years of Pakistan's existence. The most powerful language-based ethnic movement of the first few years of Pakistan was the Bengali language movement. The most detailed and incisive account of this movement, though in the context of left-wing politics and from a Marxist perspective, is by Badruddin Umar.[23]

In 1948 and 1952 a number of urban Bengalis—mostly students, intellectuals and educated people—demanded that their language, Bengali, should be a national language of Pakistan and should also be used in public domains. This movement, called the Bengali Language Movement or *Bhasha Ondolan,* was politically significant because it was a reaction to the perceived domination and injustice of West Pakistani decision makers towards the people of East Bengal. However, the Muslim League in particular, and West Pakistanis in general, saw it as a conspiracy of communists, Indian agents and enemies of Pakistan to destabilize the new state. Among the few West Pakistanis who saw it as a spontaneous response to West Pakistani hegemony were ethno-nationalist leaders who were themselves regarded as anti-state forces by the West Pakistani establishment.

The Tamuddun Majlis, a private social organization, demanded Bengali as the language of instruction, administration and means of communication in East Bengal as early as September 1947, only a month after Pakistan was established. However, it was ignored till December of that year when it was feared that Urdu alone would be the language of the state. The language movement started off in earnest in 1948 when Mohammad Ali Jinnah, or Quaid-i-Azam (the Great Leader) as he is called in Pakistan, declared on 19 and 21 March, 1948 that the state language of Pakistan is "going to be Urdu and no other language."[24] Jinnah made that statement on the assumption that one language unites a new nation and that nobody, except anti-Pakistan agitators, was against Urdu. Later, in 1952, Khwaja Nazimuddin, the then prime minister of Pakistan, repeated these sentiments in Dhaka.[25] After this, the language movement really gathered momentum. The students of Dhaka University were the leaders of the movement, who organized processions in favor of Bengali every day. On 21 February, 1952 the police fired on the students who had decided to defy Section 144 by coming out of the University in batches of four and five. As a result of this firing, according to the police report given to the inquiry conducted by Justice Ellis of the Dhaka High Court, there were "nine casualties of whom three were students and six outsiders."[26] This day, called *Ekushe*, became a significant symbol of Bengali defiance of the West Pakistani ruling elite and evokes strong sentiments even today. The language movement appeared to come to an end in 1954 when Bengali was accepted as one of the national languages—the other being Urdu— by the constituent assembly.[27] However, the sentiments it had created lingered on and formed the basis of Bengali nationalism, which led to the creation of Bangladesh in 1971. In short, the Bengali language movement remains crucial for the understanding of identity formation, ethnicity, nationalism and the clash of elites and proto-elites in multilingual aspiring nation states.

The conditions of East Bengal parallel those of Sindh. Like Sheikh Mujibur Rahman, the leader of Bangladesh, G. M. Syed, the nationalist leader of Sindh, also advocated the creation of an autonomous state of Sindhu Desh.[28] However, this demand for autonomy was sometimes accompanied by veiled threats of secession. Here too Sindhi has been the medium of instruction in government schools as well as that of the judiciary and the administration at the lower levels, just as Bengali was in East Bengal. Thus the ruling elite's policy of favoring Urdu, which is the mother tongue of the *mohajirs* of the cities of Sindh, is strongly resented. The *mohajirs*, a non-assimilationist minority proud of their urban Mughal culture, of which Urdu is a symbol, resist all attempts at promoting Sindhi. In 1970 when the Sindh University and the Board of Intermediate and Secondary Education made Sindhi compulsory for *mohajirs*, they protested and there were riots in January–February 1970 in the cities of Sindh.[29] In 1972, when the provincial PPP tried to pass a bill to increase the use of Sindhi and make *mohajirs* learn it, there were riots again.[30] The situation nowadays, ever since 1984, is that the *mohajirs* see themselves as an ethnic group like the Sindhis and claim power in Sindh on the basis of this distinct identity. In other words the question is really which community will rule Sindh—Sindhis or

mohajirs? This makes Sindh a potential battleground for a vicious civil war.

Balochistan is a multilingual province because some parts of Afghanistan were included in it in British days. Thus, besides Balochi and Brahvi, Pashto too is fairly widely spoken in Balochistan. As the Balochi-speaking and Brahvi-speaking people define themselves as Baloch, they insist on common origin rather than language as a marker of identity. However, there has been a Balochi language movement since 1951 which aims at preserving the Baloch cultural identity. Balochi identity is expressed by coining words of Baloch origin and, indeed, by writing in a language which has little official patronage.[31] Baloch ethnicity, which includes Brahvis also, is expressed mostly through armed resistance, as in 1948, 1960s, mid-1970s, and at present (2006 onwards). This is probably because the educated elite is so small that a language movement is hard to sustain.

In Balochistan as well as in the North-West Frontier Province (NWFP), Pashto serves as an identity symbol. It was the moral code of the Pathans, *Pashtoonwali,* which was such a symbol in pre-modern times. The efforts of Khan Abdul Ghaffar Khan (1890–88), the anti-British Pakhtun nationalist leader, made Pashto such a symbol.[32] Earlier, Persian was the language of culture and prestige and was used by the Persian-speaking population of northern Afghanistan and the ruling Pakhtun elite. After the 1930s, the ruling elite promoted Pashto as a means of creating nationalism and unity among tribes which were divided and understood only their extended kinship system and tribal loyalties. Thus Pashto was the new symbol, like the national flag and other centralizing icons, used to create the Afghan nation out of a mere collection of tribes.

In both cases, Pashto was used for political purposes under modern political conditions. However, because of the Afghan claim to Pakhtunistan, the ruling elite was mistrustful of Pashto despite the fact that the Pakhtun nationalist NAP (National Awami Party) chose Urdu as the official language of the frontier in

235

its brief rule in 1972. It is only recently that the Pakhtun elite has been co-opted by Pakistan's ruling elite and the threat of the secession of the NWFP has disappeared. Pashto still remains an identity marker and part of Pakhtun nationalism as expressed politically by the Awami National Party (ANP, the new name for the NAP), which continues to challenge the domination of the center. The events of 9/11 formed a watershed in Pakistan ethnic politics. By this time Pashto had come to be associated with the Taliban who were ruling Afghanistan while Persian, once the major bureaucratic language and elitist symbol of Afghanistan, was associated with the anti-Taliban Northern Alliance. Thus, when the coalition forces attacked Afghanistan in October 2001, the Pakistani Pakhtuns supported their Afghan "brethren" out of religious as well as ethnic (linguistic) affinity. The ANP failed to defend Pakhtun ethnic interests and at least part of the Pakhtun ethnic vote went to the religious coalition MMA (Mutahadda Majlis-e-Amal or United Congress for Action) rather than the ANP.[33] In short, in the Pashto-speaking areas at least a certain fusion of religious and ethnic feeling appears to have taken place.

The southern part of Punjab is under-developed and the leaders of this area blame the Punjabi ruling elite for this under-development. From the 1960s they have labeled their language Siraiki and have standardized it for purposes of writing. The language had been written even in the nineteenth century, but different writers used different orthographic symbols of the Urdu script. The choice of the term Siraiki in the 1960s meant that the people of southern Punjab could identify with one identity symbol instead of calling their language by local names such as Multani, Derewali, Riasati, and so on. Since a famous conference in Multan in 1975 a number of institutions—like the Siraiki Lok Sanjh—have been promoting the language, with the support of Siraiki ethnic political parties.[34]

While the Siraiki movement is clearly a response to perceived Punjabi domination and internal colonialism, the Punjabi language movement is hard to understand. The Punjabis occupy most of the powerful positions in the apparatus of the state: the federal government, legislature, and especially the army and the bureaucracy, and oppose the use of Punjabi even in primary schools. They do so presumably because they have internalized the low status given to Punjabi by all former rulers of Punjab and feel that this language cannot be used in formal domains. Possibly, they also feel that if the use of Punjabi is allowed in formal domains, the speakers of the other languages, which are also ethnic identity symbols, will increase the pressure on the state to give even more importance to their languages. This, they reason, will lead to the intensification of ethnic sentiments and the weakening of the federation of Pakistan. But this attitude of the Punjabi elite is precisely why there is such a movement. The activists of the movement claim that the price of Punjabi domination over Pakistan is the denial of the Punjabi ethnic identity. In fact, by teaching only English and Urdu to the Punjabi elite, Punjabi language and culture have been suppressed. This culture shame, they feel, should go; Punjabis should learn to be proud of their Punjabi identity. This is only possible if the state uses Punjabi in the domains of power. But if the state does that, the ethnonationalist argument of using all the other indigenous languages in these domains too would be strengthened. Thus the status quo continues.[35]

The theoretical insights used in this account of the relationship between language and ethnic identity are constructivist. Language is not a primordial given but something which, under certain circumstances, gains salience as an icon. In short, an identity is imagined and language—along with shared myths, artifacts, and history—help to "imagine" it.[36]

From this theoretical perspective it appears that in all language movements, except the Punjabi one, language has been more or less consciously manipulated by leaders for instrumental, rational, goal-seeking reasons: the creation of a pressure group to obtain greater power, goods and services from the state; to redress a situation of internal colonialism which is perceived as being unjust. In the Punjabi language movement, however, the major motivation is sentimental or extra-rational. It is the desire for self-respect; for the acceptance of one's identity without culture shame; for psychological fulfillment without adopting the language and behavior of another culture.

However, this instrumentalist explanation would be misleading if the emotional or extra-rational motivation of the actors in a movement were not taken into account. For, in the heat of the moment, people are ready to die or kill not for something as prosaic as a job or admission in a college but for honor, vengeance, love, hatred, and self-respect. This extra-rational aspect of movements is difficult to analyze unless one observes the deep emotion of the actors and finds out their subjective truth.

But, if language movements are part of ethnic assertions meant to counter perceived domination and injustice, only linguistic policies will not be helpful. A language will remain ghettoized and will be resisted even by its own speakers—as mother tongue schooling was in South Africa[37] and the indigenous languages in the NWFP[38] and Balochistan—if it is not used in the domains of power and powerful jobs are not available in it or if it is otherwise despised socially. To create a secure country where ethnicity is no longer a threat, a truly federal (or even a confederal) political order may be necessary. That will mean that there will be five national languages in the country with Urdu as a language of inter-provincial communication and English for international communication. And, even more important, it will mean that the provinces, which may be rearranged along ethnic and linguistic lines, will be genuinely empowered. In such a political system, no federating unit would want to opt out of the system because it would then be responsible for its fate and would no longer be dominated by the center. Only then can ethnicity be used to create a state with a rich and pluralistic culture.

Language and class conflict

Besides being symbolic of ethnic identity, language is also part of a divide along socio-economic class lines. This is because certain varieties and styles of a language, in the words of Pierre Bourdieu, "can function as linguistic capital, producing a *profit of distinction* on the occasion of each social exchange."[39] If a language is used in the domains of power—of the state or the corporate sector—it can be exchanged for wealth, power and prestige. That is why the educational system sells it and consumers buy it. Bourdieu puts it as follows:

> The position which the educational system gives to the different languages (or the different cultural contents) is such an important issue only because this institution has the monopoly in the large-scale production of producers/consumers, and therefore in the reproduction of the market without which the social value of the linguistic competence, its capacity to function as linguistic capital, would cease to exist.[40]

Pakistan's educational system gives the highest value to English followed by Urdu and Sindhi. However, Sindhi is restricted to the province of Sindh and that too to mostly rural areas and small towns. English, Urdu, and Sindhi are, therefore, the media of instruction in schools corresponding to a class-based division of Pakistan society. The Ministry of Education declares officially that Urdu is the medium of instruction in government schools. At the higher level, while English in used in scientific and technical subjects, most students opt for teaching and examinations in Urdu. Parallel to this stream of ordinary students and teachers is the elitist stream which studies in English-medium schools, colleges and universities. The elitist English medium schools, where the teachers really teach in English and the students come from elitist backgrounds with exposure to English, are so expensive as to exclude lower middle and working-class pupils. The Urdu and Sindhi medium schools, as well as the few schools where Pashto is the medium of instruction at the lower levels, are run by the state and are quite affordable for most Pakistanis. Medium of instruction actually serves as an indicator of socioeconomic class with the most affluent going to the English medium schools, the lower middle classes to the vernacular medium ones and the poorest people, as well as people in remote, rural areas, studying in the *madrasahs*. Data concerning the number of schools according to their medium of instruction, as provided by the ministry of education, are given in Table 16.1.

The most affordable educational institutions—because they often provide free board and lodging—are religious seminaries or *madrasahs* reported by the ministry of education to number 12,979 in 2006. The *madrasahs* preserve Arabic more as a symbol of continuity with the past and of Islamic identity than a living language; most of their graduates cannot function in Arabic. They do, however, function in Urdu which has spread through the *madrasah* network ever since the nineteenth century and is now associated with Islam and Muslim identity in both Pakistan and India.[41] In the NWFP and parts of rural Sindh, Pashto

and Sindhi are used to explain concepts but the language of examination is Urdu.[42]

The role of English in Pakistan has been studied by Sabiha Mansoor[43] and Tariq Rahman.[44] Mansoor has conducted two major surveys on the attitudes of students towards languages. The first survey, conducted in Lahore in 1992, suggests that students have a linguistic hierarchy in mind, with English at the top followed by Urdu, with their mother tongue (in this case Punjabi) at the bottom. She also found that English is associated with modernity and efficiency while Punjabi is associated with informality and intimacy.[45] The second survey provides a detailed analysis of the role of English in higher education. Both studies confirm positive attitudes towards English among Pakistani students, their teachers and parents, and university administrators.

English is the language of globalization. The international corporate sector, bureaucracies (such as the United Nations and the World Bank), foreign-funded NGOs, the service sector and the internet work predominantly in English in Pakistan. This is of enormous advantage for the Pakistani elite, whose members are very proficient in English. Consequently, lucrative private sector employment is almost entirely dominated by the

Table 16.1 Educational institutions in Pakistan by medium of instruction

Type of management	No. of institutions	Medium of instruction			
		Urdu (%)	English (%)	Sindhi (%)	Others* (%)
Total	227,791	64.6	10.4	15.5	9.5
Boys	57,868	77.3	2.9	6.7	13.2
Girls	48,475	78.3	2.6	9.3	9.8
Mixed	121,448	53.1	17.1	22.2	7.6
Public	151,744	68.3	1.4	22.4	7.9
Boys	50,265	82.2	1.2	7.5	9.1
Girls	41,878	80.6	1.4	6.7	11.3
Mixed	59,601	48.0	1.6	43.4	7.0
Private	76,047	57.2	28.4	1.8	12.7
Boys	6,597	63.7	10.7	2.6	23.0
Girls	7,602	44.4	1.4	1.3	52.9
Mixed	61,847	58.0	32.1	1.7	7.7

Note: * includes Pashto, Balochi, Arabic, etc.

Source: GOP Highlights, Table 23, p. 37

English-using elite while the vernacular educated proto-elite is increasingly joining public-funded institutions (the state bureaucracy, education, the judiciary, and the military).

The Pakistani elite has invested in an elitist system of education through the medium of English while allowing most Pakistanis to remain uneducated, seek *madrasah* education or remain confined to vernacular medium schooling and substandard institutions of higher education. This has created a perception of injustice, and hence anger. The elite's appropriation of English as cultural capital for themselves and a device for filtering out the less advantaged, as explained by Myers-Scotton,[46] is a political strategy which perpetuates the hegemony of the English-using elite over the upper echelons of Pakistani society.

One component of this elite, the officer corps of the armed forces, has used its power and resources to establish and control educational institutions. Initially, the armed forces established cadet colleges, which are large residential schools run along the lines of elitist British private schools (the so-called public schools, such as Eton and Harrow). These were defended by Ayub Khan, the first military ruler of Pakistan (1958–69).[47] During the 1960s, however, a number of students opposed these schools. A special commission whose mandate was to investigate the causes of the students' mobilization declared that the system was unlawful because it discriminated between citizens but, nevertheless, allowed it to continue in the name of quality. The elitist schools, therefore, kept flourishing.[48] The state spends

public money to subsidize these cadet colleges (see Tables 16.2 and 16.3) while government schools (vernacular medium) receive much less funding per student per year (see Tables 16.3 and 16.4). In the last 15 years or so the military has expanded its business activities—including banks, business firms, real estate, insurance, transportation, entertainment[49]—and has also entered the business of education. Besides controlling schools it has also set up five universities, all using English as the medium of instruction.[50] In addition to the armed forces, a number of other institutions—bureaucratic as well as corporate sector ones[51]—have established English medium schools for their employees. Even the federal government has established "model" schools and colleges which use English as the medium of instruction. Tuition and fees at these institutions, like their counterparts in the private sector, are high and either the state or the students, or both, must pay for them. In short, the state gives subsidies to the rich from public funds (see Table 16.3).

Language policy and education, as we have seen, are subordinated to the class interests of the urban, professional, English-using elite in Pakistan. For its political interests, this elite has been using the name of Islam, and has strengthened the religious lobby in the last many years. Given the state's encouragement of privatization in the recent past, this seems to be a trend which can have negative consequences for peace in South Asia and the world. Privatization, with its concomitant strengthening of English as an elitist preserve, will lead to "ghettoization" in Pakistan's public educational institutions and increase anger

Table 16.2 Expenditure on cadet colleges in Pakistan

Institution	Donation from provincial govt	No. of students	Yearly cost per student to govt
Cadet College, Kohat	5,819.800	575	10,121
Cadet College, Larkana	6,000,000	480	12,500
Cadet College, Pitaro	14,344,000	700	20,491
Laurence College	12,000,000	711	16,878
Cadet College, Hasanabdal	8,096,000	480	16,867

Source: information about donations and number of students was supplied by the offices of the respective institutions in 2003 to the present author

239

Table 16.3 Differences in costs in major types of educational institution in Pakistan (Pakistani rupees)

Institution	Average cost per student per year	Contributors	Cost to the state
Madrasahs	5,714 (includes board and lodging)	Philanthropists + religious organizations	*Rs 1.55 in 2001–02, an additional sum of Rs 28.60 for subsidies on computers, books, etc. in some madrasahs in 2003–04
Urdu medium schools (gigh)	2,264.5 (only tuition)	State	2,264.5
Elitist English medium schools	96,000 for "A" level and 36,000 for other levels (only tuition)	Parents	None reported except subsidized land in some cantonments
Cadet colleges/public schools	90,061 (tuition and all facilities)	Parents + state (average of six cadet colleges + one public school)	14,171 (average of five cadet colleges only)
Public colleges (provincial)	9,572	State + parents (parents pay Rs 1,591 per year on average)	7,981
Public colleges (federal)	21,281	Parents pay Rs 2,525 for BA on average	18,756

Note: * cost per student per year in a madrasah is calculated for all 1,065,277 students reported in 2000. In 2001–02, a sum of Rs 1,64,000 was given by the government to those madrasahs that accepted financial help. However, not all students receive this subsidy as their madrasah may refuse government help.

Source: Data obtained from several institutions by the present author in 2003

Table 16.4 Income and expenditure of educational institutions in Pakistan

PUBLIC EDUCATION

Institution	No.	Enrolment	Expenditure	Expenditure per students per year
Middle school	14,334	2,788,727	NA	NA
High school	9,471	4,544,724	NA	NA
British system school	11	5,492	NA	NA
Madrasah	354	44,780	NA	NA

PRIVATE EDUCATION

Institution	No.	Enrolment	Expenditure	Expenditure per students per year
Middle school	24,115	3,864,143	5,724,520,758	1,481.5
High school	13,484	3,778,322	14,050,542,801	3,718.7
Schools (mid and high)	37,599	7,642,465	19,775,063,559	2,587.5
British	270	143,774	1,363,779,186	9,487.6
Madrasah	11,799	1,504,462	2,723,533,797	18,10.3

Note: expenditure per student per year of public institutions (high schools 9,471, British system 11, madrasahs 354) cannot be calculated as the data are not available.

Source: GOP 2006, Tables 1, 1.1, 1.2, 3 and 49

among the non–English educated and especially the unemployed workforce of the country. This will have several consequences. First, the most educated people will lose faith in the country and give up on it. Second, the ideological polarization between the different socioeconomic classes will increase even further. And, above all, the incentive for reforming Pakistan's educational system and making it more conducive for creating a tolerant and peaceful society will decrease.

Another trend will be to strengthen the power of the military in Pakistan. As more and more elitist schools and universities pass into the hands of the military, the number of teachers, administrators, and business concerns under the patronage of the military will increase. More students will also be influenced by them. This will work in favor of the military's views about national interest, the future of the country, and economic priorities. This may dilute ideas of civilian supremacy that underpin democracies and jeopardize the chances of lasting peace in South Asia.

An even more dangerous possibility is the strengthening of political and militant Islam in the country. It is true, as pointed out by Hussain Haqqani, that the military has strengthened the Islamists in Pakistan.[52] However, it is also true

that the rank and file of the Islamists owe their existence to a failed educational system which excludes them or exposes them to pro-war, anti–India, and anti-Semitic ideas. Already resentful of the injustices of their society, they now hear of American aggression in Iraq and Afghanistan or Zionist expansion in the Middle East, which tends to radicalize them further. This includes *madrasah* students but, as pointed out by a survey of those who had gone to fight against the US in Afghanistan after 9/11, most of these militants are not from the *madrasahs*. They are from the ordinary Urdu medium schools.[53] As law and order breaks down in Pakistan and the military keeps appropriating the highest share of the country's resources, vigilante groups seeking to impose their own interpretation of Islam increase their power. The rank and file of these groups, although using the idiom of Islam, manifests the same alienation from the state as do the ethnic militants.

The present author has suggested that private, elitist, English medium schools be phased out and state-influenced ones (cadet colleges and public schools) be replaced by merit-based vernacular medium schools. Moreover, English ought not to be taught to a high standard only for the benefit of a small elite, but must be spread out as widely as possible, and, especially through innovative methods, to all schoolchildren. This will appear just to most people and reduce the perception of injustice and, hence, anger, which may create student militancy, possibly expressed through the idiom of an Islamic revolution in Pakistan. On the negative side, the author has admitted that this policy may empower the vernacular proto-elite, which may in turn strengthen traditional values and radicalize the Islamist students even further by eroding their traditional religious culture and bringing them into contact with neofundamentalist thought through the internet. While these possibilities must be recognized, the alternative hope is that the creation of a more just educational system will reduce the potential for violence within Pakistan and its possible spillover to other parts of the world.[54]

Effects of language policy on weaker languages of Pakistan

With the advent of modernity, the smaller languages of the world, being denied any role in the domains of power, began to die away. Globalization, having increased modes and speed of communication, has hastened the process. English, the major vehicle of globalization, can be seen as a world language, or, alternatively, as a "killer language"—an expression used by Tove Skutnabb-Kangas, who champions the notion of linguistic rights.[55] Indeed, so great is the concern to save the world's 6,000-plus languages that many linguists are increasingly writing about it.[56] In Pakistan, however, concerns about language death are rarely expressed.

The policy of promoting English and Urdu, in that order, at the expense of the other languages of Pakistan, has weakened Pakistani languages, even though most of them are, numerically, major languages. However, since they are not being used in the domains of power they do not have cultural capital. As mentioned earlier, languages are given a hierarchical value in the minds of Pakistanis,

with English at the top of the pyramid followed by Urdu and then the indigenous mother tongues (other than Urdu). In the NWFP and Sindh, however, Pashto and Sindhi are seen as identity markers and are spoken informally. In Punjab, contrariwise, there is widespread culture shame about Punjabi.[57] In all the elitist English medium schools the author visited, there were policies forbidding students from speaking Punjabi. If anyone spoke it, s/he was called "*paendu*" (rustic, village yokel) and made fun of. Many educated parents speak Urdu rather than Punjabi with their children. In short, UNESCO's advice on teaching in the mother tongue, at least at the elementary level, falls on deaf ears in Pakistan.[58]

Such prevailing attitudes have a negative effect on Pakistani languages. Urdu is secure because of the huge pool of people very proficient in it and especially because it is used in lower level jobs, the media, education, the court system, commerce, and other such domains in Pakistan. Punjabi is a large language and will survive despite culture shame and neglect. It is used in the Indian Punjab in many domains of power and, what is even more significant, it is the language of songs, jokes, intimacy, and informality in both Pakistan and India. This makes it the language of private pleasure and if it continues to be used in this manner, it is in no real danger.

Sindhi and Pashto are both major languages, whose speakers have a sense of pride. Sindhi is also used in the domains of power and is the major language of education in rural Sindh. Pashto is not a major language of education, neither is it used in the domains of power in Pakistan. However, its speakers see it as their identity marker and it is used in some domains of power in Afghanistan. It, too, will survive though it is under some pressure. The Pashto variety which is spoken in cities in Pakistan is now adulterated with Urdu words. Moreover, educated Pakhtuns often code switch between Pashto and Urdu or English. Thus, the language is under some pressure.

Baloch and Brahvi are small languages under much pressure from Urdu. However, there is awareness among educated Balochi that their languages must be preserved. Although they are not used in the domains of power, they will survive as informal languages in the private domain. Nevertheless, the city varieties of these languages will become very "Urdufied." About 55 very small languages of Pakistan, mostly in the northern part, are under tremendous pressure.[59] The Karakorum Highway linking these areas to the plains has placed much pressure on these languages. In the city of Karachi, Gujarati is being abandoned, at least in its written form, as young people seek to be literate in Urdu and English, the languages used in the domains of power. A number of smaller languages have disappeared altogether and others are under threat.

Conclusion

The language policies of Pakistan's ruling elite have referred to the ideologies of nationalism and modernization for legitimacy. Nationalism has been used to declare Urdu the national language of the country and authorize its use in the domains of non-elitist schooling, radio, TV and some functions of the government at the lower level. Modernization is used for promoting English as a language of elitist schooling, science education and elitist domains, both public and private. These policies have led to the use of the indigenous languages of the country as markers of ethnic identity. Such usage is mostly instrumental, i.e., to mobilize a pressure group in order to obtain a certain share in the goods and services available in the country. However, the participants in language-based ethnic movements find motivation for their personal actions in notions which have an emotional or extra-rational appeal, i.e., notions of self-respect, justice, love, hatred, vengeance and group honor, etc.

The application of discriminatory language-based policies to education have also strengthened the class-based differences in the country expressed through—among other indicators—the medium of instruction one can afford to buy. Yet another effect is the weakening of the indigenous languages of Pakistan, which are looked down on and are becoming weaker as the forces of globalization invest English with far more cultural capital than ever before.

In short, the present language policies have the cumulative effect of increasing inequality and polarization in the country. While inequality was rationalized in the name of ordained fate (*kismet*) in traditional thought in Pakistan, it is now increasingly being seen as a consequence of bad governance. This creates resentment, which feeds into both ethnic and religious militancy in the country. Indeed, it appears that class conflict too is expressed in terms given currency by political Islam.[60] Thus, there is a great danger that, unless language policies are changed, their consequences will become serious threats to the well-being of Pakistan and its neighbors.

Notes

The following abbreviations have been used in the annexures and the notes and references that follow:

GOP 2006 = *National Education Census: Pakistan* (Islamabad: Government of Pakistan, 2006)

GOP Highlights = *National Education Census Highlights* (Islamabad: Government of Pakistan, 2006)

LAD-F = *Legislative Assembly Debates; North West Frontier Province* (dates and pages numbers are given parenthetically)

1 Tariq Rahman, *Language and Politics in Pakistan* (Karachi: Oxford University Press, 1996); reprint edn (Delhi: Orient Longman, 2007).
2 Tariq Rahman, *Denizens of Alien Worlds: A Study of Education, Inequality and Polarization in Pakistan* (Karachi: Oxford University Press, 2004).
3 Paul R. Brass, *Language, Religion and Politics in North India* (Cambridge: University Press, 1974).
4 Jyotirindra Das Gupta, *Language Conflict and National Development: Group Politics and National*

Language (Berkeley, CA, and London: University of California Press, 1970).

5 R. K. Agnihotri, "Identity and Multilinguality: The Case of India," in Amy B. Tsui and James Tollefson (eds), *Language Policy, Culture, and Identity in Asian Contexts* (Mahwah, NJ: Lawrence Erlbaum, 2007), pp. 185, 204; L. M. Khubchandani (ed.), *Language in a Plural Society* (Delhi: Motilal Banarsidass and Indian Institute of Advanced Studies, Shimla, 1988); E. Annamalai, *Managing Multilingualism in India: Political and Linguistic Manifestations* (New Delhi: Sage, 2001); Lachman Khubchandani, "Language and Education in the Indian Subcontinent," in S. May and N. H. Hornberger (eds), *Encyclopedia of Language and Education*, 2nd edn, vol. 1 (New York: Springer Verlag, 2008).

6 Hamza Alavi, "Politics of Ethnicity in Pakistan," *Pakistan Progressive*, Vol. 9, No. 1 (Summer 1987), cited in Hamza Alavi and John Harriss (eds), *Sociology of Developing Societies* (London: Macmillan, 1989), pp. 222–46. "Pakistan and Islam: Ethnicity and Ideology," in Fred Halliday and Hamza Alavi (eds), *State and Ideology in the Middle East and Pakistan* (London: Macmillan and New York: Monthly Review Press, 1987).

7 S. Akbar Zaidi (ed.), *Regional Imbalances and the National Question in Pakistan* (Lahore: Vanguard, 1992).

8 Tahir Amin, *Ethno-National Movements of Pakistan: Domestic and International Factors* (Islamabad: Institute of Policy Studies, 1988).

9 Alavi, "Politics of Ethnicity," p. 265.

10 Naveed Hamid and Akmal Hussain, "Regional Inequalities and Capitalist Development: Pakistan's Experience"; Hafiz A. Pasha and Tariq Hasan, "Development Ranking of Districts of Pakistan"; S. Akbar Zaidi, "The Economic Bases of the National Question in Pakistan: An Indication," in Zaidi, pp. 1–42, 43–89, 90–138.

11 Amin, p. 256.

12 Feroz Ahmed, *Ethnicity and Politics in Pakistan* (Karachi: Oxford University Press, 1998).

13 Ahmed, *Ethnicity and Politics*, p. 158.

14 Hussain Ahmad Khan, *Re-Thinking Punjab: The Construction of Siraiki Identity* (Lahore: National College of the Arts, 2004).

15 Ishtiaq Ahmed, *State, Nation and Ethnicity in Contemporary South Asia* (London and New York: Pinter, 1996); Adeel Khan, *Politics of Identity: Ethnic Nationalism and the State in Pakistan* (New Delhi: Sage, 2005).

16 Ahmed, p. 289.

17 Adeel Khan, p. 189.

18 The number of languages listed for Pakistan is 72 in Raymond G. Gordon Jr. (ed.), *Ethnologue Languages of the World*, 15th edn (Dallas: SIL International; online version 2005: http://www.ethnologue.com). The present author, however, lists 55 languages and dialects in addition to the six major languages (Punjabi, Sindhi, Pashto, Siraiki, Urdu and Balochi) given in the preceding text. This lower number is calculated as follows. The dialects of Pashto (3), Balochi (3), Hindko (3), Greater Punjabi (Pahari, Potohari) are subsumed under the language head itself. English, sign language, Badeshi (which is dead) are excluded. Marwari, mentioned twice, is counted only once. Kundal Shahi, not mentioned in the *Ethnologue*, is, however, included. See the author's list of languages in Tariq Rahman, "Multilingualism and Language Vitality in Pakistan," in Anju Saxena and Lars Borin (eds), *Trends in Linguistics: Lesser-Known Languages of South Asia: Status and Policies, Case Studies and Applications of Information Technology* (Berlin and New York: Mouton, 2006), pp. 73–104.

19 According to the *Census of Pakistan 1951* and *Census Report of Pakistan 1961* (Karachi: Government of Pakistan, 1951 and 1961), the number of Pakistanis who commonly spoke English was less than 2 percent of the population (Tables 7 and 8a and statements 5.1 and 5.5 respectively). The present author calculated the number of fluent and spontaneous speakers of English (the westernized elite) from the figures of those who appeared in British school examinations in 2003. For details see Tariq Rahman, "The Role of English in Pakistan," in Amy and Tollefson, p. 235.

20 *The Constitution of the Islamic Republic of Pakistan* (Islamabad: Government of Pakistan, 1963).

21 Nizamuddin Nizamani, "Socio-Political Unrest and Vulnerable Human Security in Balochistan," in *At the Cross Roads: South Asian Research, Policy and Development in a Globalized World* (Islamabad: Sustainable Development Policy Institute, 2007), pp. 245–55.

22 *Declaration of the Oppressed Nations Movement*, adopted on 2 November, 1998, Islamabad, cited in Hussain Khan, p. 115.

23 Badruddin Umar, *The Emergence of Bangladesh: Class Struggles in East Pakistan (1947–1958)* (Karachi: Oxford University Press, 2004),

pp. 190–229. Also see Anwar Dil and Afia Dil, *Bengali Language Movement to Bangladesh* (Lahore: Ferozsons: 2000), pp. 131–91.

24 The negative reaction of students to these statements is given in Tariq Rahman, *Language and Politics*, pp. 87–88.

25 *Pakistan Observer* (Dhaka English daily), 29 January, 1952.

26 "Report of the Enquiry into the Firing by the Police at Dacca on 21 February 1952," in B. Umar (Comp.), *Bhasha Ondolan Prasanga: Katipay Dolil* (The Language Movements: Some Documents), vol. 2 (Dhaka: Bangla Academy, 1986), pp. 43, 48.

27 *Dawn*, 8 May, 1954.

28 M. S. Korejo, *G. M. Syed: An Analysis of His Political Perspectives* (Karachi: Oxford University Press, 1998). Also see his *A Testament of Sindh Ethnic and Religious Extremism: A Perspective* (Karachi: Oxford University Press, 2002).

29 Details in *Dawn, Hilal-e-Pakistan, Pakistan Times,* etc.

30 Feroz Ahmed, op. cit., pp. 41–60.

31 Carina Jahani, *Standardization and Orthography in the Balochi Language* (Upsalla, Sweden: Almquist and Wiksell, 1989), p. 233.

32 M. S. Korejo, *The Frontier Gandhi: His Place in History* (Karachi: Oxford University Press, 1993), p. 18.

33 Mohammad Waseem, *Democratization in Pakistan: A Study of the 2002 Elections* (Karachi: Oxford University Press, 2006), p. 196.

34 Husain Khan.

35 Rahman, *Language and Politics*, ch. 11. For the role of history in the marginalization of Punjab and its language and literature, see Tahir Kamran, "Imagined Unity as Binary Opposition to Regional Diversity: A study of Punjab as a 'Silenced Space' in the Pakistani Epistemic Milieu," in *At the Cross Roads*, p. 302.

36 Benedict Anderson, *Imagined Communities: Reflections on the Origin and Spread of Nationalism* (London and New York: Verso, 1983). Also see Anthony D. Smith, "The Nation: Real or Imagined," in E. Mortimer (ed.), *People, Nation and State: The Meaning of Ethnicity and Nationalism* (London: IB Tauris, 1999).

37 B. Hirson, "Language in Control and Resistance in South Africa," *African Affairs*, Vol. 60, No. 319 (1981), pp. 219–37.

38 For Pashto, see LAD-F 12 October, 1932, p. 132; for Baluchi, Brahvi and Pashto in Balochistan see Tariq Rahman, *Language and Politics*, p. 168.

39 Pierre Bourdieu, *Language and Symbolic Power*, trans. Gino Raymond and Matthew Adamson (Cambridge: Polity Press, 1992), p. 55.

40 Bourdieu, p. 57

41 Tariq Rahman, "Urdu as an Islamic Language," *Annual of Urdu Studies*, 21 (2006), pp. 101–19.

42 Tariq Rahman, *Language, Ideology and Power: Language-Learning Among the Muslims of Pakistan and North India* (Karachi: Oxford University Press, 2002), pp. 7–8, 16–18.

43 Sabiha Mansoor, *Punjabi, Urdu, English in Pakistan: A Sociolinguistic Study* (Lahore: Vanguard, 1993); *Language Planning in Higher Education: A Case Study of Pakistan* (Karachi: Oxford University Press, 2005).

44 Tariq Rahman, "The Role of English in Pakistan with special Reference to Tolerance and Militancy," in Amy and Tollefson, pp. 219–39.

45 Mansoor, *Punjabi, Urdu, English*, pp. 51–56.

46 Carol Myers-Scotton, "Elite closure as a Powerful Language Strategy: The African Case," *International Journal of the Sociology of Knowledge*, 103 (1993), pp. 149–63.

47 Ayub Khan, *Friends Not Masters* (Karachi: Oxford University Press, 1967), p. 25.

48 *Report of the Commission on Student Problems and Welfare: Summary of Important Observations and Recommendations* (Islamabad: Government of Pakistan, Ministry of Education, Central Bureau of Education, 1966), pp. 17–18.

49 Ayesha Siddiqa, *Military Inc: Inside Pakistan's Military Economy* (London: Pluto Press, 2007).

50 Rahman, *Denizens*, pp. 53–56 (schools), 123–25 (universities).

51 GOP 2006, Table 6, p. 61.

52 Hussain Haqqani, *Pakistan: Between Mosque and Military* (Lahore: Vanguard Books, 2005).

53 Sohail Abbas, *Probing the Jihadi Mind* (Islamabad: National Book Foundation, 2007), pp. 90–95.

54 For details see Rahman, "The Role of English in Pakistan," in Amy and Tollefson, pp. 231–33.

55 Tove Skuntabb Kangas, *Linguistic Genocide in Education or Worldwide Diversity and Human Rights?* (Mahwah, NJ, and London: Erlbaum, 2000), p. 46. The major work on the imperialistic role of English is by Roberet Phillipson, *Linguistic Imperialism* (Oxford: University Press, 1992).

56 David Crystal, *Language Death* (Cambridge: University Press, 2000); David Nettle and Suzanne Romaine, *Vanishing Voices: The Extinction of the World's Languages* (New York: Oxford University Press, 2000).

57 Mansoor, *Punjabi, Urdu, English*, pp. 51–56.

58 UNESCO, *Position Paper: Teaching in the Mother Tongue* (Paris: UNESCO, 2003).

59 A list of these languages; including written material in them and the domains in which they are used is in Tariq Rahman, "Language Policy and Language Vitality in Pakistan," in Anju Saxena and Lars Borin, pp. 73–104.

60 Olivier Roy, *Globalized Islam: The Search for a New Ummah* (New York: Columbia University Press and Centre d' Études et de Recherche Internationales, Paris, 2004).

Part V

Crises of national unity

17

Crises of national unity in India

Punjab, Kashmir, and the northeast

Gurharpal Singh

Introduction

The recent sixtieth anniversary of India's independence (August 2007) was marked by the absence of the usual angst about national unity[1] that has all too often been expressed in familiar anxieties about territorial integration, separatist violence, and fissiparous tendencies.[2] Instead, the occasion was notable for the celebration of India as an emerging economic power that is redefining conventional assumptions about its polity and helping to shape a new architecture of peace and development in South Asia. In this changed environment, which by happenstance has coincided with better relations with Pakistan (post-9/11) and China, some of the old intractable issues—Jammu and Kashmir, the Indo-China border and northeastern states, and the periodic regional tensions in Punjab—have begun to unravel while other concerns such as energy, development, and reservations' policy now dominate the national agenda. Indeed, as India's economic development proceeds apace, it can reasonably be conjectured that the issue of national unity, which has traditionally been associated with the management of the peripheral regions in the northwest and the northeast, might begin to diminish in political salience.

While most serious students of Indian national unity are likely to be weary of such an optimistic reading, noting the importance of events like Kargil (1999) or the potential of resurgent Hindu nationalism to decouple such long-term trends, any meaningful understanding of contemporary—and likely future—developments in this area needs to address *how* the Indian state has dealt with crises of national unity in the 1980s and 1990s. The rest of this chapter will review the literature on this subject. It then examines these approaches in more detail with reference to Punjab, Jammu and Kashmir and the northeastern states, each of which has followed different trajectories. Finally, the chapter assesses whether we have entered a new phase in the understanding of India's national unity.

Understanding the crises of national unity

In the 1980s and 1990s, the peripheral states within the Indian Union became the battlegrounds for ethnonationalist and regionalist struggles. In a period of almost 20 years (1980–2000), nearly 100,000 people were killed in terrorist and counterinsurgency violence as these regions tied down the majority of India's armed forces.[3] Such conflicts created a state of high anxiety concerning violence "against the nation," giving rise, among other things, to a virulent form of Hindu nationalism led by the BJP, which grew from a marginal force in the early 1980s to a national governing party by the late 1990s. This meteoric rise was not unrelated to the inability of BJP's opponents—whether the Congress or non-Congress parties—to manage the troubled borderland states, and climaxed in two dramatic showdowns with Pakistan as well: the Kargil war and the nuclear standoff between the two countries in 2002. External threats to national unity and internal politics of religious identity became inextricably intertwined, resulting in official promotion of cultural nationalism, violence against religious minorities (for example, pogroms against Muslims in Gujarat and elsewhere), and efforts to restructure the politics of the peripheral regions. The election of a congress-led United Progressive in Alliance coalition administration in 2004 marked something of a turning point but also coincided with external events (particularly the regional implications of 9/11) that have had profound consequences for India's relations with its neighbors.

Given these developments, in what ways has scholarship addressed the crises of national unity since the 1980s? How do the approaches utilized provide meaningful insights into the way these crises have been managed as well as indicators of future developments? In the section that follows, we review some of the approaches identified.

Crises of national unity as result of "external threat"

Perhaps the most common approach to the subject is to argue that the difficulties of managing the peripheral states arise principally from "external threats"; that is, historically the malevolent policies of India's neighbors, principally Pakistan and China, but also on occasions, Nepal and Bangladesh, with whom India has territorial disputes.[4] Violent secessionist

and militant nativist movements that have flourished in these states off and on since Independence are regularly associated with "asymmetrical warfare" and targeted "terrorism" directed against India from foreign countries and designed to wrest these territories from Indian control. During the Cold War, moreover, the polar alignments of South Asian states turned the peripheral states into battlegrounds for "proxy wars." For Pakistan, the humiliation of the loss of Bangladesh, it is frequently argued, has resulted in renewed efforts since 1971 in support of insurgents in India, whether they were operating in Kashmir, Punjab, or the northeast. For China, the territorial dispute that led to the 1962 war, and remains largely unresolved, led to support for secessionist groups in the northeast. In more recent years, the Nepalese and Bangladeshi authorities have also been accused of harboring dissidents who have been instrumental in acts of violence and terrorism in the borderlands.[5] In addition, the transnational diasporas from these peripheral borderlands—the Kashmiris, Sikhs, Nagas, and communities settled in the developed countries, for example—are seen to be especially active in promoting the external threat by mobilizing resources, "soft power," and diplomacy against Indian sovereignty .[6]

Crises of national unity as result of regional factors

Although most commentators recognize the importance of external factors in the instability that has reigned in the peripheral regions, some emphasize the primacy of regional factors as the principal causes of the failures of these states to develop along the lines of "mainstream"[7] states. In Punjab, for instance, the militancy of the 1980s and 1990s was seen as the direct outgrowth of the consequences of the Green Revolution, which accelerated the process of agricultural modernization but also produced a Sikh political leadership frustrated with the limited economic developmental opportunities for the state. That this agitation eventually took the form of religious discrimination and ultimately turned violent was due to the particular dynamics of social and political formation in the state.[8] Similarly, in Jammu and Kashmir, the uniquely contested political heritage of the state notwithstanding, the mismanagement of the Abdullah-Farrouq dynasty in the 1980s is seen as the root cause of the Kashmiri *intifada* which began after the rigged elections of 1987. As in Punjab, the religious and social dynamics of Kashmir political life transformed regional dissent into a generalized revolt that was subsequently *exploited* by external influences.[9] And, also as in Punjab, external intervention by Pakistani-sponsored groups occurred *after* a prolonged period of conflict among the major political forces within the state over competing visions of governance. A similar pattern prevails also in the northeast, a region that is desperately underdeveloped and beset by perennial conflicts between locals and new migrants, between settled populations and tribals, and between those who have cornered the scarce resources of development and the rest. Most commentators agree that these conflicts have not, by and large, been contained by "developmental federalism,"[10] that is, the gradual establishment of various subnational units and institutions for this region, which is home to myriad social groups, but rather have been exacerbated with the onset of modernization as ethnic group competition has intensified. Heavy-handed interventions by New Delhi have, more often than not, added fuel to the fire. In short, the regionally based accounts highlight the need to focus on regional processes in the peripheral states which, because of the unique social, religious and political formations, often reinforce cumulative cleavages and, as a consequence, quickly assume an exaggerated national importance.[11]

Crises of national unity as result of national factors

The main political science explanation put forward for the crises of national unity in the peripheral regions is that it is an acute manifestation of the centralizing tendencies unleashed by the post-Nehruvian leadership, in particular Indira Gandhi. Whereas the objective tendencies within Indian politics since the mid-1960s were towards regionalism, pluralism, and decentralization,[12] the response of the national leadership to these pressures was to centralize power in New Delhi, a process that coincided with the destruction and "deinstitutionalization"[13] of the Congress party from the early 1970s onwards and climaxed with the emergency (1975–77). It is alleged that Mrs Gandhi both undermined the historic congress organization and turned the conventional relationship between congress and religious minorities on its head by courting a Hindu majoritarian vote bank during her last administration. In most mainstream states, the growth of powerful regional parties had mediated these centralizing pressures, but in the peripheral states the unstable competition between the regional, and often religious and ethnic parties and Congress frustrated such a development with the consequence that Congress's pursuit of regional and national dominance drove the main political formations in these areas, which were essentially moderate, first into agitational politics, and, subsequently, the arms of militants. Although the dynamics of these developments were substantially different in Punjab, Kashmir, and the northeast, what distinguished the center's policy were repeated impositions of President's Rule, efforts to undermine regional parties, and virulent rhetoric against these parties on the grounds that they were anti-national. The key to reversing this process, it was argued, lay essentially in restructuring center–state relations to better reflect India as a diverse, regional, multicultural, and de facto multinational society.[14]

Inevitability of crises of national unity due to "wrongsizing" of India's borders and because India is an "ethnic democracy"

Although the centralization thesis is clearly valid in some cases, it fails to explain the persistence and resilience of ethnonationalist movements in the peripheral regions. Reflecting more critically on these movements as well as the failure of the center to manage them, one school of thought has suggested its roots might lie in the wrongsizing of India at independence, referring to the inheritance of undemarcated colonial borders and borderlands over which the Indian National Congress exercised limited influence before 1947.[15] However, the partition seared the "lineaments of India's territorial boundaries deep into the national consciousness . . . [through] the popular sacralization of territory,"[16] and in so doing created enduring dilemmas concerning how these regions were to be governed. Post-1947 experience suggests that governance in these regions has veered between authoritarianism and "violent control," that is, where Indian nation and state building has been accompanied by regional "nation destroying." The distinction between peripheral and mainstream states, moreover, corresponds to a religious divide in that the former have non-Hindu majorities: (Kashmir [Muslim], Punjab [Sikh], Nagaland, Mizoram, Meghalaya [Christian], Arunachal Pradesh [Buddhist], Manipur [Christian and Nativist], Tripura [a majority tribal population classified in the census as "Hindu"] and Assam [similarly with a "Hindu" majority that includes a substantial tribal/native population]). The religious composition of these regions has led some to suggest that India is in fact a de facto ethnic democracy accommodating majoritarian Hindu sentiment while violent control is exercised over religious minorities in the peripheral states. The inbuilt, structured predominance of Hindu majoritarianism within Indian democracy—whether articulated through congress or BJP—creates a perpetual momentum to administer the peripheral states through the "official regime"[17] and violent control. In fact, because Indian and Hindu nationalism substantially define themselves largely in terms of territory, crises of national unity arising out of the management of peripheral states are inevitable.[18]

Crises of national unity after 9/11

Post-9/11, the war in Afghanistan and Pakistan's emergence as a frontline state in the "war on terror" have marked something of a turnabout in the relations among South Asian states. Coming as these events do on the back of the latest wave of globalization and national polices directed towards economic liberalization, they have been seen as an opportunity for rethinking the fraught relations among South Asian states that have all too often been characterized by territorial disputes and nation-building failures. Central to this change has been the normalization of relations between India and Pakistan, which has led to the de-escalation of hostilities, a peace process involving the disputed issue of Jammu & Kashmir, and a reemphasis in both states on economic development. To what extent these changes mark a fundamental shift in priorities remains to be seen, and one might question whether it will be possible in the long term to place territorial disputes such as Jammu & Kashmir on the backburner while development imperatives further strengthen the processes of normalization and mutual economic dependency. Despite these reservations, the positive example of improved Indo-China relations suggests that there are possibly new avenues for redefining the Indo–Pakistan relationship in ways that would provide a more enduring settlement of the crises of governance in the peripheral regions while also disarming the powerful religious nationalisms in both countries that have undergirded state and nation formations since partition.[19]

Punjab, Kashmir, and the northeast

The general approaches outlined earlier are useful as overarching explanations but need to be contextualized with reference to regional specificities and histories since 1947. It will be argued that their main value lies in providing useful insights into *how* crises of national unity have been constructed, especially by institutions and parties at the center of Indian politics, while the role of regional institutions and actors—the more important dimension—has been largely overlooked, if not deliberately misrepresented. In this section we reassess the events in Punjab, Kashmir, and the northeastern states in light of the literature reviewed at the beginning of the chapter and what has happened after post-crisis phases in each case.

Punjab

Apart from the wars with Pakistan (1948, 1962, 1965, 1971, 1999), it is often argued that the Punjab crisis (1984–93) was the most serious challenge to India's national unity since Independence. The campaign for regional autonomy led by the main Sikh political party, the Akali Dal, from 1982 onwards, climaxed in Operation Blue Star (June 1984) in which the Indian Army stormed the Golden Temple, the Sikhs' holiest shrine. The fallout from this event led to the assassination of Mrs Indira Gandhi, pogroms against Sikhs in several places in Delhi and elsewhere, and almost a decade of sustained militant and counterinsurgency violence in which, by conservative estimates, some 25,000 people were killed. The number of involuntary disappearances and illegal detainees was never ascertained, although the latter were estimated to vary between 20,000 and 45,000.[20] At the height of the insurgency in the early 1990s, almost a quarter of a million military and paramilitary personnel were engaged in counterinsurgency operations against groups campaigning for a separate Sikh state of Khalistan. These groups were not without significant popular support: in the 1989 Lok Sabha elections, their representatives or supporters won 10 of the 13 parliamentary seats from Punjab and captured the majority of popular support; and in June 1991, had the newly elected national congress government not postponed the impending assembly elections in Punjab, the militants would certainly have won and made a declaration for a new independent state of Khalistan. In the event,

Congress aborted these polls, launched an aggressive counterinsurgency operation against the militants, and held elections in extremely difficult circumstances that were boycotted by the Sikh militants and moderates, resulting in a Congress landslide that was used as pretext to intensify the "war on Sikh separatism." By the end of 1993, most leading Sikh militants and their organizations had been eliminated, the moderates had been muzzled, and Punjab was being hailed as a model for combating separatism.[21]

The conventional explanation of the Punjab crisis is to argue that it was mainly the outcome of centralization pressures unleashed by Mrs Gandhi. Brass, in his systematic review of the subject, argues convincingly that Mrs Gandhi deliberately engineered the Punjab problem in order to cover the weaknesses of her party, which had become increasingly personalized, as well as to cultivate a new constituency of Hindu majoritarianism. In so doing, Mrs Gandhi subverted the unwritten rules of ethnic conflict management that had been carefully crafted by her father.[22]

There are, however, a number of limitations with this approach. First, it does not satisfactorily explain why centralization drives should have *disproportionately* adverse consequences for India's religious minorities, especially a minority like the Sikhs, who were so effectively integrated into state structures (notably the army and bureaucracy). Second, the differences in the centralization drives of Nehruvian and post-Nehruvian leadership were one of degree rather than kind: a more critical reading of the Nehruvian era in Punjab (and Kashmir and the northeast) reveals, even by a set of objective criteria, the high degree of "bossism," constitutional subversion, and authoritarian rule. Third, few scholars, Brass included, recognize that underpinning the Sikh demand for autonomy was a parallel claim to sovereignty which would have been difficult to accommodate within the existing structure of Indian federalism. Indeed, the Sikh Magna Carta, the Anandpur Sahib Resolution, around which Sikh demands for autonomy were articulated, called for confederalism rather than neofederalism. And fourth, the Punjab crisis was managed without a restructuring of center–state relations. To be sure, a number of developments since the early 1990s—economic liberalization, the legal obstacles to the imposition of direct rule from New Delhi by means of the imposition of President's Rule, and the regionalization of Indian political formations—have undercut the pressures towards centralization, if not reversed them, but these secular changes are still unable to accommodate Sikh demands, which remain largely unrealized.[23]

Given the obvious shortcomings of the centralization thesis, how can we better understand the causes and consequences of the Punjab crisis?

In a historically based account, I have argued that events that led up to 1984 and unfolded afterwards have to be situated in a broader context that recognizes how claims of Sikh ethnonationalism have been accommodated within the Indian Union since 1947.[24] Such accommodation has tried to undercut Sikh claims to sovereignty by exercising hegemonic control, which makes an "overtly violent ethnic contest for state power either 'unthinkable' or 'unworkable' on [the] part of the subordinated communities," and has co-existed with the formal structures of democracy.[25] When hegemonic control has broken down, as after 1984, violent control has been imposed, although not as often as in other peripheral states.

In Punjab after 1947, hegemonic control was exercised by Congress, which successfully divided Sikh elites by co-option, accommodation, and symbolic agreements while thwarting, until 1966, the linguistic reorganization of the state. However, the reorganization was subsequently hemmed in by so much conditionality that it led to the autonomy agitation that climaxed in Operation Blue Star. This agitation marked the culmination of Sikh ethnonationalist resistance, a "freedom movement," which reopened the Sikh national question by drawing on the cumulative failures to achieve Sikh national aspirations in post-Independence India. This failure was also indicative of a type of statecraft used by the Indian state to manage ethnic conflict in Punjab. Repetitive symbolic accommodation was used in place of real tangible concessions, with special emphasis on the co-option of Sikh political leadership. Between 1982 and 1984, as the negotiations with the Center proved futile, Bhindranwale, a charismatic leader, was able to revive a vision of Sikh nationhood by drawing on a rich pool of Sikh religious and historic symbolism that cut the ground from under moderate Akali politicians. Of course, this occurred at a time when there was a rapid commercialization of Punjab's agriculture, external support to Sikh militants from Pakistan, and growing involvement in Punjab affairs by the Sikh diaspora, but these were auxiliary factors which, on their own, could not have marshaled the resources of Sikh ethnonationalism.

Similarly, the role of the central congress government needs to be reassessed against traditional explanations. By the 1980s the creation of a Punjabi-speaking state had provided a bridgehead for resistance against hegemonic control, which had become increasingly thin. The Nehruvian approach of disarming Sikh ethnonationalism through accommodation, co-option, and symbolic agreements that were never implemented, had more or less exhausted the limits of statecraft by the mid-1960s. Mrs Gandhi's innovations included more direct interventions in Punjab politics, coupled with a search for an alternative hegemonizing ideology in the form of Hindu revivalism. If the Akali agitation of 1982–84 ultimately led to disaster, it was mainly because Mrs Gandhi was hemmed in by the compulsions of national politics and could not entertain making concessions to Akalis that would have meant dismantling hegemonic control and surrendering to the discourse, and potential realities, of autonomy and secession.

Although, after 1984, attempts were made to re-establish hegemonic control with the Rajiv-Longowal Accord (1985), the failure of the center to deliver on the terms of the accord undermined the newly elected moderate Akali government while emboldening militants to declare an open campaign for a Sikh state. Thereafter the center quickly reverted to violent control in which counterinsurgency operations practiced in the northeastern states were heavily utilized, with minimal regard for political legitimacy in the region, resulting in well-publicized human rights abuses. From the mid-1980s to the early 1990s, the annual death toll from militant and counterinsurgency violence regularly hovered around 4,000 to 5,000 as the state became an area of darkness, with the virtual collapse of the civilian administration and the rule of paramilitaries and the police. In a crescendo of violence in 1992 involving 250,000 military and paramilitary personnel, the militants were eliminated and the khaki assembly elections held that restored a Congress administration to the state.

The return to normalcy in Punjab through the use of violent control by successive union governments between 1986 and 1993 had one primary objective: to restructure Sikh politics within the framework of hegemonic control that had characterized the pattern of Punjab politics since 1947. Sikh ethnonationalism, which had underpinned the politics of the militants, was intellectually discredited and physically smashed, with the result that, given the limited resources available for Sikh nation-building, a return to hegemonic control was the only realistic strategy open to Sikh political leadership, although this would occur only after some time given Congress investment in violent control.[26] Indeed, this is precisely what happened with the return of the Akali Dal to power in the state in the assembly elections of 1997. The Akali Dal not only eschewed a renewal of a campaign of demands for autonomy that have so far remained unrealized, but also formed a strategic alliance with the BJP to secure a national patron against the center's continued intervention in the state. Since 1997, the Akali Dal and congress have alternated in power in the state while the leadership of both parties has sought to deflect Sikh

ethnonationalist aspirations into the discourse of development in light of the post-Green Revolution collapse of agriculture and the new opportunities opened up by economic liberalization. Nevertheless, these efforts to erase the Punjab problem underestimate its potential to evoke a multiplicity of unsettling memories for the Sikh community, which could yet undermine the foundations of hegemonic control, especially if large sections of Punjab's peasantry remain unable to secure gains from the growth of the non-agricultural sector of the economy.[27]

Jammu & Kashmir

As in Punjab, developments in Kashmir in the 1980s and 1990s posed a serious challenge to national unity. Yet most of the literature that has addressed this subject focused on either the changes in national government policy in New Delhi or regional factors as the main drivers of this threat.[28] Although this approach recognized the rupture caused by the rigged elections to the regional assembly in 1987, it fails to address adequately the periodic oscillations between violent control and hegemonic control, or the new dimension created by the intensity of violent control and its intersection with developments in Afghanistan since the withdrawal of the Soviet forces and the engagement of Pakistani-based *jihad* groups in the Kashmiri insurgency. The latter undoubtedly further internationalized the insurgency, leading to Kargil (1999) and, indirectly, the nuclear confrontation between India and Pakistan in 2002, but in retrospect it also provided a new point of departure in Indo–Pak relations after 2002 that hold the potential to unlock the dispute that has blighted relations between the two countries since Independence.

The decision of the Hindu ruler of a Muslim majority kingdom to accede to India in October 1947 resulted in hostilities between India and Pakistan, United Nations intervention, and a de facto division of the province in January 1949 along the ceasefire line. Jammu

& Kashmir's accession to India was secured by concessions to Kashmiri nationalism, most notably Article 370 of the Indian constitution that provided a substantial measure of autonomy. However, at the time of United Nations intervention in the dispute, this article was projected as a transitional measure towards the exercise of self-determination by Kashmiris. Nehru personally gave an open pledge to ensure that the "fate of Kashmir is to be ultimately decided by the people," and accepted the Security Council resolution of April 1948 that the dispute should be "decided through democratic method of free and impartial plebiscite." Nevertheless, this commitment soon waned as Congress first promoted National Conference of Kashmir nationalists, led by Sheikh Abdullah, and then, in a volte face as a result of Hindu nationalist pressure in 1952–53, Nehru began the piecemeal integration of Jammu and Kashmir into the Indian Union. Abdullah, the "Lion of Kashmir," was interned for almost two decades while a compliant state legislative assembly, established by extensive vote rigging, opted for merger with the Indian Union in 1956. Thereafter, India's response to renewal of the Security Council resolution (in March 1957) for a "free and impartial plebiscite conducted under the auspices of the United Nations" was to cloak its integrationist intent under the pretext of the Cold War threat emanating from the US policy of encirclement that included a military alliance with Pakistan.

Three wars (Indo-China [1962], and Indo-Pakistan [1965 and 1971]) and the emergence of India as an atomic power (1974) convinced Abdullah of the unattainability of the demand for Kashmiri sovereignty. Towards the end of his life, he signed an accord with Mrs Gandhi (1975) that recognized Kashmir as a "constituent unit of the union of India" in return for the formal survival of Article 370, although its actual provisions were extensively diluted in the application of central powers to the state. The accord enabled Abdullah to nurture a political dynasty, and on his death (1982), his son Farooq took over. Farooq's tenure was marred by the need to straddle regional nationalism and the limits of autonomy imposed by New Delhi; his efforts to establish an all-India oppositional front for more autonomy resulted, first, in his dismissal, and, then, his return to power in alliance with Congress in the rigged assembly elections of 1987. It was the rigging of these elections and the unwillingness to recognize the growing support of the Muslim United Front, that triggered the uprising in the Kashmir valley from 1987 onwards. Thereafter, the separatist groups (Jammu and Kashmir Liberation Front and Hizbul Mujahideen) transformed decades of ethnic oppression, into a generalized uprising against the Indian state. Between 1990 and 1995 25,000 people were killed in Kashmir, almost two-thirds by Indian armed forces; Kashmiris put the figure at 50,000.[29] In addition, 150,000 Kashmiri Hindus fled the valley to settle in the Hindu majority region of Jammu. In 1991, Amnesty International estimated that 15,000 people were being detained in the state without trial.[30]

The Indian government's response to the Kashmir crisis has been to use violent control, justified according to four principles: that the insurgency is externally supported and directed by Pakistan; that it is rooted in Islamic fundamentalism which poses a serious threat to Indian state secularism; that the separatist movements have no legitimate claim to independence; and that the insurgency is a threat to India's overall security, territorial integrity, and nationhood.[31] In furtherance of these objectives, the Indian Army and para-militaries, aided by lumpen counterinsurgents, were unleashed against Kashmiri separatists to contain the violence and re-establish control. This strategy was partially successful and paved the way for fresh elections in September 1996, which produced a dismal turnout of less than 30 percent, and led to the reelection of Farooq.[32] But this "restoration" was soon undermined by the conflict between India and Pakistan over Kargil (1999) and the mobilization by both countries in 2002 following the terrorist attack on the Indian Parliament that brought the two countries to the brink of a nuclear war.[33] In the fallout and the emerging peace process brokered by the US,[34] new assembly elections in 2002 marked a firm rejection of the dynastic National Conference of Farooq and brought to power a Congress-PDP (People's Democratic Party, a progressive regional party) coalition that has begun a dialogue both with New Delhi and the local militant groups. The outcomes of these processes will be determined by the broader peace process with Pakistan, but India's determination not to alter the boundary or "abandon the people on the other side of Jammu and Kashmir" (Azad Kashmir) in favor of a "people-centric approach"[35] is unlikely to provide a new legitimacy for governance in the province or undermine the claims for Kashmiri self-determination, or, accession to Pakistan.

Indeed, India's response to the Kashmir dispute in the post-2002 dialogue with Pakistan has been to pursue a piecemeal approach rather than a grand settlement, one that aims to make borders irrelevant rather than redraw them. This approach, if allowed to develop to its logical conclusion by India and Pakistan, holds the potential of re-establishing political autonomy in Kashmir. However, given the bitter rivalry between the two countries for control of the state's territory, it is likely to be a punctuated process, whose outcome will be determined by the enduring difficulties of settled governance in Pakistan, on the one hand, and India's vast experience in managing a "people-centered" approach to maintain its continued sovereignty over the province, whether through hegemonic or violent control, on the other hand.

Northeastern states

In the northeastern states, Indian nation and state building have been bitterly contested since Partition. After 50 years of independence, the region is still tormented by separatist insurrection, guerrilla warfare, and terrorism, with some of the movements having been campaigning for independence since before 1947. The original inhabitants of the region, nearly half of whom are from aboriginal tribes, are uncertain of their place, whether within India or outside it. In a visit to the area in 1996, the former Prime Minister, H. D. Deve Gowda, acknowledged that people in the northeast feel New Delhi treats them like a stepmother and pledged to provide basic services to bring the region "to the standards in the rest of the country."

In August 1947 Nehru's response to self-determination movements in this region was blunt: "We can give you complete autonomy but never independence. No state, big or small, in India will be allowed to remain independent. We will use all our influence and power to suppress such tendencies."[36] Thereafter the strategic importance of this area in state expansion led to state building and "nation destroying" as the inaccessible regions were brought within the parameters of New Delhi's rule. Where economic exploitation of the region's vast natural resources resulted in indigenous opposition to migration from the mainland, a variety of administrative and constitutional provisions were adopted to placate tribal sentiment, including the creation of tribal zones and councils, autonomous districts, union territories and, eventually, new states. According to one commentator, state building in the face of separatist pressures has followed a three-step strategy: "to fight the insurgency with military force for some time; then, when the rebels seem to be tiring, offer negotiations; and finally, when the rebels are convinced that no matter what the casualties are on either side, they are not going to be able to secede, win them over with the offer of constitutional sops, invariably resulting in power being given to them in the resulting elections."[37] Although the same commentator emphasizes the *capacity* of the Indian state to control these movements, he is silent on numerous cases where constitutional rehabilitation ("sops") has been followed by renewed struggles, violence, and endemic terrorism. Since the 1950s, the histories of Assam, Mizoram, Nagaland, Tripura and Manipur have been filled with "accords" with separatist groups signed by New Delhi that remain unimplemented. In Assam, as in Punjab, much of the resentment that fuelled the separatist movement was the failure of New Delhi to deliver on the regional accord agreed in August 1985. This failure revived the fortunes of the United Liberation Front for Assam, resulting in the repeated deployment of the army to crush the movement.

Unlike Kashmir or Punjab, coercion tempered by minimal consent has been the main strategy by which New Delhi has maintained its hold on the northeastern states. In this sparsely populated region, what is surprising is not the willingness of the insurgents to accept hegemonic control in face of overwhelming odds against any other alternative, but their determination to sustain such opposition to the Indian state for so long. Current developments suggest that these states have been far from pacified or politically integrated into the Indian Union. The emergence of a first generation of educated youth among these communities combined with a growing realization of India's "internal colonialism"—Assam produces 70 percent of India's oil and the bulk of its tea— has strengthened the arguments and the support base for separatism.

As in Kashmir, geopolitical changes are likely to have a significant impact on the future of separatist and insurgency movements in this volatile region. India's increasing rapprochement with China—the territorial dispute over the Indo-China border notwithstanding—has removed one of the leading patrons of the separatist groups. Similarly, India's close relations with Burma, and efforts by both countries to develop this region economically, offer new horizons as well as potential risks in what has traditionally been India's Afghanistan, that is, a lawless borderland that has traditionally been hostile to modernization and an intrusive central state. And while the Indo–Bangladesh relationship remains fraught with persistent tension over immigration, border lines, and use of river waters, India's demand for Bangladeshi natural gas and other Bangladeshi goods are likely to exercise power-ful influences in mitigating these tensions as well as strengthening New Delhi's hold over the traditionally "ungovernable" northeast.

Conclusion: Re-assessing crises of national unity

In light of the evaluation of the three case studies, what conclusions can we draw about the contemporary understanding of crises of national unity? How are these understandings likely to shape the future course of policy in managing these crises and their potential implications for India's relations with its neighbors?

An optimistic reading would suggest that the sixtieth anniversary of India's Independence in 2007 marked a decisive turning point in the nation's history, a new age of equipoise in which a critical threshold has been crossed in which peripheral regions will become increasingly less important in setting the parameters of national policy. The significance previously attached to these regions is likely to be displaced by new concerns such as economic development and redistribution policies, particularly with the growing mobilization of *dalit*s and lower castes. India's territorial integrity, always fragile in these regions, is no longer an issue for dispute or contestation. India's emerging economic might, like that of China before it, will ensure that such contestations, as in the case of Tibet, simply wither away. It is perhaps because of this new emerging reality that India's more belligerent neighbors (notably Pakistan) have redefined their strategic relationship from hostility to diplomacy. This turn marks a decisive shift in understanding the new economic realities in South Asia, with regional economic cooperation becoming the principal driver of change, and new patterns of economic integration are also likely to be accompanied by alternative forms of regionalization and de-centralization. In the long term, these changes could also redefine for a globalized age the rigid post-1947 constructions of national unity in South Asia.

A less optimistic reading from the case studies, by the same token, would acknowledge the profound changes that have taken place both within the geopolitics of South Asia and within India politics, but would also offer more cautious insights about the potential of the Indian state to manage the peripheral regions and their capacity to invoke crises of national unity in the future. As the case studies have demonstrated, there appears to have been little innovation in the way the peripheral regions have been managed since the 1980s compared with their handling in the 1950s and 1960s. There are, of course, significant regional and historical differences, but as a general rule their administration has oscillated between hegemonic and violent control. Even the attempts to respond to post-9/11 developments are permeated with efforts to create new hegemonies, for example, by using the language of people-centered approaches, or by regularly restructuring the politics of these regions through the ballot box.

Perhaps the main reason why the peripheral regions are unlikely to decline in their ability to create issues of national unity is that Indian nationalism defines itself primarily in territorial terms that are heavily encoded with images of loss and "vivisection" at partition. Mainly because Nehru and other Congress elites were exceptionally successful in using Partition to embed beliefs about the new state's borders, the mere questioning of these beliefs subsequently became synonymous with subversion. Indeed, the self-determination movements in the peripheral regions have provided a mirror to the distorted image of Indian nation–and state–building that historically failed to command legitimacy in the Muslim majority areas, and since 1947 has struggled to accommodate effectively states with majority non-Hindu populations. Such an accommodation is possible, especially if the trends outlined in this chapter take hold. For it to be successful, however, it would have to overcome two major obstacles: Congress's historical soft *Hindutva* and the BJP's more strident vision that sometimes speaks of wrongsizing India through "akhand Bharat" (suggesting a united India that incorporates Pakistan and Bangladesh).

Notes

1   The focus of this chapter is on the crises of national unity that have posed a threat to India's territorial integrity as a result of ethnic, secessionist and/or regionalist movements in the peripheral states in the 1980s and 1990s.

2   The year 1997 provides an interesting contrast with 2007. For coverage of some of the literature and wider implications, see Gurharpal Singh, *Ethnic Conflict in India: A Case-Study of Punjab* (Basingstoke: Macmillan, 2000), ch.xii.

3   In Jammu and Kashmir and Punjab, according to widely cited figures, at least 60,000 and 25,000 were killed, respectively.

4   See Maya Chadda, *Ethnicity, Security and Separatism in India* (New York: Columbia University Press, 1997).

5   See, for example, J. N. Dixit, *India and Pakistan in War and Peace* (London: Routledge, 2002).

6   See Government of India, *White Paper on the Punjab Agitation* (New Delhi, 1984). For soft power, see Joseph Nye, *Soft Power: The Means to Success in World Politics* (New York: Public Affairs, 2004). For Nye, the term soft power is used in international relations theory to describe the ability of states to indirectly influence the behavior or interests of other political bodies through cultural or ideological means. The South Asian diasporas of these regions in the west have been quite influential in utilizing cultural and ideological means to advance their case.

7   Soon after Partition, policymakers in New Delhi, including Nehru, established a clear distinction, especially following the demands for linguistic reorganization of Indian states, between the border, or peripheral states, where special considerations applied, and the "mainstream" or "heartland states," where such considerations were unimportant. The distinction became especially popular in general discourse during Mrs Indira Gandhi's last administration (1980–84).

8   See Gurharpal Singh, "Understanding the 'Punjab Problem,'" *Asian Survey*, Vol. 27, No. 2 (December 1987), pp. 1,268–77.

9   Balraj Puri, *Kashmir: Towards Insurgency* (New Delhi: Orient Longman, 1995).

10 The term is Dasgupta's; see Jyotirindra Dasgupta, "Democracy, Development and Federalism: Some Implications of Constructive Constitutionalism in India," in Subrata K. Mitra and Ditmar Rothermund (eds), *Legitimacy and Conflict in South Asia* (New Delhi: Manohar, 1997), pp. 82–103.

11 What distinguishes the peripheral regions is their non-Hindu majorities. The religious cleavage in which violence is sometimes directed against Hindus has played a central role in the construction of threats to national unity.

12 See, in particular, Paul R. Brass, *Ethnicity and Nationalism: Theory and Comparison* (New Delhi: Sage, 1991), chs iv–vi.

13 The term "deinstitutionalization" has been used with reference to the Congress Party under the leadership of Mrs Indira Gandhi, in particular in two senses: first, with reference to the destruction of the historic Congress Party organization and, second, with reference to the enfeeblement of state institutions. For further details, see Atul Kholi, *Democracy and Discontent: India's Growing Crisis of Governability* (Cambridge: University Press, 1991).

14 Brass, pp. 212–13.

15 For an explanation of the concepts of "rightsizing" and "wrongsizing" and its application to India, see Brendan O'Leary *et al.* (eds), *Rightsizing the State: The Politics of Moving Borders* (Oxford: University Press, 2001), Introduction and ch. v.

16 Dipankar Gupta, *The Context of Ethnicity: Sikh Identity in a Comparative Perspective* (New Delhi: Oxford University Press, 1996), p. 17.

17 The "official regime" is here defined as the organizations of the Indian state in these regions and their employees (including civil servants) and political formations that lend them permanent support.

18 This argument is most clearly developed by Singh, *Ethnic Conflict in India*, chs iii and xii.

19 For useful insight into the "composite dialogue" between the two countries, see Dennis Kux, *India-Pakistan Negotiations: Is Past Still Prologue?* (Washington, DC: United States Institute for Peace, 2006).

20 Shinder S. Thandi, "Counterinsurgency and Political Violence in Punjab, 1980–1994," in Gurharpal Singh and Ian Talbot (eds), *Punjabi Identity: Continuity and Change* (New Delhi: Manohar, 1996), pp. 159–85.

21 Shekhar Gupta, *India Redefines its Role* (Oxford: University Press and IISS, 1995).

22 See Brass, *Ethnicity and Nationalism*, ch. v.

23 Gurharpal Singh, "The Punjab Crisis since 1984: A Reassessment," *Ethnic and Racial Studies*, Vol. 18, No. 3 (1995), pp. 476–93.

24 Singh, *Ethnic Conflict in India*.

25 See Brendan O'Leary and Arthur Paul, "Introduction: Northern Ireland as the Site of State- and Nation-Building Failures," in John McGarry and Brendan O'Leary (eds), *The Future of Northern Ireland* (Oxford: Clarendon Press, 1990), p. 9.

26 This point was made by Singh, "The Punjab Crisis."

27 For a detailed discussion of the challenges facing the Punjab economy, see World Bank, *Resuming Punjab's Prosperity: The Opportunities and Challenges Ahead* (Washington: World Bank, 2004).

28 See Puri, *Kashmir*; Sumit Ganguly, *The Crisis in Kashmir: Portents of War, Hopes of Peace* (Cambridge: University Press, 1997); Vernon Hewitt, *Towards the Future? Jammu and Kashmir in the 21st Century* (Cambridge: Portland Books, 2001); Sumantra Bose, *Kashmir: Roots of Conflict, Path to Peace* (Cambridge, MA, and London: Harvard University Press, 2003).

29 K. Balagopal, "Kashmir: Self-determination, Communal and Democratic Rights," *Economic and Political Weekly*, Vol. 32, No. 43 (2 November, 1997), pp. 2,916–21.

30 See Amnesty International, *India: Torture, Rape, and Death in Custody* (London, 1992).

31 Jyotindra Nath Dixit, "Kashmir: The Contemporary Geo-Political Implications for India and Regional Stability," unpublished paper presented at the School of Oriental and African Studies, London, 8 April, 1994, pp. 6–7.

32 *India Today*, 31 October, 1996.

33 Gurharpal Singh, "On the Nuclear Precipice: India, Pakistan and the Kashmir crisis," *OpenDemocracy*, 7 August, 2002, http://www.opendemocracy.net/conflict-india_pakistan/article_194.jsp, accessed 23 November, 2006.

34 Gurharpal Singh, "The Indo-Pakistan Summit: Hope for Kashmir?" *OpenDemocracy*, 16 February, 2004, http://www.opendemocracy.net/conflict-

india_pakistan/article_1738.jsp, accessed 15 November, 2006.

35 Comments of Shyam Saran, Prime Minister's special envoy on Kashmir, *The Tribune*, Chandigarh, 23 November, 2006 (online).

36 Neville Maxwell, *India, the Nagas and the North-East* (London: Minority Rights Group, 1980), p. 4.

37 Shekhar Gupta, *India Redefines its Role*, p. 25.

18

Communal and caste politics and conflicts in India

Steven I. Wilkinson

Introduction

There is often a tendency to treat caste and communal conflicts and politics as separate. In fact, however, the degree to which one of these identities is salient in politics or conflicts at a particular time is often linked to the institutional and economic incentives supporting mobilization around the other, or to another identity such as language or class.[1] André Béteille pointed out long ago for instance that communal politics seemed to take a Hindu–Muslim pattern in the north but have a caste pattern in the south, and he noted that even within the south there was substantial regional variation, with Muslim political mobilization strongest in those areas such as Kerala and parts of Andhra, where the non-Brahman movement had been weakest.[2] In the late 1980s and early 1990s, the interconnectedness between the salience of caste and communal identities became even more apparent in the violent political contest between "mandir" and "mandal": the Bharatiya Janata Party (BJP) and the Sangh Parivar, on the one hand, pushing a policy of Hindutva ("Hinduness"), and parties representing a variety of backward and lower caste interests pushing a policy of caste reservations.

The most important fact to understand about the development of caste and communal politics and conflicts since Independence is that, politically and constitutionally, caste is a privileged category, one that can deliver tangible benefits to communities and voters (e.g., reservations in education, employment, and sometimes in politics) in a way that religious identities cannot. So while attempts have been made, at various times since Independence, to use anti-Muslim, anti-Christian, and (much more rarely) anti-Sikh mobilizations and violence to create a Hindu majority for a particular political party (and that party has not always been the BJP), these attempts have only been successful in the short term, and have typically foundered on the much greater resonance of caste appeals to the state, local, and even the national electorate.[3] From 1989 to 1992, for instance, it seemed as if the Ayodhya campaign around the Babri Masjid and other "disputed" sites, which involved large-scale *yatra*s (processions) and demonstrations across India, involving millions of participants, might be capable of generating a permanent Hindu majority for the BJP. On the back of the campaign to build a Ram Mandir on the site of the Babri mosque, the BJP's representation shot up from two seats in the Lok Sabha to 88 in the December 1989 elections, and then to 120 seats in 1991. But, after the destruction of the Babri Masjid on 6 December, 1992, the national Hindutva agitation temporarily ran out of steam, as the immediate goals seemed to have been achieved, the violent destruction of the mosque and subsequent communal riots turned off many supporters, and the Congress government of P. V. Narasimha Rao imposed emergency rule on four BJP-ruled states. The BJP, contrary to its own expectations, then suffered very severe electoral reversals in 1993 state elections in these states at the hands of parties such as the Bahujan Samaj Party and Samajwadi party in UP, which promised concrete policies to particular lower castes rather than the unclear future benefits of a Hindu Raj.

Turning now to communal conflicts, the fundamental fact about communal polarization and violence in post-Independence India is that whether it happens is the outcome of political decisions. Riots are often, although not always, fomented for political purposes, and they are prevented or stopped by the state police and administration when it is in the interests of those who control the state government to do so.[4] To understand the political incentives facing the state politicians who control the 28 state governments which in turn control the police is therefore *the* most important factor in understanding why communal violence takes place.

Riots pay political dividends: they unify Hindus behind the party that seems best able to defend "Hindu" interests, they help break up the coalitions of other parties, and they temporarily make the Hindu–Muslim cleavage appear more significant than other political issues, such as caste, urban vs. rural cleavages, or development. Christophe Jaffrelot has rightly pointed out that embracing Hindutva and the organizational energies of militant organizations such as the RSS, VHP, and Bajrang Dal seems to be especially attractive to BJP leaders when the party has suffered reverses, and therefore looks unlikely to win on other issues.[5] In 2001, most notably, the BJP government in Gujarat, which had performed badly

since its election in 1998 in terms of development and rehabilitation after the January 2001 earthquake, turned decisively to a "hard" Hindutva policy to save itself after a succession of defeats in local elections pointed to likely defeat in upcoming Vidhan Sabha elections. These defeats convinced the party leadership that only a sharp turn to the right would help, and the incumbent chief minister was replaced by hardliner Narendra Modi. In March and April 2002 the Modi government reportedly fomented large scale riots and pogroms against the state's Muslim minority in order to solidify a majority behind the party in upcoming Vidhan Sabha elections. Perhaps a thousand people, mainly Muslims, died in these disturbances and tens of thousands more were forced to flee their jobs and homes.[6] The riots paid clear electoral dividends, and, in December 2002, the BJP won a crushing victory in state elections over Congress, doing especially well in riot-affected districts. Polls taken during the elections suggested that the riots were a major issue in helping swing voters decide in favor of the BJP, as well as in increasing turnout among the BJP's core supporters.[7] But, overall the anti-minority mobilization of Hindutva and communal polarization, like most other religious ideologies, makes much more sense as an oppositional ideology, a temporary way of unifying people against a clear target, than it does as a way of governing. This is because in itself it (like secularism) offers no clear roadmap to decide what Harold Lasswell long ago identified as the key questions of politics: who gets what, when and how?[8] In the absence of rules bolstering religious identities and favoring one religion over another—rules that would be unconstitutional in the secular framework created in India in 1950—religion is inherently limited as a political ideology, compared with linguistic or caste identities that do benefit from this government and institutional support.

Institutional foundations of caste politics in India

The Indian Constitution of 1950 provides certain benefits for scheduled castes and tribes, and also in a 1951 amendment specifies that benefits *may* also be provided for other backward *classes* (OBCs)—meaning, in effect, castes—a category that might potentially incorporate most of the population, since backwardness is in the eye of the political beholder. In sharp contrast, however—and understandably given that the Constitution was drafted after Congress' long struggle with the Muslim League during the campaign for India's independence, as well as the communal violence of Partition that followed—the constitution is unambiguous in its opposition to religious preferences, such as job reservations, educational reservations, or the separate constituencies that existed before 1950 for Muslim, Sikh, and Christian minorities in various provinces. The future of these religious reservations was extensively debated by the Constituent Assembly from 1947–49, and the assembly decided to abolish them, the substantial support they still enjoyed at the time from many in the Muslim and Sikh communities notwithstanding.[9]

Nehru would have liked to abolish caste reservations as well, and move away entirely from a society in which caste or religious labels were important. His ultimate goal, as he wrote to Charan Singh in 1954, was to end the caste system, which he saw as "the biggest weakening factor in our society."[10] That Nehru could not achieve this goal, however, was largely because caste was already entrenched in politics in two different ways. First, in the previous four decades there had been a very substantial "non-Brahman" movement in the south, especially in the province of Madras and in the princely states of Mysore and Travancore-Cochin, against upper caste dominance in government employment, education, and politics. This upper caste dominance had been overwhelming in the early twentieth century, with Brahmans, for instance, accounting for around 50–80 percent of

government employees in many branches of the subordinate civil service in Madras despite accounting for only 3.5 percent of the population, a percentage that reflected their much higher levels of wealth and education.[11] Further, 68 percent of the graduates of Madras University in 1918 were Brahmans.[12]

After the Second World War non-Brahman movements used their access to sympathetic policymakers in Madras and the princely administrations of Mysore and Travancore and Cochin as well as their control of the new elected provincial government in Madras (1920) to institute widespread government reservations for backward classes.[13] These reservations created large numbers of politicians, employees and voters who invested in backward caste identities—the number of castes formally recognized as backward in Madras shot up as a result from 45 to 245 by the mid-1920s—and formed a well-entrenched interest group that was able to resist legal and political challenges to the system of employment reservations after Independence.[14] In 1950 and 1951, for example, there were large and violent protests in Madras, led by E.V. Ramaswamy Naicker's Dravida Kazhagam Party, after court rulings that placed caste reservations in the state in jeopardy. These protests led the Madras government to pass a motion defending the reservations system in 1951, and soon after the Indian National Congress backed down over the issue, passing Amendment 15(4) to the constitution, which permitted reservations for "backward classes."[15]

The second way in which caste was entrenched was through a historic compromise that Congress itself had to make with Dr Ambedkar in the mid-1930s over the question of political reservations for what came to be called the Scheduled Castes. (The "Schedule" refers to a list appended to the 1935 Government of India act, specifying castes that were treated as untouchable by caste Hindus.) Congress was generally opposed to such reservations, and Gandhi in particular opposed them, seeing them as an insidious part of a more general British divide-and-rule policy. But Congress was forced to compromise over the issue in the 1932 Poona Pact. The compromise involved accepting British proposals for reserved SC seats but *not* their proposals for separate caste electorates for these seats as the price of enlisting lower caste support in the campaign for independence. The tangible electoral impact of such support at the time may not have been great, given that lower castes constituted a small share of the electorate because of the property-based franchise (around 14 percent could vote after the 1935 act), but the symbolic value was high and securing Ambedkar's support also gave the British one argument less to use when they claimed that general devolution of power had to wait until Indians were united in their demands and that granting independence would not unduly disadvantage any particular important minority.

So, even before the Constituent Assembly was elected and independence attained—and at a time when Congress leaders spoke out forcefully against the system of separate electorates for *religious* minorities—caste reservations were well entrenched in the south, and reservations for "depressed classes" (SCs) had been accepted in principle by Congress leaders in the Poona Pact. The practical political effect of so many people already being nominally included within the reservation system, at least once southern politicians successfully blocked legal efforts to end reservations in 1950–51, was that politicians representing lower and backward castes had no incentive whatsoever to end reservations, and in fact if they wanted to add supporters it was much more effective to simply extend the principle of reservation to more and more castes. This political logic played itself out very quickly in the south after Independence, as politicians recognized more and more castes as "backward" and eligible for reservations throughout the 1950s and 1960s: by the mid-1950s over 40 percent of positions in employment and education in Tamil Nadu were reserved for members of the backward and most backward castes, a proportion that

eventually rose to 69 percent. In the north, as a result of backward caste mobilization, large-scale reservations were gradually extended to the OBCs in the same way in the 1970s and 1980s, a process systematically explored in Jaffrelot''s 2003 book *India's Silent Revolution*.[16] By 1980, according to the Mandal Commission, the number of castes officially recognized as "Backward" in India had risen to 3,743, compared with 2,394 in 1955, at the time of the first backward caste commission headed by Kaka Kalelkar.[17] In some states, the rise was even more dramatic, with the number of OBCs in Tamil Nadu that qualified for reservations reportedly rising from 150 before 1970 to 310 castes in 1994.[18]

Much of this increase has come about as the result of explicit quid pro quos, as politicians have used promises of reservations to peel off supporters from larger groups allied with another party or leader, and caste leaders themselves have indicated that the support of their community can be obtained in return for reserved status. In Rajasthan, for instance, the Meena community was reportedly recognized as a Scheduled Tribe in return for the support of 13 MLAs for the chief minister during a party leadership contest in 1957.[19] In 1994 the Vokkaligas and Lingayats in Karnataka were recognized as OBCs in return for their support of Mr Veerappa Moily in the state elections.[20]

The extension of reservation to more and more jobs and positions and of reserved status to a greater share of the population has, of course, been resisted by upper castes, as well as others (such as those on the Left, at least until recently) who think that entrenching caste identities in jobs and education might not be the way to get beyond caste identities and end caste inequalities. In 1989–90, most notably, there were violent upper caste protests in large cities and on university campuses against the V. P. Singh government's proposed implementation of the Mandal Committee's nearly decade-old recommendations to extend the scope of OBC reservations in central government employment. The commission had controversially estimated the OBCs at 52 percent of the population, and the proposals involved increasing the number of reserved places in government employment and universities by 27 percent, while decreasing the number of "merit" places by a similar amount. One student at Delhi University, Rajiv Goswami, set himself on fire, and several other students across the country followed suit in angry demonstrations. And in 2006, in what became known as the "Mandal II" protests, there were renewed demonstrations by upper castes against plans to extend OBC reservations to one of the few areas not yet affected, namely, higher level graduate education, by Human Resources and Development Minister Arjun Singh. But the fact that opposition in both cases took the form of public demonstrations by groups of students without substantial political direction was, paradoxically, a sign of the anti-reservation movement's fundamental political weakness. The fact is that, in both cases, but especially in 2006, the political arithmetic in favor of reservations is simply so overwhelming that no major politician will come out openly against them. In a national survey done in 2004, 61 percent of the Indian population supported reservations and only 22 percent opposed them, proportions very close to the percentages of *dalits* and Backward Castes in the population, on the one hand, and forward castes on the other.[21] Given this overwhelming political support, violent demonstrations in urban areas where upper castes are a larger share of the population are one of the only ways, together with court cases, in which opponents can try to slow their growth.

The political currency of reservations has, however, become devalued through overuse, with the number of groups being made eligible for reservations increasing much more rapidly than the supply of government positions or other benefits. So, in response, powerful caste groups have asked for and politicians have promised more valuable forms of reservation: such as inclusion within "Most Backward Caste" classifications that offer more benefits than are available to general backward castes, or specific "quotas within quotas" that guarantee

groups that they will receive a specific share of benefits, rather than simply being included within a larger category in which better educated and wealthier *jatis* might secure most of the benefits.[22]

These efforts have, not unexpectedly, led to fierce conflicts and even some quite substantial caste violence because some castes that benefit from the current classifications seek to prevent any changes that would disadvantage their groups. As one backward caste minister who opposed such changes in UP put it in 2001: "Come what may, we will not allow anybody to take away from our share. If separate reservation is required for the most backward castes, let there be an increase in the [percentage of] reservation."[23]

Politicians and caste leaders can use various methods to block changes to the reservation system that they do not like. Politically influential backward castes in Kerala, for instance, blocked a caste census proposed in 1995 that would have increased pressure for reform of the existing reservation system by demonstrating that their own "backward" groups were in fact doing better than some "forward" groups.[24] Three years later, in September 1998, the census was finally dropped.[25] The Yadavs and other relatively well-off OBCs in Uttar Pradesh successfully blocked Rajnath Singh's proposals to create a southern-style MBC category in UP, a measure Singh hoped would split the political coalitions created by the BJP's rivals, the SP and BSP. Further, in Andhra Pradesh, Madigas and Malas have frequently come to blows since 1994 as the latter have tried—through direct action as well as their support for particular parties—to block efforts by the worse-off Madigas to reform the scheduled caste reservation system in a way that will disadvantage the Malas. In 1998 the Madiga Reservation Porata Samithi (MRPS) launched a statewide agitation in favor of the subdivision of the SC category that led, over the course of a week, to ten attempts at self-immolation (one ending in death), 1,100 arrests, several large-scale strikes, and the burning or partial burning of 86 buses.[26] This violence was largely repeated by the MRPS in 2004. Similar conflicts have also arisen, so far less violent, over subdividing reservations for OBCs and SCs, for example between the Meenas and Gujjars in Rajasthan, between Jatavs and Pasis in Uttar Pradesh, and between the Mahars and Mangs in Maharashtra. We can expect these distributional conflicts within ethnic categories to rise in number and intensity in the future, unless the private sector should quickly create large numbers of good jobs for middle and lower castes outside the reservation systems, which seems unlikely given the very poor level of state primary, secondary, and higher education to which many of them have access.

Writing in October 1991, in the aftermath of the violent street conflicts over the Mandal Commission, the eminent sociologist André Béteille rightly predicted that the economic liberalization then beginning in India would, sooner or later, be bound to collide with the system of caste reservations. The economic reforms would reduce the relative share of jobs controlled by the center and the various state governments, and the principles and mechanisms of the market would conflict with those of government planning and reservation.[27] Since 1991, despite a growing population and growing demand for jobs, the number of positions in central and many state governments has remained stable, and the massive retrenchment of many public sector units (PSUs) has also meant that the overall number of reserved places in industrial enterprises under state or central government control has also been stagnant. Overall, central government employment, in fact, dropped by 2.66 percent between 1995 and 2001, to 3,876,000.[28] So, with the number of options for expanding reservations within the state sector diminishing, the political focus of demands for reservations has, since the late 1990s, begun to shift to the private sector, which has long been a bastion of upper caste dominance. This extension of caste reservations to the private sector is not, of course, a new idea. As far back as 1990, the then Union Social Welfare Minister, Ram Vilas Paswan, floated the idea of job reservations in the private sector as a way of filling the gap between the aspirations of the backward classes and SCs and the available supply of government-controlled jobs.[29] But the cries for the extension of reservation have grown more insistent since then as the number of government jobs, their status, salaries and perquisites have failed to keep up with the obviously booming private sector, especially given the very large number of backward class parties and politicians on which coalition governments in India now survive. The privatization of public sector units (PSUs) has been a particularly big flashpoint, prompting BSP leader, Mayawati for instance to make several forceful speeches in parliament in 2001 claiming that the privatization policy and reforms were "nothing but an attempt to deprive us from getting jobs."[30]

The Congress government elected in 2004 appointed a committee (staffed with known supporters of reservations, such as Laloo Prasad Yadav and Ram Vilas Paswan) in August that year to look at the issue of whether and how private sector reservations might be implemented. But in the short term not much seems likely to happen, partly because of very substantial business resistance to reservations (the two main business federations, CBI and FICCI, both came out against formal private sector reservations) and partly because of larger questions about how such reservations would be implemented. In the near term, the most likely outcome would seem to be some voluntary affirmative action programs similar to those in some US companies, with requirements that companies doing substantial business with the government demonstrate that they employ significant numbers of SCs and OBCs. In the longer term, however, the issue looks sure to return, and has the potential to cause massive conflict between the largely upper caste-controlled business world and the increasingly OBC and SC-controlled world of politics.

One aspect of caste politics and conflicts that has not been extensively explored by sociologists is the extent to which claiming "backwardness" in the narrow context of reservations over a substantial period of time, and formally claiming kinship with other castes for instrumental political purposes, might have long-term effects on the way in which caste is practiced in other spheres, such as in social or market interactions. Srinivas, writing in the mid-1990s about the Vanniyar community in Tamil Nadu, implied that the effect of successfully claiming backwardness in a political context had only a minimal impact on other spheres, and that the community was "Janus-faced ... claiming high caste status in a traditional context and a low one in the fierce struggle for access to scarce resources."[31] It seems to be the case that some communities which cooperate in caste politics are still at loggerheads in local disputes over land and local political power. But studies of intracaste conflicts in different spheres have been few and far between, so there is little firm information on whether cooperation in one sphere will ultimately reduce conflicts more generally in areas such as disputes over intercaste marriages, caste practices, or land.

Communal politics

At independence in August 1947, few would have predicted that India's first few decades would be relatively free from communal conflict. Under the British, India had a system of communal reservations in politics and administration, and a system of "class recruitment" in the army whose effect (and its intention) was to accentuate communal divides and preserve their own rule.[32] The partition itself led to the killing of perhaps 200,000 people and the mass migration of 13 million more, in a process that was to continue well into the 1950s.[33] Congress itself was also vulnerable to pressure from the Hindu right, especially in the north and west, with both the powerful Hindu Mahasabha and Congress right wingers such as Purushottam Das Tandon pushing for a more supremacist policy towards members of the Muslim minority.[34]

But, under Nehru, the communal temperature was significantly lowered. The Muslim League was clearly a spent force, with much of the Muslim political elite having left for Pakistan. The Muslim social and economic elite left behind was largely broken by the *zamindari* reform of the 1950s and the loss of economic opportunities and discrimination so poignantly displayed in M. S. Sathyu's 1973 film *Garam Hava*. Anti-cow slaughter legislation passed in most major states in the late 1940s and 1950s, as did legislation enshrining the status of Hindi written in devanagari script as an official language of India, taking both these important symbolic issues off the political agenda after decades of conflict. Further, pressure from the right wing diminished after the 1948 assassination of Mahatma Gandhi, which allowed the temporary ban of many organizations and, more importantly, cast a very negative light over assertive support for a Hindu right agenda within the Congress party. The death of Sardar Patel in 1950 also allowed Nehru to take stronger action against hardliners within congress, most notably in his 1951 power struggle with Congress President Purushottam Das Tandon over the exclusion of a prominent Congress Muslim, Rafi Ahmad Kidwai, from the Congress Working Committee. This standoff, in which Nehru threatened to resign, ultimately led to Tandon's own resignation as Congress president in September 1951.[35]

That is not to suggest that everything was perfect with communal relations under Nehru. Periodic episodes of violence against Hindus in Pakistan led to refugee flows into India, sparking tit-for-tat violence in West Bengal on more than one occasion in the late 1940s and 1950s. In early 1950, for instance, more than 50 people were killed and 256 injured in West Bengal in strikes and riots that broke out in that state in protest at the death of perhaps 600 Hindus in Dacca, violence that was to be repeated again in 1964 in similar circumstances.[36] Although Nehru was personally secular and demanded that Muslims be treated as full citizens, he could do little about day-to-day employment discrimination against

Muslims in the states, despite urging chief ministers to address the issue in 1959 and again in 1961.[37] The Muslim proportion in state police forces and administrations declined rapidly in the decade and a half after Partition, and much of the legislation and ordinances passed to protect Muslim educational interests, such as regulations on the provision of Urdu schools, or requirements that government servants communicate in Urdu with citizens under certain circumstances, were not enforced because of political opposition.[38]

Moreover, throughout the long period of Congress dominance in the post-Independence period, there were periodic attempts by politicians (sometimes Congress ones) to whip up communal issues and instigate violence for political or electoral advantage on one pretext or another: the 1956 riots over a book with an offensive biography of the Prophet Muhammad, which Nehru thought had been engineered to help Hindu parties in the upcoming elections;[39] the anti-cow slaughter agitation in 1966 in New Delhi and elsewhere, designed to help the Jana Sangh and other communal parties in the run-up to the 1967 elections;[40] the 1967 Ranchi-Hatia riots over Urdu, designed to destabilize the coalition government in Bihar; and the horrific 1969 riots in Ahmedabad, apparently instigated by the RSS and Jana Sangh.

In the short term, the decline of Congress from the mid-1960s seemed to many to be directly related to the rise in communal violence in India, which they blamed on the absence of the steady Nehruvian hand at the center, the decline of Congress as a party organization, the growth of caste and communal parties, and the increasing marginalization of congress in state politics in some areas. But ultimately, as I have suggested elsewhere, the decline of Congress and the growth of caste politics in the states was not, as if often viewed, a bad thing for Hindu–Muslim relations. It has, in fact, been helpful for communal relations in the long term in several important ways.[41] It was in Kerala, lest we forget, that Congress first lost power (in 1957),

and in which communalization of politics into definable caste and religious parties has been most advanced, and yet Kerala has had one of the best records, compared to other states, in preventing communal violence.

The growth of OBC parties has been a good thing for Hindu–Muslim relations in two ways. First, parties such as the Dravida Kazhagam in Tamil Nadu and the Communists in Kerala specifically included Muslims within their broad concepts of "Dravidian" or "backward" in order to build coalitions capable of challenging Congress. Second, and more importantly, the growth in each state of a larger number of effective political parties created a much more competitive environment for Muslim votes, in return for which Muslims could demand that states provide them better security. Even if a coalition did not, at the moment, need Muslim votes and Muslim-supported parties, a competitive environment in which there were five or six effective parties in a state made it very likely that it *would* need such support in the future, which gave it an incentive to protect Muslims. Why should Muslims, rather than militant Hindus, benefit from such increased competition along caste lines, and become pivotal swing voters in many states? First, because Muslim demands tended not to conflict with those of caste supporters of backward caste parties because Muslims are constitutionally banned from making effective claims for reservations on the grounds of religion equivalent to those made on the basis of caste by the OBCs and SCs;[42] second, because Muslims placed a very high premium on the state providing physical security, a demand that was relatively cheap for Hindu politicians to supply, as long as they were not seen to be intervening too aggressively on behalf of Muslims.

The rise in political competition in the states as a consequence of the rise in OBC and SC parties—there are now an average of 4.4 effective parties competing in large states and the average level of electoral volatility (the seats changing hand at each election) has gone up from 20 percent in the 1957 election to 40

269

percent in the mid-1990s—has created a powerful incentive for state politicians to cultivate the large Muslim community, 13 percent of India's total population but concentrated in particular states and especially in urban areas.

The changing political incentives in the states are absolutely critical because the Indian Constitution clearly makes local law and order the responsibility of the 28 state governments, *not* local or central governments.[43] If a riot breaks out in a town or district, the army or central paramilitary forces may intervene only at the explicit invitation of the district magistrate or state government, even if there is a barracks just a few miles from the area in which the riot is taking place, as was the case for instance at Ranchi-Hatia in 1967. In theory, the central government can threaten to use its emergency constitutional powers and get rid of a state government that allows communal riots to take place. In practice, however, central governments only used this power five times between 1950 and 1996 over the issue of communal riots, despite the many large riots that took place over this period (e.g., Moradabad 1980, Ahmedabad 1969) and even then *only* in cases where the party in power in a state was not their own party, and where the center therefore had a clear electoral motivation for dismissing the state government. So, while the perceived threat of the imposition of President's Rule can occasionally be useful—as Congress threats seem to have been in persuading the Modi government to quickly call in the army when riots broke out in Vadodara in May 2006, for instance—in practical terms the security of Muslims is largely dependent on state politics and the actions of the state government.[44] This is even more true after the Supreme Court's March 1994 Bommai judgment, which severely limits the freedom of the central government to impose President's Rule in cases where there is not clear proof—subject to judicial review by the court—of the breakdown of the constitution. The effect of Bommai in restraining the center has also been magnified because the growth of central coalition governments in recent years in which many of the parties that were victims of the misuse of President's Rule in the past are important participants, make them loath to sign off on any use of Article 356 outside Kashmir.

The crucial importance of the minority support base of the party in power together with the overall level of party competition in a state, in determining whether communal violence will be controlled or not, was tragically demonstrated during the massive riots that afflicted Gujarat in 2002. In Gujarat itself, the incumbent BJP government had no Muslim support, according to 1998 exit polls done by CSDS, and Gujarat also had very low levels of party competition, in what was basically a straight fight between the BJP and Congress. The Modi government, unconcerned about losing Muslim support and standing to gain all the support that fell away from Congress as a result of the riots, acted in a biased and partisan way throughout, even going so far as to transfer 27 officials for taking too aggressive a stance towards Hindu rioters.[45]

Outside Gujarat, though, the state political environments in 2002 were all favorable to controlling communal violence. Every state government in 2002 either relied heavily on Muslim voters directly, as for instance was the case in Madhya Pradesh and Rajasthan, or else was in a state that was very competitive in terms of overall levels of party competition.[46] Bihar, for instance had 7.7 effective parties, Maharashtra had 5.64, Uttar Pradesh 4.99, and Tamil Nadu 4.84 (compared with 2.97 in Gujarat).[47] These governments, therefore, had an enormous incentive to act strongly to prevent violence when the RSS, VHP and Bajrang Dal organized massive demonstrations, protests and strikes in the aftermath of the Godhra massacre of 57 Hindus in Gujarat on 27 February, 2002. In Gujarat, these demonstrations were a prelude to the pogroms of March and April. Outside Gujarat, however, owing to very decisive police action, including preventive arrests of thousands and, in some cases, deadly firing on rioters, large-scale anti-Muslim pogroms were completely avoided. In

Rajasthan, for instance, a state adjacent to the violence in Gujarat, the state police force used deadly force to prevent riots from breaking out in Gangapur and Silwara.[48] In Andhra Pradesh, the state police force successfully prevented riots from breaking out in the highly sensitive capital of Hyderabad, that city's long history of communal riots notwithstanding, which one might have thought would predispose it to violence.[49]

Conclusion

None of this is meant to imply that communal relations in India are satisfactory. There has been a creeping communalization in many state administrations, with the growing display of Hindu symbols and fraternization of state servants with members of Hindu nationalist organizations such as the RSS and VHP. There have also been periodic attempts to rewrite school textbooks to accentuate the conflictual and anti-Muslim strands of Indian history rather than its more hopeful aspects: more Aurangzeb and temple destruction, in other words, and much less about Akbar and other rulers who employed many non-Muslims in their administrations and endowed temples across the land. And social and physical segregation are still realities in many places across India, with anti-Muslim prejudice and fears preventing many upwardly mobile members of the Muslim minority from obtaining housing outside of recognizable "ghetto" areas in the major cities.

But ultimately India's strong caste, regional and linguistic cleavages, and above all the institutionalized nature of caste identities through the Constitution, reservations, and political parties have sharply undercut the likelihood of massive polarization along religious lines, despite the occasional terrible episodes such as Gujarat. The way in which strong lower and backward caste identities crosscut Hindu identities, and provide massive support for an overall "secular majority" in India is quite nicely demonstrated by recent

survey data on support for majoritarian versus pluralist policies among Indian voters. In a large 2004–05 survey of the *State of Democracy in South Asia*, 5,389 Indians were asked if they agreed with the statement that "minorities should adopt the ways of life of the majority community." Overall the good news is that there is a substantial pro-diversity majority among the Indian population, defined by the pollsters as the ratio of those who strongly disagreed with the statement compared to those who agreed with it.[50] In India this "pro-diversity ratio" was 3.56. The corresponding ratio in Bangladesh, just for comparison, was 2.78 and in Pakistan a very depressing 0.60, indicating considerably more supporters of majoritarianism in that country than those who supported a more pluralist policy. Among Indian Hindus, though, the poll found considerable variation in terms of support for majoritarianism. Support is highest for a pro-majority policy among upper caste Hindus (prodiversity ratio of 1.79) and lowest among OBCs (2.77) and dalits (4.90).[51] Thus, whether because of their own lower and backward caste ideologies, their association of Hindutva with upper castes, or the lack of tangible benefits that Hindutva supplies to them, the middle and lower castes seem to be strongly resisting majoritarian ideologies.

Notes

1 In Madras, for instance, the Hindu–Muslim divide before the late 1930s was crosscut by the divide between Brahmans and non-Brahmans; see Eugene Irschick, *Tamil Nationalism in the 1930s* (Madras: Cre-A, 1986). In Bihar, the Hindu–Muslim divide was crosscut in the same period by the conflict between Biharis and Bengalis over the latter community's disproportionate share of government employment. See, e.g., the questions asked about Bengali overrepresentation in the police in *Bihar: Legislative Assembly Debates Official Report*, Vol. 4, No. 37 (26 April, 1937), pp. 2443–44.

2 André Béteille, *Castes: Old and New* (Bombay: Asia Publishing House, 1969), p. 50.

3 Some have argued that Hinduism does not work as a unifying identity in Indian politics because it is cross cut by other identities such as caste and language. It is certainly correct that religious identity in India is both diverse and is crosscut by multiple other identities, but this seems to me less important than the institutional benefits available to people who mobilize on the basis of caste rather than religion. In fact, *all* potential identities in India are crosscut in some way or the other, so intragroup differentiation is not a sufficiently good argument to explain why religion does not work but caste or language (both of which can offer tangible benefits) do, and, further, religion was, of course, highly salient as a unifying identity in Indian politics before 1947, when it *was* institutionalized by the British through separate elections and employment reservations.

4 This fundamentally political view of riots, in opposition to the more local and sociological view taken in Varshney (2002), is put forward in both Brass, *The Production of Hindu–Muslim Violence in Contemporary India* (Seattle: University of Washington Press, 2003) and in Wilkinson, *Votes and Violence: Electoral Competition and Ethnic Riots in India* (Cambridge: University Press, 2004).

5 Jaffrelot presentation on Hindu nationalism, Michigan State University, April 2003.

6 See the three volumes of the *Concerned Citizens Tribunal—2002* for the most complete account of the violence, available at http://www.sabrang.com/tribunal/.

7 Sanjay Kumar, "Gujarat Assembly Elections 2002: Analyzing the Verdict," *Economic and Political Weekly*, Vol. 38, No. 4 (25 January, 2003), pp. 270–75.

8 Harold Lasswell, *Politics: Who Gets What, When, How* (New York: McGraw-Hill, 1936).

9 Members of religious minorities within Congress generally supported reservations for their communities in employment and politics before Independence, although they opposed the separate electorates insisted on by the Muslim League. Opinion surveys conducted among Muslim legislators in the 1960s suggested that many were still in favor of separate electorates and employment reservations; Theodore P. Wright, "The Effectiveness of Muslim Representation in India," in Donald E. Smith (ed.), *South Asian Politics and Religion* (Princeton, NJ: University Press, 1966), pp. 102–37.

10 Sarvepalli Gopal, *Jawaharlal Nehru: An Anthology* (Delhi: Oxford University Press, 1983), pp. 324–25.

11 S. Saraswathi, *Minorities in Madras State: Group Interests in Modern Politics* (Delhi: Impex India, 1974), p. 48.

12 Saraswathi, p. 49.

13 See Irschick, *Tamil Nationalism in the 1930s*; David Washbrook, *The Emergence of Provincial Politics, The Madras Presidency 1870–1920* (Cambridge: University Press, 1976), pp. 271–87.

14 Irschick, pp. 36–37.

15 P. Radhakrishnan, "Backward Class Movements in Tamil Nadu," in M. N. Srinivas, *Caste: Its Twentieth Century Avatar* (New Delhi: Viking, 1996), pp. 110–34, 120–22.

16 Jaffrelot, *India's Silent Revolution: The Rise of the Lower Castes in North India* (New York: Columbia University Press, 2003).

17 Srinivas, p. xxviii.

18 "Racketeering in Quotas," *India Today*, 15 November, 1994, pp. 36–42.

19 "Racketeering," p. 37.

20 "Racketeering," pp. 36–42.

21 A poll of 17,885 voters conducted 26 July–5 August, 2004. "Mood of the Nation-Poll," *India Today*, international edn (New Delhi), August 30, 2004, pp. 16–23.

22 The category of "most backward class" was created in Madras in 1954 by Congress Chief Minister Kamaraj as a compromise way of addressing demands by backward class Dhobis and barbers that they be listed as scheduled castes, which would have entitled them to more benefits; *Report of the Backward Classes Commission Tamil Nadu Volume I–1970* (Madras: Government of Tamil Nadu, 1974) (Chairman S. Sattanathan), p. 54.

23 "Uttar Pradesh: The Reservation Plank," *Frontline*, 1–14 September, 2001.

24 M. Vijayanunni, "Caste and the Census of India," unpublished paper, 2003, pp. 10–11.

25 Vijayanunni, p. 11

26 S. Ramakrishna, "Reservation Wars," *Indian Express*, 20 June, 1998.

27 André Béteille, *The Backward Classes in Contemporary India* (New Delhi: Oxford University Press, 1992), pp. 108–10.

28 Ministry of Labor, Government of India, *Census of Central Government Employees, 2001* (New Delhi: Ministry of Labour, Directorate General of Employment and Training, 2003).

29 "Reservation in Private Sector Likely: Paswan," *Times of India*, 22 June, 1990.

30 "Mayawati Presses for Quota in Pvt. Sector," *The Hindu*, 4 March, 2001

31 M. N. Srinivas, "Introduction," in Srinivas, pp. vii–viii, ix–xxxviii.

32 See, for instance, the clear support for divide and rule in the quotes from Secretaries of State Wood (1862) and Hamilton (1897) in Sumit Sarkar, *Modern India 1885–1947* (New Delhi: Macmillan, 1983) pp. 16, 21.

33 I follow the casualty estimate in Moon, *Divide and Quit* (London: Chatto & Windus, 1961), p. 269, and the refugee estimate in Keller, *Uprooting and Social Change: The Role of Refugees in Development* (Delhi: Manohar Book Service, 1975), p. 17.

34 For details of this pressure from the right, both inside and outside Congress, see William Gould, *Hindu Nationalism in Late Colonial India* (Cambridge: University Press, 2005); and Mukul Kesavan, "Invoking a Majority: the Congress and the Muslims of the United Provinces, 1945–47," *Islam and the Modern Age*, Vol. 24, No. 2 (1993), pp. 109–30.

35 Jaffrelot, p. 101.

36 *Times of India*, 24 February, 1950; 15 January, 1964.

37 G. Parthasarathi (ed.), *Jawaharlal Nehru: Letters to Chief Ministers 1947–1964, vol. 5, 1958–1964* (New Delhi: Oxford University Press, 1989), pp. 233–46, 427–32, 446–59.

38 See Wilkinson, *Votes and Violence*, ch. 4.

39 Jaffrelot, *The Hindu Nationalist Movement in India* (New York: Columbia University Press, 1996), p. 107, citing N. L. Gupta, p. 249.

40 Jaffrelot, pp. 205–10.

41 Wilkinson, *Votes and Violence*.

42 Politicians in a few states, such as Tamil Nadu, Andhra Pradesh and Kerala, have tried to get around this ban for at least some Muslims by reserving jobs and places in education for certain Muslim *jatis* on the basis of *caste* rather than *religion*.

43 In India, with only a few exceptions, all local law and order is controlled by the state police.

44 "Army Deployed in Vadodara," *The Statesman Weekly*, 98, 18 (6 May, 2006).

45 "Modi ties hands of cops who put their foot down," *Indian Express*, New Delhi, March 26, 2002, p. 1.

46 The argument here follows that in Wilkinson, *Votes and Violence* (2004) and Wilkinson, "Putting Gujarat in Perspective," *Economic and Political Weekly*, 27 April, 2002, pp. 1,579–83.

47 The effective number of parties measure (ENPV), widely used in political science, allows us to get a measure of the overall level of party competition in a state using a measure that underweights the vote share of the many small parties that secure little support in an election. In 2002 the effective number of parties in major states ranged from 2.78 in Andhra Pradesh (where the two largest parties had 85 percent of the vote) to 7.7 in Bihar (where the two largest parties had only 43 percent of the vote). For more details see Wilkinson, *Votes and Violence*, ch. 5.

48 *Rajasthan Patrika*, 27 March, 2002; "Police Firing in Rajasthan: Two Killed," *Indian Express*, 26 March, 2002.

49 "Andhra Police on High Alert," *Indian Express*, 26 March, 2002.

50 Centre for the Study of Developing Societies, *State of Democracy in South Asia: A Report* (Oxford: University Press, 2008), Table 5.5, pp. 261–62.

51 The minority communities, not surprisingly, strongly oppose majoritarianism, with pro-diversity ratios of Sikhs (5.70), Muslims (16.25), and Christians (11.30).

19

Ethnic and Islamic militancy in Pakistan

Mohammad Waseem

Introduction

In 2007, Pakistan entered into an era of suicide bombing, attacks on public rallies, government property, military personnel, police stations, and girls' schools, killing of alleged 'spies,' and abduction of government officials and foreign diplomats. Proto-Taliban elements were able to torch a large number of containers carrying supplies for NATO forces across the border with Afghanistan. They practically took over Swat valley in late 2008 and early 2009, abolished the writ of the state and forced a quarter of a million people to migrate. The army started operations against the Taliban but failed to make any headway. The government in Peshawar felt obliged to negotiate with the Taliban after the breakdown of social order in the valley. There were also incidents of sectarian violence in Quetta in Balochistan and Dera Ghazi Khan in Punjab which cost dozens of lives and created tension between the followers of *Shi'a* and *Sunni* sects.

Politics in Pakistan took a major turn towards violence under Musharraf (1999–2008) and later under Asif Zardari (2008–). The expanding profile of the building blocs of militant action in pursuit of political objectives presented a grim picture of public life in the country in 2008. This involved incidents of suicide bombing, capture of government buildings, and abduction and beheading of security officers in Swat valley in pursuit of a home-grown project of implementation of *Sharia*. In January 2009, the Swat valley was overrun by Tehrik Taliban Pakistan who issued their edicts relating to public morality and religious injunctions. A widely circulated video released by the Taliban in the tribal areas of Pakistan showed bodies of declared criminals dangling from electricity poles.[1] Other incidents included burning of video shops, closing down educational institutions for girls and stopping administration of polio drops to children, suicide bomb attacks in the garrison city of Rawalpindi near President Musharraf's office, in Sargodha on a bus carrying air force cadets, and in Karachi on a million-strong rally for Benazir Bhutto when she arrived in Pakistan after an eight-year long exile. Curiously, while there were demands to unmask the faces behind the suicide bombing on Benazir's rally, she pointed her finger at Zia's remnants within the political establishment. Others pointed to the complete failure of intelligence agencies to uncover terrorists, thus allowing them to spread from tribal to settled areas, and indirectly hinting at their possible connivance in incidents of violence. The political community and civil society generally held the Musharraf government responsible for Benazir Bhutto's assassination in a public meeting in Rawalpindi on 27 December, 2007. For its part, the government held the Taliban leader in Pakistan, Baitullah Mahsud, responsible for killing Benazir, which the latter denied.

At the other end, Balochistan continued to be in the throes of a mini-insurgency in the wake of an undeclared military operation, involving attacks on gas pipelines, railway tracks, and government buildings. The banned Baloch Liberation Army (BLA) spearheaded the militant activities. Its followers among youth also opposed the nationalist parties for participating in the February 2008 elections. They disrupted a public meeting of the nationalist leader, a former chief minister of Balochistan, Akhtar Mengal for not declaring war against the state.[2] In Balochistan, as elsewhere in Pakistan, militancy was an indirect outcome of the nation-building project, which generally dwelled on coercive strategies for unification across ethnic divisions. It was a structural requirement of the state to disallow subnational communities from claiming a share in the political and economic resources beyond the script. The inherently liberal constitutional legacy of British India, which considered mass mandate as the source of legitimacy and federalism as the principle of unity in diversity, operated against the perceived interest of the postcolonial state. Dismissal of elected governments in provinces and successive unification models of the federal government led to various ethnonationalist movements.

In contemporary Pakistan, the quantum of violence in an urban milieu is higher than in the countryside, especially if the movement is supported by a strong party organization, a well-established cult of leadership, and an electoral mandate. In consequence, politics of the bullet and politics of the ballot may not necessarily be contradictory. At the other end, religious militancy is an indirect and long-term consequence of the expanding power of the *ulema*, as they flourished due to the state's quest for, and commitment to, divine sources of legitimacy beyond the constitutional

framework. At the heart of the emergence of the Islamic establishment was the so-called *Khaki-mullah* alliance, which has operated for decades from the late 1970s to the late 2000s. The crucial input of the world of Islam perspective in bringing forth a dichotomous worldview based on Islam versus the West cannot be overstated.[3] In this context, empathy with Muslim suffering in regional conflicts ranging from Palestine to Bosnia, Kosovo, Afghanistan, and Iraq has effectively externalized political identity in Pakistan.

Ethnic revival and Islamic ascendancy draw on different sources of inspiration. However, it is possible to point to the shared political context experienced by them, which is shaped by a state system struggling to operate in an unstable regional setting characterized by wars and revolutions involving India, Afghanistan, Iran, and Iraq. The two movements have sometimes operated in succession. Thus, the Pakhtun nationalist movement, which dominated the politics of the NWFP for decades before and after Partition, gave way to a strident Islamic movement from the 1980s onwards. The latter culminated in the victory of the alliance of Islamic parties, Muttahida Majlis Amal (MMA) in NWFP in the 2002 elections. However, in the 2008 elections, MMA lost to the resurgent Pakhtun nationalist Awami National Party (ANP). Similarly, *mohajirs* (Urdu-speaking migrants) who generally supported Islamic parties, the Jamat-i-Islami (JI) and Jamiat Ulema Islam (JUP) in elections in the 1970s, overwhelmingly shifted their allegiance to a new ethnic party the Mohajir (later Muttahida) Qaumi Movement (MQM) in the 1980s. At the same time, the Islamic movement typically operated at the behest of the state authorities to contain the ethnonationalist movements in various provinces. To that extent, we need to look at Islamism as a force antithetical to ethnicity, as part of the nation-building project of the state of Pakistan. The legitimizing potential of Islam for the ruling dispensation provided a filip to the operational dynamics of *ulema* parties and groups, whereas the perceived villainy of ethnic parties, leaders and ideologies often invited the wrath of the state.

In this chapter, we plan to look into ethnic and Islamic militancy as an outcome of the project of state building. Paul Brass located state policies and elite competition at the heart of ethnonationalist movements.[4] It makes perfect sense that state policies can and do lead to consequences which can be positive or negative for the cause of national harmony. In this context, two broad policy orientations have been outlined:

1   ethno-pluralism, especially its British variety of multiculturalism, whereby the political system provides a space for multiple identities and communities, and
2   institutional pluralism whereby a variety of federal formulas emerge to provide regional autonomy to the core communities living in the federating units.[5]

This approach tends to focus on government policies.[6] It is argued here, however, that reliance on policy as an independent variable is problematic. Apart from the fact that policies do not operate effectively in the political context of a postcolonial society in which the state-building project is underway, we need to look at the context and the source of these policies.

Structural dynamics of the state

The ruling elite of post-independence Pakistan, which had pushed forward the agenda of a separate Muslim homeland in British India, embraced a set of policies that included: a foreign policy based on perceived insecurity vis-à-vis India, that sought security through Islamic unity; a constitutional policy that denied parliamentary sovereignty, and emphasized a quasi-unitarian federalism; and a policy concerning Islam as the ultimate source of legitimacy in a supralegal sense. Partition led to the emergence of a new ethnic hierarchy led by a *salariat* based on the *mohajir* and

Punjabi middle classes.[7] On the other hand, Pakhtuns, Bengalis, Sindhis, and the Baloch operated at the margins of the emergent multiethnic society. While the former group looked at Pakistan as a nation state, the latter perceived it as a "composite multination."[8] The perceived dichotomy between the *mohajir*–Punjabi salariat and all others created an ethnic bipolarity that was absent in India.[9]

The middle class shaped the authority structure of the new state through the civil bureaucracy that controlled public policy, even as the tribal and landed elite was formally represented in the national and provincial assemblies. The national project was essentially conceived and put in place by the middle class, which was ideologically Islamic modernist, ethnically *mohajir* and Punjabi, and sociologically urban-based and professionally oriented. It was socially progressive and politically conservative. Pakhtuns, Bengalis, Sindhis, and the Baloch had no sizeable middle class and thus had meager representation in the bureaucracy. Their political leadership constantly knocked at the doors of the state in a bid to open them through elections. The relatively less-developed ethnic communities, with their leadership still immersed in a cultural ethos rooted in pre-modern values and norms characterized by oppression against tribesmen, peasantry, and women, upheld the cause of electoral democracy. At the other end, the state apparatuses of army and bureaucracy, with their modern training, exposure to the West and high educational and professional standards, often sought to dispense with electoral democracy, parliamentarism, and political freedoms. This anomaly has operated throughout Pakistan's history. General Musharraf's promulgation of emergency on 3 November, 2007 reflected the middle-class ethos of controlling what was considered unbridled political participation.

It can be argued that there is need to take one step back from policy proper to the policy-creating ethnic and class dynamics of the structure of power in Pakistan in order to look for an explanation of ethnic revival and Islamic ascendancy along with potential or actual violence. The operational context for exercise of state power can be defined in terms of the grand nation-building project. Structurally speaking, Pakistan passed through four major processes of political transformation in the postcolonial period: centralization, militarization, Punjabization, and Islamization.

Centralization

The project of centralization brought in political actors from outside the parliament, especially the civil bureaucracy and later the army. Various policy-related matters in provinces were handled by the bureaucracy, which was recruited, trained, posted, and promoted by the Center. Federalism in West Pakistan was abolished when its four provinces and princely states were merged into one unit (1955–70). Presidentialism reigned supreme as the principle of unity of the nation, enshrined in the 1962 Constitution. Later, the presidency was eastablished as the supraparliamentary office under the 1985 Eighth Amendment and 2003 Seventeenth Amendment. The upper house of parliament, the Senate, emerged as a territorial chamber as late as 1973, a quarter of a century after Partition. It was supposed to give strength to the provinces vis-à-vis the centre. However, the differential in the policy scope of the two houses continued to frustrate the federalist ambitions of the smaller provinces. The Senate continued to be weak into the late 2000s. Additionally, the Centre often dismissed provincial governments led by opposition parties by using relevant constitutional provisions. This "constitutional terrorism" continued to play havoc with principles of pluralism, often involving the judiciary on the side of the federal government. A blatant example of this was the 1976 verdict of the Hyderabad Tribunal which banned an opposition party, the NAP. In February 2009, the supreme court disqualified the chief minister of Punjab, Shehbaz Sharif of the PML-Nawaz Sharif, from holding office, allegedly at the behest of President Zardari.

Militarization

The military is to Pakistan what party is to India. In common parlance, the army is considered to be a party by default, which is permanently in power overtly or covertly without being obliged to seek a mass mandate. The militarization of politics in Pakistan has followed a clear path. During a century of military recruitment from Punjab after 1857, the province provided half of the British Indian army, and thus laid the basis of the new myth of martial races cultivated by the British.[10] During the interwar years, the soldiery acquired proprietary rights through an ambitious scheme for allotment of canal-irrigated lands to men at arms. It also enjoyed preferential treatment in voting rights for the Punjab Legislative Assembly under the prevalent system of restricted franchise.[11] Thus, Pakistan inherited the most militarized province of India, which soon emerged as the power base of the new country. At the heart of the partition of India lay the partition of Punjab. The demobilized soldiery, belonging to the rival Muslim, Sikh, and Hindu communities, perpetrated violence on opponents in an organized and professional way.[12] This more than anything else brought about the exodus of Muslims from East Punjab and Hindus and Sikhs from West Punjab. The butchery during the partition riots and the bloody process of migration in 1947 left deep scars on the twin communities now living across the newly drawn international borders. However, unlike India where (East) Punjab was a mere peripheral state, in Pakistan Partition deeply securitized the national vision because Punjab played a central role in the country

While Punjabis on both sides of the new border committed acts of murder, arson, and rape on the rival communities fleeing their homes and hearths, the two governments of India and Pakistan put together military evacuation organizations to escort refugees safely across the border.[13] In Pakistan, army units were exposed to the misery of Muslims fleeing from East Punjab and living in temporary refugee camps on their way to a life of extreme uncertainty in their new homeland. This further militarized politics and greatly weakened the principle of civilian supremacy over the armed forces even before the latter formally took power in 1958. The strategic vision of the army moved to the center stage of all policy-making activity in the civilian sector, thus drawing the contours of political imagination along the ends and means of national security. Not surprisingly, centralization of the command structure, a unitary state model, the presidential form of government and a non-sovereign parliament have represented the leading aspects of the state elite's political thinking for six decades. At the other end, the idea of a diversity of authoritative institutions based upon principles of federalism, parliamentarism, provincial autonomy and a pluralist framework of politics in general continued to characterize the political vision of various ethnic communities not effectively represented in the state. In 2007–08, Musharaf, as both a serving and later a retired army general, on the one hand and a coterie of politicians including Nawaz Sharif and Benazir Bhutto—later Asif Zardari—on the other, characterized the divide in national thinking along civil–military lines.

Punjabization

The demographic makeup of Pakistan has been such that various policy measures relating to federalism have focused on a concern that one province may come to dominate all. For a quarter of a century after Partition, East Pakistan had a majority (around 55 percent) of the country's population. However, its demographic strength could not be reflected politically because general elections were postponed repeatedly. The power elite typically comprising *mohajirs* and Punjabis, failed to reconcile to the idea of a Bengali-dominated parliament and government. This concern led to the idea of inter-wing parity and thus to constitutional engineering. Lahore, the capital of Punjab, became the capital of the "One Unit," comprising the whole of West Pakistan.

Other provincial capitals, namely, Peshawar, Quetta, and Hyderabad lost their pivotal positions in their respective areas. This policy of coercive de-ethnicization of politics led to the emergence of rampant anti-Punjab feelings. The erstwhile smaller provinces reacted sharply to the One Unit "steamroller," which had disregarded popular ethnoregional aspirations and identities.[14] After the 1958 military coup, the Punjab-based army put a lid on the federalist ambitions of the smaller provinces. Later, Ayub shifted the capital of Pakistan from Karachi to Islamabad. Thus, both the federal and provincial capitals were located in Punjab from 1960 to 1970, when finally Yahya restored the four provinces. The ill-conceived constitutional project to meet the challenge of demographic imbalance between the two wings ran adrift at a considerable cost to the cause of national harmony in the form of resurgent ethnic movements.

After the emergence of Bangladesh, Pakistan again faced the one-province-dominates-all situation. Now it was Punjab that enjoyed a numerical preponderance at around 58 percent of the total population. During the following decades, Punjab emerged at the heart of the new ethnic discourse.[15] In the 1960s Punjab had emerged as the hub of the Green Revolution. With 66 percent of tubewells and 62 percent of tractors operating in Punjab, the province progressed rapidly. It enjoyed huge government subsidies for fertilizer, pesticides, seeds, and agricultural machinery.[16] By the late 1960s Punjab had overtaken Sindh in its manufacturing potential as well, especially in the textile industry. Apart from the lion's share going to Punjab in both agricultural and industrial development, that province increasingly dominated the bureaucracy. By the 1980s it occupied nearly 55 percent of the jobs in the public sector as opposed to its nearest rival, the *mohajir* community, whose share declined from a whopping 30 percent to less than 18 percent, with Sindhis at 5.4 percent, NWFP at 13.4 percent, and Balochistan at 3.4 percent.[17] The army has been both numerically and symbolically Punjabi, initially with 79 percent of the men in uniform coming from that province. The military operations against Bengalis (1971), the Baloch (1973–77), Sindhis (1983) and *mohajirs* (1992–94 and 1995) spread anti-Punjab sentiment all around. The fact that Pakhtuns and *mohajirs* also have a disproportionately high share of the army's officer cadre is generally not part of the public imagination of non-Punjabis. Neither are they conscious of the underprivileged groups, communities and regions within Punjab. The story of ethnic militancy in Pakistan is one of reaction to the perceived Punjabization of the state in economic, political, cultural, administrative, and military terms.

Islamization

Islam in Pakistan has played a role in mobilizing the public as a means towards acquiring or retaining power. The selection and use of Islamic symbols and provisions changed according to the prevailing situation in relation to the objectives of political actors. Over decades, the state establishment followed a strategy of depoliticizing the public by appropriating Islamic sources of legitimacy in addition to, or in lieu of, a mass mandate as a source of constitutional legitimacy. Reetz has outlined four major constituents of the legacy of Islam inherited by Pakistan:[18] street agitation in pursuit of Islamic causes from the *khilafat* and *hijrat* movements (1920s) onwards; institutions of Islamic learning, especially in UP, which recreated the glory and the pristine message of Islam and led to a century of anti-Western intellectual discourse; Wahhabist and Deobandist orientations rooted in a purifying mission at one end and reaction to heretical interpretations of religious classics by Ahmadis at the other; and *mulla* activism in the Pakhtun belt along the border of Afghanistan in the form of a tribal rebellion against the modern state, which was perceived to be ungodly and immoral. Examples of this near-xenophobic tribal movement are the Wana rebellion in the 1970s, the Tehrik Nifaz Shariat Mohammadi movement in Swat in the early 1990s and

again in 2007–09, and the Taliban and proto-Taliban movements in the middle and late 2000s.

The Islamic legacy skirted around mainstream politics led by the Muslim League, first in pursuit of a Muslim homeland and later as part of its nation-building project. Ishtiaq Ahmad has suggested a fourfold typology to define the relationship between Islam and the state in Pakistan:[19]

- the sacred state excluding human will
- the sacred state admitting human will
- the secular state admitting divine will
- the secular state excluding divine will.

The independence generation of the political and intellectual elite implicitly, and Justice Munir professedly, believed in the fourth model which envisaged disengagement between church and state.[20] Jinnah declared: "You may belong to any religion or caste or creed, that has nothing to do with the business of the state . . . Hindus would cease to be Hindus and Muslims would cease to be Muslims, not in the religious sense because that is personal faith of each individual, but in the political sense as citizens of the state."[21]

The 1956 Constitution represented a compromise between the *ulema* and the ruling elite whereby the non-Islamic provisions would be taken off the statute book and the sovereignty of Allah would be exercised in Pakistan through public representatives.[22] In other words, the elite settled for the model of a secular state while admitting the divine will into the scheme. At the other end, the two variations of the sacred state model continued to knock at the doors of the state even as, curiously, support from the public for this model has been scant. The JI and the conservative intelligentsia in general deliberated on the need for establishing an Islamic state, acknowledging the agency of human will in keeping with the requirements of the modern age. However, the two decades of the Afghan war in the 1980s and 1990s greatly strengthened the Islamic establishment in

Pakistan, which recruited, trained and armed *mujahideen* for Afghanistan, as well as for Kashmir from 1989 onwards. Pakistan's involvement in Kashmir came to an end in 2003–04 as the composite dialogue with India moved ahead under Washington's auspices. But, the spillover of Taliban from Afghanistan into the tribal areas and beyond brought the fourth model of the sacred state without human will into full action. This has become socially embedded through the Islamization of the Pakhtuns and their rigid adherence to rituals on the two sides of the Pak-Afghan border during the last quarter of the twentieth century. This was part of an emergent Islamic vigilante culture formalized through the 2006 Hasba Bill passed by the NWFP Assembly under the MMA government (2002–07).

During the six decades since Independence, Pakistan moved from a position in which the state defined religion to one in which religion defined the state. As the 1970 election campaign brought forth the leftist and Bengali nationalist movements in West and East Pakistan respectively, Yahya's military government aligned itself with Islamic parties, especially the JI. This alliance was further cemented during the civil war in East Pakistan in 1971. A *mulla*–garrison alliance came into being, which operated both covertly, for example in opposition to the three PPP governments (1971–77, 1988–90, 1993–96) and overtly as under Zia (1977–88) and selectively under Musharraf (1999–2008). Islamic parties and groups gained tremendous patronage from the army. They were catapulted into prominence as contenders of power in their own right. They shared the military establishment's political vision based on anti-Indianism, anti-secularism, relative intolerance for subnational identities rooted in ethnic sentiments and, until recently, the presidential form of government as a mechanism of unity by command. Not that everything fit well. The centrality of Islam as part of the state system demanded by Islamists was never on the agenda of the state. Conversely, despite the post-9/11 anti-US sentiment of Islamic parties belonging

to MMA, the pro-US Musharraf government formed a coalition government with them in Balochistan (2003–07). It also appointed the Jamiat Ulema-e-Islam (JUI-F) chief, Fazlur Rehman, as leader of the opposition in the National Assembly even though he enjoyed the support of only a minority from the opposition. Moreover, the army displayed a bias in favor of Sunni sectarian groups. This bias was operationalized in the backdrop of the largely Sunni-based Islamization program of the Zia government; support for the largely Sunni–Deobandi Afghan *mujahideen*; and the need to stem the tide of the much-feared revolutionary fervor of Shi'as in Pakistan after the Iranian revolution.[23]

As a typically weak postcolonial state, characterized by a quasi-unitary form of authority system within a federalist framework, Pakistan faced ethnonationalist movements in four out of five provinces. While the establishment sought to pursue its agenda for nation building, it co-opted Islamic forces in order to activate the divine sources of legitimacy. These initiatives ended up strengthening Islamic movements directly by way of patronage and ethnic movements indirectly by alienating their leaders still further. In 2009, the government was criticized both at home and abroad for appeasement of Islamic militants by entering into negotiations and signing ceasefire agreements with the Taliban leadership of Islamic insurgency in FATA (Federally Administered Tribal Areas) and Swat valley.

Ethnic violence

Pakistan emerged as a migrant state. The migration of more than seven million Muslims from India to Pakistan provided a source for the nationalist movements of both Sindhis and *mohajirs*. Jinnah and Liaqat were both migrants from India, along with the majority of the members of the Muslim League Council and Central Working Committee. The civil bureaucracy was dominated by migrants from UP and East Punjab, while the business community drew overwhelmingly from Bombay. Refugees from India accounted for 20 percent of the population in West Pakistan in 1951. The migratory elite had a profound impact on the literary, artistic, cultural, administrative, and political aspects of public life in Pakistan. Urdu became the national language even though only three percent of the population had it as its mother tongue. Islamic literature was written predominantly in Urdu. The leaders of Islamic parties were typically Urdu-speaking migrants, including Shabbir Ahmad Usmani (JUI), Maududi (JI) and later Noorani Mian (JUP). In the new ethnic hierarchy, the Urdu-speaking migrants were on top. As early converts to the cause of Pakistan and voters for the Muslim League in the 1937 elections, *mohajirs* mistrusted the popular leadership of the Pakistan areas proper who voted for Jinnah's Pakistan only in 1946 as late converts. The former cultivated a higher legitimacy for themselves than for their lesser compatriots.[24]

It is true that migrants suffered through the tragedy of leaving their homes and hearths behind, along with the breakdown of family and clan ties in many cases. However, it was a migrant-dominated administration at the other end of their journey that welcomed refugees, arranged for their safe passage from India, provided them shelter on arrival, allotted them urban property and agricultural land evacuated by the outgoing Hindus and Sikhs, and extended loans to them for starting their businesses. Migrants, especially those from minority provinces, who generally cultivated a self-image as makers of Pakistan, were territorially agnostic in their political vision. For them, Pakistan was a Muslim homeland, the end product of a struggle for political survival in India that was rapidly moving towards a majoritarian democracy. The actual territory and peoples of their land of migration were never part of their imagination. In the post-Partition years, deification of the state emerged as the leading political attitude of migrants, as they started their new life in an "alien" society. They shunned ethnic and linguistic identities and embraced an ideology

of "all-Pakistanism."[25] Islam now served to unite the disparate provinces and states of Pakistan that had never before formed a territorial state. The new Muslim homeland was conceived and projected as the "historical spatial container" of somewhat unproblematized ethnic groups, and "a sacred place set aside for God."[26]

An acute sense of national insecurity vis-à-vis India, mistrust of "local" politicians in and out of parliament, and commitment to firm leadership on top turned migrants into supporters of military governments. The larger section of migrants, almost two-thirds, who had come from East Punjab and adjoining states of India, got assimilated in West Punjab within a generation, and lost its identity. A shared legacy of language, literature, culture, administration, politics, geography, and history welded migrants and locals together. However, the one-third of migrants who had come from other parts of India outside Punjab and settled mainly in Sindh remained unassimilated in the host community. Being non-Sindhi speaking in Sindh, they soon gravitated towards the identity of an Urdu-speaking *mohajir* community that needed to carve out a niche under adverse circumstances. As they descended on Karachi from the north, south, east, and west of India in their hundreds of thousands, the Sindh government became concerned over the grim prospect that Sindhis might become a minority in their own homeland.

The Sindhi grievances against migrants continued to accumulate on several counts.[27] The central government moved to separate Karachi from Sindh to become the federal capital and, in 1948, pushed the Sindh government to Hyderabad instead. The Sindhi language was banned or discouraged at various levels as a medium of instruction. The Sindh University at Karachi was relocated at Jamshoro near Hyderabad. The assets of the provincial government in Karachi were arbitrarily transferred to the central government. The province of Sindh was merged with One Unit. *Mohajirs* were accused of assuming an attitude of cultural arrogance towards

Sindhis, almost bordering on racism. Karachi overnight became a *mohajir* city where Sindhis were reduced to 3.5 percent of the population. *Mohajirs* occupied government jobs in numbers grossly disproportionate to their population while representation of Sindhis in jobs in both public and private sectors was negligible. A large tract of land brought under irrigation through Guddu and Ghulam Mohammad barrages in Sindh was allotted to civil and military officers, both Punjabis and *mohajirs*. Refugees from India allegedly sponsored Hindu–Muslim riots in Karachi in 1948 with a view to pushing Hindus out of Sindh. This was resented by Sindhi Muslims who swore by tolerance between followers of the two faiths and accused *mohajirs* of bigotry. Under Yahya (1969–71) finally One Unit was disbanded, which led to restoration of the four provinces, including Sindh. Karachi once more became the capital of Sindh, and a new quota system was introduced with separate provisions for rural and urban Sindh to take care of Sindhis and *mohajirs* respectively.

The PPP government in Karachi and Islamabad (1971–77) was able to consolidate the gains of the quota system by incorporating it into the 1973 Constitution and implementing it at various levels. In a quarter century, it produced a tiny middle class among Sindhis and led to the emergence of a rudimentary Sindhi civil bureaucracy. The execution of Z. A. Bhutto by Zia in 1979 eventually led to insurgency in Sindh in 1983 as part of the agitation of the Movement for Restoration of Democracy (MRD). Zia's martial law government brutally suppressed the Sindhi agitation. An indirect consequence of the Sindhi nationalist upsurge was the emergence of a *mohajir* nationalist party (MQM) in 1984, which many among its opponents believed was the creation of Zia. At the other end, PPP operated as an ethnonationalist party in Sindh even as it had the profile of a federal party elsewhere in the country.

In this way, the province of Sindh produced two rival ethnic movements of Sindhis and *mohajirs*, based in rural and urban sectors, and led by the PPP and the MQM respectively. Sindhi nationalists have been struggling with the perceived enemies within: *mohajirs* in urban areas, Punjabis in both urban and rural milieus, and Pakhtuns in Karachi. The Sindhi nationalist leadership remained firmly in the hands of the landed elite, Sindhi intelligentsia, bureaucracy, and students. Banditry, the main form of traditional violence in Sindh, was occasionally mixed up with ethnic militancy. Being non-urban in its support base, the Sindhi ethnonational movement remained somewhat contained despite violent outbursts such as in 1983 and, to a lesser extent, in 1992.

In contrast, *mohajir* nationalism had a militant character from the start.[28] The movement was born out of the "indigenous revival" in and around 1970, expressed through Bengali and Sindhi nationalisms and the anti-establishment revolt in Punjab identified with PPP. The "migrant" state finally took roots in the territory where it was based. In post-Bangladesh Pakistan, Indus civilization became the new source of identity. The federating units were severally defined as four brothers, four cultures, and four nationalities. Mohajirs in Sindh lost in many ways during the 1970s. A quarter of a million of their counterparts in Bangladesh, called Biharis, had fled to Pakistan through Nepal and India as well as by sea. They were brutalized by years of insecurity, ethnic hatred, and separation from their families and friends back in Bangladesh. They eventually provided the core of the militant wing of the incipient *mohajir* movement in Sindh. The Sindhi nationalists reacted sharply to the prospects of another spate of migration destined to further upset the worsening demographic balance against them. At the other end, *mohajirs* had suffered under a series of reversals of fortune during the first quarter of a century after Partition, including: appropriation of jobs by Punjabis after the 1958 and 1969 military coups; shift of capital from Karachi to Islamabad in 1960; merger of Karachi back in Sindh in 1970; regionalization of the political idiom along ethnic lines; and the affirmative action policies which directly hit their potential for recruitment into government services on the basis of merit. *Mohajirs* further lost their political, bureaucratic, commercial, and cultural ascendancy under Z. A. Bhutto in the 1970s.

Mohajirs reacted to the widely cultivated idea of Karachi as a mini-Pakistan where all ethnic communities could settle and as a safe haven for foreign refugees. *Mohajir* nationalism represents a new sons-of-the-soil movement.[29] The *mohajir* community sought to shed its alien identity and develop nativist nationalism in the process of transforming itself into a distinct ethnic community. In this movement, we see ethnicity-in-making, drawing on multiple linguistic, cultural, historical, and geographical identities. *Mohajirs* shared the minimal experience of having been non-Punjabi refugees from India, dominated by the Urdu-speaking community. The peculiar resettlement process of migrants coming in successive waves resulted in nearly half of the population in Karachi living in squatter settlements by the end of the twentieth century. It is here that ethnic violence took birth in the midst of rude competition for social space, amenities, security, and habitat, largely outside the purview of law. These groups at the bottom of the social ladder hobnobbed with the criminal underworld to obtain supplies of water, electricity, and other amenities, and to fight rival groups making similar demands. This type of endemic violence spilled into the streets in a situation in which Pakhtuns controlled public transport in a *mohajir*-dominated metropolis. The famous Bushra Zaidi incident in which a young girl was killed in a road accident in 1985 brought to surface the simmering *mohajir* anger. It was followed by MQM's victory in the local bodies' elections in 1987 and successive general elections thereafter.

The MQM soon emerged as a militant party. It targeted the press for covering its militant activity by burning and looting property. It also attacked the perceived renegades from its own cause and non-conforming *mohajirs* in general, thereby seeking to impose unity by command. This "in-group policing" was carried out by application of informal sanc-

tions characterized by social pressure or even violence.[30] MQM's militant operational network approximated what Paul Brass calls an institutionalized riot system (IRS) in his explanation of Hindu–Muslim riots in Meerut.[31] Brass claims that this system leaves doors open for more riots and for their eventual acceptance by the society.[32] The military operation against MQM in 1992–94 and the so-called Rangers Operation in 1995 sought to control the party's militant politics. The government resorted to extra-judicial murder of MQM workers, ruthless searches and intensive intelligence work. Under Nawaz Sharif (1997–99), the party again joined the coalition government, but later parted ways with it on the issue of the murder of ex-governor Hakim Saeed, alleged to be the work of MQM. After an uneasy period under Musharraf's military rule (1999–2001), the MQM joined coalition governments in Karachi and Islamabad with the "king's party," Pakistan Muslim League Quaid-i-Azam (PML-Q), from 2002 to 2007 and again with the PPP in Sindh after the February 2008 elections. The party was accused of carrying out bloody attacks on the occasion of the defunct Chief Justice Iftikhar Chaudhary's arrival in Karachi on 12 May, 2007, on Benazir Bhutto's rally on 18 October, 2007, and on the lawyers' offices on 9 April, 2008.

Lack of understanding between major ethnic communities in Karachi turned the city into a powder keg. The character of violence was different in the two cases of *mohajirs* and Sindhis. The *mohajir* violence has been planned and organized, rooted in a social matrix of sustained tension between communities in the backdrop of an urban situation of extreme congestion. As opposed to this, the rural-based Sindhi violence operated from outside the mainstream social fabric, generally identified with the dacoit phenomenon. The Sindhi militancy was characterized by a lesser quantum of planning and organization, and was not based on geographical proximity between hostile communities in densely populated areas. A major reason for this difference also lay in the phenomenon of party. The MQM had well-trained and ideologically indoctrinated party cadres, who had internalized the cult of Altaf Hussain's leadership. The production of violence under these circumstances was far more efficient than in the case of Sindhis. The father of Sindhi nationalism, G. M. Syed, was unable to win popular votes or establish a cult of his leadership. He consistently lost to rival leaders, from Ayub Khuhro in the 1950s to Z. A. Bhutto in the 1970s. There was no all-Sindhi party per se, except that the PPP operated in that province along ethnolinguistic lines. At the heart of MQM's politics was "ethnic outbidding," which led to its monopoly over representation of the perceived *mohajir* interests and identity. At the heart of the PPP's politics was "ethnic underbidding" for fear of losing support in other provinces.[33]

Unlike the Sindhi, mohajir and Bengali movements, the Baloch and Pakhtun movements started from separatist agendas in the late 1940s. The congress government in NWFP was removed within days after Partition. But the province gradually moved towards integration with the rest of West Pakistan, both politically and economically. The Pakhtun leadership by Ghaffar Khan and his family of the Khudai Khidmatgars, later transformed succesively into the National Awami Party (NAP) and the Awami National Party (ANP), lost ground in a span of two generations. In contrast, Balochistan remained without a pristine Baloch Party and an all-Baloch leader. The merger of Balochistan with Pakistan took place through annexation under alleged coercion and co-option. Tribal *lashkars* (armed units) put up resistance, leading to counterinsurgency measures by successive governments. The dismissal of the NAP's popular government of Balochistan by the Bhutto government in Islamabad in 1973 led to a guerrilla war that lasted four years. It involved a major military operation, a complex judicial process known as the Hyderabad Tribunal, lengthy jail terms for the Baloch leadership, and militarization of the Baloch ethnic movement in general.

During the Afghan *jihad* against the Red Army, Baloch nationalists saw hundreds of thousands of refugees from across the border settling in their province, which turned the delicate demographic balance against the Baloch in favour of Pakhtuns. After Musharraf's coup of 1999, the old wounds were reopened. The government's accountability drive led to incarceration of several Baloch leaders. That left the field open for party cadres, student activists, and intelligentsia to take the initiative in their own hands. The rape of a female Baloch doctor, allegedly by an army officer, in 2005 finally ignited a fresh wave of violence from the Bugti tribe that spread to other areas and groups.

The most obvious targets of Baloch militant actions are: the gas pipeline, which is the symbol of nationalist resistance against the state inasmuch as a local facility serves other parts of the country, providing four-fifths of the total supply of gas; railway lines, which link Balochistan with other provinces; and military cantonments, which carry a profile of an occupying force belonging to the dominant ethnic community of Punjab. Baloch militants fired 30,000 mortars in three years from 2005 onwards, with 1,570 attacks in that year alone, backed by an armory that included Kalashnikovs, machine guns, and grenades, along with walky-talkies and satellite phones.[34] Among the militants, the BLA, mainly comprising Bugti and Marri tribesmen, consistently made news headlines. It was banned as a terrorist organization.

Another irritant for Baloch nationalists was the government's project for development of Gawadar as an international port on the Arabian coastline with the help of China. The Baloch resisted the project on various grounds: the fiercely ambitious land grab movement of military and non-military personnel from outside the province represented a colonial presence; the migration and settlement of people into the province from outside was expected to dwarf the Baloch population; the much-touted development work in Balochistan was perceived to be a conspiracy to increase the potential of the military and security agencies to control the province rather than improve the living conditions of people. The Musharraf government followed a policy of sorting out the recalcitrant tribal lords (*sardars*) led by Nawab Bugti, who was later killed in an ambush in 2006. A spate of arrests and extra-judicial killings followed, and several cases of "disappeared" persons came to the surface, allegedly involving intelligence agencies. Islamabad even sought to support the Pakhtun-based Islamic parties to counter the ethnic appeal of the Baloch nationalist parties.[35] After the February 2008 elections, the PPP Chief Minister Raisani released Akhtar Mengal and Nawab Bugti's grandson Shazain Bugti, among others. Prime Minister Gilani stopped the military operation against Baloch activists and announced a policy of dialogue with them.

Militancy in Balochistan has been considered especially dangerous because of the fear of a state-sponsored counterinsurgency based on cultivation of Islam against Baloch ethnicity, or of al-Quaeda moving in to fill the vacuum.[36] However, there are reasons to believe otherwise. First, violence itself is relatively contained. The number of militant Baloch activists has been small, reflecting the demographic weakness of Balochistan at a mere 3.5 percent of the national population, with only half of it belonging to the Baloch proper. Second, with 42 percent of the land of Pakistan, the province is sparsely populated. This made guerrilla warfare extremely difficult across hundreds of kilometers of rugged territory. Third, tribal hierarchies led by sardars and nawabs represented rival power blocs, often organized as parallel political parties or party factions. Thus, the Baloch National Party (BNP) represented Mengals, Jamhoori Watan Party (JWP) Bugtis, and Baloch Haq Talwar (BHT) Marris. This pattern circumscribed their potential of producing an all-Baloch nationalist party along the lines of MQM, and thus kept their militant activities bound to certain localities and tribes. Fourth, for decades the Baloch have been engaged in a quiet war

against Pakhtuns, the enemy within. The latter dominated the economic and cultural life of the capital city of Quetta and northern Balochistan in general. The arrival of Afghan refugees in the 1980s further changed the profile of the city and the province linguistically, culturally, demographically, and economically in favor of Pakhtuns.

Identity formation seems to be a major and continuing preoccupation of nationalists and ethnonationalists alike. In Amartya Sen's words, "imposition of singular and belligerent identities" on people can only serve to sharpen divisions in society.[37] Identity underscores the cultural construction of the fear of the other.[38] It serves the purpose of laying out the turf for a pre-emptive attack out of fear for personal and collective security.[39] As such, identity-based violence rooted in the imperatives of security has prevailed in all the current ethnic movements of Pakistan, namely, *mohajir*, Sindhi, and Baloch.

Islamic militancy

While answering the question of whether Islam provides a theory of violence, the contributors to a recent book on Islamist violence define a fundamentalist as "a messianic, death-dealing hero who sacrifices his life on the altar of God spurred by the promise of eternal salvation of his soul in paradise."[40] This may be the psychology of individual terrorists, but it hardly explains the larger phenomenon, namely, an extra-constitutional and aggressive mode of political participation through violence. Jessica Stern's exposé of Pakistan's *jihad* culture brings in the institutional background of potential terrorists emerging from *madrasahs*, the "schools of hate."[41] She sees it as a principal–agent problem whereby the agent (terrorist) has outgrown the principal (state).[42] Islamism has been widely discussed with reference to modernity from opposite perspectives. It is defined as a reaction to modernity that brought down traditional mechanisms of solidarity in Muslim communities at the hands of the Westernized elite.[43] Alternatively, it is understood in terms of serving a modern agenda relating to statehood and interstate relations reflecting "sectarian utopian orientations."[44]

Western approaches to the phenomenon of Islamic militancy focus on a reified construct of that religion as an indomitable force pushing its adherents in a certain undesirable direction of action and behavior. The clash of civilizations thesis deals with this phenomenon at a macro level, as do various analyses dealing with the current wave of Islamic militancy flowing from central to southeast Asia. However, following the research based on the World Values Study 1995–2001, Pippa Norris and Ronald Inglehart find that there is no fundamental difference of values between the Islamic world and the West, that the postcommunist European societies show far less support for democracy than Islamic societies, and that certain sub-Saharan African countries and Catholic countries of Latin America provide an even stronger role for religious authorities than do Muslim countries. By the same token, they *do* find a real difference in the realm of gender equality and sexual liberalization.[45] The typical Western scholarly approach seeks to unravel the "mystery" of Islam. The conflation of religion and state in Islam has already become an academic orthodoxy, which belies the political scene on the ground for almost the whole of the last 1,500 years in almost all Muslim societies.[46]

These views ignore the professed subjective, narrative and projective idiom of the practitioners of both politics and Islam in the Muslim world. One can argue that the world view of Muslims has been increasingly shaped by a dichotomy between the world at large dominated by the West and the mini-world of Islam conceived as two essentialisms. A pervasive world-of-Islam perspective operates through projects such as the Organization of the Islamic Conference (OIC) and support for the perceived Muslim suffering in regional conflicts ranging from Palestine to Chechnya, Afghanistan and Iraq. In other words, a dichotomous worldview provides the background against which we need to judge the understanding and action of Muslims in Pakistan. A persecution syndrome has been part of the Muslim self-image during the last half century in various geographical regions of the world.

After 9/11, Islamabad turned its back on its erstwhile allies, the Taliban in Kabul, in support of the US war effort. A large number of state functionaries, especially from intelligence agencies led by ISI, who were recruited, trained and socialized into militant action against Russian "infidels" in Afghanistan under Zia, were jolted into changing sides, although in some cases unsuccessfully. Combined with the invasion of Iraq in 2003, the latent goodwill for the Taliban among the general public was increasingly couched in anti-American terms. The top brass of the army took the "pragmatic" decision of joining the US-led war against terrorism. But, various Afghanistan-savvy ex-generals, mid-career intelligence officers, Islamic parties, remnants of pro-*mujahideen* and pro-Taliban elements from the articulate sections including academia, media, and the professions in general continued to oppose the new deal with America. They believed that the war against terrorism was fought in the American interest and not in Pakistan's interest. This led to ambiguity, confusion, and contradiction concerning religious violence among politically motivated sections of the public. Along with formal condemnation of terrorism, one finds opposition to anti-terrorist operations such as the one against the Red Mosque in Islamabad in August 2007, in Swat in October–November 2007 and January–February 2009, in South Waziristan in mid-2008 and Bajaur in February–March 2009. The legitimacy and high moral ground of the war against terrorism were lost on the way.

We can point to regional instability as a potent factor in shaping the contours of contemporary Islamic militancy in Pakistan. The Afghan resistance heavily influenced Pakhtun politics in Pakistan by discrediting the relatively secular ANP leadership in the 2002 elections. Pakhtuns moved from the ethnic project to the Islamic project, in the process leaving behind Ghaffar Khan's ideology of non-violence and embracing a militant strategy to defeat the West as well as "Westernism" at home. Like Afghanistan, the tribal areas had no colonial legacy of a constitutional state system, rule of law, rational–legal bureaucracy, political parties, elections, and independent judiciary. In the absence of an urban-based middle class committed to legal, educational, bureaucratic, and technocratic careers, tribal-based resistance in Afghanistan and in the tribal areas of Pakistan produced the Islamic project identified with the Taliban. No constraint in the way of implementation of *Shari'a* was to be tolerated by various proto-Taliban elements from north and south Waziristan and Wana. A similar pattern of Pakhtun Islamism emerged from the semi-settled areas from Swat and Dir states, which became part of the mainstream legal–administrative setup as late as 1970. The latter states targeted the central government's implements of authority and sought to take over government at the district level. In October 2007, Sufi's son-in-law, Fazlullah, launched the movement for implementation of Shari'a and took control of 59 villages in the valley. The Musharraf government launched a military operation in order to restore the government's writ. The pattern was clear: the less constitutional the state, the more the political violence.

Pakistan's military engagement with Afghanistan for two decades, first as a launching pad for guerrilla warfare and later as creator, supporter, and patron of the Taliban, produced an Islamic movement that was predominantly *Sunni*-based. Zia's own Islamization program in Pakistan bore the same character, reflecting the mainstream sectarian commitment. The Iranian revolution introduced a new factor in the whole Islamic project in the form of reinvigorated *Shi'a* dynamism, which soon led to resistance against imposition of *Sunni* jurisprudence. From the mid-1980s onwards, a sectarian war began in

various localities of Pakistan that involved targeted killing of *Sunni* and *Shi'a* leaders, throwing of hand grenades on mosques and *imambargahs*, and demonstrations and violent clashes between sectarian activists. The Zia government and the first Nawaz Sharif government (1990–93) were generally perceived to be supporters of the *Sunni* activists, who operated from the platform of Sipah Sahaba Pakistan (SSP).[47]

Apart from Afghanistan and Iran, Saudi Arabia played a significant role in shaping Islamic attitudes in Pakistan along revivalist lines. The Saudi influence operated in three distinct ways: by financing the Afghan jihad and providing it diplomatic, ideological and moral legitimacy; by supporting anti-*Shi'a* activist organizations, thus indulging in a proxy war with Iran on the soil of Pakistan; and, most significantly, by shaping the religious beliefs and practices of millions of Pakistani expatriates in Saudi Arabia along *Wahhabist/ Salafi* lines, thus seeking to reproduce a pristine Islam. The returnees from Saudi Arabia brought back petrodollars and also a commitment to Islamic glory along with hatred for the perceived enemies of Islam led by America and Israel.

The tribal and semi-settled areas along the northern borders with Afghanistan represent a political culture that is not in consonance with the style of a typical ex-British colony such as India or Pakistan. This latter style is characterized by issue formation and policy orientation and even ideological expression typically through party activity in and outside the electoral framework. In this way, parliament performed the function of taking protagonists of various causes, Islamic or ethnic, off the streets. By the same token, the tribal areas and the recently annexed princely states such as Swat, Dir, and Chitral continued to operate according to the traditions of "indirect rule." These areas have been characterized more by arbitrary rule than by adherence to the rule of codified law based on the British Common Law, a rational–legal bureaucracy, habeas corpus and other writs for protection of citizens from the state, and a general respect for the will of the majority and piecemeal accommodation of grievances. Instead, these areas exhibited an arbitrary expression of individual and group power, an unregulated public behavior, the will of a minority against that of the majority, and the power of the bullet prevailing over the power of the ballot. Democracy binds individuals to the state, prescribing duties for the former and responsibilities for the latter. It controls the flight of imagination, restricts agendas, focuses on resources, and allows only incremental change.[48] Democracies carry far more authority than authoritarian regimes, which depend on the rude exercise of naked power. Bringing the unsettled and semi-settled areas into mainstream politics requires careful planning for the transition from indirect to direct rule.[49]

Conclusion

Our observations bring out various factors that led to Islamic and ethnic violence in Pakistan in recent years. First and foremost, the character of violence needs to be defined in relation to the level of destruction, for example, by distinguishing indiscriminate killing from precisely targeted attacks and individual acts of terrorism from group participation in violence. In Pakistan, violence itself remains limited. It does not approach the level of genocide such as in Rwanda and Burundi, massacres such as in Sabra and Shatilla or in Bosnia, protracted human suffering such as in Darfur, or a life of endemic insecurity involving recurrent loss of life and property as in Iraq, Afghanistan, and Gaza. In other words, the terrorist profile of Pakistan is far higher than the reality on the ground. The enigma lies in the way the transnational Islamic networks have operated in Pakistan. Incidents of violence in the country include attacks on a perceived enemy or its symbols such as government property, railway lines, gas pipelines, holy places of other religious sects, and, most recently, defense

establishments and men in uniform especially at the hands of the Taliban. Pakistan entered the era of suicide bombing in 2007 after the army's attack on the Red Mosque in Islamabad. However, Pakistan's legal and institutional infrastructure is reasonably strong by the Third World standards, sufficiently at least to keep violence from becoming a way of life.

There is a measure of consensus in Pakistan on the normative ideal of democracy, at least in procedural terms. Ethnic conflicts often reflect a desire to safeguard the rule of public representatives against centralized rule, especially in provinces and communities other than Punjab. State elites celebrate the 1940 Lahore Resolution as a milestone on the way to establishment of a Muslim homeland. Ethnonationalist leaders seek a (con)federal arrangement on the basis of the same resolution whereby provinces would have maximum autonomy.[50] Ethnic movements drew heavily on grievances against the dismissal of the elected government in NWFP in 1947, successive elected governments in East Bengal and Sindh, and the elected government of Balochistan in 1973, obliging the NAP government in NWFP to resign in protest. In other words, violence emerged as a desperate mode of politics after exhausting all constitutional formulas and parliamentary initiatives. The failure of the Musharraf government to implement the recommendations of the two senate committees to deal with the Balochistan issue contributed to the commitment of Baloch nationalists to pursue their mission outside the constitutional framework.

At the same time, Islamists have been brought in by successive military governments to subvert the constitutional source of legitimacy derived from mass mandate. Islamist groups duly obliged the military governments and, in the process, professed and practiced an extra-constitutional agenda, while amassing small arms in pursuit of *jihad* in Afghanistan and Kashmir. The chickens came home to roost in the first decade of the twenty-first century. Public acceptance of violence outside the purview of law, even more than violence itself, is a persistant malaise of societies such as Pakistan.

Notes

1 Pervez Hoodbhoy, "It is our War," *Dawn*, 23 October, 2007.
2 *Dawn*, 11 June, 2008.
3 See Mohammad Waseem, "Islam and the West: A Perspective from Pakistan," in James Peacock *et al.* (eds), *Identity Matters: Ethnic and Sectarian Conflict* (New York: Berghahan Books, 2007), pp. 191–92.
4 Paul R. Brass, *Ethnicity and Nationalism* (New Delhi: Sage, 1991), p. 8.
5 William Safran, "Non-separatist Policies Regarding Ethnic Minorities: Positive Approaches and Ambiguous Consequences," *International Political Science Review*, Vol. 15, No. 1 (1994), pp. 63–64.
6 Michael E. Brown and Sumit Ganguli (eds), "Introduction," in *Government Policies and Ethnic Relations in Asia and the Pacific* (Cambridge, MA: MIT Press, 1997), p. 11.
7 Hamza Alavi, "Authoritarianism and Legitimacy of State Power in Pakistan," in Subrata Mitra (ed.), *The Postcolonial State in South Asia* (London: Harvester Wheatsheaf, 1990), pp. 32–33.
8 See Alain-G. Gagnon and James Tully, *Multinational Democracies* (Cambridge: University Press, 2001), p. 2.
9 James Manor, "Ethnicity and Politics in India," *International Affairs*, Vol. 72, No. 1 (1996), p. 463.
10 Tai Yong and Gyanesh Kudaisya, *The Aftermath of Partition in South Asia* (London: Routledge, 2000), pp. 206–10.
11 Yong and Kudaisya, pp. 211–12.
12 Swarna Iyer, "August Anarchy: The Partition Massacres in Punjab 1947," *South Asia*, Special issue, 18 (1995), pp. 23–24.
13 Mohammad Waseem, "Muslim Migration from East Punjab: Patterns of Settlement and Assimilation," in Ian Talbot and Thinder Shandi (eds), *People on the Move: Punjabi Colonial and Postcolonial Migration* (Karachi: Oxford University Press), p. 69.
14 Rafiq Afzal, *Political Parties in Pakistan: 1947–1958* (Islamabad: National Institute of Historical and Cultural Studies, 1998), pp. 255–58.
15 Stephen P. Cohen, *The Idea of Pakistan* (Lahore: Vanguard, 2005), pp. 207 and 223–24.
16 Mohammad Waseem, *Politics and the State*, pp. 213–16.
17 Charles Kennedy, "Pakistan: Ethnic Diversity and Colonial Legacy," in John Coakley (ed.), *The Territorial Management of Ethnic Conflict* (London: Frank Cass, 2003), Table 7.2, p. 162.
18 Dietrich Reetz, *God's Kingdom on Earth: The Contestations of the Public Sphere by Islamic Groups in Colonial India (1900–1947)*, rehabilitation thesis, Berlin University, Berlin 2001, abstract.
19 Ishtiaq Ahmed, *The Concept of an Islamic State*, PhD thesis, University of Stockholm (published) (Edsbruk, 1985), pp. 34–43.
20 See Justice (Rtd) Munir Ahmed, *From Jinnah to Zia* (Lahore: Vanguard, 1980), pp. 32–36.
21 Mohammad Ali Jinah, *Speeches as Governor General of Pakistan, 1947–48* (Karachi, n. d.), p. 9.
22 Article 198, Clause 1, *Constitution of Pakistan (1956)*; see also Fazlur Rehman, "Islam in Pakistan," *Journal of South Asian and Middle Eastern Studies*, Vol. 8, No. 4 (1985), p. 35.
23 See Vali Nasr, "Islam, the State and the Rise of Sectarian Militancy in Pakistan," in Christopher Jaffrelot (ed.), *Pakistan: Nationalism without a Nation* (New Delhi: Manohar, 2002), pp. 88–92.
24 See Mohammad Waseem, "Functioning of Democracy in Pakistan," in Zoya Hasan (ed.), *Democracy and Muslim Societies: The Asian Experience* (New Delhi: Sage, 2007).
25 Feroz Ahmed, *Ethnicity and Politics in Pakistan* (Karachi: Oxford University Press, 1999), pp. 100–02.
26 Robert J. Kaiser, "Homeland Making and the Territorialization of National Identity," in Daniel Conversi (ed.), *Ethnonationalism in the Contemporary World* (London: Routledge, 2002), p. 230.
27 Mohammad Waseem, "Political Ethnicity and the State in Pakistan," in *The Nation-State and Transnational Forces in South Asia* (Tokyo, 2001), pp. 270–71.
28 Mohammad Waseem, "Mohajirs in Pakistan: A Case of Nativisation of Migrants," in Crispin Bates (ed.), *Community, Empire and Migration: South Asians in Diaspora* (Basingstoke: Palgrave, 2001), p. 245.
29 See, for comparison, Myron Weiner, *Sons of the Soil: Migration and Ethnic Conflict in India* (Princeton, NJ: University Press, 1978), pp. 6–7.
30 Brubaker and Laitin, p. 433.

31 Paul R. Brass, "Development of an Institutionalised Riot System in Meerut City, 1961 to 1982,"
Economic and Political Weekly, Vol. 39, No. 44
(30 October–5 November, 2004), pp. 4,839–48.

32 Brass, "Development of an Institutionalised
Riot System," p. 4,845.

33 See Brubaker and Laitin, p. 434.

34 Massoud Ansari, "Between Tribe and Country,"
Himal (Khatmandu), Vol. 20, No. 5 (May 2007),
pp. 23, 27.

35 International Crisis Group (ICG), *Pakistan: The
Worsening Conflict in Baluchistan*, Report No. 119
(Islamabad, 2006), p. 21.

36 Fredrick Grare, *Pakistan: The Resurgence of Baluch
Nationalism*, Carnegie Papers, No. 65, 6 January,
2006; and Rajshree Jetly, "Resurgence of the
Baluch Movement in Pakistan: Emerging
Perspectives and Challenges," paper for
International Symposium on Pakistan, Institute
of South Asian Studies (ISAS) National
University of Singapore, 24–25 May, 2007, p. 8.

37 Amartya Sen, *Identity and Violence: The Illusion of
Destiny* (London: Allen Lane, 2006), p. 2.

38 Brubaker and Laitin, p. 442.

39 Stuart J. Kaufman, *Modern Hatreds: The Symbolic
Politics of Ethnic War* (Ithaca, NY: Cornell
University Press, 2001), p. 19.

40 Hamadi Redissi and Jan-Erik Lane, "Does Islam
Provide a Theory of Violence?" in Amélie Blom
et al. (eds), *The Enigma of Islamist Violence*
(London: Hurst & Company, 2007), p. 45.

41 Jessica Stern, "Pakistan's Jihad Culture," *Foreign
Affairs* (November/December 2000), p. 118.

42 Stern, p. 16.

43 Ira M. Lapidus, "Islamic Revival and Modernity:
The Contemporary Movements and the
Historical Paradigms," *Journal of Economic and
Social History of the Orient*, Vol. 40, No. 4 (1997),
p. 444.

44 S. N. Eisenstadt, *Fundamentalism, Sectarianism,
and Revolution* (Cambridge: University Press,
1999), pp. 2–3.

45 Pippa Norris and Ronald Inglehart, *Islam and
the West: Testing the Clash of Civilizations Thesis*,
KSG Working Paper (April 2002), No. RWP02,
pp. 14–15.

46 Dale F. Eickleman and James Piscatori, *Muslim
Politics* (Princeton, NJ: University Press, 1996),
pp. 47–48.

47 See Vali Nasr, "The Rise of Sunni Militancy in
Pakistan: The Changing Role of Islamism and
the Ulema in Society and Politics," *Modern Asian
Studies*, Vol. 34, No. 1 (2000), pp. 145–54.

48 See Philippe C. Schmitter and Terry Lynn
Karl, "What Democracy is . . . and is Not,"
Journal of Democracy (1991), pp. 50–54.

49 Brubaker and Laitin, p. 428.

50 See Mohammad Waseem, "Pakistan Resolution
and the Ethnonationalist Movements," in Kaniz
F. Yusuf *et al.* (eds), *Pakistan Resolution Revisited*
(Islamabad: National Institute of Historical and
Cultural Studies, 1990), pp. 522–27.

20

Ethnic conflict and the civil war in Sri Lanka

Jayadeva Uyangoda

Beginning of the civil war

The transition of Sri Lanka's ethnic conflict into a civil war between the state and Tamil nationalist groups began in the late 1970s, and accelerated in the early 1980s, particularly after the anti-Tamil ethnic riots of July 1983.[1] There is a pre-civil war phase to the ethnic conflict, running back to the early post-independence years. Since political independence in 1948, Sinhalese–Tamil relations, specifically the relations between the state and the minority Tamil community, had been characterized by tension and conflict. The Tamil community's experience of discrimination and political exclusion had produced a particular project of minority aspirations translated into a demand for federalist regional autonomy. It is perhaps fair to say that Sri Lanka's ethnic minorities were "unreconciled to the constitutional arrangements" that came along with political independence; but only a "few expected that the majority rule would be so quickly followed by discriminatory legislative measures."[2] The peaceful and parliamentary agitation for autonomy rights continued until the late 1970s, but with little success. As Kearney, Roberts, Wriggins, and Wilson have documented and commented on in great detail, there were many barriers to interethnic accommodation

through political reforms.[3] The failure of the Bandaranaike-Chelvanayakam agreement of 1957 and the Senanayake-Chelvanayakam agreement of 1965 were crucial landmarks in the ethnic politics of accommodation failure. The inflexibility of Sinhalese nationalism in responding to minority ethnic grievances and aspirations as well as the electoral politics of "ethnic outbidding" have been crucial in shaping the breakdown of Sinhalese–Tamil ethnic relations throughout these years.[4]

The immediate circumstances that saw the transition of Tamil ethnic politics from a demand for regional autonomy to secession evolved in the late 1970s. The promulgation of a strictly unitary republican constitution in 1972 by the United Front government, ignoring the Tamil demands for regional autonomy, created conditions for a decisive rupture of Tamil trust in the Sinhalese political class. The resultant tension between the Tamil nationalist Federal Party and the United Front regime had produced some violence that included police killing of Tamil civilians and assassinations by Tamil radical activists. These incidents marked a shift towards confrontation in state–Tamil relations. At the parliamentary election of 1977, the newly formed Tamil United Liberation Front (TULF) contested the seats in the Tamil-dominated Northern and

Eastern Provinces, seeking a mandate from Tamil voters to campaign for independence. This was the beginning of the struggle for "Eelam," a separate Tamil ethnic state. The TULF, having won 17 of the 19 parliamentary seats in the two provinces, seemed to have expected the ruling United National Party (UNP) to initiate negotiations so that some measure of autonomy could be won for the Tamils. But the UNP government under President Junius Jayewardene was not willing to concede regional autonomy to the Tamils. Instead, the government offered in 1981 limited administrative decentralization by establishing a system of district development councils (DDCs). The growing violence between incipient Tamil armed groups and the state in the Northern Province had by this time created an atmosphere of increasing tension in government–Tamil relations. The government's resort to emergency law and the enactment of the Prevention of Terrorism Act in 1979 indicated that its priority was to defeat "Tamil terrorism" by means of law and order measures, rather than addressing the political demands of the Tamil minority.[5] The government's deployment of violence against Tamils in 1981 in Jaffna, the symbolic heartland of northern Tamil society, during the elections to the DDCs, sent the worst possible signal to the Tamils: the Sinhalese political establishment was not willing to concede even administrative decentralization to the Northern and Eastern Provinces. This provided the context for greater radicalization of Tamil nationalist politics. Thus, the politics of bargaining that the TULF had been practicing, even after obtaining an electoral mandate from the Tamil electorate, was increasingly replaced by the politics of "armed struggle" for "national self-determination."

It was against such a backdrop of increasing tension in state–Tamil relations that the anti-Tamil violence occurred in July 1983. This ethnic violence appeared to have been sponsored by sections linked to the UNP regime and even tolerated by the government and its leaders. Sinhalese mobs, backed by

nationalist groups, and often encouraged by sections of the state apparatus, attacked, wounded, killed, and even burnt alive Tamil citizens in the Sinhalese majority areas, including the capital city of Colombo. Property belonging to Tamil families, including houses and commercial establishments, were set on fire and destroyed almost as if in accordance with a premeditated plan. The most troubling aspect of this anti-minority violence was the government's inaction to control mob violence for a few days. It indeed gave the impression that the government saw the violence as a politically necessary development in order to control a politically assertive ethnic minority. During the violence spread over a week in the month of July 1983 many thousands of Tamil citizens were displaced as internal refugees. The government sent many of them to the Tamil majority Northern Province, ostensibly for their safety. But it also gave the Tamils the unfortunate signal that the state could not protect them outside the Northern Province.[6]

The atrocities of July 1983 widened the chasm between the Sri Lankan state and the Tamil community. It also led to the effective replacement of parliamentary Tamil nationalist politics by an armed struggle for separation. Tamil militant groups that were active in sporadic guerrilla operations against the government found the post-July 1983 situation most favorable to claims for their legitimacy and the validity of their tactics. With support and solidarity from the Tamils in southern India, and access to new sources of recruitment and material support, a number of militant groups relaunched their "national liberation armed struggle," seeking the establishment of the state of Eelam in the Northern and Eastern Provinces.

Trends in the Tamil armed struggle

In the early days of the Tamil nationalist insurgency in Sri Lanka in the late 1970s, there was no unified resistance movement as such.

There were a number of armed groups with different ideological commitments and organizational identities. All were Tamil nationalist in ideological persuasion, but some were Left–oriented. The Left–nationalist groups were the Eelam People's Revolutionary Liberation Front (EPRLF), Eelam Revolutionary Organization of Students (EROS) and People's Liberation Organization of Tamil Eelam (PLOTE). The Liberation Tigers of Tamil Eelam (LTTE) was the most nationalist of all the militant groups. After July 1983, all these organizations operated from southern India where they had obtained either political asylum or enjoyed the status of guests. Almost all these militant groups are reported to have received training in guerrilla warfare while in India. Some sources say that the Indian intelligence agencies were instrumental in providing military training for these groups, as well as weapons and material support, an allegation officially denied by India.[7]

In August 1984 the Tamil militant groups formed a united front to take part in the peace talks held in Thimpu, the capital of Bhutan. These talks were facilitated by the Indian government. The Tamil militant groups and the TULF, which was in exile in India at the time, seemed to be relying more on the outcome of the armed struggle than a compromise through negotiations. In the same vein, the Sri Lankan government showed no interest in meeting Tamil nationalist aspirations through negotiations. From the perspective of the dynamics of the civil war, it was too early for either party to move away from unilateral outcomes which they pursued through military means. The government's overall objective was to defeat the Tamil insurgency militarily and "unify" the state. By the same token, the Tamil militant groups were committed to an armed struggle for secession. Thus, negotiations did not mean much for the strategies of either the government or the Tamil nationalist rebels. Although the Thimpu talks failed to produce an outcome leading to ethnic conflict resolution, the talks were significant in the sense that the Tamil groups formulated four principles which, from

their perspective, were to constitute the essential framework for a negotiated settlement:

1   recognition of the Tamils as a distinct nationality in Sri Lanka
2   recognition of a Tamil homeland
3   recognition of the right of the Tamil people for self-determination
4   recognition of the right to full citizenship of all Tamils living in the island.[8]

The role of the Indian government in altering the trajectory of Sri Lanka's ethnic conflict in the early and mid-1980s is crucial to an understanding of the ways in which the Tamil nationalist insurgency developed in that period. Although the Indian government of Prime Minister Indira Gandhi gave covert support to Tamil militants, there was also the apprehension among policy circles in New Delhi that the Tamil insurgency might become an unmanageable conflict with regional consequences. The Thimpu talks arranged on the initiative of Prime Minister Rajiv Gandhi gave a clear indication that the Indian political and bureaucratic elites were exploring a negotiated political settlement to the civil war. The Indian engagement with both the Sri Lankan government and the Tamil nationalist groups through diplomatic channels eventually led to the Indo-Lanka Accord of July 1987. The accord was signed in Colombo by the Indian prime minister and the Sri Lankan president.[9] It proposed for the Sri Lankan government to establish a system of "devolution of power" in exchange for laying down of their arms by the Tamil militant groups, disbanding their guerrilla units, and joining the political "mainstream." The Indian government was to act as the guarantor of the implementation of the accord. At the time it was signed, the accord appeared to be a major breakthrough in the direction of resolving the ethnic conflict by political–constitutional means.

The success of the Indo–Lanka Accord depended on two crucial factors: the willingness of the Sri Lankan government to constitutionalize the devolution framework and of the Tamil militant groups to accept the peace deal and give up the armed struggle. The government, despite resistance from within it and oppositionist Sinhalese nationalist forces, established provincial councils through a constitutional amendment before the end of 1987. Most of the Tamil militant groups also accepted the accord, surrendered their weapons, and agreed to join the parliamentary political process. The leading groups among them were the EPRLF, PLOTE, EROS, and TELO, but not the LTTE. The last had by this time emerged as a powerful military entity. The LTTE did not surrender weapons or accept the framework of political solution offered by the Indo–Lanka Accord. Instead, it continued the armed struggle. In October 1987 the Indian army was inducted in Sri Lanka, in accordance with the terms of the accord, to ensure the surrender of weapons by the LTTE. That engagement soon led to a new phase of Sri Lanka's civil war between the Indian peacekeeping troops and the LTTE, which lasted until March–April 1990 when the new Sri Lankan government forced the Indian government to withdraw from its military engagement on the island.[10]

The Indian involvement in 1987 through the Indo-Lanka Accord in a way resulted in a significant transformation of Tamil militant politics in Sri Lanka. While it created conditions for the TULF to return to Sri Lanka from exile in India and re-enter parliament, it also provided political space for a number of Tamil militant groups to give up the armed struggle for secession. They came to the conclusion that a separate Tamil state was no longer a viable political goal. In 1988, the EPRLF became the governing party of the first provincial council of the Northern and Eastern Provinces. Subsequently, the EPRLF as well as the PLOTE, EROS and TELO, and the newly emerged Eelam People's Democratic Party (EPDP) took part in parliamentary elections and their representatives were elected to parliament. The EPDP even became members of the SLFP-led cabinet. This transformation of Tamil militant groups stands in sharp contrast to the LTTE's continuing commitment to the goal of Eelam, a separate Tamil state, through armed struggle.

Negotiations and their outcomes

Sri Lanka's civil war has also been interspersed with a number of attempts at a negotiated political settlement.[11] The first attempt, as already noted, was made in 1984. The Thimpu talks did not produce an outcome. The second attempt was the Indo–Lanka Accord of July 1987, with the involvement of the Indian and Sri Lankan governments. It produced a constitutional framework for a political solution—the provincial council system—and created conditions for a number of Tamil militant groups to give up the armed struggle and join parliamentary politics. But it did not lead to the termination of the civil war or the resolution of the ethnic conflict.

The third attempt at a negotiated solution was made in 1989–90 by President Ranasinghe Premadasa, who assumed office in January 1989 amidst a massive political crisis.[12] The war between the Indian peacekeeping troops and the LTTE was raging and the armed insurgency led by the JVP against the government was at its peak. In April 1989 President Premadasa called on both the LTTE and the JVP for talks. While the JVP refused the invitation for talks, the LTTE responded positively. The two sides held talks for about a year. During these talks, the JVP intensified its armed attacks on the state in the belief that it could push the government out of power in the midst of the crisis. However, utilizing the breathing space created by the talks with the LTTE, the Premadasa regime launched a massive and ruthless counterinsurgency war against the JVP. By the end of 1989, the government managed to crush the JVP insurgency with deadly efficiency, resulting in 40,000–50,000 deaths. Meanwhile, the negotiations between the Premadasa regime and the LTTE during this counterinsurgency war seemed to be guided merely by the tactical consideration of both sides and not by any serious commitment to a negotiated settlement. The Premadasa regime's immediate tactical goal was the management of the political crisis by defeating the JVP insurgency and sending the Indian peacekeeping troops back to India. The LTTE's tactical goal was to make use of the Premadasa regime to get rid of the Indian peacekeeping troops, which had risen above 75,000 in numbers. When both sides were satisfied that they had achieved their separate objectives, there was no need for them to produce a tangible outcome from the talks or even to continue them. In June 1990, the LTTE broke the unofficial ceasefire with the government and resumed hostilities. Thus began the so-called Third Eelam War in Sri Lanka that continued till the next ceasefire of January 1995.

The change of government in 1994 led to another round of negotiations between the government and the LTTE. The newly formed People's Alliance, led by the Sri Lanka Freedom Party (SLFP) with some Left parties as coalition partners, campaigned for the parliamentary election of August 1994 and the presidential election of November that year on a "peace platform." The initial talks between the two sides that began in September 1994 led to a formal Cessation of Hostilities Agreement (CHA), signed in January 1995. Although the two sides then held three rounds of direct talks and exchanged many letters, this engagement too failed to produce any agreement to bring the civil war to an end. Citing as its reasons the government's lack of commitment to the restoration of peace, the LTTE unilaterally abrogated the CHA on 19 April, 1995. That created immediate conditions for the two sides to relapse into war. In this new face of the conflict, the People's Alliance government, led by President Chandrika Kumaratunga, adopted a dual strategy of constitutional reforms and war. The constitutional reform package, announced in August 1995, promised greater devolution of power to the existing provincial councils in a framework approximating semi-federalism. The military

dimension of the government strategy had two objectives. Weakening the LTTE militarily was the first. The government expected that a militarily weakened LTTE would eventually return to the negotiation table and then the government's offer for enhanced devolution would constitute the basis for negotiations and a settlement agreement. The second objective was to appeal directly to the Tamil people and the non-LTTE Tamil parties to accept the government's unilateral offer and then eventually isolate the LTTE both politically and militarily. None of these objectives was achieved. The war continued till the year 2001 with huge human, material and battlefield costs. Although the government succeeded in capturing the Jaffna peninsula from the control of the LTTE, the LTTE retreated to the Vanni jungles located south of Jaffna and engaged the state armed forces in a protracted war that combined both the guerrilla tactics and conventional warfare.

The next round of peace talks began in early 2002 after the change of government occasioned by the parliamentary elections of December 2001. The new United National Front government, led by Prime Minister Ranil Wickramasinghe, signed a ceasefire agreement (CFA) with the LTTE on 22 February, 2002 and held five rounds of negotiations. The peace talks of 2002 set three specific conditions that were absent in previous negotiations. First, a ceasefire agreement jointly signed by the prime minister and the LTTE leader and monitored by an international (Nordic) monitoring committee provided a framework for managing violence. Second, a third party, the Royal Norwegian government, acted as the facilitator and mediator for the CFA as well as negotiations. Third, the international community, coordinated by the EU, the US, and Japan, came forward to provide direct economic assistance to peace building to encourage the parties to move towards a comprehensive peace agreement. Something closer to a breakthrough in the negotiations occurred in December 2002 when, during the Oslo talks, the government

295

and the LTTE agreed to "explore" a solution to the ethnic conflict based on a "federal" framework within a "united" Sri Lanka. However, that exploration did not go far when the LTTE decided in March–April 2003 to suspend its participation in negotiations, alleging that the UNF government was slow in implementing promises made at negotiations. Attempts made by the international actors, local civil society groups and the government to persuade the LTTE to return to the negotiation table throughout 2003 did not succeed.

Meanwhile, in October 2003, the LTTE presented to the government a set of proposals for an interim self-governing authority (ISGA). The LTTE expected these proposals to be the basis for the resumption of stalled negotiations. In the ISGA proposals, the LTTE envisaged a framework of self-rule and autonomy for the Northern and Eastern Provinces that went beyond Sri Lanka's existing constitution and even the conventional understanding of federalism. The ISGA proposals actually approximated a confederal model, although the LTTE described them as a framework for an "interim" solution. Soon after these proposals were submitted, a political crisis developed in Colombo, leading to the dissolution of the government by the president. At the parliamentary elections held in April 2004, the UNF, which had so far engaged the LTTE politically, lost power. A new Sinhalese nationalist coalition, led by the SLFP, won the parliamentary election after a campaign that portrayed the UNP–LTTE negotiations and the CFA as having endangered national security, state sovereignty, and the state capacity to fight terrorism by military means. In the new conditions of severe polarization of political forces on the question of war or peace, there was hardly any space for the new government and the LTTE to resume political engagement. The return to war by either side or both was prevented only by the CFA, monitored by the Sri Lanka Monitoring Mission (SLMM).

The year 2004 saw the steady erosion of the peace process that began in early 2002.

Violations of the CFA by both sides went on unabated. The ceasefire monitors blamed the LTTE more than the government for the violations. In such a context of growing unease and tension in conditions of "no war–no peace," the tsunami disaster occurred on 26 December, 2004. Coastal communities in areas under the control of the government as well as the LTTE suffered massive destruction. The great humanitarian tragedy of the tsunami offered an opportunity for both the government and the LTTE to resume engagement on humanitarian grounds. But they failed to take that opportunity forward to resume formal negotiations for ethnic conflict resolution. Even the initiative taken by the two parties to set up a joint mechanism for humanitarian cooperation through a post-tsunami operational mechanism (P-TOM) was thwarted by the judiciary, backed by the Sinhalese nationalist forces.[13] The subsequent change of government that occurred after the presidential election of December 2005 did not lead to resumption of the peace process as such, even though two rounds of peace talks were held in Geneva. The period after 2006 saw a steady re-escalation of violence leading to full-scale war. The government and the LTTE fought an "undeclared war" until early 2007. When the government withdrew from the CFA in early 2007, the international monitoring too ceased to exist.

A question of state

At the heart of Sri Lanka's ethnic conflict, civil war, and violence is the question whether state power should or should not be shared among Sinhalese, Tamil, and Muslim ethnic communities.[14] The capture of the state by the ethnic majority and the exclusion of the ethnic minorities from exercising state power were developments that led to the consolidation of a postcolonial Tamil nationalist project in the immediate post-Independence years. The formulation of a federalist demand took place as early as 1951, within three years of political independence, on the argument that the unitary state needed to be reformed to accommodate minority aspirations. The citizenship and franchise legislation of 1948 and 1949 enacted by the first post-Independence regime in fact discriminated against the Tamil-speaking minorities. The making of Sinhalese the official language of the state further entrenched the majoritarian character of the postcolonial Sri Lankan state. When the Tamil leaders formed the Federal Party in 1951, one key political assumption on which the demand for regional autonomy was formulated was that the Sri Lankan Tamils constituted a separate "nationality," not just an ethnic minority. In the Tamil nationalist imagination, a separate nationality had the right to share state power in a federal framework. The notion of self-determination, in its initial phase, was interpreted in the Tamil nationalist project as the right to regional autonomy.[15]

It is precisely this demand by the Tamil minority for sharing state power on the basis of ethnicity that generated much resistance in the majority Sinhalese polity. Thus, the Sinhalese nationalism of the post-Independence years came to be defined not only in opposition to the European ex-colonial powers, but also against the politics of the Tamil ethnic minority. The competing projects of postcolonial state building had two perspectives and paths that were mutually exclusive: centralized unitary state or decentralized federal state. The Eelam demand, which the Tamil nationalists developed in the late 1970s, gave an extreme interpretation to the concept of national self-determination, namely, the right to form a separate territorial state. This transition of the Tamil nationalist goal from regional autonomy to statehood constituted the key dimension that characterized Tamil politics after the late 1970s. The civil war that began in the early 1980s highlighted the incompatibility of these two state formation projects.

A third dimension of state formation developed in the 1980s in the midst of the war between the state and Tamil rebels. That was the aspiration of the Muslim community for regional autonomy. The Muslims in Sri Lanka are a dispersed minority, but in the Amparai district of the Eastern Province, they constitute a regional majority. In the Batticaloa district of the Eastern Province, too, there is a sizeable concentration of a Muslim population. There have been such Muslim concentrations in the Northern Province as well. Conventionally, the Tamil nationalists had developed the formulation, "Tamil-speaking people in Sri Lanka" to include the Muslim community whose language was Tamil. However, in the context of repeated violence which the Tamil militant groups had unleashed against the Muslims in the north and east, a new Muslim political leadership emerged in the late 1980s to argue for a separate Muslim ethnic and political identity. Consequently, the Sri Lanka Muslim Congress was formed in 1988. Subsequently, a number of other Muslim political groups also emerged to campaign for Muslim rights in the conflict areas. A key argument developed by these Muslim groups is that Muslims should be a direct party to any negotiated settlement to the ethnic conflict and that, in any power-sharing arrangement between Sinhalese and Tamil political elites, regional autonomy to the Muslims in the north and east should be included. The Muslim demand for regional autonomy has been developed into the idea of a non-contiguous Muslim-majority unit in the Northern and Eastern Provinces.

One of the reasons why negotiations for a political solution to the conflict have repeatedly failed in Sri Lanka is the complexity of the question of state power that the negotiations failed to address. The Sinhalese political establishment that represented the Sri Lankan state was initially reluctant to reform the state at all in response to minority demands. They were committed to preserving and maintaining the unitary and centralized state with administrative decentralization granted to the periphery. Reforming the state in response to ethnic minority demands was seen by the Sinhalese political establishment as conduct unbecoming of the leadership of the majority ethnic community. The federalist demand of a relatively small ethnic minority was seen by the majority as an unreasonable demand. Meanwhile, the Tamil nationalists thought that the Tamils constituted a nation, or a nationality, that deserved an equal share of state power through a federal constitutional arrangement. When the Sinhalese political leadership began to show some willingness to consider power sharing, which occurred in response to the armed rebellion, the Tamil nationalists had by then moved far away from power sharing towards secession. During negotiations in the mid-1980s and after, the gulf between the framework of solution acceptable to the Sinhalese political establishment and the Tamil nationalist actors was vast. A middle ground on which a compromise could be worked out could have been a framework of federalism, which was beyond the acceptable framework for the Sinhalese majority and much less than what the Tamil nationalism of the LTTE would have accepted as an alternative to secession. As a middle ground, a federalist framework still remains unwanted.

The Muslim demand for recognition and autonomy in the conflict has introduced a third dimension to the central question of state power to be settled in the process of a negotiated political solution. As mentioned earlier, the Muslim community in the Eastern Province demands territorial autonomy. The basis of their demand is that a two-party solution that would grant the Tamil community regional autonomy would make them, the Muslims, a permanently disempowered regional minority. A tripartite settlement, as they envisage it, would empower Muslims as a regional minority. The Sinhalese and Tamil political classes are quite reluctant to acknowledge this Muslim demand for a share of state power.

One key issue that has made political negotiations between the Sri Lankan government and the LTTE quite complex is the self-representation of the LTTE as the ruling stratum of an emerging or parallel "state" of the Tamil "nation." The LTTE's own concept of "equality of status" with the Sri Lankan government in negotiations was defined in this notion of a parallel state, which no Sri Lankan government or international actor has even acknowledged. Thinking and even acting like a parallel state, the LTTE took part in peace processes with a particular vision of a possible political solution, that is, winning regional statehood through negotiations.[16] The ISGA proposals of October 2003, to which we have already made reference, were obviously conceived in this framework of thinking and acting like a parallel state. Such a maximalist perspective could hardly constitute the basis for negotiations for a settlement acceptable to the Sri Lankan government. Sri Lanka's political reform agenda thus remained entrapped in the minimalism of the Sinhalese political class and the maximalism of the Tamil political class.

Can ethnicity-based state reforms provide a sustainable basis for a political settlement to Sri Lanka's ethnic conflict? This question has emerged in Sri Lanka's political debate from time to time. Some argue that ethnicity-based devolution will further polarize the already divided ethnic communities, create ethnic enclaves and make interethnic reconciliation difficult. Others argue that devolution or federalism without a strong human rights framework would only create regional entities of authoritarianism in the name of peace. This constitutes a major dilemma in the conflict resolution process in Sri Lanka. The ethnic conflict and the protracted war have repeatedly reinforced the ethnic identities, ethnic politics, and ethnicized political visions. Sri Lanka's ethnic communities see political emancipation from ethnic eyes. Ethnicity is a political reality that cannot be wished away. At the same time, solutions to ethnic conflicts may not necessarily be ethnic ones. Ethnic conflicts, as the debate over Sri Lanka's future suggests, require democratic solutions.

Political economy of war

In discussing the dynamics of the reproduction of war and violence in Sri Lanka, some analysts have pointed out that the protracted war produced a specific culture and economy of war. Rajasingham-Senanayake is among the earliest commentators to make the argument that the armed conflict had generated a specific logic and momentum, exceeding the ethnic roots of the conflict.[17] This logic and momentum are also propelled forward by what has been termed a "hidden economy of war" that has provided violence and war with an internal momentum of its own. Rajasingham-Senanayake makes the further argument that the hidden economy of war moved the conflict away from its ethnic foundations: the war was not just about ethnic identities and ethnic agendas, but it propelled forward for its own sake.

Sri Lanka's political economy of war seemed to possess a number of key dimensions, some open and others hidden. The capacity of the national economy to adjust itself to the continuing war amidst macroeconomic liberalization and structural adjustment programmes of the 1980s and the 1990s is noteworthy. As some economists point out, the war did not create a major economic crisis leading to the necessity of war termination.[18] Bastian argues that Sri Lanka's greater integration with the global economy after economic liberalization that began in 1977 had been a major factor that paradoxically protected the economy from war-induced crisis.[19] The donor policy towards Sri Lanka during the conflict was to promote liberalization of the economy along with liberal political reforms. Humanitarian assistance and peace promotion, along with macroeconomic support from bilateral and multilateral sources, were fairly consistent throughout the period of civil war. Donor assistance for peace promotion was a particularly significant policy plank that became salient after the mid-1990s.[20] In this context, it is important to recall that the argument for a peace dividend, highlighted in 1994–2000 and 2002–2003 by

peace constituencies, failed to convince the policymakers, the bureaucracy or the citizens that there was a strong economic argument for termination of the civil war through a negotiated political settlement.

The hidden economy of war has generated another logic in conflict areas which can be explained in the language of Charles Tilly.[21] It is about the emergence of informal regimes of illegal taxation, extortion networks, and protection rackets. In the conflict areas and in the so-called border areas where there is no clear political–military authority, these networks and rackets have emerged in the context of state collapse. The LTTE's so-called parallel state could be considered as an institutionalization of this hidden political economy of war in a context of relative absence in some conflict areas of the Sri Lankan state, except in the form of its war machine. In the "border" regions, the agents of the hidden economy of war were multiple, including especially the military and a variety of paramilitary groups.

Future of the conflict?

Concerning how Sri Lanka's ethnic conflict should end, there were five clearly discernible perspectives. Two of them were unilateral and extreme solutions. The LTTE's goal of secession by mean of a protracted armed struggle and the Sinhalese nationalist goal of restoring the unitary state by militarily defeating the LTTE and Tamil militancy were the two extreme perspectives. A confederalist constitutional framework of two nations within one state having two political systems would have been the LTTE's option to reconsider the secessionist goal. But as a model of a political solution, it had no takers outside the LTTE, certainly not in Sinhalese society. A federal framework was the fourth perspective, which had support among non-LTTE Tamil groups and in Sri Lanka's civil society. It sought to expand the present framework of devolution by granting more regional autonomy to the provinces. The fifth was minimalist devolution that did not go beyond a limited imple-mentation of the existing Thirteenth Amend-ment and the provincial councils. The formulation developed by Sri Lanka's present government, "maximum devolution within a unitary state," encapsulated this position. Whether any of these five options will even-tually be adopted now that the LTTE has been defeated and its leaders killed is a difficult question.

The trajectories of Sri Lanka's conflict have shown that its turns and developments were characterized by a strong element of unpredictability. Political scientists and conflict resolution professionals were particularly vulnerable to the temptation of predicting the future paths of the conflict, and specifically outcomes of peace negotiations. A sober lesson to learn from the past experience is that conflict outcomes are difficult to predict because every conflict has a specific dynamism with a constant propensity and capacity to redefine and reconstitute itself. For example, ceasefire agreements and peace negotiations did not lead to conflict mitigation or settle-ment, but to redefining the dimensions of the conflict, bringing new actors into the equa-tion, new contradictions to the process, new fears and anxieties about the outcomes, and new priorities to the agenda. Inconclu-sive peace attempts reinforced the arguments for giving war another, fresh chance. Similarly, peace was never a clear concept throughout the conflict, although those committed to peace continued to believe in it as a shared moral goal for all. In fact, Sri Lanka's experience has demonstrated that peace is intensely contested as a process, as an outcome and as a goal. For example, what the govern-ment envisioned as peace is not what the Tamil nationalists sought as peace. In the same vein, what the international actors perceived as peace in Sri Lanka was not what the domes-tic actors wanted as peace. In Sri Lanka's civil war, both war and "peace" were mutually sustaining processes. In the absence of a commitment to a shared understanding of peace as a process, as an outcome and as a

political goal, the conflict seems to possess the potential to reproduce itself for quite some time to come.

Summoning all the knowledge and experi-ence one may have gained trough observing the ways in which Sri Lanka's ethnic conflict and civil war progressed, one can say only that de-linking the ethnic conflict from war and violence would have been a crucial pre-condition for ethnic peace.

Notes

1 The literature on the beginnings of the civil war is quite large. Some key writings are Keteshwaran Loganathan, *Sri Lanka, Lost Opportunities: Past Attempts at Resolving Ethnic Conflict* (Colombo: University of Colombo Press, 1996); K. M. De Silva, *Reaping the Whirlwind: Ethnic Conflict and Ethnic Politics in Sri Lanka* (New Delhi: Penguin, 1998); A. J. Wilson, *Break up of Sri Lanka: The Sinhalese–Tamil Conflict* (London: C. Hurst & Co., 1988); and John Richardson, *Paradise Poisoned: Learning about Conflict, Terrorism and Development from Sri Lanka's Civil Wars* (Kandy: International Centre for Ethnic Studies, 2004). Anton Balasingham, *War and Peace in Sri Lanka, Armed Struggle and Peace Efforts of Liberation Tigers* (Mitcham: Fairmax, 2004) provides the Tamil nationalist—or rather the LTTE—perspectives on the origins and spread of Sri Lanka's civil war.
2 Neelan Tiruchelvam, "The Politics of Federalism and Diversity in Sri Lanka," in Yash Ghai (ed.), *Autonomy and Ethnicity: Negotiating Competing Claims in Multi-ethnic States* (Cambridge: University Press, 2000), p. 198.
3 See Robert Kearney, *Communalism and Language in the Politics of Ceylon* (Durham, NC: Duke University Press, 1967; Wilson; Howard Wriggins, *Ceylon: Dilemmas of a New Nation* (Princeton, NJ: University Press, 1960); Michael Roberts, "Ethnic Conflict in Sri Lanka and Sinhalese Perspectives: Barriers to Accommodation," *Modern Asian Studies*, Vol. 12, No. 3 (1978), pp. 353–76.
4 For a detailed study of the politics of ethnic outbidding in the context of Sri Lanka's party politics and electoral competition, see Neil DeVotta, "From Ethnic Outbidding to Ethnic Conflict: The Institutional Bases for Sri Lanka's

Separatist War," in P. Sahadevan and Neil DeVotta (eds), *Politics of Conflict and Peace in Sri Lanka* (New Delhi: Manak, 2006), pp. 3–29.

5   N. Manoharan, *Counterterrorism Legislation in Sri Lanka: Evaluating Efficacy, Policy Studies No. 28* (Washington, DC: East-West Center, 2006) provides a very useful account of the counter-terrorism legislation introduced in Sri Lanka in the context of armed insurgencies in the 1970s and 1980s and their contribution to the overall political process in the country.

6   For some useful accounts of the anti-Tamil violence of 1983, see V. Kanapathipillai, "July 1983: The Survivors' Experience," in Veena Das (ed.), *Mirrors of Violence: Communities, Riots and Survivors in South Asia* (New Delhi: Oxford University Press), 1990; James Manor (ed.), *Sri Lanka in Change and Crisis* (London: Croom Helm, 1984); and Jonathan Spencer, "Collective Violence and Everyday Practice in Sri Lanka," *Modern Asian Studies*, 24 (1990), pp. 603–23.

7   Academic literature in English on Sri Lanka's Tamil militant groups is extremely thin. However, there are useful accounts written by journalists who have had access to some of these organizations and their leaders. Two important works are Anita Pratap, *Island of Blood* (Bombay: Penguin, 2001) and M. R. Swamy Narayan, *Tigers of Lanka: From Boys to Guerrillas* (New Delhi: South Asia Books, 1995).

8   Loganathan (pp. 104–05) provides the best available account on the Thimpu talks. He was a participant at these talks, representing the EPRLF.

9   The Indian intentions and motives in pushing for the accord have been given different interpretations. For a firsthand account of it, see J. N. Dixit, *Assignment Colombo* (New Delhi: Konark, 1998). Dixit was India's High Commissioner in Colombo during these crucial months. Krishna provides an academic critique of Indian motives, basically arguing that it was a part of the Indian ruling elite's pre-occupation with replicating its own political and nation-state model in South Asia; Sankaran Krishna, *Postcolonial Insecurities: India, Sri Lanka and the Question of Nationhood* (Minneapolis, MN: University of Minnesota Press, 1999). For a set of Sri Lankan perspectives on the theme see Shelton U. Kodikara, *Indo–Sri Lanka Accord of July 1987* (Colombo: University of Colombo Press, 1989).

10 Literature on the Indian political and military engagement in Sri Lanka in 1980s is quite extensive. Some key texts are Dixit; Krishna; and S. D. Muni, *Pangs of Proximity: India's and Sri Lanka's Ethnic Crisis* (New Delhi: Sage Publications, 1993).

11 There is a growing body of literature on peace negotiations in Sri Lanka. The two-volume anthology edited by Rupesinghe is most useful; Kumar Rupesinghe (ed.), *Negotiating Peace in Sri Lanka: Efforts, Failures and Lessons* (Colombo: Foundation for Co-Existence, 2006).

12 The literature on Premadasa government–LTTE negotiations is quite thin, but both Jayatilleke and Weerakoon provide some useful accounts of these talks; Weerakoon and Jayatilleka were insiders of the Premadasa regime. See Dayan Jayatilleke, "Premadasa-LTTE Talks: Why they Failed and What Really Happened," in Kumar Rupesinghe (ed.), *Negotiating Peace in Sri Lanka: Efforts, Failures and Lessons,* 2nd edn, vol. I (Colombo: Foundation for Co-Existence, 2006), pp. 141–56; and Bradman Weerakoon, "Government of Sri Lanka and LTTE Peace Negotiations 1989/90," in Rupesinghe, pp. 111–28.

13 Sri Lanka's failure to use the humanitarian space of the tsunami disaster for peace building stands in sharp contrast to the experience in Indonesia where the government and the GAM rebels (Gerakan Aceh Merdeka or Free Aceh Movement) signed a peace agreement to end the civil war. For a discussion of the political contro-versies surrounding the post-tsunami attempts at peace in Sri Lanka, see Jayadeva Uyangoda, "Ethnic Conflict, the Tsunami Disaster and the State in Sri Lanka," *Inter-Asia Cultural Studies*, Vol. 6, No. 3 (September 2005), pp. 341–52.

14 This point is further developed in Jayadeva Uyangoda, *Ethnic Conflict in Sri Lanka: Changing Dynamics* (Washington, DC: East-West Center, 2007).

15 The concepts "ethnicity" and "ethnic minority" entered Sri Lanka's academic and political discourse only in the early 1980s. "Racial minorities" was the term previously used to refer to ethnic minorities. Similarly, "communalism" was the term used to describe what later came to be described as "minority nationalism" or "ethnic politics."

16 There has been an interesting discussion on the issue of the LTTE's building up of state-like structures in the areas under its control. Stokke's

characterization of them in the language of state building has been passionately resisted by Muthukrishna; see Kristian Stokke, "Building the Tamil Eelam State: Emerging State Institutions and Forms of Governance in LTTE-controlled Areas in Sri Lanka," *Third World Quarterly*, Vol. 27, No. 6 (2006), pp. 1021–40; and Muttukrishna Sarvananthan, "In Pursuit of a Mythical State of Tamil Eelam: Rejoinder to Kristian Stokke," *Third World Quarterly*, Vol. 28, No. 6 (2007), pp. 1185–95.

17 See, Rajasingham-Senanayake (1998) and her subsequent writings.

18 See, for example, Saman Kelegama, "Economic Costs of Conflict in Sri Lanka," in Robert Rotberg (ed.), *Creating Peace in Sri Lanka: Civil War and Reconciliation* (Washington, DC: Brookings Institution, 1999) and "Transformation of a Conflict via an Economic Dividend: The Sri Lankan Experience," in Kumar Rupesinghe (ed.), *Negotiating Peace in Sri Lanka: Efforts, Failures and Lessons, Vol. II* (Colombo: Foundation for Co-existence 2006), pp. 205–39.

19 Sunil Bastian, "Foreign Aid, Globalization and Conflict in Sri Lanka," in Markus Mayer *et al.* (eds), *Building Local Capacities for Peace: Rethinking Conflict and Development in Sri Lanka* (Delhi: Macmillan, 2003); and Sunil Bastian, *The Politics of Foreign Aid in Sri Lanka: Promoting Markets and Supporting Peace* (Colombo: International Center for Ethnic Studies, 2007).

20 The literature that provides discussions on the donor policy towards Sri Lanka amidst conflict and civil war are Bastian, *The Politics of Foreign Aid*; Kelegama, "Managing the Sri Lankan Economy" and "Transformation of a Conflict"; and David Dunham and Sisira Jayasuriya, "Economic Crisis, Poverty and War in Contemporary Sri Lanka: On Ostriches and Tinderboxes," *Economic and Political Weekly*, Vol. 33, No. 49 (5 December, 1998) pp. 3,151–56; and Arve Ofstad, "Countries in Violent Conflict and Aid Strategies: The Case of Sri Lanka," *World Development*, Vol. 30, No. 2 (2002), pp. 165–80.

21 Tilly counterposes the idea of state as a "social contract," with the suggestion that at least in the European contexts, war making and state making have been analogous to organized crime. In civil war contexts, as repeatedly demonstrated in Sri Lanka, the practices of agents of the state and other multiple agents of war, violence, and terror approximates on Tilly's characterization of war and state making. See Charles Tilly, "War Making and State Making as Organized Crime," in Peter B. Evans *et al.* (eds), *Bringing the State Back In* (Cambridge: University Press), pp. 169–91.

Part VI

Political economy

21

The political economy
of development in India
since Independence

Stuart Corbridge

Introduction

India has been acclaimed in recent years as an information technology (IT) superpower and perhaps even as a major new player in the world economy. The Indian economy has been growing at around 5 or 6 percent per annum since 2003, adjusted for population growth, and there are good reasons to suppose that similar rates of growth of gross domestic product (GDP) per capita might be sustainable over the next 20 years. Savings rates are very high in India. Indeed, at just over 30 percent of GDP, gross domestic savings are approaching East Asian levels. The economy sits well inside its total factor productivity frontier, in large part because of low levels of human capital formation, and the country now has the chance to reap a demographic dividend. The ratio of dependants to workers is set to decline from just over 0.6 in 2000 to just under 0.5 in 2025.[1] The launch in January 2008 of the Tata Nano seemed like icing on this cake of economic success. Much was made in the west about a car selling for $2,500, but in India the marketing of a car for Rs 1 lakh (100,000) spoke to the existence of a mass middle class. It also signaled the rise of a small group of Indian capitalists and entrepreneurs who could bestride the global stage. Four-lane highways packed with Nanos

offered a vision of India far removed from one of pot-holed roads shared by bullock carts, scooters, and state-built Ambassador cars. In the words of Gurcharan Das, India had been unbound.[2] It had escaped from a Kafkaesque world of bureaucratic red tape to take its place in the global information age.

There are clearly nuggets of truth in accounts of India's political economy that hinge around 1991, as Das's book largely does. Yet the notion that all was bad or sick before "the reforms," or that all has been good or healthy since, fails to provide a nuanced picture of economic development in India since independence. Recent academic work points out that high rates of economic growth are now being achieved in India in part because of past legacies, some more intended than others, and not wholly in spite of them. Investments in higher education and basic industries are two cases in point.[3] Recent work also points out that economic reform did not begin overnight in 1991, but was prefigured in important respects by the pro-business agendas pursued by Prime Ministers Indira Gandhi and Rajiv Gandhi in the 1980s. In any case, the real turning point in India's trend rate of economic growth was 1980–81, not the early 1990s, although there are signs that the trend rate has improved again since 2003–04.[4]

We also need to acknowledge that post-reform growth in India has reduced absolute poverty less quickly than might have been expected, particularly through the 1990s. The incidence of absolute poverty is much less now than it was at the end of the 1970s, when something like 50 percent of Indians were poor, but a Tata Nano driven from Delhi to Kolkata still takes its riders through the epicenter of world poverty. The government of India (GOI) uses a particularly brutal measure of absolute poverty, one that is more basic even than the "one dollar a day" definition used by the leading multilateral institutions.[5] Yet even on this measure some 260 million people in India are finding it hard to keep body and soul together—fewer than 100 million people less, in total numbers, than the figure of 350 million in 1980.

Social and spatial inequalities have also increased sharply since 1990. Rising inequality levels are inevitable in a country escaping a low-level equilibrium trap, a point made by Simon Kuznets many decades ago.[6] We can refer to "good inequality" where it is based on higher rewards to talent and entrepreneurship. But there is also "bad inequality," and this occurs when people are locked out of markets, or from the schools, roads and other routes that lead to the acquisition of human capital and other transferable skills, perhaps on the basis of gender or caste or ethnicity. What is worrying about recent developments in India is the abundance of bad inequality and unemployment. Governments continue to invest meagerly in the provision of public goods, particularly in the eastern part of the country. Naxalism is one index of pervasive government failure in a group of states running south from Bihar to Andhra Pradesh. For rural people in these states, as the World Bank has recently reminded us, living standards are about on a par with living standards in rural areas of sub-Saharan Africa.[7] They are a long way removed from the living standards of India's urban middle classes. In contrast, as the World Bank also points out, the richer parts of New Delhi, Mumbai, and Bangalore can reasonably be described as India's "Latin Americas."

These inequalities are holding back economic and social development in post-reform India. They led John Harriss and me to conclude that economic reform in India in the 1990s had taken the form of an "elite revolt" against those aspects of the *dirigiste* state that most constrained a loose coalition of business groups and the urban middle classes.[8] That revolt has wrought some important and much needed changes in India's economy. It has also helped to rework key political relations between the central state and the provinces and between the state and its citizens. But the reform process remains highly uneven, both in its mainsprings and in its consequences. I shall argue here that the term "elite revolt" still works well as a descriptor of the contradictory dynamics of political and economic change in India over the past two decades.

Political economy of growth in India, 1950–80

When the British quit India in 1947 they left behind an economy scarred by two centuries during which first preference was given to imperial interests. It is true that the British invested heavily in a railway system that linked most of the major towns and cities in South Asia. They also sank considerable sums of money into the canal colonies of Punjab and provided new systems of property rights and commercial law in both rural and urban areas. The British could even maintain in 1947 that they had built India into the world's tenth largest industrial power. There were large textile industries in Ahmedabad and Bombay, and an iron and steel industry in Bihar and Orissa (thanks mainly to Jamsetji Tata). But what this rosy picture neglects is the involution of the countryside in Bengal that followed the Permanent Settlement of 1793—a settlement that promoted rack-renting landlordism rather than capitalist farming—and the undermining of many of India's craft industries as imports flooded in from Lancashire and elsewhere. The grim truth of British misrule was apparent in a series of famines that hit India at the end of the nineteenth century, and which culminated in the deaths of three million people in the Bengal famine of 1943–44. Alan Heston has estimated that average living standards in the Indian countryside barely improved from 1900 to 1947.[9] There were always significant regional variations within this general picture, but it is likely that as many as two in three Indians lived in absolute poverty at the mid-point of the twentieth century.

Against this backdrop, and given the loss in 1947 of the jute economy of East Bengal (now Bangladesh), as well as the loss of the major port city of Karachi, it is not surprising that India's first plans for economic development took shape in an atmosphere of crisis. The first five-year plan (1951–56) was something of a damp squib and remained broadly neutral as between the agricultural and non-agricultural sectors. After the assassination of Mahatma Gandhi in January 1948, the remaining "tall men" of India's nationalist elite were forced to occupy themselves mainly with nation building in a broader sense, with Sardar Patel working hard to ensure the de facto integration of India's 565 princely states into the new republic, while B. R. Ambedkar and Jawaharlal Nehru oversaw work on the constitution. It was clear by 1950 that India would be a federal democratic republic in which universal suffrage would be coupled to the establishment of a central state with considerable executive and emergency powers and matching geographical reach. Ambedkar and Nehru agreed that the social and economic modernization of India would have to be secured by vigorous planned actions emanating from New Delhi. Conservative politicians sitting in the states would need to be disciplined by wiser and more far sighted men sitting in the country's capital. Modernization was conceived as a diffusion process wherein great pulses of social and economic change— ultimately liberating and uplifting, if often disruptive of established ways of being in the short run—would push outwards from India's major cities to its smallest towns before reaching into the countryside.[10]

Ambedkar would break with Nehru over the failure of his government to transfer surplus lands specifically to so-called untouchable (or *dalit*) families. Ambedkar had warned at the end of the Constituent Assembly debates that India was about "to enter a life of contradictions. In politics we will have equality and in social and economic life we will have inequality." In his view, the failure to redistribute landed wealth in India would put "our democracy in peril."[11] It seems likely that Nehru shared this view, although he had more faith than Ambedkar in the economically empowering effects of political equality. In any case, by 1951 Nehru was unchallenged in his leadership of the Indian National Congress. His ascendancy followed the death of Patel in December 1950 and the defeat of Patel's close supporter, Purushottam Das Tandon, in a struggle for the presidency of the Indian National Congress. But Nehru still had to secure consent for his project of social and economic modernization, and this meant that he had to deal with precisely those state Congress bosses who would conspire against his plans for land-to-the-tiller land reforms in the 1950s.[12]

In retrospect, we can see that Nehru sought to manage the modernization of India by pursuing a development model that was being widely touted by economists even as the second five-year plan was drafted. Early development economics took shape in the 1940s and 1950s around three key ideas. First, there was a critique of comparative advantage theory. Hans Singer and Raoul Prebisch took issue with the idea that latecomer countries could develop effectively as primary goods producers.[13] There were both theoretical and empirical reasons to suppose that prices of non-primary goods rose faster over time than the prices of primary commodities. Developing countries had to build up local (infant) industries as a priority, even if this meant erecting tariff barriers to protect the domestic economy.[14] Second, this commitment to import substitution industrialization (ISI) implied in the short term a run of balance of trade deficits. Developing countries first had to import the machine tools and other goods that would help them build up local manufacturing capacity. A foreign exchange constraint would become especially compelling in a country like India where ISI privileged the production of capital goods (iron and steel, chemicals, heavy engineering, etc). Flows of foreign direct investment were thin on the ground in the 1950s and 1960s, and probably would not have been very welcome in India. A surplus on the capital account would thus have to be achieved by large and continuing inflows of foreign aid. Nehru's ability to position India at the head of the nonaligned movement helped in this respect. India was able to build a steel mill at Bokaro (Bihar) with assistance from the USSR and another at Rourkela (Orissa) with help from West Germany. Third, the very scarcity of foreign exchange in the 1950s and 1960s, coupled with poorly formed local stock markets and often weak private trading systems (some of which were coded as "oppressive" or exploitative), inclined the Government of India (GOI) to think of economic development as a project that had to be planned for and delivered by a beneficent state. Ronald Inden exaggerates only a little when he says that, in the Nehru–Mahalonobis universe, planning came to substitute for religion as the new godhead.[15] Nehru's faith in reason and modernity complemented a more general mid-century faith in technology and progress, both of which needed support from good (or at any rate strong) government.

Thus conceived, India's model of development through most of the 1950s and 1960s made a virtue of deferred gratification. Nehru and Mahalanobis believed that high rates of economic growth would depend on high rates of personal and government savings (equivalent to present consumption foregone), and their efficient mobilization for purposes of large-scale industrialization. By definition, this first wave of capital goods-based production would not be labor intensive; it would not create large numbers of goods for the underemployed peasants who wished (or needed) to leave the countryside to find more productive jobs in the modern sector. This Lewisian transformation would have to await the second stage of India's industrial revolution.[16] Cheap steel, chemicals and power could then be plugged into a plethora of efficient Indian-run companies that would produce bikes, radios, two-wheel tractors and such like for the final consumer.

Put another way, the Nehru–Mahalanobis model presupposed that India would be governed by a developmental state, of the sort that would soon take shape in East or Southeast Asia. This would be a state that was relatively autonomous of privileged local classes, as Marxist theoreticians liked to put it. In India, it would be embodied in the planning commission and the five-year plans. The state would specify a social welfare function for the future (5, 10, 15 or 25 years away) and then devise the best economic and statistical instruments to match inputs to outputs. The model further supposed that the GOI could funnel resources from the agricultural sector to the non-agricultural sector without provoking a backlash among India's rural population. Nehru believed that he could square this circle in two main ways: first, by making use of food aid from the US, and second, by means of land ceilings legislation that would break up unproductive estates and enfranchise efficient small farmers. India's countryside would be bought off not with state funds, but with resources from abroad and by institutional reform at home. Agriculture was the "bargain basement" that would free up scarce resources for use elsewhere in the developing economy.[17] Except it did not, or not as Nehru had hoped.

By the early 1960s it was apparent that increases in grain production were barely keeping pace with population growth. Food supply growth in the 1950s came mainly from increases in the area under cultivation, and now the land frontier was closing. By the mid-1960s many farmers were bemoaning their lot. The great *jat* farmers' leader, Charan Singh, had opposed Nehru's plans for cooperative farming in the 1950s. In 1967, he defected from the Congress, setting up the Bharatiya Kranti Dal in 1969. Charan Singh, in his extensive writings on agriculture and agricultural policy in India, anticipated Michael Lipton's later claim that India was suffering from high levels of urban bias.[18] Government spending decisions were denounced as inequitable, inefficient and unsustainable. In a country where more than 75 percent of the people still lived in the countryside—agriculture's share of GDP was as high as 58 percent in 1950, and not much less than 50 percent in the mid-1960s—it made little sense to waste capital on inefficient urban and industrial projects. The need instead was to fund new irrigation systems and off-farm employment growth in the countryside.

This view gained currency at the end of the 1960s, following the failures of the 1965 and 1966 monsoons and in the wake of new data showing that the incidence of absolute poverty in the Indian countryside had increased between 1961 and 1969.[19] Nehru died before the crisis of India's agriculture was fully exposed and before the suspension of planning in 1966–69. But his death also came after a disastrous war with China in 1962, and these events taken in the round would continue to infect the poisonous political and economic atmospheres in which first Lal Bahadur Shastri (1964–66) and then Indira Gandhi had to make their way as prime ministers.

Indira Gandhi has many times been compared unfavorably with her father (Nehru), and very often for good reason. She deserves to be condemned above all for the disastrous way that she fought religious fire with fire in Punjab in the early 1980s, when she covertly supported Sant Jarnail Singh Bhindranwale, and for her government's suspension of democratic rule in India during the Emergency (1975–77). But what is sometimes forgotten in these comparisons is that Mrs Gandhi came to power at a time when India's democracy was deepening, when the dominance of the Congress system was for the first time being challenged in New Delhi and the states, and when state–society relations more generally, in the words of Lloyd and Susanne Rudolph, had

moved from a pattern of "command politics" to one of "demand politics."[20] The new political landscape of the 1970s and 1980s saw not only the deinstitutionalization of Congress and the rise of credible opposition parties; it also marked a period in India's political economy when a prospectively developmental state imploded.[21] That state had always been an uneasy construct in India, as Partha Chatterjee and Sudipta Kaviraj have several times reminded us.[22] Nehru mobilized large sections of the English-speaking "progressive" elite in support of his modernizing agenda. But this elite was fated to see its ambitions translated at local level by power brokers who rarely shared its commitments to the "greater good" or the "long run." Local worlds were more often vernacular worlds, or worlds where commitments were most often forged at the level of a household, kin group or caste community. As Kaviraj so memorably puts it, India's high modernist state "had feet of vernacular clay."[23]

Worse, the developmental state model presupposes an executive state that is autonomous from a country's dominant proprietary elites. Such was the case, for example, in Taiwan, where the ruling elite after 1949 was transplanted from mainland China and was later funded as much by the US as by rental incomes from land. "Land-to-the-tiller" land reform worked in Taiwan, just as it did in South Korea in the 1950s. Regime changes ensured that a developmental state was not confronted by entrenched powers elsewhere in the land. In India, in contrast, as scholars as diverse as Francine Frankel, Pranab Bardhan, and Jagdish Bhagwati have all shown, the developmental state was captured by three interlocking groups: India's richer farmers (who blocked agrarian reform), its industrial bourgeoisie (business houses that took advantage of state-induced scarcities and blocked competition and innovation), and the country's leading bureaucrats (many of whom earned large rental incomes from the "permit-license-quota Raj" built up around ISI, and almost all of whom enforced unproductive rent-seeking behavior on smaller businesses and ordinary citizens).[24]

309

The so-called "Hindu rate of growth" that dogged India in the 1970s reflected the squeeze placed on the country's developmental state by aggressively sectional interests. The state was now forced to accommodate to the demands of these interest groups, no matter whether they acted for the greater good or not. Average GDP growth in the 1970s was 2.9 percent per annum, which was barely positive in per capita income terms. In some accounts, too, the greater costs of participating in India's competitive politics led some politicians to finance their campaigns illegally and/or through abuses of office. Civil servants, for example, were forced to stump up greater rents to acquire a desirable posting, or to head off an undesirable one. Criminals, for their part, moved into politics, both to milk the system and to head off unwelcome attention from the justice system. The criminalization of politics became particularly marked in parts of north India from the 1970s and posed yet another barrier to economic reform there.

Lobbying, of course, is endemic to all political systems, and what is called lobbying in Washington or London is all too routinely described as corruption in New Delhi or Dhaka. Corruption also comes in many forms, and when it takes the form of speed money payments it can grease the wheels of an economic system that otherwise tends to atrophy or entropy. And it is at this systemic level, as economic reformers like Bhagwati and Srinivasan have consistently pointed out, that the bigger picture lies.[25] The failure of the Congress party in the 1950s and 1960s to support an executive/developmental state left India's economy between two stools. On the one hand, the state was not strong enough to force the commanding heights of the economy to be lean and mean, let alone to dispense with the subsidies and protectionist barriers that were meant to provide them with *temporary* support. Neither management nor organized labor believed that governments in the 1970s or 1980s had the guts to get tough with them. On the other hand, the central role occupied by the state in India's productive economy—

from steel to cars to banking—was so great that it suffocated innovation and new startups in the organized private sector. Even into the mid-1980s, India's leading industrial houses were happy to connive in the reproduction of this world of the second or third best. For that to change, or so this argument goes, the contradictions of *dirigiste* development in India would necessarily come to a head, as they did with the fiscal and balance of payments crises of the early 1990s. Only then would politicians and leading businesspeople in India be forced to reform the economy and the systems of politics that had supported economic mismanagement on a grand scale.

Political economy of reform in India

As ever, it is not difficult to recognize the truth of some of these claims. But what this narrative of rise, decline and recovery cannot account for is the upturn in India's rate of economic growth post-1980. The fact is that per capita incomes in India grew on average at 3.8 percent in the 1980s, or at more or less the same rate as they grew in the 1990s. There are three main reasons why this was so. To begin with, as Atul Kohli has argued, the governments of Indira Gandhi and Rajiv Gandhi (1980–89) began to tilt economic policy more clearly in the direction of big business.[26] The courting of foreign direct investment was still not a priority through the 1980s, although a few joint ventures were brokered in the autos sector. Nevertheless, the strongly anti-capital (especially, anti-foreign capital) rhetoric that Indira Gandhi had deployed in the 1970s was toned down. New initiatives were introduced that favored established Indian producers. In place of *garibi hatao* (an end to poverty), the political platform on which Indira Gandhi made her name in the early 1970s, the Congress governments of the 1980s retired those parts of the Monopolies and Trade Practices Act that made it hard for big business to expand in core sectors like chemicals and cement. Some efforts were also made to liberalize credit for large companies. Perhaps most importantly, both Indira and Rajiv Gandhi took steps to tame labor activism in the organized sector, and to encourage private sector investments with limited tax concessions.

Kohli argues that a major effect of these policy changes was to shift the balance of capital formation in India through the 1980s. Albeit at the margin, it was the private corporate sector that now began to contribute more to economic development, while capital formation in the public sector stabilized after a period of rapid growth in the 1970s. It seems likely, too, that the growth-inducing effects of a pro-business tilt were augmented by the gradual diffusion of Green Revolution technologies out of Punjab, Haryana, and parts of south India. West Bengal now became a Green Revolution heartland, following significant government investment in irrigation and electricity supply.

Poor people in the countryside generally escape from poverty by migrating to towns or cities, or by winning more work in the countryside at higher real wage rates. There is some evidence that labor markets tightened in the 1980s in several states, including West Bengal, Andhra Pradesh, and Karnataka. By 1989–90, the percentage of people in India living in absolute income poverty had reduced to just under 39 percent from 51 percent in 1977–78. The GOI in the early 2000s liked to claim that the rate of poverty reduction accelerated after the reforms of 1991. Most scholars, however, have discounted the suggestion of the 55th round of the National Sample Survey (NSS) that just 26 percent of people were absolutely poor in 1999–2000—an astonishing decline of 10 percent from six years earlier. The 55th round of the NSS broke with the long-established convention of estimating household spending on a uniform reporting period basis. Under this system, respondents recall their spending on all items over a period of 30 days. The 55th round instead introduced a mixed reporting period of weeks, months, and years. This made sense for all sorts of reasons (greater

accuracy of recall, most notably), but it undermined the GOI's efforts to track poverty trends on a consistent basis. Adjustments made to the 55th round data by Angus Deaton and Jean Drèze suggest that the rate of poverty reduction in the 1990s was probably no greater than the rate of poverty reduction in the 1980s.[27] Others, notably Abhijit Sen and Himanshu, have argued that the 1990s was a lost decade for poverty reduction.[28]

Why then, "economic reform"? The usual answer is that the economic growth that led to poverty reduction in the 1980s was unsustainable. Huge subsidies into and out of the agricultural system (cheap fertilizer, water and power in – cheap food out via the public distribution system) ensured that India's growth spurt in the 1980s would push the country into the linked fiscal and balance of payments crises that erupted in 1991. Limited tax concessions to big business in the 1980s, combined with pervasive tax evasion, also forced both Congress party and National Front (1980–91) governments to raise revenues by deficit financing and by borrowing more at home and abroad. Worse, the underlying structures of the Indian economy remained as sclerotic and irrational as ever. India had some of the highest rates of effective protection anywhere in the world. These barriers encouraged Indian business to provide goods and services that were increasingly unwelcome at home and that no one else in the world would buy. Early proponents of reform wondered aloud why Indians at home were condemned to poor service and poor jobs at the hands of the permit-license-quota Raj while Indians abroad were acclaimed for their hard work and innovation.

By circa 1990 it was clear that some elements within India's business communities, led by the Confederation of Indian Industry (CII), as well as significant parts of the urban middle class, were fed up with forms of economic mismanagement that discouraged innovation and which limited choice in the shops. They objected to the pro-farming agendas of the National Front government, and they resented Prime Minister V. P. Singh's attempts to reward his mainly rural, mainly "Backward Classes" support base by extending systems of reservation (for government and public sector jobs and places in educational institutions) upwards from the Scheduled Castes and Tribes to those designated as Other Backward Classes. By this time, too, the battles won by the likes of Margaret Thatcher in the UK and Ronald Reagan in the US were changing the landscapes of international economic thinking. The disintegration of the Soviet Union in 1991 also had profound effects in India. These were felt first in terms of a loss of export markets and foreign assistance. Later on they helped push India closer to the US and the World Trade Organisation.[29] In the early 1990s the economist John Williamson felt able to describe a new Washington Consensus on "sensible" macroeconomic management. Development economics was already out of fashion by then.[30] Deepak Lal had charged in 1983 that it was precisely a first generation of planners and development economists who had done the most damage in the "third world."[31] These were the "guilty men" who had stalled economic progress in India by 20 years or more. Washington, for its part, used the debt crisis in Latin America to launch a broader assault on *dirigiste* forms of economic management. Developing countries needed to return to basics: to sound monetary and fiscal policies and to open trade and capital accounts. The elite revolt that led to Finance Minister Manmohan Singh's famous budget of 1991, and to the devaluation of the rupee that year by 18–20 percent against leading currencies, was as much an echo of this thinking as it was a practical response to the balance of payments crisis that so damaged India's reputation for economic competency.

By the early summer of 1991 India's fiscal deficit stood at nearly nine percent of GDP and the country had sufficient foreign currency reserves to finance only two weeks' worth of imports. Moody's and Standard & Poor had downgraded India's international credit rating. Finance Minister Manmohan Singh's budget was designed first and foremost to stabilize this situation. Cuts in defense spending and in subsidies for exports, sugar, and fertilizers were meant to bring the fiscal deficit down to 6.5 percent of GDP in the 1991–92 tax year.[32] Thereafter, the government of Narasimha Rao moved steadily—but not at any great pace—to "adjust" the deeper structures of the economy. Efforts were made to liberalize India's trading regime, but even as late as 2000, despite considerable progress, tariffs in India still averaged close to 30 percent and the ratio of international trade to GDP remained under 25 percent (low by global standards). More progress was made with industrial policy. The system of industrial licensing that had taken shape since the 1950s was "dismantled in all but 18 designated industries (including drugs and pharmaceuticals, cars, and sugar), and for all locations save for 23 cities with populations above one million people where licenses were still required for new ventures or project expansion."[33] Perhaps most significantly of all, "the reforms," as they soon became known, opened the door to greater foreign direct investment in India's economy. Inward investment by western multinationals became a major part of the new "Shining India" that was trumpeted by the Bharatiya Janata Party-led (BJP) National Democratic Alliance ahead of the Lok Sabha elections in 2004. McDonald's in Delhi and Mumbai, along with IBM and Infosys in Bangalore, signaled India's connections to the new landscapes of globalization that had gathered pace in the 1990s, and which were strongly registered in the telecommunications revolution that swept through middle-class India.

No one now expects India to return to the *dirigiste* models that it pioneered more than half a century ago. Significantly, Congress used the rise of the BJP in the 1980s, and the destruction of the Babri Masjid in Ayodhya in December 1992, as a foil for its economic agenda. Leftist parties were warned that strong opposition to that agenda would cause the Rao government to fall, and that this in turn would bring the Hindu nationalists to power in New Delhi.[34] As things worked out, the BJP did come to power in India in 1998 and ruled the country until 2004. By then, however, the BJP had made its peace with globalization and reform. It gently retired its rhetoric of "swadeshi liberalization" and its support for "microchips but not potato chips." By 2000 it was an enthusiastic advocate for a continuing process of economic liberalization that offered clear advantages to some of its supporters in the urban middle class.

Even the Communist Party of India (Marxist) (CPM) came to embrace liberalization. The CPM has continued to speak out against some aspects of the national reform agendas now being pressed by Prime Minister Manmohan Singh (from 2004). But in its West Bengal heartland it has embraced that agenda vigorously and with surprisingly little concern for its traditional support bases in the countryside and among government workers. In 2007, the public face of economic reform in India was focused for a while on Nandigram, a rural area in the Medinipur district of West Bengal. In March 2007, 14 people were killed in Nandigram after the ruling Left Front government in Kolkata instructed CPM cadres and the police to break resistance to their plans to expropriate 10,000 acres of local farming land. The land was earmarked for a Special Economic Zone (SEZ) to be developed by the Salim group of Indonesia. The Left Front government argued that a linked group of chemical works in Nandigram would create up to 100,000 jobs in West Bengal. They further noted that they had to do battle with eight other states to host a joint venture with the Salim group.

The killings at Nandigram have taken on a significance that few in the Left Front government could have anticipated when contracts were signed. On the one hand, and most immediately, they advertised the willingness of the state in West Bengal to embrace what Marxists call "accumulation by dispossession."[35] In doing so, they dramatized the violence of the accumulation process in other parts of India —along the Narmada river valley, for example, where resistance to large

dams continues, or wherever poor people are "tidied out" of street environments marked for improvement and upgrading (as they have been in many of India's leading cities, including through the grotesquely named "Operation Sunshine" in Kolkata).[36] Development is never easy or painless, whatever the platitudes offered to the contrary by politicians or real estate developers.

On the other hand, Nandigram provides insight into changing geographies of power in India. Nehru found to his cost in the 1950s that he could not enforce land-to-the-tiller reforms in the countryside, where power resided mainly with richer farmers. (Agricultural policy was handed to the states in the Constitution of India, adopted in 1950.) Nevertheless, the federal settlement that was worked out between 1946 and 1949 placed India's states in a dependent relationship with the Center.[37] President's Rule can be imposed on states under Article 356 of the constitution, and the inelasticity of major state revenues often forced them to seek extra funding from New Delhi in the form of grants-in-aid under Article 275.

In the 1990s, in contrast, and more so in the 2000s, many of India's states have been able to improve their bargaining position against the center. Rob Jenkins has argued that the reform process has empowered states to behave as "competition states."[38] Instead of competing with one another to draw down funds from New Delhi, states like Maharashtra, Karnataka, Tamil Nadu, or West Bengal now fight with one another to host foreign direct investment or the funds of non-resident Indians (NRIs). In Jenkins' view, the real momentum of economic reform in India now lies in the states. A process of "provincial Darwinism" has taken hold, he argues, that compels states to compete with one another for the foreign funds that will reduce their fiscal deficits and dependence on New Delhi. Forcible evictions of peasants and harsher labor laws are just two instruments deployed by business-oriented state elites to attract capital to their states. In some cases, too—and Nandigram illustrates this very

313

well—states are being encouraged to free up extensive parcels of land as de facto fiefdoms of private capital: this, in effect, is the remit and purpose of the roughly 300 Special Economic Zones that were formed between 2005 and 2007 under the act of that name.

Causes and consequences of uneven growth

The privatization of space is a necessary complement to the way the ongoing process of economic reform in India is being negotiated. To date, that process has been focused on the non-agricultural economy, and in towns and cities. There are sound political reasons for this, and it is widely agreed that successive governments in India since 1991 have managed the reform process with levels of determination and skill that evaded policy-makers in the 1960s and 1970s. This in turn is causing observers of India to rethink their understandings of state–society relations. It is not simply that power is being leached from New Delhi to state capitals, important though this is. It is also becoming clear that a modern-izing elite in India, pushed on no doubt by big business and the international community, but ably fronted by a band of far sighted techno-crats, first used the politics of crisis and now uses the politics of success to create a climate for ongoing reform that is nonetheless at odds with market fundamentalism or the Washington Consensus. This is the real and considerable achievement of the CII and men like Manmohan Singh, Montek Singh Ahluwalia, and Palaniappan Chidambaram. If the reform agenda in India can be criticized for its partiality and unevenness, even for its slow speed, it can also be hailed as a success story that has avoided the pitfalls of the big bang approach to liberalization.[39] A lot of progress has been made by stealth, and this has involved all manner of deals between different members of India's business and political elites. But the reform process in India has also been advanced by the careful building of coalitions,

and by the bringing on side of politicians as well as "rent-seeking" elites in the states, many of whom had benefited from the permit-license-quota Raj and who might have been expected to slow down changes to it. Significantly, too, the ongoing process of eco-nomic reform in India has led to a sharpening of the technical competency of some leading departments of government. Arguably, that competency was not there in the 1950s or 1960s to support the Nehru-Mahalanobis model of development.

The net effect of the reforms has been to widen the gulf between rich and poor people in India, and between rich and poor regions, but that was always going to be the case. The strongest arguments in the pro-reform locker are these: (a) that rates of average per capita income growth in India have been rising since 2003–04 beyond the 3.5–4.0 percent levels recorded in the 1980s and 1990s; and (b) that such rates of growth would not have been recorded without economic reform. Put another way, low levels of economic growth are no friend of the poor, neither are forms of economic management based on populist politics and deficit financing. In the short run, this argument has it, economic growth must promote higher levels of income inequality— not that Indian levels are yet on a par with those of Brazil or China. Richer people will pull ahead as the economy rewards talent and scarce skills, as for example in the IT sector.

Meanwhile, the gap between the western and eastern states in India is opening up not because the latter are getting poorer, but because the former are getting richer. Again, we are seeing talent, or good economic policies, being rewarded. By the same token, poor people in Bihar are the victims of more than two decades of economic mismanage-ment. Lalu Prasad Yadav built a political coalition that rewarded Yadavs and Kurmis with dignity (*izzat*), and Muslims with pro-tection, no mean feats both, but what he did not promote was a politics of development aimed at tightening labor markets (thus raising real wages) or attracting inward investment.

Per capita net state domestic product at constant 1993–94 prices actually fell in Bihar from Rs 4,474 in 1990–91 to Rs 3,396 in 2003–04 (in part because of the loss of Jharkhand), while the residents of Uttar Pradesh, including the richer western parts of that state (but not Uttaranchal), saw their real incomes rise from Rs 5,342 in 1990–91 to a meager Rs 5,975 in 2003–04. In the western state of Maharashtra, meanwhile, the corresponding figures show more than a 60 percent increase in real terms over 13 years, from Rs 10,159 and Rs 16,765. In Gujarat, the rate of economic expansion was even greater, with a per capita net state domestic product of Rs 8,788 nearly doubling in 2004–05 to Rs 16,878.[40]

What is now evident in India, even more so than previously, is the yawning gulf between the country's haves and have-nots. For the former, India is shining brightly. It is a land of Tata Nanos and shopping malls. It is a country that seems to be leapfrogging the industrial revolution to land talented people directly in those jobs—in IT, information processing, and finance—that connect India to the globalizing world outside. This is precisely the land of SEZs, the Golden Quadrilateral, Gurgaon, the Bandra Kurla complex in Mumbai, and various technopoles in Bangalore, Chennai, and Hyderabad. Henri Lefebvre reminds us that capitalism advances "by occupying space, by producing [abstract] space," or by sweeping away those legal, cultural or political forces which conspire to slow down the circulation time of capital.[41] This is what we are beginning to see in India: the building of new urban and regional geographies that trumpet the country's modernity. Boosters of reform argue, furthermore, that the benefits of higher average rates of growth must in time trickle down to the poor. After a decade (the 1990s) when the rate of poverty reduction in India seemed to slow down, there are signs now that economic growth is again driving considerable reductions in the headcount incidence of absolute poverty. Even in Bihar, changes appear to be underway, with Chief Minister Nitish

Kumar advertising a business-friendly climate at some remove from the policies of his predecessor, Lalu Yadav. More tellingly, perhaps, the mushrooming growth of private, English-language schools in Bihar suggests an appetite on the part of some parents there to see their offspring join the circuits of economic growth and enrichment that are on offer elsewhere in India.

But here too is the rub. The anti-growth policies that have held back large parts of Bihar and Uttar Pradesh have more to do with state-level politics than with deliberate neglect on the part of New Delhi. If Rob Jenkins is right, pressures will grow even in these two states, particularly among the middle classes, for their ruling elites to embrace the reform agenda (as the CPM is doing in West Bengal). But there are also significant path dependencies at work here, a point sometimes lost on those urging Bihar to be more like Maharashtra. Aseema Sinha makes this point very well in her book on the regional roots of development politics in India.[42] We need to recognize that India's recent experiments with high-tech growth depend in part on earlier (Nehruvian) rounds of investment in tertiary education (notably the institutes of technology and management) and other forms of colonial and postcolonial support for private sector capitalist development in western India. In parts of eastern India, in contrast, slow growth may have been caused in large part by bad governance. But the governance systems in place there also reflect the continuing legacies of the permanent settlement and the more recent consequences of a Freight Equalization Act that worked strongly to the disadvantage of states in India's resource triangle by reducing the cost of coal, iron, and steel in non-producing regions of India. Tim Besley and his colleagues note that the poverty-reducing effects of a given unit of GDP per capita growth in India are much less than in East Asia, where the distribution of landed wealth since circa 1950 has been much more even. Poverty elasticities in East Asia and the Pacific are greater than −1 (that is, 1 percent growth produces more than a 1 percent reduction in poverty), whereas in South Asia they are close to −0.6. But Besley and his collaborators also note that poverty elasticities in India vary from a high of −1.23 in Kerala to a low of −0.30 in Bihar.[43] Even if economic growth does come to Bihar, their research suggests, the unevenness of land holdings, together with poor levels of existing infrastructure and primary education, will conspire to limit such poverty-reducing effects as it might and should have.

And here is a second difficulty. While it may be true that New Delhi has not set out to hold back Bihar since circa 1980 or 1991, the particular way in which India's urban and industrial elites have pushed forward the agenda of economic reform has done few favors for the eastern part of the country. To begin with, there is the matter of the agricultural economy. What is needed in Bihar, still, is agrarian reform, but this is not on the mainstream agenda. What we observe instead, as across India, is a crisis of profitability in agriculture. Young people are leaving the countryside in droves, driven out by poor rates of return on farming and pulled to the cities by the prospect of less onerous work. Close to 60 percent of Indians still find some employment in agriculture and allied sectors, but the share of the agricultural economy in India's GDP is now below 20 percent. It will move down further over the coming decades. The countryside is also becoming the preserve of women, as more young men earn the major part of their livelihoods in the urban economy. More so than in the 1950s and 1960s, the cities of India really do represent the "modern" and there is every reason to suppose that an increase in education supply in the countryside will push young men (and some young women) even faster to those places where they can wear western clothes and hanker after office jobs.[44]

Whether decent jobs for high school or college graduates will be on offer is another matter.[45] There are worries that India's reform trajectory is bringing with it jobless growth and the urbanization of poverty. It is sometimes forgotten that the IT sector accounts for only

2 percent of total services in India and only 1 percent of GDP (although it contributes around 5 percent of export earnings).[46] That said, the manufacturing sector has been doing better than many critics have recognized, and there has been enormous growth in employment since circa 1990 in the household industry sector. What is clear looking ahead is that the mass movement of people from rural to urban India has only just begun. We will see much more of it over the next 20 or 30 years, as the agricultural sector continues to shrink as a supplier of employment and as a contributor to GDP. When the GOI does finally turn its reforming spotlight on the countryside it will reduce the remaining subsidies that agriculture enjoys. It will also encourage the consolidation of larger farms, a process that is already under way in northwest India.

Finally, there is the matter of public goods provision, broadly defined. The most serious impediment to continued high rates of economic growth in India is the undersupply of infrastructure, from schools and hospitals to roads, railways and ports. The World Bank estimates that "India must invest around 3–4 percent more of GDP on infrastructure to sustain growth of around 8 percent, address existing gaps and meet policy-driven coverage goals."[47] This is a considerable sum of money to find in a country that is still returning significant fiscal deficits at both central and state levels (albeit that considerable progress has been made since circa 2004), and which still tolerates high levels of tax evasion.[48] It is also not clear there is the political will yet in India to finance improvements in public sector health care and education provision. The preference is for people to pay for such goods in the private sector, an elite-driven policy choice that is hugely damaging to poorer families.

Much less widely recognized outside India, although it has been referred to with some regularity by Prime Minister Manmohan Singh, is the worsening security situation in large swathes of eastern India, particularly in the so-called tribal belt. The retreat of functioning local government in parts of more than

150 of India's 602 Districts has opened the door to a Naxalite movement that does on occasions seek to provide both security and basic goods for disadvantaged local people. It is unlikely that the Indian state will lose control of these territories in the same manner that the government of Nepal lost almost all of the hill areas outside Kathmandu in the years from 1996 to 2006. But any attempt to win back these blocks and districts will take time, and might be bloody. In the meantime, they are no-go areas for economic development. Private investment will not flow to regions lacking clear property rights or an established rule of law. For better or worse, these red zones promise to be a significant brake on the production of abstract space—that is, functioning spaces for capital and modernization—in large parts of Bihar, Orissa, Jharkhand, Chhattisgarh, and Andhra Pradesh, not to mention in some of the northeastern states.

Conclusion

The transformation of the Indian economy since 1980 has surprised most observers and deserves a positive press. The Indian economy will be the third largest economy in the world sometime in the mid-2030s (trailing only the US and China). It is already in third place once adjustments are made for purchasing power parities (PPPs). Nominal average per capita incomes in India were just over $1,050 in 2007, rising to $4,550 in PPP terms: still placing India in the World Bank's band of low income countries, but edging it closer to middle income status. Moving forwards, Rodrik and Subramanian note that: "Over a 40-year period, a 5.3 percent [per capita] growth rate would increase the income of the average person nearly eight-fold."[49] There are reasons to believe that India is now hitting a target rate of growth of GDP of 7 percent, and that such growth rates can be continued at least up to 2025 (if not to 2040 or 2045, by which time some decline in the rate of growth is to be expected, as capital–output ratios increase).

The incidence of absolute poverty, measured by income, should fall sharply in the wake of high growth and will likely induce improvements in other measures of poverty and deprivation, including in respect of sanitation, child health, and gender equality. These are all areas where India is behind its millennium development goal (MDG) targets.

But nothing is guaranteed. India is still less dependent on world market conditions than many other emergent developing countries, but that dependence is set to grow. India is not immune to global crises, whether stock market crashes, rising energy prices or adverse climate change. Internally, the GOI has major political issues to negotiate in future, not just with regard to forms of cultural nationalism, including a possible backlash against "westernization," but also in regard to gender issues (the role of women in the workforce, most notably) and the management of urban poverty or the containment of urban unrest. As things stand, all leading political parties in India support the agenda of economic reform. There is a growing sense that India's reform agenda is being driven by a culture of success, rather than by the politics of fear or even necessity. The fruits of that initial success have gone overwhelmingly to India's elites and its urban middle classes, and upper castes, as was always bound to be the case. The challenge now, however, is for India to move on from a reform agenda inspired by elites in revolt against the permit-license-quota Raj. Opportunities need to be provided for poor and excluded people to participate in the new circuits of growth, not least if they are to be deterred in some regions from the paths of unrest, rebellion and/or secession.

The political enfranchisement of India's poorest groups might still be the country's long-term salvation, much as Nehru once imagined. It is equally possible, however, that the politics of exclusionary growth will be reinforced. As yet, rapid economic growth does not seem to be binding rich and poor Indians closer together. The privatization of space in India's cities surely hints at another future as well: that of the Latin America city, with all its glitz, crime, segregation, and violence. Whichever way it goes, the future for economic development and social change in India is intimately bound up with its cities, and with the politics of urban management. Of that we can be certain.

Notes

1 Dani Rodrik and Arvind Subramanian, "Why India Can Grow at 7 Percent a Year or More: Projections and Reflections," *IMF Working Paper*, 04/118 (2004), p. 6.

2 Gurcharan Das, *India Unbound: The Social and Economic Revolution from Independence to the Global Information Age* (New York: Anchor, 2002).

3 Kalpana Kochar *et al.*, "India's Pattern of Development: What Happened, What Follows," International Monetary Fund, *Working Paper* WP/06.02, www.imf.org/external/pubs/ft/wp/2006/wp0622.pdf (2006); see also Abhijit Banerjee, "The Paradox of Indian Growth: A Comment on Kochar *et al.*" (Mimeo: MIT, available at www.mit.edu/faculty/download_pdf.php?id+1340, 2006).

4 After writing a first draft of this essay I was able to read Arvind Panagariya's spirited and upbeat account of *India: The Emerging Giant* (Oxford: University Press, 2008). Panagariya accepts that India's growth rate stepped up in the 1980s (to 4.8 percent per annum 1981–88), but further argues that the growth rate stepped up again—to 6.3 percent—from 1988. Given that the run of annual GDP growth rates from 1987–88 to 1993–94 are 3.8 percent, 10.5 percent, 6.7 percent, 5.6 percent, 1.3 percent, 5.1 percent, and 5.9 percent, I find the cutoff date of 1988 (or 1988–89: the year of 10.5 percent growth) unconvincing, if not indeed rather arbitrary.

5 Work for the World Bank's 1990 World Development Report proposed an international poverty line of $1 per day at 1985 PPPs (purchasing power parities). At that time, India used an official poverty line of $0.75 per day. In 2008 the World Bank proposed a new international poverty line of $1.25 per day, using 2005 data on PPPs. India's official poverty lines for 2004–5 were Rs. 17.71 in urban areas and Rs. 11.71 in rural areas, which translate to just

£1.03 against 2005 PPPs. For discussion, see Chen and Ravallion 2008.

6 Simon Kuznets, *Modern Economic Growth: Rate, Structure and Speed* (New Haven, CT: Yale University Press, 1966).

7 World Bank, *India: Inclusive Growth and Service Delivery—Building on India's Success* (Development Policy Review, Report No. 34580-IN) (Washington, DC: World Bank 2006), Figure 1.12 and text.

8 Stuart Corbridge and John Harriss, *Reinventing India: Liberalization, Hindu Nationalism and Popular Democracy* (Cambridge: Polity Press, 2000).

9 Alan Heston, "National Income," in Dharma Kumar and Meghnad Desai (eds), *Cambridge Economic History of India,* vol. II (Cambridge: University Press, 1982), pp. 376–462.

10 André Béteille, *Caste, Class and Power: Changing Patterns of Stratification in a Tanjore Village* (Berkeley, CA: University of California Press, 1965).

11 Quoted in Sunil Khilnani, *The Idea of India* (London: Hamish Hamilton, 1997), p. 35.

12 See the chapter by Jan Breman in this volume.

13 Hans Singer, "The Distribution of Gains Between Investing and Borrowing Countries," *American Economic* Review, 40 (1950), pp. 478–96; and Raúl Prebisch, *The Economic Development of Latin America and Its Principal Problems* (Lake Success, NY: United Nations, 1950).

14 Dadabhai Naoroji anticipated this argument in his *Poverty and Un-British Rule in India* (London: Swan Sonnenschein, 1901).

15 Ronald Inden, "Embodying God: From Imperial Progresses to National Progress in India," *Economy and Society,* 24 (1995), pp. 245–78.

16 William Arthur Lewis, "Economic Development with Unlimited Supplies of Labour," *The Manchester School,* 22 (1954), pp. 139–91.

17 John Harriss, "Does the 'Depressor' still work? Agrarian Structure and Development in India: A Review of Evidence and Argument," *Journal of Peasant Studies,* 19 (1992), pp. 189–227.

18 Michael Lipton, *Why Poor People Stay Poor: A Study of Urban Bias in World Development* (London: Temple Smith, 1977). Charan Singh's views permeate much of his writings, but see esp. *India's Economic Policy: The Gandhian Blueprint* (New Delhi: Vikas, 1978), ch. v; and *Economic Nightmare of India: Its Cause and Cure* (New Delhi: National 1981), chs vi–viii.

19 V. M. Dandekar and Nilkanth Rath, "Poverty in India: Dimensions and Trends," *Economic and Political Weekly* [*EPW*], Vol. 6, No. 1 (2 January, 1971), pp. 25–48, 106–46.

20 Lloyd Rudolph and Susanne Hoeber Rudolph, *In Pursuit of Lakshmi: The Political Economy of the Indian State* (Chicago, IL: University of Chicago Press, 1987).

21 Atul Kohli. *Democracy and Discontent: India's Growing Crisis of Governability* (Cambridge: University Press, 1990).

22 Partha Chatterjee, *A Possible World: Essays in Political Criticism* (New Delhi: Oxford University Press 1977); also his *The Politics of the Governed: Reflections on Popular Politics in Most of the World* (New York: Columbia University Press, 2004). Sudipta Kaviraj, "On the Crisis of Political Institutions in India," *Contributions to Indian Sociology*, 18 (1984), pp. 223–43; also his "On State, Society and Discourse in India," in James Manor (ed.), *Rethinking Third World Politics* (Harlow: Longman, 1991), pp. 72–89.

23 Kaviraj, "Crisis of Political Institutions," p. 227.

24 Francine Frankel, *India's Political Economy, 1947–1977: The Gradual Revolution* (Princeton, NJ: University Press, 1978); Pranab Bardhan, *The Political Economy of Development in India* (Oxford: Blackwell, 1984); Jagdish Bhagwati, *India in Transition: Freeing the Economy* (Oxford: Clarendon, 1993).

25 Bhagwati, *India*; Thirukodikaval Nilakanta Srinivasan, "Reform of Industrial and Trade Policies," *EPW*, Vol. 26, No. 37 (14 September, 1991), pp. 2,143–45.

26 Atul Kohli, "Politics of Economic Growth in India, 1980–2005, Parts I and II," *EPW*, Vol. 41, No. 13 (1 April, 2006), pp. 1,251–59 and 14 (8 April, 2006), pp. 1,361–70.

27 Angus Deaton, and Jean Drèze, "Poverty and Inequality in India: A Re-examination," *EPW*, Vol. 37, No. 36 (7 September, 2002), pp. 3,729–48.

28 Abhijit Sen and Himanshu, "Poverty and Inequality in India-I," *EPW*, Vol 39, No. 38 (18 September, 2004), pp. 4,247–63 and "Poverty and Inequality in India-II," 39, pp. 4,361–75.

29 Kohli, "Politics of Economic Growth," p. 1,362.

30 John Williamson, "Democracy and the 'Washington Consensus,'" *World Development*, 21 (1993), pp. 1,329–36.

31 Deepak Lal, *The Poverty of 'Development Economics'* (London: Institute of Economic Affairs, 1993).

32 Drawing on Corbridge and Harriss, *Reinventing India*, p. 152.

33 Corbridge and Harriss, *Reinventing India*, p. 153.

34 See Ashutosh Varshney, "Mass Politics or Elite Politics? India's Economic Reforms in Comparative Perspective," in Jeffrey Sachs *et al.* (eds), *India in the Era of Economic Reforms* (New Delhi: Oxford University Press, 1999), pp. 222–60.

35 David Harvey, *The New Imperialism* (Oxford: Clarendon Press, 2003).

36 On Narmada, see Amita Baviskar, *In the Belly of the River: Tribal Conflicts Over Development in the Narmada Valley* (New Delhi: Oxford University Press, 1995). On Operation Sunshine, see Chatterjee, *Politics of the Governed*, p. 61.

37 See Paul R. Brass, *The Politics of India Since Independence*, 1st edn (Cambridge: University Press, 1990).

38 Robert Jenkins. "The Developmental Implications of Federal Political Institutions in India," in Mark Robinson and Gordon White (eds), *The Democratic Developmental State* (Oxford: University Press, 1998), pp. 187–214. See also Lawrence Sáez, *Federalism Without a Centre: The Impact of Political and Economic Reforms on India's Federal System* (Thousand Oaks, CA: Sage, 2002).

39 See Bradford De Long, "India since Independence: An Analytical Growth Narrative," in Dani Rodrik (ed.), *In Search of Prosperity: Analytic Narratives on Economic Growth* (Princeton, NJ: University Press, 2003), pp. 184–204. See also Rob Jenkins, *Democratic Politics and Economic Reform in India* (Cambridge: University Press, 1999).

40 Government of India, *Economic Survey, 2006–7* (New Delhi: GOI, Ministry of Finance, 2007), Table 10.4.

41 Henri Lefebvre, *The Survival of Capitalism* (New York: St. Martin's Press, 1976), cited in David Harvey, *Spaces of Capital* (Edinburgh: University Press, 2001), p. 376.

42 Aseema Sinha, *The Regional Roots of Development Politics in India: A Divided Leviathan* (Bloomington, IN: Indiana University Press, 2005).

43 Tim Besley *et al.*, *Operationalising Pro-Poor Growth: A Country Case Study on India* (Mimeo: Working Paper of Department of Economics, London School of Economics, www.lse.ac.uk/collections/LSEIndia/pdf/propoorgrowth.pdf, 2004), p. 13.

44 An important word of caution here. The feminization of the countryside in states like Haryana and Punjab is taking place in a context where child sex ratios indicate there are now fewer than 850 girls for every 1,000 boys aged 0–6. Amartya Sen has argued that there are more than 100 million missing from the world today. Perhaps as many as 30 million of these women are missing from India; Amartya Kumar Sen, "More Than 100 Million Women Are Missing," *New York Review of Books*, 20 December, 1990.

45 See Craig Jeffrey *et al.*, *Degrees Without Freedom? Education, Masculinities and Unemployment in North India* (Stanford, CA: University Press, 2008).

46 Jim Gordon and Poonam Gupta, "Understanding India's Services Revolution," paper prepared for IMF-NCAER Conference, New Delhi, November 2003 www.imf.org/external/np/apd/seminars/2003/newdelhi/gordon.pdf.

47 World Bank, *India*, p.15.

48 See Barbara Harriss-White, *India Working: Essays on Society and Economy* (Cambridge: University Press, 2003).

49 Rodrik and Subramanian, *Why India Can Grow*, p. 6.

22

The political economy of agrarian change in India

Jan Breman

Settling the agrarian question

At the time of Independence, in the middle of the twentieth century, India could firmly be classified as a peasant society. The rural-based mode of existence had remained dominant from generation to generation, and the large majority of the population continued to live in the countryside and work in agriculture. A series of village monographs, most of which were published between the 1950s and 1970s as the outcome of anthropological research, showed that the habitat of peasants included a wide variety of non-agrarian households and that, moreover, the peasantry was highly differentiated. A major point of departure in the populist course steered by the nationalist leadership was the restoration of a social order which had been eroded under colonial rule. The owner–cultivator, reported to have steadily lost ground in the transition to a market economy, was to be shored up as the backbone of agricultural production. Solving the agrarian question stood high on the political agenda of the Congress movement, which came to power at both central and state level. In preparation for the takeover of government a national planning committee (NPC) was set up under the chairmanship of Jawaharlal Nehru, with the task to frame the

main outlines of economic policy after decolonization. Radhakamal Mukerjee drafted a paper on the land issue which was first discussed in his working group on agriculture and then endorsed by experts and politicians in a plenary meeting of the NPC at the end of June 1940. Landlordism was to be abolished and ownership rights transferred to the actual tillers of the soil. The family farm would remain the main unit of cultivation and its size should be neither larger nor smaller than an economic holding. It should provide adequate employment and income for the family without making use, at least not permanently, of outside labour.

The architects of the postcolonial era clearly envisaged an agricultural economy of self-cultivating owners. In their directives the planners seemed to have ignored the existence, in most parts of the subcontinent, of a vast agrarian underclass completely bereft of landownership. Their disregard for this landless mass was operationalized in the decision not to include them in the redistribution of the surplus land that would become available with the fixation of a ceiling on land ownership and the abolition of absentee ownership. By way of consolation, the planning document suggested that agricultural labourers be allowed access to land not yet under cultivation, village commons and other wasteland waiting to be taken into production. Perhaps not by the straightforward handing out of individualized ownership rights but indirectly, through the establishment of land-tilling cooperatives in which various agrarian classes would join and collaborate.

The cooperative model was one of the vaguely phrased socialist ideas which appealed to some sections of the Congress movement but which were never taken seriously in the execution of mainstream policies firmly heading in a capitalist direction. Of similar symbolic value was the promise that agricultural laborers would be released from bondage when they had been indebted to landowners for more than five years. A large-scale, nationwide survey of agricultural labor conducted a few years after Independence showed that a substantial segment worked in a state of attachment that took away their freedom of employment.[1] The land reform operation was closely monitored. Thorner was one of many observers who came to the conclusion that the redistribution of property rights, both in making the design for a new agrarian blueprint and in the subsequent stage of implementation, fell short of what had been promised in the decades leading up to Independence by Congress leadership.[2] Myrdal minced no words when he concluded halfway in his three-volume *Asian Drama* (1968) that the opportune moment for a radical reshaping of the agrarian structure had passed. The land reforms, he wrote, have bolstered the political, social, and economic position of the rural better-off segments on which the postcolonial government depended for crucial support. The policy was not merely tilted in favor of the more well to do but had an anti-poor bias as well.

Measures that would deprive the upper strata in the villages of land and power, and would genuinely confer dignity and status on the underprivileged and the landless, are among the last that those in power would find acceptable.[3]

Practising land reforms: Gujarat

What was the shape and outcome of the agrarian question in the villages of south Gujarat where I started my fieldwork in the early 1960s? Under the provisions of the Bombay Tenancy and Agricultural Lands Act of 1948 the Maratha *inamdar* (landholder), who lived in Baroda, lost most of the agrarian property which his family had held in Gandevigam village for many generations. The Anavil Brahmans, who were already the dominant landowners, received the title deeds for the plots which they used to cultivate as his tenants. *Bania* moneylenders and urban traders forfeited whatever land they had taken over from farmers indebted to them. The same happened in Chikhligam, the second site of my fieldwork. For the Brahmans, Tillers' Day—April 1957—heralded their consolidation as the landed elite in the region. By the same token, the subaltern castes—in Gandevigam, the Kolis, and in Chikhligam, the tribal Dhodhias—lost out in the land transfer deals. In the past, local Anavil farmers had leased out plots to them on a sharecropping basis and, under the new legislation, the low-caste cultivators could lay a claim to these fields. To avoid losing property, the main landowners decided to discontinue most sharecropping arrangements even though their clients swore that they would never dare to register their names in the local record of rights. The land-poor were only beneficiaries if the land they worked belonged to owners not residing in the village. A land ceiling, fixed in 1960 and scaled down in 1974, could have threatened the privileged position of the Anavil Brahmans, but because of the many exemptions and loopholes in the act, the members of this dominant caste—which to the present day average no more than 15 percent of the village population—managed to appropriate two-thirds to three-quarters of the total arable land in the locality.

The landless were, of course, excluded from the reallocation of the meager amount of surplus land which became available. One of the reasons given for their non-qualification was that they had never been, even in their own memory, owner–cultivators. Their huts used to be built on land owned by the Anavil landlords who had tied them as farm servants in a relationship of bondage, which was passed on from father to son. In the years between Independence and the enactment of the land reform, they were thrown out of the plots they inhabited in their masters' fields. When I came for the first round of my research nearly half a century ago, I found them living on the outskirts of the village, occupying homesteads for which they had not been issued title deeds. The withholding of a legal status, either as owners or tenants, meant that the landless could be blamed for having invaded as squatters the public domain kept as a reserve open to the local community at large for grazing cattle, cutting grass, collecting firewood, and, not least, for defecation. The promise made by the national planning committee that members of the agrarian underclass be given access to the still undivided land under the control of the village *panchayat* was more often broken than honored.

On the contrary, in a subsequent round of land reform, the commons were privatized, surreptitiously and in collusion with the local bureaucracy, resulting in the registration of ownership rights for what had always been communal property in the names of the dominant caste. As one of my informants in Chikhligam caustically commented: "Even when I go for shitting to the field where I always have been doing that in the morning I stand accused of trespassing." And when the agricultural laborers went on strike in Gandevigam in their fight for higher wages, the landowners retaliated with the threat that they would stop the landless women and children gathering firewood on "their" land. One last effort was made to hand out land to the landless for self-cultivation. Acharya Vinoba Bhave started the *Bhoodan* (land gift) campaign in the 1950s to deradicalize agrarian struggles such as the agitation that had been going on in Telangana. In his opinion the Gandhian approach would persuade the well-endowed

elite to part with their surplus land. The movement turned out to be a failure,[4] although it was quite popular for some time in south Gujarat where a network of Gandhian institutions had become firmly entrenched in the late colonial era. Social activists were told that agricultural laborers lacked the wherewithal and discipline to work the land on their own account. There was, however, a more genuine argument why the landless segment should not benefit from restructuring of the agrarian order. The widely held verdict was that it made no sense to burden households with a tiny piece of land, which would, in any case, be inadequate for them to make a decent living. It would simply act as an obstacle to their mobility.

Swami Sahajanand, the national leader of the *kisan sabha*, the peasant union, had come to the same conclusion. He pointed out that the agricultural economy was unable to provide enough employment for the mass of agricultural labor.[5] At least half of them would have to get out and seek a better future in the urban industries that were going to emerge after independence. This was also the destiny which the national planning committee had in mind for the large number of households at the bottom of the village economy.[6] It was in line with what Sardar Patel had advised the Dublas of south Gujarat to do towards the end of the 1930s if they wanted to be free: to go elsewhere.[7] All those who said that they were guided by what would be best for the rural underclass suggested that a more dignified life was awaiting these hapless people outside agriculture. Migration to the cities and factory employment were thus highlighted as an end to the misery of the landless and the final solution for the agrarian question.

Social profile of the landless proletariat

The large majority of the agricultural laborers in south Gujarat are Dublas (or *Halpatis*, as they came to be called later). Their earlier name had been given a derogatory meaning and *sala*

Dubla[8] is still a common curse. The denigration resonated in the suggestion that the word Dubla was to be understood as weakling, a reference to the inferior character ascribed to the members of this community. Classified as a scheduled tribe in the colonial bookkeeping, the Dublas had been tied to high-caste landowners such as the anavil Brahmans for many generations. Their work as farm servants included using the plow, which their employers had to avoid to retain their purity. Although they were bonded, the Dublas were not ranked as unclean and both men and women performed household chores, releasing their masters from having to do such demeaning work themselves. In my initial fieldwork, I still found traces of the earlier bondage. My investigations focused on the changes that had come about in the relations between these landowning and landless castes-cum-classes at opposing ends of the social hierarchy. In my opinion, the fading away of bondage in the preceding decades was more the result of internal dynamics—on one side, landowners shedding clients whom they no longer wished to grant full employment and, on the other side, agricultural laborers refusing to consider themselves debt bonded to masters who impinged on their freedom of movement—than outside intervention. The external forces at work were either the state unwilling to condone any longer practices of unfree labor or civil agencies, Gandhian activists in particular, attempting in the late colonial era to uplift the Dublas.[9] There is no doubt that Mahatma Gandhi himself had tried to elevate their social standing by renaming them Halpatis, lords of the plow, to try to eradicate their dismal history as Dublas. Summing up my findings, I reported in my fieldwork account that while features of patronage had disappeared over time the dimension of exploitation had remained as strong as ever.[10]

The agricultural laborers continued to live in deep poverty because of the extremely low wages they received for their work: less than a rupee a day in the early 1960s. It was far less than they needed to meet their basic needs.

Outside agriculture, there was hardly any work available in the village. In the slack season their already low food intake declined further and many families could not still their hunger for days on end. Undernourishment, a lack of clothes to cover the bodies of adults and children, and inadequate shelter in huts that gave no protection against cold and rain made them vulnerable to health risks, leading to high morbidity, particularly for the youngest and oldest age groups. Only a handful of children would attend school for a few standards, but illiteracy was the general state of affairs. The Minimum Wage Act, announced in 1948, was not put into effect and this did not change when the first and second Agricultural Labour Enquiries, held in 1950–51 and 1955–56 respectively, provided abundant evidence of the deprivation of the lowest class in the rural economy. In 1966 a panel of experts urged the government of Gujarat to fix a floor price for agricultural labor to prevent tensions which had been building up in several parts of the state from boiling over into open clashes. A better deal could not wait for much longer, the committee's report warned, in order to pre-empt organized political radicalism from surfacing.[11] It took six more years of deliberation and consultation before a legal minimum rate was finally introduced, later and lower than the downright conservative advisors had deemed both wise and fair. Further delay would have risked losing a major vote bank of the Congress party: the landless electorate that made up more than half (55 percent in 1982) of the agrarian workforce in south Gujarat. Gandhian activists had begun to mobilize the Halpatis in the late colonial era and remained active as political agents who delivered the votes of these downtrodden people to the Congress party in the early decades after Independence. The well-established landowners who had rallied behind Congress in the struggle for independence did not appreciate the mainstream party voicing and articulating the interests of the rural poor. This was one of the major reasons why Mahatma Gandhi never became a popular figure in his own home state,

THE POLITICAL ECONOMY OF AGRARIAN CHANGE IN INDIA

in contrast to the strong-handed Sardar Patel who became idolized as the hero of the Bardoli *satyagraha*.[12] Already at this early stage, the elite formations in the countryside began to distance themselves from Congress stalwarts and backed candidates who canvassed for Jan Sangh and Swatantra. My informants among the dominant caste insisted that giving Halpatis the right to vote, as ordained by the principle of universal suffrage, had been a grave blunder. Such lowly people had fewer needs than full citizens—a major argument why their wages should not be fixed above reproduction level— and should have remained excluded from participating in the regular political process. While the New Congress "high command" did not go beyond paying mere lip service to the *garibi hatao* (ban poverty) slogan when it was coined after the split in the party, it was good enough reason for the landed interests to side with veterans such as Morarji Desai who established their leadership of the old Congress party (Congress-O) in opposition to Indira Gandhi, whose new Congress party came to be called Congress (I) (I for Indira). The rupture between the rural rich and poor further escalated when the main landowners transferred their allegiance first to Janata and, after the failure of that intermezzo at central and state level, to the Bharatiya Janata Party (BJP), which appealed to the rapidly spreading mood of Hindu fundamentalism in the 1980s and 1990s. Extending their power base to the upwardly mobile castes helped the BJP and its front organizations to tackle and defeat the political strategy of new congress which had formed the KHAM alignment, carrying for some time the vote banks of Kshatriyas, Harijans, Adivasis, and Muslims.

The failure of the Gandhian gospel

In the shifting political constellation during the last quarter of the twentieth century the Halpatis by and large remained faithful to the Congress party. Their voting behavior was more inspired by confronting the successive choices made by their caste-cum-class oppo-

nents, who cast their votes for candidates belonging to opposition parties. The Halpatis never wavered from their loyalty to Congress, although not out of gratitude for concrete material gains. The minimum wage legislation came too late and offered too little to be hailed as clear proof of successful representation. In a violent incident which took place in 1976 in a village close to the sites of my research, two Halpatis were killed by *zim rakhas*, private guards hired by the landlords to protect their fields against crop theft. A committee of inquiry reported that the agricultural laborers had become restive because they were paid much less than the prescribed legal wage. Heeding these signals, the government of Gujarat set up a rural labor inspectorate in 1981 with the mandate to check whether farmers paid for the labor they utilized in accordance with the law. But, during their rounds, the government labor inspectors collected bribes rather than fines, so that employers could buy off prosecution for noncompliance.[13] Nevertheless, Indira Gandhi has remained a cult figure in the Halpati milieu until the present day. If *Mataji* could not deliver what she promised, freedom from exploitation and oppression, it was because of the collusion between the vested interests at local level and the officials in charge of the district and subdistrict bureaucracies. This political– bureaucratic front of high caste domination had prevented the rural landless from making their numerical weight felt. There was the famous statement made by one congress minister who, when *gherao*ed (surrounded) by angry farmers protesting against a rise in the minimum wage rate for agricultural labor, went on public record saying: "Some laws are not meant to be implemented." However, when I came back in the late 1980s for a restudy of my initial fieldwork villages, I noticed some signs of progress in the landless quarters. Huts had become houses, and although they were not *pakka* (well-made of brick), they were definitely better than the shacks in which I had found them before. Floor space had not increased much but the walls were higher and the thatched roofs were now tiled or covered with asbestos or corrugated iron sheets. Not having to bend down low in order to pass through the opening and to be able to stand erect once inside testified to an increase in dignity.

Housing programs were a major instrument with which congress bought the support of the rural poor. The Halpatis required public subsidies to build their accommodation in the new colonies because they needed at least four-fifths of their daily income for food intake. What helped in that respect was the public distribution system, which provided a monthly ration of low-price grain to households officially declared as living below the poverty line. As a consequence, the number of days without at least one meal decreased. More children had started going to school, to some extent motivated by the introduction of a noon meal scheme. Although the dropout rate remained high, a small minority managed to complete their basic education. Disease and debilitation were still rampant, but access to public health care helped to moderate the impact of chronic or recurrent illness. The primary health centers opened in subdistrict towns played an important role in bringing down morbidity.

The *Halpati Seva Sangh* (HSS), founded in 1946 by Gandhian activists and led by them ever since, became a useful instrument for spreading the public welfare benefits among the landless of south Gujarat. The staff of social workers belonging to the *ujliparaj*, the higher castes, considered themselves to be engaged in a mission to civilize the tribal communities. Acting as a front organization for congress, the HSS was rewarded for its mobilizing role in election campaigns with large grants spent on a network of boarding schools and social welfare schemes. Propagating vegetarianism and abstinence from drinking country liquor, a favorite pastime among the landless, the HSS leadership tried to convert its clientele to a Hinduized way of life and, by strengthening communal sentiments, to instill in the Halpatis a sense of caste identity. The leaders of this social movement firmly refused to turn it into a trade union fighting for freedom from bondage and higher wages for agricultural laborers. Its ideological stance was based on preaching harmony. Whenever conflicts broke out, caused by the antagonistic relationship between landowners and landless, the Gandhian missionaries rushed to the scene and appealed to what they considered to be their flock to abstain from militant confrontation. The aim of their mediation was to reach a compromise, which invariably meant systematically understating and misrepresenting the interests of the dominated class.[14] This leads me to conclude that the role played by civil society in raising the visibility of the landless mass and in helping them to acquire better political representation has been more negative than positive.

Opening up the countryside and modernizing the forces of production

Equally important as the efforts made by various state agencies in the 1970s and 1980s to alleviate poverty somewhat was the accelerated diversification of the rural economy arising on account of road building and motorized transport. Distances could be bridged much easier than before and new modes of communication resulted in more information about what was going on beyond the local boundaries. I have never endorsed the view that, in the past, there had been a closed labor market at the village level, but it would be difficult to deny that agricultural laborers became more mobile than they had been before. They started to operate in a wider and more fluid labor market and moved around both in spatial terms, going to sites of employment which had been beyond their reach in the past, and in finding access to other economic sectors than agriculture. Not only did seasonal migration increase, but also daily commuting to the industrial estates that had sprung up in most district towns. Gaining access to these new employment niches was only possible for those who owned a bicycle, which thus became a major asset also for the younger generation of landless who continued to work as agricultural laborers. What I found quite striking was that only a few Halpatis left the village to settle down in the urban localities alongside the railway line, which rapidly expanded from the 1980s onwards. Migration became circulatory, with laborers leaving home to work, but coming back at the end of the day, every few weeks or at the onset of the monsoon. Urbanization, in the sense of staying on more indefinitely in the town or city, required, apart from access to low-cost housing, a modicum of educational qualifications and proper skills, a network of contacts to find shelter, and a regular job. That kind of social capital was rare in the bottom of the rural milieu. Consequently, the Halpatis had no other option but to remain footloose, hired and fired according to the needs of the moment at a wage level which was not much higher than that paid by the farmers. Leaving the village had become easier, but in and outside their home base the landless mass turned into a reserve army of labor dependent for irregular work and low income on the steadily expanding informal sector of the economy.[15] Their hopes for a better future lay in the prospect that a process of formalization would eventually take place that would absorb the surplus labor redundant in agriculture into the better paid and more skilled jobs that were bound to become available, if not in the village then elsewhere.

In the second half of the twentieth century, agricultural production became less dependent on rainfall. The construction of, first, the Kakrapar Dam and then the Ukai Dam in the Tapti River led to a significant extension of the irrigated area in the central plain of south Gujarat. Crops could now be cultivated throughout the year. The lengthening of the agrarian cycle resulted in a growing demand for labor, although this was somewhat lessened by the mechanization of farming operations and transport—the introduction of tractors and power tillers. More damaging for the local landless, however, was the influx of seasonal labor from the remote hinterland. Throughout the region, sugarcane became the major cash crop and the agro-industry managing its production and processing recruited harvesting gangs from far off destinations for the duration of the season. Elaborating on the political economy of labor migration, I pointed out that the decision to bring in these outsiders was not caused by a local shortage of labor but was conditioned by an employment strategy that reduced the cost of the brutal work regime to the lowest possible level.[16] Labor migrants are easy to discipline, are not allowed to bring dependants along, can be put to work day and night, and have to leave the region again when their presence is no longer required. While the local landless have to remain at home idle, an army of more than 100,000 men, women, and children camp along the roadside or in the open fields from October to June to cut the cane and take it to the cooperative sugar mills that have been set up in nearly every *taluka* (subdivision of a district).

As I was able to observe in Bardoligam, which became the third village of my field-work at the end of the 1970s, growing sugarcane has been a very profitable business for the landowners whose prosperity has significantly increased in the last half century. The houses in which they used to live have been replaced by *haveli*s mansions two or even three storeys high, with well-furnished interiors designed to demonstrate the wealth of the inhabitants. They no longer use mopeds or scooters to get around, but are the proud owners of motor cars, preferably expensive foreign models. The members of the dominant castes had already given up working in the fields one or two generations ago, and their growing detachment from agriculture is expressed in an unwillingness to invest time and money in farming. In recent decades, milk cattle have followed draught animals in disappearing from the high-caste neighborhoods. When I asked why, I was told that keeping them was too much of a nuisance, despite the fact that looking after the animals and cleaning the stables were chores done by the farm servants and maids anyway. Anavil Brahmans and Kanbi patidars have dissociated themselves from the agrarian lifestyle of their ancestors. Settling down in towns and cities has become increasingly popular among the younger generations and attending college in a nearby town helps them to prepare for a life oriented more towards the world beyond the village. Sons and, more particularly, daughters do not see a future for themselves living in the village and working in agriculture. They really want to become embedded in an urban environment, but because of the soaring prices of real estate—the cost of even a small and rather mundane apartment in the municipalities of Valsad, Navsari, Bardoli, or Surat runs to more than four *lakh* (hundred thousand) rupees—not all can afford it. Fathers complain that they find it difficult to get suitable girls to marry their sons because coming to the village inevitably implies having to take up the role of the dutiful daughter-in-law. For the rich, their rural lifestyle has become sufficiently urbanized, with all the modern gadgets and conveniences until recently only available in the town. The infrastructure has been upgraded and distances can be easily bridged by scooter or motor car. It is, therefore, nowadays acceptable to continue to live in the village, also for the younger generation, but it is important to have a proper urban job, i.e., white collar and in the managerial ranks or, preferably, having your own business so as to be your own boss. It is interesting to note that the trend away from agriculture at the higher end of the village hierarchy rarely leads to land being sold off. A new class of "absentee" landlords has emerged who own most of the land but desist from plowing their earnings back to raise production. They manage their property by remote control and in a leisurely fashion—having fruit orchards and growing sugarcane—rather than as active, let alone innovative, agrarian entrepreneurs.

Widening divide between winners and losers

The members of the village elite are, however, not content to just shed their rurality. Their real ambition is to settle abroad and join their caste mates as NRIs (non-resident Indians). Leaving for other shores is not a new phenomenon in south Gujarat, but the number of migrants going overseas has increased enormously in the last quarter century. An earlier generation went to East Africa and later on to the UK, but nowadays the US is the favored destination. Getting hold of a green card to send a son or daughter to America is a high priority in many well-established households. What they do there depends on the educational qualifications of the migrants. Running your own business is the dream of every patidar youngster and the popular saying *hotel-motel-patel*, in which the community at large takes pride, illustrates the strength of their presence in this branch of trade. Much less widely known is that at least part of the money spent on buying a motel somewhere in the US comes from the profits reaped from agriculture at home. Sugarcane, in particular, has been a real moneyspinner, and the Rs 500 shares which a farmer had to buy many years ago to register himself as member of the cooperative agro-industry processing the cane are now sold for not less than Rs 150,000–250,000 on the open market. The landowners not only indulge in conspicuous consumption but also help to provide the cash their sons need to buy the overseas property which has made them such successful emigrants. If it comes to the crunch they are even willing to sell a piece of land because they see it as an investment in the future well-being of their children and grandchildren abroad. To that extent the NRIs regard themselves as frontrunners in building up a globalized identity, not afraid to move themselves and their capital around in the pursuit of happiness. They come home to relax, to charge their religious batteries, to find marriage partners, to check on the family property, to seek medical care (the cost of which is much lower than in the US) or to spend their retirement, but not to engage in business. The dominant castes are strong, even vehement, supporters of the BJP. Narendra Modi, the *Hindutva* supremo and prime minister of Gujarat, is their hero. They affectionately call him *chhote sardar,* the little lion, who has stepped into the shoes of his famous namesake, Sardar Patel. Patel was a close associate of Gandhi in the struggle for independence, but was strongly opposed to the doctrine of piety preached by the Father of the Nation and his steadfast concern for upliftment of the poor.[17] So far, however, Modi has not been successful in his appeal to the NRIs to bring their overseas profits back to the state where they were born and bred. It has been made clear to him that a precondition to their willingness to build and run hotels and motels in Gandhi's homeland would be the repeal of prohibition. Given the huge illegal intake of alcohol in all quarters, that moment may actually not be far off.

In the ongoing discussion on the shape and magnitude of the current stagnation in agrarian investment and production, most if not all attention has usually been given to economic factors. I have argued already that an important feature of the crisis is that the main owners of agrarian property are distancing themselves from active farming, a way of life with which they no longer feel comfortable. For totally different reasons the class of agricultural laborers is also turning away from what has been, until now, the primary economic sector. They are being pushed out from cultivating the land because they get neither enough work nor a wage that enables them to satisfy their basic needs. Lack of sufficient employment has reached the point at which the rural landless in south Gujarat cannot be occupationally classified any longer as spending most of their working days in agriculture. What have conventionally been registered as subsidiary sources of income in other sectors of the economy have become the main ones. It boils down to a wide assortment of unskilled jobs, such as digging, hauling, and lifting work, which taxes their bodily strength and stamina

and for which they get a wage not much higher than that paid by the farmers: in 2005–06, that was Rs 30–40 for eight hours, and less even than that if their presence was required for only half a day.

Have the poor become poorer since my investigations in Gandevigam and Chikhligam nearly half a century ago? That statement would be difficult to substantiate if only because their condition then could hardly have been worse than the intense misery in which I found them: steeped in hunger, prone to illness, having only one set of clothes, without adequate shelter. As I have already pointed out, in all these respects some progress has been made. But today, with a few exceptions, the Halpatis are still stuck firmly below the poverty line. It seems that more progress was made in the 1970s and 1980s than since. The annual income of most households does not rise above Rs 15,000–20,000. That means that an average household of four to five members can spend at best Rs 50–60 a day on their basic needs, which is less than 40¢ a day for each of them. My informants in the landless colonies are not impressed when I tell them that their parents and grandparents were even poorer than they are now. "How does that help us today?" they reply. "We know it was very bad then but that does not mean that our condition is much better now." They are right of course; they should not be compared with the indigence of an earlier generation, but with the highly visible comfort, if not luxury, in which their employers live. What they experience is relative deprivation, an acute awareness that those who were already much better off in the past have appropriated most of the fruits of economic growth. All stakeholders acknowledge that the cake has become bigger, but the way it is cut up shows even greater inequity than before. And why not, is the widely held opinion in the milieu of those who have become much better off. They have no problem arguing that the poor masses are non-deserving because of their defective way of life.

Policies of exclusion

While in the past the landless used to live in the shadow of the landowners, who kept a close check on their bonded servants, the demise of the beck-and-call relationship meant that having a permanent and abundant supply of agricultural labor had become more of a nuisance than a comfort. In all the sites of my fieldwork the Halpatis were thrown off their master's land and became squatters on the waste land at the outskirts of the village. As already noted, the houses in which they live— although an improvement on the earlier huts— are small, jerry-built and lack the basic amenities, such as drinking water and drainage, which have upgraded the accommodation of the non-poor. Electricity lines reach the landless colonies but many households cannot afford to have a meter installed and pay the price of the two-monthly subscription. The uneven terrain on which the colonies are built makes them difficult to access and the *kachha* (rough) roads leading to the outskirts are not properly maintained, making them difficult to walk or ride on, particularly in the monsoon. What I am describing are nothing less than slums. For no good reason at all, this term is reserved for labeling the settlements in which the urban poor congregate. Such quarters in the countryside may be smaller and somewhat less congested, but they are otherwise similar to the deficient habitat of those who live a down-and-out existence in the urban milieu. The inhabitants buy their daily provisions in small shops or *galla*s, roadside cabins in their own neighborhood which sell a narrow range of commodities, since in terms of both quantity and quality the customers have to be modest in their purchases. Also in this respect, the contrast with mainstream society stands out because the non-poor are not shy in demonstrating their ability to consume more and better. All this contributes to making the gap in material well-being more visible than ever.

Living in slums and being constantly exposed to the deprivations that are inherent to such a dire existence is only part of a more comprehensive policy of exclusion that has turned the landless into a new class of untouchables. The deterioration of public health care over the last two decades, in the wake of the drive towards privatization, has made the Halpatis more vulnerable to disease. Because of the prohibitive cost, they delay seeking medical help. Only if the problem becomes unbearable do they consult professionals with lower qualifications than the doctors, clinics and hospitals frequented by the non-poor. Finally, segregation is a prominent feature in seeking access to education. Although the percentage of Halpati children going to school has steadily increased, still only half of them at best complete primary school. A small minority go on to secondary school, but they too tend to drop out after the first few standards. If they have become literate, their ability to read and write soon wanes again because of lack of practice. By and large, the children belonging to the higher castes continue their education for much longer. Moreover, the route they follow is different from the very beginning. The school in the village is nowadays only attended by the local poor. The high-caste parents send their children to private schools in town, which are considered to offer better quality. Apart from better teachers, the return on the investment is also growing up in the company of peers who share a similar elevated caste–class identity. The growing apartheid of the rural underclass is the inevitable outcome of a policy of exclusion in all walks of life.

Absence of collective action

To cope with deprivation is a full-time occupation and most people living precariously do not have much energy left for engaging in joint activities leading to redemption from their indigence. I am not suggesting that the Halpatis' way of life comes close to, or actually is, a culture of poverty. Their behavior is indeed marked by improvidence but this is mainly because the demand for their labor power is intermittent and the employment for which they qualify as unskilled or self-skilled workers is casual rather than regular, and is invariably paid on piece rates at the lowest possible level. Due to a chronic shortage of income many Halpatis have no other option than to ask for payment in advance. They refuse, however, to consider themselves subservient to one or more employers who have bought a claim on their labor power at some later stage. Nevertheless, using debt as an instrument for what I have called practices of neo-bondage adds to the dependency that is a major feature of poverty itself. Resistance against oppression and exploitation is difficult to organize when the supply of labor is structurally so much higher than the demand for it. The vested interests, by way of contrast, face fewer problems in taking a united stand when their domination is challenged. This does not mean that the Halpatis accept with docility the harsh treatment meted out to them. Agrarian relations are fragile as well as tense, and what begins as a quarrel may escalate into a regular fight. I reported on one such incident which began when an agricultural worker was beaten to death to punish him for his impudence.[18] Strikes do break out every now and then to articulate claims for a higher wage. But they tend to be spontaneous, rather then well planned, usually remain localized instead of spreading to other villages, and are short in duration because the landless have no reserves to live on. Lack of food brings them back to work after only a couple of days, and if this does not happen, the landowners back up their refusal to bargain by bringing in outside labor. It is true that the opening up of the rural economy has made the landless more mobile, but going out of the village or trying to gain access to regular work outside agriculture is not so easy. A proper job is difficult to come by since the eagerly awaited formalization of informal sector employment has not taken place. On the contrary, labor has become firmly informalized in all sectors of the economy.[19] Instead of changing their occupational profile from agricultural to industrial workers the landless masses remain footloose, but in a fluid and already saturated labor market. It is a workforce without skills, social capital and political leverage, a reserve army stuck in their rural slums, pushed out for some time and then pushed back again. They are fragmented over a wide range of short-term work niches and continually rotate among them. The pretension that they are self-employed in whatever they do at any moment needs to be addressed critically. Their mode of employment is a contractualized and casualized waged labor relationship, but one which makes it difficult to unite them in solidarity for concerted action.

Pauperism

Of the many problems I have with the great debate on poverty, as it is complacently called by a closed shop of number-crunching economists,[20] the major one is the fixing of a highly debatable poverty line and then clustering together all those who live beneath it as if they constitute a more or less homogeneous segment.[21] This kind of incomprehension shows the lack of insight concerning the various layers of deprivation, ranging below and above a decent livelihood, and of the differences among them. The households inhabiting the rural slums are differentiated from each other in composition and size as well as in levels of consumption. Reducing these variations to average figures would ignore a range of lifestyles, running from coping with adversities without being overwhelmed by them to having lost even minimal control over the circumstances conditioning one's life and giving up the fight for a better existence.

In contrast to the vast amount of literature on poverty, not much has been written on pauperism, but this is what strikes the eye when going around the landless colonies in the villages of my fieldwork: Gandevigam, Chikhligam and Bardoligam. It is expressed in symptoms suggesting that planning for today or tomorrow, let alone investment in future well-being, is impossible. Income from work is haphazardly spent without giving priority to the most basic needs, in particular a sufficient and adequate intake of food. Addiction to drink means that up to a quarter or even half of the wages earned is set aside for the purchase of illegally distilled alcohol. Quarrels with neighbors or within the household are a frequent occurrence. Husband and wife fall out with each other, unable to handle the misery in which they find themselves, and because of desertion or neglect children already have to fend for themselves at a very young age. Sometimes, the men are unable or unwilling to be the main providers for their households, but in other cases it is the women who default on their role as caretakers. Outside intervention to avoid the situation getting worse is rare. Neighbors or relatives are often too much bothered by their own problems to spend time on mediation or giving support to the victims. "We can't afford to live and act in solidarity," one of my halpati informants remarked. Communal institutions, such as the *panch*, which used to play an important role in maintaining social mores, arranging the celebration of religious festivals and settling internal disputes, have disappeared and have not been replaced by new conventions cementing togetherness in the landless milieu. Certainly, there is a section aspiring to achieve more respectability, to gain in dignity by demonstrating behavior expressive of the desire to belong to mainstream society. Women seem more than men to be at the forefront of that endeavor. Their ambition is to run a self-contained, well-ordered and sober household, to avoid abuse or being abused, to live within one's means and not to indulge in consumerism, to encourage their children to get educated beyond primary school, to economize on the inevitable *rites de passage*, to consolidate what they have and to reach out for more. Their presence is significant because it shows that not all the inhabitants of the landless colonies can be classed as lumpen. Having said that, I also want to emphasize that, among the Halpatis, the "deserving poor" are a minority segment. They swim against the tide

of deprivation and discrimination, and reaching where they want to be, out of indigence, is a long haul. Sliding back proves to be easier than moving up.

A dangerous class?

Mass poverty tends to be seen as a political risk to the established order. In this line of thinking the reserve army of labor does not remain sunk in apathy but can be mobilized for all kinds of subversive activities which put the security and comfort of well-established citizens at risk. It has been argued that the threat the restive and unwieldy lumpenproletariat posed to political stability was a major reason for giving this underclass access to mainstream society. To defuse their nuisance value, the poor had to be given a fair deal and be co-opted into the social security and other benefits which became available. This is why and how, according to de Swaan, the welfare state came into being during the restructuring of western economies from a rural–agrarian to an urban–industrial mode of production.[22] Is it possible to discern such a sobering reappraisal in the code of conduct of those who are better off and who see themselves not only as the driving force of "Shining India" but also as its natural beneficiaries? Are they genuinely making an effort to divide the spoils of economic progress between the haves and the have-nots a in a more balanced way than has been done so far? In the context of my fieldwork in south Gujarat I observe a trend in the opposite direction: not a narrowing but a widening of the gap between the people at the top from those at the bottom of the heap.

The landowning elite feel neither compassion nor anxiety about the misery in which the Halpatis live. Incidents do occur, when the local landless from the colonies on the outskirts attack members of the dominant caste and their property in the village, but these are irregular mishaps which do not escalate into a kind of class war, spilling over into neighboring localities. Moreover, the district police can be relied on to deal firmly with the mischief makers. How could the landless in their slums challenge the social fabric from which they have been excluded? Or rather, from which they are said to have excluded themselves. Because that is how Anavil Brahmans and Kanbi patidars tend to qualify the subhuman existence of Halpatis. Among those who are better off, the received wisdom is that poverty is the result of a defective way of life. In this view the landless have themselves to blame for remaining stuck in misery. This particular instance of blaming the victims is justified by various kinds of rationalizations, which elaborate on the indolence, irresponsibility, deceit, and malevolence of the Halpatis. These are all traits typically associated with criminality-prone lumpen behavior. I ventured to conclude a short essay on the relevance of the doctrine of social Darwinism with the remark that the relatively low level of technology which characterized the early phase of industrialization in the west ultimately enabled the laboring masses, until then written off as superfluous, to demand to become gainfully and decently employed:

> The industrial reserve army proved to be much more than useless ballast. Schooling put an end to the combination of hidden employment and too low wages. Around the turn of the [nineteenth] century and in the early years of the twentieth century, the poor succeeded in becoming full-fledged participants in the labour process of Western societies and contributed to growth in prosperity. Greater political representation was a logical outcome of this development.[23]

That same transformation does not appear to be the course giving shape and direction to the process of change that is currently under way in large parts of the world. Globalization is not for all those subjected to it a path towards more and better inclusion.

Mine is a dismal account, one which I need to qualify on two scores. In the first place, I have not discussed what has happened to the middle ranks in the countryside of south Gujarat. My experience, based on recurrent fieldwork, is that many of these people, holding some land or other productive assets, have been able to find somewhat more room for manoeuver. Having said that I would like to point out that the trend of change is set by the two classes at the poles of village society: the main landowners and the landless. They are at the forefront when it comes to finding out who has won and who has lost. Besides, as I have argued, in figuring out the sum total, the interdependency of the component parts needs to be stressed. The misery of the Halpatis can be understood only by tracing the dynamics of their subordination to the village elite. A second qualification which is required concerns the tricky issue of generalization. I immediately grant that landless labor elsewhere in the South Asian subcontinent may have fared better than the segment of this class in south Gujarat. There are reliable reports showing that where members of the rural proletariat were able to increase their bargaining strength by finding regular employment in the new industrial workshops or as construction workers in urban localities, farmers had no other choice but to raise agricultural wages in order to motivate at least part of the workforce to stay on. However, such success stories must also be seen in a wider perspective. They cannot be held up either as a disclaimer to the outcome of my research or as confirmation that the regional variation is so enormous that any generalizations are untenable. My findings are not unique; they have a relevance which goes beyond the villages I have closely investigated over a long period of time.[24] Moreover, the condition of poverty on which I have focused is not caused by backwardness. Gujarat is one of the fastest-growing states in the country and the landless I have been talking about belong to the heartland of the capitalism that has come to maturation here. In a new and vibrant stage, yes, but also ferocious and predatory in its impact.

The retreat of the state and the urgent need to bring back public space

An understated feature in my analysis of the political economy of agrarian change so far has been the role of the state. In propelling market fundamentalism, which has become the cornerstone of economic policy, the state surrendered the agency it earlier claimed as a balancing force between the interests of capital and of labor. "Inspection *raj* has gone," proclaimed Prime Minister Manmohan Singh, the head of what is misleadingly called the National Progressive Alliance. His rallying cry ended all pretension to insist on a minimum wage rate. The market would realize what the state failed to achieve: to raise more and more people above the poverty line. Statistics are being produced to vindicate the righteous choice made in favor of this most dogmatic brand of free enterprise. In Gujarat, the number of people below the poverty line has—in state-produced statistics—plummeted from 41.9 percent in 1983 to 14.2 percent in 2004–05. But on the Human Development Index, Gujarat ranks much lower than its official economic record would suggest. Traveling around urban and rural Gujarat it takes more than mere wishful thinking to accept the government's claim that the problem of indigence is on the verge of being solved. It requires the observer not to look behind the Potemkin façade that has been erected. The statistical tally is engineered by sending instructions from the commanding heights in the state to the district and subdistrict authorities not to issue new BPL (below poverty line) identity cards and to unregister households owning some durable assets, thus taking away their right to buy a monthly food ration at a subsidized price. Poverty has become a phenomenon which needs to be kept out of sight and out of the government's bookkeeping. Scaling down the size and intensity of misery, if not in reality then at least on paper, is part of the "Shining India" operation.

The retreat of the state in keeping a check on how the economy is run has not only resulted in a policy of deregulation aimed at repealing a host of restrictions on the free interplay of the forces of production, but has also led to an erosion of the public domain. The proponents of this approach maintain that privatization is the ultimate solution and that the state has no business in poverty alleviation. People living in that condition have to avail themselves of economic incentives which give a higher return to their labor power. In this perception, appealing to self-interest is the best route to upward mobility and the reward for heeding that message is crossing the poverty line. Nevertheless, in the face of immense misery due to underemployment, low wages, failing health or old age, by no means everyone is convinced by the logic of the free market and its supposed benevolence. In the National Alliance which is currently (2008) in power at the central level, Congress has been put under pressure to generate employment by carrying out public works, introducing social security benefits for the more than 90 percent of the total labor force working in the informal sector of the economy, and upgrading labor standards in order to safeguard workers against hazards to health and well-being. One of the measures suggested under the latter scheme put forward in a report of the National Commission of Enterprises in the Unorganized Sector (NCEUS), is the introduction of a minimum wage.[25] The proposal seems to acknowledge that the unbridled working of the market needs to be tamed by public action. It is rather naive, to put it mildly—after having given in to the strong pressure for a thorough informalization of the economy and endorsing the verdict that the formalization of employment is the root cause of sustained poverty—to suggest that the consequences of this policy can be repaired with state-sponsored regulations that are in stark contrast to the spirit of market fundamentalism. Paying lip service to the rights of workers and the promise to provide security for them at times of illness or old age may very well be an electoral ploy. One wonders if the political will does exist to restore the public domain and bring the state back into the promotion of social welfare. My strong reservations about such an emancipatory course of action taking place in south Gujarat are in the last instance based on the fact that the devolution of political power has not been able to break through the closed front of vested interests. In my longstanding fieldwork experience it has remained an exercise in pseudo-democratization. The landowning elite, working hand in glove with the local state bureaucracy, has consistently frustrated attempts to include the rural poor. In a report on one of my field trips a quarter of a century ago, I described what had become of the *gram majur kalyan kendra* (rural workers' welfare center) set up by the government a few years before.[26] These centers are still there, as ineffective as before, and the new welfare schemes are meant to be launched from these nodal points of social action for poverty alleviation. Going by their past performance, it is not so difficult to predict that the outcome will again be negative.

Conclusion

My conclusion is that, if space is not provided for political empowerment of the rural poor, their inclusion in mainstream society is bound to remain a mere figment of the imagination, nothing but an illusion which may well turn into a fascist nightmare. The doctrine of market fundamentalism and an ingrained ideology of social inequality are a deadly combination. The upshot of that reactionary regime is that the landless caste–class should not be included. From the vantage point of the well-to-do, they get no less and no more than what they deserve: exclusion from a decent existence, leading their lives on the village outskirts and on the margins of the economy. In this chapter, I have expressed my skepticism that a reversal in the trend towards exclusion is in the offing. But what about the long-term perspective for emancipation of the rural underclass? One needs a historicizing mindset to remain hopeful. A

definite step forward was when the Halpatis managed to find redemption from age old bondage half a century ago. Mere blinking at an egalitarian mirage was how D.A. Low summed up the outcome of the populist interlude in India and other third world countries during the second half of the twentieth century.[27] Indeed, for large parts of mankind living in decency and dignity is a faraway dream. But have the landless in south Gujarat lost all hope that such a day will come? Monitoring the milieu at the bottom of the village economy in the past decades at close quarters, I have found no symptoms of an internalization of subordination and a passive acceptance of the doctrine of inequality. The mood in the rural slums is sultry, inspired more by sullenness, resentment, and anguish than by docility. To be sure, those feelings are not converted into concerted action. But is it not only after the event, in retrospect, that the turning point from disguised resistance to open and more sustained revolt can be identified?

Notes

1 Government of India, *All India Agricultural Labour Enquiry Report on Intensive Survey of Agricultural Labour. . ., 1950–51*, Vol. 1 (Delhi: Manager of Publications [MOP], 1955).

2 Daniel Thorner, *The Agrarian Prospect in India: Five Lectures on Land Reform Delivered in 1955 at the Delhi School of Economics*, 2nd edn (Bombay: Allied, 1976).

3 Gunnar Myrdal, *Asian Drama: An Enquiry into the Poverty of Nations*, Vol. II (New York: Twentieth Century Fund, 1968), p. 1,375.

4 See Thorner, 1976, pp. 70–71.

5 Walter Hauser, *Sahajanand on Agricultural Labour and the Rural Poor* (Delhi: Manohar, 1994). Also Walter Hauser, *Culture, Vernacular Politics and the Peasants* (Delhi: Manohar, 2006).

6 See Jan Breman, "The Study of Indian Industrial Labour in Post-Colonial India," in Jonathan Parry *et al.* (eds), *The Worlds of Indian Industrial Labour* (New Delhi: Sage, 2002).

7 Jan Breman, *Labour Bondage in West India: From Past to Present* (Delhi: Oxford University Press, 2007), p. 168.

8   *Sala*, literally brother-in-law, is very commonly used also as a term of abuse, so the meaning here is, more or less, "miserable weakling," but is really much stronger than that in Hindi and Gujarati.

9   I have elaborated on these issues in Breman, *Labour Bondage*.

10 Jan Breman, *Patronage and Exploitation: Changing Agrarian Relations in South Gujarat* (Berkeley, CA: University of California Press, 1974).

11 Government of Gujarat, *Report of the Minimum Wages Advisory Committee for Employment in Agriculture* (Ahmedabad: Government of Gujarat, 1966).

12 See "The Agrarian Question in the Struggle for National Independence," in Breman, *Labour Bondage*.

13 See Jan Breman, "I am the Government Labour Officer," *Economic and Political Weekly* [*EPW*], Vol. 20, No. 24 (15 June, 1985), pp. 1,043–55. Reprinted in Jan Breman, *Wage Hunters and Gatherers* (Delhi: Oxford University Press, 1994), ch. iv.

14 I have seen no reason to change my assessment on the role played by the HSS after my first critical report in Jan Breman, "Mobilisation of Landless Labourers; Halpatis of South Gujarat," *EPW*, Vol. 9, No. 12 (23 March, 1974), pp. 489–96.

15 This was the theme of my fieldwork in south Gujarat during the last decade of the twentieth century; see Jan Breman, *Footloose Labour: Working in India's Informal Economy* (Cambridge: University Press, 1996).

16 Jan Breman, *Peasants, Migrants and Paupers: Capitalist Production and Labour Circulation in West India* (Oxford: Clarendon Press and Delhi: Oxford University Press, 1985).

17 See chapters 3 and 4 in Breman, *Labour Bondage*.

18 Jan Breman, "Silencing the Voice of Agricultural Labourers," in *The Labouring Poor in India* (Delhi and Oxford: University Press, 2003), ch. ii.

19 See Jan Breman, "A Question of Poverty," in Breman, *The Labouring Poor*, ch. vi.

20 See Angus Deaton and Valerie Kozel (eds), *The Great Indian Poverty Debate* (Delhi: Macmillan, 2005).

21 The only concession made in part of the literature is to separate the poor from the very poor or destitute, a distinction in which the latter category is identified as having less than three-quarters of the amount of the cutoff point for the poverty line.

22 Abram de Swaan, *In Care of the State: Health Care, Education and Welfare in Europe and the USA in the Modern Era* (Cambridge: Polity Press, 1988).

23 Jan Breman, "Return of Social Inequality: A Fashionable Doctrine," *EPW*, Vol. 39, No. 35 (28 August, 2004), p. 3,872.

24 See Jan Breman, *The Poverty Regime in Village India: Half a Century of Work and Life at the Bottom of the Rural Economy in South Gujarat* (Delhi: Oxford University Press, 2007). Factual evidence backing up my reading of rural dynamics can be found in a large number of empirical studies. To name but a few: Government of India, Ministry of Labour, New Delhi, *Report of the National Commission on Rural Labour*, Vols I and II (1991). See also Stuart Corbridge *et al.*, *Seeing the State: Governance and Governmentality in India*, Part III The Poor and the State, pp. 219–74; and Barbara Harriss-White, *India Working: Essays on Society and Economy* (Cambridge: University Press, 2003), ch. ii; Arun Sinha, *Against the Few; Struggles of India's Rural Poor* (London: Zed Books, 1991); P. Sainath, *Everybody Loves a Good Drought; Stories from India's Poorest Districts* (New Delhi: Penguin Books, 1996). Specifically on rural labor, see the Special Issue on Rural Labour published by the *Journal of Peasant Studies*, Terrence Byres *et al.* (eds), Vol. 26, Nos 2–3 (1999).

25 National Commission for Enterprises in the Unorganized Sector, *Report on Social Security for Unorganized Workers* (New Delhi, 2006); see also *Report on Conditions of Work and Promotion of Livelihoods in the Unorganised Sector* (New Delhi, 2007).

26 See Jan Breman, "State Protection for the Rural Proletariat," in *Wage Hunters and Gatherers*, ch iv. When I recently paid a visit to one of these centers located close to Chikhligam I found that nothing had changed at all. Window dressing is the best way to explain why they have not been closed down.

27 D. Anthony Low, *The Egalitarian Moment: Asia and Africa 1950–1980* (Cambridge: University Press, 1996).

23

Economic development and sociopolitical change in Sri Lanka since Independence

W. D. Lakshman

Historical backdrop

The beginnings of the modern economic history of Sri Lanka are conventionally traced to the commencement (in the 1840s) of organized cultivation of export crops and the related development of "modern" trading, transport, communication, and financial activities under British colonial rule. Based initially on capital from Britain, capitalist development in the colony gradually gave rise to a capitalist class of domestic origin.[1] Workers brought from southern India to work in plantations as indentured labor formed the core of the working class, which gradually expanded in numbers as well as in terms of trade union organization, drawing in workers from other growing sectors.[2]

The overall result of these developments since the beginnings of plantation agriculture has been the emergence of such conditions in Sri Lanka as would make it an export economy par excellence. Around the time of Independence in 1948, export earnings formed an estimated 30 percent of national product according to the country's initial national accounting statistics.[3] Three primary commodities—tea, rubber and coconut—formed more than 95 percent of these exports, with tea alone contributing as much as 60 percent. The corollary

to this production pattern, in which a substantial part of the country's natural and human resources was devoted to export production, was an excessive dependence on imports, not only for manufactured, but also for agricultural goods. A dominant share of imports consisted of essential food items. Some described the economy at the time, therefore, as an "export–import economy."

In the transformation of the system of colonial rule, there was an experimental stage of "partial self-government" (1931–48).[4] The practice of taxing part of the "surplus" generated in the export economy and using it for social development expenditures of the government—particularly to expand educational and health facilities—was developed during this period.[5] Among these social expenditure programs, the most far reaching— and virtually unique in the colonial world— were the free education and free medical facilities programs in relevant governmental institutions. To these social expenditures, a program of rationed distribution of certain essential food items, like rice at subsidized prices, was added during the Second World War. These social policy innovations were influenced by a widely prevailing political philosophy of social democracy, actively promoted by a group of Marxist intellectuals turned politicians, who initiated a vibrant socialist movement in the country.[6] The resulting sociopolitical and economic state of affairs in the country at Independence was the Sri Lankan variety of a welfare state. For its sustenance, it depended on continued economic prosperity of the country and the ability of the state to tax the well-to-do classes without adverse effects on their earning capacity. It was not a welfare state system integrally bound to the system of production, employment and income generation.

Having become used to free services, subsidies, and handouts from the government, the electorate had learnt to expect all elected governments to continue the practice. The majority in the electorate probably had neither the knowledge nor the common sense to be concerned about who pays for these services. Political parties contesting elections have developed the practice of pledging more "welfare" services at election times, to learn— if and when the implementation time came— that the required sources of finance are not easy to find. This is the sociopolitical foundation for some of the problems widely discussed during the post-Independence period in relation to development policy, namely, short-term policy horizon, lack of long-term consistency in vision, the electoral policy cycle, sacrifice of logic and sense to populism in policymaking and so on.

Another implication was that the ruling class, to whom the British transferred the responsibility of managing Sri Lankan affairs after their departure and the members of which were elected to governmental power in the immediate aftermath of Independence, was enamored with the socioeconomic results of colonial policy experience, that is to say, reasonably successful economic growth based on export-oriented primary production together with impressive state-engineered human development. These governments did not consider it prudent to change track. Economic policy began to change only when post-war world market conditions began to change, producing forces inimical to the continued success of export-oriented primary production. The principal symptom of this change, seen after the mid-1950s, was the secular deterioration in the country's commodity terms of trade, namely the ratio of export prices to import prices. The deterioration of a country's terms of trade indicates a decline in the amount of imports it can purchase with a unit of its exports. The deterioration in these terms from 1950 = 520 to 1990 = 100 was indeed catastrophic.[7] Sri Lanka moved in the direction of import substitution industrialization— so common in the rest of the third world after the Second World War—only about a decade after Independence.

Economic development since the late 1970s

I have examined the character of development Sri Lanka has achieved since political Independence in some detail in an earlier publication.[8] I provide here only a brief sketch of the development processes during the more recent half of the 60-year period since Independence, namely the period since 1977 when Sri Lanka moved into a package of neoliberal economic policies. A violent separatist movement of ethno-political origin ran through the most part of this period. It was spearheaded by a group from the minority Tamil community – the Liberation Tigers of Tamil Elam (LTTE) – which gradually evolved into a fascistic-terrorist outfit* of significant domestic and international influence. This rebellion was eventually put down and the LTTE annihilated by the country's armed forces through a military campaign ending on 18 May, 2009. This defeat of the LTTE is likely to become a critical watershed in post-Independence Sri Lankan history, opening up as it does great opportunities for accelerated national development.

Economic growth in Sri Lanka, in terms of real GDP or real GDP per capita, in the first three decades after Independence was consistent but slow. Because of sluggishness in its rate of expansion, a number of Asian countries, formerly at similar or lower standing, have surpassed Sri Lanka economically.[9] Great concern has been expressed in many circles about this relative stagnation of the country. Moving into a regime of neoliberal policies in the late 1970s was motivated—aside from the ideological predilections of those in power— by a desire to accelerate economic growth. Yet Sri Lanka's performance in terms of long-term economic growth even under neoliberal policies has been lackluster, significantly less than in what the World Bank calls "high performing economies" in Asia.[10] Growth during this period, contrary to expectations, was never higher than 8.2 percent per annum—that too in one single year (1978), soon after liberalization of the economy, perhaps indicating an element of "beginner's luck."[11] The period average of the growth rate was substantially lower at 5.0 percent during the entire period of 1978–2008. In the sub-periods 1978–87, 1988–97, and 1998–2008, the average growth rates were respectively 5.2, 4.8, and 5.0 percent. The average growth rate of the last-mentioned sub-period would have been higher if not for negative growth (–1.6) recorded in 2001. Growth rate remained above 6 percent after 2005.

This lackluster growth scenario reflects the working of a complex array of underlying economic, technological, social, and political factors. These constraints have been reflected in some important imbalances, leading often to serious short-term instability as well as imposing limits on long-term economic growth. Capital formation as a proportion of GDP, lower than in many fast growth countries in East and Southeast Asia, was nevertheless significantly higher than the domestic saving ratio. For example, in 2008 these two ratios were respectively 28 and 14 percent. In almost every year during this period, domestic savings fell short of investment, making the country heavily dependent on "foreign" savings (from foreign aid, foreign direct investments and remittances from migrant workers) to maintain the higher rate of investment. Two related

imbalances in the system have been observed in the balance of payments and the government budget. The current account deficit in the balance of payments (as percent of GDP) averaged –5.5 percent during 1978–2008 and ranged between –0.4 percent in 2003 and –16.4 percent in 1980. The budget deficit averaged 10.9 percent of GDP during 1978–2008 and ranged between 7.5 percent in 1999 and 23.1 percent in 1980. These savings, current account, and budget deficits have figured prominently in the country's macroeconomic management over almost the entirety of the last three decades, making the movement on to a higher growth trajectory problematic and difficult.

The modest economic growth of this period was coupled with considerable structural change. The share of primary (agricultural and related) activities in the economy has declined substantially to reach 13 percent of GDP in 2008. Their contribution to total employment in 2008 was 33 percent indicating, among other things, the relatively low productivity, on average, of those engaged in primary activities. These numbers for 2008, compared to a 30 percent GDP proportion for 1978 and a 53 percent employment proportion for 1978–79,[12] are indicative of substantial declines in relevant percentages. The peculiarity of the pattern of structural change in Sri Lanka, considering the fact that the country is still at a low level of economic attainment, is that the declining agriculture share was offset not so much by a rising industry/manufacturing share[13] but by a substantial increase in the share of the services sector. In 2008, the share of services in GDP was 57 percent. These services included highly remunerative activities like banking, financial, and IT services, not so well paid but quite secure jobs in government administration, and rather poorly remunerated personal services.

Another important aspect of structural change is reflected in shifts in the composition of foreign trade. The significance of the trio of agricultural exports—tea, rubber, and coconut—has declined drastically, from 77 percent in 1978 to 19 percent in 2008. Their proportional drop was offset by a rise in industrial exports (76 percent in 2008) among which textiles and garments occupy the key position. The share of textiles and garments— 4 percent in 1978 and 43 percent in 2008—is only a few percentage points less than the 49 percent share of tea in 1978. In terms of the extent of commodity concentration of exports, Sri Lanka has been transformed from its "tea country" position to a "garments country" position. The increase in export values and the significant structural transformation of exports over time have not been sufficient to meet the growing import needs of people and production sectors. The entire period of three previous decades was characterized by large annual trade deficits. In 2008 this was as large as 14.4 percent of GDP. Commodity composition of imports too changed. The proportion of consumer goods in total imports declined. This decline was compensated almost fully by a corresponding increase in the share of intermediate goods. The proportion of investment goods in the total has remained virtually constant. The import proportion of intermediate goods, with petroleum and textiles occupying large individual shares, was as high as 62 percent in 2008.

The pattern of economic growth and structural change appears to have been "employment friendly," perhaps because of pressures emanating from prevailing sociopolitical forces. The rate of unemployment had its ups and downs during the last three decades, but since around 1990 its trend has been downward—from around 15–16 percent in the early 1990s to 5.2 percent in 2008. As has been normal in Sri Lanka, the unemployment rate has been higher for women than for men, for the young (15–24 years of age) members of the labor force than for the older (above 25 years of age) members and for the more educated than for the less educated. The pattern of distribution of the unemployed, described by the International Labor Office (ILO) in 1971[14] as indicating a structural mismatch between aspirations and available opportunities, continues to prevail, although to

a lesser extent than in the 1970s. Extensive unemployment, often of long duration, among the educated youth has proved to be extremely destabilizing socially and politically.

An unemployment rate of around 5 percent is historically the lowest recorded in Sri Lanka since the beginnings of the practice of collecting detailed employment-related data from the late 1960s when the labor force and socioeconomic survey of 1969–70 was conducted.[15] Allowing for frictional unemployment,[16] an unemployment rate of 5 percent may be interpreted as a condition very close to full employment. Whatever it may be, the production contribution of a large proportion of the employed can be expected to have been very small. Several points may be noted in this regard.

First, given the stage of development of the country, self-employment or own account work has always been a major source of employment for Sri Lankan workers. Own account workers as a percentage of total employment during 1990–2007 ranged between 25 and 31 percent. The relevant percentages for male workers were 30 and 35. Under neoliberal policies, both governmental and non-governmental organizations have actively promoted self-employment. The bulk of the self-employment opportunities opened up are likely to have been subsistence/survival-type activities of low productivity.

Second, since 2005—after a period of restrictions on recruitments to public service— tens of thousands of relatively more educated youth have been recruited to government service, already known for its overstaffing problems. The expansion of employment in public administration, and often also in state-owned enterprises, is likely to have added to "underemployed" full-time workers, implying that the service delivery could be maintained, both in quantity and quality terms, with substantially lower employment numbers.

Third, a very large proportion of total employment—this time too in the public sector—comes from the armed services. This is the legacy of the 30-year armed conflict with the LTTE, which ended on 18 May, 2009.

The armed forces are likely to continue as a large employer for some more years to come as, for purposes of national security, those recruited at the time of armed conflict are retained in service together with a significant number of new recruits. The government continues to be concerned about the threats to security coming from remaining elements of the LTTE, from both within and outside Sri Lanka. The production contribution of armed forces, at the time of armed conflict, would have been at best dubious.[17] At the present time with hard-earned peace, however, the armed forces personnel are increasingly being used in numerous developmental projects, in addition to their normal national-security-related responsibilities, particularly in the formerly LTTE-controlled areas in the north and the east of the country .

To summarize, the average rate of economic growth has been around five percent per annum over the last three decades and the economy has moved gradually toward virtual full employment conditions. Yet, as the average productivity of a large proportion of workers in employment has remained low, total production in the country is most likely to have been less than potential. Given the political economy conditions as described earlier, the sharing of whatever was produced came to be determined partly in markets and partly in the political system. Market forces under neoliberal policies, as elsewhere in the world, have produced conditions that favor a heavy concentration of incomes and wealth in the hands of the rich classes—owners and managers of capital and large land holdings, holders of remunerative positions, and so on. The structural transformations observed in the last three decades have also produced a change in activity areas from which the country's wealthy have accumulated their riches. Many of those who became rich through large land holdings and plantations in a different era continued to wield power, but the richest stratum in the country during the last three decades has come from activity areas like banking and finance, export-oriented manufacturing (e.g., garments), and

trade.[18] Investments in the private sector providers of social services like health and education are also seen as sources of wealth for the rich classes. Those who could exercise power over markets, due to large market shares controlled by them, have accumulated more. The political mechanism, as it operated in Sri Lanka, has added an additional dimension to this market-led process of income and wealth concentration. The politically powerful and their helpers and cronies, often in collaboration with the bureaucracy, used their political/administrative clout to gain financially from income- and wealth-generating processes in the country. They gained in numerous ways. Undue personal gains have been made in the execution of tenders involving construction or purchase contracts in government-funded projects. Going by intelligent guesswork and "whistleblowers" in the system, the practice of commission-taking and bribery has been rampant among the politically and bureaucratically powerful elements. There have also been many cases of bribery investigated and proven against, normally, lower level officials in bribery commission investigations but only a very few against the powerful. The politically powerful have indeed become a very rich stratum in society alongside owners and managers of capital and land.

Coupled with relatively slow economic growth and the economy remaining at less than its production potential, there has been significant social change. Society, including communities in areas rather remote from the metropolis, has been subject to varying degrees of globalization influences. The spread of mass communication facilities, particularly television, and the extensive phenomenon of migration of domestic workers to foreign countries have been significant factors in this social transformation. The preponderance of women in household service jobs abroad constitutes a major element in this labor migration phenomenon. During the time of the armed conflict with the LTTE, people in the affected areas of the north and the east were, to a large extent, cut off from globalization influences. Yet large numbers of people have migrated abroad from these areas, not completely severing their links with kith and kin left behind.

The important point here is that people in Sri Lanka, including the relatively not so well-to-do, were aware of what they were missing in terms of basic necessities of life that are available in more affluent societies. The influence this awareness has had on people's aspirations has obviously been strong. The prevailing high level of literacy and relatively high school participation rates at all primary, junior secondary and senior secondary levels have strengthened the process of social change, particularly those arising out of growing aspirations. There was, furthermore, the experience gained by many people at even low income levels from participation in various social movements—village-level voluntary associations, electoral processes, trade unions and political protests. The experience in the exercise of universal adult franchise at national and subnational level elections for as many as 75 years and that of changing governments through ballot on many occasions have perhaps given a sense of power to the electorate, although this would have been deceptive when taken out of the context of distribution of real power in the society.

The point to be highlighted is that all this has added another dimension to the process of contest for a share of the available resources and opportunities. Ordinary people do not have any organizational or other power to influence markets in their favor. But over the years, they have learnt to use the available political mechanisms to gain and retain economic and social benefits provided by government. Without this political mechanism, these social welfare benefits would have been denied to or withdrawn from them.

In spite of the plea from Washington institutions advising the government to reduce the scale of government activities, domestic political compulsions have been such that Sri Lanka has retained much of the social welfare network built up over the years, even at the cost of large budget deficits. Provision of certain services free of charge—e.g., water supply for domestic use—was abandoned, but free education and free health services (in relevant public sector institutions) have been retained, in spite of discussions at policymaking levels about the need for charging user fees.[19] Various populist measures have been introduced to satisfy the electorate—for example, "poverty alleviation programs"—although at the implementation level these have often failed to reach the stated goals. Subsidies on consumer essentials as well as for weaker production sectors like agriculture were also implemented. As noted, the combined operation of the market and political mechanisms has made the rich richer. According to data from the Consumer Finances Surveys of the Central Bank, the Gini coefficient for spending units has increased during the period of neoliberal policy reforms from 0.35 in 1973 to 0.46 in 2003–04. The ratio of the income share of the highest quintile to that of the lowest changed from nine times in 1973 to 14 times in 2003–04.[20] Suspicion has often been expressed concerning whether the poor actually gained from programs maintained ostensibly for their benefit. But these programs were anyway offered mainly to satisfy these classes in order to win their support at elections and to gain their acquiescence to maintain relative social peace.

In the multiethnic Sri Lankan society, these policies worked fairly satisfactorily most of the time in regions dominated by the majority community, the Sinhalese.[21] This was not so in regions—northern and eastern—dominated by the principal minority communities of the country. The armed separatist struggle in these regions, led by the LTTE had many causes. The failure of market and political mechanisms to provide a fair deal to the country's north and east appears to have been a major causal factor. The strong bias of neoliberal policies toward regional inequality is widely known. The Western Province,[22] with a population share of 29 percent, produces as much as half of the GDP. Of the nine provinces in the country, the market mechanism has left several underdeveloped but the political mechanism operated to lessen the disadvantages suffered by those provinces dominated by the Sinhalese community. Several special programs were implemented to ease the degree of regional underdevelopment there. The political mechanism, however, did not operate so favorably within the Northern and Eastern Provinces. The people in these provinces, particularly the Tamils, voted mostly for political groups which stood against the ruling party in the central administration on many key issues. The government has therefore taken very little action of positive discrimination in favor of people in these regions.

Constitutional and political processes

Sri Lanka gained political Independence in 1948 after four-and-a-half centuries of European colonialism: Portuguese, Dutch, and British. The Independence movement, not as intensively carried out as, for example, in India, reached its goals largely on the basis of negotiations between the British government and the politically prominent elites in Sri Lanka. In this process, at the last stages of British colonial rule, in 1931, the people in Sri Lanka were introduced to the principle of electing their "rulers" through universal adult franchise. This was perhaps an experiment on the part of the British government at the time as there was hardly any concerted agitation locally for universal adult franchise. At Independence, in any case, the adult population of Sri Lanka had already gained the experience of exercising their voting right for the election of legislators over a period of 15 years.

Independent rule commenced with a Westminster-type of parliamentary and cabinet government. Sri Lankan elites at the time opted for dominion status within the British Commonwealth, with the British monarch as the head of state represented by an appointed governor-general. The prime minister, commanding a majority in the lower house in the bicameral parliament, was the executive head

of government. The constitutional changes of 1972 had introduced a republican constitution with an appointed president as head of state. The parliamentary/cabinet system of government was, however, retained. In a second far-reaching constitutional reform in 1978, a presidential system of government was introduced, with an elected president as both head of state and government. Under this constitution, the president enjoys enormous constitutional power. The electoral system too was changed from an electorate-based system of electing candidates on the first-past-the-post-principle to a district-based system of proportional representation.

Until 1987, Sri Lanka had a highly centralized form of government. Responding to Tamil demands for self-government and pressures exercised at the time by the Indian government, a system of provincial councils (PCs) was introduced in 1987 in a significant amendment to the constitution. The purpose was to introduce an element of devolution of power. Within the country's highly centralized political culture, however, the system of PCs has so far failed to devolve powers significantly. The center has been hesitant to give up its powers to PCs and PCs also were not agitating strongly enough to win over what is their constitutional right. To make matters worse, the center has systematically encroached into even the areas of jurisdiction entrusted to PCs by the 1987 constitutional amendment.[23]

However, when compared to the failures of many postcolonial states to retain representative forms of government, the maintenance of a system of representative democracy for over half a century in Sri Lanka, under the trying conditions of overall sociopolitical and economic underdevelopment, extensive armed conflict, and increasing militarization of society, is remarkable. Yet, shortcomings in the exercise of electoral democracy have become quite prominent in more recent times such that discussions today would often highlight these negative elements, neglecting the positive achievements of Sri Lankan democracy. The practice of politics is a contest for power.

The character of participants in this contest at the leadership level, the manner in which this contest is carried out, and the rules of the game guiding the contestants have undergone significant change over time. In early post-Independence times, persons who had already achieved elite status in society through birth, wealth, or education prevailed in the political contest for power. In more recent times, the practice of politics has become a path to achieve elite status in society. In contrast to the past, when many who came to practice politics were interested in social/national service, today many in politics appear to use political power to accumulate personal wealth. After a couple of violent anti-state movements, the society has achieved in May 2009 conditions of relative peace. Law and order situation and conditions of human security have improved tremendously. An element of the process of militarization of society that operated during the time of civil war [24] may prevail for some more time. As a result of conflict-laden conditions of the last three decades, electoral politics too has become characterized by extensive use of violence. With transparency and accountability becoming less highly valued in the use of political power, issues of poor governance have come to be highlighted by many domestic and international commentators on Sri Lankan politics. There is, unfortunately, no simple formula to strengthen practices of good governance, in the same way as there is no simple formula and short cut to sustainable and balanced development.

Human development

The operation of market and political mechanisms of allocation, discussed earlier, has brought about important socioeconomic transformations, producing distinct and notable changes in the quality of life of ordinary people. Absolute poverty for the whole country, measured by the familiar headcount ratio, was at or above 23 percent in the preceeding quarter century but had come down signi-

ficantly to 15 percent by 2006/07 – the latest year of data availability. The inequality in the distribution of incomes and wealth, however, remains, with the poverty ratio also varying significantly as between different regions and social segments. Sociopolitical forces, which generated the Sri Lankan welfare state, were also referred to earlier. The superior human development record of Sri Lanka, in terms of such measures as the Physical Quality of Life Index (PQLI) and the Human Development Index (HDI) and various disaggregated social indicators, amidst relatively low per capita income conditions, has received attention in the development literature for about four decades. [25] Life expectancy at birth at around 73 years, a population proportion of 93 percent with access to health services, an adult literacy rate of 96 percent, an infant mortality rate of 16 per 1,000 live births, primary school enrolment rate of 98 percent are some of these human development achievements at a per capita GNP of US $1,969. This is the foundation of the well-known Sri Lankan policy achievement in terms of social indicators, often described as the country's "outlier status" in inter-country comparisons. At a relatively low level of economic attainment in terms of per capita income, Sri Lankans have come to enjoy a level of human development corresponding to substantially higher income levels. It may be also noted that Sri Lanka has either already achieved or on target to achieve the bulk of the Millennium Development Goals (MDG). [26] Also noted in this literature is the lower relative inequality in distribution of income until about the end of the 1970s. The significant tendency toward income and wealth concentration during the three recent decades of neo liberal policies has already been noted.

"Social indicators," being aggregative in nature, have their weaknesses and limitations as measures of living conditions of ordinary people. Averages do hide distributional inequalities. It was through different types of "public action," sometimes complementary to market forces, and sometimes contradictory, that the country managed to achieve this outlier status in terms of human development achievements. A significant factor to be noted in this regard is the relative equality of the status of men and women in terms of these human development achievements. There has also been substantial upward mobility in society, a consequence of education, coupled with hard work and good fortune. All this is indicative of the social democratic directions in which the contest for resources and opportunities has been resolved in political and market processes.

Conclusion

As noted, Sri Lanka's per capita income in 2008 was US $1,969. Over the last several years it has been grouped into the "lower middle income" category of countries in the World Bank country classification. It has been undergoing a process of economic liberalization over the last three decades. Although the main objective behind liberalization has been to accelerate economic progress, the rate of economic growth during this period averaged a moderate five percent. As has happened so often elsewhere, the neoliberal policy package has led to increased inequality in both income distribution and regional development. The poverty head count ratio, however, had come down to 15 percent in 2006/7. This is the lowest level to which the poverty headcount ratio has dropped since regular computation of poverty statistics began in the 1980s.

Yet Sri Lanka stands out among developing countries for its high average levels of human development, whether measured by the HDI or by social indicators taken separately. Sri Lanka is ranked among countries with "medium human development" in terms of HDI. Its HDI ranking has consistently been higher, that is to say, better than its GDP per capita ranking. It has been described as an outlier in intercountry comparisons of social indicators vis-à-vis per capita GDP levels. The argument in this chapter has been that Sri Lanka's superior performance in terms

of human development has been largely a consequence of public action intervening in market processes.

It was argued earlier that the unusual results of the development process in Sri Lanka have occurred through a combined operation of two mechanisms, which determined resource allocation and income distribution patterns, namely, the market mechanism and the political mechanism. Patterns of allocation and distribution result from a contest among different social groups and different economic activities for available opportunities, resources, and benefits. These contests are resolved through *both* markets and the political system. Distribution no doubt favored the rich but welfare-oriented public action has persisted because of the pressures of a politically conscious electorate. People seem to treat certain welfare services provided by the state free of charge as part of their fundamental rights. The best examples in this sense are educational and health services provided by the state free of charge for those who care to use them. The government too has come to view these social welfare expenditures as indispensable to secure and maintain social peace, an essential prerequisite for the achievement of accelerated economic growth.

Notes

* The editor does not agree with this designation for the Tamil Tigers.

1 Kumari Jayawardena, *Nobodies to Somebodies: The Rise of the Colonial Bourgeoisie in Sri Lanka* (Colombo: Social Scientists Association and Sanjiva Books, 2007); S. B. D. De Silva, *The Political Economy of Underdevelopment* (London: Routledge & Kegan Paul, 1982); Donald R. Snodgrass, *Ceylon: An Export Economy in Transition* (Homewood, IL: Richard D. Irwin, 1966).

2 Kumari Jayawardena, *The Rise of the Labor Movement in Ceylon* (Colombo: Sanjiva Books, 2004).

3 Since the economic product of many "traditional" sectors of the economy is likely to have been significantly underestimated, this export

percentage would overestimate the contemporary contribution of exports to national product.

4   This was perhaps a unique experience in the entire British colonial history. People in Sri Lanka were given the right of universal adult suffrage and a system of government in which seven out of the ten members in the executive— the board of ministers—came from elected representatives in the state council. The other three ministers were British government officials.

5   Patricia Alailima, "The Human Development Perspective," in W. D. Lakshman and C. A. Tisdell (eds), *Sri Lanka's Development Since Independence: Socio-economic Perspectives and Analyses* (New York: Nova Science, 2000).

6   Y. Ranjith Amarasinghe, *Revolutionary Idealism and Parliamentary Politics: A Study of Trotskyism in Sri Lanka* (Colombo: Social Scientists Association, 1998).

7   By 1990, the trade pattern had undergone substantial change. Sri Lanka became a developing country exporting manufactured goods. Terms of trade movements after this year, more complex than before, are not taken up for comment here.

8   W. D. Laksham and C. A. Tisdell (eds), *Sri Lanka's Development since Independence: Socio-economic Perspectives and Analyses* (New York: Nova Science, 2000), pp. 1–10.

9   W. D. Laksham (ed.), *Dilemmas of Development: Fifty Years of Economic Change in Sri Lanka* (Colombo: Sri Lanka Association of Economists, 1997), pp. 13–16.

10 World Bank, *The East Asian Miracle: Economic Growth and Public Police* (Oxford: University Press, 1993), p. 21.

11 W. D. Lakshman, "State Policy in Sri Lanka and its Economic Impact 1970–85: Selected Themes with Special Reference to Distributive Implications of Policy," *Upanathi*, Vol. 1, No. 1 (January 1986), p. 21.

12 Central Bank of Ceylon, *Report on Consumer Finances and Socio Economic Survey 1981/82 Sri Lanka* (Colombo: Central Bank of Sri Lanka, 1984), Table 4.18, p. 136.

13 Industry share in 2006 was 27 percent and that of manufacturing 16 percent. The relevant 1977 proportions were, respectively, 29 and 17 percent. The national accounting data for the two years, however, are of doubtful comparability.

14 International Labour Organisation (ILO), *Matching Employment Opportunities and Expectations: A Programme of Action for Ceylon: Report* (Geneva: ILO, 1971).

15 Sri Lanka Government, Department of Census and Statistics (DCS), *Socio-economic Survey of Sri Lanka, 1969/70* (Colombo: DCS, 1971).

16 Due to normal institutional rigidities in an economy, a person laid off by one employer has to remain temporarily unemployed until he/she finds a job with another employer. Such unemployment is called frictional unemployment.

17 The usual argument would be that armed forces do not contribute to production. I formulated my argument as in the text because when areas have been freed, even partially, from "terrorism" through the efforts of armed forces, there is an indirect contribution to production, as production workers would begin to use those regions for agricultural and other productive activities.

18 The website wiki.answers.com/Q/Who_is_the_richest_person_in_Sri_Lanka indicates names of richest individuals/families in different periods. Names like Maharajahs, Lalith Kotalawala, Sohli Captain, Anthony Page, and H. K. Dharmadasa are mentioned in this connection for the 1990s, and Harry Jayawardena, Dhammika Perera, Amaleans, and Selvanathans for the 2000s. These individuals and families have accumulated their wealth in the activity areas mentioned in the text.

19 The comment must be added that because of certain elements of the neoliberal package, shifts in budget allocations took place leading to significant modifications in the free supply of education and health services in the public sector. There is no space here for details.

20 To save space the data from the surveys for 1978–79, 1981–82, 1986–87, and 1996–97 have not been cited here.

21 Even with the majority community it did not work so well in the second half of the 1980s when there were increasingly violent protests from among its members against the regime in power.

22 The Western Province consists of three Districts—Colombo, Gampaha, and Kalutara. Commercial and adminnistrative capitals of the country, as well as most large industrial and service enterprises are located in these districts.

23 Asoka Gunawardena and Weligamage D. Lakshman, "Challenges of Moving into a

Devolved Polity in Sri Lanka," in Fumihiko Saito (ed.), *Foundations for Local Governance: Decentralization in Comparative Perspective* (Heidelberg: Physica-Verlag, 2008), pp. 113–36.

24 Neloufer De Mel, *Militarizing Sri Lanka: Popular Culture, Memory and Narrative in the Armed Conflict* (New Delhi: Sage, 2007).

25 Paul Isenman, "Basic Needs: The Case of Sri Lanka," *World Development*, Vol. 8, No. 3 (March 1980), pp. 237–58; W. D. Lakshman, "Economic Growth and Re-distributive Justice as Policy Goals: A Study of the Recent Experience of Sri Lanka," in *Modern Ceylon Studies*, Vol. 6, No. 1 (1975), pp. 64–87; Lal Jayawardena, "Sri Lanka," in H. B. Chenery *et al.* (eds), *Redistribution with Growth* (London: Oxford University Press, 1970), pp. 273–79. Amartya K. Sen, "Public Action and Quality of Life in Developing Countries," *Oxford Bulletin of Economics and Statistics*, Vol. 43, No. 4 (1981).

26 United Nations, ECOSOC, *National Development Strategies and Commitments to Achieve the Internationally Agreed Development Goals, Including Millennium Development Goals: Sri Lanka National Report*, Report No. E/2009/111. Available at the following website: www.un.org/ecosoc/newfunct/amrnational 2009.shtml.

Part VII
Comparative chapters

24

The militaries of South Asia

Stephen P. Cohen

Introduction

South Asia contains some of the largest and most important military organizations in the world today. The Indian Army is the world's second largest, Pakistan's is the world's sixth, and both countries have a growing stock of nuclear weapons.[1] The Bangladesh Army is active in UN peacekeeping activities and plays an important political role in that country, although not as great as that of the Pakistan Army, which has directly or indirectly dominated Pakistan for more than half of its 60-year history.

While these three armies have much in common—notably a shared origin in the British Indian Army—the subcontinent is home to other military forces with divergent beginnings. These include the navies and air forces of India, Pakistan, and Bangladesh, the three Sri Lankan services, and importantly, because of their political role and rapid growth over the last 20 years, South Asia's many paramilitary organizations. The latter include both government forces and the proto-armies of numerous separatist, terrorist, and autonomist groups. One such non-state military force, the Liberation Tigers of Tamil Eelam (LTTE) of Sri Lanka, challenged the state itself, and others, such as Nepal's Maoist para-

militaries, may be given official or semi-official status in the future.

This chapter focuses on the origins and roles of the three major subcontinental armies—India, Pakistan, and Bangladesh—and in passing discusses other South Asian forces.[2] While their roles in politics will be emphasized (in the Indian case, the absence of such a role is notable), it should be borne in mind that all armies are complex state bureaucracies that perform several functions. Their stated purpose is to apply force in a war against a foreign enemy, or to use force at home to maintain law and order. Yet South Asia's armies (far more than its air forces or navies) have a complex relationship to their respective societies, especially to their many ethnic, caste, and linguistic groups. They may also play a role in decision making, and their budgets are often the state's single largest expenditure. Finally, militaries (again, especially armies) often play a role in shaping both state and national identities.

British roots

Over a nearly 200-year period, the British evolved a military structure in India to serve their own purposes. At first this was to establish control over the territories they ruled directly and indirectly. Later, as part of a larger imperial project, the British deployed Indian-based forces throughout Asia and Europe which played a critical role in both world wars. This structure and these policies have shaped the present-day armies of India, Pakistan, and Bangladesh.

The first building block in the construction of the British Indian Army was the "sepoy" system. The first regiment of what was to evolve into the Indian army was raised in 1748 by Colonel Stringer Lawrence.[3] Ironically, the idea was borrowed from the French, then the leading European rival to Britain in India.[4] The sepoys (derived from the Persian *sipahii*; after Independence they were renamed *jawan*, or youth) were drawn from rural and tribal India, and trained along modern, professional lines under the command of British officers. Sepoys were recruited on the basis of merit and some were often as professionally competent as the officers of the British Army. This system allowed the British to raise large and loyal "native" forces, with which they defeated the French, various Indian rulers, and, ultimately, the Mughal Empire itself.[5]

A second major innovation came in response to the Mutiny of 1857 when Hindu and Muslim troops rose against their officers and nearly succeeded in routing the British. Recruitment was subsequently restricted to the most loyal regions, castes, and ethnic groups; members of those groups ("classes" in Indian Army parlance) that were deemed disloyal were discharged.[6] They also reduced recruitment from those regions, such as the south, which had been pacified, justifying both steps in terms of a freshly invented theory that deemed only some classes to be martial. The designation of "martial races" shifted over the next 100 years, and some groups, thought to be martial in the middle of the nineteenth century (such as Oudh Brahmans and Tamils) saw their numbers markedly reduced.[7]

In reorganizing the army after the Mutiny, the British reinforced the regimental system, which tightly bound officers and soldiers together. The importance and utility of the regimental system is evident in the comparison between Gurkha units in the British and Indian armies and those in the Royal Nepal Army, which have proved militarily ineffective, as seen in their recent failure to take the field against Maoist insurrectionists.

The British also saw to it that each ethno-linguistic class was balanced by a social rival. All Indian units were also balanced by British forces, which retained control over artillery, the era's most advanced military technology.[8] The railways, built with an eye towards the strategic unification of the subcontinent more than its economic development, were also placed in the hands of a loyal Anglo-Indian community. The one class that did not have its own regiment was Muslims. During both world wars, Punjabi Muslims were the largest single class recruited to the army. Fearing another uprising, the British dispersed their Muslim soldiers among regional regiments, such as the Punjab Regiment, where they were balanced by Sikh and Hindu soldiers. Today, the Indian Army's Punjab Regiment is still "mixed," but that of the Pakistani army is overwhelmingly Punjabi, although some regiments have Pashtuns. This presented problems in dealing with insurgencies in the FATA, where all-Punjabi units sent there found themselves ill-equipped to deal with local issues.

Lord Kitchener, the British commander-in-chief in India at the turn of the twentieth century, turned the primarily constabulary and border force into an expeditionary one, giving the Indian Army a greater role outside the subcontinent. This coincided with a growth in strength from 155,000 to 573,000 soldiers during the First World War, when the army was employed in France and Gallipoli, and to 2.5 million during the Second World War, when it fought in North Africa and Burma. Kitchener's reforms also brought larger numbers of Indians into the officer corps, effectively nationalizing the army before India's Independence. When British India was partitioned on the eve of Independence in 1947, a new Pakistan Army was formed out of units of the old, and officered by those Muslim Indians who opted for Pakistan. Subsequently, the Indian and Pakistani armies began to diverge markedly, especially in their political roles.

India and civilian primacy

In 1905 Kitchener forced the resignation of the viceroy, Lord Curzon, after the two disagreed over the extent to which Indian forces would be used to protect imperial, as opposed to Indian interests, in what was possibly the last assertion of military power in India. While Kitchener won the political battle, the British Indian government evolved a system of fiscal and political control over the army that ensured civilian supremacy.

By the time of Independence, civilian control was firmly established, although operational matters remained in the hands of the military. That the last two viceroys—Wavell and Mountbatten—were from the military largely obscured the degree of civilianization that had taken place. Indian defense budgets were hotly contested in the nascent Indian assembly by Indian representatives, who were also critical of the way in which the military was used to support imperial goals. Directed by India's first prime minister, Jawaharlal Nehru, the relative power of civilians was further enhanced. The position of commander-in-chief was abolished (the president of India is now the titular commander-in-chief). Control over the armed forces was lodged in the civilian cabinet under the prime minister, and the status of the officer corps vis-à-vis the civil service as well as elected and appointed public officials was sharply downgraded.

While in retrospect the bargain between the nationalist movement and the Indian officer corps—effectively brokered by the British—seems inevitable, at the time there were other viable possibilities. During the war, Nehru's rival, Subhas Chandra Bose, raised the Indian National Army (INA) out of captured Indian Army personnel in Southeast Asia. Bose's force was militarily ineffective but ideologically potent—he challenged the martial races theory

and there was no pretense that the INA was anything but a revolutionary army. Bose died in an air crash in 1945, but had he lived, or had the Japanese succeeded in invading India, the role of the army might have turned out quite differently. As it was, the INA officers were praised by Nehru and other politicians as great heroes, but were effectively denied re-entry into the army.

Civilian control was further tightened after the 1958 coup in Pakistan, as were contacts with foreign armies. Nehru believed that the Pakistan military's coup had been facilitated by ties to its American and British counterparts. The Indian government had two other major policies in the immediate post-Independence era: it attempted to "democratize" the army by effectively doing away with the martial race theory and it kept military matters away from public scrutiny.

As for organizational patterns, India's new leaders, encouraged by the British, permitted the army to retain its colonial structure, but emphasized loyalty to the new government. One consequence of the way civilian control was imposed in post-Independence India was that the political leadership stayed away from military matters while the military leadership remained institutionally frozen. This implicit bargain—internal autonomy in return for political supremacy over the armed forces—was strengthened by the events of the 1962 war against China. India's defeat in the conflict was squarely blamed on political interference. Prior to the war, Nehru and his defense minister V. K. Krishna Menon had promoted politically pliable generals, requiring them to pursue a risky "forward strategy," a move that had clearly backfired. Later wars in 1965 and 1971 reinforced military autonomy. In 1971, in the war that led to the independence of Bangladesh, General Sam Maneckshaw, the army chief, asked for operational freedom and came back with the country's only outright military victory. This further ensured that political leaders remained wary of interfering in the internal matters of the military so long as the armed forces accepted political supremacy. In later crises, notably with Pakistan in 1999 and 2001–02, civilians called the shots. The stalemated 2001–02 crisis led to some re-examination of the essentially eighteenth-century army structure, the archaic defense budgeting system, and the absence of real "jointness" between the services and among the various civilian agencies responsible for national security policy.[9]

While India's robust civil–military arrangement is different from virtually every other ex-colonial or developing society, it does not mean that it is optimal.[10] Civil "control" has been achieved, the military is politically docile, but India has not really had a debate on the purpose and role of the Indian Army, let alone its relationship to Indian society, and civilians generally lack the professional expertise or experience to make informed decisions when it comes to the use of force, training, or weapons acquisition. Rather than institute real reform, India prefers to expand its forces.

The absence of a sound methodology for making important strategic and military decisions has been often noted by India's most influential strategic writer, K. Subrahmanyam.[11] While he and others have urged that a modern mechanism be established to develop and implement strategic policy, there is an unwillingness to make the changes necessary.[12] The move to create a national security council only wrapped existing institutions in new cloth. Efforts to establish a chief of defense staff position have been stillborn. India also lacks an effective, transparent defense acquisition process.

The Indian military is expected to modernize significantly over the next few years, an effort that is backed by an explosive growth in India's defense budget enabled by a rapidly expanding economy.[13] India's defense budget grew by 75 percent between 2002 and 2007. However, it remains under 3 percent of India's GDP, less than China's allocation of about 5 percent. Between 1999 and 2006 India was also the largest recipient of military equipment by value, importing $22.4 billion worth of arms. While the military has some input in acquisitions, decisions ultimately remain in politicians' and bureaucrats' hands. The defense acquisition process has also been tainted over the years by major scandals. Allegations that former Prime Minister Rajiv Gandhi received kickbacks from Swedish armament manufacturer Bofors for a major howitzer contract resulted in his losing the 1989 general election. In 2001 Defense Minister George Fernandes resigned after a media investigation uncovered large-scale corruption related to defense acquisition.

Internal security and the rise of the paramilitaries

Over the last 20 years, the Indian army has become enmeshed in the gargantuan task of maintaining internal security. An increase in domestic violence has taken place in most of the South Asian states. While the immediate causes may be different from state to state, or even from region to region in India, Pakistan, Sri Lanka, Bangladesh, and Nepal, the general trend is the same. In an era of rapid social change and dislocation, caused in part by the impact of globalization on traditional societies, more and more young men (and women) find themselves educated to the point where they no longer have a place in traditional society, but are unable to find a role in the slow-growing modern sectors.

In India, this trend is especially notable in an eastern belt stretching northwards from Andhra Pradesh through Chhattisgarh, Bihar, and Orissa, and extending into the north-eastern states, where discontent has led to a significant rural leftist militancy, called the Naxalite movement. By government admission, over a quarter of India's districts are affected by Naxalite activity. There are also regions of endemic insecurity in Kashmir. Other uprisings have been dealt with more successfully by the Indian government. The massive Sikh uprising in Punjab in the 1980s was contained by the Punjab police action, and there has been some success in containing separatist and autonomist groups in Nagaland and Mizoram.

Partly to meet such challenges, the Indian Army has been dragged into an internal security role. The only time the army was called on for internal security during the Raj, after Britain's European rivals and rebellious princely states had been defeated, was during "aid to the civil" operations, such as quelling a communal riot or containing a political demonstration that had got out of hand. In such cases, ultimate authority remained in the hands of the local civilian magistrate who directed the local army commander when and where to apply force. While there were notable excesses, such as the Jallianwala Bagh massacre, the army's role remained limited.

Recent army history has been as much about internal security as it has been about fighting external enemies. Indeed, the importance of internal security is reflected in the dominance of the army over the other services. Twelve of the Indian Army's 18 major campaigns between 1947 and 1998 were fought on Indian soil.[14] Constabulary duties in counterinsurgency campaigns in the country's northeastern states, Punjab, and Jammu & Kashmir, eroded the country's ability to project power outside. In addition, long and arduous internal duty led to soldiers from armored and air defense units being rotated through counterinsurgency formations.

The government's response to the expanding internal security challenge was to turn to the army, and then, when the army resisted, to create new paramilitary forces. These now outnumber the army 1.3 million to 1.1 million.[15] The major paramilitary forces include the Border Security Force (208,422) and the Central Reserve Police Force (229,699). There are also about 450,000 state armed police forces. The Indian paramilitaries fall under the control of the home ministry, and India's home minister commands one of the world's largest armies, albeit one of its most unruly, with a long record of abuse, disobedience, and even mutiny. Yet, the paramilitary task is so important that the army has created its own paramilitary force, the Rashtriya Rifles, which is manned by regular officers and soldiers who rotate through it from regular army units.

Thus, the army in India suffers from an identity crisis. It really is a three-in-one force: a counterinsurgency army fighting primarily in Kashmir and the northeast, backing up the generally unreliable paramilitary forces; a mountain defense force guarding against a Chinese incursion, divided between the borders in the north and the northeast, with some elements, particularly in the latter, also engaged in counterinsurgency; and a mechanized and armored strike force, focused on the next war with Pakistan along the western border, but now made less relevant because of nuclear weapons.

The air force, navy, and nuclear forces

India's other two services, the air force and the navy, never acquired as many of the colonial trappings as the Indian Army. They do not recruit on the basis of caste or language, are keyed to advances in military technology, and play no role in Indian politics. For both these services, however, acquiring and deploying modern equipment has been a paramount problem, and their share of the Indian defense budget has always been very small, compared with that of the politically more sensitive army. In 2004, for example, the army was allocated 41.9 percent of the defense budget while the Indian Navy's share was 14.7 percent and that of the Indian Air Force was 24.7 percent.[16]

Finally, it is important to consider the impact of the introduction of nuclear weapons on the role of the armed forces in India, and the accompanying potential for miscalculation or misjudgment. On the ground, there is a slow but steady introduction and integration of nuclear weapons in the military arsenal. Based on its fissile material production capacity, India probably has somewhere between 50 and 100 nuclear weapons of proven design and the aircraft to deliver them.[17] In the future, there are plans for missile-delivered nuclear warheads,

355

and even a nuclear navy, which would be able to range widely, delivering nuclear weapons onto targets many thousands of miles from the Indian mainland. The Indian government has tried to apply the principle of civilian supremacy in the use of these weapons, has a designated chain-of-command in emulation of western nuclear powers and the Soviet Union, and has built secure shelters to protect key decision makers in a crisis. Yet, there appears to be no integrated service nuclear doctrine, and the government has not faced up to the problem of command and control and delegation of authority during a crisis in which nuclear weapons might be used. In the recent history of the subcontinent, three crises (in 1990, 1999, and 2001–02) involved nuclear threats, and possibly the movement of nuclear assets.[18]

The Pakistan army

It has been said that Pakistan has an army in control of a state, and the army's dominant role is unlikely to soon change. The Pakistan army is unique among armies of the world in its combination of size, military professionalism, a dominant political role, and its possession of nuclear weapons. It still reflects its British Indian Army origins, and thus has much in common with the Indian and Bangladesh armies, as well as many western armies. Perhaps the most important aspect of this inheritance, however, is that it more closely resembles the military-centered Raj of the nineteenth century than the civilizing Raj of the early twentieth century.

Beginning in 1954, the Pakistan Army's political role expanded rapidly and General Ayub Khan seized power in a bloodless coup in 1958. He unsuccessfully "civilianized" himself and, as a result of domestic unrest, was displaced by General Yahya Khan in 1969. Following Zulfikar Ali Bhutto's chaotic period of governance (1971–77), General Zia-ul-Haq seized power in a third coup, and governed with an iron fist until he died in an air crash in 1988. Zia built on Bhutto's attempts to Islamize

Pakistan, and the army became more overtly "Islamic" than at any time in its history. After ten years of erratic democracy, the army again seized power in 1999, and Pakistan was until 2008 governed by General Pervez Musharraf. Most of Zia's efforts to Islamize the army have been rolled back, although the army retains close ties to some Islamist groups, and Islamic dimensions of the army's identity are still taught in army schools.

Why did the army assume power in Pakistan, when it stayed on the sidelines in India? There were three main factors that pushed the army into the role of Pakistan's dominant political force.

First, Pakistan very early lost whatever competent civilian leadership it had. Mohammed Ali Jinnah, the founding leader of Pakistan, died only one year after Independence and there was no follow-on leadership of equivalent stature. Neither was there another leader with proficiency in strategic and military affairs, such as Jinnah had developed early in his career. The only Pakistani civilians with professional skills of a high order were the bureaucrats, and Pakistan was initially dominated by a coalition of senior civil servants and army officers.

Second, the Pakistan Army came to see itself as the only force that stood between Pakistan and destruction by a hostile India, and was accepted as such by the people. Jinnah had argued that Pakistan would be a homeland for oppressed Indian Muslims. The army came to the view that this homeland had to assume the shape of a fortress, besieged by a malevolent India, and that the army best knew how to prepare these defenses. Echoes of this view were also heard in President Musharraf's declaration that the Pakistan army knew best what Pakistan's "national interest" really was. Because of the army's central role in Pakistani politics, certain military formations are politically very relevant. This includes the 10 Corps, based in Rawalpindi, and its 111 Brigade. Also politically critical are the corps in or near Pakistan's major cities, Karachi and Lahore.[19]

Third, the army was strongly influenced by its contacts with Washington, which equipped

THE MILITARIES OF SOUTH ASIA

it in the 1950s and 1960s mainly to serve as a bulwark against the Communist threat in Asia. With US aid and encouragement, the Pakistan Army grew from approximately 150,000 in 1947 to 320,000 in 1970, and 550,000 in 2006. During the 1980s, China supplanted America as a major supplier of military equipment, but the US role was revived when a massive military aid program was instituted after 9/11 and Pakistan assumed the role of a frontline state in the so-called "war on terror."

Other than its gradual Islamization under Zia, the Pakistan Army has not changed very much in 60 years. Its corps and divisional structure, the hierarchy of ranks, and its military schools would be familiar to western (or Indian) visitors. Neither has the officer–other rank relationship changed very much. Officers are drawn increasingly from Pakistan's middle classes and are overwhelmingly Punjabi, but they are part of Pakistan's ruling elite. Other ranks are still predominantly rural and peasant in their origin and most come from a few districts in Punjab. Unlike India, where political power is widely dispersed among geographical regions, in Pakistan it is concentrated in dominant Punjab, which is home to more than half the country's population.

Despite its role in the "war on terror," Pakistan's army is largely deployed to meet an Indian conventional military threat. In the past, the Afghan border was lightly covered, and the army relied on frontier and paramilitary forces for local security arrangements. But with the rise of Islamic militancy in the North-West Frontier Province, and separatist sentiments still in evidence in Balochistan, this is fast changing, and the Pakistan Army has moved several divisions from the eastern front to fight insurgents in the NWFP.

A balance sheet of the army's stewardship over the state of Pakistan would show that while it has done well in some endeavors, it was average in others, and was grossly deficient in a few areas. The army has engaged in a number of international peacekeeping operations, often under United Nations auspices,

and these can be judged an unqualified success. The professionalism of the officer corps, the discipline of the other ranks, and its considerable experience have earned the army praise from many quarters. When it comes to conventional military operations—all against India—it has acquitted itself well militarily. The 1965 war resulted in a standoff, despite the greater numbers on the Indian side. Pakistan's conventional capabilities were also used to good effect in the 1987 "Brasstacks" crisis, when it maneuvered in such a way as to force the Indians to abandon what might have been a pre-emptive strike.

Since 1990 all of Pakistan's conflicts with India carry with them the threat of escalation to nuclear war. In this regard, the army has presided over a nuclear weapons program with some success, involving the covert acquisition of technology from many countries, including the United States, Germany, Holland, and China. Pakistan now has at least 80 nuclear weapons, enough to deter any significant Indian attack.

Pakistan's covert military operations have been a mixed success. In the 1980s it worked with China, the US, and some Middle East states to support the anti-Soviet *mujahiddin* in Afghanistan. This support was effective, but Pakistan suffered the consequences of "blowback" as drugs, weapons, and Islamic extremism filtered back into Pakistan itself, destabilizing several parts of the country, including Karachi. Subsequently, the army supported *jihadi* elements in Indian-administered Kashmir, and the Taliban in Afghanistan. India and Pakistan fought a mini-war in 1999 in the Kargil region of Kashmir when Pakistan-supported Islamic *jihadi*s, operating alongside army units, infiltrated across the Line of Control, triggering a violent Indian response, and bringing the United States to support India's side. The 9/11 attacks forced Pakistan to nominally withdraw its support to Kashmiri separatists and the Taliban, although there are still allegations that the Pakistan Army tolerates Taliban operations that are directed against US and NATO forces in Afghanistan. In Kashmir, the support seems to have declined, but a major terrorist incident, especially one that is traced back to Pakistan, could lead to another crisis.

The two areas in which the Pakistan Army can be judged to have consistently failed are in the political management of the state of Pakistan and in counterinsurgency operations on its own territory.

The story of the Pakistan army's involvement in politics is an oft-told tale. Three extended military regimes, those of Ayub Khan, Zia ul-Haq, and Pervez Musharraf, have each left the state worse off than it was before the military took over. The army maintains a firm front against civilian rule, and this façade will have to crack before there is any real progress in transitioning from a chronically inadequate system of military rule to something that approximates a competent civilian-led government. No change is in sight: the army still believes that it is Pakistan's savior, and that the civilians will ruin the state. The prognosis is that a stable transition is highly unlikely, and that Pakistan will lurch from domestic crisis to domestic crisis. This will be manageable as long as Pakistan receives significant amounts of economic and political help from its major outside supporters, such as Saudi Arabia, China, and the United States.

The army's failure to manage domestic insurgency is paradoxical because Pakistani intelligence services and home-grown *jihadis* have been successful in destabilizing Pakistan's neighbors, notably parts of India and Afghanistan, and Pakistan-based Islamic extremists have operated in China's western provinces as well. Historically, the army's operations against Bangladeshi separatists were ineffective, and the army should never have allowed the situation to deteriorate to the point where it was faced with a massive Indian-supported movement. Subsequently, its operations against insurrectionists in Balochistan failed to effectively combine political and military elements. This problem is evident today in Balochistan and in large swaths of the North-West Frontier Province,

where the army, after being attacked by Islamist extremists, discovered that it lacked either a counterinsurgency doctrine or an understanding of growing social dislocation.

As in India, Pakistan has responded to social dislocation and the breakdown of law and order by increasing paramilitary forces, which now number well over 300,000, compared to the army's 550,000. Yet social turmoil, stemming in part from political incompetence and from the effects of globalization on a hitherto conservative social order, continues to grow, and is critical in the NWFP. So great is the problem that the army is now faced with a three-front war: in the east with India, in the northwest against Taliban-like militants, and in Punjab, against rising sectarian terrorist violence. Ironically, some of the militants were trained by Pakistan's own intelligence services and shielded over the years.

This confronts the army, and the state of Pakistan, with a deep existential crisis.[20] Can the army engage in effective counterinsurgency without the support of its own population? Can a largely Punjabi army deal with a Pashtun or Baloch separatist movement, the former reinforced by Islamist extremism, the latter by subnationalist passions? Army leaders have no clear answer to this, but Pakistan's politicians argue that only they, with a popular mandate, can exert the force necessary to tackle these extremist and separatist groups. They draw on classic British counterinsurgency doctrine, which teaches that fighting an insurgency is 80 percent political and economic and only 20 percent military.

One strategic conclusion that can be drawn is that Pakistan may be driven into an arrangement with India regarding Kashmir, and that the long-cherished goal of prising Kashmir from India will have to be abandoned. Some Pakistan army officers have reached this conclusion, and embedded in Musharraf's unsuccessful peace overtures towards India was an understanding that Pakistan itself cannot afford to "bleed" India as it is itself facing a major threat of its own in the North-West Frontier Province, the FATA, and the Punjab itself.

The army's political role is unlikely to change dramatically in the near future. The army is in the peculiar position of being unable to comprehensively run Pakistan, but not letting civilians do it either. It regards Pakistan's civilian politicians, not entirely without reason, as self-seeking, corrupt and incompetent. Under Musharraf, the army further dismantled Pakistan's civilian bureaucratic institutions. It is attempting to reconstruct the entire educational system. It tries to contain the spread of Islamist extremism while partnering with radical Islamist parties. Since the army lacks the expertise and training to actually administer Pakistan, or to move it ahead economically, its penetration of administrative and economic sectors will eventually be costly. The army is skilled at playing "balance of power" games with Pakistan's political parties, but it cannot substitute for political parties that can broker compromises among Pakistan's contending class, ethnic, sectarian, and regional elements. The contradictions in the army's position became increasingly evident and, as of 2008, Musharraf's position as Pakistan's leader had been undermined and the army's position as the state's most important institution had come under attack.

The Pakistan Amy faces challenges it is not prepared to meet. The question suggests itself: can a professional army with conventional roots fight a major counterinsurgency war against diverse enemies, prepare for both a conventional and nuclear war with India, remain the dominant political force in Pakistan, and oversee Pakistan's economic, educational and administrative institutions? No army in history has ever successfully coped with such a wide range of tasks over a long period. The Pakistan Amy is unlikely to do so either.

The Bangladesh experiment

Until 1971, East Pakistan, like West Pakistan, was dominated by the Pakistan Army. A civil war, followed by indirect and then direct Indian military intervention led to the army's surrender on 16 December, 1971 and the establishment of Bangladesh.

When the Bangladeshi liberation struggle broke out in March 1971, officers and men from Pakistan army units were among the very first to turn against the West Pakistanis. Most of the Bengal Regiment's battalions had been trapped in the west, but enough were in the east to form the core of military resistance. They were joined by the Bengali elements of the East Pakistan Rifles, a paramilitary border force which had many non-Bengali officers. These regulars and irregulars were led by commissioned Pakistan army officers, all of relatively low rank, but who eventually formed the backbone of the Bangladesh Army.

A second component of the new Bangladesh Army consisted of veterans of various "*bahinis*," or forces, which thrived during the nine-month liberation struggle. The regular Bengali soldiers who were brought together as a resistance force were first known as the Mukti Fauz and then as the Mukti Bahini. Meanwhile, thousands of civilians had formed themselves into guerrilla groups of varying degrees of competence and training. The Indian government covertly assisted these groups, often via Indian Bengali officers who temporarily resigned their commissions to lead the *bahini*s.

The Bangladesh government in exile had only limited control over the *bahini*s. Some came under the control of the Awami League's student group. Others such as the Quader Bahini, named after its leader Quader "Tiger" Siddiqui, operated independently and retained their identity after independence.

Unlike India and Pakistan, the new Bangladesh government began with a clean slate in creating an army. Its forces consisted of regular Bengali officers from the Pakistan army officers and *jawan*s, plus the *bahini*s. However, there were also strains between former Pakistan army officers who fought with the *bahini*s and those who were prisoners during the war, who returned after liberation. In addition, there were tensions between those who favored a military establishment along Pakistani lines and were suspicious of India, and those who understood that large armored forces were unnecessary and were willing to accommodate the much larger India, especially given Bangladesh's dependence on Indian economic assistance.

With Indian encouragement, the decision was made to stick as close to the British military model as possible, and in a few years the *bahini*s were terminated and a new Bangladesh army was established. This decision echoed that of Jawaharlal Nehru and his Home Minister Sardar Vallabhbhai Patel when they rejected the idea of folding the Indian National Army into the regular Indian Army. Eerily, however, Bangladesh soon began to replicate the tortuous civil–military relationship that had plagued Pakistan since the 1950s.

The first prime minister of Bangladesh, the charismatic Sheikh Mujibur Rahman, elevated himself to president in 1975 after launching a scheme of nationalizing key industries, one that paralleled the policies pursued in Pakistan by Zulfikar Ali Bhutto.[21] Mujib was assassinated later in the year, along with most of his family, and General Zia Rahman assumed the presidency, creating a political party, the Bangladesh National Party (BNP) to rival Mujib's Awami League. He lifted martial law in 1979, but was assassinated during an abortive military coup in 1981. After a period of further instability and chaos, General H. M. Ershad assumed power in a 1982 coup, suspending the constitution and political parties. Ershad assumed the presidency and, to India's consternation, Islam became the state religion. Ershad was forced to step down eight years later and was convicted and jailed on corruption charges, returning to politics on his release, but with little success.

Civilian rule returned, albeit shakily, when Begum Khaleda Zia became prime minister in 1991 and the presidency returned to ceremonial status. From this time onward, the military played no overt role in politics, but there remained a divisive rivalry between Begum Zia, General Zia's widow, and Sheikh Hasina Wajed, one of Mujib's surviving daughters. The two women traded places as prime minister and opposition leader for much of the following decade, while Bangladesh's internal security situation steadily deteriorated. The military remained vital, and was called on repeatedly to deal with general strikes, mass bomb blasts, and the rise of Islamic militancy.

There were several attempts in late 2006 to draw the military into politics, but the army resisted the temptation, intervening only in January 2007 when it moved to neutralize the two major parties, possibly preventing massive civil strife. A state of emergency was declared and the scheduled national election was postponed. The interim government—urged on by the generals—restricted the freedom of movement of both Khaleda Zia and Sheikh Hasina, and continued to govern Bangladesh. Since then, the armed forces have worked with the civilian administration to tackle corruption and maladministration, but remained overtly subservient to civilian authority.

The Bangladesh Army, unlike its Pakistani counterpart, is reluctant to get deeply involved in politics and openly govern again. Yet, it is fearful of continuing violence, and behind the scenes has urged discipline and calm on the political community. One reason why it has refrained from again intervening in domestic politics is that it plays a major role as an international peacekeeper. Bangladesh earns a good deal of its foreign exchange through such peacekeeping missions, currently contributing about 9,000 peacekeepers to eleven different countries, the largest contribution of any state.[22]

Another consequence of a potential military coup could be sanctions that would reduce aid programs to Bangladesh. Thus, civilian government is maintained in part by the concerns of the international community, whose aid programs keep Bangladesh solvent.

In addition, the military maintains a self-imposed distance from politics. It understands the vast scale of Bangladesh's developmental and sectarian problems. Two failed experiments by Generals Zia and Ershad seem to have deterred the current generation of officers from attempting a third spell of military rule.

The Aspirants: Non-state armies

An important development in the military history of all South Asian states is the emergence of significant paramilitary forces, on the one hand, and non-state forces, some approximating professional armies in terms of their capabilities, equipment, and discipline, on the other hand.

Sri Lanka presents the most important case of a non-state military challenging the state itself, and holding the government's forces at bay. Ostensibly a political party, the Liberation Tigers of Tamil Eelam (LTTE), which claimed to speak on behalf of the island's ethnic Tamils, was also an army with a political agenda, engaged in a permanent war against the Sri Lankan state.[23] Unlike some of the Indian non-state groups or Nepal's Maoist insurgents, the Tigers sought the practical dissolution of the Sri Lankan state and its transformation into a federal state to give the LTTE control of slightly under one-third of the country as part of an ethnic Tamil homeland. Further, the Tiger ideology would not stop at the water's edge, for the LTTE at times articulated aspirations for a much larger Tamil nation, to include the much more populous Indian state of Tamil Nadu.

The LTTE was by far the most sophisticated non-state army in South Asia, perhaps in the world. It pioneered the technique of suicide bombing, successfully assassinating Indian Prime Minister Rajiv Gandhi, Sri Lankan President Ranasinghe Premadasa, and senior Sri Lankan general Parami Kulatunga in that manner.[24] The LTTE had an extensive overseas support network that relied on expatriate Tamils, and it maintained offices, like a state, around the world. Although declared a terrorist group in a number of countries, it still managed to extract, willingly or otherwise, a huge amount of money from expatriate Tamils to purchase weapons, retain an army of about 8,000–11,000 fighters in the field, maintain a small fleet of ships (the "Sea Tigers"), and even a tiny air force, made up of a few light aircraft purchased abroad and assembled in the jungle fastness of northern Sri Lanka.

Facing them was the Sri Lankan army of about 150,000 troops, largely Sinhala, although there have been leading Tamil and Burgher officers over the years. The Sri Lankan government has a small air force that it sent on air strikes irregularly. Its tiny navy was barely able to monitor the comings and goings of the Tamil Sea Tigers, and Sri Lanka relied on Indian help to detain or sink supplies coming to the LTTE from abroad.

Despite being immersed in a vicious civil war for nearly 20 years, the Sri Lankan state avoided the pitfall of militarization. Key decisions were made by civilians, and the parliamentary system worked as best it could under near-wartime conditions.

Postscript

In Bangladesh the army yielded power to civilians at the end of 2008, and Sheikh Hasina once again became Prime Minister. Bangladesh's paramilitary border guards mutinied in February 2009, only to be put down by the army, but the mutineers slaughtered many of their officers.

Pakistan's President Musharraf resigned after nine years in office, on 18 August, 2008, leaving behind a weaker economy, domestic political chaos, a chastened army, and a raging insurgency in the federally administered areas (FATA) and the North-West Frontier province. He was eventually succeeded by Benazir Bhutto's widower, Asif Ali Zardari, who has presided over further chaos. A reluctant army is likely to step in again before the year is up. A crisis with India was narrowly averted after ten (or more) Pakistan-based terrorists launched attacks on several Mumbai hotels, a railroad station, and a Jewish center. The event was televised globally over a three-day period, which, along with the murder of nationals from over twenty states, contributed to heavy international intervention in an attempt to avoid escalation and to identify and bring the perpetrators to justice. Despite its achievements in other spheres, India displayed supreme incompetence in coping with this attack before, during and after the event.

In Sri Lanka a fresh assault, aided by Tamil Tiger defectors, led in early 2009 to a comprehensive military victory, but the Tigers will probably revert to guerrilla war.

The Nepali Maoists were the more successful of the non-state paramilitaries, and have come to uncertain power in a debilitated Nepal. They abolished the monarchy and are attempting to supplant the Nepal army.

Notes

1 Throughout this entry figures on numbers of troops, paramilitary forces, and other armed groups, as well as defense budgets, are drawn from the authoritative Institute for Strategic Studies, *The Military Balance, 2006* (London: International Institute for Strategic Studies, 2007).

2 For a comparative study of the role of the army in these three countries, see Veena Kukreja, *Civil–Military Relations in South Asia: Pakistan, Bangladesh and India* (New Delhi: Sage, 1991).

3 For three different histories of the British Indian army, see Stephen P. Cohen, *The Indian Army: Its Contribution to the Development of a Nation*, rev. edn (New Delhi: Oxford University Press, 1990); Philip Mason, *Matter of Honour: An Account of the Indian Army, Its Officers and Men* (London: Jonathan Cape, 1974); and Lt. Gen. S.L Menezes, *Fidelity and Honour: The Indian Army from the Seventeenth to the Twenty-first Century* (New Delhi: Oxford University Press, 1999).

4 For a summary of the important French contribution, see Lt. Gen. Gurbir Mansingh, *French Military Influence in India* (New Delhi: Knowledge World and United Services Institution of India, 2006); also see John A. Lynn, *Battle: A History of Combat and Culture* (Boulder, CO: Westview, 2003).

5 There is a vast literature on the battles of the British Indian Army. For an historically informed and accessible description of the way in which it was used alongside the British Army in India, see the Sharpe series of novels by Bernard Cornwell, the first three of which cover the battles of Seringapatam, Assaye, and Gawilghur.

6 The Indian army's use of the word "class" does not refer to economic or social stratification, but to the various castes, religious groups, and even regions that contribute men to the military. Each class had its own quota. Thus, before Partition, Punjabi Muslims and Punjabi Hindus were two separate classes for purposes of recruitment.

7 The British compiled a series of handbooks in which the special qualities of each recruited class were narrated. See Nicholas B. Dirks, *Castes of Mind: Colonialism and the Making of Modern India* (Princeton, NJ: University Press, 2001).

8 For details of army expansion, see Bisheshwar Prasad (ed.), *Official History of the Indian Armed Forces in the Second World War: Expansion of the Armed Forces and Defence Organization, 1939–1945* (New Delhi: Combined Inter-Services Historical Section, India and Pakistan, 1965), p. 298.

9 Perhaps the most scathing criticism of the decision-making system was that of the Kargil Review Committee, a quasi-official body appointed by the government in 1999; it whitewashed the army's performance but did offer some useful suggestions regarding defense organization.

10 For a comparison of the Indian and Pakistani armies, see Cohen, *The Indian Army*, and Stephen P. Cohen, *The Pakistan Army* (Berkeley, CA: University of California Press, 1984 and Karachi: Oxford University Press, 1992; rev. edn, Oxford University Press, 1998).

11 For a definitive collection of his writings on strategy, defense organization, and civil–military relations see K. Subramanyam, *Shedding Shibboleths: India's Evolving Strategic Outlook* (Delhi: Wordsmiths, 2005).

12 For a discussion of Subrahmanyam's views see P. K. Kumaraswamy (ed.), *Security Beyond Survival: Essays for K. Subrahmanyam* (New Delhi: Sage, 2004).

13 For a comprehensive overview of the relationship of the armed forces to Indian society and politics, and their search for a strategic framework, see Verghese Koithara, *Society, State and Security: The Indian Experience* (New Delhi: Sage, 1999).

14 Jaswant Singh, *Defending India* (Basingstoke: Macmillan and New York: St. Martin's Press, 1999).

15 For authoritative details, see *The Military Balance*, 2007, pp. 230–35.

16 *The Military Balance 2007* (London: International Institute for Strategic Studies), p. 310.

17 Accurately estimating the strength of India's nuclear arsenal is notoriously difficult. See George Perkovich, *India's Nuclear Bomb: The Impact on Global Proliferation* (Berkeley, CA: University of California Press, 1999), p. 430; and David Albright, "India's Military Plutonium Inventory, End 2004," Institute for Science and International Security, 7 May, 2005.

18 For a comprehensive overview of the role of nuclear weapons in these and other crises, see P. R. Chari *et al.*, *Four Crises and a Peace Process: American Engagement in South Asia* (Washington: Brookings, 2007).

19 The creation in 2007 of three army commands, each encompassing several corps, may change the hitherto critical role of the corps commanders.

20 For an attempt to describe Pakistan's possible futures, see Stephen P. Cohen, *The Idea of Pakistan* (Washington: Brookings, 2004).

21 For a survey of the relationship between the politicians and the military, see Talukder Maniruzzaman, *Politics and Security of Bangladesh* (Dhaka: University Press, 1994).

22 *The Military Balance 2007*, p. 314.

23 For studies of the Tigers and the Sri Lankan dilemma see Rohan Gunaratna, *Sri Lanka's Ethnic Crisis and National Security* (Colombo: South Asian Network on Conflict Research, 1998); and, by the same author, *International and Regional Security Implications of the Sri Lankan Tamil Insurgency* (Colombo: Taprobane, 1997).

24 A remarkable film, *The Terrorist* (1999), traces the recruitment of a female Tamil fighter to the ranks of a suicide squad, and her journey to (presumably) India to carry out a mission against a foreign politician.

25

Corruption and the criminalization of politics in South Asia

Stanley A. Kochanek

Although corruption is a universal and persistent global phenomenon, it has tended to be more pervasive in developing countries. Most global measures of corruption have repeatedly ranked the countries of South Asia at the top of the list of the most corrupt countries in the world. The level of corruption in the region, however, has varied considerably and appears to be somewhat more pervasive in some countries than others. While Pakistan and Bangladesh, for example, repeatedly appeared at the top of the list of the most corrupt countries in the world, India and Sri Lanka ranked much lower.

Although the states of South Asia share a common history, bureaucratic tradition and British colonial heritage, since independence in 1947 the countries of the region have followed divergent paths of political, bureaucratic, and institutional development. British rule left behind two quite distinct governing traditions. On the one hand, British liberal democratic values, educational policy, and the gradual introduction of elections and representative institutions in South Asia created a new western-educated, urban middle class that developed a strong commitment to British-style liberal democracy. On the other hand, the British vice-regal system of colonial rule and the paternalism of the colonial civil service created an equally strong legacy of centralized authoritarian rule.

Like many former colonies, the major states of South Asia began independence as liberal democracies. Some states, however, quickly succumbed to vice-regal authoritarian rule. The liberal democratic tradition has proved to be most enduring in India and Sri Lanka, while the vice-regal system has come to dominate Pakistan and Bangladesh.

Despite divergent patterns of political development, the historical legacies in the region have helped to shape character of governance, the growth of corruption, and the increasing criminalization of politics.

The current state of political development in South Asia was summarized in a study published by the London *Economist* in 2006. The study constructed a democracy index that was used to rank 165 independent states and two territories that together represented most of the world's population. The variables used to construct the democracy index included the frequency of elections, levels of political participation, the state of civil liberties, the character of political culture, and the quality of governmental performance.[1]

As seen in Table 25.1, India and Sri Lanka, South Asia's two longest-functioning democracies, ranked well above the other countries in South Asia on the *Economist's* democracy index. While India ranked 35th and Sri Lanka 57th out of the 167 states and territories included in the study, Bangladesh was ranked 75th, Pakistan 113th, and Nepal 126th. As we shall see numerous parallel studies have also shown that the type of political system tends to be highly correlated with levels of political corruption. Given their shared colonial heritage, a study of the post-Independence development of India, Pakistan, and Bangladesh may provide helpful clues to our understanding of the causes, scope, forms and styles, economic costs, and political consequences of corruption and strategies for dealing with the growth of corruption and the growing criminalization of politics in the region.

The study of corruption and its causes

Definitions of corruption vary considerably. The World Bank has defined corruption as "the abuse of power for personal or group benefit."[2] The United Nations Development Program (UNDP) defines it as "the abuse of public power for private benefit through bribery, extortion, influence peddling, nepotism, fraud or embezzlement."[3] While the Swedish economist Gunnar Myrdal defined corruption as "the improper or selfish exercise of power or influence attached to public office,"[4] others have come to see corruption as a form of narrative that focuses on what is or is not proper moral behavior. Most definitions of corruption focus especially on the intersection between public and private spheres of activity. Some critics, however, insist that the issue of corruption should not be confined solely to the public sector. Corruption, they argue, can also be seen as a form of rent whereby the private sector manipulates markets to secure rewards that exceed normal market returns.[5]

Table 25.1 Index of Democracy for South Asia, 2006

Country	Rank	Score
India	35	7.68
Sri Lanka	57	6.58
Bangladesh	75	6.11
Pakistan	113	3.92
Nepal	126	3.42

Source: Economist Intelligence Unit, Index of Democracy: www.theworldin.com

In short, corruption involves the abuse or misuse of power by public officials to provide benefits to individuals and groups in return for financial benefits, public sector jobs, or political support. It takes a variety of forms including the direct payment of bribes, the use of patronage in the allocation of public sector jobs on a non-merit basis, the awarding of non-competitive government contracts, and the payment of "speed money" to ensure timely decisions. Corruption also entails a variety of traditional modes of behavior in societies dominated by a web of patron–client relations, which entails a reciprocal exchange of benefits. In India, this reciprocal exchange involves giving as *bakshish*. In Pakistan, the exchange of benefits is based on friendship and close social relations known as *safarish* (friendship and pleading on behalf of someone). In the highly traditional social setting of Bangladesh, patron–client relations rest on a complex web of connections known as *tadbir* (connections).

The causes of corruption and its impact on politics and development have generated considerable debate among economists. Initially, most economists tended to treat corruption as a benign force or even as a positive device for overcoming bureaucratic slough in developing countries. Increasingly, however, the growing pervasiveness of corruption has led economists to portray the growth of corruption as a cancer that distorts development priorities, heightens economic uncertainties, aggravates inflation, hurts the poor, slows the rate of economic growth, and leads to ineffective governance and political decay. Although countries have succeeded in sustaining rapid growth despite high levels of corruption, most economists insist that rampant corruption entails significant costs that slow economic growth and distort public choice.[6]

Renewed interest in the study of corruption has produced a variety of conflicting assessments of its causes, modes of measurement and impact. While Marxists see corruption as inherently rooted in capitalism, World Bank studies have associated corruption with socialism and the developmental state. Gunnar Myrdal blames the growth of corruption on government instability; Fred Riggs saw it as a concomitant of development; and a survey of Indian administrators blamed it on moral weakness, economic deprivation, and structural strains.[7] Still others see corruption as rooted in the traditional culture of patron–client relations, poverty, and low levels of development or as a form of discourse. The idea of corruption as discourse focuses on corruption as a form of narrative that determines what are considered proper or improper forms of behavior and provides a cultural code designed to make sense of the political world.[8]

Whatever its causes, the widespread existence of corruption has proved very difficult to document or measure. Attempts to quantify the level of corruption in various countries rely heavily on the results of indirect measures based on survey research. Survey research has focused primarily on public perceptions of corruption in an effort to measure its scope and impact in various countries around the world. The most comprehensive surveys of public perceptions of corruption have been conducted by Transparency International (TI), a Berlin based non-governmental organization (NGO). Transparency International conducts annual global surveys that it uses as the basis of its Corruption Perception Index (CPI). The CPI is based on a scale of 1 to 5 with a score of 1 reflecting the existence of a very high level of corruption and a score of 5 indicating very low levels of corruption.[9]

As seen in Table 25.2, the 2006 Transparency International survey of perceptions of corruption in South Asia showed considerable varia-

Table 25.2 Corruption Perceptions Index for South Asia, 2006

Country	Rank	Score
India	70	3.3
Sri Lanka	84	3.1
Nepal	121	2.5
Pakistan	142	2.2
Bangladesh	156	2.0

Source: Transparency International, Corruption Perceptions Index, 2006

tion among the countries in the region. The most striking feature of the survey was the significant difference in the perceived levels of corruption between democratic and non-democratic states. In the 2006 Transparency International survey of corruption, India and Sri Lanka, which were ranked high on the democracy index of the London *Economist,* were also found to have much higher CPI scores than authoritarian countries. On a scale of 1 to 5, India received a CPI score of 3.3 and was ranked 70th out of a total of the 163 countries surveyed. Sri Lanka received a CPI score of 3.1 and was ranked 84th. By contrast, Nepal, Pakistan and Bangladesh, which ranked much lower on the democracy index, were ranked at the bottom of Transparency International's list of the most corrupt countries. Nepal was ranked 121st with a CPI score of 2.5, Pakistan was ranked 142nd with a CPI score of 2.2 and Bangladesh was ranked 156th with a CPI score of 2.0.

Pakistan and Bangladesh have had a long history of authoritarian rule and high levels of corruption. During most of the 1990s, Transparency International ranked Pakistan as one of the most corrupt countries in the world. As a result of a military coup in 1999 led by General Pervez Musharraf, Pakistan initially improved its CPI score. The Musharraf government introduced a range of economic reforms, established a National Accountability Bureau and enacted a comprehensive national anti-corruption strategy. As a result of these reforms Pakistan's CPI score rose from 2.2 in 1999 to 2.6 in 2002 and Pakistan's global ranking went from 88 out of 99 countries surveyed in 1999 to a ranking of 81 out of 105 countries in 2002. As a result of continued military rule and the partial restoration of democracy in 2004, however, Pakistan's CPI score and its global ranking began to decline. In 2006 Pakistan received a CPI score of 2.2 and the country ranked 142 out of the 163 countries surveyed.[10]

Despite the end of military rule and the restoration of democracy in Bangladesh in 1991, the country has faced a very difficult process of democratic consolidation. The country developed a highly polarized politics, was faced by repeated anti-government movements designed to topple elected governments, and developed extremely high levels of political corruption. As a result of these developments, Bangladesh had the dubious distinction of being ranked by Transparency International as the most corrupt country in the world from 2001 to 2005. Bangladesh finally succeeded in improving its global ranking in the 2006 report as a result of a major political crisis that led to the creation of a military-backed neutral caretaker government (NCG). The NCG took a series of important steps that were designed to reduce corruption. These steps included the introduction of major economic reforms; the reconstitution of the country's ineffective Anti-Corruption Commission (ACC); and filing of numerous court cases against corrupt politicians, bureaucrats, and businessmen.[11]

Transparency International's Political Corruption Index provides useful comparative data for measuring perceptions of corruption at the global, regional, and country level. The existence of these differences also raises several important questions. How does one explain the variation in the scope of corruption from country to county? How do forms and styles of corruption differ from state to state? How does one explain differences in the pattern of corruption in the region? And are there any common elements that can account for the pervasiveness of political corruption in South Asia?

Development of corruption in India

The existence of corruption in India is not a recent phenomenon. Because of its dual civilian and commercial activities, the British East India Company was plagued by corruption during most of its history. The introduction of recruitment to East India Company's Indian Civil Service (ICS) by a process of open competition in 1853 and the end of company rule in 1858 led to major improvements in colonial administration. Under direct crown rule, the ICS was transformed into a cadre of some 1,000 or so professional "covenanted officers" who became the administrative "steel frame" of British India.[12] While the small, elite ICS became renowned for its efficiency and high levels of integrity, the same was not the case for the vast army of "unconvenanted" Indian officers who staffed the lower levels of bureaucracy. These officials were accustomed to receiving traditional gifts, payments, and perks as part of the routine performance of their duties. They staffed the revenue services, police, excise and public works departments which became especially known for their high levels of corruption.[13]

Despite its reputation for integrity, the quality and performance of even the higher levels of the civil service in India gradually began to deteriorate under the stress of the First World War, the depression of the 1930s and, especially, the outbreak of the Second World War. The introduction of wartime controls, growing shortages, sharp increases in government expenditures, and the explosion of government contracting and procurement resulted in widespread governmental corruption during the war years from 1939 to 1945 that carried into the postcolonial era.[14]

Following Independence in 1947 the leaders of India's freedom movement attempted to set a high standard of integrity and honesty and even minor transgressions were dealt with severely. In the early years of Congress rule, for example, India's finance minister resigned immediately when the propriety of one of his actions was called into question, a Congress

367

member of parliament was reprimanded for acting on behalf of a client and even Congress-controlled state governments were censured by national Congress leaders for improper bidding and tender practices in the allocation of government contracts.[15]

Over time, however, the rapid expansion of the size of government and government programs, persistent scarcity of goods and services, the weakening of the bureaucracy because of the loss of experienced British and Muslim ICS officers, a flood of new recruits into the newly created Indian Administrative Service (IAS) and a rising tide of popular demands for government services contributed to a series of major scandals in the 1950s. These scandals included the purchase of jeeps by the Indian military, the famous Mundhra affair involving improper transactions between an industrialist and the government-controlled Life Insurance Corporation of India, and allegations of corruption against Pratap Singh Kairon, the former chief minister of Punjab. These incidents combined to begin to tarnish the image of the ruling Congress Party.[16]

Faced by repeated charges of Congress corruption and growing public criticism, Prime Minister Nehru complained that the media were devoting far too much time and attention to these wild allegations and became increasingly reluctant to investigate charges of wrongdoing. The problem, however, did not go away. Corruption became increasingly widespread as a result of the emergence of a socialist-oriented developmental state, centralized planning, comprehensive government control, and regulation of the economy, the growth of public sector enterprises and popular demands for government services and subsidies. The massive expansion of the role of the state was compounded by the Congress Party's need to raise more and more funds in order to be able to fight increasingly competitive elections. By the early 1960s the corruption issue was so pervasive that the government felt compelled to appoint a special commission to study the problem. Although the Santhanam Committee on the Prevention of Corruption

submitted a comprehensive report in April 1964, its impact proved limited.[17]

The death of Nehru in May 1964, followed by that of his successor, Lal Bahadur Shastri, in January 1966, the erosion of congress popularity, the historic split in the party in 1969, and the rise of personalized, dynastic rule under Indira Gandhi further compounded the problem. By the early 1970s India was faced with a rapidly rising tide of official corruption. As money and muscle began to play a more important role in Indian politics, Congress was also forced to change its methods of raising funds to fight elections. During the freedom movement and for most of the Nehru-Shastri era, the Indian business community provided generous support to the Congress Party. For the most part, money for elections was collected by a small group of Congress leaders with close ties to India's large private sector business houses. Businessmen and industrialists willingly contributed to Congress coffers as a way of guaranteeing ready access to ministers and party leaders, keeping the Indian Communist Party at bay, and providing insurance that their interests would be protected. Contributions were made by individual business leaders, major business houses, and other companies, facilitated by laws allowing such donations to be tax deductible.

The financing of political parties in India, however, was significantly altered in the early 1970s as a result of the introduction of a legal ban on company donations to political parties, a historic split in the dominant Congress Party, the rise of competitive politics, and the sharply escalating costs of election campaigns. The results were an increasing reliance on the patronage capabilities of the developmental state to raise campaign funds and the use of money and muscle to ensure victory at the polls. While the growing reliance on money and muscle to win elections led to an increasing criminalization of politics, the use of what became known as the "permit-license-quota Raj" (PLQR) as the basis of campaign finance led to a new era of "briefcase politics," which relied very heavily on the vast reservoir of unreported "black money" in the Indian economy.[18]

Under Indira Gandhi's leadership from 1966 to 1977 the PLQR was gradually transformed into a major source of leverage to extract funds from India's business community. Those businessmen who willingly cooperated by generously providing financial support to the ruling congress were allowed to amass huge fortunes. Those industrialists who resisted or failed to cooperate were faced with excruciating delays, tax raids, and government harassment.[19]

Under the leadership of Rajiv Gandhi, who succeeded his assassinated mother as prime minister in the early 1980s, the leverage provided by the PLQR was supplanted by the huge commissions that could be demanded in the awarding of large government contracts.[20] The result was a series of defense procurement scandals involving the purchase of German submarines and a billion-dollar scandal involving the purchase of Swedish Bofors 155mm howitzers[21] that tarnished Rajiv's Mr Clean image and contributed to his defeat in the 1989 parliamentary elections.

The massive defeat of the Congress Party in the 1989 elections brought about an end to one-party dominance and the temporary eclipse of dynastic rule and ushered in a new era of coalition politics. While some of the post-1989 coalition governments were in office for far too short a time to suffer from major scandals, others were not. The coalition governments of V. P. Singh from 1989 to 1990, H. D. Deve Gowda from June 1996 to April 1997, and the I. K. Gujral government from April 1997 to 1998 were largely free of major scandals. The government of Chandra Shekhar from 1990 to 1991, the Congress-led government of P.V. Narashima Rao from 1991 to 1996 and the BJP-led government of Atal Bihari Vajpayee from 1998 to 2004, however, all faced a series of devastating scandals.[22]

Although the new era of coalition politics failed to reverse the trend toward increased levels of corruption, it did result in opening the political system to greater transparency. The Indian media, the courts, and NGOs began to focus greater public attention on the problem of corruption by exposing an increasing number of scandals and demanding accountability and reform. While greater transparency has not led to an end to corruption in India, it has led to a series of new initiatives that have attempted to limit its impact, such as the recently enacted Freedom of Information Act.

While the brief Chandra Shekhar government was saved from disastrous scandals by the intervention of the President of India, who repeatedly blocked the award of major government contracts, the government of Narashima Rao faced a rash of corruption scandals that directly implicated the prime minister himself. If Indira Gandhi and Rajiv were said to have presided over an era of "briefcase politics," the government of Narashima Rao was charged with introducing a new era of "suitcase politics" as a result of the Harshad Mehta financial scandal. Mehta, a Bombay stockbroker who faced charges relating to a banking and securities fraud, claimed he had delivered a suitcase containing Rs 10 million to the prime minister's residence on 4 November, 1991 in an effort to secure patronage and support from Rao's government. The Harshad Mehta financial scandal was only one of a series of major scandals that came to plague the government of Narashima Rao. These scandals included the Jain *hawala* scandal, the Jharkhand Mukti Morcha (JMM) scandal, the Pathak bribery case, the St Kitts affair, and the Sukh Ram scandal. The Jain Hawala scandal came to light when on 16 January, 1996 the CBI accused some 100 prominent politicians and administrators, including three senior ministers in Rao's government, of receiving Rs 650 million from three Delhi businessmen in return for favors between January 1988 and April 1991. The Pathak bribery case involved an allegation by a British businessman of Indian origin who claimed that he that he had paid Rao $100,000 as a bribe to secure a government contract in 1983. The JMM scandal involved a charge that Prime Minister Rao had bribed four JMM

MPs to gain their support on a no-confidence vote in 1993. The St Kitts affair involved a charge that Rao had orchestrated the forgery of documents designed to implicate the son of V. P. Singh in an illegal transaction on the Caribbean island of St Kitts. The Sukh Ram affair involved Rao's minister of telecommunications, who was caught with millions of rupees in cash in his house that was believed to have been obtained from the allocation of telecommunications licenses. From Narasimha Rao's perspective the most devastating scandal proved to be the Pathak case. As a result of Pathak's allegations, P.V. Narasimha Rao became the first prime minister in Indian history to be convicted of bribery by an Indian court. His conviction, however, was overturned eight years later by a higher court.[23]

The formation of a BJP-led government in March 1998 brought to power a Hindu nationalist party that claimed to be "a party with a difference." During its six years in office from 1998 to 2004, however, a series of corruption scandals led to charges that the corruption under Indira Gandhi paled in comparison to the systemic graft of the BJP-led NDA government.[24] Naresh Chandra, a former cabinet secretary, went so far as to charge that corruption under the BJP had "reached such unbelievable proportions that almost nobody believes that there is anything that they can do about it."[25]

Among the major scandals that erupted during the period of BJP rule were the March 2001 "Tehelka.com" corruption case, a sting operation involving the BJP chief minister of Chhattisgarh, and the Delhi petrol pump scandal. The Tehelka corruption scandal resulted from a sting operation initiated by an internet news service. Posing as arms dealers, Tehelka.com journalists videotaped the president of the BJP and other coalition party leaders accepting bribes to facilitate the prospects of obtaining a defense contract. Two years later, in another sting operation, the BJP candidate for chief minister of Chhattisgarh was caught taking bribes in return for the allocation of leases on protected forest lands in

the state. The Delhi scandal involved the allocation of petrol pumps in the city.[26]

Studies of corruption in India by Transparency International and its local chapter provide a composite picture of the prevalence of corruption in India. In 2006 India was ranked as moderate on Transparency International's global Integrity Index which assesses the existence and effectiveness of anti-corruption mechanisms that promote public integrity.[27] Similarly, Transparency International's Global Corruption Barometer 2006 survey that explores the larger issue of how petty corruption affects ordinary people found that corruption in India affects the lives of some 31 to 50 percent of the population.[28] An earlier study of 11 public services in 20 major states conducted in 2005 by Transparency International India found that Indian citizens paid a total of Rs 21,068 crores in bribes in order to secure public services. The eleven services surveyed included the police (crime/traffic), the judiciary, land administration, municipal services, government hospitals, electric supply, income tax assessment, water supply, schools, rural financial institutions, and the public distribution system (PDP) that is charged with issuing ration cards and supplies. The survey found that the police, lower courts, and land administration were considered to be the most corrupt government agencies in the country. Government hospitals, public sector electric supply corporations, and the PDP ranked next in line. While some states like Kerala were found to be relatively free of corruption, the state of Bihar was found to be far and away the most corrupt state in India.[29] Despite the existence of high levels of corruption in India, P.V. R. Rao, a retired civil servant, insists: "The normal individual can live and carry on his vocation without succumbing to graft, though he may have to put up with frustrations and delays."[30]

Corruption in Pakistan

Despite a common British colonial heritage and similar development policies, the chaos surrounding the birth of Pakistan and Bangladesh, the absence of an established political and administrative infrastructure, the organizational weakness of their political parties, and extended periods of military–bureaucratic rule have led to higher levels of corruption in both countries. Compared to India, Pakistan and Bangladesh have been repeatedly ranked among countries with the highest levels of corruption in the world in Transparency International's surveys.

Unlike India which inherited the infrastructure of the British Raj, the new state of Pakistan emerged with a near non-existent governmental infrastructure, limited administrative capabilities and a divided polity. The very weakness of the state limited the role of government, severely curtailed the impact of government on the country's society and economy, and enabled various economic and social groups to exercise a considerable degree of autonomy. The very survival of the state, however, forced the country's undersized and inexperienced political, bureaucratic, and military elites to develop an unstable symbiotic relationship among themselves. Muslim League politicians depended heavily on the bureaucracy to help them consolidate their power and in return provided high-level bureaucratic officials with extensive autonomy, support, and patronage. The result was the emergence of an unstable political system dominated by rampant corruption that ultimately led to a military coup in 1958 under the leadership of General Ayub Khan.

The military coup of 1958 ushered in an era of political stability, administrative consolidation, and state building in Pakistan. Under the leadership of General Ayub Khan, the country embarked on an ambitious economic development plan and a major reconstruction of the country's political system. Ayub's new economic development strategy, financed by massive amounts of foreign aid, created a large government-owned public sector; introduced a comprehensive system of bureaucratic control and regulation of the economy that granted enormous discretionary powers to

government officials; and attempted to create a state-based corporatism designed to enable the government to penetrate and control all key sectors of Pakistani society and economy. The newly created developmental state enabled the government to use its power to provide public benefits in return for political support. These distributive benefits included such things as industrial licenses, subsidized loans and import/export permits.

General Ayub Khan also embarked on a major transformation of the Pakistani political system. In the name of creating a more indigenous form of government, Ayub introduced a new political order that he called "basic democracy." The system of basic democracy was based on a complex process of direct elections at the local level and indirect elections at the provincial and national levels. Under the new system, village-level constituencies directly elected 80,000 "basic democrats" on the basis of mass franchise. These 80,000 basic democrats then formed an electoral collage to elect the provincial assemblies, the national parliament, and the president. The new system, however, was easily manipulated. It enabled local elites to maintain their dominance; it encouraged the use of the government's electoral machinery to ensure electoral success; and it enabled national and provincial politicians to buy votes in an effort to gain political power and influence.[31]

Although General Ayub Khan came to power promising to cleanse the old corrupt parliamentary system of the 1950s, the institutions of basic democracy and the emergence of a bureaucratically dominated developmental state resulted in an even more pervasive pattern of corruption. While Ayub remained personally free of corruption, the same was not the case for his friends, supporters, and relatives. His son Gohar Ayub, for example, was able to join the ranks of the lucky 22 business families that were said to dominate the Pakistani economy of the 1960s.[32] Ultimately, corruption and the resulting social and regional inequalities of Ayub's development model led to a mass uprising, the collapse of the regime, and the breakup of the country.

The breakup of united Pakistan, the authoritarian character of the newly created government of Zulfikar Ali Bhutto, and the socialist policies of the Pakistan People's Party vastly increased the power and role of the state in society and the economy. In an effort to reduce the economic power and political influence of Pakistan's 22 families, Bhutto nationalized all private sector banks, insurance companies, most large-scale private sector industries, and a large portion of domestic and international trade and commerce. Under Bhutto, the size of the public sector almost doubled overnight from 24 percent of gross domestic product (GDP) to 51 percent. The nationalization policies of the Bhutto government not only increased the size of the public sector but also substantially enhanced the capabilities of the Pakistani state to distribute benefits to private individuals and groups in return for political support.

Bhutto's attempt to renew his electoral mandate in 1977 proved to be a disaster. The massive popular vote in favor of the PPP led to opposition party charges of extensive vote rigging and a mass movement demanding new elections. The political chaos that followed the 1977 Pakistani elections was brought to a halt by a military coup led by General Zia-ul-Haq and the arrest and execution of Bhutto.[33] Despite the overthrow of the PPP government, General Zia was reluctant to upset the economic status quo and faced enormous bureaucratic resistance to any attempt to reduce the size of the public sector by reversing Bhutto's nationalization policies. Buoyed by a massive increase in foreign aid in the 1980s related to the Afghan war and a flood of foreign remittances from oversees Pakistani workers in the Middle East and Europe, Zia attempted to buy political support through the use of government benefits in an effort to establish his legitimacy. As a result, the Zia government, like its predecessors, was marked by rampant corruption.[34]

Zia's move toward the restoration of limited civilian rule and the formation of the Junejo government in March 1985 further aggravated the level of corruption in the country. From 1985 onward, noted Rizvi, every Pakistani government "has surpassed its predecessor in offering material rewards" to its followers and supporters. These rewards included cabinet posts, ministerial perks, bank loans, quotas, licenses, loan waivers, development funds, land allocations, jobs, and other government benefits.[35]

The death of General Zia and the full restoration of civilian rule in 1988 were followed by 11 years of political instability; the emergence of confrontational politics between Benazir Bhutto and Nawaz Sharif, the country's two leading politicians; and the rapid growth of pervasive corruption. Numerous studies of corruption perceptions in Pakistan from 1988 to 1999 by Transparency International revealed a steady rise in levels of corruption with each change of government. During the first Benazir Bhutto government from 1988 to 1990, only 8 percent of those surveyed considered her government to be corrupt. Corruption perceptions showed a slight increase from 8 percent under Benazir to 10 percent from 1990 to 1993 under Nawaz Sharif.

The remainder of the 1990s, however, was marked by political instability and uncertainty that seemed to alter party behavior significantly. The second government of Benazir Bhutto that ruled from 1993 to 1996 proved to be one of the most corrupt in Pakistani history. A survey by Transparency International in 1996 found that some 48 percent of Pakistanis considered Benazir Bhutto's second government to be corrupt. The survey also found that Pakistan ranked second only to Nigeria among the most corrupt countries in the world. These perceptions of the Bhutto government based on survey data were later confirmed by a study commissioned by the country's neutral caretaker government (NCG). The study conducted by Burki and Pasha, two of Pakistan's leading economists, estimated that the cost of corruption from 1993 to 1996 was equal to 20 to 25 percent of the country's 1996–97 GDP or about $15 billion.[36]

Both Benazir Bhutto and Nawaz Sharif have been accused of corruption and faced a number of cases in the Pakistani courts. Both were also known to have acquired valuable foreign properties in London and elsewhere. Bhutto, for example, purchased a 350-acre estate in Surrey in the United Kingdom, while Nawaz used bank loans and nonpayment of taxes to accumulate additional wealth. Asif Zardari, Benazir's husband, is accused of accumulating his wealth through kickbacks. During Benazir Bhutto's first term as Prime Minister from 1988 to 1990, Zardari came to be known as "Mr Ten Percent." By Bhutto's second term from 1993 to 1996, however, Zardari had become "Mr Twenty Percent."[37]

Although perceptions of corruption declined slightly during Nawaz Sharif's second term in office from 1996 to 1999, the prime minister's attempt to gain total control of Pakistani politics and his open challenge to the power of the Pakistan Army resulted in a military coup in 1999 that toppled his government and led to his exile to Saudi Arabia. The military coup led by General Parvez Musharraf promised to restore honesty, economic growth, and political stability to the country. Despite considerable success in rehabilitating the Pakistani economy and restoring high levels of growth, a survey by Transparency International revealed that some 32.69 percent of Pakistanis considered the initial years of Musharraf's rule from 1999 to 2002 to be corrupt. These corruption perceptions changed dramatically in the aftermath of the 2002 parliamentary elections when a new survey revealed that perception of corruption had reached a new all-time high. Some 67.31 percent of Pakistanis considered Musharraf's rule from 2002 to 2006 to be corrupt![38]

The current scope of corruption in Pakistan has been demonstrated by several recent assessments. A study by the World Bank in 2003, for example, found corruption in Pakistan's education, police, and judicial sectors to be much higher than in other countries in South Asia.[39] While Pakistan received the same score as India in Transparency International's 2006 Global Corruption Barometer, it was ranked much lower in the organization's 2006 Global Integrity Index.[40] In addition a Transparency International study in Pakistan in 2006 concluded that bribery in Pakistan was estimated to cost the average citizen in the country Rs 2,303 per household. The study also found that the police, the electric utility sector, the judiciary, and land administration were the most corrupt governmental sectors. Overall, petty corruption was estimated to cost the country about Rs 45 billion.[41]

Corruption in Bangladesh

The politics of patronage and corruption have plagued every government in Bangladesh since liberation. During the period of Awami League rule from 1972 to 1975, Prime Minister Sheikh Mujibar Rahman distributed government benefits and jobs to party leaders and supporters as a reward for their "suffering for the cause of the nation."[42] Awami League activists received jobs in newly nationalized industries, grew rich as smugglers, appropriated abandoned Pakistani houses and property, and sold government-allotted permits and licenses to the highest bidder. Awami League leaders, party supporters, and Mujib's relatives plundered the society in almost every way possible.[43]

The assassination of Mujib in August 1975 was followed by a series of military coups and the rise of General Ziaur Rahman. Zia dominated Bangladesh politics from 1975 until his assassination in May 1981. Under General Zia, corruption in Bangladesh became institutionalized and came to dominate all levels of government. Although personally free of corruption, Zia accepted corruption as a fact of life and publicly admitted that corruption and the misuse of power had led to the misappropriation of 40 percent of the country's development funds. Under Zia's rule, noted one critic, corruption was "converted from a crime to a habit." Under Zia's successor, Justice

Abdus Sattar, corruption became so rampant that it was invoked by General H. M. Ershad as the major justification for his military coup.[44]

But then, corruption in Bangladesh under General H. M. Ershad became all-pervasive. Petty corruption forced businessmen and citizens to pay fees to obtain routine application forms, to secure customs clearances, and even to ensure proper billing for government services. Public sector enterprises were especially known for their high levels of corruption. The Power Development Board (PDB), for example, which was responsible for the manufacture and distribution of electric power, was unable to account for as much as 50 percent of the electricity it generated. This electricity was either stolen by consumers or simply unaccounted for as PDB employees altered large utility bills in return for a substantial cut. Even public and private educational institutions were not immune from widespread corruption in student placement and teacher recruitment. Public procurement and contracting, however, were the most notorious sources of massive payoffs. During the Ershad years, major contracts for the acquisition of aircraft for the state-owned airline, government food purchases, and contracts for large development projects were all subject to the payment of massive commissions that ranged between 20 and 40 percent of cost.[45]

The end of military rule and the restoration of democracy in 1991 did not fundamentally alter levels of corruption in Bangladesh. Under both the Bangladesh Nationalist Party (BNP) governments of 1991 to 1996 and 2001 to 2006 and Awami League rule from 1996 to 2001, corruption became increasingly pervasive. Corruption in Bangladesh in 2002 was estimated to cost the country 44 billion taka ($745 million) or an estimated 10 percent of the country's budget and 67 percent of the foreign assistance received by the country. The World Bank has noted that corruption in Bangladesh reduced the country's economic growth rate by as much as 2 percent per year.[46]

Causes of corruption in South Asia

Corruption in most Asian countries, argues Jon S. T. Quah, has been driven by a multiplicity of factors, including: low civil service salaries, the massive social and economic role of the developmental state, the near absence of detection and punishment, the primacy of family, nepotism and patron–client relations, a strong tradition of gift giving, the absence of political will on the part of dominant elites in dealing with the problem, and the lack of an effective anti-corruption strategy.[47] While most of these factors also apply to the countries of South Asia, the higher levels of corruption in the region have focused special attention on the impact of the developmental state, the dominant role of family and group loyalties, the strength of clientelism and traditional patron–client relations, and the absence of effective anti-corruption strategies. These factors have not only contributed to the rise of corruption but also have contributed to the growing criminalization of politics in the region.

Impact of the developmental state

The imposition of a highly centralized, bureaucratically dominated developmental state on the decentralized, largely rural, highly traditional agrarian societies of South Asia has contributed significantly to the emergence of corruption in the region. The developmental state created by the political elites in South Asia was superimposed on an agrarian society and an antiquated bureaucratic administrative system that placed vast discretionary powers in the hands of politicians and bureaucrats. This administrative system was inherited from the British and was known as the secretariat system. The secretariat system was designed to diffuse power and responsibility. It was procedurally complex, highly inefficient and based on a case-by-case review of all governmental policies and actions regardless of size or importance.

The case-by-case decisions were reached through a complex process of bureaucratic consensus building that began at the very bottom of the bureaucratic hierarchy and slowly worked its way up to the top. Under this system, all bureaucratic actions were based on a unit of work known as the file. The file was initially assembled by a low-level clerk, who was responsible for collecting all papers and documents related to the case and preparing a note that cited all relevant government acts, rules, and regulations that were applicable. The file then moved slowly through the bureaucratic maze as each level of the bureaucracy thoroughly vetted the file, recorded its comments, and recommended appropriate action. All disagreements were settled by a painstaking system of repeated individual discussions between officials and group meetings until a consensus was achieved. Since the notations on the file reflect a bargained bureaucratic consensus, senior-level officials charged with making a final decision were extremely reluctant to overrule the agreed consensus. This complex process of decision making was extremely time-consuming and subject to inordinate delay, delegated enormous discretionary powers to government officials, and diffused responsibility and accountability.

Overcoming the delays, procedural hurdles and the ambiguity of decisions that emerged from this Byzantine system required intense lobbying at each level, close personal connections with officials, and the distribution of gifts, payments and rewards. Lower-level clerks were given *bakshish* to ensure that the case was properly prepared; and "speed money" was distributed at various levels of the bureaucracy to ensure that the file moved through the system in a timely manner. At the senior levels of the bureaucracy, small gifts, the payment of domestic and overseas travel and hotel expenses, and the provision of lavish entertainment to officials usually proved to be sufficient to facilitate the desired outcome. At the political level, money and large campaign contributions to ministers and politicians were required.[48]

Despite the economic reforms introduced in 1991, India continues to be plagued by the residues of the old order. While the Indian middle class and the large-scale industrial sector have been freed from the restrictions of the PLQR, the reforms have not reached the rest of the economy. This is especially true of the medium and small-scale sectors. Luce thought otherwise:

> Many believe, that corruption is therefore on the retreat. What is less appreciated is the extent to which India's license Raj of quotas, permits, and hairsplitting regulations continue to exist outside the "organized" economy. Beyond the manicured lawns of middle-class India, the tentacles of the License Raj continue to reach into the lives of vast numbers of Indians. Most of them tend to be poor.

Even the large-scale industrial sector has complained that the PLQR of the past has simply been replaced by the new "Inspector Raj." In short, the developmental state in India was said to be dominated by a simple formula: $M + D = C$, Monopoly plus Discretion equals Corruption.[49]

Criminalization of politics and the role of the state

The corruption generated by the rise of the developmental state in South Asia was reinforced by electoral pressures that led to a growing reliance on money and muscle to win elections; the emergence of a linkage between political parties and the underworld; and a growing criminalization of politics in the region. In the early years following independence, elections in South Asia were largely influenced by the popular appeal of nationalist leaders and not by coercion or money or the manipulation of election results. Over time, however, noted Pai Panandikar, the growth of factionalism, confrontational politics, and increased electoral competition has led to the increased use of violence, money and muscle at the polls. Muscle has been employed by candidates, political parties, locally dominant landed elites, factory owners, slum lords, and urban-based mafia dons to win elections. The growing criminalization of politics and the growth of electoral violence in South Asian politics have been reinforced by the decline of ideology and ideologically-based political parties, the growth of anti-government revolutionary movements, the desire to gain control of the patronage resources of the state, and the increasing polarization of party politics. Over time, criminals who initially were hired to help politicians get elected began to contest elections in their own right as a way of enhancing the scope of their profits from criminal activity and protecting themselves from arrest and criminal prosecution.[50]

The criminalization of politics in India began in the early1960s as the old nationalist leadership began to pass from the scene and an increasingly divided Congress Party could no longer count on the legacy of the freedom movement to win elections. Following the introduction of mass franchise, state-level Congress leaders relied heavily on local notables and caste leaders to mobilize voters. With the passage of time, however, Congress leaders in various parts of the country began to resort to the use of local thugs to disrupt the polls and stuff ballot boxes in a desperate effort to ensure victory.[51] By the late1970s and early 1980s, the practice of ballot stuffing developed into a more organized system known as "booth capturing." Although the practice was widely employed in various parts of the country, it became especially prevalent in various parts of northern India. In Bihar and Uttar Pradesh, for example, politicians paid armed gangs of thugs between Rs 50,000 and 100,000 to seize control of a polling station, frighten away potential voters, and stuff the ballot boxes as a way to ensure victory.[52]

The steady decline of the once-dominant Congress Party and the increasing use of booth capturing gradually led to a growing criminalization of politics in the country. By the mid-1980s, the very criminals and thugs who were hired by politicians to engage in booth capturing decided to secure public office for themselves. Election to the state assembly and the national parliament became a way for criminals to secure political protection for their illicit activities and guarantee safety from prosecution. Like the political bosses that came to dominate urban politics in the early part of the twentieth century in the United States, India began to develop its own mafia-style gangs and political bosses in places like the slums of Mumbai and the coalfields of Bihar.

The growing nexus between criminality and politics led the government of India to appoint a special committee to study the problem. The Vohra Committee Report issued in 1995, however, had to rely largely on anecdotal data. A more comprehensive study of criminality and politics by Paul and Vivekananda based on an analysis of data taken from affidavits submitted by MPs to the Indian Election Commission found that 23.2 percent of the 541 MPs elected to the Lok Sabha in 2004 had criminal cases registered against them or had criminal cases pending against them in court. The study also found that MPs representing smaller regional parties such as the Rashtriya Janata Dal, the Biju Janata Dal and the Shiv Sena had much higher proportions of criminal cases filed against them than was the case for MPs from large national parties like congress and the BJP. A state and regional breakdown found that MPs from the north and the west had a higher number of MPs with pending criminal cases than was the case for MPs from other regions of the country. The study also found that four north Indian states—Bihar, Uttar Pradesh, Madhya Pradesh, and Jharkhand—accounted for 50 percent of all MPs with serious criminal cases filed against them that carried a penalty of five years or more in prison.[53]

The criminalization of politics in Bangladesh has followed a somewhat different path from that of India. Since liberation, Bangladesh has experimented with several political systems and has been heavily influenced by its brief but intense Pakistani experience. The political process in the newly-created state of Bangladesh became highly centralized, popular elections were repeatedly manipulated by the government of the day, elected assemblies were largely weak and irrelevant, opposition groups repeatedly resorted to direct action and violence, and the country's leaders created a highly personalized, patrimonial, developmental state that rested on an intricate network of patron–client connections and patronage that in turn relied on control of government resources in order to remain in power.

Electoral irregularities in Bangladesh began at the time of the first post-liberation parliamentary elections held in March 1973. Although the charisma of Sheikh Mujibur Rahman and the popularity of the Awami League all but guaranteed victory for the party at the polls, the elections were marred by numerous malpractices. The Awami League's determination to win a total victory led the party to engage in a reign of terror against its opponents in prestige constituencies; opposition candidates were prevented from filing or were forced to withdraw their nomination papers, and ballot boxes were stolen and replaced by new ones stuffed with Awami League votes. The massive corruption and chaos that characterized Awami League rule contributed to the assassination of Mujib, the collapse off the Awami League government, a series of military coups, and the rise of General Ziaur Rahman.[54]

Like the Awami League, General Zia and his newly created BNP were also accused of engaging in corruption and electoral malpractices designed to ensure victory. Under Zia, the official electoral machinery was ordered to insure the victory of official party candidates and the government-controlled media announced what appeared to be tailor-made results. The New York Times characterized the 1979 Bangladesh parliamentary elections as an "election of questionable integrity" and the 1981 election led the Manchester Guardian to conclude that: "No one who knows Bangladesh well could expect an election free from foul play." Although General Zia was personally free of charges of corruption, he accepted the existence of corruption as a fact of life. Following Zia's assassination, the pervasiveness of BNP corruption was, as previously noted, used by General H. M. Ershad to justify his 1981 military coup.[55]

Elections under General H. M. Ershad were popularly referred to as "voterless elections" because of the abysmal voter turnout. Polling officials during the 1986 and 1988 elections were "instructed" to ensure victory for Ershad's Jatiya Party candidates; ballot boxes were seized on election day and stuffed with votes for ruling party candidates; and state-controlled television simply declared that the Jatiya Party candidate had won.[56]

The popular movement that led to the overthrow of the Ershad government in 1990 was followed by an election supervised by a Neutral Caretaker Government (NCG). The elections held in February 1991 were declared by both domestic and international observers to be the first truly free and fair election in Bangladesh since 1970. The successful transition to democracy in Bangladesh in 1991, however, was followed by a failed effort at democratic consolidation. Awami League and the BNP, the two major parties in Bangladesh, embarked upon a no-holds-barred struggle for power. The patrimonial character of the country's politics led to a bitter polarization of politics and a winner-take-all battle for control of the state and its resources. While the majority insisted its electoral victory granted it an absolute mandate to govern as it pleased, the defeated opposition parties countered that the elections had been rigged and took to the streets demanding new elections. The mass demonstrations, hartals (general strikes), and repeated resort to agitational politics had a devastating impact on the economy and the political stability of the country.

Even the adoption of a constitutional amendment in 1996 that mandated the creation of an NCG to conduct free and fair parliamentary elections failed to stem the tide of bitter confrontation between the two parties. Despite the constitutional mandate, once it was in power, each party did everything it could to undermine the country's election commission, the newly created NCG system, and the entire electoral process in an effort to guarantee the party's success at the polls. Efforts by the BNP government to dominate the election commission and the NCG appointed to oversee the 2006 parliamentary elections led to a major political crisis and the appointment of a military-backed NCG. In short, elections in Bangladesh have been repeatedly marred by the use of the official machinery of the state to influence election results and by a resort to money, muscle, violence, and criminal elements to ensure electoral success.

As in Bangladesh, the breakup of united Pakistan in 1971 resulted in the restoration of democracy. While Bangladesh fell under the sway of the Awami League led by Sheikh Mujibur Rahman, Pakistan fell under the control of the PPP led by Zulfikar Ali Bhutto. Unlike Mujib, Bhutto did not bother to seek a renewed electoral mandate until 1977. Although Bhutto claimed to have won a massive victory in the 1977 elections, his opponents refused to accept the results of the elections and took to the streets. Following months of mass agitation over the alleged rigging of the 1977 parliamentary elections, the Bhutto government was overthrown by a military coup.

The restoration of military rule in Pakistan in 1977 had a major impact on the country's political development. Following over a decade of military rule, democracy was restored in 1988 after the death of General Zia. Despite the restoration of democracy, however, Pakistani polities from 1988 to 1999 continued to be shaped by the military through the behind-the-scenes manipulation of the Inter-Services Intelligence (ISI) agency. The ISI was closely allied with the locally dominant landed elite and the country's religious leaders. The ISI sponsored the creation of a "king's party" by engineering defections from existing political parties; it supplied its allies with huge amounts of election funds; and, when

necessary, it manipulated the results of elections. Elected civilian governments that failed to toe the military's line or threatened military dominance were dismissed by the president of Pakistan under instruction from the military.[57] As in the case of Bangladesh, the use of the official electoral machinery of the state continues to play a critical role in determining election results.

Culture of corruption: Patron–client relations and patronage

Corruption in South Asia is deeply entangled in the cultural traditions and social structure of the countries of the region. In traditional South Asian villages, families and groups secure protection, security, and the necessities of existence through a complex network of patron–client relations. Patron–client relations depend on a comprehensive web of relations based on a reciprocal exchange of mutual dependency and obligations. Those with higher rank, wealth, and status command the services and support of those of lower rank and the lower ranks receive the support and protection from their patrons in return. These village-level relationships are integrated into a larger complex web of factions and alliances with more powerful patrons beyond the village at the district and state levels.

Patron–client relations and factional alliances divide rural society along vertical lines and are held together by hierarchical relations based on mutual obligations, reciprocity and the need for support. This clientelist system continues to dominate social relations and influence individual and group behavior in India, Pakistan, and Bangladesh. It has also played a critical role in governance. Even during the colonial era, lower level government officials felt compelled to maintain a close alliance with local landed elites and group leaders. Government officials in the region have traditionally relied on alliances, social networks, and locally powerful landlords as a

CORRUPTION AND THE CRIMINALIZATION OF POLITICS IN SOUTH ASIA

way of supplementing the organizational weakness of the state at the local level. Traditional forms of gift giving played an essential role in maintaining and sustaining these social relationships.

The rise of the state and political parties altered but did not destroy the old order. Political parties and the state simply evolved a new style of clientelism in which clients received benefits from the state in exchange for political support at the polls.[58] Although the new system continued to be based on instrumental relationships and the distribution of benefits, it was less hierarchical, more personal, more bureaucratized and more fluid than the old. The new clientelism, in short, evolved into a new style of special interest politics based on the distribution of government jobs and public resources in an effort to build and sustain political support.

The durability of patron–client relations in South Asia continues to be reflected in the relationship between the state and society. Given the tradition of bureaucratic paternalism and the emergence of the developmental state, groups and individuals in the region continued to resort to the tradition of gift giving, nepotism, patronage, money, and lobbying to secure benefits. These tactics were facilitated by traditional modes of behavior reflected in the employment of *bakshish* in India, *safarish* in Pakistan, and *tadbir* (connections) in Bangladesh. These traditions were based on the principle of reciprocity, which required that a gift be returned with a gift, a favor rendered for a favor, and favorable treatment reciprocated by favorable treatment.

Wealth, rank and status continue to play important roles in the politics of South Asia. Support for the developmental state in the region, for example, has survived the decline of socialist and communist ideologies because of the critical role it has played in the rise of the urban middle class. The developmental state, created in the name of helping the poor, developed into a system of preferential access that has primarily benefited the urban middle class. The urban middle class has used its status

and political influence to gain access to a vast array of public goods and state subsidies. Elite connections based on family, school tie, and community have continually enabled the urban middle class to jump the queue, pull strings, and secure services and benefits allocated by the bureaucracy free of charge or at highly subsidized rates. As a result, public benefits created in the name of helping the poor have tended to go largely to those who have money, status, and connections while the poor continue to pay for these services or are forced to do without. In short, drawing on the tradition of patron–client relations, the new clientelism provided the urban middle-class liberal access to public resources that gave them very little incentive to support economic reforms, demand a clamp down on corruption or change a system that has supported their private consumption.

Strategies for dealing with corruption

Although numerous World Bank Studies have concluded that there is no single solution to dealing with the problem of corruption, the most successful programs have focused on capacity building, reducing opportunities, and limiting benefits. Success depends largely on the scope of the problem, its causes, and the amount of resistance. The World Bank has concluded that the most successful anti-corruption strategies involve improved civil service supervision, public awareness campaigns, limiting the discretionary power of bureaucrats and politicians, higher civil service salaries, privatization, or public sector reform, an effective anti-corruption enforcement mechanism, and most important of all, political will on the part of senior elected officials. The most critical elements in any anti-corruption strategy are strong political will, external mechanisms to ensure accountability, and clear objectives and priorities.

Obstacles to reform

All reform programs, however, tend to encounter significant obstacles that must be overcome. The most significant obstacles to reform in South Asia vary from country to country. The most important common factors include the need to overcome the resistance of entrenched elites, the absence of incentives to change, a lack of political will, the repeated enactment of ineffective anti-corruption laws, and a refusal to reduce the role of the state in the society and economy.

While reformers admit that a major reduction in poverty in South Asia will require continued state intervention, this objective, they argue, is unlikely to be achieved by an unreformed and unaccountable state. The incentive to substantially alter the current system, however, has yet to emerge. While the growth of civil society represents an important development, civil society in South Asia has been shown to be still too weak to achieve success. So long as government continues to totally dominate the society and economy, pervasive corruption and bribery will continue to play a major role in the political, social and economic development of the region. Most reforms in South Asia in the past have been introduced largely in response to economic crisis, systemic breakdown, the rise of new social forces, international pressure, and global change. What has been absent is the required political will.

Notes

1 Laza Kekic, "A Pause in Democracy's March," *The World in 2007* (*Economist*, 2007), pp. 59–60.
2 Dieter Haller and Cris Shore (eds), *Corruption: Anthropological Perspectives* (London: Pluto Press, 2005), p. 2.
3 Rick Stapenhurst and Sahr J. Kpundeh (eds), *Curbing Corruption: Toward a Model for Building National Integrity* (Washington, DC: World Bank, 1999), p. 19.
4 Gunnar Myrdal, *Asian Drama: An Inquiry into the Poverty of Nations*, vol. II (New York: Twentieth Century Fund, 1968), p. 937.
5 School of Advanced International Studies (SAIS), Johns Hopkins University, Washington, DC, seminar on corruption, 30 March, 2007.
6 Haller and Shore, pp. 3–6.
7 Narendra Kumar Singh, *Bureaucracy: Positions and Persons* (New Delhi: Abhinav Publications, 1974), pp. 198–99.
8 Sten Widmalm, "Explaining Corruption at the Village and Individual Level in India: Findings from a Study of the Panchayati Raj Reforms," *Asian Survey* (September–October 2005), pp. 756–76. See also Akhil Gupta, "Blurred Boundaries: The Discourse of Corruption, the Culture of Politics, and the Imagined State," *American Ethnologist*, Vol. 22, No. 2 (1995), pp. 375–402.
9 Transparency International, Corruption Perceptions Index, 2006.
10 Transparency International Pakistan, Press Release, 11 August, 2006.
11 Mahmuduk Rahman, *Economic Governance Issues and Bangladeshi Experience of Growth and Governance* (Dhaka, June 2006).
12 Judith M. Brown, *Modern India: The Origins of an Asian Democracy* (Oxford: University Press, 1994), p. 59.
13 B. B. Misra, *Government and Bureaucracy in India: 1947–1976* (New Delhi: Oxford University Press, 1986), pp. 270–71.
14 Government of India, Ministry of Home Affairs, *Report of the Committee on the Prevention of Corruption* (Santhanam Committee Report), 14 April, 1964, pp. 6–7.
15 P. V. R. Rao, *Red Tape and White Cap* (New Delhi: Orient Longmans, 1970), p. 3.
16 Basudev Panda, *Indian Bureaucracy: An Inside Story* (New Delhi: Uppal, 1978), pp. 78–101.
17 *Santhanam Committee Report.*
18 Stanley A. Kochanek, "Briefcase Politics in India: The Congress Party and The Business Elite," *Asian Survey*, Vol. 27, No. 12 (December 1987), pp. 1,278–301.
19 Kochanek, "Briefcase Politics," p. 1,291.
20 R. Venkataraman, *My Presidential Years* (New Delhi: HarperCollins, 1994), p. 40.
21 B. G. Deshmukh, *From Poona to the Prime Minister's Office: A Cabinet Secretary Looks Back* (New Delhi: HarperCollins, 2004), pp. 217–26.

22 Paranjoy Thakurta and Shankar Raghuraman, *A Time of Coalitions: Divided We Stand* (New Delhi: Sage, 2004), pp. 337–44.

23 Stanley A. Kochanek, *India: Government and Politics in a Developing Nation*, 7th edn (Boston, MA: Thomson Wadsworth, 2008), pp. 304–05.

24 Francine R Frankel, *India's Political Economy: 1947–2004* (New Delhi: Oxford University Press, 2005), pp. 725–26.

25 *Financial Times Weekly* (London), 12–13 October, 2002.

26 Thakurta and Raghuraman, pp. 337–44.

27 Global Integrity Assessment Index, http://www.globalintegrity.org/data/2006index.cfm.

28 Transparency International, *Report on the Transparency International Global Corruption Barometer*, 7 December, 2006.

29 Transparency International India, *India Corruption Study 2005: To Improve Governance*, 30 June, 2005.

30 Rao, p. 198.

31 Karl Von Vorys, *Political Development in Pakistan* (Princeton, NJ: University Press, 1965), p. 265.

32 Herbert Feldman, *From Crisis to Crisis: Pakistan 1962–1969* (London: Oxford University Press, 1972), pp. 295–96.

33 Shahid Javed Burki, *Pakistan Under Bhutto: 1971–1977* (New York: St. Martin's, 1980).

34 Anita M. Weiss and S. Zulfiqar Gilani (eds), *Power and Civil Society in Pakistan* (Oxford: University Press, 2001), p. 111; and Shahid Javed Burki and Craig Baxter, *Pakistan Under the Military: Eleven Years of Zia ul-Haq* (Boulder, CO: Westview, 1991), pp. 30–31.

35 Hasan-Askari Rizvi, *Military, State, and Society in Pakistan* (London: Macmillan, 2000).

36 See Burki and Baxter, *Pakistan Under the Military*, p. 173; and Transparency International, *Global Perception Survey*, 1996.

37 Owen Bennett Jones, *Pakistan: Eye of the Storm* (New Haven, CT: Yale University Press, 2002), pp. 232–35.

38 *Global Corruption Barometer*, p. 1; and "News: Pakistan Leads in Corruption", http://puggy.symonds.net/pipermail/corruption-issues/2003-June/000346.html.

39 *Global Corruption Barometer*, p. 1.

40 Transparency International, *Integrity Index*.

41 Transparency International Pakistan, Press Release, 11 August, 2006.

42 Stanley A. Kochanek, *Patron Client Politics and Business in Bangladesh* (New Delhi/Newbury Park/London: Sage, 1993), p. 258.

43 *Kochanek, Patron Client Politics*, p. 259.

44 *Kochanek, Patron Client Politics*, p. 259.

45 *Kochanek, Patron Client Politics*, pp. 261–62.

46 See World Bank, *Taming Leviathan: Reforming Governance in Bangladesh* (Dhaka: World Bank, 2002).

47 Jon S. T. Quah, "Curbing Asian Corruption: An Impossible Dream?" *Current History* (April 2006), pp. 176–79.

48 Stanley A. Kochanek, "The Politics of Regulation: Rajiv's New Mantras," *Journal of Commonwealth and Comparative Studies*, Vol. 23, No. 3 (November 1985), pp. 189–211.

49 Edward Luce, *In Spite of the Gods: The Strange Rise of Modern India* (New York: Doubleday, 2007), pp. 66, 78–84.

50 V. A. Pai Panandiker (ed.), *Problems of Governance in South Asia* (Dhaka: University Press, 2000), pp. 355–57.

51 T. N. Seshan with Sanjoy Hazarika, *The Degeneration of India* (New Delhi: Penguin Viking, 1995), pp. 24–25, 264–65.

52 Atul Kohli, *Democracy and Discontent: India's Growing Crisis of Governability* (Cambridge: University Press, 1990), pp. 212–26.

53 Samuel Paul and M. Vivekananda, "Holding a Mirror to the New Lok Sabha," *Economic and Political Weekly*, Vol. 39, No. 45 (6–12 November, 2004), pp. 4,927–34.

54 *Kochanek, Patron Client Politics*, pp. 225–27.

55 Shamsul Huda Harun, *Bangladesh Voting Behaviour: A Psychological Study 1973* (Dhaka: University Press, 1986), pp. 220, 244.

56 *Kochanek, Patron Client Politics*, pp. 226–27.

57 Husain Haqqani, *Pakistan: Between Mosque and Military* (Washington, DC: Carnegie Endowment for International Peace, 2005).

58 See Kanchan Chandra, *Why Ethnic Parties Succeed: Patronage and Ethnic Head Counts in India* (Cambridge: University Press, 2004).

26

Radical and violent political movements

Sumanta Banerjee

Prelude to violence

The violent forms that radical movements are assuming in parts of South Asia today have a long tradition stretching back to the unresolved conflicts that were left behind in the wake of the transfer of power by the British colonial rulers to the nationalist leaders in the late 1940s. Since then, during the last half century or so, discord between the landless and the landed gentry, contention for power among different ethnic communities, and hostility between religious majority and minority groups, among other divisive matters, had off and on reached flashpoints in the postcolonial states. The governments of these South Asian states have been incapable of disentangling the roots of these conflicts which they inherited from the pre-Independence era, and have failed to resolve them through a democratic process.

Violence often becomes the ultimate and extreme response of the most desperate segments of the population who have remained deprived of the benefits of development following Independence, and who find that the prevailing ruling system has failed to fulfill its promises. The history of Communist radical movements in India testifies to the will of the poor peasantry and landless to opt for violence as the last resort in their attempt to improve their lot when all other means (such as Gandhian *satyagraha*, or parliamentary reforms) have failed.

In fact, soon after Independence in 1947, both newly formed states, India and Pakistan, apart from getting embroiled in the high-profile territorial dispute over Kashmir, had to face the less publicized Communist-led armed insurgencies, which had broken out in several areas on the eve of Independence and continued thereafter. These insurgencies were mainly confined to the rural areas, involving peasants and poor tribal people, who were fighting oppressive landlords and the police force. Communist-led uprisings by the tribal *hajongs* in Mymansingh, and *santhals* in Rajshahi against rack renting by feudal landlords in the newly independent East Pakistan, peasant guerilla movement in Kakdwip in West Bengal, and similar acts of armed resistance by the rural poor of Kishengarh in Patiala and Tanjore in Tamil Nadu in the Indian state, were extensions of pre-Independence anti-feudal struggles under Communist leadership.[1] These feudal forces were represented in the Indian countryside by an axis of upper caste landlords and orthodox religious patriarchs from all denominations, both notorious for their economic exploitation and social oppression of the poor peasants, particularly their womenfolk. The most serious challenge to the new government in New Delhi was posed by the Communist insurgency in Telangana in southern India. This area was a princely state ruled by the Nizam, who controlled vast feudatory lands and against whose oppressive practices the Communist peasant leaders had waged an armed resistance from 1946 onwards, in the course of which they carved out liberated zones over large swaths of rural territory where they distributed land among the poor, and set up *gram raj* or village soviets for governance. Even after the Nizam's rule ended with the entry of Indian troops in September 1948 and the official merger of the Nizam's state into the Indian Union, the Communists continued the armed struggle against the Indian army. The latter unleashed a military offensive that took a heavy toll of the Communist leaders and cadres. In 1951, the CPI (Communist Party of India) central leadership instructed its followers to surrender arms and withdraw the movement, following the party's decision to abandon armed struggle and join the mainstream of parliamentary politics).[2]

The continuation of old armed struggles, and initiation of new ones in the South Asian subcontinent in the years immediately following independence from British rule could be traced partly to the local internal contradictions just mentioned, and partly to the post-Second World War international strategy of Communists. This was the period when the Cold War was heating up, with the US expanding its economic and military influence over the area, and the Moscow-led international Communist movement trying to intensify national resistance against such expansion. Communists in Burma, Malaya, the Philippines, Indonesia, Indochina (today's Vietnam), were taking up the threads of their erstwhile anti-Japanese war of resistance, and were transforming their struggles into national liberation movements either against the still ruling colonial powers, or the new native rulers who were close to Washington and London. Representatives from these

various Communist parties gathered in Calcutta in March 1948 to attend the second party congress of the CPI there. It is believed that sections of the then CPI leadership were inspired to a large extent by the experiences of militancy narrated by these Southeast Asian Communist delegates, and news of the approaching victory of the Chinese Communists, in adopting a policy of armed insurrection to overthrow the Congress government, which it considered to be an agent of "Anglo–American imperialism."[3]

The insurrectionary program adopted by the CPI at its second party congress in 1948 led to a string of urban actions, including armed clashes between students and the police and destruction of government properties in cities like Calcutta and Bombay, seizure of factories by Communist unions, an abortive railway strike, and jail breaks among other similar isolated and sporadic acts of militancy, which were soon suppressed by the police. In contrast to the swift collapse of the CPI's armed insurrection in the cities, its program for the rural areas—guerrilla warfare—was to find a more lasting echo in the ongoing armed peasant struggles in Kakdwip in West Bengal, and more importantly in Telangana where the Communists were able to build up and sustain their liberated zones for quite some time. As mentioned earlier, the Telangana peasant guerrillas laid down their arms only in 1951 after being advised by their party leaders. This inaugurated a new phase in the strategy and tactics of the Indian Communists, which was marked by a shift of emphasis from armed insurrection to participation in parliamentary politics, towards their final aim of capturing state power.

Intermission

The period spanning the mid-1950s to the mid-1960s could be described as a rather peaceful interlude which was highlighted by Communist participation in the parliamentary system, both in the role of the opposition, led by able legislators and orators such as Hiren Mukherjee, A. K. Gopalan, and others in parliament, and as a ruling party in the first-ever Communist state government (in Kerala) in 1957. But, in Kerala, when the Communists tried to implement land reforms, they faced tremendous opposition from entrenched feudal landlords. When they attempted reforms in the educational sector to provide access to the underprivileged, they faced equally aggressive opposition from the religious orthodoxy (the Catholic church in this case) which had been running schools on commercial lines and felt threatened by the reforms that would curtail their power. This again represented the typical axis of landlords and religious patriarchs—a manifestation of the type of feudalism current in modern India, to which I have drawn attention earlier. These privileged sections, which had a vested interest in the status quo, were mobilized by the Congress party in a violent agitation to topple the Communist government in Kerala. The then Congress party President Indira Gandhi (who later as India's Prime Minister in 1975–76 was to impose emergency rule to suppress all democratic rights) played a major role in fostering this anti-Communist agitation, and persuading a Congress-led government at the center (headed by her father Jawaharlal Nehru) to dismiss the Communist government in Kerala in July 1959 (on the plea of the breakdown of law and order), although the Communists still enjoyed a majority in the legislature.

During the years that followed, the erosion of the credibility of the ruling national Congress at the center through such undemocratic acts, was accompanied by an equally steady decline in popular faith in its ability to bring about land reforms and stem the degradation of the rural masses. The Communist Party of India itself also went through an agonizing phase of self-introspection during this period. While one section of the leadership and cadres felt that the party should continue to support the ruling congress at the center (primarily because of its pro-Soviet foreign policy), their opponents were getting increasingly strident in their criticism of the congress government's failures on the domestic front and were moving closer to the Chinese Communist Party's critique of the Nehruvian policies. From the late 1950s onwards, the international Communist movement was showing signs of splitting. The Chinese Communists attacked the Soviet leader Khrushchev for enunciating the theory of "peaceful co-existence" with the capitalist west, and upheld instead the Maoist theory of the intensification of class struggles against the US-led western camp. The international Communist policy to be adopted towards the Indian government became one of the major issues in the Sino-Soviet ideological debate. China's leaders, who were embroiled in a border dispute with India, were peeved by the Soviet Union's support to Nehru, who, in the opinion of the Chinese Communists, was granting increasing concessions (like tax benefits to the private sector and collaboration with the US in business) to the Indian "big bourgeoisie" and "imperialism."[4]

Echoes of these global Communist dissensions reached Indian Communists when, in October 1962, war broke out between India and China over the disputed border. Although the conflict lasted only a few days and ended with a humiliating defeat of the Indian Army and a status quo of sorts imposed by China, it aggravated the fissures within the Communist Party of India. While the pro-Moscow section steadfastly supported India's anti-China stand, their opponents pleaded for unconditional negotiation with China, which led to their being branded as "Chinese agents" by their rivals. Soon after, the police arrested the radical leaders of the CPI's National Council, who were opposing the party's official pro-government line, and swooped down on their followers.

Return to violence

After their release from jail in 1964, these Communist dissidents got together, and the same year they broke away from their parent CPI to form the CPI (Marxist). Although, in their program, the latter pledged to set up a "revolutionary" party dedicated to the task of establishing a "people's democracy," they also maintained, like their rival CPI, that they would strive to achieve their objective through "peaceful means." This dissatisfied the radicals in the party, who began to propagate among the ranks their views in favor of armed struggle. In under three years, the politics of violence reemerged on the agenda of the Indian Communist movement, leading to yet another split in its leadership and ranks.

The contemporary economic and political context needs to be explained in this connection. By the late 1960s, agrarian tensions had surged to a boiling point with newspapers reporting incidents of deaths from starvation and sporadic pillaging of food warehouses in different parts of India. In May 1966 Prime Minister Indira Gandhi was compelled to admit that 46.6 million people spread over 117 districts from north to south and west to east (a little over one-tenth of the total population), were suffering from "scarcity conditions"—an euphemistic term for famine used in Indian government documents. The mood of popular discontent was reflected in the fourth general elections held in March 1967, when voters in many states rejected the hitherto one-party Congress rule, and ushered in a new phase in Indian politics. Since Congress was reduced to a minority in several state legislatures, non-Congress coalitions of various political hues captured power in these states. In West Bengal, a similar coalition termed the United Front Government, was sworn in on 2 March, 1967. A left-of-center government, it consisted of breakaway groups from Congress, as well as the CPI (M), the CPI, and some other leftist parties.

It was against this backdrop that the first spark of violent protest by a disgruntled peasantry, reminiscent of the days of Communist insurgency of the 1940–50 period, was kindled in May 1967 in a place called Naxalbari. Ironically, the spot happened to be in West Bengal, and the outbreak occurred when the Land and Land Revenue Ministry of the newly installed United Front government there was being headed by the veteran CPI (M) peasant leader Harekrishna Konar. The events in Naxalbari revealed the complex tensions between the radical aspirations of the rural poor and the obligations and compulsions of a leftist ruling party, which had agreed to administer a state within a constitutional and parliamentary system that is heavily loaded against these poor sections, offering little representation for their interests. That these tensions continue to plague the Indian parliamentary Left even 40 years after the Naxalite uprising is evident in the recent turmoil in the West Bengal countryside following the Left Front government's plans for taking over land for industrialization (a subject to which we shall return later). It indicates the still unresolved conflict of political and economic priorities among the Indian Left that continues to manifest itself in violent conflagrations.

Naxalbari and its ripples

Let us look more closely at the events at Naxalbari in May 1967. Situated in the northeastern tip of West Bengal, it was populated primarily by poor tribal peasants and tea plantation labor among whom the Communists had a strong base built over years of struggles against local landlords and plantation owners. The uprising in May was led by local leaders of the CPI (M), prominent among whom were Charu Mazumdar and Kanu Sanyal. Their immediate aim was to end the feudal landlord system, redistribute land through peasants' committees, and arm the peasants to resist landlords who opposed such reforms. But Charu Mazumdar, the ideologue, nursed a long-term strategy to carve out "liberated zones" through such tactics, following the Maoist model of the Chinese revolution. In fact, Mazumdar had been working on the strategy since 1965, and by

1967 he and his comrades had built up a well–knit organization of militant peasant cadres. Within two months of the United Front's coming to power in West Bengal, in May 1967, these peasants occupied land, cancelled all debts and interest owed by them to moneylenders, passed death sentences on oppressive landlords, formed armed bands and set up a parallel administration to look after the villages.[5] After a series of clashes between peasants and the police and landlords, the CPI(M) ministers fell in with the government's decision to launch a massive police action in Naxalbari in July 1967, as a result of which the rebellion was soon snuffed out. But it engendered a lasting and acrimonious relationship between the CPI (M) and the Maoist Communists to the detriment of the leftist movement in India.

Although the rebellion in Naxalbari lasted hardly a couple of months and collapsed in the face of a police offensive, future events were to show that, although the Indian state won the battle in Naxalbari, it was not able to win the war that was to follow, which still continues. The sequence of developments that came on the heels of the Naxalbari upsurge was to change the course of the radical Communist movement in India. First, when the Communist rebels were still in control in Naxalbari, on 28 June, 1967, Communist China's official mouthpiece, Radio Peking, welcomed the rebellion as "the front paw of the revolutionary armed struggle launched by the Indian people under the guidance of Mao Tse-tung," and dismissed the West Bengal United Front government (of which the CPI (M) was a part) as a "tool of the Indian reactionaries to deceive the people." The Chinese Communist Party's support for the CPI (M) dissidents in Naxalbari was motivated primarily by its then foreign policy of opposition to the Indian government (a carryover from the 1962 Sino-Indian border dispute), as well as its ideological dispute with the Soviet party mentioned earlier. The Chinese support bolstered courage among dissenters in the CPI (M) in other parts of India. In the middle of

November 1967, they met in Calcutta and decided to form the All-India Coordination Committee of Communist Revolutionaries, and issued a statement in their mouthpiece, *Liberation*, referring to the Naxalbari uprising and "revolutionary peasant struggle [that were] breaking out or going to break out in various parts of the country," and giving a call to "all revolutionary elements inside and outside the party" to develop and lead these struggles by coordinating their activities to build up a revolutionary party.[6]

This brings us to the second development that followed closely after the Naxalbari events, namely, the "revolutionary peasant struggles" referred to in an earlier statement. Sure enough, after news of the Naxalbari uprising spread, there was a noticeable increase in peasant agitations in the Indian countryside, spreading from Assam, Tripura, and Manipur in the northeast, to Punjab in the northwest, and to the central states of Madhya Pradesh, Rajasthan, and Maharashtra down to the eastern and southern states of Orissa, Tamil Nadu, and Andhra Pradesh. They were serious enough to compel the home ministry of the then government of India to compile a report in 1969 in which it acknowledged that the land reform measures undertaken by the government till then had "not benefited the actual tiller," and the failure "provided [a] breeding ground for various political movements." Usually spontaneous, or led by local militant groups, these agitations were marked by occupation of land by the landless, forcible harvesting of crops by evicted sharecroppers, demonstrations demanding increase in wages of agricultural workers, and protest actions against higher taxes among other features.[7]

Close on the heels of these incidents was the third major development. Soon after the Naxalbari uprising, an agitation by forest tribals (known as girijans) living in the jungle-clad hilly region of Srikakulam in Andhra Pradesh in south India spread like wildfire towards the end of 1967. It was again led by radicals in the Andhra Pradesh CPI (M), who organized the girijans to carry out raids on the houses of landlords, seize crops, and burn promissory notes that were obtained from the debt-bound tribals by the landlords, thus following the familiar trends that marked peasant *jacqueries* in the past. By 1968, however, the leaders of the agitation, who had been facing reprisal from the state armed police, had switched over to guerilla actions with the objective of "seizing political power." They also got in touch with the Naxalbari leader, Charu Mazumdar, and the All-India Coordination Committee of Communist Revolutionaries. By 1969, the militant Communists in Srikakulam were claiming control over some 300 villages, from where the landlords had been forced to flee, and which were being administered by the *Ryotanga Sangrama Samithi* or peasants' revolutionary committees. The guerrilla movement also expanded to the neighboring tribal areas of Orissa, bordering Andhra Pradesh.[8]

The first phase: A decade of ups and downs

The spread of peasant agitations, including spontaneous uprisings and organized armed struggles, inspired radicals in the CPI (M) to make a final break with their parent party, and on 22 April, 1969, they formed the CPI (Marxist-Leninist). Describing the Indian state as run by big landlords and comprador[9] bureaucratic capitalists, the new party stated its main objective as seizing power through armed struggle of the peasants, the basic form of which would be guerrilla warfare. In May the next year, the party held its congress and came out with a program, reiterating the path of armed struggle, and stressing that the "principal contradiction" of the period was that between feudalism and the broad masses of the Indian people, the resolution of which would lead to the resolution of the other three contradictions: (i) between imperialism and the Indian people; (ii) between capital and labor; and (iii) among the ruling classes.

The formation of the CPI (M-L) ushered in the first phase of a new radical Communist uprising in India, which came to be known as the Naxalite movement. It traced its ideological beginnings to the middle of the 1960s (when Charu Mazumdar and other Maoist leaders tried to frame a strategy of agrarian revolution through guerilla warfare), and it could sustain itself till the mid-1970s (when both internal dissensions and severe police repression put an end to it). During this period, the CPI (M-L)-led peasant struggles were mainly concentrated in parts of Andhra Pradesh and Orissa in the south, Bihar and West Bengal in the east, and a few pockets in Punjab and Uttar Pradesh in the north.

Significantly enough, the movement was also able to draw a large number of urban youth and intellectuals, who were inspired by its egalitarian values, and, more importantly, by its restoration of revolutionary humanism in the Indian Communist movement that valorized individual courage, and readiness to sacrifice for a cause. They left their homes, schools and colleges, abandoned their careers, and went to the villages and joined the peasants in guerilla struggles. In cities like Calcutta, students took part in armed attacks on the police and government establishments. The role of urban youth in the Naxalite movement needs to be understood in the context of the international situation in the late 1960s. This was the period of the growing anti-war movement in the US in the background of the Vietnam liberation war; the anti-establishment student agitations in Paris, Rome, Berlin, and other parts of Europe; and Che Guevara's heroic self-sacrifice in the jungles of Bolivia in pursuit of the old dream of international solidarity of all revolutionaries. In India, youth found in the Naxalite movement an echo of the international rebellious spirit of the times.

The movement recorded some successes as well as failures. Their efforts to establish temporary "liberated zones" in the tribal-inhabited forest belt of Andhra Pradesh, the villages of Birbhum and Medinipur in West Bengal, and the plains of Bhojpur in Bihar, were soon defeated, primarily because of their inability to build up a strong armed resistance to protect them from the onslaught of a militarily far superior state, as well as because of divisions within their leadership and ranks.[10] Although the CPI (M-L) claimed to adopt Maoist guerrilla tactics as the means to achieve their goal, they ignored two basic tenets of the Maoist military strategy: (i) the choice of a favorable terrain to create a stable liberated zone from whence to expand; and (ii) the building up of a people's liberation army to take on the enemy.[11] The imposition of "emergency" authoritarian rule in the entire country by Congress Prime Minister Indira Gandhi on 26 June, 1975, was the decisive blow that brought to an end the first phase of the Maoist movement. Along with the stifling of the growing popular discontent against her policies (which found expression in an all-India agitation headed by the Gandhian socialist leader Jayaprakash Narayan), it also smothered the last embers of the Naxalite armed struggle.

Looking back at the brief but tumultuous phase of the Naxalite movement in the 1960s' period, a contemporary political observer cannot but acknowledge that it was a watershed in the recent history of India in more than one sense. For the first time in post-Independence India (barring the short-lived Telangana struggles in 1947–51, mentioned earlier), the movement set forth the demands of the poor and landless peasantry in a way that shook the atrophied Indian political scene. The violent outbreak sensitized the rest of society to the problems of the hitherto downtrodden sections of the population. This was to lead to the development of a robust social activism among the Indian middle classes, after the Emergency was lifted. It continues in the shape of non-government voluntary organizations working for the empowerment of the dispersed underprivileged and dispossessed groups; intervention of the media in exposing atrocities on the depressed castes and tribal peoples by the upper-caste landlords; affirmative actions by human rights activists to protect citizens against police repression and illegal acts of the state. Second, by openly asserting the right of armed resistance against the Indian

state, the CPI (M-L) squarely placed violence as a persistent method of action in Indian politics. It became a precedent for armed offensives by other groups, albeit ideologically different, such as militants from religious and ethnic minority communities, who were to crop up in the 1980s (e.g., Khalistanis of Punjab, JKLF (Jammu and Kashmir Liberation Front) and Islamic secessionists of Kashmir, ULFA (United Liberation Front of Assam), and similar separatist groups in Assam and the northeast).

But the main achievement of this first phase of the CPI (M-L) movement was not its physical occupation and administrative control over territory, but its success in spreading its ideological message of people's power and the right of self-defense among the rural poor. It continues to arouse the latter to protest and take up arms against their old landlord oppressors and new industrial predators encroaching on their lands, and to take on the Indian state whenever it sends its police to protect these powerful interests, whether in the villages of Bihar and Jharkhand in the east, or the tribal hamlets of Chhattisgarh in central India, or the hills and forests of Andhra Pradesh in the south.

The second phase: Continuity and change

This brings us to the later history of the Maoist movement in India. Following the setback in the 1970s, survivors of the state repression got a reprieve during the non-Congress Janata government (a coalition of heterogeneous rightist, centrist and social democratic parties) that came to office in 1977. Both the old timers (who were released from jails, or resurfaced from years of underground) and a new generation of revolutionary ideologues and activists began to pick up the threads left by their predecessors in the Naxalite movement, trying to gather and rebuild the broken pieces.

Although the newly elected non-Congress government at the center restored democratic rights, which led to the release of the Naxalites, it did not lead to any change in the traditional oppressive land relations or any betterment in the conditions of the rural poor. In fact, many of the parties in the ruling coalition were dominated by landlords. This posed a challenge to the Naxalite movement. There were two broad trends discernible in the movement in the late 1970s and early 1980s: one preferring to fight for their old demands through participation in parliamentary elections and trade union activities, which were rejected in the past by the Charu Mazumdar-led CPI (M–L), and the other returning to the path of armed struggle. The first trend was represented by Santosh Rana, (a leader of the 1969–70 Naxalite upsurge in Debra-Gobipallavpur in West Bengal) who contested the 1977 state assembly elections from his old area of revolutionary activities, and won the electoral contest after campaigning on the same demands of the peasants (e.g., land redistribution, higher wages for agricultural laborers, end to usury) that he had sought ten years earlier to gain through an armed battle.[12]

The second trend was reflected in the activities of a number of radical groups and their leaders in Bihar and Andhra Pradesh, who believed that the basic problems of the peasantry could never be solved within the prevalent parliamentary system that was heavily loaded in favor of their oppressors. In Bihar, three Naxalite groups resumed armed struggle by regrouping members of the old guerrilla squads and recruiting new members from among the peasants: (i) one led by Vinode Mishra under the aegis of the CPI (M–L); (ii) the CPI (M–L) Party Unity group; and (iii) the Maoist Communist Centre (MCC), which did not join the CPI (M–L) at the time of its formation in 1969. By the end of the 1980s, all these groups had expanded their activities from the traditional stronghold of Bhojpur to further north in Patna, Arrah, and down in the south to Gaya, Jehanabad, and Aurangabad in Bihar. They drove landlords from the villages, occupied their lands, distributed the harvested crops among the agricultural laborers and peasants, and set up rudimentary units of

administration in what they described as "liberated zones." Control over these clusters of villages, however, often changed hands, with the police frequently raiding and taking them over, to be followed soon by Naxalites, who recovered them. In Andhra Pradesh, two groups of Communist revolutionaries resumed armed struggle in the hill forests of Telangana spread over the three districts of Khammam, Karimnagar, and Warangal. One group came to be known as the People's War Group of the CPI (M–L) led by Kondapally Sitaramayyah, and another as the Central Committee of the CPI (M–L) headed by Chandra Pulla Reddy. They mobilized daily laborers from among the forest tribals (the girijans) around struggles over immediate demands such as better wages and end to extortions by forest officials. They recruited the younger tribals to form armed squads, in order to resist the police who came to suppress their movement. Visiting one of these Naxalite strongholds in Khammam in early 1980, the Swedish author Jan Myrdal wrote as follows:

[D]uring one week we moved around with the (Communist) armed platoon through the forest district [where] 20,000 policemen have been brought to restore order. We slept in the villages, completely secure; people keep the platoons informed about the movements of police, but don't say a word to the police troops about where the platoons are.[13]

By the end of the 1980s, the armed Naxalites had spread far and wide in different parts of India. Reports prepared by the home ministry of the Indian government in 1988 indicated that they were operating in 12 districts spread over Andhra Pradesh (in the south), Madhya Pradesh (in the center), Maharashtra (in the west), and Bihar and Orissa (in the east). The authorities were more concerned about the situation in Andhra Pradesh, where in 1987 the guerrillas kidnapped a group of civil servants, including the senior S. R. Sankaran, and succeeded in securing the release of their arrested comrades.[14]

389

Besides expanding their traditional base in Andhra Pradesh, during the 1980s, the People's War Group (PWG), established new guerrilla zones in the tribal belts of Bastar (in the present state of Chhattisgarh), Garchiroli and Chandrapur in Maharashtra, and Koraput and Malkangiri in Orissa, all contiguous to its base in the northern part of Andhra Pradesh. Thus, by the 1990s, a wide stretch spanning large tracts of forest and hilly villages in at least four states came under the control of armed Naxalites. During this period, other changes were taking place in the Naxalite movement in West Bengal and Bihar. West Bengal, the cradle of the movement, gradually receded from the scene. The old Naxalite bases of the early 1970s in the state—including Naxalbari itself (from which the movement took its name)—changed from armed citadels of militant peasant uprisings into electoral bulwarks for the parliamentary CPI (Marxist) party, which, along with other leftist parties, had formed the Left Front government in the state in 1977. The transformation of the mood of the erstwhile militant peasantry, who formed the bulk of the voters in these areas, in favor of parliamentary politics in the 1980s, can be explained to a large extent by the Left Front government's success in distributing land among the landless, guaranteeing the rights of sharecroppers, increasing the minimum wages for agricultural laborers, devolution of power at the grassroots level through the *panchayat* system, among other agrarian socioeconomic reforms, the demand for which initially drove the rural poor to join the Naxalites. These reformist measures neutralized the violent potentialities for rural unrest in West Bengal, and forestalled a resurgence of the Naxalite movement.

At the same time, in Bihar, two different trends were observable among the Naxalites. The Vinode Mishra group—known as CPI (M-L) Liberation—was thinning out its armed squads, dismantling its underground apparatus and increasingly moving towards parliamentary politics by taking part in elections, and setting up open mass fronts and trade unions. The other two Naxalite groups, the CPI (M-L) Party Unity and the MCC (Maoist Communist Center), continued to carry out armed guerilla warfare in the villages of Bihar, and succeeded in carving out guerrilla zones in Gaya, Aurangabad, Jehanabad, and neighboring districts. By the turn of the millennium, both the Bihar armed groups had joined together to form a single party and build up a network with the CPI (M-L) People's War Group (PWG) of Andhra Pradesh, and to engage in joint operations in large parts of Bihar, Jharkhand, Orissa, Andhra Pradesh, Maharashtra, Chhattisgarh, and other states. They also established links with various Communist radical groups in other parts of the world. In July 2003 these Indian Naxalite groups hosted a South Asia Regional Conference of the Parties and Organizations of the Revolutionary Internationalist Movement, in a guerilla zone located in what they described as the "Bihar-Chattisgarh-Orissa-Jharkhand Special Area." It was attended by delegates from the Communist Party of Nepal (Maoist), and various Maoist groups from Bangladesh and Bhutan, who narrated their experiences and exchanged views regarding future coordination.[15]

Underlying the expansion of the armed Maoist movement during this period were two major changes, one in the class character of its local level leadership, the second in the broadening of its influence in civil society. Over the years, activists from the poor peasant and tribal communities took over as leaders not only of guerrilla squads, but also as members of the CPI (Maoist) state and central committees. Thus, a new generation of "organic" leaders (in the Gramscian sense) has emerged in the Maoist movement. This is corroborated by newspaper and police reports, which revealed that the Maoist leaders arrested or killed in Andhra Pradesh and Chhattisgarh in recent years, were mostly from the rural depressed classes and the downtrodden tribal communities, in contrast to the overwhelming middle class character of the leadership in the 1970s. The second change in the movement is the setting up of mass fronts—cultural groups, students' and women's organizations, and others—which allow the Maoists to operate and propagate their views in society.

The birth of the CPI (Maoist)

On 21 September, 2004, in one of their base areas, the leaders and cadres of all the various armed Naxalite groups met, and decided to form a single revolutionary party, called the Communist Party of India (Maoist). The program drafted by their leaders, harked back to the 1970 party program of the CPI (M–L), describing the Indian state as run by big landlords and a comprador bureaucratic class, reiterating that the contradiction between feudalism and the broad Indian masses remained "principal," and that armed peasant guerilla war was the main form of struggle towards its goal of creating a "people's democratic state."[16] The CPI (Maoist) has today emerged as a formidable armed opponent of the Indian state, its network spread over 160 odd districts in at least ten states of India, spanning some 400,000 square kilometers, equivalent to one-eighth of the total Indian land mass. It effectively controls a long corridor of both forests and plains, stretching from the northern states bordering Nepal along Bihar in the east, through Jharkhand further south and Chhattisgarh, Madhya Pradesh, and Maharashtra in the west, down to Orissa and Andhra Pradesh in the south. The corridor is twice the size of the geographical region of the other two insurgency-affected areas, that is, the five states of the northeast (Assam, Manipur, Nagaland, Meghalaya, Tripura) and Jammu & Kashmir in the northwest. The population inhabiting the corridor is five times as great. Little wonder then that the Indian prime minister, at a conference in New Delhi in July 2006, described it as the "single biggest internal security challenge."

The present situation

In the guerrilla zones in this corridor, the Maoists have been able to set up a parallel administration of sorts. Visiting some of these zones in the Jharkhand area some years ago, a journalist from a national newspaper observed that the Maoists had driven out the big landlords, and set up revolutionary peasant committees (known in local parlance as KKC, or Krantikari Kishan Committee) to redistribute land among the poor, ensure the running of schools and health centers, and settle disputes among villagers. These committees also undertook development projects such as building roads and erecting dams. From where did they get funds to sustain their activities? The journalist found that in areas where the Maoists had seized land from the landlords and distributed it among the villagers, "one-fourth of the produce from land, orchards and ponds go to the KKC as tax." He added: "From contractors engaged in building of roads and bridges, 20 percent of the project cost has to be given to the KKC. In case of dams, the tax levied is 10 percent." In order to resist the police, who often raided these villages, the Maoists set up defense squads for every village, apart from full-fledged platoons (each consisting of three guerrilla squads), armed with self-loading rifles, light machine guns, mortars and mines. Ironically, most of these weapons were seized by the guerrillas from the police. "The more the police use sophisticated arms," one of the Jharkhand Maoist leaders told the journalist, "the better for us."[17]

Even more spectacular has been the success of the Maoists in the Dandakaranya area of central India. Covered by thick forests, hills, and rivers, this huge expanse is inhabited by several tribal groups, and is spread over 11 districts in the states of Madhya Pradesh, Chhattisgarh, Maharashtra, Andhra Pradesh, and Orissa, spanning an area of over 110,000 square kilometers. The Maoists began working here from the 1980s, organizing the tribal laborers against big landlords and contractors (who denied them their wages and socially exploited them by abducting their women and selling them off to brothels—a business which had been thriving in the tribal areas for years), industrial enterprises (which tapped the vast mineral wealth of their habitat without giving them their dues), and forest officials (who denied them access to the forest produce to which they had been traditionally entitled). They were soon able to build up guerilla squads from among the tribal youth, drive out the forest officials and landlords, compel the contractors to pay higher wages, and set up a new organ of power called the GRC or Gram Rajya Committee (village administrative committee) for day-to-day governance in the guerilla zones. Reports by Maoist activists working in Dandakaranya in 2000 indicated that they had succeeded in setting up such parallel organs of administration in vast stretches of the area. They set up "people's courts" to try and adjudicate local disputes, and also carried out campaigns against superstitious practices and introduced modern medicines among the tribal population. As in Jharkhand, in the Dandakaranya area also, the Maoists undertook several development projects, including construction of tanks for irrigation and drinking water, setting up of schools and health centers, and forming agricultural cooperatives among other things.[18]

Even in West Bengal, where short-term economic benefits and limited land reforms by the Left Front government, blunted the edge of peasant militancy from the early 1980s till the late 1990s, the Naxalites appear to be staging a comeback now. Tensions are brewing on two issues. First, the tribal poor in the backward districts of Bankura, West Medinipur, and Purulia, who had been bereft of such benefits during the last three decades of Left rule, are getting restive and are gravitating towards the CPI (Maoist) cadres who have renewed their activities in these areas. Second, the Left Front government's policy of acquiring fertile land for setting up industrial enterprises in Singur (for a motor car factory) and Nandigram (for a chemical industrial hub) has hit large sections

of the agricultural community. Although their agitations at the moment (in 2007) are being led by non-Communist organizations, both the parliamentary Naxalites of the CPI (M-L) Liberation group and the armed cadres of the CPI (Maoist) are reported to have stepped in. The ruling left in West Bengal is today in a catch-22 situation. Its land reforms process has reached a plateau, unable to offer further economic benefits to the villagers. The present progeny of the earlier beneficiaries of land reforms are facing unemployment. In the industrial sector, closure of old factories that were dependent on outmoded machinery, which could not compete with new technology, has thrown thousands of workers on the streets. The Left Front government in West Bengal is, therefore, seeking its next leap in an industrial revival. But, having accepted the prevailing global economic model of development, it is compelled to agree to the norms laid down by both the Indian big business houses and multinational companies that are willing to invest in West Bengal even if it leads to displacement of thousands from their homelands, and establishment of special economic zones (enclaves owned by big industrial houses who are given land at throwaway prices and offered tax waivers, among other concessions) where workers are denied their traditional trade union rights. Thus, popular discontent in the agrarian sector and working-class disgruntlement in the new industrial zones, are likely to fuel the resurgence of the Maoist movement in some parts of West Bengal. However, much depends on the Indian state's political will for resolving these conflicts that are in the making.

Indian state's response

Ever since the beginning of the Naxalite movement in 1967, the approach of the Indian state towards it had been marked by a contradiction. While at the level of policy discussion it grudgingly admits that it is rooted in popular socioeconomic grievances, at the ground level, instead of eradicating these grievances, it treats the Naxalite outbursts against them as a law and order problem by deploying the police to suppress them. Bureaucrats and police of the Maoist-affected states meet at regular intervals and admit that prolonged neglect of the complaints of the rural poor is driving them towards the "extremists," an admission that their predecessors made some 40 years ago in the 1969 Home Ministry report entitled *The Causes and Nature of Current Agrarian Tensions* (referred to earlier in this chapter). If, after four decades, they continue to reiterate the same view, it shows how little the Indian state has progressed, and how it has learnt still less from past failures in resolving socioeconomic conflicts in vast stretches of the Indian countryside. At the same time, instead of correcting the wrongs of the past by addressing the demands of the rural poor, the Indian state continues to devise ever more militarist methods to suppress the Maoists. In Jharkhand, the government has come out with a Rs 3.4 billion proposal to set up a special air force to be deployed against the Maoist bases in the inaccessible terrain.[19] In Andhra Pradesh, the police have been given a free hand to raid the homes of tribals suspected of harboring Naxalites, arrest their men folk, and kill their sympathizers in fake "encounters."[20] In Chhattisgarh, the administration has set up an organization of vigilantes by arming a section of the tribals, described as Salwa Judum,[21] and unleashing them on the Maoist tribals, thus leading to internecine warfare among the tribal community and displacement of thousands of villagers.[22] All these areas are at present undergoing a period of violent reprisal and counter-reprisal, marked by razing of tribal hamlets and false encounters by the police, on the one hand, and retaliatory killing of policemen by Maoist guerrillas on the other hand.

In the course of the past few years efforts have been made by civil society groups to bring an end to this recurring cycle of destruction and killings, each year seeing between 300 and 400 deaths on an average. In Andhra Pradesh, one such group called the Committee of Concerned Citizens, headed by S. R. Sankaran (the senior bureaucrat, who as mentioned earlier, was kidnapped by the Naxalites in 1987) and consisting of human rights activists, eminent advocates, and journalists initiated a process of dialogue between the state government and the Naxalites. After five years of patient negotiations with the two adversaries, the committee succeeded in bringing them together for talks in June 2002. Although the first round of deliberations between representatives of the then PWG of the CPI (M-L) and ministers of the Andhra Pradesh government were marked by exchanges of conflicting views and demands, the contending parties agreed on a sort of ceasefire for at least a month, until July, when they were expected to meet for the second round of talks. But even before the expiry of the period, the Andhra Pradesh police resumed its repressive policies by killing four members of the PWG, including a senior leader, on 2 July. Quite understandably, the PWG withdrew from the talks, declaring that the ceasefire was no longer operative.[23] Undeterred, the committee continued with its efforts, and, in October 2004, succeeded again in persuading the leaders of the CPI (Maoist) and the Andhra Pradesh government to sit together. The talks ended with an agreement on a ceasefire till 16 December that year, during which period the government promised to consider the main Maoist demand for distribution of land among the landless. When the state failed to keep the promise, the Maoists began to forcibly distribute the land, an action that immediately invited retaliation by the police, who gunned down several Maoists in January 2006. The CPI (Maoist) leaders came out with a public statement blaming the state police for violating the norms of the October truce and withdrew from the talks. Following this, things went back to square one as the cycle of violence renewed its deadly course.

From all available indications, it is evident that, at the present moment, the option of dialogue has been discarded by the Indian state in favor of intensified military offensive against the Maoists. But the militaristic policy is flawed in several respects. First, as the history of the last four decades has shown, police repression may curb Maoist insurgency in a few pockets for a while, but cannot prevent its spread to wider areas and its resilience over longer periods, as long as the basic socioeconomic grievances that give rise to the insurgency remain unaddressed. This brings us to the second problem with the militarist policy. By laying stress on armed retaliation, the Indian state has refused to recognize the distinct ideological character of the CPI (Maoist), namely, its concerns about economic inequity and social injustice, and the program of setting up a secular and socialist society in India, which are radically different from the sectarian or religious fanatical belief systems and terrorist manifestations of other insurgent groups (such as the ethnic-based secessionists in the northeast, or the Islamic militants in Kashmir and elsewhere).

But that apart, the state's anti-Maoist militarist policy has had damaging effects on vast sections of Indian society (e.g., arrest and torture of innocent citizens as suspected Naxalites; persecution of human rights activists; ban on newsmen covering Maoist activities) which threaten the democratic rights of the Indian people, and have quite predictably drawn censure from global institutions like Amnesty International.

Future of the CPI (Maoist) movement

Given the relentless militarist offensive that has been launched by the Indian state, how can the Maoist movement resist it, sustain its existing bases and extend them in future? These are questions that are being deliberated by the CPI (Maoist) leaders. But as observers from outside, we can hazard a few guesses while critiquing the movement.

First, let us examine the actual power of the Maoists in terms of changing the course of India's national policies (compared particularly

with the recent success of their counterparts in Nepal). As of now, the Indian Maoists are confined to a narrow stretch of territory. Although larger in area and covering more states than the other insurgency-affected states in the border areas of the northeast and Jammu & Kashmir, the Maoist "red corridor" is of less strategic importance to the Indian state. It is a hilly and forest belt that had remained inaccessible and under-administered for years, thus offering a favorable terrain to the rebels. But increasing state-sponsored industrial development and projects like roads and bridges are reducing the protective forest cover and opening up the hitherto unreachable territory to the police. It is significant that the latest targets of the Maoists are contractors working on these road communications and industrial enterprises, their aim being subversion of official plans to reach these areas. Thus, unlike Nepal, where the Maoists were in control of two-thirds of the country and were in a position to encircle the capital of Kathmandu during the anti-monarchy movement, thereby disrupting the supply of essential commodities to the capital for days together, what the Indian Maoists control can be described as only a bypass that is encircled and besieged from either side by the Indian state's powerful armed apparatus. The Maoists have not yet acquired the decisive striking capacity that their comrades in Nepal enjoy.

Further, in the coming years, besides losing their military advantage, the Maoists will also have to contend with the options being offered by the development projects to their followers among the rural poor and tribal population, who may be swayed by promises of a better deal such as jobs as unskilled laborers. Apart from the loss of the favorable terrain, their political support base may also erode in the future in these areas. A sense of panic generated by such apprehensions is already evident in the increasing tendency among the Maoists to kill individuals or families in villages on the mere suspicion that they may be police informers, or working for the government. This is threatening to alienate the movement from the local people, sections of which are already being wooed by the government with promises of jobs, or are being recruited into vigilante squads (such as the already mentioned Salwa Judum organization in Chhattisgarh).

The Maoists have, of late, suffered a serious setback in Andhra Pradesh, from where most of their central leadership comes (including their general secretary Ganapathy, who apparently till now has escaped capture by the police). In the hill and forest areas of Andhra Pradesh, which had been the main Maoist base all these years, the killing of several important leaders by the police and the surrender of a large number of disillusioned cadres by the end of 2007, have eroded that stronghold to a large extent. It is becoming increasingly evident that confinement to a narrow geographical terrain and within sections of the poor tribal and *dalit* (the underprivileged castes) people alone, cannot sustain the movement for long. The history of the movement suggests that its achievements and failures at different points of time and in different areas were due to a combination of several factors. In the 1969–70 period in Srikakulam in Andhra Pradesh, for instance, it could draw on the long tradition of tribal militancy in that area and at the same time attract a large number of middle-class intellectuals who spread their message among the urban populace, thus creating a widespread sympathetic support base. In the 1970–80 period in the plains of Bihar, they could bring together the small farmers and the poor peasants from the underprivileged castes on the common issue of oppression by upper-caste landlords, and drive out the latter from the villages where, for a limited period, they set up alternative administrative units. Interestingly, unlike their comrades in Andhra Pradesh, who mainly operated among the tribals in the hilly and forest terrain, the Bihar Maoists mobilized all sections of the rural poor in vast stretches of the plains area during the peak of their struggle, thus indicating the possibility of breaking out from the model of the tribal-based insurgency with which the Indian Maoist movement is usually associated, as well as

confirming the persistence of popular grievances among other sections of the poor, which can take the form of armed resistance. By the turn of the twenty-first century, although the Maoists had lost most of their strongholds in the Bihar plains (which were vulnerable to easy attacks by the state police), they succeeded in expanding their bases to areas that had till then remained outside their influence, including Malkangiri in Orissa, the forests of Jharkhand, Garchiroli and Chandrapur in Maharashtra, and Bastar in Chhattisgarh.

All these new Maoist strongholds are based among the poorest tribal people who inhabit these areas, and who are economically exploited by local landlords and socially deprived of basic amenities like medical facilities, nutrition, and education, among other things. But, one cannot conclude from this that the Maoist movement covers all the Indian tribal population. It has not been able to extend its influence to other tribal poor in different parts of the country (like the tribal district of Dangs in Gujarat in western India, where the rightist religious Hindu group, the Bharatiya Janata Party (BJP) has managed to muster the tribals to vote it to power in the recent December 2007 legislative elections, or in the northeast of India, where the Maoists have no presence at all among the various tribal groups who are fighting for secession from the Indian state). Let alone the tribals, the Maoists have failed to spread their influence to other sections of the Indian poor and under-privileged people in the rest of India. This is due to several factors. First, the non-uniform socioeconomic situation in India, where religious and caste differences and ethnic diversities prevent the poor from becoming a homogeneous consolidation capable of responding to the class-based call for a radical transformation of the political system and society. Second, the uneven levels of political consciousness of the poor, varying from a tradition of militancy among the tribals to that of fatalistic submission among sections of the underprivileged. Third, the indifference of the Maoists to the task of building up mass

395

movements in the vast stretches of the countryside and urban areas by politicizing the rural poor, the industrial workers, and the middle classes.

Along with these factors, because of their strategy of selecting particular spots (which are militarily suitable) to set up liberated zones, the Maoists' bases remain confined to hill and forest areas, where lack of roads and modern communication systems works to their advantage. The unapproachable tiny hamlets here, which are in close proximity with each other, cutting across the state borders, but untouched by the modern market economy, provide a militarily advantageous terrain and a supportive bulwark of poor inhabitants. But in the absence of a wider hinterland of popular sympathy and backing of a mass movement (which the Maoists in Nepal enjoyed), it will be difficult for the Maoists in India to expand their bases and retain their present "liberated zones" for long. Like their predecessors in the hills and forests of Andhra Pradesh, today's Maoist revolutionaries, confined in the red corridor of the forests of Jharkhand, Malkangiri and Bastar, may soon fall victims to the more powerful Indian military forces that are closing in on them from all sides.

However, even if the Maoists lose their existing strongholds in the red corridor, it may be a temporary setback for their cause. Like the legendary phoenix rising from the ashes, they have always bounced back, and with greater intensity and larger expanse than in the past, as evident from the history of the Naxalite movement described so far. New zones of conflict are emerging in different parts of India in the wake of the government's neoliberal policies that force out villagers from their lands and homes for the establishment of special economic zones, industrial enclaves, or some development projects. Instead of meeting their demands, the state machinery is resorting to militarist retaliation against their protests (e.g., police firing on protesters in Kalinganagar in Orissa, Nandigram in West Bengal in 2006 and 2007). Invariably, such repressive actions are provoking violent public retaliation.

Maoists are stepping into the scene, trying to mobilize these disgruntled people and initiate them into their ideological beliefs. Their exposure to the popular needs and demands of these wider sections of the people may help them to come out from the underground of the tribal-based and territorially confined militaristic tactics that they had been following till now, and integrate themselves with the popular movements (e.g., environmental, feminist, etc.) which have been marking the Indian political landscape in recent decades.

The options: Confrontation or negotiation?

Since negotiated settlement of conflicts is the cornerstone of democratic practice, one expects the Indian state to resolve its conflicts with its opponents on those lines. But, paradoxically enough, the Indian state, despite its swearing by the Gandhian doctrine of non-violence, has been following the Maoist doctrine of "power flowing from the barrel of the gun," judging by the record of its bloody repression of popular protests. In response, those among its opponents who seek radical changes have subscribed to the same doctrine and taken up arms to challenge the state's monopoly over violence. One of the longest insurgencies led by such opponents, with an unbroken record, is that of the Nagas in the northeast, who began their struggle for an independent homeland soon after the Indian state was born in 1947. Only after repeated failures to suppress their movement, the Indian officials today have been compelled to sit with the same leaders of the NSCI (Isak-Muivah),[24] whom they denounced in the past as "secessionist terrorists," trying to chalk out a settlement that would satisfy the aspirations of the Naga people. The Indian state is even opening doors for talks to groups of recent insurgent movements, such as the secessionists in Jammu & Kashmir and ULFA (United Liberation Front of Assam) in Assam. What then prevents the Indian state from taking up the threads of the dialogue with the Maoists, interrupted in 2004? In fact, the Maoist program of establishing a socialist and secular society is more consistent with the Indian Constitutional commitment to that goal than the programs of the various terrorist groups, which follow the design of dividing the Indian people along religious, regional and linguistic lines. Besides, we have to acknowledge that the Maoist movement has acted as a major catalytic agent, sensitizing the nation to the lot of the rural poor, the tribals and *dalits*, and compelling the ruling powers to give some relief to them.

However, a dialogue can succeed only when both sides are willing to give up their maximalist positions and meet halfway. In order to enter a dialogue with the Maoists, the Indian state must stop using the police to restore the rule of landlords in villages where the Maoists have already established a parallel socio-economic order that allows the rural poor to enjoy rights to their land and forest produce, and that offers them educational and medical facilities. The Indian state will have to acknowledge that the battle it is fighting against the Maoists is over issues that should have been solved years ago, especially land reforms and social justice for the rural poor. It cannot hope to suppress the grievances of the poor by continuing to ignore these issues. It is a no-win situation where both the state and the Maoists will have to think of new ways to come to terms with the reality. As for the Maoists, they should have a second look at their hitherto-followed strategy and tactics. They cannot hope to clone a Mao-led Chinese revolution in today's India, neither can they expect (like the Nepali Maoists) to wield power over the country's vast plains and cities in the immediate future, given the resilience of faith (however grudgingly vested) by the majority of Indians in the present parliamentary system. At best, they can create a few autarkic enclaves. A ceasefire is therefore necessary, not only in their enlightened self-interest for an intermission to allow them self-introspection, but mainly in the humanitarian interest of the thousands of poor and innocent families who have been caught in the crossfire

between the police and the Maoists in the affected areas.

But in the long-term perspective, there is the more fundamental need for a new political leadership at the helm of affairs in India. It has to be a leadership that is courageous enough to break out of the militarist paradigm and negotiate with the Maoists by giving due recognition to their ideology (even when disagreeing with their tactics) and which is bold enough not only to destroy the age-old entrenched order of oppressive landlords and religious orthodoxy by implementing the laws that provide for land reforms and social equality in the rural areas, but also to resist the domination of domestic corporate magnates and foreign multinationals in the Indian economy in the garb of special economic zones that are threatening the livelihood of thousands. This putative leadership must also be innovative enough to chart out an alternative model of development that would give priority to the demands of the vast alienated and deprived sections of the Indian people for equitable distribution of wealth, social justice, access to education and medical facilities, democratic rights, and protection of their environment.

Notes

1 Moni Sinha, *Jeebon Sangram* (Dhaka: Jatiya Sahitya Prakashani, 1983); and Amit Kumar Gupta, *The Agrarian Drama: The Leftists and the Rural Poor in India* (New Delhi: Manohar, 1996).
2 P. Sundarayya, *Telengana* [sic] *People's Struggle and Its Lessons* (Calcutta: CPI [Marxist], 1972); and Sumanta Banerjee, *In the Wake of Naxalbari* (Calcutta: Subarnarekha, 1980).
3 Gene D. Overstreet and Marshall Windmiller, *Communism in India* (Bombay: Perennial, 1960).
4 *People's Daily*, 6 May, 1959.
5 Kanu Sanyal, *Report on the Terai Peasants' Movement* (Calcutta: CPI (M-L), 1969).
6 *Liberation*, December 1967.
7 Government of India, Ministry of Home Affairs, *The Causes and Nature of Current Agrarian Tensions* (New Delhi: GOP, 1969).

8 *Liberation*, May 1968 and June 1969.

9 A term used to denote agents of foreign commercial interests exploiting Indian human resources both economically and politically.

10 Sumanta Banerjee; Shankar Ghosh, *The Naxalite Movement* (Calcutta: Firma K. L. Mukhopadhyay, 1971); Biplab Dasgupta, *The Naxalite Movement* (New Delhi: Allied, 1973); Ashis Kumar Roy, *The Spring Thunder and After* (Calcutta: Minerva, 1975); Kalyan Mukherjee and Rajendra Singh Yadav, *Bhojpur: Naxalism in the Plains of Bihar* (New Delhi: Radha Krishna, 1980); Rabindra Ray, *The Naxalites and their Ideology* (Delhi: Oxford University Press, 1988); Marius Damas, *Approaching Naxalbari* (Calcutta: Radical Impression, 1991).

11 Mao Tse-Tung, *Selected Works*, vol. I (Peking: Foreign Languages Press, 1965).

12 Partha N. Mukherjee *et al.*, *Left Extremism and Electoral Politics: Naxalite Participation in Elections* (New Delhi: Indian Council of Social Science Research, 1979).

13 Jan Myrdal, "Seven Days with Telengana [*sic*] Naxalites," *New Delhi Magazine* (29 September, 1980), pp. 16–20.

14 Sankaran, after his retirement, was to become an important campaigner for human rights and play a major role in peace talks between the government and the Naxalite leaders in 2002, a development that is discussed later in this chapter.

15 *People's March* (Ernakulam, Kerala), Vol. 4, No. 10 (October 2003).

16 Central Committee (P), CPI (Maoist), *Party Programme*, 2004.

17 Aloke Banerjee, *Inside MCC Country* (Calcutta: K. Das, 2003), pp. 5–9.

18 Biplabi Yug Publication, *New People's Power in Dandakaranya* (Calcutta: Biplabi Yug, 2000); *People's March*, August and December 2003.

19 *The Telegraph*, 4 February, 2006.

20 Committee of Concerned Citizens, *Third Report: 1997–2002* (Hyderabad: S. R. Sankaran, 2002).

21 "*Salwa*" is the local *gondi* tribal word for the water that is sprinkled on a patient to cure him/her of illness, and "*judum*" is the word for collective hunting, the term *salwa judum* thus meaning a purification hunt meant to cure tribal society of the Maoist "illness."

22 People's Union for Democratic Rights, Delhi, *et al.*, *When the State Makes War on Its Own People: A Report on Violation of People's Rights during the Salwa Judum Campaign in Dantewada, Chhattisgarh*, April 2006, Delhi.

23 Committee of Concerned Citizens, *Third Report, 1997–2002* (Hyderabad: S. R. Sankaran, 2002).

24 National Socialist Council of India, led by Isak Scu and Thuengaling Muivah, which had been carrying on an armed insurgency against the Indian government since 1975 to set up a sovereign, independent Nagaland which would be "socialist and Christian" in character.

27

International politics of South Asia

Vernon Hewitt

Since the Partition and Independence of the British Indian Empire in 1947, and the subsequent Independence of Ceylon in 1948, academic literature on the international politics of South Asia has proliferated, especially since the 1998 nuclear tests. Issues such as nuclear weaponisation, religious and ethnic violence, revolutionary movements, Islamic "terrorists," and "failing states" have informed—or distorted—debates on what constitutes South Asia, prospects for peace and stability in the states of the region, and how and to what extent events and policies can be effectively influenced by outside sources—primarily the west, and specifically, US administrations.[1]

Although characterized by a series of diverging theoretical positions, this literature has been predominantly realist or neorealist in orientation. This has had a peculiar and unfortunate effect on the significance of South Asia in and of itself, reducing it to a systemic understanding of the international system as seen primarily from somewhere else.[2] This predominantly static and ahistorical approach precludes any interesting or relevant discussion between, say, the nature of state formation in South Asia, the links between the state and domestic politics, how domestic politics is influenced directly by international non-state actors (and vice versa), or the role of cultural or

ideational factors on policy or process.[3] The view that South Asian elites have of the international system itself is deemed irrelevant since all states are the same, and the determining factor is international anarchy and the way this determines state behavior.[4] Even within neoliberal and behavioral approaches, "states have fixed identities and interests . . . they are rational egoists that seek to maximize their long-term utility gains and . . . this can best be achieved when states harness themselves to cooperative norms"[5] through international organizations and conventions.

This chapter will argue that the "naturalization" of the state is, for South Asia, singularly unhelpful in dealing with a part of the world where state formation has been derivative, and where formal sovereignty was granted (or won) at a unique moment in the international system, namely, the end of European primacy, the rapid retreat from empire, and the rise of bipolarity.[6] Scholarship in the 1990s has, reassuringly, moved to problematize the links among the states, territoriality, sovereignty, nationalism, and community in ways that take history seriously and open the way for a more sociologically informed debate as to how "state–society complexes are agents that both constitute and are in turn constituted by, sociodomestic and international global structures,"[7] This dialectic interest in agency–structure–agency must also consider non-materialist sources of power, such as culture and religion, if it is to have any real utility.

Influenced by post-structural and post-modern trends within international relations, recent scholarship has sought to "recover the roots of social constructs and categories of action by tracing the knowledgeable activities of culturally inscribed but strategic actors and the sometimes accidental turns that underline and define historical processes."[8] This is vital for an area of the world where "the artificial vivisection of British India created two states, India and Pakistan, with several nations and parts thereof, as well as multiple ethnies within them."[9] The "constructivist" turn in nationalist literature shows how nationalist elites inherited states that were, in effect, created by the colonial powers, and gave priority to the challenges of state and nation building posed for societies that were extremely pluralistic. It also reveals the social and cultural impact of colonial modernity that synchronized the emergence of local, regional, and "national" imaginations of the community at around the same historical moment.[10] As such, the dynamics that drive the international politics of South Asia are not primarily derived from the international system but almost equally "rooted in contending national and ethnic claims and the failure of the state to capture the loyalty of its citizens."[11]

The state is a constructed and contested concept. The degree and nature of this contestation critically affects the foreign policy of the states of South Asia, which must be concerned as much with securing the state from its own populations as from other states, and from competing subnationalist claims and ethnic separatism.[12] In deconstructing the state, the study of international relations has begun to accommodate the rich ethnographic and subaltern approaches that stress the significance of domestic politics and identity formation, how the state is "experienced and perceived" by local elites competing for scarce cultural and material resources. As Jeremy Gould recently noted: "[T]he state in recent anthropological interest is less an efficacious regulatory force, than a quasi mythical entity with which competing actors attempt to associate and thus legitimate their claims to public authority."[13] Such recent turns within the field of international relations have done much to end the static ahistoricism and crude positivism of the Waltzian "real world" approach to studying international politics, although one may still puzzle why it took quite so long.

State formation and the end of empire

The impact of British colonialism on South Asia was contradictory and profoundly uneven. From 1857 onwards, part of the modernizing project was to reform society along lines already experienced in the west, including the creation of elected, institutionalized forms of government, representative of the subcontinent's religious, ethnic, and social diversity as initially conceived by the British, while protective of British material interest.[14] Another part was a desire to shield aspects of so-called "traditional" society from the impact of modernity and the "inappropriateness" of capitalism and majoritarian forms of democratic practice. Informed partly by preconceived notions of Orientalism, the importance of religion, and the distinctiveness of a Hindu majority from minority Muslim practices, and partly by what was evidently important to social elites and communities collaborating with the British state, the path of colonial reform by the early twentieth century thus faced in two quite contradictory directions.[15]

The British created a powerful state with a commitment to democracy and individual rights, but rights that were also subordinated to collective or communal identities. These were defined through separate electorates, nomination to legislative bodies, and the preservation of so-called traditional rulers. The British created a state that was administratively centralized, but in other ways federal, in which individual provinces or states were guaranteed rights in a written constitution interpreted by a supreme court. Yet they also created a state that contained, until the final moments of Independence, pre-Westphalian sovereign entities known collectively as Princely India, the most significant one being the Princely State of Jammu & Kashmir. Two-fifths of the British Indian Empire consisted of feudal entities embedded within the Raj. In the cases of Nepal, Bhutan, and Sikkim, the British sought solely to protect traditional societies rather than modernize and transform them.

The consequences that followed from these conflicting ideologies of the Raj[16] led, at Independence, to the formation of a regionalized state system, and not, as the British had hoped, a single sovereign state cemented to Britain through an active, militarily-defined commonwealth that would ensure Britain's continuing role as a great power.[17] The Partition of India was a product of elite negotiation among leaders, the status of some of whom had been defined in relation to communal categories recognized by the British; disagreements between Muslim minority and majority provinces; and intra-elite disputes over the spoils of central office. It created two states that were to have quite differing capacities to govern themselves, and two quite different personalities within the international system. The driving process behind colonial disengagement was the speedy collapse of British authority and will to govern as much as it was the mass resistance to British colonial authority.[18] This collapse was in part a product of the Second World War, and increased US pressure on British colonial reformers from the late 1930s, but it was structured by a massive victory in Britain for a socialist Labor government committed to granting India full sovereign independence as quickly as possible. Independence was facilitated by the change in the international system from one dominated by a European empire to one shaped by the emerging Cold War.[19]

The carving out of East and West Pakistan, between June and August 1947, as a separate state for the Muslims of South Asia, seems now less the product of Jinnah's articulation of the two-nation theory, premised on Muslim minority fears of Hindu domination, than a bungled attempt by the Muslim League to assure a weakly federal India with significant power vested in the provinces.[20] It was not desired in principle by the British or, in its actual form—the creation of two widely separated new states comprising in both wings much less territory than claimed—by the Muslim leadership. The territorial configuration of Pakistan did not even map onto areas of electoral support for the League, or to areas that shared any cultural or linguistic similarities other than that they were majority Muslim areas defined crudely by the two boundary commissions coordinated and entirely dominated by Sir Cyril Radcliffe.

In some areas, such as the North-West Frontier Province (NWFP), the League was a relatively marginal political actor with little legitimacy. Even if it is accepted that Jinnah wanted a separate state, he was ambiguous about what the Muslim "nation" would be: religious or secular, pluralist or homogenous. Where societal pressures existed to mobilize support for Muslim separatism, it did so independently of the League's central leadership.[21] The process of state formation left a significant minority of Muslims behind in India, even after approximately nine million *mohajirs* (refugees), Urdu speakers, migrated to a "homeland" that was largely unknown. As such, Pakistan was founded by an émigré nationalist movement, and facilitated by the end of empire that created an impasse between regional and national identities as well as disputes over federal and confederal ideas of sovereignty.[22] The formation of India and Pakistan thus prefigured the difficulties of ethnic irredentism that would characterize Africa from the late 1950s, where cartographic lines crossed cultural and linguistic communities, and where notional territorial sovereignty did not match the much weaker coercive, extractive, and institutional attributes of the Weberian state.[23]

"Fixing" the boundary was bewildering. Disputes followed between Pakistan and Afghanistan, with particular reference to the Pathan-speaking areas in the NWFP, with Iran over Baloch nationalist identities, and with India over several areas in Gujarat, the Thar desert, and in the northeast with reference to Assam and the Chittagong Hill Tracts (CHT). India and China disputed significant areas of India's northeast (tucked in behind East Pakistan), the status of Tibet, and the role of both states with reference to Nepal. Preliminary drafts of the boundary commission gave Chittagong and Lahore to India, while the final award, published the day after Independence, left numerous ethnic enclaves such as Gurdaspur and Sylhet arguably in the "wrong" state. Even on the island of Ceylon, the close proximity of the Tamils of southern India, from the Jaffna peninsula through the Palk straits, troubled Sinhalese Buddhists concerning Tamil nationalism as much as it concerned Nehru over Dravidian separatism in the South. But the critical divide was Partition itself.

India and Pakistan were born amid animosity, recrimination over the partition of the Raj's financial and military resources, and with an actual armed conflict taking place in the Jhelum Valley. The regional state system was heavily dominated by India, which inherited over 70 percent of the territory of the British Indian Empire, and over 77 percent of its industrial and institutional capacity. Whatever the contradictions and tensions within the Indian National Congress over issues of secularism, the role of language, and the exact constitutional balance within an inherited federal structure, it was a more homogenous entity than the League[24] and it had greater legitimacy and a more coherent (albeit improvised) idea of what it wanted its nation to look and feel like.[25] Both states were relatively poor, but the physical imbalance between them was telling even in 1949. Each remained linked to the British Commonwealth, but British impartiality and weakness failed to resolve their disagreements, and their disagreements further marginalized the relevance of the commonwealth in South Asia.[26]

Kashmir, Pakistan, and India

Kashmir

The Kashmir conflict of 1947–49 illustrated the tensions inherent in seeking to fix state boundaries free of any pre-existing local or regional consensus, and where loyalties to the prince were overlapping, feudal in origin, and in the case of the Poonch district, in active rebellion.[27] Social and political movements acting to their own agenda, even with covert support from a neighbor, reveal the dynamics of state and non-state agency that were to bedevil the region through to the 1999 Kargil conflict, and beyond. Kashmir remains central to understanding the emergent relationship between India and Pakistan, and how the lines of foreign alliances radiated out from the centrality of this conflict to the international system.

The process of resolving princely India was botched by the British, who, having shored up the princes as a bulwark against nationalist sentiment, swiftly abandoned them in 1946. Having been reassured that, once their treaty obligations to the British were laid aside, they would revert to sovereign entities, the British political department proceeded to bully the princes into deciding which one of the two proto-dominions they wanted to join. The decision appeared to be one of princely fiat, but even this degree of agency was compromised by the overriding demand for geopolitical contiguity for the new states that was demanded by both the Congress and the League.[28] Where the princes were of a differing religious persuasion from their subjects, these two principles clashed. The Nawab of Deccan Hyderabad was a Muslim presiding over an overwhelming by Hindu population. He was also situated in the middle of Indian territory. To Nehru's outrage, he initially opted for

Pakistan, made a dash for independence, and then was finally incorporated into the Indian Union. This drama was played out in a number of locations in the panic and drama of Independence.[29] In Kashmir, the situation was reversed, with the Dogra Rajput Hindus residing in an overwhelmingly Muslim Vale, and with diverse communities of Muslims and Buddhists throughout the kingdom. Moreover, Jammu & Kashmir was the only significant princely state that was so located as to be contiguous to both new states and thus be able, in principle, to join either India or Pakistan.[30]

The Maharaja of Jammu & Kashmir first sought independence as a sovereign state, but then, faced with ongoing unrest in Poonch, and tribal incursions from the NWFP (i.e., from Pakistan) ostensibly to aid fellow Muslims, he opted for India with the promise of imminent military aid. There followed significant confusion over the exact sequence of events, and over the exact meaning of the Indian offer to hold a plebiscite to settle the dispute once the violence in the valley had abated and Pakistani forces withdrawn.[31] The allegation that "Pakistan" instigated a covert tribal invasion is undermined by the weakness and incoherence of Pakistan at the time. The support by the National Conference Party—a popular movement in the Valley itself—for Nehru and the Congress, which is well attested in Indian historiography, meanwhile underplays the desire for independence as a sovereign socialist state, and an "idea of Kashmir" that places Sheikh Abdullah, a sunni Muslim with a secularist outlook, closer to the Hindu Maharaja and to Jinnah than to Nehru. The portrayal of Muslim interests as being pro-Pakistan likewise downplays the desires of many leading politicians, later presidents within Azad (Pakistan-administered) Kashmir, to create an independent state as well. This apparent consensus in favor of independence, however, was compromised by the fact that differing actors imagined different forms of national sovereignty.[32]

With the arrival of Pakistani troops into Baltistan, the Kashmir war became an overt "interdominion" conflict, initially—and bizarrely—involving British commanding officers on both sides. In an attempt to display international leadership, partly in the naive conviction that India's position was above reproach, Nehru referred the crisis to the UN Security Council, after which, in 1949, a ceasefire was declared that effectively partitioned the state. India was left in control of roughly two-thirds of Jammu & Kashmir, including the Vale, with its nearly 90 percent Muslim population. India resented subsequent UN involvement, suspecting US and British support for Pakistan.

Much has been made of the fact that the inclusion of a Muslim-majority province in India provided an essential litmus test of secularism, while the exclusion of such a province made a mockery of Pakistan as the state for the Muslims of South Asia. Other arguments, strategic and geopolitical, were advanced that supported either the Indian or Pakistani position, while gradually a "third way," namely the idea of a Kashmir separate from both Pakistan and India, reemerged in the 1980s and 1990s. In 1965 Pakistan launched a series of covert infiltrations across the ceasefire line on the eve of Operation Gibraltar—the code name for the Pakistani attack on Indian-administered Kashmir—but a second armed conflict failed to resolve the issue. In 1971, in response to Indian support for the Bangla rebels, Pakistan attacked parts of western India. The resulting conflict did not significantly change ground realities. The Shimla Accord of 1972 converted the ceasefire line into a Line of Control, an attempted "soft border" that sought to compromise the requirements of statehood with shared cultural and social communities on either side, and remove the issue from the clutches of the UN. Nonetheless, both India and Pakistan set about furthering the integration of their respective parts of Kashmir into their state structures and nationalist narratives. Pakistan continued to seek international support for sustaining the dispute, and to counterbalance India's perceived hegemonic strategy, making Kashmir a precondition for any discussion with India over improving bilateral relations.

Thus the Kashmir conflict provided the prism through which these two states and their elites perceived each other, and the crisis that structured Pakistan's foreign policy both within the region and towards the wider international community. Jinnah's conviction that Nehru was determined to "strangle" the Muslim state at birth remains to many Pakistanis a demonstrable fact. And in Indian eyes, Pakistan remains a state that will stop at next to nothing to revise the territorial settlement of 1972, including masterminding covert militant strikes deep inside Indian-occupied Kashmir in 1999, allegedly funding terrorist strikes against the Srinagar and New Delhi parliament buildings between 2001 and 2003.

Pakistan

Pakistan's concern over provincial instability and international vulnerability emphasized the role of the military and an alliance with the *mohajirs* around the central bureaucracy and the non-elective aspects of state power from the beginning. Military expenditure dominated Pakistan as a need to underpin domestic order and police an almost impossible territorial configuration that placed East Pakistan over 1,000 miles across an assumed hostile India. The state of martial rule had foreign and international policy implications as well as ramifications for a proclivity towards authoritarian forms of governance in which political parties were fragmented and personalized.[33] From the moment of Independence, Pakistan sought International allies willing to secure prohibitive defense requirements against India, and against Bengali, and later Sindhi and Baluchi separatism. These requirements were funded primarily by the US, and involved the apparent support by Pakistan for Soviet containment, but it also—more problematically—involved support from China. Defined as an ally in US containment policy towards the Soviet Union, and encouraged by Washington's mistrust of India's emergent non-aligned,

socialist rhetoric, Pakistan's strategic position lent itself to CENTO and SEATO membership and soft loans and grants from a variety of US administrations. By 1972, the Sino–US rapprochement seemed to cement Pakistan's ties with two key allies. Yet both these alliances were rather tenuous.

Initiated by the 1954 mutual security pact, the US commitment to Pakistan unraveled in the early 1970s, despite its rhetorical support for Pakistan in the Bangladesh war and the delay in granting diplomatic recognition to Bangladesh. To many in Pakistan, the US has been found wanting in failing to act more decisively to defend Pakistan's territorial integrity. The US commitment unraveled further with increasing US mistrust concerning Pakistan's nuclear weapons intentions, until the hapless Soviet intervention in Afghanistan in 1979–80 transformed a tenuous military government (under General Zia) back into a frontline state. China's support did not involve active military engagement in 1971 against India, and China has been equivocal in its attitude towards Pakistan's nuclear tests in 1998.

During the 1980s, a new domestic political settlement led to a search for more useful allies. This involved General Zia's espousal of an "Islamic" Pakistan, that would unite fragmentary ethnic identities into a single religious community under a unitary presidential system, and cooperation with the Arab states, especially Saudi Arabia, and until 1979, with Iran as well. It also led to an active membership within the Organization of the Islamic Conference. Stressing the religious links between the Middle East and Pakistan made some economic sense, but it also facilitated and encouraged the growth of domestic Islamic movements, which the state failed to control effectively; nor did they provide a basis for a lasting new consensus on a "mainstream," i.e., moderate Muslim identity. Often it placed Pakistan in the middle in disputes between moderate and extremist Muslim states. Seemingly as ignorant of intra-Muslim identities within Pakistan as the British were of those within British India, Zia's policies generated sectarian violence as well as the proliferation of religiously and ethnically defined non-state actors active in the region, primarily in Afghanistan, and then, from 1989 onwards, in Indian-administered Kashmir.

Until the horrors of 9/11, Zia's policies dovetailed neatly with US support for the Islamic resistance to the Soviet regime, and the strategic use of Saudi resources. However, the end of the Cold War, and of the Soviet adventure in Afghanistan, facilitated a return to democracy within Pakistan in the wake of Zia's likely assassination in a plane crash in 1988. Yet the domestic creation of the militant, anti-western Taliban within Pakistan Punjab, its involvement in executing the Pakistan Army's foreign policy in Afghanistan, and then, in fomenting the rise of religious violence in Karachi and Islamabad, meant that the restoration of democracy was problematic. Between Zia's death in 1988, and the declaration of martial rule by General Musharraf in 1999, it was Pakistan's misfortune that an emergent post-Cold War order emphasized conceptions of good governance, democratization, and civilian leadership, three areas in which Pakistan was particularly vulnerable. US concerns over Pakistan's "Islamic" bomb also resurfaced in US policy circles. During 11 years of political instability and constitutional decline, the Pakistan state—never a unitary actor—fragmented into a series of parallel and disconnected areas of political and legal authority: president against prime minister, secular against religious authority, the judiciary against the executive, the executive against the legislature. In 1993, 1997, and again in 2007–08, such rivalries paralyzed the government and threatened the state with endemic instability. The impact of such duplication and rivalry on policy and its implementation remains serious. The security threats to Pakistan's elites were diverse and diverging and they frequently collapsed distinctions between internal and external enemies.

The rise to prominence of the Inter-Services Intelligence unit within the executive, its combination of foreign and domestic intelligence and surveillance, and its dominance over the Ministry of Foreign Affairs and the office of the prime minister, indicate the weakness of democratic accountability or even the existence of established norms for foreign policy formulation. In 1999, prior to his removal in a bloodless coup, Prime Minister Sharif was significantly under-informed about the role of Pakistan's military involvement in Kargil (an area within Indian-administered territory), and confused about the role of *mujahideen* irregulars in the fighting.[34] When pressured by the Clinton administration to disengage from the conflict, Sharif appeared concerned about possible political revenge from the military, and especially from Musharraf who had headed up the Kargil operation. Earlier, in 1998, Sharif had struck a senior US negotiator as being entirely uninformed on Pakistan's emergent nuclear posture, excluded from foreign policy matters, and more concerned about the army threat to his power base.[35]

Musharaf's coup in 1999 was domestically popular, although internationally condemned. Despite having demonstrable links with Islamic militants and ISI policy in Kashmir at the time of Kargil, Musharraf urged the Pakistani army to offer complete assistance to the US Bush administration in their planned attacks on Afghanistan in 2001–02. It was argued that significant economic and military resources would be forthcoming, while active resistance would lead the US to throw their support behind India, if not to "bomb[ing] Pakistan back to the stone age."[36] Such pragmatism overturned earlier army support and diplomatic recognition of the Taliban government, and was pressed home in the face of open hostility toward the US by domestic religious groups and communities, especially in the frontier and tribal areas of Pakistan.[37] The paradox of a Pakistani state supporting Islamic militants, while drawing on the US as a principle ally in the US "war on terror," was not lost on India, and provided the backdrop to a sustained crisis in Indo–Pakistan relations from 1998 through to 2002–04. By 2004–05,

US State Department officials were increasing pressure on the Pakistani leader to demonstrate he was being tough on Islamic organizations operating within Pakistan, and active against unlicensed *madrasah* schools alleged to be training militants drawn from the wider Muslim diaspora.[38]

By 2006–07, US pressure was also aimed at improving Musharraf's democratic credentials, by coercing him into a dialogue with Pakistani politicians, especially Benazir Bhutto, in the run-up to scheduled elections in early 2008. That US foreign policy was pushing Pakistan in two differing directions seemed lost on the US State Department. Even the British Foreign Office continuously downplayed the generic weaknesses of the Pakistan People's Party (PPP) as a democratic social movement, ignoring the basically feudal, over-personalized elite that surrounded Ms Bhutto. The Washington–London axis thus compelled Musharraf into a political accord with Benazir Bhutto that alienated sections of his own army, and angered Muslim hardliners, especially in the NWFP and areas affected by the influx of Pathan refugees.[39] The assassination of Ms Bhutto in December 2007 fragmented opposition to the regime, and further underlined the systemic fragility within Pakistan and the extent to which the domestic compulsions of its foreign policy are ill conceived and little understood.[40]

India

Ayesha Jalal has argued that the tendency to compare democratic–civilian India with an authoritarian–military Pakistan, ignores the shared political and institutional legacy between them. At crucial moments, each country has demonstrated very similar forms of political dynamism, such as authoritarian populism during the 1970s, the institutional decline of party structures, and high levels of social violence. Gujarat in 2002–03, and the widespread communal violence associated with the rise of the BJP to power in the early to mid-1990s clearly indicate how volatile

India can be, and the extent to which the cliché of the world's "largest democracy" should not be taken at face value. Insurrections in the northeast, as well as Kashmir, and Punjabi violence throughout the 1980s do compel comparison with Pakistan. However, to draw too many parallels with Pakistan significantly misrepresents the extent to which India's political elite has managed to connect an inherited state structure to emergent, and indeed diverging, sections of civil society, and given the state ideological and national cohesion. Important differences between the Muslim League and the Indian National Congress as national movements, and the differences in their leadership (or crudely put, between Jinnah and Nehru) translated into very different international "personalities" and very different foreign policy aspirations.

More geographically cohesive, less traumatized by Partition, and less hamstrung by its own internal security concerns, India's political leaders were able to initially articulate a foreign policy premised less on survival than on an ideological commitment to internationalism, nonalignment, and an active solidarity with colonial peoples. From the outset, India's political and intellectual elite set their ambitions apart from Pakistan, indeed arguably from South Asia itself.[41] Individuals such as Nehru, Krishna Menon, and K. M. Panikkar came from a westernized intelligentsia that inherited from the British a conception of "great power" status, and the belief that India, by virtue of its size and ancient civilization would quickly assume a position of global responsibility. Such apparent continuities in the view of Indian greatness led Nehru to refer the nascent Kashmir issue to the United Nations as a sign of India's commitment to internationalism, and to engage with China in lengthy debates over the status of Tibet and India's northeastern and northwestern borders, despite the fact that such idealism yielded few results. Yet nonalignment was certainly not a pacifist stance, and the rhetoric of third world solidarity was to give India a high profile within the British Commonwealth on matters of African and Asian decolonization, and as an active member of the UN General Assembly important enough to influence the voting behavior of many member states.[42]

Yet the sophistication of the Nehruvian view of India's place in the world was lost on various US administrations, irritated by the equation between oppressive neocolonialism and US foreign policy and, by the late 1960s, the growing collusion between India and the Soviet Union. India's position on the Nuclear Non-Proliferation Treaty further irritated Washington. Nehru's socialism and his suspicions of capitalism contrasted sharply with that of Pakistan, as did his condemnation of apartheid and Israel. As the formalized nonaligned movement continued to merge with Soviet allies such as Cuba, Iraq, and Libya, US concerns about India's tilt towards Moscow were expressed more stridently, and were reflected as well in diminishing economic support. Although military humiliation at the hands of China in 1962—and another draw in the second Indo-Pakistan war of 1965— undermined much of Nehru's naive illusions about the effectiveness of diplomacy, the search for military aid did not soften India's criticism of the US. Neither did India allow the US to broker any deals over Kashmir, or provide any support for US global aims and objectives in East Asia, as during the Vietnam War, or over disputes concerning UN recognition of Cambodia. Subsequent difficulties over Indian socioeconomic planning, the forced devaluation of the rupee, and the conditional US food imports created resentment and concerns over Indian self-reliance.

The nadir of New Delhi's relationship with Washington came in 1970–72, especially when Indira Gandhi signed a 25-year friendship treaty with the Soviet Union in 1971, and was able to utilize this effectively in the wake of the 1971 Indo-Pakistan War to checkmate US–Chinese support for Pakistan. Misread by US analysts as a mutual defense pact, and distorted by US global strategy aimed at using Pakistan to facilitate an opening with China, the State Department ignored the excesses committed by the Pakistan army in their attempt to suppress the movement of Bengali speakers in the eastern wing of the country, and interpreted India's military incursion into East Pakistan as a Soviet-sponsored enterprise. In fact, the Soviets were as anxious to constrain India as the US, and were evidently relieved when India declared a unilateral ceasefire in the west following the surrender of Pakistan at Dhaka.[43]

India's peaceful nuclear explosion (PNE) in 1974 deepened tensions with Pakistan. Moreover, India continued to challenge the US over whether the Non-Proliferation Treaty (NPT) was an arms control or arms elimination agreement. India's objections to the NPT were both principled and pragmatic. They were principled in that they argued that the NPT was discriminatory in preventing non-nuclear weapon states from acquiring a legitimate means to defend themselves, while not compelling existing nuclear weapon states to eliminate their nuclear weapons. Indeed, the vertical proliferation of nuclear weapons throughout the 1980s confirmed to India that the treaty was worthless. Delhi's objections were also pragmatic in that China's status as a nuclear weapons state created a security dilemma that was of regional significance to India, especially in the context of a Pakistan–China alliance. India's allegations of US support for (or at least indifference to) a covert Pakistan bomb program, as well as criticisms over the Pakistan–China security relationship, blighted any attempts to improve US relations while the Cold War lasted.

The Soviet invasion of Afghanistan in 1979–80 heightened tensions with the US, while seriously compromising India's understanding with Moscow. Again misinterpreted by the US, India was not so much complicit in the Soviet move as angered by the attack against a fellow member of the nonaligned movement, and at a time when Mrs Gandhi was the chairperson of the organization. India realized that Pakistan's subsequent realignment with the US would have significant financial and military implications for the South Asia region, and increase the chances for Pakistan to acquire nuclear weapons covertly.[44]

The subsequent implosion of Afghanistan, and the support by the US and Pakistan for Islamic *mujahideen* fighters was to have regional and domestic consequences for India as well. In 1989–90, the situation in Kashmir took a dangerous turn when longstanding grievances against New Delhi's disregard for the region's autonomy, and its willful intervention into the political processes of the state's ruling party, coincided with the rise of insurgency from Pakistan's NWFP in protest over the Line of Control. Such insurgency marked in part a conscious Pakistan design to use covert forces in an asymmetrical campaign against India, especially in the wake of the Paris Peace Accords that ended the Afghan conflict. Yet it also marked the rise of non-state actors with their own socio-religious and political agendas acting both on Pakistan and within both Azad Kashmir and the Indian State of Jammu & Kashmir.

Although India supported the restoration of party politics in Pakistan after 1988, and Pakistan's subsequent return to the Commonwealth, the irony remained that Indo–Pakistan relations tended to deteriorate during such democratic interludes. The rise of coalition governments often compromised mainstream politicians such as Benazir Bhutto and Nawaz Sharif, who found themselves dependent on the support of Islamic parties with extreme agendas concerning Kashmir. From 1989 onwards, with the exception of the Rao congress government, coalition politics weakened India as well, but less extensively on issues of foreign policy than on matters of regionalism and local autonomy.

The prolonged crisis in Kashmir during the years 1989 to 1996 especially, and India's deteriorating relationship with Pakistan throughout the 1990s[45] coincided with a profound political change within the Indian political system. Socioeconomic and political violence in the name of religion, associated with the rise of Hindu nationalism, challenged the basis of Nehru's secularist state. Also for the first time, Nehruvian foreign policy was publicly attacked for allegedly leading to "50 wasted years."[46] The rise of the BJP to power in the central government coincided with a more overtly strident use of great power language. In 1998, the new BJP-led National Democratic Alliance (NDA) government authorized a series of nuclear tests. Unlike the PNE of 1974, and in part provoked by Washington's move towards a comprehensive test ban treaty that threatened to delegitimize any future Indian move to go nuclear, the 1998 tests were aimed at overt weaponization, and were justified by reference to China, and later Pakistan. The significance of China's support for the Pakistan missile program was not lost on Indian intelligence, and the greater challenge that China posed to Indian ambitions was not lost on western analysts either.

A series of statements made it clear that India now claimed the de facto status of a nuclear weapons state (NWS). The move required an immediate reciprocal move by Pakistan, despite concerted efforts by the Clinton administration to prevent it.[47] In the face of international condemnation and sanctions imposed by the US and other members of the OECD, India and Pakistan had succeeded in undermining the NPT and the ability of the US to prevent the horizontal proliferation of nuclear weapons. Both India and Pakistan had sufficient expertise in the development and refinement of delivery systems to make deployment a reality, with India having a notable edge in domestic ballistic technologies, including guidance systems and software and satellite capabilities.

Although the unilateral declaration by India of its status as an NWS appeared at one level to indicate a significant ideological and policy break from previous governments, there was much continuity behind India's policy on nuclear capability broadly defined, in which possession of nuclear weapons was less a matter of practical value than a symbolic emblem of great power status. Indian attempts to assert its moral superiority by claiming that New Delhi would renounce nuclear weapons once global nuclear disarmament was restored to the heart of the NPT regime, was a rhetorical gesture, a figleaf hardly able to hide India's realist intentions.[48] Yet, as always, the allegations of western and US moral duplicity struck their targets. The BJP leadership was candid, if not slightly crude, in recognizing that, armed with nuclear weapons, India would by definition become overnight an influential power whose views would be difficult to ignore or patronize. Opinion polls revealed that over 70 percent of the population supported the move by the Indian government to the status of a NWS. This support was not affected by the growing realization that Pakistan too had visibly increased its international profile, and by the growing risk of a nuclear arms race not only in South Asia but in the entire East Asian region.[49]

The complexity of the tradeoffs between status and security became apparent in 1999, when India and Pakistan engaged in open conflict over Kargil. As Kundu has noted, "the Kargil conflict, the first armed confrontation between . . . states equipped with nuclear weapons, [was] fought without either side having established a formal tactical or strategic doctrine for their use."[50] Subsequent allegations that "unauthorized" movements of Pakistan's nuclear weapons took place during the conflict heightened tensions by revealing the very real lack of transparency or even defined procedure within the Pakistan chain of command. Many western observers were struck by the distressing level of "nuclear threats" uttered by statesmen on both sides in 1999, and in the subsequent crisis that followed Islamic terrorist attacks on the Kashmir parliament and then the Indian national parliament.

However, by 2003–04, both India and Pakistan had moved to clarify their nuclear doctrines, and had to some extent created or revised institutional arrangements to house, oversee, and ultimately authorize the use of nuclear weapons. In the meantime, ongoing negotiations with the Clinton administration aimed at putting the genie back in the bottle moved towards condoning some sort of "limited" Indian nuclear deterrent. In the wake of Clinton's successful visit to India in 2000 (by

far the most successful visit by a US president), the nuclear gamble of 1998 appeared, paradoxically, to have transformed the US–Indian relationship (or as one analyst stated, to have finally "lanced the boil" of the NPT issue once and for all).[51] By contrast, the sight of a US president lecturing the Pakistanis on democracy boosted the BJP realist view as both appropriate and necessary for Indian success. By 2003–04, a more complex analysis of the security dilemma post-1998 implied that nuclear weapons might have prevented the Kargil incident from escalating into a full international conflict. While there remained concerns that India and Pakistan might use the threat of nuclear war to encourage low-intensity conflict, there was some room for optimism that it would proscribe the overall use of force in pursuit of political and strategic aims. However, the role and influence of armed non-state actors, and their proliferation and association with international militant groups linked to global terrorism against the west, would soon become of increased concern.

The election of George W. Bush, and the new international era that emerged in the wake of 9/11, hampered the Indian momentum towards rapprochement with the US because of Pakistan "outbidding," but it did not stop it. While it restored Pakistan to US favor, it did not undo the gains that New Delhi had made from 1998 or blight the emergent symmetry between western concerns over Islamic terrorism and Indian concerns over "Pakistani"-backed terrorism. While retaining links with the Russians, and pursuing independent initiatives aimed at Iraq prior to the invasion by the coalition, India strengthened its new found understanding with Washington by forging an alliance with Israel. A series of intelligence and arms deals with this country opened the way for the modernization of some of India's aging Soviet-era military hardware, while neo-conservative rhetoric from within the Bush administration complemented Indian concerns over China's continuing economic and military growth. Indo–US relations have continued to develop, despite India's refusal to participate in the Iraq involvement without a UN mandate.

The successful transformation of the US–Indian relationship cannot be underestimated. It has paved the way for the recent and, to some, surprising recognition of India as a great power by a British prime minister and open support for an Indian seat on a revised UN security council. Yet such views reflect not so much the success of the BJP's "outing" of Pakistan's nuclear capability, but more significantly, the economic transformation that has been gathering pace since the early 1990s. India's economic "takeoff" and its ability to combine a nationalist strategy with the neoliberal compulsions of globalization are complex and open to dispute,[52] but they have been transformative, both on the nature of the Indian federal system itself, and the role that India is playing in international entities such as the World Trade Organization (WTO), the World Bank, and the International Monetary Fund (IMF). Taken as a whole, it is the degree of Indian economic prosperity that has commanded US and western attention as much if not more than its status as an NWS. During the late 1990s, India–US trade grew by a staggering 264 percent, with the US providing a market for one-fifth of Indian exports. Moreover, India is the second largest source of immigrants to the US after Mexico and has begun to generate a societal presence in the US, and a powerful lobby that is creating a domestic constituency that may influence US policy towards India in the future. More significantly still, the need to sustain economic growth and to deepen economic cooperation in the region as a whole, has improved the position of the troubled South Asian Association of Regional Cooperation, and led to significant moves towards enhancing India's role in the Association of South East Asian Nations (ASEAN) as well.[53]

India's recent willingness to talk "trade" with Pakistan without pre-conditional posturing over Kashmir, overcoming the deadlock of the Agra summit in 2001, seems to imply a recognition that regional instability undermines Indian claims to greatness. It also follows that India needs a stable and workable "idea of Pakistan" and not a failing Pakistani state that would destabilize the entire Central and South Asian region.

Bangladesh, Nepal, Sri Lanka, and the international system

India dominates the South Asian subcontinent, and presides over a regional state system that shares numerous ethnic, religious, and linguistic identities. These states are constantly mediating, resisting or encouraging specific forms of social identity. It has been argued in this chapter that such dynamics blur the anodyne distinctions made in IR literature among domestic, regional, and international politics. I wish to conclude this chapter by a brief overview of the regional dynamics of cooperation and resistance, and their consequences for the smaller states of South Asia.

The state elites of South Asia use resources gleaned from the international community—both material and ideological—to forward domestic ideas of the nation, and to shape the regional state system to their own liking and for their own security. The search for security is often as much a domestic one as it is international. As we have seen, shared sociocultural and religious identities facilitate such strategies, as well as encourage the risk of blowback. Both India and Pakistan have intervened in the internal conflicts within the other state, covertly or overtly. India has intervened in Bangladesh, Sri Lanka, and the Maldives. It has also sought almost continuously to influence and control the domestic and foreign policy of Nepal. India's bilateral relations with the smaller states of South Asia have often been in competition with Pakistan, but also with China, especially in the sensitive areas of northeast India. Bhutan and—until its integration into India—the state of Sikkim, occupied curious positions as quasi-sovereign states under implicit forms of "trusteeship" that have had more in common with ideas of

British paramountcy than with notions of Westphalian statehood. All have felt the attempted assertion of India's primacy, and all have sought to challenge it.

Bangladesh

In 1971–72, Pakistan became the first post-Second World War state to disintegrate.[54] East Pakistan, containing a bare majority of its population, emerged from almost 25 years of economic and social discrimination against its Bengali-speaking community, to stake a claim to statehood. Delivered by Indian intervention, and conscious of a shared language and community that united it with West Bengal, Bangladesh has curiously mirrored Pakistan's own political and social instability in trying to establish a national community congruent with the territorial state. This has involved a shift from a secular, socialist democracy to an Islamic republic, premised on *sharia* law that implies an important role for the *mullahs*. It too has veered from prime ministerial to presidential systems of government, and from civilian to military dictatorship. These struggles have been driven in the main by different images of the nation held by competing elites, who have used domestic, regional, and international resources to seize state power.[55] A short but brutal civil war generated a radicalized, pro-Maoist liberation movement, a more orthodox Bengali secularist movement premised around the Awami League, and a pro-Pakistan movement linked to religious parties associated with ex-patriot officers and soldiers returned to Bangladesh after the war.[56] The last group, exemplified by General Ershad, who held power between 1982 and 1990, had been influenced by Pakistani army views on Islam, and been removed from the profoundly galvanizing experiences of the civil war itself. Political parties quickly formed around each potential national signifier—Islamic and secular linguistic—despite the dominance of the Awami League, and although the Jamaat-i-Islami (JI) was proscribed in Bangladesh until 1976. Neighboring states supported one

preferred option over another, India a secular version of Bangladesh derived from its own experiences, and Pakistan a more Islamic version. And behind them emerged their international allies in turn.[57] Intense party competition and social mobilization complicated and compromised these options further, especially following the restoration of party politics in 1990.

Indian support for the Awami League and Bangladesh's first secular and socialist constitution of 1973 backfired. It was alleged that India was bullying Bangladesh on matters of economic assistance and trade, even implying that Bangladesh was a satellite of India. The murder of Mujibur Rehman brought to power an army that turned Bangladesh back towards Pakistan, and a strategic alliance with the US, Saudi Arabia, and the Gulf states, and away from India and the Soviet Union. This occurred despite the fact that the US was initially hostile to the Awami League and was pro-Pakistan throughout the civil war. This foreign policy shift, brought about by General Ziaur Rehman (in power 1976–81), went along with a move to construct a conservative Muslim—but not necessarily Islamist—nationalism led by the newly formed BNP, and through the rehabilitation of former so-called Pakistani collaborators. Gulf remittances into the Bangladesh economy made a significant contribution to state revenue, but also furthered external Islamic influences that competing elites charged were alien to Bengali Islamic traditions.

In the mid-1980s, during the presidency of Ershad, Bangladesh played a critical role in setting up the South Asian Regional Cooperation Council (SAARC) in the hope of getting away from India's domination through collaboration with other smaller states anxious over Indian designs. At the same time, difficulties within Bangladesh, especially with reference to the ongoing insurgency within the Chittagong Hill Tracts, and the dispute over the sharing of water resources from the Ganges (especially in the wake of India's completion of the Farakka Barrage in 1974), compelled

411

cooperation with India, regardless of emerging ideological differences. Throughout the 1980s, Indo–Bangladeshi relations were bitter and confrontational. However, despite issues of illegal migration from Bangladesh into India's northeastern states, and India's attempt to construct a border fence, bilateral relations improved under I. K. Gujral's brief policy of close cooperation between India and its immediate neighbors. Relations were also improved through SAARC, and in part by a more sophisticated appreciation by India of the internal constraints of its neighbor.

The termination of military rule in Bangladesh was facilitated by the end of the Cold War and by democratic restoration in Nepal, which momentarily demonstrated the power of mass protest. Still, although the restoration of elected government from 1990 fits to some extent within the so-called "third wave" of democratization, the results have been more complex and more disappointing than the democratization literature would have us suppose.[58] Intense competition between the Awami League and the BNP has led to a degree of Islamic outbidding, similar to the experience of Pakistan between 1988 and 1999. The refusal of political elites to abide by electoral verdicts within Bangladesh has led to outside attempts at mediation from such diverse actors and organizations as the British Commonwealth, British labor politicians and US ambassadors. The extent of instability has led to Indian concerns over the role of Islamic groups, and also has raised concerns within the international community over issues of good governance and corruption, especially following the intense electoral instability since 2006.

Bangladesh's extraordinary dependence on international aid, at a time of reluctance on the part of aid givers to commit to future grants, as well as increased conditionality on proposed loans, threatens to alienate domestic opinion concerned over compromising national sovereignty. Such concerns also have the potential to strengthen Islamicist parties that denounce western intervention. Between 1972

and 2006, Bangladesh has received approximately $45 billion in grants, and $44 billion in soft loans. These grants and loans have constituted between 12 and 25 percent of all government expenditure. Yet, some argue that up to 75 percent of this glut of external funding has failed to reach its targeted project or constituency.[59] By 2005 pledges of further aid had declined considerably.

Nepal

Given the role of Maoist parties in the formation of Bangladesh, and the location of the new state close to regions and territories contested between India and China, Bangladesh has proved relatively immune to Sino-Indian rivalry. Nepal, in contrast, has often found itself in the position of a "yam between two boulders." Nepal shares the complex social and cultural pluralism of the rest of South Asia, as well as the preservation of feudal-like political structures within a modern territorially defined state.[60] Its traditional elites are drawn from Hindu migrants who left India from the fourteenth century onwards, establishing themselves in and around Kathmandu. These elites supported a particularly orthodox Hinduism not found throughout the rest of Nepal or, for that matter, in modern India. The Bahun families dominated courtly politics, retaining hereditary offices such as head priest and prime minister, and managing non-Bahun clans through a form of amoral familism,[61] in the form of strategic patron–client linkages known as the *chakari* system. Superimposed on, and refracted through such alliances, was an older division between the hills and the plains or the *tarai*, dominated by Hindus who migrated from the nineteenth century onwards, and influenced by social and cultural reforms stimulated in India during British colonial rule.

Nepal emerged after the British withdrawal as an independent state, but with India concerned over the former's proximity to Tibet and, later, with Chinese collusion with Pakistan. Indian influence in Nepal was facilitated by shared sociocultural and development goals and, between 1948–61, close cooperation between the Indian National Congress and the Nepali Congress. However, in 1961, the monarchy banned political parties and imposed a Panchayat Raj scheme of local governance, which provoked tensions with India. As Sino–Pakistan relations solidified in the wake of the first and second Indo-Pak wars, Nepal's fragmented elite came to resent India's talk of nonalignment as a cover to support pro-democracy movements within the kingdom, and isolate Nepal from Pakistan. Chinese offers of developmental aid were also accepted as a counterbalance, but the construction of the strategically vital Karakorum Road linking China to Pakistan, especially following a border agreement between Pakistan and China over territory claimed by India, led to direct Indian pressure on Nepal. Bilateral relations deteriorated dramatically in the late 1980s, when various transit deals on commodities were held up by New Delhi, with immediate and serious consequences for the Nepal economy. SAARC provided a much needed opportunity for Nepal to negotiate with Bangladesh and Pakistan to try and reduce transit costs as alternatives to India's control of the border through airlifting supplies from its two neighbors. Following the restoration of party politics in 1990, India has continued to support the Nepal Congress and assist in a series of bilateral aid and trade deals, while China tended to support the main Marxist opposition, but resisted supporting the Maoist insurrection. The fragmentation of the Nepali Left in the wake of the Cold War, and China's own reform and moderation from the 1990s onwards, led to a lessening of overt Chinese antagonisms against India, and limited Chinese intervention within Nepalese domestic politics during the recent insurgency. In 1996, the decision by the Maoist Communist Party of Nepal to quit the institutions of parliamentary government and head a people's rebellion paralyzed the constitutional monarchy. At one stage, the Maoists controlled over 70 percent of the territory of Nepal, but it did so

without China's backing. The struggle among king, parliament, and rebels led to a bewildering set of competing alliances (after 2005, increasingly between a fragmented parliament aligned with the rebels, against the absolutism of King Gyanendra), with the king seeking to reestablish local institutions of government in an attempt to undermine parliament's claims to represent the will of the people. Such a move aimed at retaining the power of the monarchy incurred the risk of alienating support from both the US and India, both of whom favored party-based governance as a requirement for socioeconomic reform. Although China strangely remained more sympathetic to the king, its refusal to support the Maoists indicated a significant degree of conversion among the US, India, and China on regional politics in general and Nepal in particular.

Sri Lanka

Finally, the regional dynamics of state formation over and above shared senses of community and belonging can be dramatically illustrated with reference to the crisis and tensions within Ceylon (Sri Lanka after 1972) and their consequences for regional and international politics. Despite a very different colonial heritage from that of India and Pakistan, and despite a very different route to independence, Sri Lanka has been beset by internal conflict over the nature of national identity, what kind of state it supports, and what foreign policies such a state should pursue. Separate Tamil kingdoms, centered on the Jaffna peninsula, linked the island to India's Dravidian south, while its long exposure to maritime trade brought diverse influence from Southeast Asia and ultimately Europe. Although administered separately from India, the transportation throughout the nineteenth century of indentured Tamil laborers to work the tea plantations added another connection that threatened Sri Lanka's Sinhala Buddhist majority with the fear of Indian dominance.

Unitary in origin, and initially elitist and solidly pro-western, pro-Commonwealth and pro-US in foreign policy, the formation of exclusively Sinhalese political parties (the United National Party, and later the Sri Lanka Freedom Party) led to ethnic mobilization based on xenophobic Sinhala-Buddhist majoritarianism that resulted in a civil war that for long dominated an otherwise wealthy and successful polity. Sinhala-dominated governments sought to accommodate Tamil political parties while abjuring federalism or even acknowledging the cultural diversity of the northern and eastern parts of the country in particular. The consequence was to create the very Tamil separatist movement they most feared and compelled the very Indian intervention they most desired to avoid.

During Rajiv Gandhi's term in office, India sought forcibly to impose a settlement on the island, moved as much by electoral fallout for Congress in southern India, especially in Tamil Nadu where pro-Tamil sympathies were high. The ill-fated Indo–Sri Lankan Accord that led to Indian intervention between 1987 and 1990 seriously undermined India's attempts to broker a deal, revealing that it could not act to disarm the Tigers, influence the Sri Lankan government to negotiate seriously, or prevent Tamil support in India for an independent Eelam. India lost more troops during its intervention in Sri Lanka during the peace accord than it did during its intervention in East Pakistan in 1971. The incident reinforced Sri Lankan mistrust of India as a regional hegemon and resulted directly in the assassination of Rajiv Gandhi in 1991. Such adventurism proved costly to Indian claims to be an emergent great power with global responsibilities, instead underlining its inability to influence events in its own backyard.

Active in SAARC, supportive of ties with China and with ASEAN, Sri Lanka has continued to view Indian ambition with concern, and has in particular remained a critic of the nuclearization of the subcontinent since 1998. Nonetheless, changes in the US–India relationship, as well as between India and Israel, have complemented India and Sri Lanka's search for a more nuanced and intimate

bilateral relationship by providing intelligence and support for "counterterrorist" operations. Sri Lanka remains the most consistently pro-western, pro-US ally in the region. The recent stress on the need for economic growth, and the "Look East" (i.e., to East Asia) policies of recent governments in New Delhi, have also complemented Sri Lanka's East Asian connections, especially with reference to Japan, Thailand and the newly emerging economies of Vietnam and Cambodia. The breakdown in the ceasefire, and the intense warfare that therefore developed, imperils had the potential wealth of the island, and the role that SAARC and global wealth can play in providing resources to buy off separatist national claims. They can only play such a role, in any case, if domestic political institutions are redesigned to substantially devolve economic, social, and cultural power.

Conclusions

This chapter set out to show that an understanding of the international politics of the states of South Asia requires an awareness of the contingent nature of state formation, and the role played by elite competition in forming national communities that are congruent with state boundaries. Only a historically grounded, constructivist approach to South Asia can reveal the dynamics working themselves out among the states of India, Pakistan, and Nepal. International forces have constrained the foreign policy of state elites, but less so than might at first be imagined. The search for security has often as not entailed realigning domestic forces and institutions as much as changing foreign allies. And it has most often required the pragmatic use of external ideological quarrels, especially those of the US during the Cold War, and even the Bush administration's ill-named "War on Terror," for domestic and regional purposes. The roots of conflict are, often as not, domestic, but changes within the international system have enabled them either to have sustained themselves or threatened them with a scarcity of resources.

What of the future? Globalization, and the convergence of elites around the search for economic wealth through market-based solutions open up some scope for regional accommodation and cooperation even as they reveal new arenas of competition and risk. At the heart of the crisis of state formation in South Asia lies the strategic standoff between India and Pakistan over Kashmir, with both India and Pakistan preoccupied with identity and stability. India's search for global power is still an irritant to China and a stark challenge to the status and prospects of Pakistan and the smaller states of South Asia. However, the prospects of economic growth and shared markets may well erode the crude assertions of power as a form of mercantilist, zero-sum assertion of "hard" power. Economic wealth not only complements hard power, it actually pays for it, and in the long term may actually be more sustainable.

In his work on the states of the Middle East, Michael Barnett analyzes how, despite shared religious and linguistic identities that challenged the premise of the modern Westphalian state, elites nonetheless managed to institutionalize their states in such a way that re-imagined Arab nationalism as complementary to a stable system of Arab states.[62] Can any insights be taken from the Middle East and added to that of South Asia? Given the contingent nature of state formation, nationalist elites need to structure interaction around processes that share cultural and economic activity in ways that increase cooperation. Can political structures be created that facilitate sharing resources among states, such as soft borders, social and cultural movements, free trade zones in place of foreign donor conditionality? It is ironic that the western powers have paid more attention to an India with a sustained and impressive growth rate, than an India with nuclear weapons.

It remains the dominant challenge within South Asia whether the ideas of sovereignty can be made to work without generating domestic or regional conflict. State formation entails violence, but it also entails a search for order and stability. If states, nations and communities are creative acts of political imagination, if they exemplify agency and not ahistoric, fixed and essentialized entities, then however difficult and demanding, solutions are possible because they lie firmly in the hands of elites and subalterns themselves.

Postscript

The political formation of the Zardari coalition in Pakistan throughout 2008, and the on going proliferation of Taliban forces within the areas of Gilgit and Hunza continue to create tensions within the Pakistan state, and between Pakistan and India. The terrorist attacks on Mumbai in late 2008 reiterate much of the dynamics of state-nation-international system discussed in this chapter. The events in Mumbai exposed the extent to which non-state and state actors are either complicit in acts of social and political violence, ot powerless to prevent them. Despite immediate denials, subsequent US pressure from the newly elected Obama administration led to Pakistan's acceptance of Indian findings that a majority of the operatives in the attack—members of *Lashkar-e-Toiba*—prepared for the attack within Pakistan, and drew on a wide range of resources from international Islamist groups as far away as Spain and the US itself. While Pakistan denied actively deploying the terrorists as a covert state-sponsored act of terrorism, India remains skeptical of the claim and of the ability of the Pakistani state to bring the sole surviving terrorist to justice, questioning the control the state has over non-state actors working within its jurisdiction. Furthermore, President Zardari's decision to compromise with Islamic extremists in Swat by allowing the application of Shari'a law and ending military activity against the extremists undermines Pakistan's internal sovereignty and the ability of the state to prevent the forcible and violent implementation of a form

415

of medievalism that is neither Islamic nor popular. These two facets of the crisis of Pakistan: internal and external, domestic and foreign, are part of the on going struggle over what sort of social order the state wants to construct, and how successful the resulting state shall be in achieving regional peace.

Notes

1 See Stephen Cohen, *The Idea of Pakistan* (Washington, DC: Brookings, 2004).

2 See Vernon Hewitt, *The New International Politics of South Asia* (Manchester: University Press, 1997).

3 See R. B. J. Walker, *Inside/Outside: International Relations as Political Theory* (Cambridge: University Press, 1992).

4 See introduction to S. Hobden and John M. Hobson, *Historical Sociology of International Relations* (Cambridge: University Press, 2002). Exceptions to this exclusion of elites came, until recently, in "crisis" situations where the psychological or personal prejudices of leaders might be important, but even then these were not seen as requiring a societal perspective; see Richard Little and Steve Smith, *Belief Systems and International Relations* (Oxford: Blackwell, 1988), pp.10–12.

5 Hobden and Hobson, p. 11.

6 Partha Chatterjee, *The Nation and its Fragments: Colonial and Postcolonial Histories* (Princeton, NJ: University Press, 1993).

7 Hobden and Hobson, p. 21

8 Michael Barnett, "Historical Sociology and Constructivism," in Hobden and Hobson, p. 101. The sociological turn within IR has led to an intriguing debate between constructivists and postmodernists; see Alexander Wendt, *Social Theory of International Politics* (New York: Cambridge University Press, 1999).

9 T. K. Oommen, "New Nationalisms and Collective Rights: The Case of South Asia," in Stephen May *et al.* (eds), *Ethnicity, Nationalism and Minority Rights* (Cambridge: University Press, 2004), p. 128.

10 Ayesha Jalal, *Democracy and Authoritarianism in South Asia: A Comparative and Historical Perspective* (Cambridge: University Press, 1995).

11 Michael Barnett "Sovereignty, Nationalism and Regional Order in the Arab State System," in

12 See Christopher Clapham's innovative *Africa and the International System: The Politics of State Survival* (Cambridge: University Press, 1996); also Paul R. Brass "National Power and Local Politics in India: A Twenty Year Perspective," *Modern Asian Studies,* Vol. 18, No. 1 (February 1984), pp. 89–119; and his *Ethnicity and Nationalism: Theory and Comparison* (New Delhi: Sage, 1991); and Subrata K. Mitra and R. Alison Lewis (eds), *Subnational Movements in South Asia* (Boulder, CO: Westview, 1995).

13 Jeremy Gould, "Anthropology," in Peter Burnell (ed.), *Democratization through the Looking-Glass* (Manchester: University Press, 2003), pp. 24–40. For a further discussion of this, see Vernon Hewitt, *Political Mobilisation and Democracy in India: States of Emergency* (Oxford: Routledge, 2008), esp. the introduction and chapter 2.

14 Thomas. R. Metcalf, *Ideologies of the Raj* (New York: Cambridge University Press, 1994).

15 C. A. Bayly, *Empire and Information: Intelligence Gathering and Social Communication in India, 1780–1870* (Cambridge: University Press, 2000).

16 Metcalf.

17 R. J. Moore, *Churchill, Cripps, and India, 1939–1945* (Oxford: Clarendon Press, 1979).

18 Maulana Azad, *India Wins Freedom* (London: Sangam, 1988).

19 A. W. Brian Simpson, *Human Rights and the End of Empire: Britain and the Genesis of the European Convention* (Oxford: University Press, 2001).

20 Ayesha Jalal, *The Sole Spokesman: Jinnah, the Muslim League and the Demand for Pakistan* (Cambridge: University Press, 1994). See also the very useful edited work by Mushirul Hasan (ed.), *India's Partition: Process, Strategy and Mobilisation* (New Delhi: Oxford University Press, 1993).

21 See David Gilmartin, *Islam and Empire: Punjab and the Making of Pakistan* (Berkeley, CA: University of California Press, 1995).

22 Gilmartin.

23 See the final chapter of Clapham.

24 See Ayesha Jalal, *Authoritarianism and Democracy in South Asia: A Comparative and Historical Perspective* (Cambridge: University Press, 1995). Jalal seeks, perhaps too emphatically, to correct the view that India is a "success" and Pakistan a "failure."

25 See Sunil Khilnani, *The Idea of India* (London: Hamish Hamilton, 1997).

26 See R.J. Moore, *Making the New Commonwealth* (Oxford: Clarendon Press, 1987).

27 For one particular take on the Poonch rebellion, see Alistair Lamb, *Kashmir: A Disputed Legacy: 1846–1990* (Hertingfordbury: Roxford, 1991).

28 For a discussion of the Standstill Agreements and the Treaty of Accession, see Vernon Hewitt, *Reclaiming the Past? The Search for Political and Cultural Unity in Jammu and Kashmir* (London: Portland Books, 1995).

29 See Vernon Hewitt, "Ethnic Construction, Provincial Identity and Nationalism in Pakistan: The Case of Baluchistan," in Mitra and Lewis, pp. 43–67.

30 See S.R. Ashton, *British Policy Towards the Indian States, 1905–1939* (London: Curzon Press, 1982).

31 Obviously the entire narrative of the Kashmir crisis from 1947–49 is contested. For a discussion on the holding of all the plebiscites at the ending of the British Indian Empire, see Michael Brecher, *India and World Politics: Krishna Menon* (Oxford: University Press, 1959).

32 See Vernon Hewitt, "Never Ending Stories: Recent Trends in the Historiography of Jammu and Kashmir," *History Compass*, Vol. 5, No. 2 (2007), pp. 288–301.

33 Ayesha Jalal, *The State of Martial Rule: The Origins of Pakistan's Political Economy of Defence* (Cambridge: University Press, 1990).

34 Strobe Talbott, *Engaging India: Diplomacy, Democracy and the Bomb: A Memoir* (Washington, DC: Brookings, 2004).

35 Talbot, pp. 108–9.

36 Owen Bennett-Jones, *Pakistan: Eye of the Storm* (New Delhi: Viking, 2002), ch. i.

37 Bennett-Jones, pp. 27–9.

38 This was a particular concern for the British, in the wake of terrorist attacks in London in 2005, which linked British Muslims with religious seminaries and "camps" in Pakistan. See also Waheguru Pal Singh Sadu *et al.*, *Kashmir: New Voices, New Approaches* (Boulder, CO: Lynne Rienner, 2006).

39 Care needs to be taken when trying to analyze the exact reasoning for this animosity to elected politicians and parties; some has genuinely to do with corruption and incompetence. See Samina Ahmed, "The Fragile Base of Democracy in Pakistan," in Amita Shastri and A.

Jeyaratnam Wilson, *The Post-Colonial States of South Asia: Democracy, Development and Identity* (New York: Palgrave, 2001), pp. 41–68; see also Ian Talbot, *Pakistan: A Modern History* (London: Hurst, 1998), part iv.

40 See Katharine Adeney, "What Comes After Musharraf?," *Brown Journal of World Affairs*, Vol. 16, No. 1 (Fall/Winter 2007), pp. 41–49.

41 In this sense, whatever their differences, Nehru would have agreed with Jaswant Singh's rebuke to Strobe Talbott in 1997 condemning the US habit of always hyphenating India with Pakistan; Talbott, p. 85.

42 See Vernon Hewitt, *New International Politics*, ch. ii.

43 Nixon's "that bitch" statement is now pretty legendary. See Walter Isaacson, *Kissinger: A Biography* (London: Faber & Faber, 1992); also Katherine Frank, *Indira: The Life of Indira Nehru Gandhi* (London: HarperCollins, 2001), pp. 339–40.

44 The argument here was along the lines of covert "selective" proliferation (such as in the case of Israel), by the US, in defiance of the logic of the NPT.

45 Vernon Hewitt, "Creating a Common Home? Indo–Pakistan Relations and the Search for Security in South Asia," in Shastri and Wilson.

46 Jaswant Singh, *Defending India* (Basingstoke: Macmillan, 1999).

47 William Walker, "International Nuclear Relations after the Indian and the Pakistani Test Explosions," *International Affairs*, Vol. 74, No. 3 (July 1998), pp. 505–28; see also Vernon Hewitt, "Containing Shiva: India, Non-Proliferation, and the Comprehensive Test Ban Treaty," *Contemporary South Asia*, 9 (2000), pp. 25–39.

48 Confirmed by recent Indian discussions over Iranian nuclear ambitions and India's support for US sanctions.

49 See Apurba Kundu, "The NDA and National Security," in Katharine Adeney and Lawrence Sáez (eds), *Coalition Politics and Hindu Nationalism* (London: Routledge, 2005), ch. iv.

50 Kundu, p. 219.

51 See C. Mohan, *Crossing the Rubicon: The Shaping of India's New Foreign Policy* (New Delhi: Viking Press, 2003); also Dennis Kux, *Estranged Democracies: India and the United States 1941–1991* (New Delhi: Sage, 1993).

52 See Rob Jenkins, *Democratic Politics and Economic Reform in India* (Cambridge: University Press, 1999).

53 See Rob Jenkins, "The NDA and the Politics of Economic Reform," in Adeney and Sáez, pp. 173–92.

54 Cohen, p. 2.

55 See Tazeen M. Murshid, "State, Nation and Identity: The Quest for Legitimacy in Bangladesh," in Shastri and Wilson, pp. 158–82.

56 Richard Sisson and Leo Rose, *War and Secession: India, Pakistan and the Creation of Bangladesh* (Princeton, NJ: University Press, 1989). There is some evidence that Indian intervention was in part determined by radical Left movements within the civil war making common cause with the Left in West Bengal; see Tariq Ali, *Can Pakistan Survive?* (Harmondsworth: Penguin, 1983).

57 See D. Hugh Evans, "Bangladesh: South Asia's Unknown Quantity," *Asian Affairs*, 75 (1988), pp. 306–16; and D. Hugh Evans, "Bangladesh: An Unsteady Democracy," in Shastri and Wilson, pp. 69–87.

58 Much of this literature derived from Latin America and Eastern Europe. For representative application to South Asia, see John M. Richardson, Jr. and S. W. R de A. Samarasinghe (eds), *Democratisation in South Asia: The First Fifty Years* (Kandy: International Center for Ethnic Studies, 1998).

59 World Development Report, *Development and the Next Generation* (Washington, DC: World Bank, 2007).

60 See Leo E. Rose, "The National Political Culture and Institutions in Nepal," in Shastri and Wilson, pp. 114–38; also Rishikesh Shaha, *An Introduction to Nepal* (Kathmandu: RPB, 1976).

61 See Edward C. Banfield, *The Moral Basis of a Backward Society* (New York: Free Press, 1958).

62 Michael Barnett, "Sovereignty, Nationalism and the Regional Order in the Arab State System," in Biersteker and Weber, pp. 148–89.

Glossary

Adivasi Literally "original dweller," it is taken as equivalent to the English "indigenous"; some use it loosely as equivalent to Scheduled Tribe and in some places both "ST" and "Adivasi" designate the same people, but in fact usage is very varied across India: some STs either reject or are ignorant of the Adivasi label and, v.v., some who claim to be Adivasis do not have ST status.

Article 356 An emergency provision of India's constitution under which the central government can remove a state government and institute President's rule for a period up to six months on a finding by the Governor that the government of the state cannot be carried on in accordance with the provisions of the constitution. Until the mid-1990s it was often used for political purposes.

bakshish gift; gratuity

Bangla Bhai Brother of Bengal (name of an Islamic militant in Bangladesh)

Bharatiya Janata Party (BJP) Hindu nationalist party which led the National Democratic Alliance (NDA) coalition that governed India from 1999 to 2004.

bhasha formal language

bhasha ondolan Bengali language movement

boli colloquial speech

Cabinet Mission Plan An effort by the postwar Labour Government of British Prime Minister Clement Atlee to resolve the conflict between the Indian National Congress and the Muslim League and other long-standing constitutional problems that stood in the way of realizing the Labour Government's commitment to Indian independence. Its proposal of a multi-layered federal state with a weak center and strong provinces was rejected by Nehru and the Congress leadership, who wanted a strong activist state.

Center/Centre The term used throughout South Asia to refer to the central government.

Centrally Sponsored Schemes (CSS) Central government transfer of funds to the states to realize national objectives in areas allocated to the states. The funds must be utilized according to the priorities established by the central government. CSS schemes are an expanding form of central intervention that can dictate state choices with respect to subjects that are constitutionally allocated to the states.

419

Congress Party   Common alternative form of referring to the Indian National Congress, founded in 1885 to lead the nationalist movement. It was transformed in the 1920s into a mass organization by Mohandas Gandhi. At Independence in 1947 it was able to form majority governments from the first national election in 1952 until the ninth in 1989. Thereafter it has led coalition governments in 1991–1996 and 2004–2009.

CPN-M   Nepal Communist Party (Maoist), the name adopted in 1995 by one of the two factions into which the Communist Party of Nepal (Unity Centre) had split the previous year; it launched its "People's War" in February 1996; following the Second People's Movement of April 2006, it entered mainstream politics and won the largest number of votes (nearly 30 percent) in the elections of April 2008; from January 2009, having merged with another small Maoist party, it became known as the CPN-UM ("unified").

CPN-UML   Nepal Communist Party (Unified Marxist-Leninist), the main parliamentary opposition party in Nepal between 1991 and 2002, which formed a minority government on its own for nine months from 1994 to 1995 and was later a partner in coalitions; despite the name and the communist history and affiliation, it is essentially a social democratic party; came third in the elections of April 2008.

crore   ten million (10,000,000) Indian rupees

dalit   Modern term for ex-untouchables, the lowest category in the caste system, outside and below the four varnas; literally "the oppressed".

Dravida Munnetra Kazagam (DMK)   Tamil Nadu regional party lending crucial support to the United Progressive Alliance (UPA) which formed the national government in 2004.

Emergency   The authoritarian government instituted between 1975 and 1977 by Prime Minister Indira Gandhi.

Finance Commission   An autonomous, constitutionally mandated commission appointed every five years to make recommendations to the Parliament of India with respect to the distribution between the union and the state governments, as well as among the states, of how the net proceeds of taxes are to be divided.

garibi hatao   "abolish poverty." A slogan used in Indira Gandhi's election campaigning in 1971.

girijans   forest tribals

Government of India Act,1935   Enacted by the British Parliament twelve years before independence, the act continued the effort, launched in 1909 and advanced in 1919, to realize responsible government in India. It provided for a federal system, and strongly influenced the 1950 constitution of free India.

Gram Rajya Committee   village administrative committee

Halpati Seva Sangh   Halpati Service Organization

haris   laborers

hartal   general strike

Hindutva   Hinduness

hung parliament   A parliament in which no party achieves a majority of seats following a national election.

Jamaat ul-Mujahedeen Bangladesh (JMB)   Assembly of Holy Warriors of Bangladesh

Janajati   Originally a Hindi neologism coined to translate "tribe" in the 1930s, it was adopted in Nepali at the very end of the 1980s and gained currency after 1990 to refer to tribal groups in Nepal.

Jan Andolan   People's Movement (Nepal); the commonly accepted name for the revolution of 1990 that overthrew the Panchayat regime; the revolution of 2006 is known as Jan Andolan II.

jawan   Literally youth, usually for army personnel.

khadi   homespun cloth

kisan sabha   peasant association

lashkar   armed unit

Madhesi   Literally "an inhabitant of Madhes/Madhyades," it has become a highly contested new ethnic category within Nepal for inhabitants of the Nepalese Tarai who share language and cultural heritage with Indians on the other side of the border, principally castes such as Yadavs, Rajputs, and Brahmans. Other groups, such as Muslims and Tharus, have been listed as Madhesis by the Nepalese state and are claimed as Madhesis by Madhesi political parties and activists, but their own activists organized vociferously during 2009 to insist that they should be considered indigenous Tarai-dwellers and a religious minority respectively instead of Madhesis.

Magar   Largest of the Janajati groups in Nepal with a population of 1,622,399 (7.2 percent) according to the 2001 census.

mastaan   thug

matru bhasha   mother tongue (Hindi)

mohajirs   Urdu-speaking migrants

Mukti Sena   liberation army (Nepal)

National Democratic Alliance (NDA)   A coalition of 22 small and regional parties, led by the Bharatiya Janata Party (BJP), which constituted the central government from 1999 to 2004.

Nepal Sadbhawana Party   A regionalist party based in the Nepalese Tarai.

panchayat/Panchayat   (i) Literally and originally "rule of five [elders]," i.e., supposedly "traditional" local or caste councils widely found across South Asia; hence the name was adopted for (ii) democratically elected local councils, the new institutions of local self-government in India after independence; it was also adopted as (iii) the name both of specific local (village, district) and national councils and the national legislature in the period of "partyless democracy" (1960–1990) in Nepal; hence (iv) it is also used as the name of the regime and period in Nepal of that time.

panchayati raj   Literally "rule by panchayats," it is the Indian term used for local government with elected bodies (panchayats) at the levels of village (*gram*), block (*kshetra*), and district (*zilla*).

Parbatiya   Literally "hill person" (cf. Pahadia), now an ethnic term; it can be used for anyone of hill provenance, but is often used more restrictively in the Nepalese context to refer to the high castes, Bahuns and Chetris, and associated Dalit service castes, as opposed to Janajatis and Madhesis.

People's War   (*jan yuddha*) The name given by the Maoists to their insurgency, begun in Nepal in 1996.

pracharak   Whole-time party worker (term especially used by the RSS).

President's Rule   Imposition of rule of a state government in India by an appointee of the central government, as authorized by article 356 of the Constitution of India.

Quaid-i-Azam   Great leader, always in reference to Mohammad Ali Jinnah.

Rajya Sabha   Council of States; upper house of the Indian parliament; represents the states of India's federal system on the basis of population.

Rana   Surname assumed by the family (previously named Kunwar) who provided the hereditary prime ministers of Nepal from 1845–1951; hence the name of the period of Nepalese history when the Shah kings were reduced to figureheads without real power.

RPP   Rashtriya Prajatantra Party a.k.a. Nepal Democratic Party (post-1990 Nepal): rightist party led by prominent politicians who had participated in the Panchayat regime.

RSS   Rashtriya Swayamsevak Sangh or National Volunteers Association, founded in 1925 by K.B. Hedgewar as a national movement of Hindus for social welfare; RSS members were involved in the murder of Gandhi and the RSS was banned for a year thereafter.

safarish   Friendship and pleading on behalf of someone.

Sangh Parivar   The "family" of associations pursuing Hindu cultural nationalism.

Sanskritization   Term introduced by Indian anthropologist M.N. Srinivas to label the process of attempted upward group mobility through imitation of the "purer" Brahmanical customs (e.g., banning widow remarriage, alcohol, meat-eating) by lower-ranked castes.

Sarkaria Commission   Appointed in 1983 by Indira Gandhi, to ward off mounting pressure to strengthen the federal system, it reported in 1988. Prime Minister V.P. Singh made an effort to implement many of its recommendations in 1990, but his government fell before being able to do so.

Scheduled Castes (SC)   Official Indian term for those formerly untouchable castes placed on a schedule that entitles members of the caste to preference in admission to educational institutions and in government jobs, and other positions, i.e., positive discrimination.

Scheduled Tribes (ST)   Official Indian term for those tribal groups placed on the "schedule" and entitled to "reservations," i.e., positive discrimination.

Shiv Sena   Literally "the army of Shiva" (i.e. Shivaji): a political party founded by Bal Thackeray in 1966, it has ruled Mumbai for the last twenty years on a Mumbai for Maharashtrians platform; it is often in alliance with the BJP.

Special Economic Zones   Enclaves of land owned by big industrial houses, allotted to them by government for purchase at well-below market prices, along with tax waivers and other concessions.

tadbir   connections

Tarai (Terai)   Strip of Gangetic plains territory belonging to Nepal and bordering India, now home to half the Nepalese population; the term is also used for the territories on the Indian side of the border, usually not capitalized, and commonly referring to previously marshy, mosquito-ridden (and, therefore, malarial) land.

Telugu Desam (TDP)   The Andhra Pradesh regional party which lent crucial support to the BJP-led National Democratic Alliance (NDA) between 1999 and 2004.

VHP   Vishwa Hindu Parishad or World Hindu Council, founded in 1964, with the involvement of the RSS; ostensibly non-political, its aim is "to promote Hindu values"; it pressurizes the BJP and acts in concert with the RSS (e.g., over the Ramjanam Bhumi/Ayodhya mosque issue) and campaigns for the "re-conversion" of Muslims and Christians.

yatra   procession

Bibliography

Abbas, Sohail. *Probing the Jihadi Mind*. Islamabad: National Book Foundation, 2007.

Adams, Vincanne. *Doctors for Democracy: Health Professionals in the Nepal Revolution*. Cambridge: University Press, 1998.

Adeney, Katharine. "What Comes after Musharraf?," *Brown Journal of World Affairs*, Vol. 6, No. 1 (Fall/Winter 2007), pp. 41–9.

Adeney, Katharine. *Federalism and Ethnic Conflict Regulation in India and Pakistan*. New York: Palgrave Macmillan, 2007.

Afzal, Rafiq. *Political Parties in Pakistan: 1947–1958*. Islamabad: National Institute of Historical and Cultural Studies, 1998.

Aggarwal, S. *Three Language Formula: An Educational Problem*. New Delhi: Gian, 1991.

Agnihotri, R. K. "Identity and Multilinguality: The Case of India," in Amy B. Tsui and James Tollefson (eds), *Language Policy, Culture, and Identity in Asian Contexts*. Mahwah, NJ: Erlbaum, 2007.

Agrawal, Arun. "The Indian Parliament," in Devesh Kapur and Pratap Bhanu Mehta (eds), *Public Institutions in India: Performance and Design*. Delhi: Oxford University Press, 2005.

Ahluwalia, Isher J. and Wahiduddin Mahmud (eds). "Economic Transformation and Social Development in Bangladesh," *Economic Political Weekly*, Vol. 39, No. 36 (4 September, 2004), pp. 4,009–52.

Ahmad Khan, Hussain. *Re-thinking Punjab: The Construction of Siraiki Identity*. Lahore: National College of the Arts, 2004.

Ahmadi, A. M. "Federalism Revisited," in Pran Chopra, *The Supreme Court versus the Constitution: A Challenge to Federalism*. New Delhi: Sage, 2006.

Ahmed, Feroz. *Ethnicity and Politics in Pakistan*. Karachi: Oxford University Press, 1998.

Ahmed, Feroz. *Ethnicity and Politics in Pakistan*. Karachi: Oxford University Press, 1999.

Ahmed, Ishtiaq. "The Concept of an Islamic State." Ph.D. dissertation, University of Stockholm; published by Edsbruk, 1985.

Ahmed, Ishtiaq. *State, Nation and Ethnicity in Contemporary South Asia*. London and New York: Pinter, 1996.

Ahmed, Munirm. *From Jinnah to Zia*. Lahore: Vanguard, 1980.

Ahmed, N. and Sheikh Z. Ahmad, "The Parliamentary Elections in Bangladesh, October 2001," *Electoral Studies*, Vol. 22, No. 3 (2003), pp. 503–9.

Ahmed, Naimuddin. "The Problems of the Independence of the Judiciary in Bangladesh," in Bangladesh Institute of Law and International Affairs (BILIA), *Human Rights in Bangladesh: A Study of Standards and Practices*. Dhaka: BILIA, 2001.

Ahmed, Nizam. "Bangladesh," in Dieter Nohlen, Florian Grotz and Christof Hartmann (eds), *Elections in Asia and the Pacific: A Data Handbook*, Vol. 1: *Middle East, Central Asia, and South Asia*. New York: Oxford University Press, 2001, pp. 515–52.

Ahmed, Nizam. "From Monopoly to Competition: Party Politics in the Bangladesh Parliament (1973–2001)," *Pacific Affairs*, Vol. 76, No. 1 (2003), pp. 55–77.

Ahmed, Raisuddin. "Rice Economy of Bangladesh: Progress and Prospects," *Economic and Political Weekly*, Vol. 39, No. 36 (4 September, 2004), pp. 4,043–52.

Ahmed, Raisuddin, Steven Haggblade and Tawfiq-e-Elahi Chowdhury (eds), *Out of the Shadow of Famine: Evolving Food Markets and Food Policy in Bangladesh*. Baltimore, MD: Johns Hopkins University Press, 2000.

Ahmed, Samina. "The Fragile Base of Democracy in Pakistan," in Amita Shastri and A. Jeyaratnam Wilson (eds), *The Post-colonial States of South Asia: Democracy, Development and Identity*. New York: Palgrave, 2001, pp. 41–68.

Alailima, Patricia. "Social Policy in Sri Lanka," in W. D. Lakshman (ed.), *Dilemmas of Development: Fifty Years of Economic Change in Sri Lanka*. Colombo: Sri Lanka Association of Economists, 1997.

Alailima, Patricia. "The Human Development Perspective," in W. D. Lakshman and C. A. Tisdell (eds), *Sri Lanka's Development since Independence: Socio-economic Perspectives and Analyses*. New York: Nova Science, 2000.

Alam, Javeed. *Who Wants Democracy?* Delhi: Orient Longman, 2004.

Alam, Muzaffar. *The Crisis of Empire in Mughal North India: Awadh and the Punjab, 1707–1748*. Delhi: Oxford University Press, 1986.

Alam, S. M. Nurul. *Whose Public Action? Analysing Inter-sectoral Collaboration for Service Delivery*. Dhaka: International Development Department, 2007. Available at: http://www.idd.bham.ac.uk/service-providers/downloads/Bangladesh History.pdf (accessed 12 August, 2007).

Alavi, Hamza. "Pakistan and Islam: Ethnicity and Ideology," in Fred Halliday and Hamza Alavi (eds), *State and Ideology in the Middle East and Pakistan*. London: Macmillan, and New York: Monthly Review Press, 1987.

Alavi, Hamza. "Politics of Ethnicity in Pakistan," *Pakistan Progressive*, Vol. 9, No. 1 (Summer 1987), pp. 4–25.

Alavi, Hamza. "Authoritarianism and Legitimacy of State Power in Pakistan," in Subrata Mitra (ed.), *The Postcolonial State in South Asia*. London: Harvester Wheatsheaf, 1990.

Alavi, Hamza and John Harriss (eds). *Sociology of Developing Societies*. London: Macmillan, 1989.

Albright, David. "India's Military Plutonium Inventory, End 2004," Institute for Science and International Security, 7 May, 2005.

Ali, Chaudhri Muhammad. *The Emergence of Pakistan*. New York: Columbia University Press, 1967.

Ali, Fazal *et al. Report of the States Linguistic Reorganization Commission*. New Delhi: Government of India, 1955.

Ali, Imran. *The Punjab under Imperialism, 1885–1947*. Princeton, NJ: University Press, 1988.

Ali, Tariq. *Can Pakistan Survive?* Harmondsworth: Penguin, 1983.

All India Judges' Association v Union of India (2002) 4 SCC 247.

Amarasinghe, Y. Ranjith. *Revolutionary Idealism and Parliamentary Politics: A Study of Trotskyism in Sri Lanka*. Colombo: Social Scientists Association, 1998.

Ambedkar, B. R. *Thoughts on Linguistic States*. Bombay: Popular Prakashan, 1955.

Amin, Tahir. *Ethno-national Movements of Pakistan: Domestic and International Factors*. Islamabad: Institute of Policy Studies, 1988.

Amnesty International. *India: Torture, Rape, and Death in Custody*. London: Amnesty International, 1992.

Anand, S. "Sanskrit, English and Dalits," *Economic and Political Weekly*, Vol. 34, No. 30 (24 July, 1999), pp. 2,053–56.

Anderson, Benedict. *Imagined Communities: Reflections on the Origin and Spread of Nationalism*. London and New York: Verso, 1983.

Anderson, Perry. *Lineages of the Absolutist State*. London: New Left Books, 1974.

Annamalai, E. "Language Choice in Education: Conflict Resolution in Indian Courts," *Language Science*, Vol. 20, No. 1 (1998), pp. 29–43.

Annamalai, E. *Managing Multilingualism in India: Political and Linguistic Manifestations*. New Delhi: Sage, 2001.

Annamalai, E. "Medium of Power: The Question of English in Education," in James W. Tollefson and Amy B. M. Tsui (eds), *Medium of Instruction Policies: Which Agenda? Whose Agenda?* Mahwah, NJ: Lawrence Erlbaum Associates, 2004.

Annual Report of the Sindh Provincial Muslim League for 1943–4, Shamsul Hasan Collection 1:24 (private collection held in Karachi).

Anonymous. "Is the Union Budget a Federal Budget?," *Economic and Political Weekly*, Vol. 43, No. 10 (8 March, 2008), p. 5.

Ansari, Massoud. "Between Tribe and Country," *Himal* (Kathmandu), Vol. 20, No. 5 (May 2007).

Ansari, Sarah. *Life after Partition: Migration, Community and Strife in Sindh 1947–1962.* Karachi: Oxford University Press, 2005.

Arab Ahmadhia Abdulla v *Arab Bail Humuna Saiyadbhai*, AIA (1988) Guj 141.

Arasaratnam, Sinnappah. Review of *Sri Lanka: From Dominion to Republic*, by Lucy M. Jacob, *Pacific Affairs*, Vol. 47, No. 4 (Winter 1974–75), pp. 567–8.

Ashton, S. R. *British Policy towards the Indian States, 1905–1939.* London: Curzon Press, 1982.

Associates in Rural Development (ARD). *Bangladesh: Knowledge, Attitudes and Practices: National Survey Covering Democracy and Governance Issues.* Burlington, VT: ARD, for USAID/Bangladesh, 2004.

Austin, Granville. *The Indian Constitution.* Oxford: Clarendon Press, 1966.

Austin, Granville. *Working a Democratic Constitution: The Indian Experience.* Oxford: University Press, 1999.

Azad, Maulana. *India Wins Freedom.* London: Sangam Books, 1988.

Bailey, Frederick G. "Politics and Society in Contemporary Orissa," in Cyril Phillips (ed.), *Politics and Society in India.* London: Allen & Unwin, 1963.

Bailey, Sydney D. *Far Eastern Survey*, Vol. 17, No. 21 (3 November, 1948), pp. 251–54.

Bakht, Farid. "Army Entrenches Itself in Bangladesh," *Economic and Political Weekly*, Vol. 42, No. 29 (21 July, 2007), pp. 2991–92.

Balagopal, K. "Kashmir: Self-Determination, Communal and Democratic Rights," *Economic and Political Weekly*, 2 November, 1997, pp. 2,916–21.

Balasingham, Anton. *War and Peace in Sri Lanka: Armed Struggle and Peace Efforts of Liberation Tigers.* Mitcham, UK: Fairmax, 2004.

Banavar, Pavithra and Nicholas Howenstein. "The Future of Democracy in Bangladesh," USI Peace Briefing, United States Institute of Peace, Washington, DC, March 2007.

Bandaranaike v *Weeraratne* (1981) 1 SLR 10.

Bandhua Mukti Morcha v *Union of India* (1984) 3 SCC 161.

Banerjee, Abhijit. "The Paradox of Indian Growth: A Comment on Kochar *et al.*," Mimeo, MIT, 2006. Available at www.mit.edu/faculty/download_pdf.php?id+1340.

Banerjee, Aloke. *Inside MCC Country.* Calcutta: K. Das, 2003.

Banerjee, Mukulika. *The Pathan Unarmed.* Oxford: James Currey, 2000.

Banerjee, Sumanta. *In the Wake of Naxalbari.* Calcutta: Subarnarekha, 1980.

Banfield, Edward C. *The Moral Basis of a Backward Society.* New York: Free Press, 1958.

Bangladesh, cases, *Aftabuddin* v *Bangladesh* 48 (1996) DLR HCD 1.

Bangladesh, cases, *Aftabuddin* v *Habibul Awal*, Writ Petition No. 6219 of 2007, judgment dated 18 February, 2007.

Bangladesh, cases, *Anwar Hossain Chowdhury* v *Bangladesh, Jalaluddin* v *Bangladesh, Ibrahim Shaikh* v *Bangladesh* (1989) BLD (1) Special.

Bangladesh, cases, *Bangladesh* v *Idrisur Rahman* (1999) BLD (AD) 1.

Bangladesh, cases, *Commissioner of Taxes* v *Justice S. Ahmed* 42 DLR (AD) 163 (exemption of Supreme Court judge's salary from payment of tax).

Bangladesh, cases, *Dr. Ahmed Hossain* v *Shamsul Huq Chowdhury* 48 DLR 155.

Bangladesh, cases, *Idrisur Rahman* v *Bangladesh* (1999) BLD 29.

Bangladesh, cases, *Idrisur Rahman* v *Bangladesh*, Writ Petition No. 1543 of 2003.

Bangladesh, cases, *Idrisur Rahman* v *Secretary, Minister of Law, Justice and Parliamentary Affairs*, Writ Petition No. 1543 of 2003, judgment dated 17 July, 2008.

Bangladesh, cases, *Masdar Hossain* v *Bangladesh* (2000) BLD (AD) 104 Per Mostafa Kamal J.

Bangladesh, cases, *Maulvi Tamizuddin Khan* v *The Federation of Pakistan*, PLD (1955) Sind 96.

Bangladesh, cases, *Md. Idrisur Rahman* v *Bangladesh and Others*, Writ Petition No. 3228 of 2008.

Bangladesh, cases, *Secretary, Ministry of Finance* v *Md. Masdar Hossain and Others*, 20 BLD (2000) (AD) 141.

Bangladesh Judicial Service Code of Criminal Procedure (Amendment) Ordinance 2007.

Bangladesh Judicial Service Commission Rules, 2004 (notified on 28 January, 2004).

Bangladesh Judicial Service (Pay Commission) Rules 2007.

Bangladesh Judicial Service (Posting, Promotion, Leave, Control, Discipline and Other Service Conditions) Rules 2007.

Bangladesh Judicial Service (Service Constitution, Composition, Recruitment and Suspension, Dismissal and Removal) Rules 2007.

Baral, Lok Raj. *Oppositional Politics in Nepal.* New Delhi: Abhinav Publishing House, 1977.

425

Baral, Lok Raj. *Nepal: Problems of Governance.* New Delhi: Konark Publishers, 1993.

Baral, Lok Raj. *The Regional Paradox: Essays in Nepali and South Asian Affairs.* Delhi: Adroit, 2000.

Baral, Lok Raj, Krishna Hachhethu and Hari Sharma. *Leadership in Nepal.* New Delhi: Adroit, 2001.

Bardhan, Pranab. *The Political Economy of Development in India.* Oxford: Blackwell, 1984.

Bardhan, Pranab. *The Political Economy of Development in India,* 2nd edition. Delhi: Oxford University Press, 1998.

Barlas, Asma. *Democracy, Nationalism and Communalism: The Colonial Legacy in South Asia.* Boulder, CO: Westview, 1995.

Barnett, Michael. "Sovereignty, Nationalism and Regional Order in the Arab State System," in Thomas J. Biersteker and Cynthia Weber (eds), *State Sovereignty: A Social Construct.* Cambridge: University Press, 1996, pp. 148–89.

Barnett, Michael. "Historical Sociology and Constructivism: An Estranged Past, a Federated Future?," in Stephen Hobden and John M. Hobson, *Historical Sociology of International Relations.* Cambridge: University Press, 2002, pp. 99–119.

Bastian, Sunil. *Ideology and the Constitution.* Colombo: International Centre for Ethnic Studies, 1996.

Bastian, Sunil. "Foreign Aid, Globalization and Conflict in Sri Lanka," in Markus Mayer, Darini Rajasingham-Senanayake and Yuvi Thangarajah (eds), *Building Local Capacities for Peace: Rethinking Conflict and Development in Sri Lanka.* Delhi: Macmillan, 2003.

Bastian, Sunil. *The Politics of Foreign Aid in Sri Lanka: Promoting Markets and Supporting Peace.* Colombo: International Center for Ethnic Studies, 2007.

Baviskar, Amita. *In the Belly of the River: Tribal Conflicts over Development in the Narmada Valley.* New Delhi: Oxford University Press, 1995.

Baxi, Upendra. "Taking Suffering Seriously: Social Action Litigation in the Supreme Court of India," in Rajeev Dhavan, R. Sudarshan and Salman Khurshid (eds), *Judges and the Judicial Power.* Bombay: Tripathi, 1985.

Baxi, Upendra. "The Rule of Law in India," *SUR— Revista Internacional de Direitos Humanos,* Vol. 6, No. 4 (2007), pp. 6–27.

Baxter, Craig. *Bangladesh: From a Nation to a State.* Boulder, CO: Westview Press, 1997.

Bayes, Abdul. "Beneath the Surface: Why Is the Price of Rice So High?," *Daily Star,* 24 August, 2008.

Bayly, C. A. *Rulers, Townsmen and Bazaars: North Indian Society in the Age of British Expansion, 1770–1780.* Cambridge: University Press, 1983.

Bayly, Christopher Alan. *Empire and Information: Intelligence Gathering and Social Information in India, 1780–1870.* New York: Cambridge University Press, 1996.

Bayly, Christopher. *Origins of Nationality in South Asia.* Delhi: Oxford University Press, 1998.

Beames, John. *Memoirs of a Bengal Civilian.* London: Eland, 2003 [1961].

Begum Nusrat Bhutto v The Chief of Army Staff and Federation of Pakistan, PLD (1974) Lahore 7.

Belge, Ceren. "Friends of the Court: The Republican Alliance and Selective Activism of the Constitutional Court of Turkey," *Law and Society Review,* Vol. 40, No. 3 (2006), pp. 653–92.

Benazir Bhutto v Federation of Pakistan and Another, PLD (1988) Supreme Court 416.

Benazir Bhutto v Federation of Pakistan and Another, PLD (1989) Supreme Court 66.

Bendix, Reinhard. *Kings or People: Power and the Mandate to Rule.* Berkeley: University of California Press, 1978.

Bennett-Jones, Owen. *Pakistan: Eye of the Storm.* New Delhi: Viking, 2002.

Besley, Tim, Robin Burgess and Berta Esteve-Volart. "Operationalising Pro-Poor Growth: A Country Case Study on India," Mimeo, Working Paper of Department of Economics, London School of Economics, 2004. Available at: www.lse.ac.uk/collections/LSEIndia/pdf/propoor growth.pdf.

Béteille, André. *Caste, Class and Power: Changing Patterns of Stratification in a Tanjore Village.* Berkeley: University of California Press, (1965).

Béteille, André. *Castes: Old and New.* Bombay: Asia Publishing House, 1969.

Béteille, André. *The Backward Classes in Contemporary India.* New Delhi: Oxford University Press, 1992.

Bhagwati, Jagdish. *India in Transition: Freeing the Economy.* Oxford: Clarendon Press, 1993.

Bhaurao Lokhande v State of Maharashtra, AIA (1965) SC 1564.

Bhushan, Prashant. "Judicial Accountability or Illusion?," *Economic and Political Weekly,* Vol. 61, No. 47 (25 November, 2006), pp. 4,847–48.

Biplabi Yug. *New People's Power in Dandakaranya.* Calcutta: Biplabi Yug, 2000.

Blair, Harry. "Sheikh Mujib and Déjà Vu in East Bengal: The Tragedies of 25 March," *Economic and Political Weekly,* Vol. 6, No. 52 (25 December 1971), pp. 2,555–62.

Blair, Harry. "Politics, Civil Society and Governance in Bangladesh," in Rounaq Jahan (ed.), *Bangladesh: Promise and Performance*. London: Zed Books, and Dhaka: University Press, 2000, pp. 181–217.

Blair, Harry. "Civil Society and Pro-poor Initiatives at the Local Level in Bangladesh: Finding a Workable Strategy," *World Development*, Vol. 33, No. 6 (2005), pp. 921–36.

Blair, Harry, Robert Charlick, Rezaul Haque, Manzoor Hasan and Nazmul Lalimullah. *Democracy and Governance: Strategic Assessment of Bangladesh*, Report for USAID/Bangladesh. Burlington, VT: ARD, October 2004.

Borre, Ole, Sushil Raj Pandey and Chitra Krishna Tiwari. *Nepalese Political Behaviour*. New Delhi: Sterling, 1994.

Bose, Ashish. "Beyond Population Projections: Growing North–South Disparity," *Economic and Political Weekly*, Vol. 42, No.15 (14 April, 2007), pp. 1,327–29.

Bose, Sumantra. *Kashmir: Roots of Conflict, Path to Peace*. Cambridge, MA and London: Harvard University Press, 2003.

Bourdieu, Pierre. *Language and Symbolic Power*, trans. Gino Raymond and Matthew Adamson. Cambridge: Polity, 1992.

Boustany, Nora. "Bombings Force Bangladesh Envoy Home," *Washington Post*, 19 August, 2005.

Brass, Paul R. "Party Systems and Government Stability in the Indian States," *American Political Science Review*, Vol. 71, No. 4 (December 1977).

Brass, Paul R. *Caste, Faction, and Party in Indian Politics*, Vol. II: *Election Studies*. New Delhi: Chanakya, 1985.

Brass, Paul R. *The Politics of India since Independence*. Cambridge: University Press, 1990.

Brass, Paul R. *Ethnicity and Nationalism: Theory and Comparison*. New Delhi: Sage, 1991.

Brass, Paul R. "Pluralism, Regionalism and Decentralizing Tendencies in Contemporary Indian Politics," in A. Jeyaratnam Wilson and Dennis Dalton (eds), *The States of South Asia: Problems of National Integration*. London: Hurst, 1982, pp. 223–64; updated in Paul R. Brass, *Ethnicity and Nationalism: Theory and Comparison*. New Delhi and Newbury Park, CA: Sage, 1991.

Brass, Paul R. *The Politics of India since Independence*, 2nd edition. Cambridge: University Press, 1994.

Brass, Paul R. *The Production of Hindu–Muslim Violence in Contemporary India*. Seattle: University of Washington Press, 2003.

Brass, Paul R. "Development of an Institutionalised Riot System in Meerut City, 1961 to 1982," *Economic and Political Weekly*, Vol. 39, No. 44 (30 October, 2004), pp. 4,839–48.

Brass, Paul R. *Language, Religion and Politics in North India*. Cambridge: University Press, 1974; reprint edition, Lincoln, NE: iUniverse, 2005.

Brecher, Michael. *India and World Politics: Krishna Menon*. Oxford: University Press, 1959.

Breman, Jan. "Mobilisation of Landless Labourers: Halpatis of South Gujarat," *Economic and Political Weekly*, Vol. 9, No. 12 (23 March, 1974), pp. 489–96.

Breman, Jan. *Patronage and Exploitation: Changing Agrarian Relations in South Gujarat*. Berkeley: University of California Press, 1974.

Breman, Jan. *Peasants, Migrants and Paupers: Capitalist Production and Labour Circulation in West India*. Oxford: Clarendon Press, and Delhi: Oxford University Press, 1985.

Breman, Jan. *Wage Hunters and Gatherers*. Delhi: Oxford University Press, 1994.

Breman, Jan. *Footloose Labour: Working in India's Informal Economy*. Cambridge: University Press, 1996.

Breman, Jan. "The Study of Indian Industrial Labour in Post-colonial India," in Jonathan Parry *et al.* (eds), *The World of Industrial Labourers in India*. New Delhi: Sage, 2002.

Breman, Jan. *The Labouring Poor in India*. Delhi and Oxford: University Press, 2003.

Breman, Jan. "Return of Social Inequality: A Fashionable Doctrine," *Economic and Political Weekly*, Vol. 39, No. 35 (28 August, 2004), pp. 3,869–72.

Breman, Jan. *Labour Bondage in West India: From Past to Present*. Delhi: Oxford University Press, 2007.

Breman, Jan. *The Poverty Regime in Village India: Half a Century of Working and Life at the Bottom of the Rural Economy in South Gujarat*. Delhi: Oxford University Press, 2007.

Brown, Judith M. *Gandhi's Rise to Power: Indian Politics, 1915–1922*. Cambridge: University Press, 1972.

Brown, Judith M. *Modern India: The Origins of an Asian Democracy*. Oxford: University Press, 1994.

Brown, Judith M. *Modern India: The Origins of an Asian Democracy*, 2nd edition. Oxford: University Press, 1995.

Brown, Michael E. and Sumit Ganguly. "Introduction," in Michael E. Brown and Sumit Ganguly (eds), *Government Policies and Ethnic*

Relations in Asia and the Pacific. Cambridge, MA: MIT Press, 1997.

Brown, T. Louise. *The Challenge to Democracy in Nepal: A Political History.* London: Routledge, 1996.

Burki, Shahid Javed. *Pakistan under Bhutto, 1971–77.* London: Macmillan, and New York: St. Martin's, 1980.

Burki, Shahid Javed. *Pakistan: A Nation in the Making.* Boulder, CO: Westview, 1983.

Burki, Shahid Javed and Craig Baxter. *Pakistan under the Military: Eleven Years of Zia ul-Haq.* Boulder, CO: Westview, 1991.

Butalia, Urvashi. *The Other Side of Silence: Voices from the Partition of India.* New Delhi: Penguin, 1998.

Byres, Terrence *et al.* (eds), Special issue on rural labour, *Journal of Peasant Studies,* Vol. 26, Nos. 2–3 (1999).

Cameron, Charles M. "Judicial Independence: How Can You Tell It When You See It? And, Who Cares?," in Stephen B. Burbank and Barry Friedman (eds), *Judicial Independence at the Crossroads: An Interdisciplinary Approach.* Thousand Oaks, CA: Sage, 2002.

Centre for the Study of Developing Societies. *State of Democracy in South Asia: A Report.* Delhi: Oxford University Press, 2008.

Chadda, Maya. *Ethnicity, Security and Separatism in India.* New York: Columbia University Press, 1997.

Chakrabarty, Prafulla. *The Marginal Men: The Refugees and the Left Political Syndrome in West Bengal.* Kalyani: Lumière Books, 1990.

Chanda, Ashok. *Federalism in India: A Study of Union–State Relations.* London: Oxford University Press, 1966.

Chandra, Kanchan. *Why Ethnic Parties Succeed: Patronage and Ethnic Head Counts in India.* Cambridge: University Press, 2004.

Chari, P. R., Pervaiz Iqbal Cheema and Stephen P. Cohen. *Four Crises and a Peace Process: American Engagement in South Asia.* Washington, DC: Brookings Institution Press, 2007.

Chatterjee, Partha. *A Possible World: Essays in Political Criticism.* New Delhi: Oxford University Press, 1977.

Chatterjee, Partha. *The Nation and its Fragments: Colonial and Postcolonial Histories.* Princeton, NJ: University Press, 1993.

Chatterjee, Partha. *Nationalist Thought and the Colonial World.* New Delhi: Oxford University Press, 1998.

Chatterjee, Partha. *The Politics of the Governed: Reflections on Popular Politics in Most of the World.* New York: Columbia University Press, 2004.

Chauhan, R. S. *The Political Development in Nepal 1950–70: Conflict between Tradition and Modernity.* New Delhi: Associated Publishing House, 1971.

Chen, S. and Martin Ravallion. "The Developing World is Poorer than we Thought, but no less Successful in the Fight against Poverty." World Bank, Policy Research Working Paper 4703, 2008.

Chhibber, Pradeep and John R. Petrocik. "Social Cleavages, Elections, and the Indian Party System," in Richard Sisson and Ramashray Roy (eds), *Diversity and Dominance in Indian Politics,* Vol. 1. New Delhi: Sage, 1990.

Chiriyankandath, James. "Bounded Nationalism: Kerala and the Social and Regional Limits of Hindutva," in Thomas Blom Hansen and Christophe Jaffrelot (eds), *The BJP and the Compulsions of Politics in India.* Delhi: Oxford University Press, 1998.

Chiriyankandath, James and Andrew Wyatt. "The NDA and Indian Foreign Policy," in Katharine Adeney and Lawrence Sáez (eds), *Coalition Politics and Hindu Nationalism.* London: Routledge, 2005, pp. 193–212.

Chopra, Pran. *The Supreme Court v. the Constitution.* New Delhi: Sage, 2001.

Choudhary, Sujit and Claire E. Hunter. "Measuring Judicial Activism on the Supreme Court of Canada: A Comment on Newfoundland (Treasury Board) v. Nape," *McGill Law Journal,* Vol. 48 (2003).

Clapham, Christopher. *Africa and the International System: The Politics of State Survival.* Cambridge: University Press, 1996.

Cmd 3131, Command papers 3131. *Ceylon: Report of the Special Commission on the Constitution of Ceylon,* July 1928. London: His Majesty's Stationery Office, 1928.

Code of Criminal Procedure (Bangladesh), 1898.

Code of Criminal Procedure (East Pakistan Amendment) Act (Act XXXVI of 1957). Hamoodur Rahman Law Commission 1967–1970.

Cohen, Craig and Derek Chollet. "When $10 Billion Is Not Enough: Rethinking U.S. Strategy toward Pakistan," *Washington Quarterly,* Vol. 30, No. 2 (2007), pp. 7–19.

Cohen, Stephen P. *The Indian Army: Its Contribution to the Development of a Nation*, revised edition. New Delhi: Oxford University Press, 1990.

Cohen, Stephen P. *The Pakistan Army*. Berkeley: University of California Press, 1984, and Karachi: Oxford University Press, 1992; revised edition 1998.

Cohen, Stephen P. *The Idea of Pakistan*. New Delhi: Oxford University Press, 2004, Washington, DC: Brookings Institution Press, 2004 and Lahore: Vanguard, 2005.

Cohen, Stephen P. and Sunil Dasgupta. *Indian Military Modernization*. Washington, DC: Brookings Institution Press, forthcoming.

Cohn, Bernard S. "The Command of Language and the Language of Command," in Ranajit Guha (ed.), *Subaltern Studies IV: Writings on South Asian History and Society*. Delhi: Oxford University Press, 1988.

Coll, Steve. *Ghost Wars: The Secret History of the CIA, Afghanistan, and Bin Laden, from the Soviet Invasion to 10 September, 2001*. New York: Penguin, 2004.

Committee for History of Andhra Movement. *History of Andhra Movement* (2 vols.). Hyderabad: Government of Andhra Pradesh, 1985.

Committee of Concerned Citizens. *Third Report, 1997–2002*. Hyderabad: S. R. Sankaran, 2002.

Coomaraswamy, Radhika. *Sri Lanka: The Crisis of Anglo-American Constitutional Traditions in a Developing Society*. New Delhi: Vikas, 1984.

Coomaraswamy, R. "Devolution, the Law, and Judicial Construction," in Sunil Bastian (ed.), *Devolution and Development*. Colombo: International Centre for Ethnic Studies, 1994.

Coomaraswamy, Radhika and Neelan Tiruchelvam. *The Role of the Judiciary in Plural Societies*. Delhi: Palgrave Macmillan, 1987.

Coppedge, Michael. *Strong Parties and Lame Ducks: Presidential Partyarchy and Factionalism in Venezuela*. Stanford, CA: University Press, 1994.

Corbridge, Stuart and John Harriss. *Reinventing India: Liberalization, Hindu Nationalism and Popular Democracy*. Cambridge: Polity Press, 2000.

Corbridge, Stuart, Glyn Williams, Manoj Srivastava and René Véron. *Seeing the State: Governance and Governmentality in India*. Cambridge: University Press, 2005.

Coupland, Reginald. *The Indian Problem* [in three parts]. New York: Oxford University Press, 1944.

CPI (Maoist), Central Committee (P), *Party Programme*, 2004.

Crystal, David. *Language Death*. Cambridge: University Press, 2000.

Dalrymple, William. *The White Mughals: Love and Betrayal in Eighteenth Century India*. New Delhi: Penguin, 2002.

Damas, Marius. *Approaching Naxalbari*. Calcutta: Radical Impression, 1991.

Dandekar, V. M. and Nilkanth Rath. "Poverty in India: Dimensions and Trends," *Economic and Political Weekly*, Vol. VI, No. 1 (2 January, 1971), pp. 25–48, 106–46.

Daniel, E. Valentine. *Charred Lullabies: Chapters in an Anthropography of Violence*. Princeton, NJ: University Press, and New Delhi: Oxford University Press, 1997.

Das, Gobind. "The Supreme Court: An Overview," in B. N. Kirpal, Ashok H. Desai, Gopal Subramanium, Rajeev Dhavan and Raju Ramachandran (eds), *Supreme but not Infallible: Essays in Honour of the Supreme Court of India*. New Delhi: Oxford University Press, 2000.

Das, Gurcharan. *India Unbound: The Social and Economic Revolution from Independence to the Global Information Age*. New York: Anchor, 2002.

Dasgupta, Biplab. *The Naxalite Movement*. New Delhi: Allied, 1973.

Dasgupta, Jyotirindra. *Language Conflict and National Development*. Berkeley and London: University of California Press, 1970.

Dasgupta, Jyotirindra. "Democracy, Development and Federalism: Some Implications of Constructive Constitutionalism in India," in Subrata K. Mitra and Ditmar Rothermund (eds), *Legitimacy and Conflict in South Asia*. New Delhi: Manohar, 1997, pp. 82–103.

Deaton, Angus and Jean Drèze. "Poverty and Inequality in India: A Re-examination," *Economic and Political Weekly*, Vol. 37, No. 36 (7 September, 2002), pp. 3,729–48.

Deaton, Angus and Valerie Kozel (eds) *The Great Indian Poverty Debate*. Delhi: Macmillan, 2005.

De Long, Bradford. "India since Independence: An Analytical Growth Narrative," in Dani Rodrik (ed.), *In Search of Prosperity: Analytic Narratives on Economic Growth*. Princeton, NJ: University Press, 2003, pp. 184–204.

De Mel, Neloufer. *Militarizing Sri Lanka: Popular Culture, Memory and Narrative in the Armed Conflict*. New Delhi: Sage, 2007.

Deshmukh, B. G. *From Poona to the Prime Minister's Office: A Cabinet Secretary Looks Back*. New Delhi: HarperCollins and India Today, 2004.

De Silva, C. R. "The Independence of the Judiciary under the Second Republic of Sri Lanka, 1978–88." Unpublished paper presented at the Eleventh Conference of the International Association of Historians of Asia, Colombo, 1–5 August, 1988.

de Silva, K. M. (ed.). *History of Ceylon*, Vol. III. Colombo: Colombo Apothecaries, 1973.

de Silva, K. M. "Sri Lanka: D. S. Senanayake and the Passage to Dominion Status, 1942–1947," *Sri Lanka Journal of Social Sciences*, Vol. 3, No. 2 (December 1980), pp. 1–14.

de Silva, K. M. (ed.), *British Documents on the End of Empire: Sri Lanka. Part II. Towards Independence (Series B: Volume 2) 1945–1948.* London: Institute for Commonwealth Studies, 1997.

de Silva, K. M. *Reaping the Whirlwind: Ethnic Conflict and Ethnic Politics in Sri Lanka.* New Delhi: Penguin, 1998.

de Silva, K. M. "Ivor Jennings and Sri Lanka's Passage to Independence," in K. M. de Silva (ed.), *Sri Lanka's Troubled Inheritance.* Kandy: International Centre for Ethnic Studies, 2007, pp. 97–117.

De Silva, S. B. D. *The Political Economy of Under-development.* London: Routledge & Kegan Paul, 1982.

Dessallien, Renata Lok. "Press Statement by UN Resident Coordinator, Ms Renata Lok Dessallien, Dhaka." Media release, Office of the United Nations Resident Coordinator in Bangladesh, Dhaka, 11 January, 2007. Available at: http://www.undp.org.bd/media%20releases/2007/UN%20Resident%20Coordinator%20Statement%20-%2011%20Jan%202007.pdf (accessed on 16 August, 2007).

de Swaan, Abram. *In Care of the State: Health Care, Education and Welfare in Europe and the USA in the Modern Era.* Cambridge: Polity Press, 1988.

Devarajan, Shantayanan. "Two Comments on 'Governance Indicators: Where Are We, Where Should We Be Going?'" by Daniel Kaufmann and Aart Kraay," *World Bank Research Observer*, Vol. 23 (2001), pp. 31–36.

Devine, Joe. "Wellbeing, Democracy and Political Violence in Bangladesh". Paper for the 57th Political Studies Association Annual Conference, University of Bath, UK, 11–13 April, 2007.

DeVotta, Neil. "Illiberalism and Ethnic Conflict in Sri Lanka," *Journal of Democracy*, Vol. 13 (2002), pp. 84–98.

DeVotta, Neil. "Sri Lanka's Political Decay: Analysing the October 2000 and December 2001 Parliamentary Elections," *Journal of Commonwealth and Comparative Politics*, Vol. 41 (2003), pp. 115–42.

DeVotta, Neil. *Blowback: Linguistic Nationalism, Institutional Decay, and Ethnic Conflict in Sri Lanka.* Stanford, CA: University Press, 2004.

DeVotta, Neil. "Explaining Political and Societal Violence in Sri Lanka," in Laksiri Fernando and Shermal Wijewardene (eds), *Sri Lanka's Ethnic Conflict in the Global Context.* Colombo: University of Colombo Faculty of Graduate Studies, 2006, pp. 113–26.

DeVotta, Neil. "From Ethnic Outbidding to Ethnic Conflict: The Institutional Bases for Sri Lanka's Separatist War," in P. Sahadevan and Neil DeVotta (eds), *Politics of Conflict and Peace in Sri Lanka.* New Delhi: Manak, 2006, pp. 3–29.

DeVotta, Neil. *Sinhalese Buddhist Nationalist Ideology: Implications for Politics and Conflict Resolution in Sri Lanka*, Policy Studies 40. Washington, DC: East–West Center, 2007.

DeVotta, Neil and Jason Stone. "*Jathika Hela Urumaya* and Ethno-Religious Politics in Sri Lanka," *Pacific Affairs*, Vol. 81 (2008), forthcoming.

Dewey, Clive. "The Rural Roots of Pakistani Militarism," in D. A. Low (ed.), *The Political Inheritance of Pakistan.* Basingstoke: Macmillan, 1991, pp. 255–84.

Dhavan, Rajeev. *Justice on Trial: The Supreme Court Today.* Allahabad: A. H. Wheeler, 1980.

Dhavan, Rajeev. "The Supreme Court and Group Life," in B. N. Kirpal, Ashok H. Desai, Gopal Subramanium, Rajeev Dhavan and Raju Ramachandran (eds), *Supreme but not Infallible: Essays in Honour of the Supreme Court of India.* Delhi: Oxford University Press, 2000.

Diamond, Larry. *Developing Democracy: Toward Consolidation.* Baltimore, MD: Johns Hopkins University Press, 1999.

Diamond, Larry. "Thinking about Hybrid Regimes: Elections without Democracy," *Journal of Democracy*, Vol. 13, No. 2 (2002), pp. 21–35.

Diamond, Larry. "The Democratic Rollback: The Resurgence of the Predatory State," *Foreign Affairs*, Vol. 87 (2008), pp. 36–48.

Dil, Anwar and Afia Dil. *Bengali Language Movement to Bangladesh.* Lahore: Ferozsons, 2000.

Dirks, Nicholas B. *Castes of Mind: Colonialism and the Making of Modern India.* Princeton, NJ: University Press, 2001.

Dixit, Jyotindra Nath. "Kashmir: The Contemporary Geo-political Implications for India and Regional Stability." Unpublished paper presented at the School of Oriental and African Studies, London, 8 April, 1994.

Dixit, J. N. *Assignment Colombo*. New Delhi: Konark, 1998.

Dixit, J. N. *India and Pakistan in War and Peace*. London: Routledge, 2002.

Dorosh, Paul A. "Trade, Food Aid and Food Security: Evolving Rice and Wheat Markets," *Economic and Political Weekly*, Vol. 39, No. 36 (4 September, 2004), pp. 4,033–42.

Downing, Brian M. *The Military Revolution and Political Change: The Origins of Democracy and Autocracy in Early Modern Europe*. Princeton, NJ: University Press, 1992.

Dunham, David and Sisira Jayasuriya. "Economic Crisis, Poverty and War in Contemporary Sri Lanka: On Ostriches and Tinderboxes," *Economic and Political Weekly*, Vol. 38, No. 49 (5 December, 1998), pp. 3,151–56.

Economist Intelligence Unit (EIU). *Bangladesh Country Report, April 2007*. London: EIU, 2007.

Economist Intelligence Unit. *Bangladesh Country Report, July 2007*. London: EIU, 2007.

Edrisinha, Rohan. "In Defence of Judicial Review and Judicial Activism." Unpublished paper presented at the Eleventh Conference of the International Association of Historians of Asia, Colombo, 1–5 August, 1988.

Edrisinha, Rohan. "Sri Lanka: Constitutions without Constitutionalism—A Tale of Three and a Half Constitutions." Unpublished paper.

Eickleman, Dale F. and James Piscatori. *Muslim Politics*. Princeton, NJ: University Press, 1996.

Eighty-fifth Report of the Parliamentary Standing Committee on Home Affairs on Legal Delays, Rajya Sabha, India.

Eisenstadt, S. N. *Fundamentalism, Sectarianism, and Revolution*. Cambridge: University Press, 1999.

Elliott, Carolyn M. (ed.). *Civil Society and Democracy: A Reader*. New Delhi: Oxford University Press, 2003.

Emerson, Rupert. *From Empire to Nation: The Rise to Self-Assertion of Asian and African Peoples*. Boston, MA: Beacon, 1960.

Epp, Charles. *The Rights Revolution*. Chicago: University of Chicago Press, 1998.

Evans, Hugh D. "Bangladesh: South Asia's Unknown Quantity," *Asian Affairs*, Vol. 75 (1988), pp. 306–16.

Evans, Hugh D. "Bangladesh: An Unsteady Democracy," in Amita Shastri and A. Jeyaratnam Wilson (eds), *The Post-colonial States of South Asia: Democracy, Development and Identity*. New York: Palgrave, 2001, pp. 69–87.

Farooqui, M. I. "Judiciary in Bangladesh: Past and Present," in 48 DLR (1996) Journal 65.

Feldman, Herbert. *From Crisis to Crisis: Pakistan 1962–1969*. London: Oxford University Press, 1972.

Feldman, Noah. *Fall and Rise of the Islamic State*. Princeton, NJ: University Press, 2008.

Frank, Katherine. *The Life of Indira Nehru Gandhi*. London: HarperCollins, 2001.

Frankel, Francine. *India's Political Economy, 1947–1977: The Gradual Revolution*. Princeton, NJ: University Press, 1978, 2nd edition 2004.

Frankel, Francine R. *India's Political Economy, 1947–2004*. New Delhi: Oxford University Press, 2005.

Freedom House. *Freedom in the World*. Washington, DC: Freedom House, various years. Available at: www.freedomhouse.org.

Gadbois, George. "The Supreme Court of India as a Political Institution," in Rajeev Dhavan, R. Sudarshan and Salman Khurshid (eds), *Judges and the Judicial Power*. Bombay: Tripathi, 1985.

Gagnon, Alain-G. and James Tully. *Multinational Democracies*. Cambridge: University Press, 2001.

Gaige, Frederick H. *Regionalism and National Unity in Nepal*. New Delhi: Vikas, 1975.

Gandhi, Mohandas K. *Thoughts on National Language*. Ahmedabad: Navajivan, 1956.

Ganguly, Sumit. *The Crisis in Kashmir: Portents of War, Hopes of Peace*. Cambridge: University Press, 1997.

Ganguly, Sumit. *India as an Emerging Power*. London: Routledge, 2003.

Garg, Subhas Chandra, "Transformation of Central Grants to States: Growing Conditionality and Bypassing State Budgets," *Economic and Political Weekly*, Vol. 61, No. 48 (2 December, 2006), p. 4,982.

Geertz, Clifford. *Negara: The Theatre State in Nineteenth-Century Bali*. Princeton, NJ: University Press, 1980.

Gellner, David N. "Caste, Communalism, and Communism: Newars and the Nepalese State," in D. N. Gellner, J. Pfaff-Czarnecka and J. Whelpton (eds), *Nationalism and Ethnicity in a Hindu Kingdom*. Amsterdam: Harwood, 1997, pp. 151–84.

Gellner, David N. "Caste, Ethnicity and Inequality in Nepal," *Economic and Political Weekly*, Vol. 42, No. 20 (19 May, 2007), pp. 1,823–28.

Gellner, David N. "Democracy in Nepal: Four Models," *Seminar,*Vol. 576 (2007), pp. 50–56.

Gellner, David N. and Mrigendra Bahadur Karki. "Democracy and Ethnic Organizations in Nepal," in D. N. Gellner and K. Hachhethu (eds), *Local Democracy in South Asia: The Micropolitics of Democratization.* Delhi: Sage, 2008, pp. 105–27.

Gellner, David N., Joanna Pfaff-Czarnecka and John Whelpton (eds). *Nationalism and Ethnicity in a Hindu Kingdom: The Politics of Culture in Contemporary Nepal.* Amsterdam: Harwood, 1997.

Ghosh, Shankar. *The Naxalite Movement.* Calcutta: Firma K. L. Mukhopadhyay, 1971.

Gilmartin, David. *Islam and Empire: Punjab and the Making of Pakistan.* Berkeley: University of California Press. 1995.

Gopal, Sarvepalli. *Jawaharlal Nehru: An Anthology.* Delhi: Oxford University Press, 1983.

Gordon, Jim and Poonam Gupta. "Understanding India's Services Revolution." Paper prepared for IMF-NCAER Conference, New Delhi, November 2003. Available at: www.imf.org/external/np/apd/seminars/2003/newdelhi/gordon.pdf.

Gordon, Raymond G., Jr. (ed.). *Ethnologue Languages of the World*, 15th edition. Dallas: SIL International, 2005. Online version 2005 available at: http://www.ethnologue.com.

Gould, Harold A. "The 12th General Election in Karnataka: The BJP Achieves its Southern Beachhead," in Ramashray Roy and Paul Wallace (eds), *Indian Politics and the 1998 Election: Regionalism, Hindutva and State Politics.* New Delhi: Sage, 1999.

Gould, Harold and Sumit Ganguly (eds). *India Votes: Alliance Politics and Minority Governments in the Ninth and Tenth General Elections.* Boulder, CO: Westview, 1993.

Gould, Jeremy. "Anthropology and Democratisation," in Peter Burnell (ed.), *Democracy through the Looking Glass.* Manchester: University Press, 2002, pp. 21–40.

Gould, William. *Hindu Nationalism in Late Colonial India.* Cambridge: University Press, 2005.

Government of Tamil Nadu. *Rajamannar Report on Centre–State Relations.* Madras: Government of Tamil Nadu, 1971.

Government of West Bengal. *Views on Centre–State Relations.* Calcutta: Department of Information and Cultural Affairs, Government of West Bengal, 1978.

Grare, Frederic. *Pakistan: The Resurgence of Baluch Nationalism,* Carnegie Papers No. 65 (January 2006).

Griswold, Eliza. "The Next Islamist Revolution?" *New York Times Magazine,* 23 January, 2005.

Guha, Ramachandra. *India after Gandhi: The History of the World's Largest Democracy.* New York: HarperCollins, 2007.

Gujarat Government. *Report of the Minimum Wages Advisory Committee for Employment in Agriculture.* Ahmedabad: Government Press, 1966.

Gunaratna, Rohan. *International and Regional Security Implications of the Sri Lankan Tamil Insurgency.* Colombo: Taprobane, 1997.

Gunaratna, Rohan. *Sri Lanka's Ethnic Crisis and National Security.* Colombo: South Asian Network on Conflict Research, 1998.

Gunatilleke, Godfrey. *Welfare and Growth in Sri Lanka,* Marga Research Studies No. 2. Colombo: Marga Institute, 1974.

Gunatilleke, Godfrey. *Development and Liberalisation in Sri Lanka: Trends and Prospects.* Colombo: Marga Institute, 1993.

Gunawardena, Asoka and Weligamage D. Lakshman. "Challenges of Moving into a Devolved Polity in Sri Lanka," in Fumihiko Saito (ed.), *Foundations for Local Governance: Decentralization in Comparative Perspective.* Heidelberg: Physica-Verlag, 2008, pp. 113–36.

Gupta, Amit Kumar. *The Agrarian Drama: The Leftists and the Rural Poor in India.* New Delhi: Manohar, 1996.

Gupta, Anirudha. *Politics in Nepal: A Study of Post-Rana Political Developments and Party Politics.* Bombay: Allied, 1964.

Gupta, Dipankar. *The Context of Ethnicity: Sikh Identity in a Comparative Perspective.* New Delhi: Oxford University Press, 1996.

Gupta, Shekhar. *India Redefines its Role.* Oxford: University Press, 1995.

Gupta, Vijay K. *Decision Making in the Supreme Court of India.* Delhi: Kaveri, 1995.

Gurung, Harka. "Representing an Ethnic Mosaic," *Himal* (May–June 1992), pp. 19–21.

Habib, Irfan. *The Agrarian System of Mughal India (1556–1707).* London and Bombay: Asia Publishing House, 1963.

Hachhethu, Krishna. "Mass Movement 1990," *Contributions to Nepalese Studies,* Vol. 17, No. 2 (1990), pp. 177–201.

Hachhethu, Krishna. *Party Building in Nepal: Organization, Leadership and People, A Comparative*

Study of the Nepali Congress and the Communist Party of Nepal (Unified Marxist-Leninist). Kathmandu: Mandala Book Point, 2002.

Hachhethu, Krishna. State of Democracy in Nepal: A Survey Report. Kathmandu: SDSA/Nepal and International IDEA, 2004.

Hachhethu, Krishna. "Civil Society and Political Participation," in Lok Raj Baral (ed.), Nepal: Quest for Participatory Democracy. New Delhi: Adroit, 2006.

Hachhethu, Krishna, with Sanjay Kumar and Jivan Suvedi. Nepal in Transition: A Study on the State of Democracy. Stockholm: International IDEA, 2008.

Haider, Mahtab. "The Rise and Fall of Bangla Bhai," Slate (monthly magazine of New Age, Dhaka) (April 2007).

Haller, Dieter and Cris Shore (eds). Corruption: Anthropological Perspectives. London: Pluto Press, 2005.

Hamid, Naveed and Akmal Hussain. "Regional Inequalities and Capitalist Development: Pakistan's Experience," in S. Akbar Zaidi (ed.), Regional Imbalances and the National Question in Pakistan. Lahore: Vanguard, 1992.

Hangen, Susan I. Creating a "New Nepal": The Ethnic Dimension. Washington, DC: East–West Center, 2007.

Hansen, Thomas Blom. The Saffron Wave: Democracy and Hindu Nationalism in Modern India. Princeton, NJ: University Press, 1999.

Hanson, A. H. The Process of Planning. London: Oxford University Press, 1966.

Haqqani, Husain. Pakistan: Between Mosque and Military. Washington, DC: Carnegie Endowment for International Peace, 2005, and Lahore: Vanguard Books, 2005.

Harriss, John. "Does the 'Depressor' Still Work? Agrarian Structure and Development in India: A Review of Evidence and Argument," Journal of Peasant Studies, Vol. 19 (1992), pp. 189–227.

Harriss, John. "Comparing Political Regimes across Indian States," Economic and Political Weekly (27 November, 1999), Vol. 34, No. 48, pp. 3,367–77.

Harriss, John. "Antinomies of Empowerment: Observations on Civil Society, Politics and Urban Governance," Economic and Political Weekly, Vol. 42, No. 26 (30 June, 2007), pp. 2,716–24.

Harriss-White, Barbara. India Working: Essays on Society and Economy. Cambridge: University Press, 2003.

Harun, Shamsul Huda. Bangladesh Voting Behaviour: A Psychological Study 1973. Dhaka: University Press, 1986.

Harun-or-Rashid. The Foreshadowing of Bangladesh: Bengal Muslim League and Muslim League Politics, 1936–1947. Dhaka: Research Society of Bangladesh, 1987.

Harvey, David. Spaces of Capital. Edinburgh: University Press, 2001.

Harvey, David. The New Imperialism. Oxford: Clarendon Press, 2003.

Hasan, Mushirul (ed.). India's Partition: Process, Strategy and Mobilisation. New Delhi: Oxford University Press, 1993.

Hasan, Mushirul. Legacy of a Divided Nation: India's Muslims since Independence. Delhi: Oxford University Press, 1997.

Hauser, Walter. Sahajanand on Agricultural Labour and the Rural Poor. Delhi: Manohar, 1994.

Hauser, Walter. Culture, Vernacular Politics and the Peasants. Delhi: Manohar, 2006.

Hazra, Arnab Kumar and Bibek Debroy (eds). Judicial Reforms in India: Issues and Aspects. New Delhi: Academic Foundation, 2007.

Heath, Anthony and Yogendra Yadav. "The United Colors of Congress: Social Profile of Congress Voters, 1996 and 1998," Economic and Political Weekly Vol. 34, Nos 34 and 35 (21 August, 1999) pp. 2,518–28.

Heller, Patrick. "Social Capital as Product of Class Mobilization and State Intervention: Industrial Workers in Kerala, India," World Development, Vol. 24, No. 6 (1996), pp. 1,055–71.

Heston, Alan. "National Income," in Dharma Kumar and Meghnad Desai (eds), Cambridge Economic History of India, Vol. 2. Cambridge: University Press, 1982, pp. 376–462.

Hewitt, Vernon. Reclaiming the Past? The Search for Cultural and Political Unity in Contemporary Jammu and Kashmir. London: Portland Books, 1995.

Hewitt, Vernon. "Ethnic Construction, Provincial Identity and Nationalism in Pakistan: The Case of Baluchistan," in S. K. Mitra (ed.), Sub-nationalist Movements in South Asia. Boulder, CO: Westview Press, 1997, pp. 43–67.

Hewitt, Vernon. The New International Politics of South Asia. Manchester: University Press, 1997.

Hewitt, Vernon. "Containing Shiva: India, Non-proliferation, and the Comprehensive Test Ban Treaty," Contemporary South Asia, Vol. 9 (2000), pp. 25–39.

Hewitt, Vernon. "Creating a Common Home? Indo-Pakistan Relations and the Search for Security in South Asia," in Amita Shastri and A. Jeyaratnam Wilson (eds), *The Post-colonial States of South Asia: Democracy, Development and Identity.* New York: Palgrave, 2001.

Hewitt, Vernon. *Towards the Future? Jammu and Kashmir in the 21st Century.* Cambridge: Portland Books, 2001.

Hewitt, Vernon. *Political Mobilisation and Democracy in India: States of Emergency.* Oxford: Routledge, 2008.

Hirschl, Ran. *Towards Juristocracy: The Origins and Consequences of the New Constitutionalism.* Cambridge, MA: Harvard University Press, 2004.

Hirson, Baruch. "Language in Control and Resistance in South Africa," *African Affairs* (1981), Vol. 80, No. 319, pp. 219–37.

Hobbes, Thomas. *Leviathan,* ed. Richard Tuck. Cambridge and New York: Cambridge University Press, 1991.

Hobden, Stephen and John M. Hobson. *Historical Sociology of International Relations.* Cambridge: University Press, 2002.

Hodson, H. V. *The Great Divide.* New York and Karachi: Oxford University Press, 1971.

Hoftun, Martin, William Raeper and John Whelpton. *People, Politics, and Ideology: Democracy and Social Change in Nepal.* Kathmandu: Mandala Book Point, 1999.

Hossain, Moazzem. "Bangladesh: 'Home-Grown' Democracy," *Economic and Political Weekly,* Vol. 41, No. 9 (4 March, 2006), pp. 791–93.

Human Rights Watch. *Recurring Nightmare: State Responsibility for "Disappearances" and Abductions in Sri Lanka.* Available at: http://hrw.org/reports/2008/srilanka0308/ (accessed on 8 March, 2008).

Huntington, Samuel P. *The Third Wave: Democratization in the Late Twentieth Century.* Norman: University of Oklahoma Press, 1991.

Huque, Ahmed Shafiqul and M. Taiabur Rahman. "From Domination to Alliance: Shifting Strategies and Accumulation of Power by the Bureaucracy of Bangladesh," *Public Organization Review: A Global Journal,* Vol. 3 (2003), pp. 403–18.

Hutt, Michael (ed.). *Nepal in the Nineties.* Delhi: Oxford University Press, 1994.

Hutt, Michael (ed.). *Himalayan People's War: Nepal's Maoist Rebellion.* London: Hurst, 2004.

Inden, Ronald. "Embodying God: From Imperial Progresses to National Progress in India," *Economy and Society,* Vol. 24 (1995), pp. 245–78.

India, cases, *ADM Jabalpur* v *Shiv Kant Shukla* (1976) 2 SCC 52.

India, cases, *Bommai* v *Union of India* (1994) 3 SCC 1.

India, cases, *Daniel Latifi* v *Union of India* AIR (2001) SC 3958.

India, cases, *IR Coelho (dead) by LRs* v *State of Tamil Nadu and Others* (2007) 2SCC1.

India, cases, *Keshavananda Bharati* v *State of Kerala* AIR (1973) SC 1461.

India, cases, *Kodeswaran* v *Attorney General,* 70 NLR 121.

India, cases, *Kodikam Pillai* v *Mudanayake,* 54 NLR 433).

India, cases, *Koolwal* v *State of Rajasthan* AIR (1988) Raj 2.

India, cases, *Minerva Mills* v *Union of India* (1980) 3 SCC 625.

India, cases, *Mohd. Ahmad Khan* v *Shah Bano Begum* AIR (1985) SC 945.

India, cases, *Mudanayake* v *Sivagnasunderam* (53 NLR 25).

India, cases, *Ravindra Kumar, Advocate and Another* v *State of UP,* Writ petition M/S 1746 of 1998, Allahabad HC.

India, cases, *S. P. Gupta* v *Union of India* AIR (1982) SC 149.

India, cases, *Sarla Mudgal* v *Union of India* (1995) SCC 635.

India, cases, *Shahar Ali* v *AR Chowdhury,* Sessions judge, 32 DLR (1980) 142.

India, cases, *Supreme Court Advocates on Record Association* v *Union of India* (1993) Supp 2 SCR 659.

India, cases, *Waman Rao* v *Union of India* (1981) 2 SCC 362.

India, Government. *All India Agricultural Labour Enquiry Report on Intensive Survey of Agricultural Labour, 1950–51,* Vol. 1. New Delhi: Manager of Publications, 1955.

India, Government. *Constituent Assembly Debates: Official Report.* New Delhi: Government of India, 1966.

India, Government. *White Paper on the Punjab Agitation.* New Delhi: Government of India, 1984.

India, Government. *Economic Survey, 2006–7.* New Delhi: Government of India, Ministry of Finance, 2007.

India, Government, Ministry of Finance. "Explanatory Memorandum as to the Action Taken on the Recommendations Made by the 11th Finance Commission Report Submitted to the President on 30 August, 2000." Available at: www.fincomindia.nic.in/eleventh.ernet.htm.

India, Government, Ministry of Finance. *Economic Survey 2004–05*, Chapter 2.2. Available at: indiabudget.nic.in/es2004–05/esmain.htm (accessed on 1 November, 2008).

India, Government, Ministry of Home Affairs. *Report of the Committee on the Prevention of Corruption* (Santhanam Committee Report). New Delhi: Manager of Publications, 1964.

India, Government, Ministry of Home Affairs. *The Causes and Nature of Current Agrarian Tensions*. New Delhi: Government of India, 1969.

India, Government, Ministry of Labour. *Report of the National Commission on Rural Labour*, Vols. I and II. New Delhi: Government of India, 1991.

Institute of Public Policy. *Status of the Economy: Challenges and Opportunities*. Lahore: Institute of Public Policy, 2008.

International Crisis Group (ICG). *Bangladesh Today*, Asia Report No. 121. Brussels: ICG, 23 October, 2006. Available at: http://www.crisisgroup.org (accessed on 12 August, 2007).

International Crisis Group. *Pakistan: The Worsening Conflict in Baluchistan*, Report No. 119. Islamabad: ICG, 2006.

International Crisis Group. *Winding Back Martial Law in Pakistan*, Asia Briefing No. 70. Islamabad and Brussels: ICG, 12 November, 2007.

International Institute for Strategic Studies (IISS). *The Military Balance*, Vol. 102. London: IISS, October 2002.

International Institute for Strategic Studies. *The Military Balance, 2006*. London: IISS, 2007.

International Institute for Strategic Studies. *The Military Balance, 2007*, Vol. 107. London: IISS, 2007.

International Labour Organization (ILO). *Matching Employment Opportunities and Expectations: A Programme of Action for Ceylon: Report*. Geneva: ILO, 1971.

Irschick, Eugene F. *Tamil Revivalism in the 1930s*. Madras: Cre-A, 1986.

Isaac, T. M. T. and R. Ramakumar, "Why Do the States Not Spend?," *Economic and Political Weekly*, Vol. 41, No. 48 (2 December, 2006), p. 4,972.

Isaacson, Walter. *Kissinger: A Biography*. London: Faber and Faber, 1992.

Isenman, Paul. "Basic Needs: The Case of Sri Lanka," *World Development*, Vol. 8, No. 3 (March 1980), pp. 237–58.

Islam, Mahmudul. *Constitutional Law of Bangladesh*, 2nd edition. Dhaka: Mullick Brothers, 2002.

Islam, Nazrul. "Military Role May Bear on Dhaka's Peacekeeping," *New Age* (Dhaka) (12 January, 2007).

Iyer, Swarna. "August Anarchy: The Partition Massacres in Punjab 1947," *South Asia*, Special issue, Vol. 18 (1995), pp. 23–24.

Jacobsohn, Gary. *The Wheel of Law: India's Secularism in Comparative Constitutional Perspective*. Princeton, NJ: University Press, 2005.

Jacobsohn, Gary and Shylashri Shankar. "Constitutional Borrowing in South Asia: India, Sri Lanka, and Secular Constitutional Identity," in an edited volume. New York: Oxford University Press, forthcoming.

Jaffrelot, Christophe. *The Hindu Nationalist Movement in India*. New York: Columbia University Press, 1996.

Jaffrelot, Christophe. "The Hindu Nationalist Movement in Delhi: From 'Locals' to Refugees and Towards Peripheral Groups?," in Veronique Dupont, Emma Tarlo and Denis Vidal (eds), *Delhi: Urban Spaces and Human Destinies*. Delhi: Manohar, 2000, pp. 181–203.

Jaffrelot, Christophe. *India's Silent Revolution: The Rise of the Lower Castes in North India*. New York: Columbia University Press, 2003.

Jaffrelot, Christophe. *The Sangh Parivar: A Reader*. New Delhi: Oxford University Press, 2005.

Jahan, Rounaq. "Bangladesh in 2003: Vibrant Democracy or Destructive Politics?," *Asian Survey*, Vol. 44, No. 1 (2004), pp. 56–61.

Jahan, Rounaq. "Bangladesh in 2005: Standing at a Crossroads," *Asian Survey*, Vol. 46, No. 1 (2006), pp. 107–13.

Jahani, Carina. *Standardization and Orthography in the Balochi Language*. Uppsala: Almquist & Wiksell, 1989.

Jalal, Ayesha. *Democracy and Authoritarianism in South Asia: A Comparative and Historical Perspective*. Cambridge: University Press, 1988.

Jalal, Ayesha. *The State of Martial Rule: The Origins of Pakistan's Political Economy of Defence*. Cambridge: University Press, 1990.

Jalal, Ayesha. *The Sole Spokesman: Jinnah, the Muslim League, and the Demand for Pakistan*. Cambridge: University Press, 1994.

Jayatilleke, Dayan, "Premadasa–LTTE Talks: Why They Failed and What Really Happened," in Kumar Rupesinghe, *Negotiating Peace in Sri Lanka: Efforts, Failures and Lessons*. Colombo: Foundation for Co-existence, 2006, pp. 141–56.

Jayawardena, Kumari. *The Rise of the Labor Movement in Ceylon*. Colombo: Sanjiva Books, 2004; first published 1972.

Jayawardena, Kumari. *Nobodies to Somebodies: The Rise of the Colonial Bourgeoisie in Sri Lanka*. Colombo: Social Scientists Association and Sanjiva Books, 2007.

Jayawardena, Lal. "Sri Lanka," in H. B. Chenery *et al.* (eds), *Redistribution with Growth*. London: Oxford University Press, 1970, pp. 273–79.

Jeffrey, Craig, Patricia Jeffery and Roger Jeffery. *Degrees without Freedom? Education, Masculinities and Unemployment in North India*. Stanford, CA: University Press, 2008.

"Jela judge Podonnoti'r khetrey 16 joner biruddhey gurutoro obhijog" [Serious allegations against 16 persons recommended for appointment to district judge], *Daily Prothom Alo* [Bangladesh] (24 May, 2008).

Jenkins, Rob. "The Developmental Implications of Federal Political Institutions in India," in Mark Robinson and Gordon White (eds), *The Democratic Developmental State*. Oxford: University Press, 1998, pp. 187–214.

Jenkins, Rob. *Democratic Politics and Economic Reform in India*. Cambridge: University Press, 1999.

Jenkins, Rob. "The NDA and the Politics of Economic Reform," in Katharine Adeney and Lawrence Sáez (eds), *Coalition Politics and Hindu Nationalism*. London: Routledge, 2005, pp. 173–92.

Jennings, W. Ivor. "The Dominion of Ceylon," *Pacific Affairs*, Vol. 22, No. 1 (March 1949), pp. 21–33.

Jennings, Ivor. *The Commonwealth in Asia*. London: Oxford University Press, 1950.

Jennings, Ivor. *Some Characteristics of the Indian Constitution*. Madras and New York: Oxford University Press, 1953.

Jetly, Rajshree. "Resurgence of the Baluch Movement in Pakistan: Emerging Perspectives and Challenges." Paper for the International Symposium on Pakistan, Institute of South Asian Studies (ISAS), National University of Singapore, 24–25 May, 2007.

Jha, S., Vijayendra Rao and Michael Woolcock. "Governance in the Gullies: Democratic Responsiveness and Leadership in Delhi Slums," *World Development*, Vol. 35, No. 2 (2007), pp. 230–46.

Jinah, Mohammad Ali. *Speeches as Governor General of Pakistan, 1947–48*. Karachi, n.d.

Joshi, Bhuwan Lal and Leo Rose. *Democratic Innovations in Nepal: A Case Study of Political Acculturation*. Berkeley: University of California Press, 1966.

Jupp, James. "Constitutional Development in Ceylon since Independence," *Pacific Affairs*, Vol. 41, No. 2 (Summer 1968), pp. 169–83.

Kaiser, Robert J. "Homeland Making and the Territorialization of National Identity," in Daniel Conversi (ed.), *Ethnonationalism in the Contemporary World*. London: Routledge, 2002.

Kamran, Tahir. "Imagined Unity as Binary Opposition to Regional Diversity: A Study of Punjab as a 'Silenced Space' in the Pakistani Epistemic Milieu," in Sustainable Development Policy Institute, *At the Crossroads: South Asian Research, Policy and Development in a Globalized World*. Islamabad: Sustainable Development Policy Institute, 2007.

Kanapathipillai, V. "July 1983: The Survivors' Experience," in Veena Das (ed.), *Mirrors of Violence: Communities, Riots and Survivors in South Asia*. New Delhi: Oxford University Press, 1990, 321–44.

Kangas, Tove Skuntabb. *Linguistic Genocide in Education or Worldwide Diversity and Human Rights?* Mahwah, NJ and London: Erlbaum, 2000.

Kapur, Devesh and Pratap Bhanu Mehta. "Introduction," in Devesh Kapur and Pratap Bhanu Mehta (eds), *Public Institutions in India: Performance and Design*. Delhi: Oxford University Press, 2005.

Karim, A. Tariq and C. Christine Fair. *Bangladesh at the Crossroads*, Special Report 181. Washington, DC: United States Institute of Peace, January 2007.

Karki, Arjun and Binod Bhattarai (eds). *Whose War? Economic and Social-Cultural Impacts of Nepal's Maoist-Government Conflict*. Kathmandu: NGO Federation of Nepal, n.d.

Karki, Arjun and David Seddon (eds). *The People's War in Nepal: Left Perspectives*. New Delhi: Adroit, 2003.

Karmis, Dimitrios and W. J. Norman. *Theories of Federalism: A Reader*. New York: Palgrave Macmillan, 2005.

Kaufman, Stuart J. *Modern Hatreds: The Symbolic Politics of Ethnic War*. Ithaca, NY: Cornell University Press, 2001.

Kaufmann, Daniel Aart Kraay and Massimo Mastruzzi. *Governance Matters VI: Aggregate and Individual Governance Indicators 1996–2006,*

World Bank Policy Research Paper 4280. Washington, DC: World Bank, July 2007.

Kaur, Ravinder. *Since 1947: Partition Narratives among Punjabi Migrants of Delhi*. New Delhi: Oxford University Press, 2007.

Kaviraj, Sudipta. "On the Crisis of Political Institutions in India," *Contributions to Indian Sociology*, Vol. 18 (1984), pp. 223–43.

Kaviraj, Sudipta. "A Critique of the Passive Revolution," *Economic and Political Weekly*, Vol. 23, Nos. 45, 46, 47 (November 1988), pp. 2, 429–44.

Kaviraj, Sudipta. "On State, Society and Discourse in India," in James Manor (ed.), *Rethinking Third World Politics*. Harlow: Longman, 1991.

Kearney, Robert N. "Ceylon: A Year of Consolidation," *Asian Survey*, Vol. 4, No. 2 (1964), pp. 729–34.

Kearney, Robert. *Communalism and Language in the Politics of Ceylon*. Durham, NC: Duke University Press, 1967.

Kearney, Robert N. *The Politics of Ceylon*. Ithaca, NY and London: Cornell University Press, 1973.

Keay, John. *The Honourable Company: A History of the English East India Company*. New York: Macmillan, 1991.

Kekic, Laza. *The Economist Intelligence Unit's Index of Democracy*. Online, 2007.

Kelegama, Saman. "Economic Costs of Conflict in Sri Lanka," in Robert Rotberg (ed.), *Creating Peace in Sri Lanka: Civil War and Reconciliation*. Washington, DC: Brookings Institution Press, 1999.

Kelegama, Saman. "Managing the Sri Lankan Economy at a Time of Terrorism and War," in S. Khatri and G. Kueck (eds), *Terrorism in South Asia: Impact of Development and Democratic Process*. New Delhi: Shipra, 2003.

Kelegama, Saman, "Transformation of a Conflict via an Economic Dividend: The Sri Lankan Experience," in Kumar Rupesinghe (ed.), *Negotiating Peace in Sri Lanka: Efforts, Failures and Lessons*, Vol. II. Colombo: Foundation for Co-existence, 2006, pp. 205–39.

Keller, Stephen L. *Uprooting and Social Change: The Role of Refugees in Development*. Delhi: Manohar, 1975.

Kennedy, Charles. "Pakistan: Ethnic Diversity and Colonial Legacy," in John Coakley (ed.), *The Territorial Management of Ethnic Conflict*. London: Frank Cass, 2003.

Kesavan, Mukul. "Invoking a Majority: The Congress and the Muslims of the United Provinces, 1945–47," *Islam and the Modern Age*, Vol. 24, No. 2 (1993), pp. 109–30.

Khan, Adeel. *Politics of Identity: Ethnic Nationalism and the State in Pakistan*. New Delhi: Sage, 2005.

Khan, Mohammad Ayub. *Friends not Masters: A Political Autobiography*. London: Oxford University Press, 1967.

Khan, Mohammad Mohabbat. "State of Governance in Bangladesh," *Round Table*, No. 370 (July 2003), 391–405.

Khan, Zillur R. "Bangladesh's Experiments with Parliamentary Democracy," *Asian Survey*, Vol. 37, No. 6 (1997), pp. 575–89.

Khandker, Shihidur R. and M. Abdul Latif. *The Role of Family Planning and Targeted Credit Programs in Demographic Change in Bangladesh*, World Bank Discussion Paper No. 337. Washington, DC: World Bank, 1996.

Khilnani, Anil. *The Idea of India*. London: Hamish Hamilton, 1997.

Kholi, Atul. *Democracy and Discontent: India's Growing Crisis of Governability*. Cambridge: University Press, 1991.

Khubchandani, L. M. (ed.). *Language in a Plural Society*. Delhi: Motilal Banarsidass and Indian Institute of Advanced Studies, Shimla, 1988.

Khubchandani, Lachman. "Language and Education in the Indian Sub-continent," in S. May and N. H. Hornberger (eds), *Encyclopedia of Language and Education*, 2nd edition, Vol. 1. New York: Springer, 2008.

Kim, Joon Suk. "Making States Federatively: Alternate Routes of State Formation in Late Medieval and Early Modern Europe." Unpublished dissertation submitted to the Department of Political Science, University of Chicago, 2005.

King, Christopher R. *One Language, Two Scripts: The Hindi Movement in Nineteenth Century India*. Delhi: Oxford University Press, 1994.

King, Robert D. *Nehru and the Language Policy of India*. New York: Oxford University Press, 1997.

Kirpal, B. N., Ashok H. Desai, Gopal Subramanium, Rajeev Dhavan and Raju Ramachandran (eds). *Supreme but not Infallible: Essays in Honour of the Supreme Court of India*. New Delhi: Oxford University Press, 2000.

Kishwar, Madhu. "Gandhi on Women," *Economic and Political Weekly* (5 October, 1985), pp. 1,691–1,702.

Kochanek, Stanley A. "The Politics of Regulation: Rajiv's New Mantras," *Journal of Commonwealth and Comparative Studies*,Vol. 23, No. 3 (November 1985), pp. 189–211.

Kochanek, Stanley A. "Briefcase Politics in India: The Congress Party and the Business Elite," *Asian Survey*,Vol. 27, No. 12 (December 1987), pp. 1,278–1,301.

Kochanek, Stanley A. *Patron Client Politics and Business in Bangladesh*. New Delhi, Newbury Park, CA and London: Sage, 1993.

Kochanek, Stanley. "Bangladesh in 1996: The 25th Year of Independence," *Asian Survey*, Vol. 37, No. 2 (1997), pp. 136–42.

Kochanek, Stanley A. *India: Government and Politics in a Developing Nation*, 7th edition. Boston, MA: Thomson Wadsworth, 2008.

Kochhar, Kalpana, Utsav Kumar, Raghuram Rajan, Arvind Subramanian and Ioannis Tokatlidis. *India's Pattern of Development: What Happened, What Follows?*, International Monetary Fund Working Paper WP/06/22. Washington, DC: International Monetary Fund, 2006. Available at: www.imf.org/external/pubs/ft/wp/2006/wp0622.pdf.

Kodikara, S. U. *Indo–Ceylon Relations since Independence*. Colombo, 1965.

Kodikara, Shelton. *Foreign Policy of Sri Lanka: A Third World Perspective*. Delhi: Chanakya, 1982.

Kodikara, Shelton U. *Indo–Sri Lanka Accord of July 1987*. Colombo: University of Colombo Press, 1989.

Kohli, Atul. *Democracy and Discontent: India's Growing Crisis of Governability*. Cambridge: University Press, 1990.

Kohli, Atul (ed.). *The Success of India's Democracy*. Cambridge: University Press, 2001.

Kohli, Atul. "Politics of Economic Growth in India, 1980–2005, Parts I and II," *Economic and Political Weekly*, Vol. 41, No. 13 (1 April, 2006), pp. 1,251–59 and No. 14 (8 April, 2006), pp. 1,361–70.

Koithara, Verghese. *Society, State and Security: The Indian Experience*. New Delhi: Sage, 1999.

Korejo, M. S. *The Frontier Gandhi: His Place in History*. Karachi: Oxford University Press, 1993.

Korejo, M. S. *G. M. Syed: An Analysis of His Political Perspectives*. Karachi: Oxford University Press, 1998.

Korejo, M. S. *A Testament of Sindh Ethnic and Religious Extremism: A Perspective*. Karachi: Oxford University Press, 2002.

Kothari, Rajni. "The Congress 'System' in India," in Rajni Kothari (ed.), *Party Systems and Election Studies*. Bombay: Allied, 1967.

Kothari, Rajni. *Politics in India*. New York: Little, Brown, 1970.

Krishna, Gopal. "The Development of the Indian National Congress as a Mass Organisation, 1918–1923," in Thomas E. Metcalf (ed.), *Modern India: An Interpretive Anthology*. London: Collier, 1971.

Krishna, Sankaran. *Postcolonial Insecurities: India, Sri Lanka and the Question of Nationhood*. Minneapolis: University of Minnesota Press, 1999.

Krishnan, K. P. and T.V. Somanathan. "Civil Service: An Institutional Perspective," in Devesh Kapur and Pratap Bhanu Mehta (eds), *Public Institutions in India: Performance and Design*. Delhi: Oxford University Press, 2005.

Kukreja, Veena. *Civil–Military Relations in South Asia: Pakistan, Bangladesh and India*. New Delhi: Sage, 1991.

Kulke, Hermann and Dietmar Rothermund. *A History of India*. London: Routledge, 1999.

Kumar, Ashutosh. "Electoral Politics in Punjab: Study of Akali Dal," *Economic and Political Weekly*, Vol. 39, No. 14 (3 April, 2004).

Kumar, Dhruba (ed.). *State, Leadership and Politics in Nepal*. Kathmandu: Centre for Nepal and Asian Studies, 1995.

Kumar, Dhruba (ed.). *Domestic Conflict and Crisis of Governability in Nepal*. Kathmandu: Centre for Nepal and Asian Studies, 2000.

Kumar, Sanjay. "Gujarat Assembly Elections 2002: Analyzing the Verdict," *Economic and Political Weekly*, Vol. 38, No. 4 (25 January, 2003), pp. 270–75.

Kumaramangalam, Mohan. *India's Language Crisis*. Madras: New Century Book House, 1965.

Kumaraswamy, P. K. (ed.). *Security beyond Survival: Essays for K. Subrahmanyam*. New Delhi: Sage, 2004.

Kundu, Apuba. "The NDA and National Security," in Katharine Adeney and Lawrence Sáez (eds), *Coalition Politics and Hindu Nationalism*. London: Routledge, 2005, pp. 212–36.

Kux, Dennis. *Estranged Democracies: India and the United States 1941–1991*. New Delhi: Sage, 1993.

Kux, Dennis. *India–Pakistan Negotiations: Is Past Still Prologue?* Washington, DC: United States Institute for Peace, 2006.

Kuznets, Simon. *Modern Economic Growth: Rate, Structure and Speed*. New Haven, CT: Yale University Press, 1966.

Lakshman, W. D. "Economic Growth and Re-distributive Justice as Policy Goals: A Study of the Recent Experience of Sri Lanka," *Modern Ceylon Studies*, Vol. 6, No. 1 (1975), pp. 64–87. Reprinted in Prema-chandra Athukorala (ed.), *The Economic Development of South Asia*, Vol. III. Cheltenham: Edward Elgar, 2002, pp. 556–79.

Lakshman, W. D. "State Policy in Sri Lanka and its Economic Impact 1970–85: Selected Themes with Special Reference to Distributive Implications of Policy," *Upanathi*, Vol. 1, No. 1 (January 1986), pp. 5–36.

Lakshman, W. D. (ed.). *Dilemmas of Development: Fifty Years of Economic Change in Sri Lanka*. Colombo: Sri Lanka Association of Economists, 1997.

Lakshman, W. D. and C. A. Tisdell (eds.). *Sri Lanka's Development since Independence: Socio-economic Perspectives and Analyses*. New York: Nova Science, 2000.

Lal, Deepak. *The Poverty of "Development Economics."* London: Institute of Economic Affairs, 1993.

Lall, Marie. "Indian Education Policy under the NDA Government," in Katharine Adeney and Lawrence Sáez (eds), *Coalition Politics and Hindu Nationalism*. London: Routledge, 2005.

Lamb, Alastair. *Kashmir: A Disputed Legacy, 1846–1990*. Hertingfordbury: Roxford, 1991.

Lapidus, Ira M. "Islamic Revival and Modernity: The Contemporary Movements and the Historical Paradigms," *Journal of Economic and Social History of the Orient*, Vol. 40, No. 4 (1997), pp. 444–60.

Lawoti, Mahendra. *Towards a Democratic Nepal: Inclusive Political Institutions for a Multicultural Society*. New Delhi: Sage, 2005.

Lecomte-Tilouine, Marie and Pascale Dollfus (eds). *Ethnic Revival and Religious Turmoil: Identities and Representations in the Himalayas*. New Delhi: Oxford University Press, 2003.

Lefebvre, Henri. *The Survival of Capitalism*. New York: St. Martin's Press, 1976.

Lewis, William Arthur. "Economic Development with Unlimited Supplies of Labour," *Manchester School*, Vol. 22 (1954), pp. 139–91.

Linz, Juan J. and Alfred Stepan. *Problems of Democratic Transition and Consolidation: Southern Europe, South America, and Post-Communist Europe*. Baltimore, MD: Johns Hopkins University Press, 1996.

Lipton, Michael. *Why Poor People Stay Poor: A Study of Urban Bias in World Development*. London: Temple Smith, 1977.

Little, David. *The Invention of Enmity*. Washington, DC: United States Institute of Peace, 1993.

Little, Richard and Steve Smith. *Belief Systems and International Relations*. Oxford: Blackwell, 1988.

Loganathan, Keteshwaran. *Sri Lanka, Lost Opportunities: Past Attempts at Resolving Ethnic Conflict*. Colombo: University of Colombo Press, 1996.

Low, D. A. "The Forgotten Bania: Merchant Communities and the Indian National Congress," in D. A. Low (ed.), *Eclipse of Empire*. Cambridge: University Press, 1991, pp. 101–19.

Low, D. Anthony. *The Egalitarian Moment: Asia and Africa 1950–1980*. Cambridge: University Press, 1996.

Luce, Edward. *In Spite of the Gods: The Strange Rise of Modern India*. New York: Doubleday, 2007.

Luebbert, Gregory M. *Comparative Democracy: Policymaking and Governing Coalitions in Europe and Israel*. New York: Columbia University Press, 1986.

Lynn, John A. *Battle: A History of Combat and Culture*. Boulder, CO: Westview, 2003.

Mahinda Rajapakse v Chandra Fernando and Others, S.C. (FR) Application No. 387/2005 (also known as the *Helping Hambantota* case). Reported in Center for Policy Alternatives (CPA). *War, Peace and Governance in Sri Lanka: Overview and Trends 2006*. Colombo: CPA, 2007.

Mahmud, Simeen. "Health and Population: Making Progress under Poverty," *Economic and Political Weekly*, Vol. 39, No. 36 (4 September, 2004), pp. 4,081–91.

Mahmud, Wahiuddin. "Macroeconomic Management: From Stabilization to Growth?," *Economic and Political Weekly*, Vol. 39, No. 36 (4 September, 2004), pp. 4,023–32.

Mahmud Ali, S. *The Fearful State: Power, People and Internal Wars in South Asia*. London: Zed, 1993.

Malik, I. H. "Ethno-Nationalism in Pakistan: A Commentary on Muhajir Qaumi Mahaz (MQM) in Sindh," *South Asia*, Vol. 18, No. 2 (1995), pp. 49–72.

Mallikarjun, B. "The Eighth Schedule Languages: Critical Appraisal," in R. S. Gupta, Anvita Abbi and Kailash S. Aggarwal (eds), *Language and the State: Perspectives on the Eighth Schedule*. New Delhi: Creative Books, 1995.

Manik, Julfikar Ali. "Judiciary Freed from the Executive Fetters Today," *Daily Star* (Dhaka) (1 November, 2007).

Manik, Julfikar Ali and Shamim Ashraf. "Tyrant Bangla Bhai Finally Captured," *Daily Star* (Dhaka) (7 March, 2006).

Maniruzzaman, Talukder. *The Bangladesh Revolution and its Aftermath*, 2nd edition. Dhaka: University Press, 1988.

Maniruzzaman, Talukder. *Politics and Security of Bangladesh*. Dhaka: University Press, 1994.

Manoharan, N. *Counterterrorism Legislation in Sri Lanka: Evaluating Efficacy*, Policy Studies No. 28. Washington, DC: East–West Center, 2006.

Manor, James (ed.). *Sri Lanka in Change and Crisis*. London: Croom Helm, 1984.

Manor, James. "Parties and the Party System," in Atul Kohli (ed.), *India's Democracy: An Analysis of Changing State–Society Relations*. Princeton, NJ: University Press, 1988.

Manor, James. "Ethnicity and Politics in India," *International Affairs*, Vol. 72, No. 1 (1996).

Manor, James. "Southern Discomfort: The BJP in Karnataka," in Thomas Blom Hansen and Christophe Jaffrelot (eds), *The BJP and the Compulsions of Politics in India*. Delhi: Oxford University Press, 1998.

Manor, James. "Center–State Relations," in Atul Kohli (ed.), *The Success of India's Democracy*. Cambridge: University Press, 2001.

Manor, James. "The Presidency," in Devesh Kapur and Pratap Bhanu Mehta, *Public Institutions in India: Performance and Design*. Delhi: Oxford University Press, 2005.

Mansingh, Gurbir. *French Military Influence in India*. New Delhi: Knowledge World and United Services Institution of India, 2006.

Mansoor, Sabiha. *Punjabi, Urdu, English in Pakistan: A Sociolinguistic Study*. Lahore: Vanguard, 1993.

Mansoor, Sabiha. *Language Planning in Higher Education: A Case Study of Pakistan*. Karachi: Oxford University Press, 2005.

Mao Tse-tung. *Selected Works*, Vol. I. Peking: Foreign Languages Press, 1965.

Marasinghe, Lakshman. "An Outline for a Constitutional Settlement in Sri Lanka," Address at the International Center for Ethnic Studies, Colombo, 2003.

Mason, Philip. *A Matter of Honour: An Account of the Indian Army, its Officers and Men*. London: Jonathan Cape, 1974.

Matthews, Bruce. "District Development Councils in Sri Lanka," *Asian Survey*, Vol. 22 (1982), pp. 1117–34.

Maxwell, Neville. *India, the Nagas and the North-East*. London: Minority Rights Group, 1980.

McCully, Bruce. *English Education and the Origins of Indian Nationalism*. New York: Columbia University Press, 1942.

McGilvray, Dennis B. and Mirak Raheem. *Muslim Perspectives on the Sri Lankan Conflict*, Policy Studies 41. Washington, DC: East–West Center, 2007.

McGrath, Allen. *The Destruction of Pakistan's Democracy*. Karachi: Oxford University Press, 1996.

McMillan, Alistair. "The BJP Coalition: Partisanship and Power-Sharing in Government," in Katharine Adeney and Lawrence Sáez (eds), *Coalition Politics and Hindu Nationalism*. London and New York: Routledge, 2005.

Mehta, Pratap Bhanu. *The Burden of Democracy*. Delhi: Penguin, 2003.

Menezes, S. L. *Fidelity and Honour: The Indian Army from the Seventeenth to the Twenty-first Century*. New Delhi: Oxford University Press, 1999.

Menon, V. P. *The Transfer of Power in India*. Princeton, NJ: University Press, 1957.

Metcalf, Thomas. R. *Ideologies of the Raj*. New York: Cambridge University Press, 1994.

Meyer, Eric. *Sri Lanka: Entre Particularisme et Mondialisation*. Paris: La Documentation Française, 2001.

Migdal, Joel. "State Building and the Non-Nation State," *Journal of International Affairs*, Vol. 58, No. 1 (2004).

Misra, B. B. *Government and Bureaucracy in India: 1947–1976*. New Delhi: Oxford University Press, 1986.

Mitra, Subrata K. "The NDA and the Politics of 'Minorities' in India," in Katharine Adeney and Lawrence Sáez (eds), *Coalition Politics and Hindu Nationalism*. London and New York: Routledge, 2005.

Mitra, S. K. and R. A. Lewis (eds), *Sub-nationalist Movements in South Asia*. Boulder, CO: Westview Press, 1997.

Mohan, C. *Crossing the Rubicon: The Shaping of India's New Foreign Policy*. New Delhi: Viking, 2003.

Moon, Penderel. *Divide and Quit*. London: Chatto & Windus, 1961.

Moore, Mick. "Thoroughly Modern Revolutionaries: The JVP in Sri Lanka," *Modern Asian Studies*, Vol. 27, No. 3 (July 1993), pp. 593–642.

Moore, R. J. *Churchill, Cripps, and India, 1939–1945*. Oxford: Clarendon Press, 1979.

Moustafa, Tamir. "Law versus the State: The Judicialization of Politics in Egypt," *Law and*

Social Inquiry, Vol. 28, No. 4 (Fall 2003), pp. 883–93.

Mukarji, Nirmal K. and Balveer Arora. *Federalism in India: Origin and Development*. New Delhi: Vikas, 1992.

Mukherjee, Kalyan and Rajendra Singh Yadav. *Bhojpur: Naxalism in the Plains of Bihar*. New Delhi: Radha Krishna, 1980.

Mukherjee, Partha N. *et al. Left Extremism and Electoral Politics: Naxalite Participation in Elections*. New Delhi: Indian Council of Social Science Research, 1979.

Muni, S. D. *Pangs of Proximity: India's and Sri Lanka's Ethnic Crisis*. New Delhi: Sage, 1993.

Muni, S. D. *The Maoist Insurgency in Nepal: The Challenge and the Response*. New Delhi: Rupa & Co., 2003.

Muralidhar, S. "Implementation of Court Orders in the Area of Economic, Social and Cultural Rights: An Overview of the Experience of the Indian Judiciary," First South Asian Regional Judicial Colloquium on Access to Justice, New Delhi, 1–3 November, 2002.

Murshid, Tazeen M. "State, Nation and Identity: The Quest for Legitimacy in Bangladesh," in Amita Shastri and A. Jeyaratnam Wilson (eds), *The Postcolonial States of South Asia: Democracy, Development and Identity*. New York: Palgrave, 2001, pp. 158–82.

Myers-Scotton, Carol. "Elite Closure as a Powerful Language Strategy: The African Case," *International Journal of the Sociology of Knowledge*, No. 103 (1993), pp. 149–63.

Myrdal, Gunnar. *Asian Drama: An Enquiry into the Poverty of Nations*, Vol. II. New York: Twentieth Century Fund, 1968.

Myrdal, Jan. "Seven Days with Telengana [*sic*] Naxalites," *New Delhi Magazine* (29 September–12 October, 1980).

Naoroji, Dadabhai. *Poverty and Un-British Rule in India*. London: Swan Sonnenschein, 1901.

Nasr, Vali. "The Rise of Sunni Militancy in Pakistan: The Changing Role of Islamism and the Ulema in Society and Politics," *Modern Asian Studies*, Vol. 34, No. 1 (2000), pp. 145–54.

Nasr, Vali. "Islam, the State and the Rise of Sectarian Militancy in Pakistan," in Christophe Jaffrelot (ed.), *Pakistan: Nationalism without a Nation*. New Delhi: Manohar, 2002, pp. 88–92.

National Commission for Enterprises in the Unorganized Sector. *Report on Social Security for Unorganized Workers*. New Delhi: National Commission for Enterprises in the Unorganized Sector, 2006.

National Council for Educational Research and Training. *Sixth All India Educational Survey: Main Report*. New Delhi: National Council for Educational Research and Training, 1999.

National Democratic Institute (NDI). *Report of the National Democratic Institute (NDI) Pre-election Delegation to Bangladesh's 2006/07 Parliamentary Elections*. Dhaka: NDI, 11 September, 2006.

Nawaz, Shuja. *Crossed Swords: Pakistan, its Army, and the Wars Within*. Karachi: Oxford University Press, 2008.

Nayar, Kuldip. *Between the Lines*. New Delhi: Allied Publishers, 1969.

Nehru, Jawaharlal. *The Question of Language*. Allahabad: Congress Political and Economic Studies, 1937.

Nettl, J. P. "The State as Conceptual Variable," *World Politics*, Vol. 20 (July 1968), pp. 559–92.

Nettle, David and Suzanne Romaine. *Vanishing Voices: The Extinction of the World's Languages*. New York: Oxford University Press, 2000.

Newberg, Paula R. *Judging the State: Courts and Constitutional Politics in Pakistan*. Cambridge: University Press, 1994.

Nissanka, H. S. S. *Sri Lanka's Foreign Policy: A Study in Non-Alignment*. New Delhi: Vikas, 1984.

Nizamani, Nizamuddin. "Socio-Political Unrest and Vulnerable Human Security in Balochistan," in Sustainable Development Policy Institute, *At the Crossroads: South Asian Research, Policy and Development in a Globalized World*. Islamabad: Sustainable Development Policy Institute, 2007.

Norris, Pippa and Ronald Inglehart. "Islam and the West: Testing the Clash of Civilizations Thesis," KSG Working Paper No. RWP02, April 2002.

Nurullah, S. and J. P. Naik. *A History of Education in India (during the British Period)*, 2nd edition. Bombay: Macmillan, 1951.

Nye, Joseph. *Soft Power: The Means to Success in World Politics*. New York: Public Affairs, 2004.

Oberoi, Harjot. *The Construction of Religious Boundaries: Culture, Identity and Diversity in the Sikh Tradition*. Chicago: University of Chicago Press, 1994.

Oberst, Robert C. "Proportional Representation and Electoral System Change in Sri Lanka," in James Manor (ed.), *Sri Lanka in Change and Crisis*. London: Croom Helm, 1984, pp. 118–33.

441

Oberst, Robert C. "Government Structure," in Craig Baxter, Yogendra K. Malik, Charles H. Kennedy and Robert C. Oberst (eds), *Government and Politics in South Asia*, 5th edition. Boulder, CO: Westview Press, 2002.

O'Donnell, Guillermo. "The Perpetual Crises of Democracy," *Journal of Democracy*, Vol. 18, No. 1 (2007), pp. 5–11.

Ofstad, Arve. "Countries in Violent Conflict and Aid Strategies: The Case of Sri Lanka," *World Development*, Vol. 30, No. 2 (2002), pp. 165–80.

Ogura, Kiyoko. "Maoists, People, and the State as Seen from Rolpa and Rukum," in H. Ishii, D. Gellner and K. Nawa (eds), *Political and Social Transformations in North India and Nepal*. New Delhi: Manohar, 2007.

Ogura, Kiyoko. "Maoists' People's Governments, 2001–05: The Power in Wartime," in D. N. Gellner and K. Hachhethu (eds), *Local Democracy in South Asia: Microprocesses of Democratization in Nepal and its Neighbours*. Delhi: Sage, 2008.

O'Leary, Brendan and Arthur Paul. "Introduction: Northern Ireland as the Site of State and Nation-Building Failures," in John McGarry and Brendan O'Leary (eds), *The Future of Northern Ireland*. Oxford: Clarendon Press, 1990.

O'Leary, Brendan, Ian S. Lustick and Thomas Callaghy (eds). *Right-sizing the State: The Politics of Moving Borders*. Oxford: University Press, 2001.

Oommen, T. K. "New Nationalisms and Collective Rights: The Case of South Asia," in Tariq Madood and Judith Squires (eds), *Ethnicity, Nationalism and Minority Rights*. Cambridge: University Press, 2004, pp. 121–43.

Overstreet, Gene D. and Marshall Windmiller. *Communism in India*. Bombay: Perennial Press, 1960.

Pai Panandiker, V. A. (ed.). *Problems of Governance in South Asia*. Dhaka: University Press, 2000.

Pakistan, cases, *Darwesh M. Arbey, Advocate v Federation of Pakistan through the Law Secretary and 2 Others*, PLD (1980) Lahore 206.

Pakistan, cases, *Dosso and Another v The State and Others*, PLD (1957) (W.P.) Quetta 9.

Pakistan, cases, *F. B. Ali v The State*, PLD (1975) Lahore 999.

Pakistan, cases, *Fazlul Quader Chowdhry and Others v Mr. Muhammad Abdul Haque*, PLD (1963) Supreme Court 486.

Pakistan, cases, *Federation of Pakistan and Others v Haji Muhammad Saifullah Khan and Others*, (1988) PSC 338.

Pakistan, cases, *Federation of Pakistan et al. v Moulvi Tamizuddin Khan*, PLD (1955) FC 240.

Pakistan, cases, *Government of East Pakistan v Mrs. Rowshan Bijaya Shaukat Ali Khan*, PLD (1966) Supreme Court 286.

Pakistan, cases, *Haji Ahmed v Federation of Pakistan through Secretary, Ministry of Justice and Parliamentary Affairs and 88 Others*, Constitutional Petitions D-76, 163, 168 of 1989.

Pakistan, cases, *Islamic Republic of Pakistan through Secretary, Ministry of Interior and Kashmir Affairs, Islamabad v Mr. Abdul Wali Khan MNA*, No. 1 of 1975.

Pakistan, cases, *Malik Ghulam Jilani v The Government of West Pakistan*, PLD (1967) Supreme Court 373.

Pakistan, cases, *Mohammed Ayub Khuro v Federation of Pakistan*, PLD (1950) Sind 49; Reference by His Excellency the Governor-General, PLD 1955 Federal Court 435.

Pakistan, cases, *Muhammad Bachal Memon v Government of Sind*, PLD (1987) Karachi 296.

Pakistan, cases, *Usif Patel and 2 Others v The Crown*, PLD (1955) Federal Court 387 (Appellate Jurisdiction).

Pakistan, cases, *Zafar Iqbal v Province of Sind and 2 Others*, PLD (1973) Karachi 243.

Pakistan, cases, *Zia-ur Rahman v The State*, PLD (1972) Lahore 382.

Pakistan Government. *Census of Pakistan 1951*. Karachi: Government of Pakistan, 1951.

Pakistan Government. *Census Report of Pakistan 1961*. Karachi: Government of Pakistan, 1961.

Pakistan Government. *The Constitution of the Islamic Republic of Pakistan*. Islamabad: Government of Pakistan, 1963.

Pakistan Government. *Report of the Commission on Student Problems and Welfare: Summary of Important Observations and Recommendations*. Islamabad: Government of Pakistan, Ministry of Education, Central Bureau of Education, 1966.

Pakistan Government. *National Education Census: Pakistan*. Islamabad: Government of Pakistan, 2006.

"Pakistan's Dilemma," *Civil and Military Gazette*, 6 March, 1955, p. 4.

Panagariya, Arvind. *India: The Emerging Giant*. Oxford: University Press, 2008.

Panda, Basudev. *Indian Bureaucracy: An Inside Story*. New Delhi: Uppal, 1978.

Pandey, Gyanendra. *The Construction of Communalism in Colonial India*. Delhi: Oxford University Press, 1990.

442

Pandey, Gyanendra. *Remembering Partition: Violence, Nationalism and History in India.* Cambridge: University Press, 2001.

Papanek, Gustav F. *Pakistan's Development: Social Goals and Private Incentives.* Cambridge, MA: Harvard University Press, 1967.

Parthasarathi, G. (ed.). *Jawaharlal Nehru: Letters to Chief Ministers 1947–1964,* Vol. 5: *1958–1964.* New Delhi: Oxford University Press, 1989.

Pasha, Hafiz A. and Tariq Hasan. "Development Ranking of Districts of Pakistan," in S. Akbar Zaidi (ed.), *Regional Imbalances and the National Question in Pakistan.* Lahore: Vanguard, 1992.

Patel, Dorab. *Testament of a Liberal.* Karachi: Oxford University Press, 2000.

Paul, Samuel and M. Vivekananda. "Holding a Mirror to the New Lok Sabha," *Economic and Political Weekly,* Vol. 34, No. 45 (12 November, 2004), pp. 4,927–34.

Peiris, G. L. "Judicial Review of Legislative and Administrative Action." Unpublished conference paper, 28 August, 1988.

People's Union for Democratic Rights, Delhi and People's Union for Civil Liberties, Chhattisgarh. *When the State Makes War on its Own People.* Delhi: People's Union for Democratic Rights and People's Union for Civil Liberties, 2006.

Perkovich, George. *India's Nuclear Bomb: The Impact on Global Proliferation.* Berkeley: University of California Press, 1999.

Philips, C. H. and W. Wainwright (eds). *The Partition of India: Policies and Perspectives, 1935–1947.* London: Allen & Unwin, 1970.

Phillipson, Robert. *Linguistic Imperialism.* Oxford: University Press, 1992.

Political Science Association of Nepal (POLSAN). *Political Parties and the Parliamentary Process in Nepal: A Study of the Transitional Phase.* Kathmandu: POLSAN, 1992.

Prasad, Bisheshwar (ed.). *Official History of the Indian Armed Forces in the Second World War: Expansion of the Armed Forces and Defence Organization, 1939–1945.* New Delhi: Combined Inter-Services Historical Section, India and Pakistan, 1965.

Pratap, Anita. *Island of Blood.* Bombay: Penguin, 2001.

Prebisch, Raoul. *The Economic Development of Latin America and its Principal Problems.* Lake Success, NY: United Nations, 1950.

Puri, Balraj. *Kashmir: Towards Insurgency.* New Delhi: Orient Longman, 1995.

Quah, Jon S. T. "Curbing Asian Corruption: An Impossible Dream?," *Current History* (April 2006), pp. 176–79.

Radhakrishnan, P. "Backward Class Movements in Tamil Nadu," in M. N. Srinivas, *Caste: Its Twentieth Century Avatar.* New Delhi: Viking, 1996, pp. 110–34.

Radhakrishnan, S. *Report of the University Education Commission.* New Delhi: Government of India, 1977.

Rahman, Latifur. "Judicial Independence and the Accountability of Judges and the Constitution of Bangladesh," in 52 DLR (2000) Journal 65.

Rahman, Mahmuduk. *Economic Governance Issues and Bangladeshi Experience of Growth and Governance.* Dhaka, 2006.

Rahman, Tariq. *Language and Politics in Pakistan.* Karachi: Oxford University Press, 1996; reprint edition, Delhi: Orient Longman, 2007.

Rahman, Tariq. *Language, Ideology and Power: Language-Learning among the Muslims of Pakistan and North India.* Karachi: Oxford University Press, 2002.

Rahman, Tariq. *Denizens of Alien Worlds: A Study of Education, Inequality and Polarization in Pakistan.* Karachi: Oxford University Press, 2004.

Rahman, Tariq. "Multilingualism and Language Vitality in Pakistan," in Anju Saxena and Lars Borin (eds), *Trends in Linguistics: Lesser-Known Languages of South Asia: Status and Policies, Case Studies and Applications of Information Technology.* Berlin and New York: Mouton, 2006.

Rahman, Tariq. "Urdu as an Islamic Language," *Annual of Urdu Studies,* No. 21 (2006), pp. 101–19.

Rahman, Tariq. "The Role of English in Pakistan with Special Reference to Tolerance and Militancy," in Amy B. Tsui and James Tollefson (eds), *Language Policy, Culture, and Identity in Asian Contexts.* Mahwah, NJ: Lawrence Erlbaum, 2007, pp. 219–39.

Rai, Alok. *Hindi Nationalism.* Hyderabad: Orient Longman, 2001.

Rajagopalachari, C. *The Question of English.* Madras: Bharatan, 1962.

Ram, Mohan. *Hindi vs. India: The Meaning of DMK.* New Delhi: Rachna Prakashan, 1968.

Ramachandran, Raju. "The Supreme Court and the Basic Structure Doctrine," in B. N. Kirpal, Ashok H. Desai, Gopal Subramanium, Rajeev Dhavan and Raju Ramachandran (eds), *Supreme but not Infallible: Essays in Honour of the Supreme Court of*

India. New Delhi: Oxford University Press, 2000, pp. 107–33.

Ramachandran, V. K. "On Kerala's Development Achievements," in Jean Drèze and Amartya Sen (eds), *Indian Development*. Delhi: Oxford University Press, 1996.

Ramasubramaniam, K.A. "Historical Development and Essential Features of the Federal System," in Nirmal Mukarji and Balveer Arora (eds), *Federalism in India: Origins and Development*. New Delhi: Vikas, 1992.

Rao, P. V. R. *Red Tape and White Cap*. New Delhi: Orient Longman, 1970.

Rao, V. K. R. V. *Many Languages, One Nation: The Problem of Integration*. Bombay: Mahatma Gandhi Memorial Research and Library, 1978.

Rashiduzzaman, M. "Political Unrest and Democracy in Bangladesh," *Asian Survey*, Vol. 37, No. 3 (1997), pp. 254–68.

Rashiduzzaman, M. "Bangladesh in 2001: The Election and a New Political Reality?," *Asian Survey*, Vol. 42, No. 1 (2002), pp. 183–91.

Rau, B. N. *India's Constitution in the Making*. Bombay: Orient Longman, 1960.

Rauch, James and Peter Evans. "Bureaucratic Structure and Bureaucratic Performance in Less Developed Countries," *Journal of Public Economics*, Vol. 75, No. 1 (2000), pp. 49–71.

Ray, Rabindra. *The Naxalites and their Ideology*. Delhi: Oxford University Press, 1988.

Redissi, Hamadi and Jan-Erik Lane. "Does Islam Provide a Theory of Violence?," in Amélie Blom, Laetitia Bucaille and Luis Martinez (eds), *The Enigma of Islamist Violence*. London: Hurst, 2007.

Reetz, Dietrich. "God's Kingdom on Earth: The Contestations of the Public Sphere by Islamic Groups in Colonial India (1900–1947)." Rehabilitation thesis, Abstract, Berlin University, Berlin, 2001.

Rehman, Fazlur. "Islam in Pakistan," *Journal of South Asian and Middle Eastern Studies*, Vol. 8, No. 4 (1985).

Rennell, James. *Memoir of a Map of Hindoostan: or the Mogul Empire: with an introduction, illustrative of the geography and present division of that country*. London: printed by M. Brown, 1788.

Riaz, Ali. "Islamist Parties and Democracy in Bangladesh," Paper prepared for the Annual Meeting of the American Political Science Association, Chicago, 30 August–2 September, 2007.

Rice, Eugene and Anthony Grafton. *The Foundations of Early Modern Europe, 1460–1559*. New York: W.W. Norton, 1994.

Richardson, John. *Paradise Poisoned: Learning about Conflict, Terrorism and Development from Sri Lanka's Civil Wars*. Kandy: International Centre for Ethnic Studies, 2004.

Richter, Melvin. *The History of Political and Social Concepts: A Critical Introduction*. New York: Oxford University Press, 1995.

Rishikesh. Shaha. *An Introduction to Nepal*. Kathmandu: RPB, 1976.

Rizvi, Hasan-Askari. *Military, State, and Society in Pakistan*. London: Macmillan, 2000.

Roberts, Michael (ed.). *Documents of the Ceylon National Congress and Nationalist Politics in Ceylon, 1929–1950* (4 vols.). Colombo: Department of National Archives, 1977.

Roberts, Michael. "Ethnic Conflict in Sri Lanka and Sinhalese Perspectives: Barriers to Accommodation," *Modern Asian Studies*, Vol. 12, No. 3 (1978), pp. 353–76.

Robinson, Francis. *Separatism among Indian Muslims: The Politics of the United Provinces' Muslims 1860–1923*. Cambridge: University Press, 1975.

Robinson, Marguerite. *Local Politics: The Law of the Fishes—Development through Political Change in Medak District, Andhra Pradesh (South India)*. Delhi: Oxford University Press, 1988.

Rodden, Jonathan and Steven Wilkinson. "The Shifting Political Economy of Redistribution in the Indian Federation." Preliminary draft prepared for the Annual Meeting of the International Society for New Institutional Economics, Tucson, AZ, 30 September–3 October, 2004.

Rodrik, Dani and Arvind Subramanian. *Why India Can Grow at 7 Percent a Year or More: Projections and Reflections*, IMF Working Paper 04/118. Washington, DC: International Monetary Fund, 2004.

Rose, Leo. E. "The National Political Culture and Institutions in Nepal," in Amita Shastri and A. Jeyaratnam Wilson (eds), *The Post-colonial States of South Asia: Democracy, Development and Identity*. New York: Palgrave, 2001, pp. 114–38.

Rosenberg, Gerald N. *The Hollow Hope: Can Courts Bring About Social Change?* Chicago: University of Chicago Press, 1991.

Rosenberg, Gerald N. "The Real World of Constitutional Rights: The Supreme Court and the Implementation of the Abortion Decisions," in Lee Epstein (ed.), *Contemplating Courts*. Washington, DC: CQ Press, 1995.

Rousseau, Jean-Jacques. *The Social Contract*, trans. Maurice Cranston. New York: Penguin, 2006.

Roy, Ashis Kumar. *The Spring Thunder and After*. Calcutta: Minerva Associates, 1975.

Roy, Olivier. *Globalized Islam: The Search for a New Ummah*. New York: Columbia University Press and Centre d'Études et de Recherches Internationales, 2004.

Rubinoff, Arthur G. "Conflicting Ambitions in Goa's Parliamentary Elections," in Ramashray Roy and Paul Wallace (eds), *Indian Politics and the 1998 Election: Regionalism, Hindutva and State Politics*. New Delhi: Sage, 1999.

Rudolph, Lloyd I. "The Faltering Novitiate: Rajiv at Home and Abroad in 1988," in Marshall M. Bouton and Philip Oldenburg (eds), *India Briefing, 1989*. Boulder, CO: Westview Press, 1989.

Rudolph, Lloyd I. "Tod vs Mill: Clashing Perspectives on British Rule in India and Indian Civilization," in Giles Tillotson (ed.), *James Tod's Rajasthan*. Mumbai: Marg, 2007.

Rudolph, Lloyd I. and John Kurt Jacobsen. "Historicizing the Modern State," in Lloyd I. Rudolph and John Kurt Jacobsen (eds), *Experiencing the State*. New Delhi and New York: Oxford University Press, 2006, pp. xi–xxix.

Rudolph, Lloyd I. and Susanne Hoeber Rudolph. *The Modernity of Tradition*. Chicago: University of Chicago Press, 1967, 1984.

Rudolph, Lloyd and Susanne Hoeber Rudolph. *In Pursuit of Lakshmi: The Political Economy of the Indian State*. Chicago: University of Chicago Press, 1987.

Rudolph, Lloyd and Susanne Hoeber Rudolph. "Redoing the Constitutional Design: From an Interventionist to a Regulatory State," in Atul Kohli (ed.), *The Success of India's Democracy*. Cambridge: University Press, 2001.

Rudolph, Susanne Hoeber. "The Imperialism of Categories: Situating Knowledge in a Globalizing World," *Perspectives on Politics*, Vol. 3, No. 5 (March 2005), pp. 5–14.

Rudolph, Susanne Hoeber and James Piscatori (eds). *Transnational Religion and Fading States*. Boulder, CO: Westview Press, 1997.

Rudolph, Susanne and Lloyd Rudolph. *In Pursuit of Lakshmi*. Chicago: University of Chicago Press, 1996.

Ruggie, John Gerard. "Territoriality at Millennium's End," in John Gerard Ruggie, *Constructing the World Polity: Essays on International Institutionalization*. London: Routledge, 1998.

Rupesinghe, Kumar (ed.). *Negotiating Peace in Sri Lanka: Efforts, Failures and Lessons*. Colombo: Foundation for Co-existence, 2006.

Saddiqa, Ayesha. *Military Inc. inside Pakistan's Military Economy*. London: Pluto Press, 2007.

Sáez, Lawrence. *Federalism without a Centre: The Impact of Political and Economic Reforms on India's Federal System*. Thousand Oaks, CA: Sage, 2002.

Safran, William. "Non-separatist Policies Regarding Ethnic Minorities: Positive Approaches and Ambiguous Consequences," *International Political Science Review*, Vol. 15. No. 1 (1994).

Sahni, Sati. *Center–State Relations: Proceedings of a Meeting of Leaders*. New Delhi: Vikas, 1984.

Sainath, Palagummi. *Everybody Loves a Good Drought: Stories from India's Poorest Districts*. New Delhi: Penguin India, 1996.

Saleem, Ali. "Inaccessible Justice in Pakistan," Asian Legal Resource Center, Hong Kong, 11 August, 2004.

Samad, Yunas. *A Nation in Turmoil: Nationalism and Ethnicity in Pakistan, 1937–58*. New Delhi: Sage, 1995.

Samad, Yunas. "Pakistan or Punjabistan: Crisis of National Identity," in Gurharpal Singh and Ian Talbot (eds), *Punjabi Identity: Continuity and Change*. New Delhi: Manohar, 1995, pp. 61–87.

Sanmugathasan, N. *Political Memoirs of an Unrepentant Communist*. Colombo: Colombo Apothecaries, 1989.

Sanyal, Kanu. *Report on the Terai Peasants' Movement*. Calcutta: CPI(M-L), 1969.

Saran, P. *The Provincial Government of the Mughals, 1526–1658*, 2nd edition. London: Asia Publishing House, 1973.

Saran, Shyam. "Prime Minister's Special Envoy on Kashmir," *Tribune*, Chandigarh, 23 November, 2006 (online).

Saraswathi, S. *Minorities in Madras State: Group Interests in Modern Politics*. Delhi: Impex India, 1974.

Sarkar, Sumit. *Modern India 1885–1947*. New Delhi: Macmillan, 1983.

Sarkar, Sumit. "Indian Democracy: The Historical Inheritance," in Atul Kohli (ed.), *The Success of India's Democracy*. Cambridge: University Press, 2001.

Sarvananthan, Muttukrishna. "In Pursuit of a Mythical State of Tamil Eelam: Rejoinder to Kristian Stokke," *Third World Quarterly*, Vol. 28, No. 6 (2007), pp. 1,185–95.

Sathe, S. P. *Judicial Activism in India*. Delhi: Oxford University Press, 2002.

Sayeed, K. B. *Pakistan: The Formative Phase, 1857–1948*. London: Oxford University Press, 1968.

Schmitter, Philippe C. and Terry Lynn Karl. "What Democracy Is . . . and Is Not," *Journal of Democracy* (1991), pp. 50–54.

Scott, David. *Refashioning Futures: Criticism after Postcoloniality*. Princeton, NJ: University Press, 1999.

Seervai, H. M. *Constitutional Law of India*, 3rd edition. New Delhi: N. M. Tripathy, 1983.

Sen, Abhijit and Himanshu. "Poverty and Inequality in India I," *Economic and Political Weekly*, Vol. 39, No. 38 (18 September, 2004), pp. 4,247–63.

Sen, Abhijit and Himanshu. "Poverty and Inequality in India II," *Economic and Political Weekly*, Vol. 39, No. 39 (25 September, 2004), pp. 4,361–75.

Sen, Amartya K. "Public Action and Quality of Life in Developing Countries," *Oxford Bulletin of Economics and Statistics*, Vol. 43, No. 4 (1981).

Sen, Amartya Kumar. "More than 100 Million Women Are Missing," *New York Review of Books*, Vol. 37, No. 20 (20 December, 1990).

Sen, Amartya. *Identity and Violence: The Illusion of Destiny*. London: Allen Lane, 2006.

Sen, Ronojoy. "Tilting at Windmills: Indian Historians and the Contestation over 1857," *Biblio: A Review of Books*, Special issue on "The Uprising of 1857: 150 Years Later," Vol. 12, No. 3–4 (March–April 2007).

Seneviratne, H. L. *The Work of Kings: New Buddhism in Sri Lanka*. Chicago: University Press, 1999.

Seshan, T. N. with Sanjoy Hazarika. *The Degeneration of India*. New Delhi: Penguin Viking, 1995.

Shah, A. B. (ed.). *The Great Debate*. Bombay: Lalvani, 1968.

Shah, Rishikesh. *Essays in the Practices of Government in Nepal*. New Delhi: Manohar, 1982.

Shah, Sajjad Ali. *Law Courts in a Glass House: An Autobiography*. Karachi: Oxford University Press, 2001.

Shankar, Shylashri. *Scaling Justice: India's Supreme Court, Anti-Terror Laws and Social Rights*, forthcoming.

Shanmugam, S. V. (in Tamil) *mozhi vaLarcciyum mozhi uNarvum: canka kaalam* [Language development and language awareness: Sangam period]. Madras: Manivasagar Patippakam, 1989.

Sharma, Prayag Raj. "Ethnicity and National Integration in Nepal: A Statement of the Problem," *Journal of Nepalese Studies*, Vol. 1 (July–December 1987), pp. 23–30.

Sharma, Prayag Raj. "How to Tend this Garden," *Himal* (May–June 1992), pp. 7–9.

Shastri, Amita. "Sri Lanka's Provincial Council System: A Solution to the Ethnic Problem?," *Asian Survey*, Vol. 32 (1992), pp. 723–43.

Shastri, Amita. "Estate Tamils, the Ceylon Citizenship Act of 1948 and Sri Lankan Politics," *Contemporary South Asia*, Vol. 8, No. 1 (1999), pp. 65–86.

Shastri, Amita. "Channelling Ethnicity through Electoral Reform in Sri Lanka," *Journal of Commonwealth and Comparative Politics*, Vol. 43 (2005), pp. 34–60.

Shugart, Matthew and John Carey. *Presidents and Assemblies: Constitutional Design and Electoral Dynamics*. Cambridge: University Press, 1992.

Siddiqa, Ayesha. *Military Inc.: Inside Pakistan's Military Economy*. London: Pluto, 2007.

Sidhu, Waheguru Pal Singh, Bushra Asif and Samii, Cyrus. *Kashmir: New Voices, New Approaches*. Boulder, CO: Lynne Rienner, 2006.

Simpson, A. W. Brian. *Human Rights and the End of Empire: Britain and the Genesis of the European Convention*. Oxford: Clarendon Press, 2001.

Singer, Hans. "The Distribution of Gains between Investing and Borrowing Countries," *American Economic Review*, Vol. 40 (1950), pp. 478–96.

Singh, Gurharpal. "Understanding the 'Punjab Problem,'" *Asian Survey*, Vol. 27, No. 2 (December 1987), pp. 1,268–77.

Singh, Gurharpal. "The Punjab Crisis since 1984: A Reassessment," *Ethnic and Racial Studies*, Vol. 18, No. 3 (1995), pp. 476–93.

Singh, Gurharpal. *Ethnic Conflict in India: A Case-Study of Punjab*. Basingstoke: Macmillan, 2000.

Singh, Gurharpal. "On the Nuclear Precipice: India, Pakistan and the Kashmir Crisis," *openDemocracy* (7 August, 2002). Available at: http://www.open democracy.net/conflict-india_pakistan/article_194.jsp (accessed on 23 November, 2006).

Singh, Gurharpal. "The Indo-Pakistan Summit: Hope for Kashmir?," *openDemocracy* (16 February, 2004). Available at: http://www.opendemocracy. net/conflict-india_pakistan/article_1738.jsp (accessed on 15 November, 2006).

Singh, Jaswant. *Defending India*. Basingstoke: Macmillan, and New York: St. Martin's Press, 1999.

446

Singh, Narendra Kumar. *Bureaucracy: Positions and Persons*. New Delhi: Abhinav, 1974.

Sinha, Arun. *Against the Few: Struggles of India's Rural Poor*. London: Zed Books, 1991.

Sinha, Aseema. *The Regional Roots of Development Politics in India: A Divided Leviathan*. Bloomington: Indiana University Press, 2005.

Sinha, Moni. *Jeebon Sangram*. Dhaka: Jatiya Sahitya Prakashani, 1983.

Sisson, Richard and Leo E. Rose. *War and Secession: India, Pakistan and the Creation of Bangladesh*. Berkeley: University California Press, 1990.

Smith, Anthony D. "The Nation: Real or Imagined," in E. Mortimer (ed.), *People, Nation and State: The Meaning of Ethnicity and Nationalism*. London: Tauris, 1999.

Snodgrass, Donald R. *Ceylon: An Export Economy in Transition*. Homewood, IL: Richard D. Irwin, 1966.

Sobhan, Rehman. "Structural Dimensions of Malgovernance in Bangladesh," *Economic and Political Weekly*, Vol. 39, No. 36 (4 September, 2004), pp. 4,101–08.

Spencer, Jonathan. "Collective Violence and Everyday Practice in Sri Lanka," *Modern Asian Studies*, Vol. 24 (1990), pp. 603–23.

Spencer, Jonathan (ed.). *Sri Lanka: History and the Roots of Conflict*. London: Routledge, 1990.

Spruyt, Hendrik. *The Sovereign State and its Competitors: An Analysis of System Change*. Princeton, NJ: University Press, 1994.

Sri Lanka, cases, *Daramitipola Ratnasara Thero v P. Udugampola* (1983) 1 Sri LR 461.

Sri Lanka, cases, *EFL v UDA* FR 47/2004.

Sri Lanka, cases, *In Re The Thirteenth Amendment to the Constitution and Provincial Councils Bill*, S.C. 7/87 (Spl) TO S.C. 48/87 (Spl).

Sri Lanka, cases, *J. Dandaniya and Edirimuni Samith de Silva v Sri Lanka*, C.A. Appeal 66/2006.

Sri Lanka, cases, *Sinharasa v Sri Lanka*, Case No. 1033/2004.

Sri Lanka Government, Department of Census and Statistics (DCS). *Socio-economic Survey of Sri Lanka, 1969/70*. Colombo: DCS, 1971.

Sridharan, Eswaran. "Principles, Power and Coalition Politics in India: Lessons from Theory, Comparison and Recent History," in D. D. Khanna and Gert W. Kueck (eds), *Principles, Power and Politics*. New Delhi: Macmillan, 1999.

Sridharan, Eswaran, "Coalitions and Party Strategies in India's Parliamentary Federation," *Publius: The Journal of Federalism*, Vol. 33, No. 4 (Fall 2003).

Srinivas, M. N. *Caste: Its Twentieth Century Avatar*. New Delhi: Viking, 1996.

Srinivasan, Thirukodikaval Nilakanta. "Reform of Industrial and Trade Policies," *Economic and Political Weekly*, Vol. 26, No. 37 (14 September, 1991), pp. 2,143–45.

Stapenhurst, Rick and Sahr J. Kpundeh (eds). *Curbing Corruption: Toward a Model for Building National Integrity*. Washington, DC: World Bank, 1999.

Stein, Burton. *Thomas Munro: The Origins of the Colonial State and his Vision of Empire*. Delhi and New York: Oxford University Press, 1989.

Stern, Jessica. "Pakistan's Jihad Culture," *Foreign Affairs*, Vol. 79, No. 6 (November–December 2000).

Stokes, Eric. *The English Utilitarians and India*. New Delhi: Oxford University Press, 1989.

Stokke, Kristian. "Building the Tamil Eelam State: Emerging State Institutions and Forms of Governance in LTTE-Controlled Areas in Sri Lanka," *Third World Quarterly*, Vol. 27, No. 6 (2006), pp. 1,021–40.

Stulligross, David. "A Piece of Land to Call One's Own: Multicultural Federalism and Institutional Innovation in India." Ph.D. dissertation, Department of Political Science, University of California, Berkeley, 2002.

Subramanyam, K. *Shedding Shibboleths: India's Evolving Strategic Outlook*. Delhi: Wordsmiths, 2005.

Sundarayya, P. *Telangana People's Struggle and its Lessons*. Calcutta: CPI (Marxist), 1972.

Sury, M. M. *Fiscal Federalism in India*. Delhi: Indian Tax Institute, 1998.

Swamy Narayan, M. R. *Tigers of Lanka: From Boys to Guerrillas*. New Delhi: South Asia Books, 1995.

Talbot, Ian. *Punjab and the Raj, 1849–1947*. New Delhi: Manohar, 1988.

Talbot, Ian. *Khizr Tiwana, the Punjab Unionist Party and the Partition of India*. London: Curzon, 1996.

Talbot, Ian. *Pakistan: A Modern History*. London: Hurst, 1998.

Talbot, Ian. *India and Pakistan: Inventing the Nation*. London: Arnold, 2000.

Talbot, Ian. *Divided Cities: Partition and its Aftermath in Lahore and Amritsar 1947–1957*. Karachi: Oxford University Press, 2006.

Talbott, Strobe. *Engaging India: Diplomacy, Democracy and the Bomb—A Memoir*. Washington, DC: Brookings Institution Press, 2004.

Tambiah, S. J. "Ethnic Representation in Ceylon's Higher Administrative Services, 1870–1946,"

University of Ceylon Review, Vol. 13, No. 2–3 (April–July 1955), pp. 113–34.

Tambiah, Stanley. *World Conqueror and World Renouncer: A Study of Buddhism and Polity in Thailand against a Historical Background.* Cambridge and New York: Cambridge University Press, 1976.

Tambiah, Stanley J. *Sri Lanka: Ethnic Fratricide and the Dismantling of Democracy.* Chicago: University of Chicago Press, 1986.

Tate, C. Neal and Torbjörn Vallinder. "The Global Expansion of Judicial Power: The Judicialization of Politics," in C. Neal Tate and Torbjörn Vallinder (eds), *The Global Expansion of Judicial Power.* New York: University Press, 1995, pp. 1–24.

Thakurta, Paranjoy and Shankar Raghuraman. *A Time of Coalitions: Divided We Stand.* New Delhi: Sage, 2004.

Thandi, Shinder S. "Counterinsurgency and Political Violence in Punjab, 1980–1994," in Gurharpal Singh and Ian Talbot (eds), *Punjabi Identity: Continuity and Change.* New Delhi: Manohar, 1996, pp. 159–85.

Thapa, Deepak (ed.). *Understanding the Maoist Movement of Nepal.* Kathmandu: Martin Chautari, 2003.

Thapa, Deepak and Bandana Sijapati. *A Kingdom under Siege: Nepal's Maoist Insurgency, 1996 to 2003.* Kathmandu: Print House, 2003.

Thapar, Romila. *A History of India.* Harmondsworth: Penguin, 1966.

Thirumalai, M. S. (comp.). "Constitution of India: Provisions Relating to Language," *Language in India*, Vol. 2, No. 2 (2002). Available at: www.languageinindia.com.

Thirumalai, M. S. (comp.). "The Official Language Act, 1963 (As Amended, 1967)," *Language in India*, Vol. 2, No. 2 (2002).

Thirumalai, M. S. "Early Gandhi and the Language Policy of the Indian National Congress," *Language in India*, Vol. 5, No. 4 (2005).

Thirumalai, M. S. and B. Mallikarjun (comps.). "The Evolution of Language Policy in the Constituent Assembly of India," Compilation of extracts from Constituent Assembly debates, Government of India, New Delhi, 1949, *Language in India*, Vol. 6, No. 2 (2006).

Thorner, Daniel. *The Agrarian Prospect in India: Five Lectures on Land Reform Delivered in 1955 at the Delhi School of Economics*, 2nd edition. Bombay: Allied, 1976.

Tilly, Charles. "War Making and State Making as Organized Crime," in Peter B. Evans, Dietrich Rueschemeyer and Theda Skocpol (eds), *Bringing the State Back In.* Cambridge: University Press, 1985, pp. 169–91.

Tiruchelvam, Neelan. "The Politics of Federalism and Diversity in Sri Lanka," in Yash Ghai (ed.), *Autonomy and Ethnicity: Negotiating Competing Claims in Multi-ethnic States.* Cambridge: University Press, 2000, pp. 197–218.

Transparency International (TI). *Corruption in South Asia: Insights and Benchmarks from Citizen Feedback Surveys in Five Countries.* Berlin: TI, December 2002.

Transparency International. *Corruption Perceptions Index, 2006.* Available at: http://www.transparency.org.

Transparency International. *Global Integrity Index, 2006.* Available at: http://www.globalintegrity.org/data/2006index.cfm.

Transparency International. *Report on the Transparency International Global Corruption Barometer.* Berlin: TI, 7 December, 2006.

Transparency International India. *India Corruption Study 2005: To Improve Governance.* New Delhi: Transparency International India, 30 June, 2005.

Umar, Badruddin (comp.). *Bhasha Ondolan Prasanga: Katipay. Dolil*, Vol. 2. Dhaka: Bangla Academy, 1986.

Umar, Badruddin. *The Emergence of Bangladesh: Class Struggles in East Pakistan (1947–1958).* Karachi: Oxford University Press, 2004.

UNESCO. *Position Paper: Teaching in the Mother Tongue.* Paris: UNESCO, 2003.

United Nations. "Contributions to United Nations Peacekeeping Operations, as of 31 January 2007." Available at: http://www.un.org/Depts/dpko/dpko/contributors/2007/jan07_1.pdf (accessed on 1 August, 2007).

Unnikrishnan v State of AP (1993) 1 SCC 645.

U.S. Department of State, Bureau of Democracy, Human Rights, and Labor. "Sri Lanka: Country Reports on Human Rights Practices—2007." Available at: http://www.state.gov/g/drl/rls/hrrpt/2007/100620.htm (accessed on 12 March, 2008).

Uyangoda, Jayadeva. "The State and the Process of Devolution in Sri Lanka," in Sunil Bastian (ed.), *Devolution and Development in Sri Lanka.* Colombo: International Centre for Ethnic Studies, 1994.

Uyangoda, Jayadeva. *Questions of Sri Lanka's Minority Rights*, Minority Protection Monograph, South

Asia Series 2. Colombo: International Center for Ethnic Studies, Unie Arts, 2001.

Uyangoda, Jayadeva. "Ethnic Conflict, the Tsunami Disaster and the State in Sri Lanka," *Inter-Asia Cultural Studies*, Vol. 6, No. 3 (September 2005), pp. 341–52.

Uyangoda, Jayadeva. *Ethnic Conflict in Sri Lanka: Changing Dynamics*. Washington, DC: East–West Center, 2007.

Van Dyke, Virginia. "'Jumbo Cabinets,' Factionalism, and the Impact of Federalism: Comparing Coalition Governments in Kerala, Punjab, and Uttar Pradesh," in Paul Wallace and Ramashroy Roy (eds), *India's 2004 Elections: Grassroots and National Perspectives*. New Delhi: Sage, 2007.

Varshney, Ashutosh. "Mass Politics or Elite Politics? India's Economic Reforms in Comparative Perspective," in Jeffrey D. Sachs, Ashutosh Varshney and Nirupam Bajpai (eds), *India in the Era of Economic Reforms*. New Delhi: Oxford University Press, 1999, pp. 222–60.

Varshney, Ashutosh. "Is India Becoming More Democratic?," *Journal of Asian Studies*, Vol. 59, No. 1 (2000), pp. 3–25.

Venkataraman, R. *My Presidential Years*. New Delhi: HarperCollins, 1994.

Venkatesan, V. "Judicial Challenge," *Frontline* (9 February, 2007).

Vijayanunni, M. "Caste and the Census of India." Unpublished paper, 2003.

Viswanathan, Gauri. *Masks of Conquest: Literary Study and British Rule in India*. New York: Columbia University Press, 1989.

Vithal, B. P. R. and M. L. Shastry. *Fiscal Federalism in India*. New Delhi: Oxford University Press, 2001.

Vittachi, Tarzie. *Emergency '58: The Story of the Ceylon Race Riots*. London: André Deutsch, 1958.

Vivienne Gunawardene v Hector Perera (1983) S.C. Application 20/83.

Von Vorys, Karl. *Political Development in Pakistan*. Princeton, NJ: University Press, 1965.

Wade, Robert. "The Market for Public Office: Why the Indian State Is Not Better at Development," *World Development*, Vol. 13, No. 4 (1985), pp. 467–97.

Walker, R. B. J. *Inside/Outside: International Relations as Political Theory*. Cambridge: University Press, 1993.

Walker, William. "International Nuclear Relations after the Indian and the Pakistani Test Explosions," *International Affairs*, Vol. 74, No. 3 (July 1998), pp. 505–28.

Waseem, Mohammad. *Politics and the State in Pakistan*. Lahore: Progressive, 1989.

Waseem, Mohammad. "Pakistan Resolution and the Ethnonationalist Movements," in Kaniz F. Yusuf, M. Saleem Akhtar and S. Razi Wasti (eds), *Pakistan Resolution Revisited*. Islamabad: National Institute of Historical and Cultural Studies, 1990, pp. 522–27.

Waseem, Muhammad. *The 1993 Elections in Pakistan*. Lahore: Vanguard, 1994.

Waseem, Mohammad. "Mohajirs in Pakistan: A Case of Nativisation of Migrants," in Crispin Bates (ed.), *Community, Empire and Migration: South Asians in Diaspora*. Basingstoke: Palgrave, 2001.

Waseem, Mohammad. "Political Ethnicity and the State in Pakistan," in *The Nation-State and Transnational Forces in South Asia* (Tokyo, 2001), pp. 270–71.

Waseem, Mohammad. "Muslim Migration from East Punjab: Patterns of Settlement and Assimilation," in Ian Talbot and Thinder Shandi (eds), *People on the Move: Punjabi Colonial and Postcolonial Migration*. Karachi: Oxford University Press, 2004.

Waseem, Mohammad. *Democratization in Pakistan: A Study of the 2002 Elections*. Karachi: Oxford University Press, 2006.

Waseem, Mohammad. "Functioning of Democracy in Pakistan," in Zoya Hasan (ed.), *Democracy and Muslim Societies: The Asian Experience*. New Delhi: Sage, 2007.

Waseem, Mohammad. "Islam and the West: A Perspective from Pakistan," in James L. Peacock, Patricia M. Thornton and Patrick B. Inman (eds), *Identity Matters: Ethnic and Sectarian Conflict*. New York: Berghahn Books: 2007.

Washbrook, David. *The Emergence of Provincial Politics: The Madras Presidency 1870–1920*. Cambridge: University Press, 1976.

Weerakoon, Bradman. "Government of Sri Lanka and LTTE Peace Negotiations 1989/90," in Kumar Rupesinghe (ed.), *Negotiating Peace in Sri Lanka: Efforts, Failures and Lessons*. Colombo: Foundation for Co-existence, 2006, pp. 111–28.

Weerawardena, I. D. S. "The Minorities and the Citizenship Act," *Ceylon Historical Journal*, Vol. 1, No. 3 (1951).

Weiner, Myron. *Sons of the Soil: Migration and Ethnic Conflict in India*. Princeton, NJ: University Press, 1978.

Weiner, Myron. "Congress Restored: Continuities and Discontinuities in Indian Politics," *Asian Survey*, Vol. 22 (1982).

Weiss, Anita M. and S. Zulfiqar Gilani (eds). *Power and Civil Society in Pakistan*. Oxford: University Press, 2001.

Welikala, Asanga. "Towards Two Nations in One State." Unpublished conference paper, EURO Regions Summer University of the Institute of Federalism, University of Fribourg, Switzerland, 21 September, 2002.

Welikala, Asanga. *The Menzingen Determination and the Supreme Court: A Liberal Critique*. Colombo: Center for Policy Alternatives, 2008.

Wendt, Alexander. *Social Theory of International Politics*. New York: Cambridge University Press, 1999.

Whaley, Joachim. "Federal Habits: The Holy Roman Empire and the Continuity of German Federalism," in Maiken Umbach (ed.), *German Federalism: Past, Present, and Future*. Basingstoke: Palgrave, 2001.

Wickramaratne, Jayampathy. *Fundamental Rights in Sri Lanka*. Pannipitiya, Sri Lanka: Stamford Lake, 2006.

Wickramasinghe, Nira. *Ethnic Politics of Colonial Sri Lanka, 1927–47*. New Delhi: Vikas, 1995.

Wickramasinghe, Nira. "Politics of Nostalgia: The Citizen as Peasant," Delhi School of Economics Occasional Paper (New Series), No. 2 (2005).

Wickramasinghe, Nira. *Sri Lanka in the Modern Age: A History of Contested Identities*. London: Hurst, 2006.

Widmalm, Sten. "Explaining Corruption at the Village and Individual Level in India: Findings from a Study of the Panchayati Raj Reforms," *Asian Survey* (September–October 2005), pp. 756–76.

Wijenayake, Lal. *Independence of the Judiciary in Sri Lanka since Independence*. Pannipitiya, Sri Lanka: Stamford Lake, 2005.

Wilkinson, Steven I. "Putting Gujarat in Perspective," *Economic and Political Weekly*, Vol. 37, No. 17 (27 April, 2002), pp. 1,579–83.

Wilkinson, Steven I. *Votes and Violence: Electoral Competition and Ethnic Riots in India*. Cambridge: University Press, 2004.

Williamson, John. "Democracy and the 'Washington Consensus,'" *World Development*, Vol. 21 (1993), pp. 1,329–36.

Wilson, A. Jeyaratnam. *Break-Up of Sri Lanka: The Sinhalese–Tamil Conflict*. London: C. Hurst, 1988.

Wilson, A. Jeyaratnam. *The Gaullist System in Asia: The Constitution of Sri Lanka (1978)*. London: Macmillan, 1980.

Woodruff, Philip. *The Men Who Ruled India*, Vol. I: *The Founders*. London: Jonathan Cape, 1953, 1957.

World Bank. *The East Asian Miracle: Economic Growth and Public Policy*. Oxford: University Press, 1993.

World Bank. *Taming Leviathan: Reforming Governance in Bangladesh*. Dhaka: World Bank, 2002.

World Bank. *Resuming Punjab's Prosperity: The Opportunities and Challenges Ahead*. Washington, DC: World Bank, 2004.

World Bank. *Bangladesh Economics and Governance of Nongovernmental Organizations in Bangladesh*, Report No. 35861-BD. Washington, DC: World Bank, 16 April, 2006.

World Bank. *India: Inclusive Growth and Service Delivery—Building on India's Success*, Development Policy Review, Report No. 34580-IN. Washington, DC: World Bank, 2006.

World Bank. *Development and the Next Generation*, World Development Report. Washington, DC: World Bank, 2007.

Wriggins, Howard. *Ceylon: Dilemmas of a New Nation*. Princeton, NJ: University Press, 1960.

Wriggins, Howard W. "Impediments to Unity in New Nations: The Case of Ceylon," *American Political Science Review*, Vol. 55 (1961), pp. 313–20.

Wright, Theodore P. "The Effectiveness of Muslim Representation in India," in Donald E. Smith (ed.), *South Asian Politics and Religion*. Princeton, NJ: University Press, 1966, pp. 102–37.

Yadav, Yogendra. "Reconfiguration in Indian Politics: State Assembly Elections 1993–95," *Economic and Political Weekly*, Vol. 31, Nos. 2–3 (13 January, 1996), pp. 95–104.

Yadav, Yogendra. "The New Congress Voter," *Seminar*, No. 526 (2003). Available at: http://www.india-seminar.com/2003/526/526%20yogendra%20yadav.htm.

Yong, Tai and Gyanesh Kudaisya. *The Aftermath of Partition in South Asia*. London: Routledge, 2000.

Zaidi, S. Akbar (ed.). *Regional Imbalances and the National Question in Pakistan*. Lahore: Vanguard, 1992.

Zaidi, S. Akbar. "The Economic Bases of the National Question in Pakistan: An Indication," in S. Akbar Zaidi (ed.), *Regional Imbalances and the National Question in Pakistan*. Lahore: Vanguard, 1992.

Ziring, Lawrence. *Bangladesh from Mujib to Ershad: An Interpretive Study*. Dhaka: University Press, 1992.

Zohir, Sajjad. "NGO Sector in Bangladesh: An Overview," *Economic and Political Weekly*, Vol. 39 (4 September, 2004), pp. 4,109–13.

Index

Page numbers in *italics* denotes a table

SAARC (South Asian Regional Cooperation
    Council) 411, 412, 413, 414
Saeed, Hakim 283
Sahajanand, Swami 323
St Kitts affair 370
Samajwadi Party 79, 263
Sangh Parivar 262
Sankaran, S.R. 389, 393
Sanskrit 224, 226
Santhanam Committee 368
Sanyal, Kanu 385
Sathe 171, 173
Sattar, Abdus 100, 374
Saudi Arabia 106, 287, 404
Sayeed, Khalid bin 29
Scheduled Castes (SCs) 264–5, 269
self-employment: Sri Lanka 340
Sen, Amartya 285
Senanayake, D.S. 43, 44, 46, 47, 48, 50, 119, 124
Senanayake, Dudley 119, 124
Senanayake-Chelvanayakam agreement (1965)
    291
sepoy system 352
Seven Party Alliance see SPA
Shah Bano case 170–1
Shamsher, Subarna 134
Sharif, Nawaz 94, 181, 185–6, 283, 287, 372,
    373, 405
Sharif, Shehbaz 277
Sharma, Shankar Dayal 63
Shastri, Lal Bahadur 58, 62, 168
Shekhar, Chandra 135, 369
Shimla Accord (1972) 403
Shiromani Akali Dal see Akali Dal
Sikh Magna Carta 253–4
Sikhs 74, 77, 410; campaign for autonomy in
    Punjab 253–5
Silva, K.M. de 50
Sindh 96, 242, 281–2
Sindhi (language) 11, 218, 224, 235, 237, 238,
    242, 281
Sindhis 181–2, 276, 278, 279, 280
Sing, V.P. 311–12
Singer, Hans 307
Singh, Ajit 68, 78
Singh, Charan 78, 150, 308–9
Singh, Manmohan 62–3, 312, 334
Singh, V.P. 55, 60, 74, 369
Singh, Zail 63
Sinha, Aseema 154, 315
Sinhala Heritage Party (SU) 124
Sinhala Maha Sabha 44

Sinhalese Buddhists 43–4, 122, 123
Sinhalese language 297
Sinhalese-Tamil relations 10, 16, 43, 118, 119,
    123, 205, 291
Sipah Sahaba Pakistan (SSP) 287
Siraiki language 236
Siraiki Lok Sanjh 236
Sitaramayyah, Kondapally 389
Skutnabb-Kangas, Tove 242
SLFP (Sri Lanka Freedom Party) 6, 119, 120,
    122, 123, 124, 295
SLMC (Sri Lanka Muslim Congress) 125,
    297
Solarz, Stephen 135
Soulbury Constitution (1947) 45–6, 48, 49,
    118, 204
South Asia Intelligence 22
South Asian Regional Cooperation Council
    see SAARC
Soviet Union 384; collapse of 151, 312; and
    India 22, 407; invasion and occupation of
    Afghanistan (1979–80) 88, 404, 407
SPA (Seven Party Alliance) 139, 141
S.R. Bommai vs Union of India 168
Sri Lanka 5–6, 41–50, 118–28; agriculture 47,
    339; armed forces 47; balance of payments
    339; and Buddhism 2, 6, 10, 119, 120, 206;
    budget deficit 339; caste politics 121;
    citizenship issue 48–9; civil service 47–8;
    class politics 46; colonial impact and legacy
    41, 47, 50, 237, 343; Constitution (1972)
    204, 206, 343; Constitution (1978) 120,
    204–5, 206, 343; constitutional and political
    processes 343–4; constitutions and judicial
    independence 204–5; corruption 6, 123,
    364, 366, *366*; crushing of JVP insurgency
    294; Defense Agreement with Britain
    (1948) 50; and democracy 6, 55, 119, 343,
    365, *365*; devolution 7, 126–8, 207, 343;
    district development council (DDC)
    scheme 126; Donoughmore Constitution
    42–3, 46, 118, 123; economy 19, 47, 121,
    299, 338–43, 345; elections and electoral
    system 46–7, 120, 122, 124, 343; ethnic
    conflict and civil war 10, 15–17, 49, 121–2,
    124, 128, 207, 291–300, 342, 414, 1126;
    anti-Tamil measures and riots 119, 120,
    124, 291, 292; continuing of civil war by
    LTTE 294; events leading to civil war
    291–2; future 299–300; and Indo-Lanka
    Accord (1987) 124, 126–7, 203, 207, 220,
    249, 254, 256, 293–4, 414; negotiations